Barcelona

timeout.com/barcelona

Time Out Guides Ltd
Universal House
251 Tottenham Court Road
London W1T 7AB
United Kingdom
Tel: +44 (0)20 7813 3000
Fax: +44 (0)20 7813 6001
Email: guides@timeout.com
www.timeout.com

Published by Time Out Guides Ltd, a wholly owned subsidiary of Time Out Group Ltd.
Time Out and the Time Out logo are trademarks of Time Out Group Ltd.

© **Time Out Group Ltd 2009**
Previous editions 1996, 1998, 2000, 2001, 2002, 2003, 2004, 2005, 2006, 2007, 2008.

10 9 8 7 6 5 4 3 2 1

This edition first published in Great Britain in 2009 by Ebury Publishing.
A Random House Group Company
20 Vauxhall Bridge Road, London SW1V 2SA

Random House Australia Pty Ltd 20 Alfred Street, Milsons Point, Sydney, New South Wales 2061, Australia

Random House New Zealand Ltd 18 Poland Road, Glenfield, Auckland 10, New Zealand

Random House South Africa (Pty) Ltd Isle of Houghton, Corner Boundary Road & Carse O'Gowrie, Houghton 2198, South Africa

Random House UK Limited Reg. No. 954009

For further distribution details, see www.timeout.com.

ISBN: 978-1-84670-070-5

A CIP catalogue record for this book is available from the British Library.

Printed and bound by Firmengruppe APPL, aprinta druck, Wemding, Germany.

The Random House Group Limited supports The Forest Stewardship Council (FSC), the leading international forest certification organisation. All our titles that are printed on Greenpeace approved FSC certified paper carry the FSC logo. Our paper procurement policy can be found at http://www.rbooks.co.uk/environment.

Time Out carbon-offsets its flights with Trees for Cities (www.treesforcities.org).

Contents

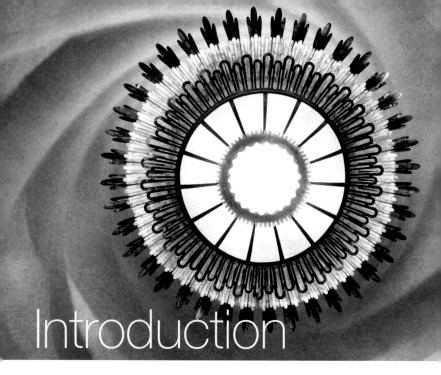

Introduction

It's not a capital. It speaks a language known only to nine million people. It's not short on attractions, but it has no Colosseum, no London Eye, no MoMA. Its nightlife lacks the dynamism of Berlin's; it has no ice hotels, no gondolas and no ornate temples. Its history is mostly one of repression. And while it's currently all the rage to compare its dining scene with that of Paris, no one's really taken in, least of all the Catalans. So why, when cities flit in and out of vogue, is Barcelona so eternally popular?

The simple answer is that the city has a panache that is all its own, and which, for many, embodies the Catalan character. It's often said that this fiercely nationalistic race is a successful synthesis of *seny,* a blend of nous and pragmatism, and *rauxa*, a passionate intensity that flirts with madness. To witness it, look at the architecture of Gaudí, the radical theatre of La Fura dels Baus, or the paintings (and, for that matter, the life) of Dalí.

It's a cliché, sure, but a cliché that works for this most multifaceted of cities. Here, a radiant pop art sculpture by Lichtenstein towers alongside a dark and sombre neoclassical arcade; serried ranks of apartment blocks in the Eixample occasionally explode in a proliferation of Modernista colour and pzazz; and the festivals involve both the *sardana*, a sedate national dance involving gentle bouncing on tiptoe, and the *correfoc*, a reckless, firework-wielding rampage through the streets.

At times, the city is so captivated by all things modern that counterculture becomes the new culture; the fanfare announcing the latest cyber-art festival is still lingering on the wind as it's suddenly pronounced passé. Even so, Barcelona never turns its back on its past. Much of its appeal to visitors stems from a respect for its heritage that gives it the best preserved medieval quarter in Europe. You could spend a day mooching around this labyrinth, escaping the heat in shadowy alleyways while seagulls wheel overhead in an azure sky, without ever feeling the need to tick off museums or head for the beach.

In fact, we suggest you do just that. This book is packed with recommendations of sights and museums large and small, famous and obscure. But to really appreciate what keeps visitors returning time and again, you won't always need us. *Sally Davies, Editor*

Barcelona in Brief

BARCELONA IN CONTEXT
The book's opening section sets out to give the city's back story: not only with a résumé of its often bloody past, which so informs the character of the city and those born here, but also with an introduction to events that are shaping today's city. This part of the book also includes a study of Gaudí, and the attempts by some in the Catholic Church to make him a saint.
▶ For more, see pp15-53.

SIGHTS
A stay here without at least a taste of Gaudí would be a missed opportunity, but there's more to the city than his architectural exuberance. While you're here, dip into the city's extraordinary variety of museums; take in a selection of its ancient churches, elegantly landscaped parks and bleeding-edge architecture; and, above all, wander its enticing, eclectic neighbourhoods.
▶ For more, see pp55-119.

CONSUME
Our Consume section details scores of places, both ancient and modern, in which to slake your thirst, linger over lunch or feast on a blowout dinner. Also here, you'll find a selection of deluxe five-star hotels, short-term apartments, budget boutiques and other accommodation options, along with an extensive list of Barcelona's more fascinating shops, markets and malls.
▶ For more, see pp121-221.

ARTS & ENTERTAINMENT
Thanks in part to a tradition of visual theatre born in Franco's era when the Catalan language was banned, Barcelona's arts scene is more accessible to non-natives than you might expect. It's also the best town in Spain to hear live music, from symphony orchestras to death metal groups. The best venues are all listed here, as are the city's leading nightclubs, cinemas, galleries and festivals.
▶ For more, see pp223-282.

ESCAPES & EXCURSIONS
Though there's plenty to keep you in the city, Barcelona is within such easy reach of mountains, beaches and vineyards that it seems a shame not to head outside its borders. The Catalan hinterland is a trove of discoveries that includes perfectly preserved Cistercian monasteries, Dalí's best work, Roman remains and a network of leafy routes for walking, cycling or driving.
▶ For more, see pp283-306.

Barcelona in 48 Hrs

Day 1 From Past to Future

9AM Start the day with a quiet stroll down La Rambla, the city's most famous boulevard, before the crowds, the living statues and the pickpockets arrive. Halfway along, duck into **Cafè de l'Opera** (*see p182*) for coffee and a breakfast *ensaimada*, a spiral of flaky pastry dusted with icing sugar.

Another couple of hundred yards or so down La Rambla, heading towards the sea, you'll see the **Plaça Reial** off to your left. Turn in to admire its elaborate lampposts, an early council commission for Gaudí; then, exiting from its northern side, head right along C/Ferran to the grand Plaça Sant Jaume, skirting round the back of the Generalitat to the **Cathedral** (*see p61*).

This is the heart of the Barri Gòtic. Allow at least half an hour to mooch around its magnificent cloister and take the lift up to the roof for a great view of the city. Come out of the Cathedral and head east, crossing the Via Laietana to the **Palau de la Música** (*see p73*). Take a guided tour or simply marvel at the fantastical Modernista façade.

2PM Having worked up an appetite, head down into the Born proper (with a quick look at the roof of the **Mercat Santa Caterina** en route) and tuck into some tapas outside the majestic **Santa Maria del Mar** at La Vinya del Senyor wine bar (*see p188*). It's a skip and a hop to the **Museu Picasso** (*see p73*), an easy place to while away a couple of hours.

6PM After this, wander down to the Port Vell. For the best view over the harbour, go up to the rooftop café of the **Museu d'Història de Catalunya** (*see p85*), where you can sip an early-evening beer before heading up to modernised Barceloneta and the seafront.

9PM In this part of town, there are several excellent seafood restaurants: try **Can Majó** (*see p164*) or **Kaiku** (*see p164*). And if you can't bear to go home afterwards, you could always join the glossy crowd for a late-night cocktail at **CDLC** (*see p260*), on the fringe of the beach.

NAVIGATING THE CITY

Barcelona is a breeze to navigate. Many major sights are within walking distance of each other, and the natural enclosure formed by the sea and the mountains mean it's hard to get too lost. Remember that uphill is *muntanya* (mountain) and downhill is *mar* (sea) – locals often give directions with these terms.

As well as using your feet or the cheap, user-friendly metro and bus systems, you can get around with **Go Cars** (902 31 03 33, www.gocartours.es), small yellow convertibles. During the day from March to November, you can also get around by hiring a **Trixi** rickshaw (www.trixi.com), either hailing one on the street or calling 93 310 13 79. For full details on transport, *see p308*.

PACKAGE DEALS

Articket (www.articketbcn.org, €20) gives free entry to seven major museums and galleries (one visit per venue over six

Day 2 Gaudí Galore

9AM To start a day of Modernisme, Barcelona's answer to art nouveau, breakfast in the charming **Els Quatre Gats** (*see p182*), designed by Puig i Cadafalch and a former haunt of Picasso. From here, walk up to Plaça Catalunya and continue straight ahead for the elegant **Passeig de Gràcia**, a showcase for all things Modernista. Note the Gaudí-designed hexagonal paving tiles, along with Pere Falqués' elegant wrought-iron lamp-posts.

11AM Unless you get sucked into some of the street's blend of swanky boutiques and major chains, it's a five-minute walk to the contrasting masterpieces of the **Manzana de la Discòrdia** (*see p101*). This block houses three extraordinary buildings designed by the holy trinity of Modernisme: Gaudí, Domènech i Montaner and Puig i Cadafalch. A five- to ten-minute walk further is Gaudí's **La Pedrera** (*see p108*). Backtrack to the Casa Batlló and take a metro train to Gaudí's most famous work, the spectacular **Sagrada Família** (*see p108*).

2PM Time for lunch. The area around the Sagrada Familia is strangely bereft of decent restaurants, but the adjacent Avda Gaudí has several spots with pavement terraces at which to grab a bocadillo and a beer. Once you're done, continue along the avenue for the extravagant **Hospital Sant Pau** (*see p106*), an unsung Modernista tour de force by Domènech i Montaner, then take bus no.92 to Gaudí's unmissable **Park Güell** (*see p111*).

9PM To complete a day of Modernisme, the deep-of-pocket will love dinner at **Casa Calvet** (*see p167*), a great, if pricey, restaurant set in a Gaudí-designed townhouse. If money is more of an issue, try the dining room at the **Hotel España** (*see p131*). The dishes are more ordinary, but the architectural and artistic flourishes of Domènech i Montaner and Modernista painter Ramon Casas are food for the soul. Both are most easily reached by cab from Park Güell; and both also offer easy access to other nightlife options if you're not yet ready for bed.

months): Fundació Miró, MACBA, the MNAC, La Pedrera, the Fundació Tàpies, the CCCB and the Museu Picasso. It's available from participating venues, tourist offices and www.telentrada.com.

The **Arqueoticket** (http://bcnshop. barcelonaturisme.com, €18) allows history buffs to visit five archaelogically oriented museums. It's available from the the museums and tourist offices, and is valid for unlimited visits until December 31 of the year in which it was purchased.

The **Barcelona Card** (www.barcelona card.com) allows unlimited transport on metro and buses, and gives discounts at sights, cable cars and airport buses. Costing €24 (€20 children aged 4-12) for a two-day pass, €29/€25 for three days, €33/€27 for four days and €36/€31 for five days, it's sold at the airport, tourist offices, Estació de Sants rail station, Estació Nord bus station, branches of El Corte Inglés, various attractions and www.barcelonaturisme.com.

Barcelona in Profile

BARRI GÒTIC

Combined with a wander down frenetic, commercial La Rambla, a stroll through the narrow alleyways and secluded squares of the Old City is the best possible introduction to Barcelona and the starting point for most visitors upon their arrival in the city. For a taste of the town's more grandiose architecture, Plaça Sant Jaume is flanked by two government buildings, the Renaissance palace of the Generalitat and the neo-classical façade of the Ajuntament.

▶ For more, see pp56-68.

BORN & SANT PERE

The Born and Sant Pere are two districts divided by C/Princesa. The pedestrianised Passeig del Born, the Born's main artery, is one of Barcelona's prettiest thoroughfares, bookended by a magnificent 19th-century market building and a glorious 14th-century church. Highlights of the slightly scruffier Sant Pere include Domènech i Montaner's magical Palau de la Música.

▶ For more, see pp69-76.

RAVAL

Once a no-go area for tourists, the Raval is being transformed. Some of its gems have been around for years – Gaudí's medievalist Palau Güell was an early attempt at gentrification. But others are newer: the revival began in 1995 with Richard Meier's monumental MACBA, housing the city's main collection of modern art, and carried on in 2008 with the futuristic Barceló hotel.

▶ For more, see pp77-82.

BARCELONETA & THE PORTS

The city's seafront was ignored until 1992, when it underwent a massive transformation for the Olympics. Despite initial resistance, it was wildly successful: the city now has seven kilometres of golden sands from the bustling Port Vell to the upscale Port Olímpic and beyond. Inevitably, this is also where you'll find some of the city's best seafood restaurants.

▶ For more, see pp83-89.

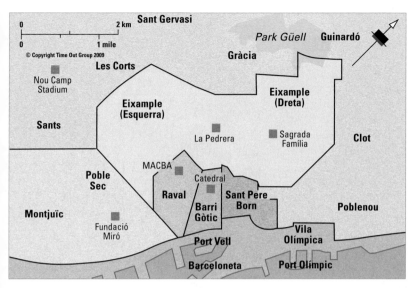

© Copyright Time Out Group 2009

MONTJUÏC

It's often left off visitors' itineraries, but the hill of Montjuïc merits a wander. In summer, the hill is a few degrees cooler than the city below, and its many parks and gardens are excellent places for a shady picnic. There are also museums: the Fundació Joan Miró is as impressive for its Corbusier-influenced building as its collection.

▶ *For more, see pp90-98.*

THE EIXAMPLE

Leaving the Old City and entering the Eixample (literally, 'Expansion'), narrow, labyrinthine streets and alleys become broad, traffic-clogged, geometrically precise roads. The area is a Modernista showcase: its buildings include the Sagrada Família, La Pedrera and the Hospital de Sant Pau.

▶ *For more, see pp99-108.*

GRACIA & OTHER DISTRICTS

Beyond the Eixample lies the low-rise *barrio* of Gràcia. Like workaday Sants and well-heeled Sarrià, it was an independent town that was swallowed up as the city spread, but it retains its own identity. Other notable areas outside the centre include the forested Collserola hills and, to the north, the former industrial neighbourhood of Poblenou.

▶ *For more, see pp109-119.*

Time Out Barcelona

Editorial
Editor Sally Davies
Copy Editors Edoardo Albert, Janice Fuscoe
Listings Editors Alex Phillips
Proofreader John Pym
Indexer Lesley McCave

Managing Director Peter Fiennes
Editorial Director Ruth Jarvis
Series Editor Will Fulford-Jones
Business Manager Dan Allen
Editorial Manager Holly Pick
Assistant Management Accountant Ija Krasnikova

Design
Art Director Scott Moore
Art Editor Pinelope Kourmouzoglou
Senior Designer Henry Elphick
Graphic Designers Kei Ishimaru, Nicola Wilson
Advertising Designer Jodi Sher

Picture Desk
Picture Editor Jael Marschner
Deputy Picture Editor Lynn Chambers
Picture Researcher Gemma Walters
Picture Desk Assistant Marzena Zoladz
Picture Librarian Christina Theisen

Advertising
Commercial Director Mark Phillips
International Advertising Manager Kasimir Berger
International Sales Executive Charlie Sokol
Advertising Sales (Barcelona) Creative Media Group

Marketing
Marketing Manager Yvonne Poon
**Sales & Marketing Director, North America &
   Latin America** Lisa Levinson
Senior Publishing Brand Manager Luthfa Begum
Marketing Designer Anthony Huggins

Production
Group Production Director Mark Lamond
Production Manager Brendan McKeown
Production Controller Damian Bennett
Production Coordinator Julie Pallot

Time Out Group
Chairman Tony Elliott
Group General Manager/Director Nichola Coulthard
Time Out Communications Ltd MD David Pepper
Time Out International Ltd MD Cathy Runciman
Group IT Director Simon Chappell
Head of Marketing Catherine Demajo

Contributors
Introduction Sally Davies. **History** Nick Rider, Sally Davies (*Profile* Edoardo Albert). **Barcelona Today** William Truini. **Architecture** Nick Rider, Sally Davies. **God's Architect** Austen Ivereigh (*Strange Truths* Sally Davies). **Sightseeing** Nadia Feddo, Sally Davies, Stephen Burgen, William Truini. **Where to Stay** Tara Stevens. **Restaurants** Sally Davies. **Cafés, Tapas & Bars** Sally Davies. **Shops & Services** Nadia Feddo (*Get All Dolled Up* Alex Phillips). **Calendar** Sally Davies (*Profile* Edoardo Albert). **Children** Sally Davies. **Film** Sally Davies. **Galleries** Alex Phillips. **Gay & Lesbian** Dylan Simanowitz, Molly Malcolm (*Marriage à la Mode* Nadia Feddo). **Music & Nightlife** Katie Addleman. **Performing Arts** Alex Phillips (*Laughter in the Dark* Nadia Feddo). **Sport & Fitness** Daniel Campi. **Escapes & Excursions** Tara Stevens (*Profile* Nadia Feddo). **Directory** Alex Phillips.

Maps john@jsgraphics.co.uk, except: pages 350-352.

Photography Greg Gladman, except: pages 3, 8 (Ciutadella), 9 (Fundació Joan Miró, La Pedrera), 15, 107 (left), 283, 284, 288, 294, 297, 301, 302, 305 Elan Fleisher; pages 7, 8 (beach), 50, 65, 70, 104 (left), 105, 291 Olivia Rutherford; pages 16, 29 Getty Images; pages 19, 21, 53, 227 Godofoto; page 22 MEPL; page 107 (right) Natalie Pecht; pages 121, 122, 126 Grand Hotel Central; page 176 (bottom) Maribel Ruiz de Erenchum; pages 176, 177 Francesc Guillamet; pages 223, 224, 228 Pep Herrero; page 237 Matt Petit/©AMPAS; page 239 DreamWorks/Photofest; page 253 Jon Santa Cruz; page 280 www.fcbarcelona.cat. The following images were provided by the featured establishments/artists: pages 44 (bottom), 203, 275.

The Editor would like to thank Laura Galisteo, Montse Planas, Montse Pozo, Sarah Barden and all contributors to previous editions of *Time Out Barcelona*, whose work forms the basis for parts of this book.

About the Guide

GETTING AROUND

The back of the book contains street maps of Barcelona, as well as overview maps of the city and its surroundings. The maps start on page 333; on them are marked the locations of hotels (**❶**), restaurants (**❶**), and cafés, tapas bars and bars (**❶**). The majority of businesses listed in this guide are located in the areas we've mapped; the grid-square references refer to these maps.

THE ESSENTIALS

For practical information, including visas, disabled access, emergency numbers, useful websites and local transport, please see the Directory. It begins on page 308.

THE LISTINGS

Addresses, phone numbers, websites, transport information, hours and prices are all included in our listings, as are selected other facilities. All were checked and correct at press time. However, business owners can alter their arrangements at any time, and fluctuating economic conditions can cause prices to change rapidly.

The very best venues in the city, the must-sees and must-dos in every category,

have been marked with a red star (★). In the Sights chapters, we've also marked venues with free admission with a **FREE** symbol.

THE LANGUAGE

Barcelona is a bilingual city: street signs, tourist information and menus may be in either Spanish or Catalan. For a language primer, see pages 323-324; in addition, there's help with restaurants on page 156.

PHONE NUMBERS

The area code for Barcelona is 93. Even if you're in the city, you'll always need to use the code. From outside Spain, dial your country's international access code (00 from the UK, 011 from the US) or a plus symbol, followed by the Spanish country code (34) and the nine-digit number. So, to reach the Sagrada Familia, dial +34 93 207 30 31. For more on phones, *see p319*.

FEEDBACK

We welcome feedback on this guide, both on the venues we've included and on any other locations that you'd like to see featured in future editions. Please email us at guides@timeout.com.

Time Out Guides

Founded in 1968, Time Out has grown from humble beginnings into the leading resource for anyone wanting to know what's happening in the world's greatest cities. Alongside our influential weeklies in London, New York and Chicago, we publish more than 20 magazines in cities as varied as Beijing and Beirut; a range of travel books, with the City Guides now joined by the newer Shortlist series; and an information-packed website. The company remains proudly independent, still owned by Tony Elliott four decades after he launched *Time Out London*.

Written by local experts and illustrated with original photography, our books also

retain their independence. No business has been featured because it has advertised, and all restaurants and bars are visited and reviewed anonymously.

ABOUT THE EDITOR

A Barcelona resident since 2001, **Sally Davies** has written, edited and contributed to a number of books on Spain. She also writes on Spanish food and culture for publications including *The Guardian*, *The Sunday Times* and *Olive*.

A full list of the book's contributors can be found opposite. However, we've also included details of our writers in selected chapters across the guide.

In Context

La Pedrera.
See p46.

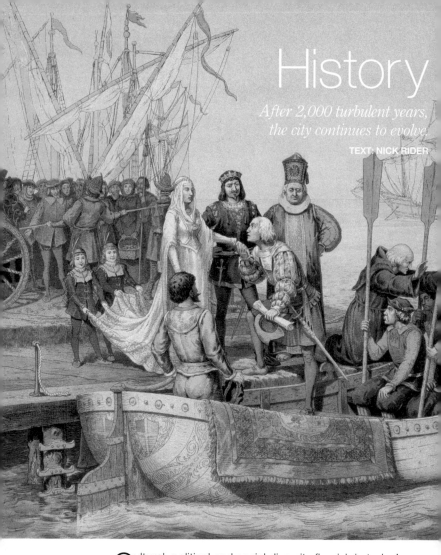

History

After 2,000 turbulent years, the city continues to evolve.

TEXT: NICK RIDER

Nick Rider wrote a Ph.D on 1930s Barcelona before becoming the first editor of Time Out Barcelona, *and has since written for several books on Spain.*

Cultural, political and social diversity flourish in today's Barcelona, but things haven't always been that way. For long periods of its history, the city was the victim of attempts by governments in Madrid to absorb Catalonia within a unified Spanish state. Under several leaders, notably Philip V in the 17th century and Franco in the 20th, these attempts resulted in a policy aimed at stamping out any vestige of Catalan culture or independence. However, the region always re-emerged from such persecutions stronger and more vibrant, with a heightened desire to show the world its distinctive character – both socially and culturally.

IN THE BEGINNING

The Romans founded Barcelona in about 15 BC on the Mons Taber, a small hill between two streams that provided a good view of the Mediterranean and which today is crowned by a cathedral. At the time, the plain around it was sparsely inhabited by the Laetani, an agrarian Iberian people who produced grain and honey, and gathered oysters. Then called Barcino, the town was smaller than Tarraco (Tarragona), the capital of the Roman province of Hispania Citerior, but it had the only harbour between there and Narbonne.

Like virtually every other Roman new town in Europe, Barcino was a fortified rectangle with a crossroads at its centre (where the Plaça Sant Jaume is today). It was also an unimportant provincial town, but the rich plain provided it with a produce garden, and the sea gave it an incipient maritime trade. It acquired a Jewish community soon after its foundation. And the people of Barcino accepted Christianity in AD 312, together with the rest of the Roman Empire, which by then was under growing threat of invasion. In response, the town's rough defences were replaced with massive stone walls in the fourth century, many sections of which can still be seen today.

Still, defences such as these couldn't prevent the empire's disintegration. In 415, Barcelona, as it became known, briefly became capital of the kingdom of the Visigoths, under their chieftain Ataülf. They soon moved on southwards to extend their control over the whole of the Iberian peninsula, and for the next 400 years the town was a neglected backwater. The Muslims swept across the peninsula after 711, crushing Goth resistance; they made little attempt to settle Catalonia, but much of the Christian population retreated into the Pyrenees, the first Catalan heartland.

Then, at the end of the eighth century, the Franks drove south, against the Muslims, from across the mountains. In 801, Charlemagne's son, Louis the Pious, took Barcelona and made it a bastion of the Marca Hispanica (Spanish March), the southern buffer of his father's empire. This gave Catalonia a trans-Pyrenean origin entirely different from that of the other Christian states in Spain; equally, it's for this reason that the closest relative of the Catalan language is Provençal, not Castilian.

When the Frankish princes returned to their main business further north, loyal counts were left behind to rule sections of the Catalan lands. At the end of the ninth century, Count Guifré el Pilós (Wilfred 'the Hairy') managed to gain control over several of these Catalan counties from his base in Ripoll. By uniting them under his rule, he laid the basis for a future Catalan state, founding the dynasty of the Counts of Barcelona, which reigned in an unbroken line until 1410. His successors made Barcelona their capital, setting the seal on the city's future.

As a founding patriarch, Wilfred is the stuff of legends, not least of which is that he was the creator of the Catalan flag. The story goes that he was fighting the Saracens alongside his lord, the Frankish emperor, when he was severely wounded. In recognition of Wilfred's heroism, the emperor dipped his fingers into his friend's blood and ran them down the count's golden shield; thus, the Quatre Barres, four bars of red on a yellow background, also known as La Senyera. Recorded facts suggest that this story probably never happened. Still, whatever its origins, the four-stripe symbol was first recorded on the tomb of Count Ramon Berenguer II from 1082, making it the oldest national flag in Europe. One other mystery: no historian has yet determined in what way Wilfred was so notably hairy.

LAYING THE FOUNDATIONS

In the first century of the new millennium, Catalonia was consolidated as a political entity, and entered an age of cultural richness. This was the great era of Catalan Romanesque art, with the building of the magnificent monasteries and the churches of northern Catalonia, such as Sant Pere de Rodes near Figueres, and the painting of the glorious murals now housed in the Museu Nacional on Montjuïc. There was also a flowering of scholarship, reflecting Catalan contacts with northern Europe and with Islamic and Carolingian cultures. In Barcelona, shipbuilding and trade in grain

Wilfred 'the Hairy'. *See p17*.

and wine grew, and a new trade developed in textiles. The city expanded both inside its old Roman walls and outside them, with *vilanoves* (new towns) appearing at Sant Pere and La Ribera.

The most significant addition, however, occurred in 1137, when Ramon Berenguer IV (1131-62) wed Petronella, heir to the throne of Aragon. In the long term, the marriage bound Catalonia into Iberia. The uniting of the two dynasties created a powerful entity known as the Crown of Aragon: each element retained its separate institutions, and was ruled by monarchs known as the Count-Kings. Ramon Berenguer IV also extended Catalan territory to its current frontiers in the Ebro valley. At the beginning of the next century, however, the dynasty lost virtually all its land north of the Pyrenees to France, when Count-King Pere I 'the Catholic' was killed at the Battle of Muret in 1213. This proved a blessing in disguise. In future years, the Catalan-Aragonese state became oriented decisively towards the Mediterranean and the south, and was able to embark on two centuries of imperialism that would be equalled in vigour only by Barcelona's burgeoning commercial enterprise.

EMPIRE-BUILDING

Pere I's successor was the most expansionist of the Count-Kings. Jaume I 'the Conqueror' (1213-76) joined the campaign against the Muslims to the south, taking Mallorca in 1229, Ibiza in 1235 and, at greater cost, Valencia in 1238 (which he made another separate kingdom, the third part of the Crown of Aragon). Barcelona became the centre of an empire that spanned the Mediterranean.

'In Catalonia, royal authority kept coming up against a mass of local rights and privileges.'

The city grew tremendously. In the middle of the 13th century, Jaume I ordered the building of a second wall along the line of La Rambla, roughly encircling the area between there and what is now the Parc de la Ciutadella; in doing so, La Ribera and the other *vilanoves* were brought within the city. In 1274, Jaume also gave Barcelona a form of representative self-government: the Consell de Cent, a council of 100 chosen citizens, an institution that would last for more than 400 years. In Catalonia as a whole, royal powers were strictly limited by a parliament, the Corts, with a permanent standing committee known as the Generalitat.

In 1282, Pere II 'the Great' sent his armies into Sicily; Catalan domination over the island would last for nearly 150 years, as the Catalan empire reached its greatest strength under Jaume II 'the Just' (1291-1327). Corsica (1323) and Sardinia (1324) were added to the Crown of Aragon, although the latter would never submit to Catalan rule and would, from then on, be a constant focus of revolt.

THE GOLDEN AGE

The Crown of Aragon was often at war with Arab rulers, but its capital flourished through commerce with every part of the Mediterranean, Christian and Muslim. Catalan ships also sailed into the Atlantic, to England and Flanders, their ventures actively supported by the Count-Kings and burghers of Barcelona and regulated by the first-ever code of maritime law, known as the *Llibre del Consolat de Mar* (written in 1258-72). By the late 13th century, around 130 consulates ringed the Mediterranean, engaged in a complex system of trade.

Unsurprisingly, this age of power and prestige was also the great era of building in medieval Barcelona. The Count-Kings' imperial conquests may have been ephemeral, but their talent for permanence in building can still be seen today. Between 1290 and 1340, the construction of most of Barcelona's best-known Gothic buildings was initiated. Religious edifices such as the cathedral, Santa Maria del Mar and Santa Maria del Pi were matched by civil buildings such as the Saló de Tinell and the Llotja, the old market and the stock exchange. As a result, Barcelona contains the most important collection of historic Gothic civil architecture anywhere in Europe.

The ships of the Catalan navy were built in the monumental Drassanes (shipyards), begun by Pere II and completed under Pere III, in 1378. In 1359, Pere III also built the third, final city wall along the line of the modern Paral·lel, Ronda Sant Pau and Ronda Sant Antoni. This gave the Old City of Barcelona its definitive shape. La Ribera, 'the waterfront', was the centre of trade and industry in the 14th century city. Just inland, the Carrer Montcada was where newly enriched merchants displayed their wealth in opulent Gothic palaces. All around were the workers of the various craft guilds, grouped together in their own streets.

The Catalan Golden Age was also an era of cultural greatness. Catalonia was one of the first areas in Europe to use its vernacular language, as well as Latin, in written form and as a language of culture. But the prosperity of the medieval period did not last. The Count-Kings had overextended Barcelona's resources, and overinvested in far-off ports. By 1400, the effort to maintain their conquests, especially Sardinia, had exhausted the spirit and the coffers of the Catalan imperialist drive. The Black Death, which arrived in the 1340s, also had a devastating impact on Catalonia, intensifying the bitterness of social conflicts between the aristocracy, the merchants, the peasants and the urban poor.

In 1410, Martí I 'the Humane' died without an heir, bringing to an end the line of the Counts of Barcelona, unbroken since Wilfred 'the Hairy'. The Crown of Aragon was

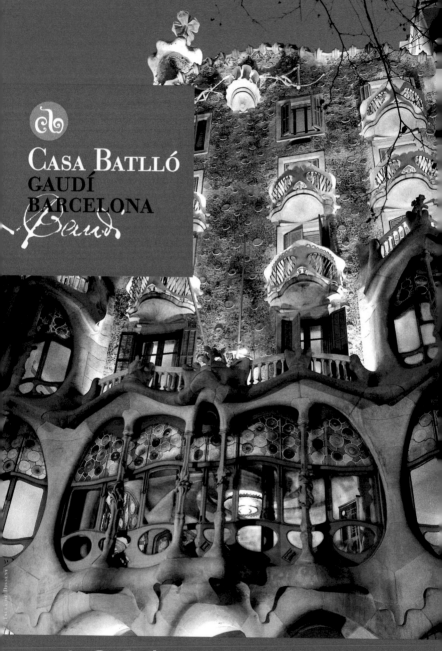

CASA BATLLÓ
GAUDÍ
BARCELONA

Gaudí

-10%
DESCUENTO / DISCOUNT

PG. DE GRÀCIA, 43
08007 BARCELONA
TEL: +34 93 216 03 06
FAX: +34 93 488 30 90
infovisites@casabatllo.cat
www.casabatllo.cat

The city mapped, in 1859

passed to a member of a Castilian noble family, the Trastámaras: Fernando de Antequera (1410-16). In the 1460s, the effects of war and catastrophic famine led to a sudden collapse into violent and destructive civil war and peasant revolt. The population was depleted to such an extent that Barcelona would not regain the numbers it had had in 1400 (40,000) until the 18th century.

In 1469, an important union for Spain initiated a woeful period in Barcelona's history; dubbed by some Catalan historians the Decadència, it eventually led to the end of Catalonia as a separate entity. In that year, Ferdinand of Aragon (1479-1516) married Isabella of Castile (1476-1504), thereby uniting the different Spanish kingdoms, even though they would retain their separate institutions for another two centuries.

As Catalonia's fortunes declined, so those of Castile rose. In 1492, Granada, the last Muslim foothold in Spain, was conquered; Isabella decreed the expulsion of all Jews from Castile and Aragon; and Columbus discovered America. It was Castile's seafaring orientation towards the Atlantic, as opposed to the Mediterranean, that confirmed Catalonia's decline. The discovery of the New World was a disaster for Catalan commerce: trade shifted away from the Mediterranean, and Catalans were officially barred from participating in the exploitation of the new empire until the 1770s. The weight of Castile within the monarchy was increased, and it soon became the clear seat of government.

In 1516, the Spanish crown passed to the House of Habsburg, in the shape of Ferdinand and Isabella's grandson, Holy Roman Emperor Charles V. His son, Philip II of Spain, established Madrid as the capital of all his dominions in 1561. Catalonia was managed by viceroys, and the power of its institutions increasingly restricted, with a down-at-heel aristocracy and a meagre cultural life.

Profile Ramon Llull

Barcelona's original troubadour – lover of God (and the ladies).

THREE TO PONDER

Llull's investigations into logic were the start of computational theory.

Llull developed voting systems centuries ahead of his time.

Llull believed that both reason and faith were needed to find the truth about God.

Writer, philosopher and holy man Ramon Llull (1232-1316) became known as the Fool of Love, thanks to a love of God that inspired him to try and convert Moorish sultans by argument; he was held prisoner in the palace toilets for his pains. However, for the first 30 years of his life, his heart was on different matters. Attached to the household of the future Jaume II of Mallorca, Llull eventually became its seneschal. But marriage and two children did nothing to cool his pursuit of the court's women, for whom he composed many songs in the troubadour style of the period.

'The more apt I found myself to sin, the more I allowed my nature to obey the dictates of my body,' he wrote later. But in the summer of 1263, while Llull was writing a song, he looked up to see 'our Lord Jesus Christ hanging upon the Cross'. His poetic flow interrupted, Llull took to his bed, but when he next picked up a pen, the figure returned. In his attempts to work out what these visions might mean, Llull devoted himself to

Christ's service by attempting to convert the 'unbelievers' (in Llull's world, this chiefly meant Muslims) by writing a book, 'the best in the world, against the errors of unbelievers', and setting up colleges to teach Arabic to missionaries.

Llull spent the next nine years in study, and only began the literary and missionary work for which he would become famous as he approached his 40th birthday. The sheer scale of his labours defies belief: as well as 265 works in Catalan, Arabic and Latin, Llull penned *Blanquerna*, a seminal Catalan novel; served as a missionary in almost constant travel between Europe and north Africa; worked as a teacher at the University of Paris, then the foremost institution of learning in Christendom; appeared as a suitor at papal and imperial courts; and originated the Ars Magna, a mammoth systematisation of... well, everything, with respect to God's attributes. He eventually became known as *Doctor Illuminatus* (the 'Illuminated Doctor'), from the series of mystical visions he had on Mount Randa in Mallorca.

At 75, Llull was on a mission to north Africa when he was 'beaten with sticks and with fists, and forcibly dragged along by his beard, which was very long, until he was locked in the latrine of the thieves' jail'. The details of his death are subject to dispute: some say he died at the hands of a Muslim mob in Tunis, others that he succumbed to disease when sailing back. But whatever the truth, his legacy is immense.

FEAR THE REAPERS

While Castilian Spain went through its 'Golden Century', Catalonia was left on the margins. However, worse was to come in the following century with the two national revolts, both heroic defeats that have since acquired a central role in Catalan mythology.

The problem for the Spanish monarchy was that Castile was an absolute monarchy and thus could be taxed at will, but in the former Aragonese territories, and especially Catalonia, royal authority kept coming up against a mass of local rights and privileges. As the Habsburgs' empire became entrenched in wars and expenses that not even American gold could meet, the Count-Duke of Olivares, the formidable great minister of King Philip IV (1621-65), resolved to extract more money and troops from the non-Castilian dominions of the Crown. The Catalans, however, felt they were taxed quite enough already.

In 1640, a mass of peasants, later dubbed Els Segadors (the Reapers), gathered on La Rambla in Barcelona, outside the Porta Ferrissa (Iron Gate) in the second wall. The peasants rioted against royal authority, surged into the city and murdered the viceroy, the Marquès de Santa Coloma. This began the general uprising known as the Guerra dels Segadors, or the 'Reapers' War'. The authorities of the Generalitat, led by its president Pau Claris, were fearful of the violence of the poor; lacking the confidence to declare Catalonia independent, they appealed for protection from Louis XIII of France. French armies, however, were unable to defend Catalonia adequately, and in 1652 a destitute Barcelona capitulated to the equally exhausted army of Philip IV. In 1659, France and Spain made peace with a treaty that gave the Catalan territory of Roussillon, around Perpignan, to France. After the revolt, Philip IV and his ministers were magnanimous, allowing the Catalans to retain what was left of their institutions despite their disloyalty.

THE REIGN IN SPAIN

Fifty years later after Barcelona fell to the Spanish army, came the second of the great national rebellions – the War of the Spanish Succession. In 1700, Charles II of Spain died without an heir, and Castile accepted the grandson of Louis XIV of France, Philip of Anjou, as King Philip V of Spain (1700-46). However, the alternative candidate, Archduke Charles of Austria, promised that he would restore the traditional rights of the former Aragonese territories, and won their allegiance. He also had the support, in his fight against France, of Britain, Holland and Austria.

But Catalonia had backed the wrong horse. In 1713, Britain and the Dutch made a separate peace with France and withdrew their aid, leaving the Catalans stranded, with no possibility of victory. After a 13-month siege in which every citizen was called to arms, Barcelona fell to the French and Spanish armies on 11 September 1714. The most heroic defeat of all, the date marked the most decisive political reverse in Barcelona's history, and is now commemorated as Catalan National Day, the Diada.

In 1715, Philip V issued his decree of Nova Planta, abolishing all the remaining separate institutions of the Crown of Aragon and so, in effect, creating 'Spain' as a single, unitary state. Large-scale 'Castilianisation' of the country was initiated, and Castilian replaced the Catalan language in all official documents. In Barcelona, extra measures were taken to keep the city under control. The crumbling medieval walls and the castle on Montjuïc were refurbished with new ramparts, and a massive new citadel was built on the eastern side of the Old City, where the Parc de la Ciutadella is today. The citadel became the most hated symbol of the city's subordination.

URBAN RENAISSANCE

Politically subjugated and without a significant native ruling class, Catalonia nevertheless revived in the 18th century. Shipping picked up again, and Barcelona started a booming export trade to the New World in wines and spirits from Catalan vineyards, and textiles, wool and silk. In 1780, a merchant called Erasme de Gómina opened Barcelona's first true factory, a hand-powered weaving mill in C/Riera Alta with 800 workers. In the next decade, Catalan trade with Spanish America quadrupled; Barcelona's population had grown from 30,000 in 1720 to around 100,000 by the end of the 18th century.

The prosperity was reflected in a new wave of building in the city. Neo-classical mansions appeared, notably on C/Ample and La Rambla, but the greatest transformation was La Rambla itself. Until the 1770s, it had been a dusty, dry riverbed where country people came to sell their produce, lined on the Raval side mostly with giant religious houses and on the other with Jaume I's second wall. In 1775, the Captain-General, the Marqués de la Mina, embarked on an ambitious scheme to demolish the wall and turn La Rambla into a paved promenade. Beyond La Rambla, the previously semi-rural Raval was swiftly becoming densely populated.

Barcelona's expansion was briefly slowed by the French invasion of 1808. Napoleon sought to appeal to Catalans by offering them national recognition within his empire, but was met with curiously little response. After six years of turmoil, Barcelona's growing business class resumed its many projects in 1814, with the restoration of the Bourbon monarchy in the shape of Ferdinand VII (1808-33).

GETTING UP STEAM

Ferdinand VII attempted to reinstate the absolute monarchy of his youth and reimpose his authority over Spain's American colonies, but failed to do either. On his death he was succeeded by his three-year-old daughter Isabella II (1833-68), but the throne was also claimed by his brother Carlos, who was backed by the country's most reactionary sectors.

To defend Isabella's rights, the Regent, Ferdinand's widow Queen María Cristina, was obliged to seek the support of liberals, and so granted a very limited form of constitution. Thus began Spain's Carlist Wars, which had a powerful impact in conservative rural Catalonia, where Don Carlos's faction won a considerable following, in part because of its support for traditional local rights and customs.

In 1832, the first steam-driven factory in Spain was built on C/Tallers, sparking resistance from hand-spinners and weavers. Most of the city's factories were still relatively small, however, and the Catalan manufacturers were aware that they were at a disadvantage in competing with the industries of Britain and other countries to the north. Complicating matters further, they didn't even have the city to themselves. Not only did the anti-industrial Carlists threaten from the countryside, but Barcelona soon became a centre of radical ideas. Its people were notably rebellious, and liberal, republican, free-thinking and even utopian socialist groups proliferated between bursts of repression.

By this time, the Catalan language had been relegated to secondary status, spoken in every street but rarely written or used in cultured discourse. Then, in 1833, Bonaventura Carles Aribau published his *Oda a la Pàtria*, a romantic eulogy in Catalan of the country, its language and its past. The poem had an extraordinary impact and is still traditionally credited with initiating the Renaixença (Renaissance) of Catalan heritage and culture. The year 1848 was a high point for Barcelona and Catalonia, with the inauguration of the first railway in Spain, from Barcelona to Mataró, and the opening of the Liceu opera house.

SETTING AN EIXAMPLE

The optimism of Barcelona's new middle class was counterpointed by two persistent obstacles: the weakness of the Spanish economy as a whole, and the instability of their own society, which was reflected in atrocious labour relations. No consideration was given to the manpower behind the industrial surge: the underpaid, overworked men, women and children who lived in appalling conditions in high-rise slums within the cramped city.

In 1868, Isabella II, once a symbol of liberalism, was overthrown by a progressive revolt. During the six years of upheaval that followed, power in Madrid would be held by the provisional government, a constitutional monarchy under an Italian prince and later a federal republic. However, workers were free to organise; in 1868, Giuseppe Fanelli brought the first anarchist ideas, and two years later, the first Spanish workers' congress took place in Barcelona. The radical forces were divided between many squabbling

Trading Places

Discovering the crafty makers of the Born.

Medieval Barcelona was dense with the noise, smell and colour of craftsmen at work: knifegrinders, weavers, tanners, cobblers, mirror makers and others. Nowhere is this more evident than in the streets of the Born, where many streets are named for particular professions that once were based on them. The **Plaça de l'Àngel**, near the Jaume I metro station, was once the site of the Plaça del Blat, the grain market. Across Via Laietana, C/Bòria leads into the evocative little **Plaça de la Llana**, the old centre of wool (*llana*) trading in the city; it's now home to a hip new Kate Moss-inspired knitting shop. Alleys to the left were associated with food trades: **C/Mercaders** ('traders', probably in grain), **C/Oli** ('olive oil') just off it, and **C/Semoleres**, where semolina was made. To the right on Bòria is **C/Pou de la Cadena** ('well with a chain'), a reminder that water was essential for textile working.

After Plaça de la Llana, the Roman road's name becomes **C/Corders** ('rope-makers') and then **C/Carders** ('carders' or combers of wool). Where the name changes, there's a tiny square, Placeta Marcús, with an even smaller Romanesque chapel, the **Capella d'en Marcús**, built in the early 12th century.

Carry on a little way along C/Carders (keeping an eye out for pickpockets and bag-snatchers, who tend to favour this area), and turn left into **C/Blanqueria** ('bleaching'), where wool was washed before spinning. At **C/Assaonadors** ('tanners'), turn right; at the end of the street, behind the Marcús chapel, is a statue of John the Baptist, patron saint of the tanners' guild.

You're now at the top of **C/Montcada**, lined with medieval merchants' palaces. A short walk down, to the right is the milliners' street, **C/Sombrerers**; opposite it is Barcelona's narrowest street, **C/Mosques** ('flies'), not wide enough for an adult to lie across, and now closed off with an iron gate because too many people were urinating in it at night. C/Montcada ends at **Passeig del Born**, a hub of the city's trading for 400 years.

Turn left: on your left is **C/Flassaders** ('blanket makers'), and to the right is **C/Rec**, the old irrigation canal. Go down Rec and turn right into **C/Esparteria**, where *espart* (hemp) was woven. Turnings off it include **C/Calders**, where smelting furnaces were found, and **C/Formatgeria**, for cheese. On **C/Vidrieria**, glass was stored and sold.

Esparteria runs into C/Ases, which crosses **C/Malcuinat** ('badly cooked'). Turn left into **C/Espaseria** ('sword-making') to emerge on to the open space of Pla del Palau. Go right, then right again into **C/Canvis Vells** ('old exchange'). There's a tiny street to the left, **C/Panses**, that has an archway above it, with an ancient stone carving of a face over the second floor. This face indicated the location of a legalised brothel.

At the end of Canvis Vells is **Plaça Santa Maria** and the parish church, **Santa Maria del Mar**. On the left-hand side is **C/Abaixadors** ('unloaders'), where porters used to unload their goods; from the square, **C/Argenteria** ('silverware') will lead back to Plaça de l'Àngel.

'The bohemians were drawn to the increasingly wild nightlife of the Raval.'

factions, while the established classes of society felt increasingly threatened and called for the restoration of order. The Republic proclaimed in 1873 was unable to establish its authority, and succumbed to a military coup less than a year later.

THE MIDAS TOUCH

In 1874, the Bourbon dynasty, in the person of Alfonso XII, son of Isabella II, was restored to the Spanish throne. Workers' organisations were again suppressed. The middle classes, however, felt their confidence renewed. The 1870s saw a frenzied boom in stock speculation, known as the *febre d'or* (gold fever), and the real take-off of building in the Eixample. From the 1880s, Modernisme became the preferred style of the new district, the perfect expression of the confidence and impetus of the industrial class. The first modern Catalanist political movement was founded by Valentí Almirall.

Barcelona felt it needed to show the world all that it had achieved, and that it was more than just a 'second city'. In 1885, a promoter named Eugenio Serrano de Casanova proposed to the city council the holding of an international exhibition, such as had been held successfully in London, Paris and Vienna. Serrano was a highly dubious character who eventually made off with large amounts of public funds, but by the time this became clear, the city fathers had fully committed themselves to the event.

The Universal Exhibition of 1888 was used as a pretext for the final conversion of the Ciutadella into a park. Giant efforts had to be made to get everything ready in time, a feat that led the mayor, Francesc Rius i Taulet, to exclaim that 'the Catalan people are the yankees of Europe'. The first of Barcelona's three great efforts to demonstrate its status to the world, the 1888 Exhibition signified the consecration of the Modernista style, as well as the end of provincial, dowdy Barcelona and its establishment as a modern-day city on the international map.

THE CITY OF THE NEW CENTURY

The 1888 Exhibition left Barcelona with huge debts, a new look and many reasons to believe in itself as a paradigm of progress. The Catalan Renaixença continued, and acquired a more political tone. A truly decisive moment came in 1898, when the underlying weakness of the Spanish state was made plain over the superficial prosperity of the first years of the Bourbon restoration. It was then that Spain was forced into a short war with the United States, in which it lost its remaining empire in Cuba, the Philippines and Puerto Rico. Industrialists were horrified at losing the lucrative Cuban market, and despaired of the ability of the state ever to reform itself. Many swung behind a conservative nationalist movement: the Lliga Regionalista (Regionalist League), founded in 1901 and led by Enric Prat de la Riba and the politician-financier Francesc Cambó, promised both national revival and modern, efficient government.

At the same time, however, Barcelona continued to grow, fuelling Catalanist optimism. Above all, it had a vibrant artistic community, centred on Modernisme, which consisted of great architects and established painters such as Rusiñol and Casas, but also the penniless bohemians who gathered round them, among them the young Picasso. These were drawn to the increasingly wild nightlife of the Raval, where cabarets, bars and brothels multiplied at the end of the 19th century. Located around the cabarets, though, were the poorest of the working classes, for whom conditions had only continued to decline; Barcelona had some of the worst overcrowding and highest mortality rates in Europe. Local philanthropists called for something to be done, but Barcelona was more associated with revolutionary politics and violence than with peaceful social reform.

In 1893, more than 20 people were killed in a series of anarchist terrorist attacks, which included the notorious incident in which a bomb was hurled into the wealthy audience at the Liceu. The perpetrators acted alone, but the authorities seized the opportunity to round up the usual suspects – mainly local anarchists and radicals. Several of them, known as the 'Martyrs of Montjuïc', were later tortured and executed in the castle above the city. Retaliation came in 1906, when a Catalan anarchist tried to kill King Alfonso XIII on his wedding day.

Anarchism was still only in a fledgling state among workers in the 1900s. However, rebellious attitudes, along with growing republican sentiment and a fierce hatred of the Catholic Church, united the underclasses and led them to take to the barricades. The Setmana Tràgica (Tragic Week) of 1909 began as a protest against the conscription of troops for the colonial war in Morocco, but degenerated into a general riot, with the destruction of churches by excited mobs. Suspected culprits were summarily executed, as was the anarchist educationalist Francesc Ferrer, who was accused of 'moral responsibility' even though he wasn't even in Barcelona at the time.

These events dented the optimism of the Catalanists of the Lliga. However, in 1914, they secured from Madrid the Mancomunitat, or administrative union, of the four Catalan provinces, the first joint government of any kind in Catalonia in 200 years. Its first president was Prat de la Riba, who would be succeeded on his death in 1917 by the architect Puig i Cadafalch. However, the Lliga's plans for an orderly Catalonia were to be obstructed by a further surge in social tensions.

CHAMPAGNE AND SOCIALISTS

Spain's neutral status during World War I gave a huge boost to the Spanish, and especially Catalan, economy. Exports soared as Catalonia's manufacturers made millions supplying uniforms to the French army. Barcelona's industry was at last able to diversify from textiles into engineering, chemicals and other more modern sectors. The war also set off massive inflation, driving people in their thousands from rural Spain into the big cities. Barcelona doubled in size in 20 years to become the largest city in Spain, and also the fulcrum of Spanish politics. Workers' wages, meanwhile, had lost half their real value.

The chief channel of protest in Barcelona was the anarchist workers' union, the Confederación Nacional del Trabajo (CNT), constituted in 1910, which gained half a million members in Catalonia by 1919. The CNT and the socialist Union General de Trabajadores (UGT) launched a joint general strike in 1917, roughly co-ordinated with a campaign by the Lliga and other liberal politicians for political reform. However, the politicians soon withdrew at the prospect of serious social unrest. Inflation continued to intensify, and in 1919 Barcelona was paralysed for more than two months by a CNT general strike over union recognition. Employers refused to recognise the CNT, and the most intransigent among them hired gunmen to get rid of union leaders. Union activists replied in kind, and virtual guerrilla warfare developed between the CNT, the employers and the state. More than 800 people were killed on the city's streets over five years.

In 1923, in response both to the chaos in the city and a crisis in the war in Morocco, the Captain-General of Barcelona, Miguel Primo de Rivera, staged a coup and established a military dictatorship under King Alfonso XIII. The CNT was already exhausted, and it was suppressed. Conservative Catalanists, longing for an end to disorder and the revolutionary threat, initially supported the coup, but were rewarded by the abolition of the Mancomunitat and a vindictive campaign by the Primo regime against the Catalan language and national symbols.

This, however, achieved the opposite of the desired effect, helping to radicalise and popularise Catalan nationalism. After the terrible struggles of the previous years, the 1920s were actually a time of notable prosperity for many in Barcelona, as some of the wealth recently accumulated filtered through the economy. It was also, though, a highly politicised society, in which new magazines and forums for discussion – despite the restrictions of the dictatorship – found a ready audience.

IN CONTEXT

A prime motor of Barcelona's prosperity in the 1920s was the International Exhibition of 1929, the second of the city's great showcase events. It had been proposed by Cambó and Catalan business groups, but Primo de Rivera saw that it could also serve as a propaganda event for his regime. A huge number of public projects were undertaken in association with the main event, including the post office in Via Laietana, the Estació de França and Barcelona's first metro line, from Plaça Catalunya to Plaça d'Espanya. By 1930, Barcelona was very different from the place it had been in 1910; it contained more than a million people, and its urban sprawl had crossed into neighbouring towns such as Hospitalet and Santa Coloma.

THE REPUBLIC SUPPRESSED

Despite the Exhibition's success, Primo de Rivera resigned in January 1930, exhausted. The king appointed another soldier, General Berenguer, as prime minister, with the mission of restoring stability. The dictatorship, though, had fatally discredited the old regime, and a protest movement spread across Catalonia against the monarchy. In early 1931, Berenguer called local elections as a first step towards a restoration of constitutional rule. The outcome was a complete surprise, for republicans were elected in all of Spain's cities. Ecstatic crowds poured into the streets, and Alfonso XIII abdicated. The Second Spanish Republic was proclaimed on 14 April 1931.

The Republic arrived amid real euphoria, especially in Catalonia, where it was associated with hopes for both social change and national reaffirmation. The clear winner of the elections in the country had been the Esquerra Republicana, a leftist Catalanist group led by Francesc Macià. A raffish, elderly figure, Macià was one of the first politicians in Spain to win genuine affection from ordinary people. He declared Catalonia to be an independent republic within an Iberian federation of states, but later agreed to accept autonomy within the Spanish Republic.

The Generalitat was re-established as a government that would, potentially, acquire wide powers. All aspects of Catalan culture were then in expansion, and a popular press in Catalan achieved a wide readership. Barcelona was also a small but notable centre of the avant-garde. Miró and Dalí had already made their mark in painting; under the Republic, the Amics de l'Art Nou (ADLAN, Friends of New Art) group worked to promote contemporary art, while the GATCPAC architectural collective sought to bring rationalist architecture to the city.

In Madrid, the Republic's first government was a coalition of republicans and socialists led by Manuel Azaña, its overriding goal to modernise Spanish society through liberal-democratic reforms. However, as social tensions intensified, the coalition collapsed, and a conservative republican party, with support from the traditional Spanish right, secured power shortly after new elections in 1933. For Catalonia, the prospect of a return to right-wing rule prompted fears that it would immediately abrogate the Generalitat's hard-won powers. On 6 October 1934, while a general strike was launched against the central government in Asturias and some other parts of Spain, Lluís Companys, leader of the Generalitat since Macià's death the previous year, declared Catalonia independent. The 'uprising' turned out to be something of a farce, however: the Generalitat had no means of resisting the army, and the new 'Catalan Republic' was rapidly suppressed. The Generalitat was suspended and its leaders imprisoned.

Over the following year, fascism seemed to become a real threat for the left, as political positions became polarised. Then, in February 1936, elections were won by the Popular Front of the left across the country. The Generalitat was reinstated, and in Catalonia the next few months were peaceful. In the rest of Spain, though, tensions were close to bursting point; right-wing politicians, refusing to accept the loss of power, talked openly of the need for the military to intervene. In July, the stadium on Montjuïc was to be the site of the Popular Olympics, a leftist alternative to the 1936 Olympics in Nazi Germany. On 18 July, the day of the Games' inauguration, army generals launched a coup against the Republic and its left-wing governments, expecting no resistance.

UP IN ARMS

In Barcelona, militants from the unions and leftist parties, on alert for weeks, poured into the streets to oppose the troops in fierce fighting. Over the course of 19 July, the military were worn down, and finally surrendered in the Hotel Colón on Plaça Catalunya (by the corner with Passeig de Gràcia, the site of which is now occupied by the Radio Nacional de España building). Opinions have always differed as to who could claim most credit for this remarkable popular victory: workers' militants have suggested it was the 'people in arms' who defeated the army, while others stress the importance of the police remaining loyal to the Generalitat throughout the struggle. A likely answer is that they actually encouraged each other.

Tension released, the city was taken over by the revolution. Militias of the CNT, different Marxist parties and other left-wing factions marched off to Aragon, led by streetfighters such as the anarchists Durruti and García Oliver, to continue the battle. The army rising had failed in Spain's major cities but won footholds in Castile, Aragon and the south, although in the heady atmosphere of Barcelona in July 1936 it was often assumed that their resistance could not last and that the people's victory was near inevitable.

Far from the front, Barcelona was the chief centre of the revolution in republican Spain, the only truly proletarian city. Its middle class avoided the streets, where, as Orwell recorded in his *Homage to Catalonia*, everyone you saw wore workers' clothing. Barcelona became a magnet for leftists from around the world, drawing writers André Malraux, Ernest Hemingway and Octavio Paz. All kinds of industries and public services were collectivised, including cinemas, the phone system and food distribution. Ad hoc 'control patrols' of the revolutionary militias roamed the streets supposedly checking for suspected right-wing agents and sometimes carrying out summary executions, although this was condemned by many leftist leaders.

The alliance between the different left-wing groups was unstable and riddled with tensions. The communists, who had some extra leverage because the Soviet Union was

IN CONTEXT

Anarchists of the **CNT militia** in 1936.

the only country prepared to give the Spanish Republic arms, demanded the integration of these loosely organised militias into a conventional army under a strong central authority. The following months saw continual political infighting between the discontented CNT, the radical Marxist party Partit Obrer d'Unificació Marxista (POUM) and the communists. Co-operation broke down totally in May 1937, when republican and communist troops seized the telephone building in Plaça Catalunya (on the corner of Portal de l'Àngel) from a CNT committee, sparking the confused war-within-the-civil-war witnessed by Orwell from the roof of the Teatre Poliorama. A temporary agreement was patched up, but shortly afterwards the POUM was banned, and the CNT excluded from power. A new republican central government was formed under Dr Juan Negrín, a socialist allied to the communists.

After that, the war gradually became more of a conventional conflict. This did little, however, to improve the Republic's position, for the nationalists under General Francisco Franco and their German and Italian allies had been continually gaining ground throughout it all. Madrid was under siege, and the capital of the Republic was moved to Valencia, and then to Barcelona, in November 1937.

Catalonia received thousands of refugees, as food shortages and the lack of armaments ground down morale. Barcelona also had the sad distinction of being the first major city in Europe to be subjected to sustained intensive bombing – to an extent that has rarely been appreciated – with heavy raids throughout 1938, especially by Italian bombers based in Mallorca. The Basque Country and Asturias had already fallen to Franco, and in March 1938 his troops reached the Mediterranean near Castellón, cutting the main Republican zone in two. The Republic had one last throw of the dice, in the Battle of the Ebro in the summer of 1938, when for months the Popular Army struggled to retake control of the river. After that, the Republic was exhausted. Barcelona fell to the Francoist army on 26 January 1939. Half a million refugees fled to France, to be interned in barbed-wire camps along the beaches.

THE FRANCO YEARS

In Catalonia, the Franco regime was iron-fisted and especially vengeful. Thousands of Catalan republicans and leftists were executed, among them Generalitat president Lluís Companys; exile and deportation were the fate of thousands more. Publishing, teaching and any other public cultural expression in Catalan, including even speaking it in the street, were prohibited, and every Catalanist monument in the city was dismantled. All independent political activity was suspended, and the entire political and cultural development of the country was brought to an abrupt halt.

The epic nature of the Spanish Civil War is known worldwide; more present in the collective memory of Barcelona, though, is the long *posguerra* or post-war period, which lasted for nearly two decades after 1939. During those years, the city was impoverished, and food and electricity were rationed; Barcelona would not regain its prior standard of living until the mid 1950s. Nevertheless, migrants in flight from the still more brutal poverty of the south flowed into the city, occupying precarious shanty towns around Montjuïc and other areas in the outskirts.

The Franco regime was subject to a UN embargo after World War II. Years of international isolation and attempted self-sufficiency came to an end in 1953, when the country was at least partially re-admitted to the western fold. Even a limited opening to the outside world meant that foreign money finally began to enter the country, and the regime relaxed some control over its population. In 1959, the Plan de Estabilización ('Stabilisation Plan'), drawn up by Catholic technocrats of Opus Dei, brought Spain definitively within the western economy, throwing its doors wide open to tourism and foreign investment. After years of austerity, tourist income at last brought the Europe-wide 1960s boom to Spain and set off change at an extraordinary pace.

After the years of repression and the years of development, 1966 marked the beginning of what became known as *tardofranquisme*, 'late Francoism'. Having made its opening to the outside world, the regime was losing its grip, and labour, youth and student movements began to emerge from beneath the shroud of repression. Nevertheless, the Franco regime never hesitated to show its strength. Strikes and demonstrations were dealt with savagely, and just months before the dictator's death, the last person to be executed in Spain by the traditional method of the garrotte, a Catalan anarchist named Puig Antich, went to his death in Barcelona. In 1973, however, Franco's closest follower, Admiral Carrero Blanco, was assassinated by a bomb planted by the Basque terrorist group ETA, leaving no one to guard over the core values of the regime. Change was in the air.

GENERALISIMO TO GENERALITAT

When Franco died on 20 November 1975, the people of Barcelona took to the streets in celebration; by evening, there was not a bottle of cava left in the city. But no one knew quite what would happen next. The Bourbon monarchy was restored under King Juan Carlos, but his attitude and intentions were not clear. In 1976, he charged a little-known Francoist bureaucrat, Adolfo Suárez, with leading the country to democracy.

The first years of Spain's 'transition' were difficult. Nationalist and other demonstrations continued to be repressed by the police with considerable brutality, and far-right groups threatened less open violence. However, political parties were legalised, and June 1977 saw the first democratic elections since 1936. They were won across Spain by Suárez's own new party, the Union de Centro Democratico (UCD), and in Catalonia by a mixture of socialists, communists and nationalists.

It was, again, not clear how Suárez expected to deal with the demands of Catalonia, but shortly after the elections he surprised everyone by visiting the president of the Generalitat in exile, veteran pre-Civil War politician Josep Tarradellas. His office was the only institution of the old Republic to be so recognised, perhaps because Suárez astutely identified in the old man a fellow conservative. Tarradellas was invited to return as provisional president of a restored Generalitat; he arrived amid huge crowds in October 1977.

IN CONTEXT

Frank Gehry's Fish. *See p32.*

The following year, the first free council elections since 1936 were held in Barcelona. They were won by the Socialist Party, with Narcís Serra appointed as mayor. The party has retained control of the council ever since. In 1980, elections to the restored Generalitat were won by Jordi Pujol and his party, Convergència i Unió, who held power for 23 years.

Inseparable from the restoration of democracy was a complete change in the city's atmosphere after 1975. New freedoms – in culture, sexuality and work – were explored, and newly released energies expressed in a multitude of ways. Barcelona soon began to look different too, as the inherent dowdiness of the Franco years was swept away by a new Catalan style for the new Catalonia: postmodern, high-tech, punkish, comic strip, minimalist and tautly fashionable. This emphasis first began underground, but it was soon taken up by public authorities and, above all, the Ajuntament, as a part of its drive to reverse the policies of the regime. The technocrats in the socialist city administration began to 'recover' the city from its neglected state, and in doing so enlisted the elite of the Catalan intellectual and artistic community in their support. No one epitomises this more than Oriol Bohigas, the architect and writer who was long the city's head of culture and chief planner. A programme of urban renewal was initiated, beginning with the open spaces, public art and low-level initiatives, such as the campaign in which hundreds of historic façades were given an overdue facelift.

This ambitious, emphatically modern approach to urban problems acquired much greater focus after Barcelona's bid to host the 1992 Olympic Games was accepted, in 1986. Far more than just a sports event, the Games were to be Barcelona's third great effort to cast aside suggestions of second-city status and show the world its wares. The exhibitions of 1888 and 1929 had seen developments in the Ciutadella and on and around Montjuïc; the Olympics provided an opening for work on a citywide scale. Taking advantage of the public and private investment the Games would attract, Barcelona planned an all-new orientation of itself towards the sea, in a programme of urban renovation of a scope unseen in Europe since the years after World War II.

Inseparable from all this was Pasqual Maragall, mayor of Barcelona from 1982 to 1997, a tireless 'Mr Barcelona' who appeared in every possible forum to expound his vision of the role of cities. He intervened personally to set guidelines for projects and to secure the participation of major international architects. In the process, Barcelona, a byword for modern blight only a few years before, was turned into a reference point in urban affairs.

ENDGAMES

The Games were held in July and August 1992 and universally hailed as an outstanding success. The cultural and architectural legacy of the games remains strong even today, with landmarks such as Frank Gehry's Fish now major tourist attractions. However, Pasqual Maragall, was to stand down amid general surprise in 1997, and went on to become the Socialist candidate for President of the Generalitat in 1999. He would not succeed until 2003, when he enjoyed a muted triumph in the regional elections. Maragall took control of the Generalitat in return for a commitment to push strongly for a new Autonomy Statute. In this he was partly successful, but many felt he should have pushed for more devolution of power, and he stepped down for the elections in November 2006, and in his place the PSC chose as candidate Andalucía-born José Montilla.

Those elections also failed to bring home an absolute winner; further negotiations resulted in the same tripartite coalition as in the previous election, therefore giving the presidency to Montilla, the first ever non-Catalan President of the Generalitat. Over at City Hall, meanwhile, Maragall had been replaced with smooth-talking Joan Clos. His successor, Jordi Hereu, brought the Socialist Party to another (slim) victory in the local elections of May 2007, having also formed a coalition with the 'eco-communists' (ICV), though not, this time, with Esquerra Republicana (ERC), the Republican left.

The Spanish general elections held in March 2008 saw a return of José Luis Zapatero and his Socialist party for a second term – meaning that the city, region and country are still in socialist hands.

Key Events

Barcelona in brief.

c15 BC Town of Barcino founded by Roman soldiers.
cAD 350 Roman stone city walls built.
719 Muslims attack and seize Barcelona.
801 Barcelona taken by the Franks.
985 Muslims sack Barcelona; Count Borrell II renounces Frankish sovereignty.
1035-76 Count Ramon Berenguer I of Barcelona extends his possessions into southern France.
1137 Count Ramon Berenguer IV marries Petronella of Aragon, uniting the two states in the Crown of Aragon.
1213 Pere I is killed; virtually all his lands north of Pyrenees are seized by France.
1229 Jaume I conquers Mallorca, then Ibiza (1235) and Valencia (1238); second city wall built in Barcelona.
1274 Consell de Cent, municipal government of Barcelona, established.
1282 Pere II captures Sicily.
1298 Work begins on Gothic cathedral.
1323-34 Conquest of Corsica, Sardinia.
1347-48 Black Death halves population.
1462-72 Catalan civil war.
1479 Ferdinand II inherits Crown of Aragon, and with his wife Isabella unites the Spanish kingdoms.
1492 Final expulsion of Jews.
1640 Catalan national revolt, the Guerra dels Segadors.
1652 Barcelona falls to Spanish army.
1702 War of Spanish Succession begins.
1714 Barcelona falls to Franco-Spanish army after siege.
1715 Nova Planta decree abolishes Catalan institutions; new ramparts and citadel built around Barcelona.
1808-13 French occupation.
1814 Restoration of Ferdinand VII.
1833 Aribau publishes *Oda a la Pàtria*, beginning of Catalan cultural renaissance. Carlist wars begin.
1836-37 Dissolution of monasteries.
1842-44 Barcelona bombarded for the last time from Montjuïc, to quell Jamancia revolt.
1854 Demolition of city walls.

1855 First general strike is suppressed.
1859 Cerdà plan for the Eixample approved.
1868 September: revolution overthrows Isabella II. November: first anarchist meetings held in Barcelona.
1873 First Spanish Republic.
1874 Bourbon monarchy restored.
1882 Work begins on Sagrada Família.
1888 Barcelona Universal Exhibition.
1899 Electric trams introduced.
1909 Setmana Tràgica, anti-church and anti-army riots.
1910 CNT anarchist workers' union founded.
1921 First Barcelona metro line opened.
1923 Primo de Rivera establishes dictatorship in Spain.
1929 Barcelona International Exhibition.
1931 14 April: Second Spanish Republic.
1934 October: Generalitat attempts revolt against new right-wing government in Madrid, and is then suspended.
1936 February: Popular Front wins elections; Catalan Generalitat restored. 19 July: military uprising against left-wing government is defeated in Barcelona.
1939 Barcelona taken by Franco's army.
1959 Stabilisation Plan opens up the Spanish economy.
1975 Franco dies.
1977 First democratic general elections in Spain since 1936; provisional Catalan Generalitat re-established.
1978 First democratic local elections in Barcelona won by Socialists.
1980 Generalitat fully re-established under Jordi Pujol.
1992 Olympics Games held in Barcelona.
1997 Joan Clos elected mayor.
2003 Coalition of left-wing parties wins control of Generalitat.
2004 PSOE (Socialist Party) wins Spanish elections.
2006 José Montilla becomes President of the Generalitat.
2007 Jordi Hereu replaces Joan Clos as mayor.

IN CONTEXT

Cocking a snook at la crisis.

TEXT: WILLIAM TRUINI

Barcelona Today

William Truini writes regularly for Barcelona Metropolitan *and has contributed to* Time Out Barcelona *since 1998. He is the translator of more than 20 books about Barcelona and Spain.*

Global economic crisis or not, Barcelona has managed to keep its head up. Surrounded by a breaking storm of negative signals from the US and the rest of Europe, life in Barcelona has merrily continued for most, almost as if the city existed on an island of its own prosperity. Here and there, however, signs have begun to pop up indicating that all is not entirely well.

The first jolt came in July 2008, when more local firms filed for bankruptcy than had done so during the entire previous year. Most of these failed ventures were linked to the construction and property industries. Fair enough, said some: the city had binged on a home-grown property boom for a decade, so it was only logical that the trend should slow. Indeed, for many younger *barcelonins* subsisting on stagnant wages and dreaming of an affordable home, a decline in property prices, however moderate, was seen as a blessing. But for others, the news is far from pleasant.

'The relationship between local residents and tourism has become tense.'

EMPTY ROOMS

Although more en venta ('for sale') signs can be seen on balcony windows around town, the city's bursting real estate bubble is perhaps most noticeable in the brand new Diagonal-Mar area. Built along the sea near the colossal, underused Fòrum complex, the zone was designed to become a major upscale residential and business centre, its two dozen or so luxury high-rises forming a scaled-down version of Miami Beach. When the high-end flats with their sea views hit the market in 2003, they sold quickly enough, but the area is now a ghost town. Less than 30 per cent of the flats are occupied; the rest were bought as investments and remain eerily empty. While the area has attracted companies looking for state-of-the-art office space, the streets are deserted after working hours.

The decline in the construction and property markets has also had an impact on city government. The latest figures indicate that in 2009, taxes paid to the city council from construction work will be down by almost €25 million. At the helm of the council, Barcelona's mayor, Socialist Jordi Hereu, holds a delicate balance of power in partnership with another left-leaning party, the environmentalist Inicativa per Catalunya-Els Verds. This two-party coalition, formed after Hereu's unconvincing victory at the polls in 2007, is the weakest left-wing government – in terms of seats and voters' support– to run Barcelona since the Socialists gained power three decades ago. The city's other left-wing party, the Catalan nationalist Esquerra Republicana, abandoned Hereu to form an unlikely alliance with the conservative Convergencia i Unió.

BUT STILL THEY COME...

Despite a tightening of belts in certain sectors, the city still enjoys a healthy revenue from its single largest industry: tourism. Although figures in mid 2008 indicated that the number of visitors to Barcelona dropped for the first time since the 1990s, revenue from these visitors was up a spectacular 20 per cent for the first half of 2008, meaning fewer visitors spent more money. And the four per cent decline in visitors in 2008 is perhaps partly explained by the unusually large numbers (seven million) who came the previous year.

Surely, a marketing genius must lurk in Barcelona's tourism office. Through strategic advertising, the city has managed to package its gastronomy, design, architecture, music and shopping facilities to appeal to a wealthier class of visitor. This campaign has also attracted more specialised congresses, notably in telecommunications, medicine and pharmaceuticals, whose well-off attendees commonly split their time between meetings, sightseeing and nights out on the town. Cruise ships are also pulling into port in greater numbers, unloading their well-tanned ranks of free-spending passengers for a day or two.

Attempts to turn the city into an upscale resort are even visible in that most popular of places: the city beach. Up until a few years ago, the beach *xiringuitos* were a motley collection of food and drink stands, many blaring popular music. Now, they've been upgraded and serve considerably more expensive fare.

As one might expect in a place that receives over four times its own numbers in visitors each year, the relationship between locas and tourism has grown tense. Residents near the Sagrada Família threw up their arms in despair in 2008, and actively protested at the daily arrival of some 200 tourist coaches rumbling up and parking in front of Gaudí's unfinished masterpiece. In the Old City, *barcelonins* have traditionally taken their Sunday stroll along La Rambla, but they're now being crowded out by hordes of sightseers, and the entire Born neighbourhood has started to resemble a tasteful if pricey outdoor boutique mall. Tourism has also aggravated the city's housing shortage: thousands of flats have been converted into short-term holiday lets, most in the city centre.

Topping things off, a glaring new symbol of the growing divide between tourist culture and local culture has appeared in the form of a shiny luxury hotel on the Rambla del Raval, a building that is literally armoured in steel mesh to protect the privacy and safety of its high-income guests in the middle of what is still a fairly rough working-class neighbourhood. Adding to the symbolism, if not the historical irony, a plaque directly across from the hotel on the corner of C/Sant Rafael commemorates the early 20th-century hero of working-class rights Salvador Seguí, *El noi del sucre* (the 'sugar boy'), who was murdered by company thugs on that very corner.

In July 2008, aware that the city may have passed the limits of sustainability both ecologically and psychologically, and simultaneously anxious to keep the flow of euro-laden visitors arriving, the city council announced the need to create a 'strategic plan for tourism'. Billed as 'a profound reflection on the city's model of tourism' and designed to save Barcelona from its own success, the scheme will run from 2010 to 2015. Exactly what measures will be taken is anybody's guess, but if the previously noted trend towards

Bike It or Not

Barcelona rediscovers pedal power.

Catalans have a knack for reinventing things. They turned art nouveau into Modernisme, champagne into cava, and nouvelle cuisine into nova cuina catalana, among other notable feats. And now the time has come for urban cycling.

For long, dark decades, Barcelona turned its back on the bike. Even up to recent years, regular cyclists in the city were a rare sight. Suddenly, however, Barcelona has rapidly and passionately rediscovered pedal power. Almost out of the blue, it's become common to see cyclists zipping through traffic, or streaming steadily along bike lines like orderly ants on the way to or from work.

In a city where heavy and constant motor vehicle traffic has created some of the most polluted air in Europe (according to a 2007 World Health Oraganisation study, Barcelona's air quality is the third worst among European cities), the appearance of so many bicycles is literally a breath of fresh air. A good measure of responsibility for the change lies with the city council's new public bike-sharing initiative, Bicing (www.bicing.com). By anyone's standards, the service has been a big hit. After just 18 months in operation, more than 130,000 people had signed up to use Bicing's 6,000 red and white bikes, which can be found all over the city.

The explosion of bikes has caused a minor social revolution. On any given day of the week, you'll easily spot dozens of middle-aged or even elderly women learning to ride bicycles in the quiet Parc de la Barceloneta. When they were young, one 58-year-old lady explained, very few girls were taught to ride because in Franco's Spain it was seen as a sin for women to do so. As the city embraces biking en masse, more and more of these women have found the courage to learn to ride. Cycling, for them, means freedom.

luxury and display is any indication of what will happen in the future, it wouldn't be at all surprising if, in ten years time, Barcelona starts to look like the new St Moritz.

RENEWING THE CITY

All this is not to say that the city isn't employing other tactics to wean itself from the easy, if potentially fickle, lure of mass tourism. The city has spent heavily on new infrastructure designed to transform Barcelona into one of the poles of the so-called 'knowledge economy'. Notable among these facilities are the €100-million Parc de Recerca Biomèdica de Barcelona (PRBB), a biomedical research centre (unmistakeable for its large horseshoe shape) that currently houses 80 international research teams as well as some 4,000 mice; and the Nexus I and II buildings on the Universitat Politècnica de Catalunya's campus, home to Europe's most powerful supercomputer, the MareNostrum. The gamble appears to be paying off, as the city has attracted some of the world's most important high-tech companies: Intel has set up its only university research lab outside the USA in Nexus II.

Plans are even in the pipeline to build a major research centre for renewable energy, something the city council has made considerable noise about as it tries to turn Barcelona into a 'sustainable city'. To this end, the council has instituted obligatory solar panels for heating water on all new buildings, and introduced a public bike-sharing service, Bicing, which has enjoyed wild popularity.

If a lot of these initiatives sound like a city trying to take responsibility for its own destiny, it's fitting that in 2008, Barcelona recovered a building that long stood as a symbol of its own lack of self-determination. After a long wait, in June 2008, the Spanish government handed over the keys of the castle of Montjuïc to the city's residents. Controlled by Madrid for most of the past 300 years, and used to dominate and occasionally bombard the city, the castle was also where the Franco regime executed political prisoners. Now, in one of the many deft about-faces for which Barcelona is known, the city has grand plans to turn the castle into an official Peace Centre.

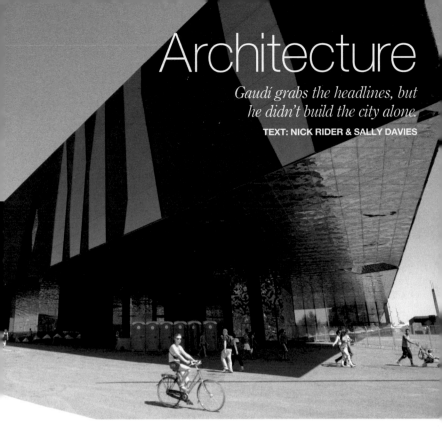

Architecture

Gaudí grabs the headlines, but he didn't build the city alone.

TEXT: NICK RIDER & SALLY DAVIES

Architecture is sometimes regarded as Catalonia's greatest contribution to art history. Catalan craftsmen have been famed since the Middle Ages for their use of fine materials and skilled finishings, while Catalan architects have long been both artists and innovators: traditional Catalan brick-vaulting techniques were the basis of visionary structural innovations that allowed later architects to span larger spaces and build higher structures. Contemporary Catalan architects such as Ricardo Bofill and Enric Miralles have inherited the international prestige of their forebears.

Unlike many European cities, Barcelona has never rested on its architectural laurels or tried to preserve its old buildings as relics. Contemporary buildings are often daringly constructed alongside or even within old ones, a mix of old and new that characterises some of the most successful recent projects seen in Barcelona. Barcelona's citizens take a keen interest in their buildings, and tourists are encouraged to do the same: a range of architectural guides is available, some in English, and informative leaflets on building styles are offered (in English) at the city's tourist offices.

Sant Pau del Camp.

ROMAN TO GOTHIC

The Roman citadel of Barcino was founded on the hill of Mons Taber, just behind the cathedral, which to this day remains the religious and civic heart of the city. It left an important legacy in the fourth-century city wall, fragments of which are visible at many points around the Old City. Barcelona's next occupiers, the Visigoths, left little, although a trio of fine Visigothic churches survives in nearby Terrassa.

When the Catalan state began to form under the counts of Barcelona from the ninth century, its dominant architecture was Romanesque. The Pyrenean valleys hold hundreds of fine Romanesque buildings, notably at Sant Pere de Rodes, Ripoll, Sant Joan de les Abadesses and Besalú, but there are very few in Barcelona. On the right-hand side of the cathedral (if you're looking at the main façade) sits the 13th-century chapel of Santa Llúcia, eventually incorporated into the later building; the church of Santa Anna is tucked away near Plaça Catalunya; and the Born is home to the Capella d'en Marcús, a tiny travellers' chapel. But the city's greatest Romanesque monument is the beautifully plain 12th-century church and cloister of **Sant Pau del Camp** (*see p82*), part of a larger monastery.

By the 13th century, Barcelona was the capital of a trading empire and had started to grow rapidly. The settlements – called *ravals* or *vilanoves* – that had sprung up outside the Roman walls were brought within the city by the building of Jaume I's second set of walls, which extended west to La Rambla. This commercial growth and political eminence set the scene for the great flowering of the Catalan Gothic style, which saw the construction of many of the city's most important civic and religious buildings. The cathedral was begun in 1298, in place of an 11th-century building. Work began on the **Ajuntament** (Casa de la Ciutat; *see p61*) and the **Palau de la Generalitat** (*see p65*), later subject to extensive alteration, in 1372 and 1403 respectively. Major additions were made to the Palau Reial of the Catalan-Aragonese kings, especially the **Saló del Tinell** of 1359-62. And the great hall of **La Llotja** (the Stock Exchange; *see p71*) was built between 1380 and 1392.

The Catalan Gothic style is distinguished from classic northern Gothic by its relative simplicity. It also gives more prominence to solid, plain walls between towers and columns, rather than the empty spaces between intricate flying buttresses that were the hallmarks of the great French cathedrals, with the result that Catalan buildings appear much larger. On the façades, as much emphasis is given to horizontals as to verticals; octagonal towers end in cornices and flat roofs, not spires. And the decorative intricacies are mainly confined to windows, portals, arches and gargoyles. Many churches have no aisles but only a single nave; the classic example of this style is the beautiful **Santa Maria del Pi** in Plaça del Pi, built between 1322 and 1453.

The Catalan Gothic style went on to establish a historic benchmark for Catalan architecture: simple and robust, yet elegant and practical. Sophisticated techniques were developed as part of the style: the use of transverse arches supporting timber roofs, for instance, allowed the spanning of great halls uninterrupted by columns, a system used in Guillem Carbonel's Saló del Tinell. The **Drassanes**, built from 1378 as the royal shipyards (and now the Museu Marítim; see p87), is really just a very beautiful shed, but its enormous parallel aisles make it one of the city's most imposing spaces.

Around this time, La Ribera (nowadays known as Sant Pere and the Born) was the commercial centre of the city. Its preeminence resulted in the construction of **Santa Maria del Mar** (see p75), the magnificent masterpiece of Catalan Gothic built between 1329 and 1384. The building's superb proportions are based on a series of squares imposed on one another, with three aisles of almost equal height. The interior is staggering in its austerity.

The architecture of medieval Barcelona, at least that of its noble and merchant residences, can be seen at its best along **Carrer Montcada** (see p71), next to Santa Maria. Built by the city's merchant elite at the height of its confidence and wealth, this line of buildings conforms to a very Mediterranean style of urban palace and makes maximum use of space. A plain exterior faces the street with heavy doors opening into an imposing patio; on one side, a grand external staircase leads to the main rooms on the first floor (*planta noble*), which often have elegant open loggias.

MARKING TIME

By the beginning of the 16th century, a period of political and economic downturn, the number of patrons for new city buildings declined. The next 300 years saw plenty of construction, but rarely in any distinctively Catalan style; as a result, these structures have often been disregarded.

The Church also built lavishly around this time. Of the Baroque convents and churches along La Rambla, the **Betlem** (1680-1729), at the corner of C/Carme, is the most important survivor. Later Baroque churches include **Sant Felip Neri** (1721-52) and **La Mercè** (1765-75; see p61). Another addition, after the siege of Barcelona in 1714, was new military architecture, since the city was encased in ramparts and fortresses. Examples include the **Castell de Montjuïc** (see p90), the buildings in the **Ciutadella** (see p75), and Barceloneta.

One more positive 18th-century alteration was the conversion of La Rambla into a paved promenade, a project that began in 1775 with the demolition of Jaume I's second wall. Neo-classical palaces were built alongside: **La Virreina** and the **Palau Moja** (at the corner of C/Portaferrisa) both date from the 1770s. Also from that time, but in a less classical style, is the **Gremial dels Velers** (Candlemakers' Guild) at Via Laietana 50, with its two-colour stucco decoration.

However, it wasn't until the closure of the monasteries in the 1820s and '30s that major rebuilding on La Rambla could begin. Most of the new constructions were in international, neo-classical styles. The site that now holds the **Mercat de la Boqueria** was first remodelled in 1836-40 as Plaça Sant Josep to a design by Francesc Daniel Molina, based on the English Regency style of John Nash; it's now buried beneath the 1870s market building, but its Doric colonnade can still be detected. Molina also designed the **Plaça Reial** (see p59), begun in 1848. Other fine examples include the colonnaded Porxos d'en Xifré, blocks built in 1836 opposite the Llotja on Passeig Isabel II by the Port Vell.

BIRTH OF THE MODERN CITY

In the 1850s, Barcelona was able to expand both physically, with the demolition of the walls, and psychologically, with economic expansion and the cultural reawakening of the Catalan Renaixença. From the start, one of the characteristics of modern Barcelona was clearly visible: audacious planning. Barcelona eventually expanded outwards and was

Casa Batlló. *See p46.*

connected to Gràcia and other outlying towns through the **Eixample** (*see pp99-108*), designed by Ildefons Cerdà. An engineer by trade, Cerdà was influenced by utopian socialist ideas, and concerned with the poor condition of workers' housing in the Old City.

With its straight lines and grids, Cerdà's plan was closely related to the visionary rationalist ideas of its time, as was the idea of placing two of its main avenues along a geographic parallel and a meridian. Cerdà's central aim was to alleviate overpopulation while encouraging social equality by using quadrangular blocks of a standard size, with strict building controls to ensure they were built only on two sides, to a limited height, and with a garden. Each district would be of 20 blocks, with all community necessities.

However, this idealised use of space was rarely achieved, with private developers regarding Cerdà's restrictions as pointless interference. New buildings exceeded planned heights, and all the blocks from Plaça Catalunya to the Diagonal were enclosed. Even the planned gardens failed to withstand the onslaught of construction. Still, the development of the Eixample did see the refinement of a specific type of building: the apartment block, with giant flats on the principal floor (first above the ground), often with large glassed-in galleries for the drawing room, and small flats above. In time, the interplay between the Eixample's straight lines and the disorderly tangle of the older city became an essential part of the city's identity.

MODERNISME

The art nouveau style was the leading influence in the decorative arts in Europe and the US between 1890 and 1914. In Barcelona, its influence merged with the cultural and political movement of the Catalan Renaixença to produce what became known as Modernisme (used here in Catalan to avoid confusion with 'modernism' in English, which refers to 20th-century functional styles).

For all Catalonia's traditions in building and the arts, no style is as synonymous with Barcelona as Modernisme. This is due to the huge modern popularity of Antoni Gaudí, its most famous practitioner, and to its mix of decoration, eccentric unpredictability, dedicated craftsmanship and practicality. Modernisme can also be seen as matching

'Although Gaudí is widely regarded as the genius of the Modernista movement, he was really an unclassifiable one-off.'

certain archetypes of Catalan character, as a passionately nationalist expression that made use of Catalan traditions of design and craftwork. Artists strove to revalue the best of Catalan art, showing interest in the Romanesque and Gothic of the Catalan Golden Age; Domènech i Montaner combined iron-frame construction with distinctive brick Catalan styles from the Middle Ages, regarding them as an 'expression of the Catalan earth'.

Art nouveau had a tendency to look at both the past and future, combining a love of decoration with new industrial techniques and materials. Even as they constructed a nostalgic vision of the Catalan motherland, Modernista architects experimented with new technology. Encouraged by wealthy patrons, they designed works made of iron and glass, introduced electricity, water and gas piping to building plans, were the first to tile bathroom and kitchen walls, made a point of allowing extensive natural light and fresh air into all rooms, and toyed with the most advanced, revolutionary expressionism.

Catalan Modernista creativity was at its peak from 1888 to 1908. The Eixample is the style's display case, with the greatest concentration of art nouveau in Europe, but Modernista buildings can be found in innumerable other locations: in streets behind the Avda Paral·lel and villas on Tibidabo, in shop interiors and dark hallways, in country town halls and in the cava cellars of the Penedès.

International interest in Gaudí often eclipses the fact that many other remarkable architects and designers worked at the same time. Indeed, Modernisme was much more than an architectural style: the movement also included painters such as Ramon Casas, Santiago Rusiñol and Isidre Nonell, sculptors Josep Llimona, Miquel Blay and Eusebi Arnau, and furniture-makers such as the superb Mallorcan Gaspar Homar. More than any other form of art nouveau, Modernisme extended into literature, thought and music, marking a whole generation of Catalan writers, poets, composers and philosophers. It found its most splendid expression in architecture, but Modernisme was an artistic movement in the fullest sense of the word. In Catalonia, it took on a nationalistic element.

GAUDÍ'S VISION

Although Antoni Gaudí i Cornet is widely regarded as the genius of the Modernista movement, he was really an unclassifiable one-off. His work was a product of the social and cultural context of the time, but also of his individual perception of the world, together with a deep patriotic devotion to anything Catalan.

Gaudí worked first as assistant to Josep Fontseré in the 1870s on the building of the **Parc de la Ciutadella** (see p75); the gates and fountain are attributed to him. Around the same time, he designed the lamp-posts in the Plaça Reial, but his first major commission was for **Casa Vicens** (see p111) in Gràcia, built between 1883 and 1888. An orientalist fantasy, the building is structurally conventional, but Gaudí's use of surface material stands out in the neo-Moorish decoration, multicoloured tiling and superbly elaborate ironwork on the gates. His **Col·legi de les Teresianes** convent school (1888-89) is more restrained, but the clarity and fluidity of the building are very appealing.

In 1878, Gaudí met Eusebi Güell, heir to one of the largest industrial fortunes in Catalonia. The pair shared ideas on religion, philanthropy and the socially redemptive role of architecture, and Gaudí produced several buildings for Güell. Among them were **Palau Güell** (1886-88; see p82), an impressive, historicist building that established his reputation, and the crypt at **Colònia Güell** outside Barcelona, one of his most structurally experimental and surprising buildings.

Profile The Starchitects

The men and women who are building Barcelona's reputation.

Architecture is something of an obsession in Barcelona, and this relatively small city boasts more than 5,000 trained architects – a staggering figure. However, with the notable exception of the late Enric Miralles, most of the architects to have won the major commissions have hailed from outside the city.

This state of affairs sits uneasily with those who take pride in the use of grand architectural projects as a means of expressing a local identity, despite the fact that Spain has looked beyond its borders for artistic and architectural talent since Moorish times. Listed here are just some of the big hitters the town planners that have arrived from around the world to work on the city.

NORMAN FOSTER
British, b.1935
Known for 30 St Mary Axe (the 'Gherkin'), the Millennium Bridge, the GLA Building and new Wembley Stadium, all in London.

In Barcelona The **Torre de Collserola** (*see p115*), and the future remodelling of the **Nou Camp** stadium (*see p114*).

FRANK GEHRY
American, b.1929
Known for Bilbao's Guggenheim Museum and the Walt Disney Concert Hall in Los Angeles, among many major projects.
In Barcelona The fish sculpture at **Port Olímpic** (*see p89*), and a proposed 34-storey titanium office complex above the planned high-speed train hub at **La Sagrera**.

ZAHA HADID
Iraqi, b.1950
Known for The Mind Zone at the Millennium Dome in London (now the O2); the London Aquatics Centre (in progress), the Phaeno Science Center in Wolfsburg, Germany; and the Bridge Pavilion in the Spanish town of Zaragoza.
In Barcelona Two buildings in progress: the **Spiralling Tower** in Diagonal-Mar (photo ❶), and the **Plaça de les Arts** in Glories.

❶

HERZOG & DE MEURON
Jacques Herzog & Pierre de
Meuron; both Swiss, b.1950
Known for Tate Modern and the
Laban Dance Centre, both in
London; the Allianz Arena in
Munich, home of Bayern Munich
FC; and Beijing National
Stadium, aka the 'Bird's Nest'.
In Barcelona The **Edifici Fòrum**
(*see p118*).

RICHARD MEIER
American, b.1934
Known for Two major
American art museums: the
Getty Center in Los Angeles,
and the High Museum of Art in
Atlanta, Georgia.
In Barcelona Another major
art museum: the Museum
d'Art Contemporani de
Barcelona, popularly known
as **MACBA** (*see p81*).

ENRIC MIRALLES
Catalan, 1955-2000
Known for The Scottish
Parliament Building
in Edinburgh.
In Barcelona
Mercat de Santa
Caterina in Sant
Pere (*see p71*);
the **Gas Natural**
building in
Barceloneta
(*see p88*); and
the **Parc de**
Diagonal
Mar (*see*
p118).

JEAN NOUVEL
French, b.1945
Known for The Institut du
Monde Arabe and the Musée
du quai Branly, both in Paris; and
the Guthrie Theater in the
American city of Minneapolis.
In Barcelona **Torre Agbar** in
Diagonal Mar (photo ❷; *see*
p117), and the **Parc Central**
de Poblenou (*see p118*).

RICHARD ROGERS
British, b.1933
Known for The Centre Pompidou
in Paris, the European court of
Human Rights in Strasbourg, and
a number of London landmarks,
among them the Lloyd's Building,
Heathrow Airport's Terminal
Five and the Millennium Dome.
In Barcelona The **Hesperia**
Tower in L'Hospitalet (photo ❸;
see p146), and the
ongoing transformation
of **Las Arenas**
bullring
(*see p91*).

IN CONTEXT

In 1883, Gaudí became involved in the design of the **Sagrada Família** (see pp104-105), which had been started the previous year. From 1908 until his death in 1926, he worked on no other projects, a shabby, white-haired hermit producing visionary ideas that his assistants had to interpret into drawings (on show in the museum alongside). Gaudí was profoundly religious, and part of his obsession with the building came from a belief that it would help redeem Barcelona from the sins of secularism and the modern era.

Although he lived to see the completion of only the crypt, apse and Nativity façade, with its representation of 30 species of plants, the Sagrada Família became the testing ground for Gaudí's ideas on structure and form. As his work matured, he abandoned historicism and developed free-flowing, sinuous expressionist forms. His boyhood interest in nature began to take over from more architectural references, and what had previously provided external decorative motifs became the inspiration for the actual structure of his buildings.

In his greatest years, Gaudí combined other commissions with his cathedral. **La Pedrera** (see p108), which he began in 1905, was his most complete project. The building has an aquatic feel about it: the balconies resemble seaweed, while the undulating façade is reminiscent of the sea, or rocks washed by it. The **Casa Batlló** (see p102; photo p44), on the other side of Passeig de Gràcia, was an existing building that Gaudí remodelled in 1905-07; the roof looks like a reptilian creature perched high above the street. The symbolism of the façade is the source of speculation: some link it to the myth of St George and the dragon, but others say it's a celebration of carnival, with its harlequin-hat roof, wrought-iron balcony 'masks' and confetti-like tiles. This last element was the work of Josep Maria Jujol, who many believe was an even more skilled mosaicist than his master.

Gaudí's fascination with natural forms found full expression in the **Park Güell** (1900-14; see p111), for which he blurred the distinction between natural and artificial forms in a series of colonnades winding up a hill. These paths lead up to the large central terrace projecting over a hall; a forest of distorted Doric columns planned as the marketplace for Güell's proposed 'garden city'. The terrace benches are covered in some of the finest examples of trencadís (broken mosaic work), again mostly by Jujol.

BEYOND THE MASTER

Modernista architecture received a vital, decisive boost around the turn of the 19th century from the Universal Exhibition of 1888. The most important buildings for the show were planned by Lluís Domènech i Montaner (1850-1923), who was both far more prominent than Gaudí as a propagandist for Modernisme in all its forms and far more of a classic Modernista architect. Domènech was one of the first Modernista architects to develop the idea of the 'total work', working closely with teams of craftsmen and designers on every aspect of a building. His admirers dubbed him 'the great orchestra conductor'.

Most of the Exhibition buildings no longer exist, but the **Castell dels Tres Dragons** in the Parc de la Ciutadella has survived. Designed as the Exhibition restaurant (it's now the Museu de Zoologia; see p73), the building demonstrated many key features of Modernista style: the use of structural ironwork allowed greater freedom in the creation of openings, arches and windows; while plain brick, instead of the stucco usually applied to most buildings, was used in an exuberantly decorative manner.

Domènech's greatest creations are the **Hospital de la Santa Creu i Sant Pau** (see p106), built as small 'pavilions' within a garden to avoid the usual effect of a monolithic hospital, and the **Palau de la Música Catalana** (see p73), an extraordinary display of outrageous decoration. He also left impressive constructions in Reus, near Tarragona, notably the ornate mansions **Casa Navàs** and **Casa Rull**, and the spectacular pavilions of the **Institut Pere Mata**, a psychiatric hospital and forerunner of the Hospital de Sant Pau.

Third in the trio of leading Modernista architects was Josep Puig i Cadafalch (1867-1957), who combined traditional Catalan touches with a neo-Gothic influence in such buildings as the **Casa de les Punxes** ('House of Spikes'; officially the Casa Terrades; see p101) in the Diagonal. Nearby on Passeig de Sant Joan, at no.108, is another masterpiece: the **Casa Macaya**, its inner courtyard inspired by the medieval palaces of C/Montcada.

Mercat de Santa Caterina. *See p49.*

Puig was also responsible for some of the best industrial architecture of the time, an area in which Modernisme excelled. The Fundació La Caixa's cultural centre recently moved from Casa Macaya to another of Puig i Cadafalch's striking creations, the **Fàbrica Casaramona** at Montjuïc, built as a textile mill (*see p95*); outside Barcelona, he also designed the extraordinary **Caves Codorniu** wine cellars. But undoubtedly his best-known work is the **Casa Amatller** (*see p102*), between Domènech's **Casa Lleó Morera** (*see p100*) and Gaudí's Casa Batlló in the extraordinary Manzana de la Discòrdia.

The style caught on with extraordinary vigour all over Catalonia, but some of its most engaging architects are little known internationally. Impressive apartment blocks and mansions were built in the Eixample by Joan Rubió i Bellver (**Casa Golferichs**, Gran Via 491), Salvador Valeri (**Casa Comalat**, Avda Diagonal 442) and Josep Vilaseca. North of Barcelona is La Garriga, where MJ Raspall built exuberant summer houses for the rich and fashionable families of the time; there are also some dainty Modernista residences in coast towns, such as Canet and Arenys de Mar. Some of the finest Modernista industrial architecture is in Terrassa, designed by the municipal architect Lluís Moncunill (1868-1931). And Cèsar Martinell, another local architect, built co-operative cellars that are true 'wine cathedrals' in Falset, Gandesa and many other towns in southern Catalonia.

THE 20TH CENTURY

By the 1910s, Modernisme had become too extreme for Barcelona's middle classes; Gaudí's later buildings were met with derision. The new 'proper' style for Catalan architecture was Noucentisme, which stressed the importance of classical proportions. However, it produced little of note: the main buildings that survive are those of the 1929 Exhibition, Barcelona's next 'big event' that served as the excuse for the bizarre, neo-Baroque **Palau Nacional** (now home to MNAC; *see p96*). The Exhibition also brought the city one of the most important buildings of the century: Ludwig Mies van der Rohe's German Pavilion, the **Pavelló Barcelona**, rebuilt near its original location in 1986. Its impact at the time was extraordinary; even today, it seems modern in its challenge to the conventional ideas of space.

Torre de Collserola.

Mies van der Rohe had a strong influence on the main new trend in Catalan architecture of the 1930s, which, reacting against Modernisme and nearly all earlier Catalan styles, was quite emphatically functionalist. Its leading figures were Josep Lluís Sert and the GATCPAC collective (Group of Catalan Architects and Technicians for the Progress of Contemporary Architecture), who struggled to introduce the ideas of Le Corbusier and of the International Style. Under the Republic, Sert built a sanatorium off C/Tallers and the Casa Bloc, a workers' housing project at Passeig Torres i Bages 91-105 in Sant Andreu.

In collaboration with Le Corbusier, GATCPAC also produced a plan for the radical redesign of the whole of Barcelona as a 'functional city', the Pla Macià of 1933-34. Drawings for the scheme present a Barcelona that looks more like a Soviet-era new town in Siberia, and few regret that it never got off the drawing board. In 1937, Sert also built the Spanish Republic's pavilion for that year's Paris Exhibition, since rebuilt in Barcelona as the **Pavelló de la República** (*see p119*) in the Vall d'Hebron. However, his finest work came much later in the shape of the **Fundació Joan Miró** (*see p95*), built in the 1970s after he had spent many years in exile in the United States.

BARCELONA'S NEW STYLE

The Franco years had an enormous impact on the city. As the economy expanded at breakneck pace in the 1960s, Barcelona received a massive influx of migrants, in a context of unchecked property speculation and minimal planning controls; the city became ringed by a chaotic mass of high-rise suburbs. Another legacy of the era are some ostentatiously tall office blocks, especially on the Diagonal and around Plaça Francesc Macià.

When a democratic city administration took over at the end of the 1970s, there was much to be done. A generation of architects had been chafing at Francoist restrictions. However, the tone set early on – above all by Barcelona's chief planner Oriol Bohigas, who has continued to design individual buildings as part of the MBM partnership with Josep Martorell and David Mackay – was one of 'architectural realism', with a powerful combination of imagination and practicality.

Budgets were limited, so the public's hard-earned funds were initially concentrated not on buildings but on the gaps between them: public spaces, a string of modern parks and squares, many of which were to incorporate original artwork. From this quiet beginning, Barcelona placed itself at the forefront of international urban design.

'The Barcelona Games provided a focus for a sweeping renovation of the city.'

Barcelona's renewal programme took on a more ambitious shape with the 1992 Olympics. The third and most spectacular of the city's great events, the Games were intended to be stylish and innovative, but they were also designed to provide a focus for a sweeping renovation of the city, with emblematic new buildings (such as Lord Foster's **Torre de Collserola**; *see p115*) and infrastructure projects linked by clear strategic planning.

The three main Olympic sites are quite different. The **Vila Olímpica** (*see p89*) had the most comprehensive masterplan: drawn up by Bohigas and MBM themselves, it sought to extend Cerdà's grid down to the seafront. The main project on **Montjuïc** (*see pp90-98*) was the transformation of the 1929 stadium, but there's also Arata Isozaki's Palau Sant Jordi and its space-frame roof. **Vall d'Hebron** (*see p119*) was the least successful of the three sites, but Esteve Bonell's Velòdrom is one of the finest (and earliest) of the sports buildings, built in 1984 before the Olympic bid had even succeeded.

AFTER THE OLYMPICS

Post-1992, the focus shifted to the Raval and the Port Vell ('Old Port'), then to the Diagonal Mar area in the north of the city. Many of the striking buildings here are by local architects such as Helio Piñón and Albert Viaplana, whose work combines elegant lines with a strikingly modern use of materials. Examples range from the controversial 1983 **Plaça dels Països Catalans** (*see 111*) to transformations of historic buildings such as the Casa de la Caritat (now the **Centre de Cultura Contemporània** (*see p79*) and all-new projects including **Maremàgnum** in the port (*see p198*).

Other contributions to post-Olympic Barcelona were made by foreign architects. In addition to the projects detailed elsewhere in this chapter (*see pp44-45* **The Starchitects**), two venerable buildings have been remodelled in recent years. The last stage of Italian architect Gae Aulenti's interior redesign of the Palau Nacional on Montjuïc created the expanded **Museu Nacional d'Art de Catalunya** (*see p96*) and the **CosmoCaixa** building in Tibidabo, which again converted a 19th-century hospice into a science museum (*see p115*). Also undergoing a major facelift, the Mudéjar-style arches of **Las Arenas** bullring are being converted by Richard Rogers into a shopping and leisure centre.

Of late, architectural projects have become increasingly circumscribed by commercial imperatives, sometimes causing tensions between local traditions and the globalisation of commerce. The huge changes to the cityscape linked to the Fòrum Universal de les Cultures 2004 are a particular case in point. The area at the mouth of the Besòs river, near where Avda Diagonal meets the sea, was transformed for the occasion, most notably by the construction of a triangular building, the **Edifici Fòrum** (*see p118*), designed by Herzog and de Meuron (of Tate Modern fame). Nearby, Enric Miralles, also known locally for his redesign of the **Mercat de Santa Caterina** (*see p71; photo p49*), created a fiercely modern and rather soulless park, the **Parc de Diagonal Mar** (*see p118*). Jean Nouvel's 2008 **Parc Central de Poblenou** (*see p118*) has been a much more popular addition to the locale, and combines futurism with nature to provide playfulness and much-needed shade.

Whether this fourth stage in the re-imagining of the city can be linked to those outbursts of Barcelona's architectural creativity in the service of urban planning is debatable. While the value of many of these buildings is unquestionable, some see the dark hand of big business behind the latest developments and dismiss the new expansions connected to the Fòrum as more about making money than art. It's also telling that many of Barcelona's most recent landmark buildings are five-star hotels (*see p134* **Designer Dreams**). Still, whatever the motives behind the city's latest reinvention, no one is denying the unique, dynamic air of its current urban fabric.

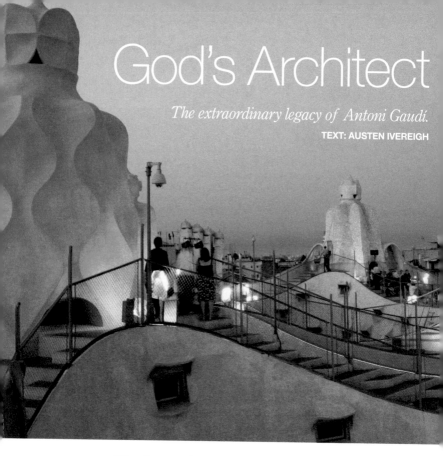

God's Architect

The extraordinary legacy of Antoni Gaudí.

TEXT: AUSTEN IVEREIGH

Genius, prophet, visionary – all these words have been used in praise of Catalan architect Antoni Gaudí. But was he also a saint? According to a dedicated group of Catholics in Barcelona, who have persuaded the Vatican to take the possibility seriously, the answer is an emphatic *sí*. The 'Cause' for Gaudí's canonisation, as considerations for sainthood are known, is already well advanced: Rome is studying the assembled evidence, and the Association for the Beatification of Antoni Gaudí says the first stage on the path to sainthood – declaring him 'blessed' – is likely to be reached in a matter of years.

If this happens, it will be a first. Despite its centuries of sponsoring great art and music, no professional artist has ever been declared a saint by the Catholic Church. (There was the 'blessed' Fra Angelico, but he was a friar who painted rather than a professional painter.) If Gaudí is canonised, then Barcelona's great architect will have broken the mould not just of architecture but of holiness.

Austen Ivereigh was deputy editor of The Tablet *and is now associate editor of* Godspy.

'Like Picasso and Dalí after him, Gaudí "was conscious of his brilliance", says Josep Maria Tarragona. "He knew that western architecture had come so far, and he was way ahead of it."'

Whether or not Gaudí is eventually canonised, the Association has already succeeded in putting the spotlight on a dimension of the architect and his work that has often been overlooked in the rush to declare him a modernist icon. Gaudí's conversion at the age of about 31 to a life of austerity and prayer was dramatic, and his art flowed directly from his relationship with God. All his works, Gaudí would later say, 'come from the Great Book of Nature'; his task was that of 'collaboration with the Creator'.

Looking around himself, Gaudí could immediately see that nature had none of the abstract geometry associated with conventional architecture. 'God's shapes' were fibrous – wood, bone, muscle – and formed by gravity. But Gaudí also observed that forms in nature served a function. If an architect looked for that same function in his work, he could arrive at beauty, whereas if he sought beauty, he would reach only abstraction. Gaudí's major works – La Pedrera, Park Güell and not least the Sagrada Família – are initially upsetting, because they are more like nature than architecture. Yet this is what makes his work both captivating and timeless.

Few could have predicted the path that Gaudí's life would later take. In his twenties, he was a wealthy dandy, dressing extravagantly and giving orders to his workmen without getting down from his horse-drawn carriage. Like Picasso and Dalí after him, Gaudí 'was conscious of his brilliance', says Josep Maria Tarragona, the author of one of the most respected books on the architect. 'He knew that western architecture had come so far, and he was way ahead of it.'

This was a recipe for the kind of egotism that befell Picasso and Dalí in their lifetimes. But fate, or God, stepped in: the young man was knocked sideways when Pepita Moreu, a beautiful, wealthy lady who fascinated Gaudí, refused his offer of marriage. A second woman to whom he proposed chose a convent life instead. Gaudí fell back on his faith. He shed his wealth, and adopted the life of a pauper and mystic. The vital moment came in 1883, when, in his early thirties, Gaudí took over the plans for the Sagrada Família: here, he believed, was the task that God had given him for the rest of his life. Every day thereafter, he worked on the Sagrada Família, read the Bible, attended Mass, and said the Rosary. He lived alone, rarely travelling, writing little (although he was a great talker) and reading almost exclusively from spiritual texts.

Yet Gaudí was no hermit. He appeared in 3,000 Barcelona newspaper and journal articles in his lifetime – an average of two a week. A Catalan nationalist, he was arrested under the dictatorship of Primo de Rivera (1922-31) for refusing to speak Castilian. He belonged to the League of Our Lady of Montserrat, a Catholic nationalist organisation that advocated a pluralistic, democratic Catalonia (as opposed to the integrists or Carlists, who spurned both Madrid and Rome). And he was active in the Cercle Artístic de Sant Lluc, a Catholic group of artists headed by Bishop Torras i Bages, a figure vital to his conversion.

The joy of artistic creation was so immense, so overwhelming, Gaudí believed, that if the artist did not respond through fasting and poverty, he would be 'over-compensated'. His asceticism could be extreme: one Lent, in 1894, Gaudí had to be told to eat by his spiritual director after a radical fast left him at death's door. 'Life is love, and love is sacrifice,' the architect used to say. 'Sacrifice is the only really fruitful thing.' Hence the Sagrada Família, which he conceived as an 'expiation' for the sins of the world.

IN CONTEXT

'The Sagrada Família was conceived as an "expiation" for the sins of the world.'

A craftsman by training, Gaudí was demanding of his workers, but endlessly kind. The site of the Sagrada Família was at the time located in one of the city's poorest *barris*, where he was loved and respected as an *obrerista* – one who identified with the working classes. They returned the compliment, protecting 'their' Sagrada Família from the anticlerical mobs who torched Barcelona's churches in 1909. After Gaudí's death in 1936, the studio containing his designs and models for the church went up in flames during the next bout of anticlerical fury; yet alone among the tombs at the Sagrada Família, Gaudí's was spared from desecration.

Even so, the move to canonise Gaudí has not been without its critics, especially those who belong to that branch of Catalan nationalism with a secular vision of Catalonia. Gaudí, an artistic genius of international fame and a hero of Catalan nationalism, belongs, they say, to the whole of humanity; and they resent what they see as the Church's attempt to muscle in and claim him for itself. Among the critics is Josep María Subirachs, one of the sculptors working to complete the Sagrada Família. 'Everyone of different religions, different beliefs, comes here to see his work,' he says. 'He should be left as he is.'

But the Association – formed in 1992 by two architects, his biographer, a priest (who has since died) and a Japanese sculptor who converted to Catholicism while working on the Sagrada Família – insists that to acknowledge the importance of Gaudí's faith to his art in no way diminishes his universal importance or appeal. Tarragona, one of the association's founders, believes that knowing Gaudí was a Catholic mystic gives the interpretative keys for understanding his art. 'That doesn't mean a non-Christian cannot understand Gaudí,' he says. 'But you cannot separate the man and his work from his faith.'

If the idea of Gaudí as saint seems strange, says Tarragona, it may be because we are accustomed to the iconic image of the artist as tortured, alienated and anarchic; the notion of an architect as both a radical modernist and a deeply prayerful, pious man therefore 'breaks the template'. That makes him doubly attractive to the Catholic Church: Gaudí's canonisation would help other professional, working people understand that they too can be holy.

The Cause was encouraged by one of the architect's admirers, Pope John Paul II, who was fascinated to discover Gaudí was an 'ordinary layman' rather than a monk or priest. In 2000 – by canonisation standards, the speed of light – he gave the go-ahead (technically, a *nihil obstat*) for the process to begin; three years later, a 1,000-page dossier was lodged in Rome. Over the next years, theologians will examine evidence of Gaudí's 'heroic virtues'. For Gaudí to be declared 'blessed', the Association needs to provide proof of a miracle: someone who has been cured in a scientifically inexplicable manner after praying to Gaudí. A number have stepped forward with tales of cures, but none so far has been sufficiently miraculous to make the grade.

Saints are not made of plaster; becoming holy is about struggling with vices and faults. Gaudí could be blunt and impatient with people who did not see things as immediately and clearly as he did. And his battle with his temper was lifelong. 'I have always fought, and I have always succeeded,' he told his spiritual director shortly before his death, 'except in one thing: in the struggle against my bad temper. This I have not been able to overcome.'

But those backing the Cause believe that while plenty of artists have been touched by divine inspiration in their work, few have exhibited the intimate personal relationship with God that Gaudí did. Unlike other artists who burn out or died young, Gaudí's greatness increased with age, as his life became ever more ordered towards prayer. 'Mozart could write the *Coronation Mass* without having a devout life,' says Tarragona. 'God gave him the grace, as of course he did with Michelangelo in the creation of the *Pietà* or the Sistine Chapel. But in Gaudí we get both divine inspiration and a personal life proper to a mystic.'

Gaudí himself was in no doubt who he was working for. When people clucked that the Sagrada Família would never be finished in his lifetime, 'God's architect' would just shrug. 'My client,' he would answer, 'is not in a hurry.'

Run over by a no.30 tram on his way to evening prayer in 1926, Gaudí was mistaken for a beggar and taken to the city's pauper hospital. When his friends found him there the next day, he refused to budge: he had always wanted to leave this world poor, he said. And he did, two days later, aged 74, mourned by a city that hailed him as an artistic genius – and a saint.

Strange Truths

Some little-known facts surrounding Barcelona's favourite son.

As a child, Gaudí was so badly afflicted by rheumatism that he would ride around on a donkey.

As a young man, he was oddly preoccupied with fashion, and would have his hats and kid gloves specially made.

For much of his life, he lived chiefly on nuts and lettuce leaves dipped in milk.

The word 'gaudy', contrary to popular belief, has nothing to do with Gaudí, and dates back to Shakespeare.

On 11 September 1924, Catalan National Day, he was arrested for refusing to speak to a policeman in anything but Catalan.

Gaudí also refused to speak in Spanish when he was introduced to King Alfonso XIII.

He was a reluctant draughtsman and would instead make models using whatever was to hand, from vegetables to mud.

Pokémon film *The Rise of Darkrai* featured a building based on the Sagrada Família, and an architect called Gaudy.

His belief in the superiority of the Catalan race led to an insistence that the model for Jesus on the Sagrada Família could be no other nationality.

Picasso and Gaudí enjoyed a mutual loathing.

He was suspicious of spectacle-wearers, and felt that poor eyesight would be cured with exercise.

George Orwell called the Sagrada Família 'the most hideous building in the world'.

Gaudí used the corpses of stillborn infants to make casts for the Massacre of the Innocents.

For various of the bird and animal figures, he would chloroform live creatures and use them as casts.

He was a firm believer in homeopathy and vegetarianism.

After he was hit by a tram, several cab drivers refused to carry his unconscious body to a hospital, suspecting he was a beggar who would be unable to pay.

In 1987, the Alan Parsons Project released an album called *Gaudí*, inspired by his life and work.

ROMÁNICOGÓTICO
MODERNISMOVANGUARDIA

MNAC — MUSEU NACIONAL D'ART DE CATALUNYA

1.000 AÑOS DE ARTE — 1,000 YEARS OF ART

Palau Nacional
Parc de Montjuïc
Barcelona
www.mnac.es

ROMANESQUE&GOTHICAR
MODERNISMEAVANT-GARDI

Sights

Barri Gòtic

Barcelona's historic core carries an indelible appeal.

An almost perfectly preserved medieval time capsule, the Barri Gòtic (Gothic Quarter) is an unmissable part of town for any visitor. History is written in stone here; the wealth of historical remains is such that visitors soon become as blasé as the locals about the large sections of Roman wall found at the back of a curry house or in a lift-shaft leading down to the metro.

In addition to the many perfectly preserved medieval palaces and Gothic churches, the Barri Gòtic holds smaller, secret histories lurking around every corner. The wall of one apartment block holds the arches of a Roman aqueduct; the back of a furniture shop is home to some arcane Jewish baths. There are surprises everywhere you look.

Map pp344-345	Cafés p182
Hotels p123	Tapas bars p183
Restaurants p152	Bars p184

SIGHTS

THE HISTORIC QUARTER

The first settlement of this 2,000-year-old city was a Roman camp set up on the gentle hill of Mons Taber, the highest vantage point on the coastal plains. Now the imposing square of Plaça Sant Jaume, this is where the Roman forum was built, at the crossroads of the main thoroughfares of the *cardo maximus* and the *decumanus* which roughly correspond to the lines traced by C/Call to C/Llibreteria and C/Bisbe to C/Ciutat today. Dominating the forum was the **Temple of Augustus**, four columns of which can still be seen in C/Pietat. The square now hosts the municipal government (**Ajuntament**) and the Catalan regional government (**Generalitat**) buildings and forms the civic heart of the city. It's also been the stage for demonstrations, speeches and key political moments, such as the proclamation of the Catalan republic in 1931.

Leading off the square, C/Bisbe has one of the locale's most photographed features: the neo-Gothic **Pont dels Sospirs** (Bridge of Sighs). It's a pastiche from 1928, when the idea

About the author
Nadia Feddo has lived in Barcelona since 1995, and works as a freelance journalist and professional tour guide.

of the area as a 'Gothic Quarter' took off. Other alterations from the same period include the decorations on the Casa dels Canonges (once a set of canons' residences, and now Generalitat offices), on the other side of the bridge. Further down C/Bisbe is the Plaça Garriga i Bachs and Josep Llimona's bronze monument to the martyrs of 1809, dedicated to *barcelonins* who rose up against Napoleon and were executed.

In C/Santa Llúcia, in front of the **cathedral**, is Casa de l'Ardiaca; originally a 15th-century residence for the archdeacon (*ardiaca*), it has a superb tiled patio. The huge square at the foot of the steps leading up to the cathedral is Plaça Nova, which houses an antiques market every Thursday (*see p217*) and is a traditional venue for festivals, concerts and *sardana* dancing (*see p60* **It's a Fair Hop**). At ground level, on the south-east corner of the square is Barcino: a visual poem by Joan Brossa installed in 1994, it refers to the ancient name for Barcelona, supposedly named by the Carthaginians after Hannibal's father, Hamil Barca. Directly above is the Roman aqueduct; the final archway of the city's two aqueducts dating from the first century AD is preserved inside the tower that defended the north-eastern side of the gate; one of these has been externally rebuilt.

Fast forward two millennia to the opposite side of Plaça Nova, dominated by one of the

La Rambla. *See p67.*

first high-rise blocks in the city: the **Col·legi d'Arquitectes** (Architects' Association) decorated with Catalan folk scenes designed by Picasso. The middle section depicts the *gegants* (giant figures who lead processions at festivals) and figures holding palm branches; the left-hand section (on C/Arcs) symbolises the joy of life, while the right-hand section on C/Capellans) depicts the Catalan flag. There are also two interior friezes depicting *sardana* dance and a wall of arches.

In front of the cathedral, on the right as you leave, is the **Museu Diocesà**, housing an excellent collection of religious art. Around the side of the cathedral, meanwhile, is the little-visited but fascinating **Museu Frederic Marès**. Further along is the 16th-century Palau del Lloctinent (Palace of the Viceroy); recently restored, it was the local headquarters for the Spanish Inquisition, from where the unfortunates were carted off to the Passeig del Born to be burnt.

Once part of the former royal palace (Palau Reial Major, not to be confused with the Palau Reial in Pedralbes), the building has another exit to the medieval palace square, the well-preserved Plaça del Rei. The square houses the **Museu d'Història de la Ciutat** and includes some of Barcelona's most historically important buildings: the Escher-esque 16th-century watchtower (Mirador del Rei Martí) and the Capella de Santa Àgata, which houses the very stone where the breasts of Saint Agatha were allegedly laid when the Romans chopped them off in Catania. Parts of the palace are said to

date back to the tenth century; there have been many remarkable additions to it since, notably the 14th-century Saló del Tinell, a medieval banqueting hall that is a definitive work of Catalan Gothic. It is here that Ferdinand and Isabella are said to have received Columbus on his return from America.

The narrow streets centred on C/Call once housed a rich Jewish ghetto (*call*) although the street names were Christianised after the 1391 pogrom. At the corner of C/Sant Domènec del Call and C/Marlet is the medieval **synagogue**, now restored and open to the public. Proving the regenerated interest in the Call, in 2008 the Centre d'Interpretació del Call research centre opened in Placeta Manuel Ribé (no.3, 93 256 21 00) as part of the Museu d'Història de la Ciutat, and has a small selection of medieval Jewish artefacts on display.

INSIDE TRACK
DO A MIRO

The **Col·legi d'Arquitectes** (Architects' Association, *see above*) is decorated with a graffiti-style sand-blasted triptych of Catalan folk scenes, designed by Picasso while in self-imposed exile in the 1950s and executed by Norwegian artist Carl Nesjar. When Picasso heard that Joan Miró was being considered for the commission, he said that he could easily 'do a Miró'.

La Mercè. See p61.

necropolis and a rare expanse of city-centre grass (although it is often fenced off). Between here and the Plaça Catalunya is the marvellous little Romanesque church of **Santa Anna**, begun in 1141 and containing an exquisite 14th-century cloister.

Head back along C/Santa Anna to emerge on the city's most crowded shopping street, the pedestrianised avenue of Portal de l'Àngel, crammed with high-street chains and the odd curiosity such as the octagonal Santa Anna drinking fountain, decorated with scowling bearded faces, which dates from 1356 and was later covered in Noucentista painted tiles. It's located to the rear of the Real Cercle Artístic housed in the Palau Pignatelli and now home to Dalí Barcelona.

From here, duck into C/Duran i Blas to see four arches from a Roman aqueduct embedded into a wall and exposed in 1988 when the neighbouring building was demolished; they date from the first century AD and brought water from the River Besòs. Back out on Portal de l'Angel, the end of the street is signposted by the famous five-storey-high **Cottet thermometer**, added in 1956 by the optician's shop beneath and greatly admired at the time as a technological marvel. Just a few metres away is the entrance to C/Montsió, which holds the world-famous **Els Quatre Gats** café (*see p182*), the legendary haunt of Picasso and other artists and bohemians. It's housed in Puig i Cadafalch's richly sculpted Casa Martí.

Back on the seaward side of the Barri Gòtic, if you walk from Plaça Sant Jaume up C/Ciutat, to the left of the Ajuntament, and turn down the narrow alley of C/Hércules, you'll come to Plaça Sant Just. This fascinating old square holds a recently restored Gothic water fountain from 1367 and the church of **Sants Just i Pastor**, built in the 14th century on the site of a chapel founded by Charlemagne's son Louis the Pious, and now looking rather unloved inside.

The once-wealthy area between here and the port became more rundown throughout the 20th century. It has a different atmosphere from the northern part of the Barri Gòtic: shabbier and less prosperous. The city authorities made huge efforts to change this, particularly in the 1990s, when new squares were opened up: Plaça George Orwell on C/Escudellers, known as the 'Plaça del Tripi (Trippy)' by the youthful party crowd that hangs out there, and Plaça Joaquim Xirau, off La Rambla. Another tactic was the siting of parts of the Universitat Pompeu Fabra on the lower Rambla.

Just above is the area's heart: Plaça Reial, known for its bars, cheap backpacker hostels and rather scuzzy atmosphere at night. It's still a popular spot for a drink or an outdoor meal

Near the centre of the *call* is the beautiful little Plaça Sant Felip Neri and its fine Baroque church, whose façade was damaged by Italian bombing during the Civil War. More than 200 people were killed, many of them refugee children on a Sunday outing. This square is another 20th-century invention; the shoemakers' guild building (now housing the **Museu del Calçat**) was moved here in 1943 to make way for the Avda de la Catedral, while the nearby tinkers' guild was moved earlier last century, when Via Laietana was driven through the district.

Close by are the attractive Plaça del Pi and Plaça Sant Josep Oriol, where there are great pavement bars and artisanal markets. The squares are separated by **Santa Maria del Pi**, one of Barcelona's most distinguished Gothic churches, with a magnificent rose window and spacious single nave. Opposite is the 17th-century neo-classical retailers' guildhall, with its colourful 18th-century sgraffiti.

Snaking up to C/Portaferrissa from the Plaça del Pi is C/Petritxol, one of the most charming streets of the Barri Gòtic, known for its traditional *granges* offering hot chocolate and cakes, and also housing the **Sala Parés** (*see p242*), the city's oldest art gallery; Rusiñol, Casas and the young Picasso all exhibited here. On the other side of C/Portaferrissa, heading up C/Bot, is the Plaça Vila de Madrid, where you'll find the excavated remains of a Roman

SIGHTS

It's a Fair Hop

The ins and outs of the Catalan national dance.

After the transporting passion and sweat of flamenco, or the athletic leaps of the Aragonese *jota*, Catalonia's emblematic folk dance can look a bit, well, wimpy. Not surprisingly, the gentle, bobbing steps of the *sardana* get a lot of stick from other regions of Spain: the mere mention of the word can result in hoots of derision, swiftly followed by an impression of a shuffling geriatric groping for the Zimmer frame. But, as any aficionado will tell you, the joy of the *sardana* is not in watching but in taking part. It's a dance of co-existence and solidarity, not spectacle.

In theory, anyone is allowed to join in a *sardana*. In practice, it's not a good idea to barge in on a circle beyond your level: choose carefully, and make sure you break into the left of a man so as not to commit the gaffe of breaking up a couple. Dancers don the traditional *tabarner* espadrille with ribbons, and join hands in a circle to begin the series of tiny, intricate steps forward and back, crossing to the left and right. Except for formal occasions, all their street shoes and belongings are piled up in the middle, sothey are, in best disco tradition, dancing around their handbags.

Sardanes, which can be lengthy, consist of interchanging sequences of 8 *curts* (short sets), when dancers hold their arms low, and 16 *llargs* (long sets), when arms are held aloft. One person in the ring takes charge of counting the sets, but the dance is also musically accompanied by a traditional band known as a *cobla*. This consists of 11 musicians playing 12 instruments: double bass, trumpets and trombones, alongside reed instruments known as the *tible* and *tenora*; the drummer also plays the recorder. To follow the structure of the *sardana*, listen out for the *flabiol* (recorder) flourishes, which mark the introduction and the counterpoints for the dancers.

Sardanes are a stock feature of all traditional festivals and also take place every weekend in front of the cathedral (Jan-Aug, Dec noon-2pm Sun; Sept-Nov 6-8pm Sat, noon-2pm Sun) and in Plaça Sant Jaume (Oct-July 6-8pm Sun). For more information and details of classes, see www.fed.sardanista.cat.

provided you don't mind the odd drunk and
re prepared to keep an eye on your bags).

In addition from the 1840s, the *plaça* has the
res Gràcies fountain in the centre, and
mp-posts designed by the young Gaudí. It's
e only work he ever did for the city council.

The grand porticos of a number of the
uildings around the church of **La Mercè**,
hoto p59) once the merchants' mansions, stand
s testament to the former wealth of the area
efore the building of the Eixample. The Plaça
e la Mercè itself was only created in 1982, with
e destruction of the houses that used to stand
ere; the 19th-century fountain was moved here
om the port. There's also a dwindling number
 lively *tascas* (small traditional tapas bars) on
'Mercè. Beyond C/Ample and the Mercè, you
merge from narrow alleys or the pretty Plaça
uc de Medinaceli on to the Passeig de Colom,
here a few shipping offices and ships'
nandlers still recall the atmosphere of decades
one by. On Passeig de Colom stands the
monolithic **Capitanía General**, the army
eadquarters. The façade has the dubious
stinction of being the one construction in
arcelona that's directly attributable to the
ictatorship of Primo de Rivera.

FREE **Ajuntament (City Hall)**

*laça Sant Jaume (93 402 70 00/special visits
3 402 73 64/www.bcn.cat). Metro Jaume I or
iceu.* **Open** *Office* 8.30am-2.30pm Mon-Fri.
isits 10.30am-1.30pm Sun. **Admission** free.
Map p345 C6.

round the left-hand corner of the city hall's rather
ull 18th-century neo-classical façade sits the old
itrance, in a wonderfully flamboyant 15th-century
atalan Gothic façade. Inside, the building's centre-
ece (and oldest part) is the famous Saló de Cent,
here the Consell de Cent (Council of One Hundred)
iled the city between 1372 and 1714. The Saló de
ròniques is filled with Josep Maria Sert's immense
ack-and-gold mural (1928), depicting the early
th-century Catalan campaign in Byzantium and
reece under the command of Roger de Flor. Full of
t and sculptures by the great Catalan masters from
larà to Subirachs, the interior of the city hall is open
r guided tours (in different languages) on Sundays.

Catedral

*a de la Seu (93 342 82 60/www.catedral
n.org). Metro Jaume I.* **Open** *Combined
cket* 1pm-5pm Mon-Sat; 2-4.45pm Sun. *Without
mbined ticket* (*Church*) 8am-12.45pm, 5.15-
pm Mon-Fri; 8am-12.45pm, 5.15-6pm Sat;
am-12.45pm, 5.15-6pm Sun. (*Cloister*) 9am-
2.30pm, 5-7pm daily. (*Museum*) 10am-12.30pm,
15-7pm daily. **Admission** *Combined ticket*
5. Church & cloister free. Museum €2. Lift
roof €2.50. Choir €2.20.* **No credit cards.**
ap p345 C5/D5.

Construction on Barcelona's Gothic cathedral began
in 1298. However, thanks to civil wars and plagues,
construction continued at a pace that makes the
Sagrada Família project look snappy: although the
architects remained faithful to the vertical Nordic
lines of the 15th-century plans, the façade and central spire were not finished until 1913. Indeed, the
façade continues to cause problems: although it's
one of the newest parts of the building, it's crumbling, and roughly a third of it is being taken down
and painstakingly rebuilt with the same Montserrat
stone that was used for the original. For the time
being, the building is shrouded in scaffolding, plastic and signs asking visitors to 'Sponsor a Stone'.

Inside, the cathedral is a cavernous and slightly
forbidding place, but many paintings, sculptures
and an intricately carved central choir (built in the
1390s) all shine through the gloom. The cathedral
is dedicated to the city's patron saint Eulàlia, an
outspoken 13-year-old martyred by the Romans in
AD 303; her remains lie in the dramatically lit crypt,
in an alabaster tomb carved with torture scenes
from her martyrdom (being rolled in a nail-filled bar-
rel down what is today the Baixada de Santa Eulàlia,
for instance). To one side, there's a lift to the
roof; take it for a magnificent view of the Old City.

The glorious light-filled cloister is famous for its
13 fierce geese – one for each year of Eulàlia's life –
and half-erased floor engravings, detailing which
guild paid for which side chapel: scissors for the
tailors, shoes for the cobblers and so on. The cathedral museum, housed is in the 17th-century chapterhouse, includes paintings and sculptures by Gothic
masters Jaume Huguet, Bernat Martorell and
Bartolomé Bermejo.

A combined ticket (*visita especial*) has a timetable
intended to keep tourists and worshippers from
bothering one another. From 1-4.30pm, the entry fee
is obligatory; howeber, ticket-holders have the run
of the cloister, church, choir and lift, and can enter
some chapels and take photos (normally prohibited).

FREE **Centre Civic Pati d'en Llimona**

C/Regomir 3 (93 268 47 00). Metro Jaume I.
Open *Exhibitions* 9am-9pm Mon-Fri; 10am-2pm,
4-8pm Sat. Closed Aug. **Admission** free.
Map p345 C6.

From the street, peer through the glass paving slabs
and windows to see the excavated foundations
of a round defence tower that dates from the earliest
Roman settlement, along with the remains of a
Roman bath and house that stood against one of
the gates of the city wall. In the 15th century, a
luxury town villa was built on the site; the courtyard
still contains various capitals with carved faces
from this period (along with a sculpture of two
female nudes by local hairdressing king, Lluís
Llongueras). The civic centre activities include
photography exhibitions, workshops, theatre shows
and poetry readings.

SIGHTS

"Me llamo Claire y vivo en Barcelona. Tengo 28 años. Me encanta aprender español."

Intensive and Extensive Spanish Courses for all levels all year rou

"I found work immediately after taking the Course at IH Barcelona. It was the best career decision I ever made."

English Teacher Training Courses including TEFL, DELTA and CE

IH BARCELON
C/Trafalgar 14,
Barcelona

932 684 511
study@bcn.ihes
www.ihes.com

Dalí Barcelona
Real Cercle Artístic

C/Arcs 5 (93 318 17 74/www.dalibarcelona.com).
Metro Jaume I or Liceu. **Open** 10am-10pm daily.
Admission €8; €6 reductions; free under-7s.
Credit AmEx, DC, MC, V. **Map** p344 C4.

This private collection of Dalí sculptures looks right
at home amid the dramatic red velvet curtains and
high, Gothic arches of the ground floor and basement of the Palau Pignatelli. In his later years, Dalí
signed his name to almost anything, but these 44
pieces are moulded by his own hands in wax by
the pool at his house in Port Lligat and show he
was just as accomplished at sculpting as painting.
Broadly divided into themes such as eroticism, Don
Quixote and mythology, they include such gems
as a small bronze that's simultaneously a swan, a
dragon and an elephant, and an erotic vision of
Dulcinea, Quixote's reluctant lady. The collection is
supplemented by more than 600 drawings, sketches, lithographs and photographs. There's also a
related temporary exhibition space (with items for
sale and free entry) which has recently included
shows by Dalí's niece, Lali Bas Dalí and his muse,
Amanda Lear. Upstairs, the Royal Art Circle wel-
comes visitors to its free exhibitions.

Museu del Calçat (Shoe Museum)

Plaça Sant Felip Neri 5 (93 301 45 33).
Metro Jaume I. **Open** 11am-2pm Tue-Sun.
Admission €2.50; free under-7s. **No credit
cards. Map** p345 C5.

Housed in what was once part of the medieval shoemakers' guild, this quirky little museum details the
cobbler's craft from practical Roman sandals to tot-
tering '70s platform boots – so that's progress. The
earlier examples are reproductions, although those
from the 17th century to the present day are originals, including clogs, swagged musketeers' boots
and even celebrity footwear such as the tiny shoes
of diminutive cellist, Pau Casals. Due to flooding, the
museum will be closed for repairs until late 2009.

Museu Diocesà

*Avda de la Catedral 4 (93 315 22 13). Metro
Jaume I.* **Open** 10am-2pm, 5-8pm Tue-Sat;
11am-2pm Sun. **Admission** €6; €3 reductions;
free under-7s. **Credit** (shop only) MC, V.
Map p344 D4.

The Diocesan Museum contains a hotchpotch of religious art, everything from 14th-century alabaster
virgins and altarpieces by Bernat Martorell to some
wonderful Romanesque murals. The building itself
is also something of a mishmash; it includes the
Gothic Pia Almoina, an almshouse and soup kitchen
founded in 1009 and stuck on to a Renaissance
canon's residence complete with Tuscan columns,
which in turn was built inside an octagonal Roman
defence tower. The museum has space for two temporary exhibitions, usually dedicated to local artists,
photographers and architects.

Museu d'Història de la Ciutat.

★ Museu d'Història de la Ciutat

*Plaça del Rei 1 (93 315 11 11/www.museu
historia.bcn.cat). Metro Jaume I.* **Open** *Apr-Sept*
10am-8pm Tue-Sat; 10am-3pm Sun. *Oct-Mar*
10am-2pm, 4-7pm Tue-Sat; 10am-3pm Sun.
Guided tours by appointment. **Admission**
Permanent exhibitions €6; €4 reductions; free
under-16s. *Temporary exhibitions* €3.50; €2
reductions. Both free 4-8pm 1st Sat of mth.
No credit cards. Map p345 D5.

Stretching from the Plaça del Rei to the cathedral are
4,000sq m (43,000sq ft) of subterranean Roman excavations – streets, villas and storage vats for oil and
wine, all discovered by accident in the late 1920s
when a whole swath of the Gothic Quarter was
upended to make way for the central avenue of Via
Laietana. The excavations continued until 1960;
today, the labyrinth is reached via the Casa Padellàs,
a merchant's palace dating from 1498, which was
laboriously moved from its original location in
C/Mercaders for the construction of Via Laietana.

Admission also allows access to the Capella de
Santa Àgata – with its 15th-century altarpiece by
Jaume Huguet – and the Saló del Tinell, at least when
there's no temporary exhibition. This majestic room
began life in 1370 as the seat of the Catalan parliament and was converted in the 18th century into a
Baroque church, which was dismantled in 1934. The
Rei Martí watchtower is still closed to the public while
it awaits reinforcement. Tickets for the museum are
also valid for the monastery at Pedralbes (*see p115*)
and the Museu Verdaguer (*see p114*).

Walk Roman Remains

Wander where the past is distinctly present.

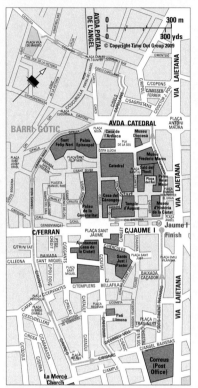

Duration: 45 minutes.

The Roman settlement of Barcino has had an unappreciated impact on the two millennia of life that followed its beginnings. Many of Barcelona's most familiar streets – C/Hospital, even Passeig de Gràcia – follow the line of Roman roads, and the best way to get an idea of the Roman town is to walk the line of its walls. Along the way sit all kinds of Roman remains, poking out from the buildings that have incorporated them or been built over them by medieval builders and those who followed them.

A good place to start a walk is at **C/Paradís**, between the cathedral and Plaça Sant Jaume, where a round millstone is set into the paving to mark what was believed to be the precise centre

of the Mons Taber. It's here that you'll find the remains of the **Temple Romà d'Augusti** (*see p67*). Where C/Paradís meets the Plaça Sant Jaume was where Barcino's two main thoroughfares once met; the road on the left, **C/Llibreteria**, began life as the Cardus Maximus, the main road to Rome. Just off this road is the Plaça del Rei and the extraordinary **Museu d'Història de la Ciutat**, below which is the largest underground excavation of a Roman site in Europe.

Rejoining C/Llibreteria, turn left at **C/Tapineria** to reach **Plaça Ramon Berenguer el Gran** and the largest surviving stretch of ancient wall, incorporated into the medieval Palau Reial. Continue along Tapineria, where you'll find many sections of Roman building, to **Avda de la Catedral**. The massive twin-drum gate on C/Bisbe, while often retouched, has not changed in its basic shape, at least at the base, since it was the main gate of the Roman town. To its left you can see fragments of an aqueduct, and at its front Joan Brossa's bronze letters, spelling out 'Barcino'.

If you take a detour up C/Capellans to **C/Duran i Bas**, you can see another four arches of an aqueduct. Heading left and straight over the Avda Portal de l'Àngel is the Roman necropolis in Plaça Vila de Madrid, with the tombs clearly visible. In accordance with Roman custom, these had to be outside the city walls.

Returning to the cathedral, turn right into **C/Palla**. A little way along sits a large chunk of Roman wall, only discovered in the 1980s when a building was demolished. C/Palla runs into **C/Banys Nous**; at no.16 is a centre for disabled children, inside which is a piece of wall with a relief of legs and feet (phone ahead for a viewing time; 93 318 14 81). At no.4 is **La Granja** (*see p182*), a lovely old café with yet another stretch of Roman wall at the back; beyond this is the junction with **C/Call**, the other end of the *cardus*, and so the opposite side of the Roman town from Llibreteria-Tapineria. The staff of the clothes wholesalers at C/Call 1 are also used to people wandering in to examine their piece of Roman tower. Carry on across C/Ferran and down **C/Avinyó**, the next continuation of the perimeter. Two sides of the cave-like dining room at the back of **El Gallo Kiriko**, the Pakistani restaurant at no.19, are actually formed by portions of the Roman wall.

From **C/Milans**, turn left on to **C/Gignás**. Near the junction with **C/Regomir** are remains of the fourth sea gate of the town, which would have faced the beach, and the Roman shipyard. Take a detour up C/Regomir to visit one of the most important relics of Barcino, the **Pati Llimona**; then, continue walking up **C/Correu Vell**, where there are more fragments of the old city wall, to reach one of the most impressive relics of Roman Barcelona in the small, shady **Plaça Traginers**: a Roman tower and one corner of the ancient wall, in a remarkable state of preservation despite having had a medieval house built on top of it. Finally, turn up **C/Sots-Tinent Navarro**, which boasts a massive stretch of Roman rampart, before finally ending the walk at Plaça de l'Àngel.

Roman necropolis.

★ Museu Frederic Marès

Plaça Sant Iu 5-6 (93 310 58 00/www. museumares.bcn.cat). Metro Jaume I. **Open** 10am-7pm Tue-Sat; 10am-3pm Sun. **Admission** €3; €1.50 reductions; free under-16s. Free 3-7pm Wed, 1st Sun of mth. **Guided tours** noon Sun. **Credit** (shop only) AmEx, MC, V. **Map** p345 D5.

Kleptomaniac and magpie, Frederic Marès (1893-1991) 'collected' everything he laid his hands on, from hairbrushes to opera glasses and gargoyles. Unlike most private 19th-century collectors, Marès didn't come from a wealthy family, but he spent every penny he earned as a sculptor and art professor on broadening his hoardings. Even when the Ajuntament gave him a palace in which to display his collection (and house himself), it wasn't enough; the overflow eventually spread to two other Marès museums in Montblanc and Arenys de Mar.

The exhibits here are divided into three main sections. The basement, ground floor and first floor are devoted to sculpture dating from the Pre-Roman era to the 20th century, including a vast array of polychromed religious carvings, tombs, capitals and entire church portals, exquisitely carved. On the second floor sits the Sentimental Museum, with objects from everyday life; look out for the Ladies' Room, filled with fans, sewing scissors and perfume flasks, and the Entertainment Room, with mechanical toys, puppets and a room dedicated to smoking paraphernalia. Also on the second floor, comprising the third main collection, is a room devoted to photography, and Marès' study and library. It's now filled with sculptures, many of them his own.

From April to September 2009, the museum will be exhibiting the works of Antoni Solà, the Catalan neo-classical sculptor.

FREE Palau de la Generalitat

Plaça Sant Jaume (93 402 46 17/www.gencat. net). Metro Jaume I or Liceu. **Guided tours** every 30-40mins approx 10.30am-1pm, 2nd & 4th Sun of mth; 9.30am-1pm Fri-Sun by appt. **Admission** free. **Map** p345 C5.

Like the Ajuntament, the Palau de la Generalitat has a Gothic side entrance that opens out on to C/Bisbe with a beautiful relief of St George (Sant Jordi), patron saint of Catalonia, made by Pere Johan in 1418. Inside the building, the finest features are the first-floor Pati de Tarongers (Orange Tree Patio), which was to become the model for many patios in Barcelona, and the magnificent chapel of Sant Jordi of 1432-34, the masterpiece of Catalan architect Marc Safont. The Generalitat is traditionally open to the public on Sant Jordi (St George's Day, 23 April), when its patios are spectacularly decorated with red roses, but queues are long. It normally also opens on 11 September (Catalan National Day) and 24 September (La Mercè). The guided tours are generally in Spanish or Catalan, so it's best to call ahead for an English-speaking guide.

SIGHTS

Sinagoga Shlomo Ben Adret

C/Marlet 5 (93 317 07 90/www.callde barcelona.org). Metro Jaume I or Liceu. **Open** 11am-2.30pm, 4-6.30pm Mon-Fri; 11am-2.30pm Sat, Sun. **Admission** €2. **No credit cards**. **Map** p345 C5.

The main synagogue of the Call until the pogrom in 1391, this tiny basement building lay abandoned for many years until its rediscovery and restoration in 1996. Once again a working synagogue, one of the two rooms is a place of worship with several interesting artefacts, the other holds the 14th-century dyeing vats used by the family that lived here until their status as crypto-Jews was discovered. The façade of the building, slightly skewing the street, fulfils religious requirements by which the synagogue has to face Jerusalem; the two windows at knee height allow light to enter from that direction.

FREE Temple Romà d'Augusti

C/Paradís 10 (93 315 11 11). Metro Jaume I. **Open** 10am-8pm Tue-Sat; 10am-3pm Sun. **Admission** free. **Map** p345 D5.

Four stunning fluted Corinthian columns dating from the first century BC soar out of their podium in the most unlikely of places: a back patio of the Mountaineering Centre of Catalonia. Part of the rear corner of the temple devoted to the Roman emperor Augustus (who after his death was elevated to the pantheon), the columns were discovered and isolated from the structure of a medieval building in 1835. The current layout is actually a slight fudging of the original as the right-hand column resided separately in the Plaça del Rei until it was slotted next to the other three in 1956. Opening hours can vary, so, call ahead.

LA RAMBLA

Whether you catch it on a Saturday night full of sombrero-wearing stags or early in the morning when the kiosk-holders are bursting open their fresh stacks of newspapers, one thing is for sure: you won't get La Rambla to yourself. And indeed, why would you want to? In the absence of any great buildings or museums, it's the people who provide the spectacle: from flower-sellers to living statues, operagoers to clubbers (imagined extras in a Fellini movie), market shoppers to tango dancers, all human life is here.

However, there's no escaping the fact that, these days, it's mostly tourists who walk the golden mile from Plaça Catalunya down to the harbour. The business of extracting as much of their money as possible, whether by fair means or foul, has had an inevitable impact on the character of the boulevard, filling it with fast food outlets, short-stay apartments, identikit souvenir shops and pickpockets. After a lot of bad press, the council is desperately trying to smarten up the city's famous boulevard, and the

prostitutes, sex shops, card sharps and fortune tellers are gradually being squeezed out. Even the famous human statues and street artists have been subjected to quality control.

La Rambla started life as a seasonal riverbed which explains both its snaking trajectory, broadening out at the sea end, and also its name, which derives from *ramla*, an Arabic word for sand. The river ran along the western edge of the 13th-century city; after it became an open sewer, it was gradually paved over, although the distinctive wave-patterned paving slabs were not added until after the Civil War. From the Middle Ages to the Baroque era, many churches and convents were built along here, some of which have given their names to sections of the road. Descending from Plaça Catalunya, La Rambla is successively called Rambla de Canaletes, Rambla dels Estudis (or dels Ocells), Rambla de Sant Josep (or de les Flors), Rambla dels Caputxins and Rambla de Santa Mònica. For this reason, many people refer to it in the plural as Les Rambles (Las Ramblas in castellano).

La Rambla also served as the meeting ground for city and country dwellers – on the far side of these church buildings lay the still scarcely built-up Raval, 'the city outside the walls', and rural Catalonia. At the fountain on the corner with C/Portaferrissa, colourful tiles depict the city gateway that once stood here (*porta ferrissa* means 'iron gate'). The space by the gates became a natural marketplace; from these beginnings sprang La Boqueria (*see p211*).

La Rambla took on its present form between approximately 1770 and 1860. The second city wall came down in 1775, and La Rambla was paved and turned into a boulevard. But the avenue only acquired its final shape after the closure of the monasteries in the 1830s, which made land available for new building. No longer on the city's edge, La Rambla became a wide path through the city's heart.

As well as having five names, La Rambla is divided into territories. The first part – at the top, by Plaça Catalunya – was long the territory of shoeshiners and groups of men who came to play chess and hold informal debates, although the sparse new single-seat benches have made it a markedly less sociable place to sit these days. The unassuming Font de Canaletes drinking fountain is beside them; if you drink from it, goes the legend, you'll return to Barcelona. Here, too, is where Barça fans converge to celebrate their triumphs. This part segues into the Rambla dels Ocells; it's named after its ranks of cacophonous bird (*ocell*) stalls, although they're slowly being weeded out by the Ajuntament in an attempt to raise the tone of the boulevard. Next comes perhaps the best-loved section, known as Rambla de les Flors for its line of flower stalls.

SIGHTS

To the right is the **Palau de la Virreina** exhibition and cultural information centre, and the superb Boqueria market. A little further down is the Pla de l'Os (or Pla de la Boqueria), the centrepoint of La Rambla, with a pavement mosaic created in 1976 by Joan Miró and recently restored to its original glory. On the left, where more streets run off into the Barri Gòtic, is the extraordinary **Bruno Quadros** building (1883); a former umbrella shop, it is decorated with roundels of open parasols and a Chinese dragon carrying a Peking lantern.

The lower half of La Rambla is initially more restrained, flowing between the sober façade of the **Liceu** opera house (*see p271*) and the more fin-de-siècle (architecturally and atmospherically) **Cafè de l'Opera** (*see p182*). On the right is C/Nou de la Rambla (where you'll find Gaudí's neo-Gothic **Palau Güell**, partially closed for renovations until at least 2010; *see p82*); the promenade then widens into the Rambla de Santa Mònica. The area has long been a haunt of prostitutes. Clean-up efforts have reduced their visibility, and renovations – including the 1980s addition of an arts centre, the **Centre d'Art Santa Mònica** – have done much to dilute the seediness of the area, but single males walking at night can still expect to be approached. Across the street is the unintentionally hilarious **Museu de Cera** (Wax Museum; *see p233*) and, at weekends,

many stalls selling bric-a-brac and craftwork. Then it's just a short hop to the port, and the Columbus column (*see p85*).

FREE Centre d'Art Santa Mònica

La Rambla 7 (93 316 28 10/www.centredart santamonica.net). Metro Drassanes. **Open** 11am-8pm Tue-Sat; 11am-3pm Sun. **Admission** free. **Map** p345 A7.

In a controversial move, the Generalitat appointed new director Vicenç Altaió to pump up the lacklustre visitor numbers for this contemporary art space. Altaió takes his position in January 2009 and has vowed to create 'a multidisciplinary centre for art, science, thought and communication', although detractors fear that the governmental hijacking of the management will mean diluted programming. After remodelling, the museum is set to reopen in March 2009 with an exhibition titled 'Architecture Without Place'. Other plans include reactivating Vilajoana's neon sculpture of the Cheshire Cat's grin across the façade and turning Drassanes metro station into a sister exhibition space.

Museu de l'Eròtica

La Rambla 96 bis (93 318 98 65/www.erotica-museum.com). Metro Liceu. **Open** *June-Sept* 10am-10pm daily. *Oct-May* 10am-9pm daily. **Admission** €7.50; €6.50 reductions. **Credit** AmEx, MC, V. **Map** p344 B4.

Despite being a condom's toss from the red-light district, the Erotic Museum is a surprisingly limp affair. Expect plenty of filler in the form of Kama Sutra illustrations and airbrushed paintings of naked maidens, with the odd fascinating item such as studded chastity belts or a Victorian walking stick topped with an ivory vagina. Genuine rarities include Japanese drawings, a painful-looking 'pleasure chair' and compelling photos of brothels in the city's Barrio Chino in the decadent 1930s.

Palau de la Virreina

La Rambla 99 (93 316 10 00/www.bcn.cat/cultura). Metro Liceu. **Open** 11am-2pm, 4-8.30pm Tue-Fri; 11am-8.30pm Sat; 11am-3pm Sun. **Admission** *Espai 2* €4.10; €3.08 reductions; free under-16s. *Espai Xavier Miserachs* free. **No credit cards**. **Map** p344 B4.

This classical palace, with Baroque features, takes its name from the widow of an unpopular viceroy of Peru, who commissioned it and lived in it after its completion in the 1770s. The Virreina houses the city cultural department, has information on events and shows, and also strong programming in its two gallery spaces. On the first floor, Espai 2 is devoted to exhibitions of contemporary art, while the free downstairs gallery, named after local photographer Xavier Miserachs, is focused on historical and contemporary photography and also hosts Barcelona's most prestigious annual photo competition: the FotoMercè, held during the Mercè in September.

SIGHTS

Museu de l'Eròtica.

Born & Sant Pere

The onetime waterfront continues to change, for better and for worse.

Both a nexus of medieval architecture and the coolest *barrio* in town, the **Born** is an old, old dog with some fashionable new tricks. Label-happy coolhunters throng the primped pedestrian streets, where museums, restored 13th-century mansions and churches alternate with cafés, galleries and boutiques.

Regeneration has come more slowly for the neighbouring area of **Sant Pere**, which maintains a slightly grungier feel despite the municipal money-pumping. Still, there have been recent large-scale improvements, such as the long Plaça Pou de la Figuera and the spectacularly reinvented Santa Caterina market. Both districts together are still sometimes referred to as **La Ribera** (the Waterfront), a name that recalls the time before permanent quays were built, when the shoreline reached much further inland and the area was contained within the 13th-century wall.

Map pp344-345	**Cafés** p185
Hotels p129	**Tapas bars** p185
Restaurants p155	**Bars** p187

AROUND LA RIBERA

La Ribera is demarcated to the east by the **Parc de la Ciutadella** and to the west by Via Laietana, both products of historic acts of urban vandalism. The first came after the 1714 siege, when the victors, acting on the orders of Philip V, destroyed 1,000 houses, hospitals and monasteries to construct the fortress of the Ciutadella (citadel). The second occurred when the Via Laietana was driven through the district in 1907, in line with the theory of 'ventilating' unsanitary city districts by creating wide avenues; it's now a traffic-choked canyon. In 2010, work is due to start on turning over some of Via Laietana's car lanes to pedestrians.

From the park's north corner, the grand gateway to the area is the **Arc de Triomf**, an imposing, red-brick arch built by Josep Vilaseca as the entrance for the 1888 Universal Exhibition. On the west side, the Josep Reynés sculptures adorning the arch represent Barcelona hosting visitors to the Exhibition, while the Josep Llimona sculptures on the east side depict prizes being awarded to the Exhibition's most outstanding contributors. Leading down to the park is the grand palm-lined boulevard of Passeig Lluís Companys, adorned with street lamps and carved stone benches by Pere Falqués. Once inside the park, it's easy to while away a morning, particularly if combined with a trip to the **Museu de Ciències Naturals** or the **Zoo** (*see p234*).

The area north of C/Princesa is centred around the 10th-century Benedictine monastery of Sant Pere de les Puelles (open for Mass only), which still stands, if greatly altered, in Plaça de Sant Pere. By the main façade is a stunning Modernista wrought-iron drinking fountain designed by Pere Falqués. For centuries, this area was Barcelona's main centre of textile production; to this day, Sant Pere Més Baix, Sant Pere Més Alt and the streets around them contain many textile wholesalers and retailers. Look out for the four low-slung Modernista warehouses of the Serra i Balet velvet manufacturers on neighbouring C/Ortigosa.

The area may be medieval in origin, but its finest monument is one of the most extraordinary works of Modernisme – the **Palau de la Música Catalana**, on C/Sant Pere Més Alt. Less noticed on the same street is a curious feature, the Passatge de les Manufactures, a 19th-century arcade that

Profile Pablo Picasso

The man, the museum, the gift shop.

SIGHTS

'There is where it all began… where I understood how far I could go,' Picasso said of his formative years in Barcelona. His family arrived here just before his 14th birthday; the nine years he was based here, before moving to Paris at 23, were to exert a lifelong influence on his work.

After training in La Llotja art school (where his father taught), the poverty-stricken Picasso lived in the port area, where he became fascinated by the underbelly of *fin-de-siècle* Barcelona – its brothels, beggars and street entertainers feature heavily in his early work. He was also a key member of the bohemian circle of artists at the Quatre Gats café, several of whom became lifelong friends. One was Jaume Sabartés, who later became Picasso's secretary and founder of the **Picasso Museum** (*see p73*).

By the time the museum opened in 1963, Picasso was world famous and the museum was housed in the prestigious Palau Aguilar. Sabartés donated his own personal collection and also united most of Picasso's pieces from the city museums. The collection has grown to fill five adjoining palaces, with more than 3,500 permanent pieces and a constant stream of high-profile temporary shows.

Rather than being an overview of the artist's work, the museum is a record of the young Picasso's vital formative years. The seamless presentation of his development from 1890 to 1904, from deft pre-adolescent portraits to sketchy landscapes to the intense innovations of his Blue Period, is unbeatable. It then leaps to a gallery of mature Cubist paintings from 1917. Those looking for hits such as *Les Demoiselles d'Avignon* (1907) and the first Cubist

paintings from the time (many of them done in Catalonia) will be disappointed. But the *pièce de résistance* is the complete series of 58 canvases based on Velázquez's *Las Meninas*, donated by Picasso himself after the death of Sabartés. Tribute is paid to Sabartés with a room dedicated to Picasso's portraits of him (best known is the Blue Period painting where he wears a white ruff), and Sabartés's own doodlings. The display ends with linocuts, engravings and some wonderful ceramics donated by Picasso's widow. Guided tours in English take place at 6pm on Thursdays and noon Saturdays and are included in the ticket price.

THREE TO SEE
A trio of other Picasso landmarks around town.

Els Quatre Gats
Former hangout of Pablo. *See p182.*

Col·legi d'Arquitectes
Picasso's frieze of Catalan folk scenes. *See p57.*

Passeig Picasso
Site of artist Antoni Tàpies' sculpture *Homage to Picasso.*

passes inside a building between C/Sant Pere Més Alt and C/Ortigosa.

Sant Pere has been renovated with the gradual opening up of a continuation of the Avda Francesc Cambó, which now swings around to meet with C/Allada-Vermell, a wide street that was formed when a block was demolished in 1994. Providing the area with some much-needed open space, the large square of Pou de la Figuera, between C/Sant Pere Més Baix and C/Carders, was completed in 2008 and houses gardens maintained by the neighbours themselves, playgrounds and a football pitch. The **Mercat de Santa Caterina**, one of the city's oldest markets, was been rebuilt to a Gaudiesque design by Enric Miralles.

In the eastern corner of the market, by the newly created square of Joan Capri, is the **Espai Santa Caterina** (open 8.30am-2pm Mon-Wed, Sat; 8.30am-8pm Thur, Fri; free), which houses a portion of the archaeological remains discovered during the market's remodelling. Viewed through a glass floor are Bronze Age buildings, layered beneath a Christian necropolis, and the foundations of the medieval Convent of Santa Caterina, which became the headquarters of the Consell de Cent (embryo of the democratic Barcelona government) and later, the Inquisition.

Another nearby convent is the Convent de Sant Agustí, which is now a civic centre, on C/Comerç. The entrance contains *Deuce Coop*, a magical 'light sculpture' by James Turrell, commissioned by the Ajuntament in the 1980s and is turned on after dark. Almost next door is the **Museu de la Xocolata** (*see p233*).

'Born' originally meant 'joust' or 'list', and in the Middle Ages, and for many centuries thereafter, the neighbourhood's main artery, the Passeig del Born, was the focal point of the city's festivals, processions, tournaments, carnivals and the burning of heretics by the Inquisition. At one end of the road is the old Born market, a magnificent 1870s wrought-iron structure that used to be Barcelona's main wholesale food market but closed in the 1970s. Plans to turn the structure into a library were thwarted by the discovery of perfectly preserved medieval remains. The foundations of buildings razed by Philip V's troops were discovered to contain hundreds of objects, some domestic and some, like rusty bombs, suggesting the traumas of the period. A viewing platform, with useful diagrams and notes, has been erected on C/Fusina and ultimately the remains will be incorporated into a cultural centre and museum, although progress is painfully slow.

Leading off the Passeig del Born is C/Montcada, one of the unmissable streets of old Barcelona. A medieval Fifth Avenue, it's lined with a succession of merchants' mansions, some of the greatest of which house the **Museu Barbier-Mueller d'Art Precolombí** and the **Museu Picasso**; the Museu Tèxtil moved uptown to the Palau Reial de Pedralbes (*see p115*) in October 2008. At its far end is the Placeta d'en Marcús, with its small 12th-century Capella d'en Marcús, built as part of an inn.

It was founded by Bernat Marcús, and said to have been the base for the *correus volants* ('flying runners'), Europe's first postal service by horse. The streets nearby were filled with workshops supplying anything from candles to hemp, and these trades are commemorated in the names of many of the streets (*see p25* **Trading Places**).

At the other end of the Passeig from the market stands the greatest of all Catalan Gothic buildings, the spectacular basilica of **Santa Maria del Mar**. Opposite the main doors is a recently renovated 13th-century drinking fountain with gargoyles of an eagle and a dragon; on the east side is a funnel-shaped red-brick square, built in 1989 on the site where it is believed the last defenders of the city were executed after Barcelona fell to the Spanish army in 1714. Called the Fossar de les Moreres (Mulberry Graveyard), the square is inscribed with a patriotic poem by Frederic Soler, and nationalist demonstrations converge here every September 11 for Catalan National Day. The red 'eternal flame' sculpture is a more recent, and less popular, addition.

From here, narrow streets lead to the Plaça de les Olles, or the grand Pla del Palau and another symbol of La Ribera, **La Llotja** (The Exchange). Its neo-classical outer shell was added in the 18th century, but its core is a superb 1380s Gothic hall, sadly closed to the public, but open doors mean you can often peer inside. Until the exchange moved to Passeig de Gràcia in 1994, this was the oldest continuously functioning stock exchange in Europe.

Museu Barbier-Mueller d'Art Precolombí

C/Montcada 14 (93 310 45 16/www.barbier-mueller.ch). Metro Jaume I. **Open** 11am-7pm Tue-Fri; 10am-7pm Sat; 10am-3pm Sun. **Admission** €3.50; €1.70 reductions; free under-16s. Free 1st Sun of mth. **Credit** (shop only) AmEx, MC, V. **Map** p345 E6.
Located in the 15th-century Palau Nadal, this world-class collection of pre-Columbian art was ceded to Barcelona in 1996 by the Barbier-Mueller Museum in Geneva. The Barcelona holdings focus solely on the Americas, representing most of the styles from the ancient cultures of Meso-America, Andean America and the Amazon region. Dramatically spotlit in black rooms, the frequently changing selection of masks, textiles, jewellery and sculpture

SIGHTS

BARCEL⊗NA M⊗DERNISME R⊗UT

New Guided Visits !!

Domènech i Montaner's **Hospital de Sant P**
Daily visits in English at 10'15 and 12'15 am

Domènech i Montaner's **Palau Montaner**
Visits in English every Saturday at 10'30 am

...and **Gaudí's Pavellons Güell**
Friday through Monday at 10'15 and 12'15 am

More information at 933 177 652 and www.rutadelmodernisme.com

 Ajuntament de Barcelona   Institut del Paisatge Urbà i la Qualitat de Vida

includes pieces dating from as far back as the second millennium BC running through to the early 16th-century (demonstrating just how loosely the term 'pre-Columbian' can be used).

Museu de Ciències Naturals (Natural History Museum)

Passeig Picasso, Parc de la Ciutadella (93 319 69 12/www.bcn.cat/museuciencies). Metro Arc de Triomf. **Open** 10am-6.30pm Tue-Sat; 10am-2.30pm Sun. **Admission** *All exhibitions & Jardí Botànic* €5.30; €3.70 reductions. *Museums only* €3.70; €2.10 reductions. *Temporary exhibitions* €4.10; €2.15 reductions. Free under-16s. Free 1st Sun of mth. **No credit cards. Map** p343 H11.

The Natural History Museum is split between Domènech i Montaner's turreted Castell dels Tres Dragons and the nearby Museu Martorell, housing the zoology and geology museums respectively. The first floor of the zoology museum is a spooky hall of stuffed animals, preserved insects and molluscs, with many of the exotic felines supplied by the nearby zoo. Several animals from the collection have enjoyed a moment of fame being lent out for TV and theatre shows and the horned Mouflon skull was the direct inspiration for the Oscar-winning faun make-up in the film *Pan's Labyrinth*. Don't expect any multimedia displays – this is a strictly old-school affair of glass cases and formaldehyde jars, although there are hands-on activities for children aged three to 12.

Over in the geology museum, the entrance contains a permanent exhibition on the geology of the local volcanic region of Olot, while the recently expanded collection in the Hall of Mineralogy and Petrology includes meteorites, gems, crystals, radioactive minerals and rocks from the Earth's lithosphere. Some 300,000 fossils reside in the Palaeontology Hall alongside 12 full-scale 1917 replicas of large extinct animals. A combined ticket also grants entrance to the Jardí Botànic (Botanic Garden) on Montjuïc (*see p96*).

Museu Picasso

C/Montcada 15-23 (93 256 30 00/www.museu picasso.bcn.cat). Metro Jaume I. **Open** (last ticket 30mins before closing) 10am-8pm Tue-Sun. **Admission** *All exhibitions* €9; €5.80 reductions. *Temporary exhibition only* €5.80; €4.80 reductions; free under-16s. Free (museum only) 1st Sun of mth. **Credit** (shop only) AmEx, MC, V. **Map** p345 E6. *See p70* **Profile**.

Palau de la Música Catalana.

★ Palau de la Música Catalana

C/Sant Francesc de Paula 2 (93 295 72 00/www. palaumusica.org). Metro Urquinaona. **Open** *Box office* 10am-9pm Mon-Sat. *Guided tours Sept-July* 10am-3.30pm daily. *Aug* 10am-6pm. **Admission** €10; €9 reductions. **Credit** (minimum €20) MC, V. **Map** p344 D3.

Commissioned by the nationalistic Orfeó Català choral society, this jawdropping concert hall was intended as a paean to the Catalan *renaixença* and a showcase for the most outstanding Modernista workmanship available. Domènech i Montaner's façade is a frenzy of colour and detail, including a large allegorical mosaic representing the members of the Orfeó Català, and floral tiled columns topped with the busts of Bach, Beethoven and Palestrina on the main façade and Wagner on the side. Inside, a great deal of money has been spent improving the acoustics, but visitors don't really come here to feast their ears: the eyes have it.

Decoration erupts everywhere. The ceiling is an inverted bell of stained glass depicting the sun bursting out of a blue sky; 18 half-mosaic, half-relief Muses appear out of the back of the stage; winged horses fly over the upper balcony. The carved arch over the stage represents folk and classical music: the left side has Catalan composer and conductor Anselm Clavé sitting over young girls singing 'Flors de Maig', a traditional Catalan song, while the right has Wagnerian Valkyries riding over a bust of Beethoven.

By the 1980s, the Palau was bursting under the pressure of the musical activity going on inside it, and a church next door was demolished to make space for Òscar Tusquet's extension, a project

SIGHTS

Walk Parc de la Ciutadella

A stroll around the city's oldest park.

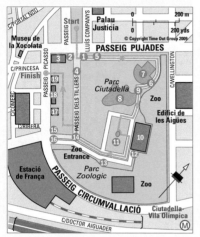

SIGHTS

Duration: 40 minutes

Ciutadella Park is named after the hated Bourbon citadel that occupied this site from 1716 to 1869, and the park came into being after the anti-Bourbon revolution of 1868, when General Prim announced that the area could be reclaimed for public use. The garrison fort was gleefully pulled down by hundreds of volunteers. Later pleasure gardens were built to host the 1888 Universal Exhibition, handsome reminders of which are scattered around the park.

The grandiose **Arc de Triomf** to the north of the park was built to mark its entrance, as was the first of the two 'Statues of Progress' erected for the Exhibition: **Commerce** (❶) is represented on the left, and **Industry** (❷) on the right. Through the entrance is Domènech i Montaner's red-brick-and-tile **Castell de Tres Dragons** (❸) on the right – this served as the exhbition café and now houses the zoology part of the **Natural History Museum** (*see p73*). Stretching ahead is the wide, leafy **Passeig dels Til·lers** (Linden-Tree Boulevard; ❹) and, to the left, Antoni Clavé's modern **Centenary Homage to the Universal Exhibition** (❺).

Continue along this path and turn right at the end: after 20 metres or so is one of the **Wallace Fountains** (❻) on the left. Philanthropist Sir Richard Wallace donated 12 of these wrought-iron drinking fountains to the city in the 19th century, but nowadays only five remain. Continuing round to the right is **La Cascada** (❼), an extravagant waterfall designed by Josep Fontseré, who was assisted by a young and unknown Antoni Gaudí.

From here the path south leads past a pretty **boating lake** (❽) on the right and, on the left, a scale model of a **mammoth** (❾). The original plan was that the much-loved mammoth would be joined by 11 other scale models of prehistoric species, but the writer and geologist behind the idea, Norbert Font i Sagué, died before the plan could be realised.

Continuing south on this path are the **Catalan parliament** (❿) buildings on the left, and the elegant Patio de Armes garden on the right. This was designed by JC Forestier in 1917, and its centrepoint is Josep Llimona's weeping woman, **Disconsolate** (⓫). At the far end of the parliament buildings, next to the former entrance to the zoo, is the **Monument to Walt Disney** (⓬), a group of leaping deer.

Turn right and soon you'll see the **Monument to the Catalan Volunteers** (⓭) on the left. The plaque reads 'To the Catalans killed in France and around the world in defence of freedom, 1914-1918/ 1939-1945'. The plaque was replaced with another, mentioning only the First World War, during Franco's rule, and the naked torso adorned with a puritanical fig-leaf, which is there to this day. Beyond this is the entrance to the zoo, in front of which stands an imposing equestrian **statue of General Prim** (⓮), the driving force behind the park. Gracing the columns either side of the park entrance beyond Prim are the other two 'Progress' statues, **Agriculture** (⓯) and **Seamanship** (⓰).

Instead of leaving this way, however, turn right up the Passeig dels Til·lers where you'll see the **Umbracle** (Shade House; ⓱). This elegant slatted wooden building, also by Fontseré, houses palms and tropical plants, though it has been closed to the public for a while pending restoration. Beside this is the neoclassical home of the geological section of the **Natural History Museum** (⓲), and then, alongside the exit leading to Passeig Picasso, the iron-and-glass, Eiffel-inspired **Hivernacle** (Winter House; ⓳).

which, combined with the extensive renovations to the old building, spanned over 20 years. Rather than try to compete with the existing façade, the new part has subtler, organic motifs in ochre brick – particularly striking are the frilled mushroom gills on the underside of the circular tower.

Guided tours are available in English every hour and start with a short film of the Palau's history. Be sure to ask questions: the guides are very knowledgeable, but unless prompted, they tend to concentrate mainly on the triumphs of the renovation.

★ FREE Parc de la Ciutadella

Passeig Picasso (93 413 2400). Metro Arc de Triomf or Barceloneta. **Open** 9am-sunset daily. **Admission** free. **Map** p343 H11/J11.

There's so much going on in this surprisingly extensive park – the zoo, the Natural History Museum, Catalan parliament buildings, a school, a church, a boating lake, a bandstand – that it's sometimes hard to find a plain, old-fashioned patch of grass. On a sunny Sunday you'll have to fight with the hordes of picnicking families, bongo players and dogs for a bit of the green stuff and even then it will be distinctly worn from serving as a back garden to the space-starved inhabitants of the Old City. *See also p74* **Walk**.

★ FREE Santa Maria del Mar

Plaça de Santa Maria (93 310 23 90). Metro Jaume I. **Open** 9am-1.30pm, 4.30-8pm Mon-Sat; 10am-1.30pm, 4.30-8pm Sun. **Admission** free. **Map** p345 E6.

One of the most perfect surviving examples of the Catalan Gothic style, this graceful basilica stands out for its characteristic horizontal lines, plain surfaces, square buttresses and flat-topped octagonal towers. Its superb unity of style is down to the fact that it was built relatively quickly, with construction taking just 55 years (1329 to 1384). Named after Mary as patroness of sailors, it was built on the site of a small church known as Santa Maria d'Arenys (sand), for its position close to the sea. In the broad, single-nave interior, two rows of perfectly proportioned columns soar up to fan vaults, creating an atmosphere of space around the light-flooded altar. There's also superb stained glass, especially the great 15th-century rose window above the main door. The original window fell down during an earthquake, killing 25 people. The incongruous modern window at the other end was a 1997 addition, belatedly celebrating the Olympics.

It's perhaps thanks to the group of anti-clerical anarchists who set the church ablaze for 11 days in 1936 that its superb features can be appreciated – without the wooden Baroque furniture that clutters so many Spanish churches, the simplicity of its lines can emerge. On Saturdays, the basilica is in great demand for weddings, and it's a traditional venue for concerts, particularly the Requiem Mass at Easter and Handel's *Messiah* at Christmas.

SIGHTS

Streetwise Carrer de la Montcada

A showground of medieval wealth.

SIGHTS

Although it was once a playground for the rich of the Middle Ages, Carrer de la Montcada's dense ranks of mansion conversions make it the most important area of Gothic and Renaissance civic architecture in the city. Its name derives from the noble Montcada family who, in the 12th century, were second only to the royal house in social status and political power; they even get a mention in Cervantes' *Don Quixote*, described as one of the noblest families in the land. They received the plot for their support to King Ramon Berenguer IV during the 1229 conquest of Mallorca, but the family palace they had built is no longer standing.

By the 15th century, the street had become the neighbourhood of choice for nobles and merchants who had made their fortunes in the maritime trade boom. But in the late 1800s, the wealthy migrated

uptown, and many of Montcada's mansions were partitioned into flats, shops and warehouses. In its modern incarnation, Montcada has been pedestrianised and exhaustively restored, and most of the *palaus* (grand town-houses) now house museums.

The street officially begins near the tiny Romanesque Marcús chapel, but is almost immediately cut through by Carrer de la Princesa, which opened in 1853. This end of Montcada is dominated by the **Picasso Museum**, which occupies a quintet of *palaus* (nos.15 to 23) and has spawned a rash of gift shops and buskers catering to all its visitors' painted crockery and Tori Amos requirements.

Of particular note is the richly carved Palau Aguilar at no.15, one of the finest examples of civil Gothic architecture in Catalonia. Berenguer d'Aguilar's coat-of-arms decorates many of the exterior and interior windows and the patio is replete with stone angels, flowers, tendrils and arched galleries. During the restoration process, a painted mural depicting the conquest of Mallorca was found and removed to the MNAC. Also part of the Picasso Museum, the Palau Finestres (no.23) is built over a Roman necropolis and is one of the oldest houses in Barcelona, with sections dating from the 12th century.

Another exceptional builidng is the Palau dels Marquesos de Lió (no.12) with its 13th-century coffered ceilings painted with griffins. In its lovely 18th-century patio is the **Tèxtil Cafè** (*see p185*); it's all that remains of its previous occupant, the Textile and Clothing Museum.

At no.20, the Palau Dalmases houses a baroque bar in a 17th-century conversion of an earlier Gothic building. It retains its Romanesque chapel and a superlative Catalan baroque staircase with twisting Solomonic columns and a frieze depicting the mythological scenes of Europa and the bull as well as Neptune's chariot.

Towards the Placeta Montcada, the **Maeght** art gallery (no.25) snags visitors freshly inspired by the Picasso Museum. It's housed in the Renaissance Palau dels Cervelló, which has the finest Gothic façade on the street, including four fearsome gargoyles.

Raval

Shedding some light on Barcelona's heart of darkness.

For at least the past century, the Raval has been the city's forbidden core, its dark other, both attracting and repelling visitors to its streets busy with the hustle of life. In the early 20th century, the area was notorious for its seedy theatres, brothels, anarchist groups and dosshouses. Gentrification has ensued in recent years, but there are still streets that the brand-conscious city council would prefer visitors not to see.

Despite decades of costly transformation (which, among other additions, have seen the arrival of a huge modern art gallery and a five-star hotel), the old red-light district still retains a busy crew of prostitutes, transsexuals, drug addicts and poor labourers. Many of these unshiftable locals could have stepped straight from the pages of Jean Genet's *The Thief's Journal*, a chronicle of the time the writer spent here as a thieving, teenaged rent boy during the 1920s.

Map p342	Cafés p188
Hotels p130	Tapas bars p189
Restaurants p160	Bars p189

Map p342 · Cafés p188 · Hotels p130 · Tapas bars p189 · Restaurants p160 · Bars p189

REVIVING THE RAVAL

Ever on the margins, Raval (*arrabal* in Spanish) is a generic word adapted from the Arabic *ar-rabad*, meaning 'outside the walls'. When a defensive wall was built down the north side of La Rambla in the 13th century, the area now sandwiched between Avda Paral·lel and La Rambla was a sparsely populated green belt of garden plots. Over the centuries, the land was to absorb the functional spillover from the city in the form of monasteries, churches, religious hospitals, prisons and virtually any noxious industry that citizens didn't want on their doorstep. When industrialisation arrived in the 18th century, the area became Barcelona's working-class district.

This was also the part of town where most land was available; more emerged after the government dissolved the monasteries in 1836, and early industries, mainly the textile mills, took the space. Workers lived in crowded slums devoid of ventilation or running water, and malnutrition, TB, scrofula and typhus kept the average life expectancy to 40 years. It's no coincidence that the city's sanatoriums, orphanages and hospitals were based here.

Then known to most people as the Quinto, or 'Fifth District', the area was also where the underclasses forged the centre of revolutionary Barcelona, a breeding ground for anarchists and other radicals. Innumerable riots and revolts began here; entire streets became no-go areas after dark. Heroin's arrival in the late 1970s caused extra problems; the semi-tolerated petty criminality became more threatening and affected the tourist trade.

Since the 1980s, city planners have done their best to open up the Raval to the rest of the city by turning the area into something of a cultural theme park, installing or rebuilding a slew of high profile cultural institutions. Spurred on by the approaching 1992 Olympics, the authorities made a clean sweep of the Lower Raval. Whole blocks with associations to prostitution or drugs were demolished, and many of the displaced families were transferred to housing estates on the edge of town, out of sight and out of mind. A sports centre, a new police station and office blocks were constructed, and some streets were pedestrianised.

However, the planners were caught by surprise by the sudden mass arrival of non-European immigrants into the area, starting in

SIGHTS

Streetwise Carrer Nou de la Rambla

Seedy sex, scruffy souvenirs and stylish shops.

C/Nou de la Rambla starts in the centre of the city but ends in the woods. From its origins on the busy Rambla, the street cuts straight through the lower Raval, crosses Avda Paral·lel and climbs Montjuïc, where it ends just as the mountain greenery takes over. In days gone by the street was one of the city's liveliest thoroughfares, known popularly as 'Fashion Avenue' for its numerous clothes shops. The street also bustled night and day with *bodegas* and low- and high-class brothels. To please the whims of wealthy clients and their mistresses, many of the clothing shops would stay open around the clock to outfit customers before they hit one of the fashionable cabarets or dance halls

nearby. Living remnants among the souvenir shops include the tiny Ara shoe store at no.4, and the J Sospedra men's outfitters at no.8. Both places design and sell their own brands.

La Emilia, the area's most famous brothel, was located directly opposite Gaudí's Palau Güell, in what is now the Hotel Gaudí. Another survivor, albeit thoroughly reformed, is the **Torres** wine shop at no.25, currently run by the third generation of the ever-friendly Torres family. Offering an excellent selection of Spanish wines and liquors, the shop has had its share of famous clients; among them were the great flamenco singer and dancer Carmen Amaya, who used to perform there for a glass of wine. Further along is the **London Bar** (*see p190*), a Modernista gem and one-time gathering place for circus types such as renowned clown Charlie Rivel.

For the sharp of eye, a rusted iron wheel is visible where the façades of buildings nos.49 and 50 meet: this relic used to connect electricity to the city tram that ran along the street until the 1940s. A little further on, the past's sleazy side is still evident at the intersection with C/Sant Ramon, lined with hookers and their clients from midday onwards. As the Nou de la Rambla nears Avda Paral·lel, an avenue once famous for its cabarets, another seedy leftover is the **Bagdad** strip club at no.103. A statue of the actress Raquel Meller at the intersection with Paral·lel pays homage to the many theatres that once existed nearby.

The street offers a few more gems after crossing Paral·lel, such as the historic **Apolo** dance hall (*see p262*) and, much higher up at no.169, **Refugi 307** (*see p98*), a restored Civil War air raid shelter.

the 1990s. These new residents have perhaps done more to transform the Raval than any of the council's best laid plans. By 2006, more than half the *barrio*'s residents were from outside Spain, the majority from Pakistan and Ecuador. The Raval is now one of the most ethnically diverse places in Europe, with more than 70 different nationalities calling it home. Shop signs appear in a babel of languages, plugging everything from halal meat to Bollywood films and cheap calls to South America.

Despite this immigration, the council continued with its ambitions to revive the area. The most dramatic plan was to create a '*Raval obert al cel*' ('Raval open to the sky'), the most tangible result of which is the sweeping, palm-lined Rambla del Raval (completed in 2000). L'Illa de la Rambla del Raval, also known as the Illa Robador, is a mega-complex halfway up the new rambla that includes a hotel, offices, protected housing, shops and the Filmoteca (due to be finished in 2009 but held up by the

SIGHTS

discovery of Bronze Age remains). The nondescript housing blocks were completed by 2007, while new office space and a luxury hotel were due to open at the end 2008. The hotel was designed, in the words of its architect Pere Puig as 'a cylindrical lamp to shed light on a dark neighbourhood'; however, after local complaints of light pollution, the building was instead coated in steel mesh, ostensibly to protect its guests' privacy. Whatever the case, the shiny armour of a high-end hotel in the middle of a once working-class district is an unbeatable symbol of the growing disconnect in the city between tourism and local neighbourhood life.

The facelift has raised the prices. Alongside the immigrants, a wealthier community of arty western expats and university students have begun to arrive, dotting the area with galleries, shops and cafés. In and around C/Lluna you'll find a good number of small, inviting boutiques stocking locally designed clothes; C/Ferlandina has its share of boho cafés; and the old industrial spaces along C/Riereta now serve as studios to more than 40 artists.

Despite its gentrification, the Raval has not lost its associations with crime and sleaze. Take care, particularly after dark in the area down towards the port. That said, as long as you exercise the usual precautions – staying off badly lit side-streets, not flaunting your new digital camera – the Raval can make for a fascinating wander.

UPPER RAVAL

From La Rambla, signposts for the MACBA carefully guide visitors along the gentrified 'tourist corridors' of C/Tallers, C/Elisabets and C/Bonsuccès to a playground of cafés, galleries and boutiques. The centre of the Upper Raval is the Plaça dels Àngels, where the 16th-century Convent dels Àngels houses both the FAD design institute and a gigantic almshouse, the Casa de la Caritat, converted into a cultural complex housing the **MACBA** and the **CCCB**.

When the clean, high-culture MACBA opened in 1995, it seemed to embody everything the Raval was not, and it was initially mocked as an isolated and isolating social experiment. But, over the years, the square has become unofficial home to the city's skateboarders and the surrounding streets have filled with restaurants and boutiques. In 2006, after seven years of building work, the university faculties of philosophy, geography and history finally opened opposite the entrance to the CCCB, and thousands of students are now changing the character of the place.

Below here C/Hospital and C/Carme meet at the Plaça Pedró, where the tiny Romanesque chapel (and ex-lepers' hospital) of Sant Llàtzer

sits. From La Rambla, the area is accessed along either street or through the Boqueria market, itself the site of the Sant Josep monastery until the sale of church lands led to its destruction in the 1830s. Behind the Boqueria is the **Antic Hospital de la Santa Creu**, which took in the city's sick from the 15th century until 1926; it now houses the Massana Arts School, a small neighbourhood library as well as the much larger Catalan National Library, the headquarters of the Institute of Catalan Studies and **La Capella**, an attractive exhibition space.

C/Carme is capped at the Rambla end by the 18th-century Església de Betlem (Bethlehem) with its serpentine pillars and geometrically patterned façade. Its name features on many shop signs nearby; older residents still refer to this part of the Raval as Betlem.

FREE Antic Hospital de la Santa Creu & La Capella

C/Carme 47-C/Hospital 56 (no phone). Metro Liceu. **Open** 9am-8pm Mon-Fri; 9am-2pm Sat. *La Capella (93 442 71 71)* noon-2pm, 4-8pm Tue-Sat; 11am-2pm Sun. **Admission** free. **Map** p344 A4.

This was one of Europe's earliest medical centres. There was a hospital on the site as early as 1024, but in the 15th century it expanded to centralise all the city's hospitals and sanatoriums (with the exception of the Santa Margarida leper colony, which remained outside the city walls). By the 1920s, it was hopelessly overstretched, and its medical facilities were moved uptown to the Hospital Sant Pau. One of the last patients was Gaudí, who died here in 1926; it was also where Picasso painted one of his first important pictures, *Dead Woman* (1903).

The buildings combine a 15th-century Gothic core with Baroque and classical additions. They're now given over to cultural institutions, among them the Massana Arts School, a neighbourhood library, the Catalan National Library (the second largest in Spain), the Institute of Catalan Studies and the Royal Academy of Medicine, which hosts occasional concerts. Highlights include a neo-classical lecture theatre complete with revolving marble dissection table (open 10am-2pm Mon-Fri), and the entrance hall of the Casa de Convalescència, tiled with lovely Baroque ceramic murals telling the story of St Paul; one features an artery-squirting decapitation scene. La Capella, the hospital chapel, was rescued from a sad fate as a warehouse and sensitively converted to an exhibition space for contemporary art. The courtyard is a popular spot for reading or eating lunch.

★ CCCB (Centre de Cultura Contemporània de Barcelona)

C/Montalegre 5 (93 306 41 00/www.cccb.org). Metro Catalunya. **Open** 11am-8pm Tue, Wed, Fri-Sun; 11am-10pm Thur. **Admission**

SIGHTS

Airline flights are one of the biggest producers of the global warming gas CO_2. But with **The CarbonNeutral Company** you can make your travel a little greener.

Go to **www.carbonneutral.com** to calculate your flight emissions then 'neutralise' them through international projects which save exactly the same amount of carbon dioxide.

Contact us at **shop@carbonneutral.com** or call into the office on **0870 199 99 88** for more details.

CarbonNeutral®flights

1 exhibition €4.50; €3.40 reductions & Wed.
2 exhibitions €6; €5.60 reductions & Wed. Free
under-16s. Free 1st Wed of mth; 8-10pm Thur.
Credit MC, V. **Map** p344 A2.
Spain's largest cultural centre was opened in 1994
at the Casa de la Caritat, a former almshouse, built
in 1802 on the site of a medieval monastery. The
massive façade and part of the courtyard remain
from the original building; the rest was rebuilt in
dramatic contrast, all tilting glass and steel, by
architects Piñon and Viaplana, known for the
Maremàgnum shopping centre (*see p197*). The
CCCB's exhibitions can lean toward heavy-handed
didacticism, but there are occasional gems.
► *The CCCB stages many literary, music and
dance festivals; see pp224-231.*

MACBA (Museu d'Art Contemporani de Barcelona)

*Plaça dels Àngels 1 (93 412 08 10/www.macba.
es). Metro Catalunya.* **Open** *last wk in June-Sept
24* 11am-8pm Mon, Wed; 11am-midnight Thur,
Fri; 10am-8pm Sat; 10am-3pm Sun. *last wk in
Sept-June 23* 11am-7.30pm Mon, Wed-Fri; 10am-
8pm Sat; 10am-3pm Sun. *Guided tours* (Catalan/
Spanish) 6pm Wed, Sat; noon Sun. **Admission**
Permanent collection €3; €2 reductions. *Permanent
& temporary exhibitions* €7.50; €6 reductions.
Temporary exhibitions €4; €3 reductions.
Wed €3.50. **Credit** MC, V. **Map** p344 A2.
The real show at the MACBA is the building itself,
Richard Meier's cool iceberg of a museum sitting
imperturbably amid the ceaseless scrape and clatter
of skateboarders on the Plaça dels Àngels. While the
museum has fattened up its holdings considerably
since opening in 1995, the shows are often heavily
political in concept and occasionally radical to the
point of inaccessibility, and queues to enter are practically unheard of. Perhaps aware of this, the
MACBA's new director, Bartomeu Mari, has
expressed the desire to put the thrill back into art.
Given, however, that Mari is an inside man, and formerly the museum's chief curator, the real excitement
will probably continue to be the skaters outside.
    The exhibits cover the last 50 years or so; although
there's no permanent collection as such, some of the
works from the museum's holdings are usually on
display. The earlier pieces are strong on artists such
as Antonio Saura and Tàpies who were members of
the Dau-al-Set, a group of radical writers and
painters, much influenced by Miró, who kick-started
the Catalan art movement after the post-Civil War
years of cultural apathy. Jean Dubuffet and Basque
sculptors Jorge Oteiza and Eduardo Chillida also feature. Works from the last 40 years are more global,
with the likes of Joseph Beuys, Jean-Michel Basquiat,
AR Penck and photographer Jeff Wall; the contemporary Spanish collection includes Catalan painting
(Ferran García Sevilla, Miquel Barceló) and sculpture
(Sergi Aguilar, Susana Solano). The MACBA's new
director also wants to expand the museum's works

from the 1980s and '90s. For 2009 shows include
German pop artist Thomas Bayrle and Brazilian
Cildo Meireles (Feb-Apr) and a retrospective of John
Cage (Oct 2009-Jan 2010). During the summer months,
the MACBA stays open until midnight (€3.50 after
8pm) and offers guided tours of the exhibitions
(8.30pm and 10pm). *Photo p82.*

LOWER RAVAL

The lower half of the Raval, from C/Hospital
downwards, is generally referred to as the
Barrio Chino (translated into Catalan as 'Barri
Xino' or simply 'el Xino'). The nickname was
coined in the 1920s by a journalist likening the
neighbourhood to San Francisco's Chinatown,
and referred to its underworld feel rather than
to any Chinese population. In those days,
drifters filled the bars, and cheap hostels lined
the streets such as Nou de la Rambla, alongside
high-class cabarets and brothels for the rich,
and cheap porn pits for the poor. A glimpse of
the old sleaze can still be found in and around
bars such as Bar Pastís and Marsella (also
known as the 'absinthe bar', *see p190*). A small
and appropriately seedy square is named after
Jean Genet, whose novel *The Thief's Journal*
(1949) describes his days as a Xino rent boy
and beggar in the 1920s and '30s.
    Just beneath C/Hospital in the Plaça Sant
Agustí lies one of the Raval's more arresting
pieces of architecture, the unfinished 18th-
century **Església de Sant Agustí** (no.2, no
phone, Mass 11am, 1pm & 8pm Mon-Fri, 11am
Sat, 11am, noon & 8pm Sun). The stone beams
and jags protruding from its left flank (on C/Arc
de Sant Agustí) and the undecorated sections
of the Baroque façade show how suddenly
work stopped when funding ran out. Inside,
the Capella de Santa Rita is packed on her feast

**INSIDE TRACK
ORPHANS' TURNSTILE**

A coat of arms, a slot for alms and a
small circular wooden framed door,
are all that remains of the façade of the
Casa de la Misericòrdia at C/Ramalleres
17. Founded as a hospice in 1583, it
later became the Casa Provincial de
Maternitat i Expòsits (Maternity and
Abandoned Children's Home), run by
nuns. From 1853 to 1931, the wooden
turnstile was a way to leave a very young
child anonymously in the nuns' care. The
infant would be placed on the revolving
surface, a screen would close behind it
and the nuns would hang a label round
his or her neck stating the date of entry.

SIGHTS

SIGHTS

day, 22 May; Rita is the patron saint of lost causes and it is to her that the unhappy and unrequited bring their red roses to be blessed.

C/Nou de la Rambla (*see p78* **Streetwise**), the area's main street, is home to Gaudí's first major project: the medievalist townhouse **Palau Güell** at no.3 (*see below*). Nearby, in C/Sant Pau, is a Modernista landmark, Domènech i Montaner's Hotel España, and at the end of the same street sits the Romanesque church of **Sant Pau del Camp**. Iberian remains dating to 200 BC have been found next to the building, marking it as one of the oldest parts of the city. At the lower end of the area were the Drassanes (shipyards), now home to the Museu Marítim (*see p87*). Along the Avda Paral·lel side of this Gothic building lies the only large remaining section of Barcelona's 14th-century city wall.

FREE Palau Güell

C/Nou de la Rambla 3 (93 317 39 74/www. palauguell.cat). Metro Drassanes or Liceu. **Open** 10am-2.30pm Tue-Sat. **Admission** free. **Map** p345 A6.

A fortress-like edifice shoehorned into a narrow six-storey sliver, the Palau Güell was Gaudí's first major commission, begun in 1886 for textile baron Eusebi Güell. After major structural renovation, it has partially reopened to the public, and is expected to fully reopen in 2010. For the time being visitors can look around the subterranean stables, with an exotic canopy of stone palm fronds on the ceiling, and the ground floor. Here the vestibule has ornate mudéjar carved ceilings from which the Güells could snoop on their arriving guests through the jalousie trelliswork; at the heart of the house lies the spectacular six-storey hall complete with musicians' galleries and topped by a dome covered in cobalt honeycomb tiles. Visitors are also shown a short video about the building. The antidote to this dark and gloomy palace lies on its roof terrace, decorated with a rainbow forest of 20 mosaic-covered chimneys.

▶ *For more on Gaudí, see pp50-53.*

★ Sant Pau del Camp

C/Sant Pau 101 (93 441 00 01). Metro Paral·lel. **Open** *Visits* 5-8pm Mon; 10.30am-1.30pm, 5-8pm Tue-Fri. *Mass* 8pm Sat; noon Sun. **Admission** *Visits* €2; €1 reductions. *Mass* free. **No credit cards. Map** p342 E11.

The name, St Paul in the Field, reflects a time when the Raval was still countryside. In fact, this little Romanesque church is over 1,000 years old; the date carved on its most prestigious headstone – that of Count Guifré II Borrell, son of Wilfred 'the Hairy' and inheritor of all Barcelona and Girona – is AD 912.

The church's impressive façade includes sculptures of fantastical flora and fauna along with human grotesques. The tiny cloister is another highlight with its extraordinary Visigoth capitals, triple-lobed arches and central fountain.

MACBA. *See p81.*

Barceloneta & the Ports

Nautical but nice: Barcelona's shoreline has spruced itself up no end.

From industrial slum to leisure port, Barcelona's shoreline transformation is the result of two decades of development, which started in preparation for the 1992 Olympics and just kept on going. The clean-up has extended to the whole seven kilometres of city seashore: this stretch is now a virtually continuous strip of modern construction bristling with new docks, marinas, hotels, cruise-ship terminals, ferry harbours and leisure areas.

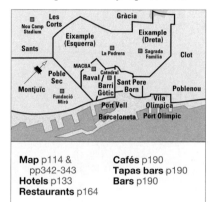

Map p114 &	Cafés p190
pp342-343	Tapas bars p190
Hotels p133	Bars p190
Restaurants p164	

The seafront got a second blast of wind in its sails from the 2004 Fòrum, which spawned a huge new swimming and watersports area, resculpted beaches and a park. The final grand project at the far end of Barcelona's waterfront is a state-of-the-art marine zoo with four different ecosystems. Despite fierce protest from environmentalists, it's due to open in 2010.

PORT VELL

The initial focus of the Olympic makeover was the area rechristened Port Vell ('Old Port'). Tearing out the railroad, warehouses and waste dumps that cut the city off from the sea, developers carved out a palm-lined promenade ringing a luxury yacht marina. Yet this was by no means the area's first major transformation.

In the Middle Ages, the area was converted from a stretch of shifting sand bars to a port befitting Barcelona's position as the dominant naval power in western Mediterranean trade. The main port was moved from the south side of Montjuïc mountain (now the container port) to the city side, which was fitted out with wharves, a large breakwater and the immense Drassanes Reials ('Royal Shipyards'). Now home to the **Museu Marítim**, the shipyards remain among the finest pieces of civilian Gothic architecture in Spain.

Barcelona's power was dealt a blow when Christopher Columbus sailed westwards and found what he thought was the East. Soon, the Atlantic became the important trade route and Barcelona went into recession. Still, the city commemorates Columbus with the **Monument a Colom**. Prosperity returned in the 19th century, when the city became the base for the Spanish industrial revolution. Trade is booming at the Moll d'Espanya ('Wharf of Spain'), an artificial island linked to the bottom of La Rambla by the wavy wooden Rambla de Mar footbridge designed by Viaplana and Piñón. The island is home to the Maremàgnum mall (*see p197*), an IMAX cinema (*see p238*) and L'Aquàrium (*see p232*) and fronted by the royal nautical and maritime clubs.

At Columbus's feet, both the **Catamaran Orsom** and the **Golondrinas** pleasure boats begin their excursions out to sea. To the right, beyond the busy ferry and cruise ports, is the

SIGHTS

Streetwise Carrer La Maquinista

Track back to the days of wagons and wheels.

With its well-kept façades and restaurants, C/Maquinista is one of the smarter streets in Barceloneta, but its beginnings were dirty, brutish and downright dangerous. The street is named after the giant factory and principal employer of the district, La Maquinista Terrestre i Marítima, which opened in 1855 and built locomotives, ships and freight cars. Until 1944, the narrow street was laid with a railway track that ferried materials between the port, the factory and the warehouses lined up along what is now the marina. The trains passed inches from the occupants' front doors and more than one of the older neighbours remembers some hairy moments with children playing in the street too close to the wagons.

All that now remains of the factory is a high stone archway at the end of the street furthest removed from the gentrified tourist promenade of Passeig Joan de Borbó. This arch was the main entrance to the factory, along with a preserved chimney and bridge crane on the other side of the perpendicular C/Salvat Papasseit.

This end of Maquinista is populated by corner shops and kebab bars, but things smarten up abruptly as the road broadens into a square dotted with bar terraces at the back entrance of the schmick new Barceloneta market. Opposite, in sharp contrast to the steel and glass of the market, is 250-year-old **Can Ramonet** at no.17 (*see p164*), painted pink and decorated with old barrels from the days when it was a wine shop, serving pricey seafood to tourists.

Past the square at no.18 is a stunning Modernista building by Domènec Boada Piera (1910) with chunky stucco carvings of curling vegetation and tendrils decorating the curved balconies and windows. A little way along at no.10 is another architectural gem, by Josep Masdeu (1929), this time with typical Noucentista details such as sgraffito depictions of mythological scenes on the façade and the chessboard ceramic patterns on the first floor parapets.

At no.8, the **Catalan Taverna d'en Pep** restaurant has grown from what used to be a tiny hole-in-the-wall delicatessen. Opposite at no.3 is the infamous **La Bombeta**, an old-school tapas bar with endless queues outside at Sunday lunchtime and full of diners inside eager to try the fiery potato *bombas*.

grandly named Porta d'Europa, the longest drawbridge in Europe, which curtains off the vast container port. Big as it is, plans are under way to enlarge the container port by diverting the mouth of the River Llobregat a mile or so to the south, doubling the port area in size by 2050. Andreu Alfaro's enormous *Onas* (Waves) greatly cheers up the gridlocked roundabout of Plaça de la Carbonera, where a grim basin of coal marks where steamboats once refuelled.

Parallel with the Passeig de Colom, the refurbished Moll de la Fusta ('Wood Wharf') boulevard was built after the city sea walls were demolished in 1878. The wooden pergolas, one of which is topped by Javier Mariscal's popular fibreglass *Gamba* ('shrimp'), are all that remain of some ill-fated restaurants and clubs, while traffic noise and congestion has been greatly reduced by passing the coastal motorway underneath the boulevard.

Just over the grassy slopes is the *Ictineo II*; it's a replica of the world's first combustion-powered submarine, created by Narcis Monturiol and launched from Barcelona port in 1862. Roy Lichtenstein's pop art *Barcelona Head* signposts the marina, with more than 450 moorings for leisure boats, and the Palau de Mar, the only remaining warehouse from the area's industrial past, which has been stylishly converted into airy offices, restaurants and the **Museu d'Història de Catalunya**. The adjoining Moll del Dipòsit ('Warehouse Wharf') is crammed at the weekends with a craft market, immigrants selling knock-off goods from blankets, and afternoon strollers.

Catamaran Orsom

Portal de la Pau, Port de Barcelona (93 441 05 37/www.barcelona-orsom.com). Metro Drassanes. **Sailings** (approx 1hr 20mins; call to confirm times) *mid Mar-Oct* noon-8pm. **Tickets** €12.50-€14.90; €6.50-€9.50 reductions; free under-4s. **No credit cards. Map** p342 F12. Departing from the jetty just by the Monument a Colom, this 23m (75ft) sail catamaran is the largest in Barcelona – it chugs up to 80 seafarers round the Nova Bocana harbour area, before unfurling its sails and peacefully gliding across the bay. There are 8pm jazz cruises from June to September or, if you don't want to fight for the trampoline sun deck, the catamaran can also be chartered for private trips.

Las Golondrinas

Moll de Drassanes (93 442 31 06/www.las golondrinas.com). Metro Drassanes. **Sailings** *Drassanes to breakwater & return (35mins): Jan-Mar, Nov, Dec* 11.45am-4pm Mon-Fri; 11.45am-5pm Sat, Sun. *Apr-June, Oct* 11am-6pm Mon-Fri; 11.45am-7pm Sat, Sun. *July-Sept* 11.45am-7.30pm daily. *Drassanes to Port Fòrum & return (1hr 30mins): Jan-Mar, Nov, Dec* 11.30am, 12.30pm,

1.20pm, 3.30pm, 4.30pm daily. *Apr-June, Oct* 11.30am, 12.30pm, 1.20pm, 3.30pm, 4.30pm, 5.30pm, 6.30pm daily. *July-Sept* 11.30am, 12.30pm, 1.20pm, 3.30pm, 4.30pm, 5.30pm, 6.30pm, 7.30pm daily. **Tickets** *Drassanes to breakwater & return* €5.50; free under-4s. *Drassanes to Port Fòrum & return* €11.50; €9 reductions; free under-4s. **Credit** MC, V. **Map** p342 F12. Since the 1888 World Exhibition, the 'swallow boats' have chugged around the harbour, giving passengers a bosun's eye-view of Barcelona's rapidly changing seascape. The traditional double-decker pleasure boats serve the shorter port tour (boats depart around every 40 minutes) while the more powerful catamarans tour as far as the Port Fòrum. The new Cine Mar tours (€25) on Friday and Saturday at 10pm show black and white films from the silent era with an authentic live piano accompaniment.

★ Monument a Colom

Plaça Portal de la Pau (93 302 52 24). Metro Drassanes. **Open** *June-Sept* 9am-8.30pm daily. *Oct-May* 9am-8pm daily. **Admission** €2.50; €1.50 reductions; free under-4s. **Credit** AmEx, MC, V. **Map** p342 F12. Inspired by Nelson's Column, and complete with eight majestic lions, the Christopher Columbus monument was designed for the Universal Exhibition of 1888. Positioned at the base of La Rambla, the monument allegedly marks the spot where Columbus docked in 1493 after his discovery of the Americas, and the carvings illustrate key moments in his voyages. Columbus's white hair comes courtesy of the city pigeons so take appropriate cover if you decide to take the tiny lift up inside the column to the vertiginous viewing platform.

Museu d'Història de Catalunya

Plaça Pau Vila 3 (93 225 47 00/www.mhcat. net). Metro Barceloneta. **Open** 10am-7pm Tue, Thur-Sat; 10am-8pm Wed; 10am-2.30pm Sun. **Admission** *All exhibitions* €5; €4 reductions; free under-7s. *Temporary exhibitions* €3; €2 reductions; free under-7s; free to all 1st Sun of mth. **Credit** (shop only) MC, V. **Map** p342 G12/F12. The Catalan History Museum spans the Lower Paleolithic era right up to Jordi Pujol's proclamation as President of the Generalitat in 1980. It offers a virtual chronology of the region's past, through two

---

INSIDE TRACK
MONUMENT A COLOM

Despite putting the city out of business, Columbus was commemorated in 1888. Consistent with the great discoverer's errant sense of direction, he's pointing not west to the Americas, but eastwards to Mallorca.

floors of text, film, animated models and reproductions of everything from a medieval shoemaker's shop to a 1960s bar. Hands-on activities, such as trying to lift a knight's armour or irrigating lettuces with a Moorish water wheel, add a little pzazz to the rather dry early history; to exit the exhibition, visitors walk over a huge 3-D map of Catalonia. Every section has a decent introduction in English; the reception desk can offer in-depth English-language museum guides free of charge, and the English website is also very complete. Excellent temporary exhibitions typically examine recent aspects of regional politics and history while the huge rooftop café terrace has unbeatable views over the city and marina.

▶ *For an overview of Catalonia's past turn to the History chapter (see pp16-33).*

★ Museu Marítim

Avda Drassanes (93 342 99 20/www.museu maritimbarcelona.com). Metro Drassanes. **Open** 10am-7pm daily. **Admission** €6.50; €5.20 reductions; free under-7s. *Temporary exhibitions vary. Combined ticket with Las Golondrinas* (35mins) €9.60; €7.40 reductions; free under-4s. (1hr 30mins) €14.40; €5.50 reductions; free under-4s. **Credit** MC, V. **Map** p342 F12.

Even if you can't tell a caravel from a catamaran, the excellent Maritime Museum is well worth a visit, as the soaring arches and vaults of vast shipyards represent one the most perfectly preserved examples of civil Gothic architecture in Spain. In medieval times, the shipyards sat right on the water's edge and were used to dry-dock, repair and build vessels for the royal fleets. The finest of these was Don Juan de Austria's galley, from which he commanded the fleet at Lepanto that defeated the Ottoman navy: a full-scale replica is the mainstay of the collection. With the aid of an audio guide, the maps, mastheads, nautical instruments, multimedia displays and models show you how shipbuilding and navigation techniques have developed over the years. Admission also covers the beautiful 1917 Santa Eulàlia schooner docked nearby in the Moll de la Fusta.

Transbordador Aeri

Torre de Sant Sebastià, Barceloneta (93 441 48 20). Metro Barceloneta. **Open** *Mid June-mid Sept* 11am-8pm daily. *Mid Sept-mid June* 10.45am-7pm daily. **Tickets** €9 single; €12.50 return; free under-6s. **No credit cards**. **Map** p342 E12/F13/G13.

These rather battered cable cars do not appear to have been touched – except for the installation of lifts – since they were built for the 1929 Expo. They provide sky-high views over Barcelona on their grinding, squeaking path from the Sant Sebastià tower at the very far end of Passeig Joan de Borbó to the Jaume I tower in front of the World Trade Center; the final leg ends at the Miramar lookout point on Montjuïc. Go late to avoid the long queues.

BARCELONETA

Fishing tackle shops are moving out and cocktail bars are moving in. The tight-knit seaside community of Barceloneta ('Little Barcelona') is metamorphosing from a working-class neighbourhood dependent on fishing and heavy industry into a node of leisured bucket-and-spade tourism with ever greater numbers of bars, restaurants and homes converted into short-stay holiday flats.

And there is more to come. As part of the Pla de Barris initiative, more than €16 million are being pumped in to improve buildings and sanitary conditions and open up the cramped interior to the main promenades; there is even talk of a new *rambla*, connecting the recently remodelled market square to the beach. It looks good on paper, but many residents are suspicious of the motives behind this vision of a shiny new Barceloneta, fearful that it's simply a municipal push to transform a neglected slice of beachfront real estate into a tourist playground.

But controversy is not new in Barceloneta. When the old maritime *barri* of La Ribera was demolished in 1714 to make way for the citadel,

SIGHTS

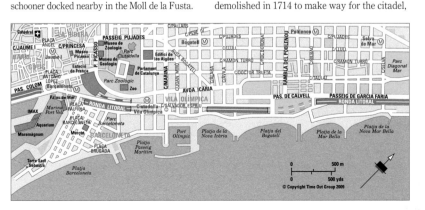

© Copyright Time Out Group 2009

Rebecca Horn's **Estel Ferit** (right).

thousands were left homeless to live in slums on the beach. The question of where to put them was solved by the broad tongue of silt that had built up after the construction of a breakwater in 1474; by the 18th century, it was solid enough to build on, and in 1753, the new district of Barceloneta was born. Military engineer Juan Martín Cermeño laid out narrow rows of cheap workers' housing set around a parade ground (now the market square). The two-storey houses became home to fishermen, sailors and dockers.

With the arrival of factories and shipbuilding yards in the 19th century, the area soon became so overcrowded with workers that the houses were split in half and later quartered. These famous *quarts de casa* typically measured no more than 30 square metres (320 square feet), had no running water until the 1960s and often held families of ten or so. Most were later built up to six or more levels, but even today, many of the flats remain cramped and in bad condition despite their brightly painted façades.

Since the Olympic clean-up, Barceloneta has had a higher profile, and current redevelopment includes university housing, Enric Miralles's glass-covered Gas Natural headquarters and, in the heart of the neighbourhood, the new market designed by Josep Miàs, a choppy composition of slats, undulating steel, solar panels and wrought iron recycled from the original 1884 structure. The new market and large central square have acted as a catalyst for small businesses which cater to the increasingly

international local population with new restaurants, food shops and boutiques.

The area has also been the beneficiary of a staggering amount of sculpture, particularly around the main promenade of Passeig Joan de Borbó. Lothar Baumgarten's *Rosa dels Vents* (Wind Rose) has the names of Catalan sea winds embedded in the pavement, and, at the other end of Passeig Joan de Borbó is Juan Muñoz's disturbing sculpture of five caged figures known as *Una habitació on sempre plou* (A Room Where It Always Rains). Monuments within the quarter include the 18th-century church of Sant Miquel del Port, with a muscular sculpture of the Archangel Michael on the façade and the Font de Carmen Amaya at the sea end of C/Sant Carles, a fountain dedicated to the famous gypsy flamenco dancer who was born in 1913 in the Somorrostro, a long-gone beach slum.

Follow the yachts moored along the Moll de la Barceloneta down to the small remaining fishing area by the clock tower (previously a beacon to guide ships into port) which is the emblem of the neighbourhood. Further down, the road leads to the Nova Bocana development, which is currently under construction. The complex will combine high-end leisure facilities and offices and is dominated by Ricardo Bofill's Hotel Vela, a towering sail-shaped luxury hotel slowly rising under a sheath of scaffolding. If you head left where Passeig Joan de Borbó passes the beach, you'll reach Rebecca Horn's tower of rusty cubes, *Estel Ferit* (Wounded

GOT YOUR PHONE?
YOUR WALLET?
YOUR TRASH?

Star), which pays homage to the much-missed *xiringuitos* (beach restaurants) that lined the sands in pre-Olympic days. The Passeig Marítim esplanade runs north from here, and is a popular hangout for skaters and strollers.

BEACHES

Barcelona never had much of a beach culture until the 1992 Olympics opened the city's eyes to the commercial potential of its location. What little sand there was before then was grey and clogged with private swimming baths and *xiringuitos* that served seafood on trestle tables set up on the sand; the rest was given over to heavy industry and waste dumps, cut off from the rest of the city by a strip of rail track, warehouses and factories.

For the grand Olympic makeover, the beaches were swiftly cleared and filled with tons of golden sand, imported palm trees and landscaped promenades. Visitors flocked, but the city beaches have become a victim of their own popularity, and keeping them clean is something of a Sisyphean task for the city council. Dubbed the Bay of Pigs by the papers, the most central area has been subjected to a massive clean-up campaign with more beachfront toilets, extra bins, and endless posters and loudspeaker announcements reminding people to pick up their rubbish.

Of the seven city beaches, the most southerly is **Platja de Sant Sebastià**, right in front of the swimming pools, popular with nudists and

anyone willing to swap an uninspiring background of industrial rubble for a bit more space. Next is **Platja de Sant Miquel**, which gets insanely crowded in the summer months; it's a slightly grubby version of Ibiza, with plenty of thongs and piercings on display, although it's quieter now the *xiringuitos* have been banned from pumping out house music.

Platja de Barceloneta provides a sandy porch for restaurants and nightclubs. The covered walkway is home to tables where old men play dominoes with all the aggressiveness of a contact sport; it also houses the new beach centre (93 224 75 71), with a small beach library that lends magazines and papers (some in English) along with beach toys and ID tags for children from June to September.

After the Port Olímpic and just down from the Ciutadella-Vila Olímpica metro station, **Platja de Nova Icària** is much broader, with plenty of space for volleyball and beach tennis, while **Platja de Bogatell** boasts the hippest *xiringuito* with torches and loungers out at night from May to October. Further north, **Platja de Mar Bella** is all about sport, with the sailing and water-sports club Base Nàutica, basketball nets, volleyball courts, table-tennis tables and a half-pipe for BMXers and skaters. It also has a small new beach library by the Bac de Roda pier. The most remote beaches are the quiet **Platja Nova Mar Bella**, which is mostly used by local families, and the newer **Platja Llevant**, which opened to the public in 2006 when the Prim jetty was removed and the platform for the future marine zoo was built.

VILA OLIMPICA

At the far end of the Passeig Marítim, the gateway to the Port Olímpic is heralded by the twin skyscrapers of the Hotel Arts (*see p133*) and the Torre Mapfre, and Frank Gehry's shimmering copper *Fish* sculpture which, when viewed straight on, also resembles the helmet of a *conquistador* in commemoration of the 500th anniversary of Columbus's discovery.

This large square of land lying up the coast was once an area of industry, but by the 1980s it had fallen into disuse and presented the perfect blank slate for the model neighbourhood of the Olympic Village for the games in 1992. Based on Cerdà's Eixample grid, it provided parks, a cinema, four beaches, a leisure marina and accommodation for 15,000 athletes.

The low population density and lack of cafés and shops, however, leaves it devoid of Mediterranean charm. Most social activity takes place in the Port Olímpic. The wide empty boulevards do, however, lend themselves to sculpture, including a jagged pergola on Avda Icària by Enric Miralles and Carme Pinós.

SIGHTS

Montjuïc

High on a hill.

Maybe it was all those years of living within its walls, but the people of Barcelona seem to prefer to huddle and jostle in the city's streets than high above the town on the hill that looks down over the city. The spectacular views across the city were revealed to the world during the 1992 Olympic Games, but few bother to step up for some fresh air on Tibidabo and Montjuïc, either of the city's remarkably underused hills.

In a city with as few parks as Barcelona, the hills of Montjuïc offer a precious escape from the stresses of urban life, along with some outstanding museums and galleries. Scattered over the landward side are Santiago Calatrava's Olympic 'needle' and many other buildings from the 1992 games; facing the sea are a lighthouse and an enormous cemetery. And at the top of the hill, all but invisible from below, is the heavily fortified Castell de Montjuïc, a dark and brooding symbol of the centuries Catalonia spent under Castilian rule.

Map pp341-342	**Cafés** p192
Hotels p134	**Tapas bars** p192
Restaurants p164	**Bars** p193

MONTJUÏC, PAST AND PRESENT

If Montjuïc is undersubscribed, it's largely because the city's constantly remodelled infrastructure has passed it by. It's relatively inaccessible; to the uninitiated, the only way up seems to be from Plaça de Espanya and the grandiose Avda Reina Maria Cristina or the vertigo-inducing cable car, though the funicular from Paral·lel is easy and convenient. Plans to convert Montjuïc into the Central Park of Barcelona involve opening up access from the locale of Poble Sec, with broad boulevards and escalators leading up to Avda Miramar.

The mists of time obscure the etymology of the name 'Montjuïc', but one widely accepted educated guess is that 'juïc' comes from the old Catalan word meaning Jewish. It is here that

About the author
Stephen Burgen *is a former Spain correspondent for* The Times. *He is currently editor of the monthly* Inside Spain *and English editor of the bilingual quarterly* Barcenova.

the medieval Jewish community buried their dead; some of the excavated headstones are now to be found in the **Museu Militar**, soon to be reincarnated as the International Peace Centre. Other headstones with Hebraic inscriptions are in to the walls of the 16th-century Palau de Lloctinent, just to the east of the cathedral; following the expulsion of all Jews from Spain by Ferdinand and Isabella in 1492, the cemetery was plundered and the stone reused. Today the **Cementiri Sud-Oest** still stands on the sea-facing side of the mountain.

The **Castell de Montjuïc** occupies a prime defensive position, with a commanding view of both the sea and the city. In reality, however, its vantage point has been used to attack the city, not to defend it. Catalan mythology has it that it was built by Philip V, after Barcelona fell to his forces in 1714, in order to keep an eye on his unwilling and rebellious subjects. In fact it was built 43 years before Philip was born and, although it has become a symbol of Spanish oppression, in 1706 the people rallied to its defence and that of its Austrian garrison against attacks from Bourbon forces. The most violent attack launched from the fortress was not the work of fascists or their precursors, but was ordered by the progressive Catalan general Joan Prim i Prats, who to this day has an entire Barcelona rambla named in his honour. Some 460 houses were damaged or destroyed in the bombardment that Prim launched on 7 September, 1843. The Franco years cemented the role of the fortress as a symbol of oppression, particularly after the Republican President Lluis Companys was executed by firing squad there in 1940. Earlier in the Civil War, however, the Republicans themselves executed some 58 people in the castle.

The 1929 Exhibition was the first attempt to turn the hill into a leisure area. Then, in the 1940s, thousands of immigrant workers from the rest of Spain settled on the hill. Some squatted in precarious shacks, while others rented brick and plaster sheds laid out along improvised streets that covered the hillside, then virtually treeless. These *barraques* thrived until the last few stragglers moved out in the 1970s, although the area still attracts intermittent waves of illegal tent and hut dwellers. Energetic visitors can follow the same steep routes these residents once took home, straight up C/Nou de la Rambla or C/Margarit in Poble Sec; the stairway at the top leaves you just a short distance from the **Fundació Joan Miró** and the Olympic stadium area.

The long axis from Plaça d'Espanya is still the most popular access to the park, with the climb now eased by a sequence of open-air escalators. In the centre of Plaça d'Espanya itself is a monument designed by Josep Maria Jujol (who created the wrought-iron balconies on La Pedrera), with representations of the rivers Ebre, Tagus and Guadalquivir. Where Paral·lel meets Plaça d'Espanya is the **Las Arenas** bullring. The last bull met its fate here in the 1970s; until 2003, the arena lay derelict. Lord Rogers is currently overseeing a huge transformation project, to be completed at some unspecified date, which will turn the ring into a circular leisure complex while restoring the existing neo-Mudéjar façade. The vision encompasses a 'piazza in the sky', a giant roof terrace that will allow for alfresco events and offer panoramic views over Barcelona. Given the current recession, and in a city already well endowed with shopping and leisure centres, this has the makings of a white elephant.

On the other side of the square, two Venetian-style towers announce the beginning of the Fira, the trade-show area, with pavilions from 1929 and newer buildings used for conventions. To the left is the former Palau d'Esports, now the **Barcelona Teatre Musical** (*see p273*) hosting large-scale musical theatre. Further up, the rebuilt **Pavelló Mies van der Rohe** contrasts sharply with the neo-classical structures nearby. Across the street, Puig i Cadafalch's Modernista factory has been converted into the excellent **CaixaForum** cultural centre. Further up the hill is **Poble Espanyol**, a model village also designed in 1929 especially to showcase Spanish crafts and architecture.

SIGHTS

CaixaForum. *See p95*.

Walk Route With a View

Step right up for the sights of the city.

Duration: 90 mins

From the gardens of the **Teatre Grec**, take the gateway to the right of the amphitheatre. From here, the **Escales del Generalife** lead up to the **Fundació Miró** (*see p95*). Named after the water gardens of Granada's Alhambra palace, this is a series of trickling fountains, flanked by stone steps, olive trees and benches for quiet contemplation. Instead of taking the steps, turn right into the **Jardins Laribal**, designed – like the Escales – by French landscape architect Jean-Claude Nicolas Forestier at the start of the 20th century. Ahead lie the **Colla de l'Arròs rose gardens**, at their best in late spring. From here a long pergola leads up to the **Font del Gat** (Fountain of the Cat), a clearing on the slope with a small restaurant designed by Josep Puig i Cadafalch, and the rather modest fountain itself.

With your back to the restaurant follow the path east towards the Miró and you'll arrive at a clearing, in the middle of which is Josep Viladomat's bronze *Noia de la Trena* (Girl with a Plait). Straight ahead is the stone *Repòs*, also by Viladomat, a scaled-up version of a Manolo Hugué figure, undertaken when Hugué was too ill to finish the commission.

Turn right on to the Avda Miramar, where, opposite the Miró museum you'll find a flight of steps which lead up and around to the **Tres Pins nursery**, where the plants are grown for the city's municipal parks and gardens. From here the Avda Miramar runs seaward, past the **Plaça Dante Alighieri**, where a bronze

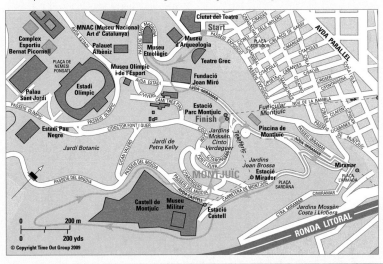

Presiding over it all is the bombastic Palau Nacional, originally built as a 'temporary exhibition' for the Expo, and now home to the **MNAC (Museu Nacional d'Art de Catalunya)**, housing Catalan art from the last millennium and recently reopened after a lengthy refurbishment. At night, the entire setting is illuminated by a water-and-light spectacular, the **Font Màgica**, still operating with its complex original mechanisms. Other nearby buildings erected for the 1929 Expo have been converted into the **Museu d'Arqueologia de Catalunya** and the **Ciutat del Teatre** (Theatre City) complex. From the same period are the nearby **Teatre Grec** (Greek theatre), used for summer concerts during the Grec Festival, and the beautifully restored Jardins Laribal, designed by French landscape architect JCN Forestier. At the top of this garden is the Font del Gat information centre. The **Museu Etnològic**, a typical 1970s construction, sits just below it.

SIGHTS

statue of the poet was presented by the city's Italian residents in 1921 to celebrate the 600th anniversary of Dantes death. In front of Dante, and in contrast to his stern salute, stands Josep Llimona's curvaceous and coquettish *Bellesa* (Beauty).

At the end of this road is the **Miramar area**, with its hotel (*see p134*), fronted by formal gardens, the station for the cable car over the port, and slightly south and below it, the **Costa i Llobera cactus gardens**. Backtracking slightly, a road leads behind the hotel up the hill towards the castle, passing the **Joan Brossa gardens** en route. These were created on the site of the old fairground, and some of the stone statues from the time (such as *Charlie Chaplin*) are still in place. Just outside the gardens is the much-photographed *Sardana*, an uplifting representation of the Catalan national dance. Cross the road here to walk up via the fountains and ceramic mosaics of the recently spruced up **Mirador de l'Alcalde**. From here the Camí del Mar, with great views out to sea, runs alongside the **castle** to the **Mirador del Migdia**, which has a wonderful outdoor café (*see p193* **La Caseta del Migdia**) far from the madding crowds and one of the few places in Barcelona where you can watch the sun set.

Take the path around the landward side of the castle, turning left just before the cable car station and following the steps and paths that wiggle down to the **Mossèn Cinto gardens**. These specialise in bulbous plants (daffodils, hyacinths and tulips) and various types of water lilies, with a series of terraced ponds running down the hillside to a small lake.

Exit from the lower side of the gardens and turn left to catch the funicular down the hill to Avda Paral·lel and the metro.

If walking isn't your thing, another way up the hill is via the funicular railway, integrated with the city's metro system, leaving from the Paral·lel station. A more circuitous way up is by the Transbordador Aeri cable car across the harbour to Miramar, a peaceful spot with unmatchable views across the city – though the tranquillity was somewhat disturbed by the opening of the swish Hotel Miramar in 2006.

Montjuïc's Anella Olímpica (Olympic Ring) is a convergence of diverse constructions all laid out for the 1992 Olympic Games. The little-used Estadi Olímpic, although entirely new, was built within the façade of a 1929 stadium by a design team led by Federico Correa and Alfonso Milà. The horse sculptures are copies of the originals by Pau Gargallo. Next to it is the most original and attractive of the Olympic facilities, Arata Isozaki's Palau Sant Jordi indoor arena, its undulating façade evoking Gaudí, and its high-tech interior featuring a transparent roof. Only 15 years after the Olympics, these two buildings are already falling into disrepair and underwent a ten-million euro renovation in 2007. In the hard, white *plaça* in front rises Santiago Calatrava's remarkable, Brancusi-inspired communications tower.

Across the square is the city's best swimming pool, the Piscines Bernat Picornell (*see p279*), while further down is the INEFC physical education institute, by architect Ricardo Bofill. Walk across the road and you look over a cliff on to a rugby pitch and an equestrian area offering pony rides. The cliff itself is a favourite for rock-climbers.

The many parks and gardens include the **Jardins Mossèn Costa i Llobera**, which abounds in tropical plants, but particularly cacti, just below Miramar, on the steep flank nearest the port. Not far above are the **Jardins del Mirador**, from where there is a spectacular view over the harbour. These gardens are also the starting point for a new path for pedestrians and cyclists, running precariously below the castle and leading to an outdoor café, **La Caseta del Migdia** (*see p193*). One of the newest parks is the nearby **Jardins de Joan Brossa**, featuring humorous, hands-on contraptions where children can manipulate water courses and practise creative adventure sports. Walk down towards the funicular station and you will reach the enchanting **Jardins Cinto Verdaguer**, with ponds filled with lotus flowers and water lilies. All these gardens play an adjunct role to the creative biospheres of the **Jardí Botànic**, just above the Olympic stadium, sharply designed and finally maturing into an important scientific collection.

Bus Montjuïc Turístic

Torres Venecianas, Plaça d'Espanya (93 415 60 20). Metro Espanya. **Open** *June, Oct* 10am-9.20pm Sat, Sun. *July-Sept* 10am-9.20pm daily. **Tickets** *Day pass* €3; €2 reductions. **No credit cards**. **Map** p341 B9.

An open-top tourist bus. There are actually two routes: the blue line runs via Plaça Espanya, the red one via Portal de la Pau, near the Monument a Colom; they coincide at the Olympic stadium and the castle. Tickets are valid for both routes. Buses pass every 40 minutes.

SIGHTS

Profile Cementiri Sud-Oest

Jump on the grave train and check out Barcelona's buried treasures.

Never ones to leave any stone unturned in their bid to attract more visitors, the Barcelona authorities have enlisted the dead in the cause of tourism. In 2004, they introduced tours of the Cementiri de Poblenou; four years later, they've launched organised tours of the larger **Cementiri Sud-Oest** (*see p95*) on Montjuïc, home to somewhat more illustrious corpses.

It's a curious-looking place. The multi-storey niches built into the hillside look from a distance like a Liliputian housing development, stacked up below the castle. However, although the dead have a Mediterranean vista that any developer would kill for, Montjuïc is not the most tranquil place to rest in peace. It overlooks one of Europe's busiest container ports and on the seaward side the cemetery is filled with the roar of traffic from the Ronda Litoral below. The cemetery is also permeated by the powerful smell of feral cat and, until the city razed the nearby Can Tunis slum, which was mostly inhabited by junkies, many of the graves had been broken into and robbed.

It is, however, a fascinating and unique place. Its roll call cannot compete with Père Lachaise in Paris – no Abelard and Héloise, no Chopin or Oscar Wilde, and certainly no Jim Morrison – but among its better-known occupants are the painters Joan Miró and Santiago Rusiñol, as well as Lluís Companys, the Catalan Republican President of Catalunya who was executed by firing squad just up the hill in the castle. The best view is from the tomb of Leandro Albareda, who designed the cemetery.

There are three suggested tours – two (the Artistic and Historic) described in multilingual leaflets, and the third, the Combined, is a free guided tour. The Artistic Route takes in 40 graves and tombs, including mausoleums and sculptures of different styles, ranging from Modernista to neo-Egyptian and neo-Gothic. The Catalan bourgeoisie commissioned their monuments to match the houses they had built for themselves in the city, and some of the family tombs are enormous.

WHEN TO VISIT
The Combined Route starts at 11am in Catalan and 11.15am in Spanish on the second and fourth Sundays of the month, visiting 37 graves and tombs of either artistic or historic interest.

★ FREE CaixaForum

Casaramona, Avda Marquès de Comillas 6-8
(93 476 86 00/www.fundacio.lacaixa.es). Metro
Espanya. **Open** 10am-8pm Mon-Fri, Sun; 10am-
10pm Sat. **Admission** free. **Credit** (shop only)
AmEx, DC, MC, V. **Map** p341 B9.

One of the masterpieces of industrial Modernisme,
this ormer yarn and textile factory was designed by
Puig i Cadafalch in 1911. It spent most of the last
century in a sorry state, acting briefly as a police
barracks and then falling into dereliction. Fundació
La Caixa, the charitable arm of Catalonia's largest
savings bank, bought it and set about rebuilding.
The original brick structure was supported, while
the ground below was excavated to house a strikingly modern entrance plaza by Arata Isozaki, a Sol
LeWitt mural, an auditorium, a bookshop and a
library. In addition to the permanent contemporary
art collection, there are three impressive spaces for
temporary exhibitions – often among the most interesting shows to be found in the city. *Photo p91.*

▶ *Other notable Puig i Cadafalch buildings in*
the city include the Els Quatre Gats café (see
p182) and the Casa Amatller (see p102).

FREE Cementiri Sud-Oest

C/Mare de Déu de Port 54-58 (93 223 16 83).
Bus 38. **Open** 9am-5pm daily. **Admission** free.

Designed by Leandro Albareda in 1880, this enormous necropolis, sits at the side of the motorway out
of town, and is a daily reminder to commuters of
their own mortality. The dead were originally placing them in four sections: one for Catholics, one for
Protestants, one for non-Christians and a fourth for
aborted foetuses. It now stretches over the south-
west corner of the mountain, with family tombs
stacked five or six storeys high. Many, especially
those belonging to the gypsy community, are a riot
of colour and flowers. The Fossar de la Pedrera
memorial park remembers those fallen from the
International Brigades and the Catalan martyrs
from the Civil War. There is also a Holocaust memorial and a mausoleum to the former president of the
Generalitat Lluís Companys.

The cemetery is much visited, in particular on All
Saints' Day, when the roads are clogged solid with
cars. In 2007, modernisation and expansion of the
facilities started in order to provide more parking
space, flower stalls, a new entrance and, eventually,
a new home for the city's collection of funeral carriages (*see p106*). *See also p94* **Profile**.

★ Font Màgica de Montjuïc

Plaça Carles Buïgas 1 (93 316 10 00). Metro
Espanya. **Shows** (every 30 mins) *May-Sept*
9.30-11pm Thur-Sun. *Oct-Apr* 7-8.30pm Fri,
Sat. **Map** p341 B9.

Still using its original plumbing, the 'magic fountain'
works its wonders with 3,600 pieces of tubing and
more than 4,500 light bulbs. Summer evenings after
nightfall see the multiple founts swell and dance to

anything from the *1812 Overture* to Freddie Mercury
and Montserrat Caballé's *Barcelona*, showing off its
kaleidoscope of pastel colours. In July 2008, a new
piece was inaugurated with the fountain choreographed to film soundtracks including *Blade Runner*,
Gladiator and *Lord of the Rings*.

★ Fundació Joan Miró

Parc de Montjuïc s/n (93 443 94 70/http://
fundaciomiro-bcn.org). Metro Paral·lel then
Funicular de Montjuïc/61 bus. **Open** *July-Sept*
10am-8pm Tue, Wed, Fri, Sat; 10am-9.30pm
Thur; 10am-2.30pm Sun. *Oct-June* 10am-7pm
Tue, Wed, Fri, Sat; 10am-9.30pm Thur; 10am-
2.30pm Sun. **Guided tours** *Temporary*
exhibitions 11.30pm Sat. *Permanent exhibition*
11.30pm Sun. **Admission** *All exhibitions* €8;
€6 reductions. *Temporary exhibitions* €4;
€3 reductions free under-14s. **Credit** MC, V.
Map p341 C11.

Josep Lluis Sert, who spent the years of the Franco
dictatorship as Dean of the School of Design at
Harvard University, designed one of the greatest
museum buildings in the world on his return.
Approachable, light and airy, these white walls and
arches house a collection of more than 225 paintings,
150 sculptures and all of Miró's graphic work, plus
some 5,000 drawings. The permanent collection,
highlighting Miró's trademark use of primary
colours and simplified organic forms symbolising
stars, the moon, birds and women, occupies the second half of the space. On the way to the sculpture
gallery is Alexander Calder's rebuilt Mercury
Fountain, originally seen at the Spanish Republic's
Pavilion at the 1937 Paris Fair. In other works, Miró
is shown as a cubist (*Street in Pedralbes*, 1917), naive
(*Portrait of a Young Girl*, 1919) and surrealist (*Man*
and Woman in Front of a Pile of Excrement, 1935).
In the upper galleries, large, black-outlined paintings from Miró's final period precede a room of
works with political themes.

Temporary shows have improved significantly,
providing an often humorous contrast to Miro.
Forthcoming exhibitions at the foundation include
American Modernity: Works from the Corcoran
Gallery (until Jan 2009) and Kiki Smith: Her Memory
(until May 2009). The Espai 13 in the basement features young contemporary artists (€2.50). Outside
is a small sculpture garden with work by contemporary Catalan artists.

★ Jardí Botànic

C/Doctor Font i Quer (93 426 49 35/www.jardi
botanic.bcn.cat). Metro Espanya/bus 50, 55, 61.
Open *Jan, Nov-Dec* 10am-5pm daily. *Feb-Mar,*
Oct 10am-6pm daily. *Apr-May, Sept* 10am-7pm
daily. *June-Aug* 10am-8pm daily. **Admission**
€3.50; €1.70 reductions; free under-16s. Free last
Sun of mth. **No credit cards. Map** p341 B11/12.

After the original 1930s botanical garden was disturbed by the construction for the Olympics, the

only solution was to build an entirely new replacement. This opened in 1999, housing plants from seven global regions with a climate similar to that of the Western Mediterranean. Everything about the futuristic design, from the angular concrete pathways to the raw sheet steel banking (and even the design of the bins), is the complete antithesis of the more naturalistic, Gertrude Jekyll-inspired gardens of England. It is meticulously kept, with all plants being tagged in Latin, Catalan, Spanish and English along with their date of planting, and has the added advantage of wonderful views across the city. There is a small space housing occasional temporary exhibitions and useful, free audio guides to lead visitors through the gardens.

▶ *Buy a combined ticket for the garden, and the Natural History and Geology Museums.*

FREE Jardins de Joan Brossa

Plaça Dante (93 205 99 12/www.bcn.cat/ parcsijardins). Metro Paral·lel, then funicular. **Open** *Dec-Feb* 10am-6pm daily; *Mar, Nov* 10am-7pm daily; *Apr, Oct* 10am-8pm daily; *May-Sept* 10am-9pm daily. **Admission** free. **Map** p341 C11.

Set in 5.2 hectares of the former fairground, Montjuïc's latest park is part-forest, with 40 species of tree, and part-urban playground. As well as a climbing frame, there are various wooden creations designed for children, allowing them to play tunes and pump water.

FREE Jardins Mossèn Costa i Llobera

Ctra de Miramar 1. Metro Paral·lel, then funicular. **Open** 10am-sunset daily. **Admission** free. **Map** p341 D12.

The port side of Montjuïc is protected from the cold north wind, creating a microclimate two degrees centigrade warmer than the rest of the city, which is perfect for 800 species of the world's cacti. This extraordinary collection has been closed to the public for some time while funding for essential maintenance is sought.

INSIDE TRACK
PARK LIFE

On the stretch of the Paral·lel opposite the city walls, three tall chimneys stand amid modern office blocks. They are all that remains of the Anglo-Canadian-owned power station known locally as **La Canadença** ('The Canadian'), and which was the centre of the city's largest general strike, in 1919. Beside the chimneys, an open space has been created and dubbed the Parc de les Tres Xemeneies (Park of the Three Chimneys).

★ MNAC (Museu Nacional d'Art de Catalunya)

Palau Nacional, Parc de Montjuïc (93 622 03 76/www.mnac.cat). Metro Espanya. **Open** 10am-7pm Tue-Sat; 10am-2.30pm Sun. **Admission** (valid 2 days) *Permanent exhibitions* €8.50; €6 reductions. *Temporary exhibitions* €3.50-€5.50. *Combined ticket with Poble Espanyol* €12. Free over-65s, under-14s and 1st Sun of mth. **Credit** MC, V. **Map** p341 B10.

'One museum, a thousand years of art' is the slogan of the National Museum, and the collection provides a dizzying overview of Catalan art from the 12th to the 20th centuries. In recent years the museum has added an extra floor to absorb the holdings of the section of the Thyssen-Bornemisza collection that was previously kept in the convent in Pedralbes, along with the mainly Modernista holdings from the former Museum of Modern Art in Ciutadella park, a fine photography section, coins and the bequest of Francesc Cambó, founder of the autonomist Lliga Regionalista, a regionalist conservative party.

The highlight of the museum, however, is still the Romanesque collection. As art historians realised that scores of solitary tenth-century churches in the Pyrenees were falling into ruin – and with them were going extraordinary Romanesque mural paintings that had served to instruct villagers in the basics of the faith – the laborious task was begun of removing the murals from church apses. The display here features 21 mural sections in loose chronological order. A highlight is the tremendous *Crist de Taüll*, from the 12th-century church of Sant Climent de Taüll. Even 'graffiti' scratchings (probably by monks) of animals, crosses and labyrinths have been preserved. The museum has recently acquired a major 13th-century Romanesque mural from the cathedral at La Seu d'Urgell.

The Gothic collection is also excellent and starts with some late 13th-century frescoes that were discovered in 1961 and 1997, when two palaces in the city were being renovated. There are carvings and paintings from local churches, including works of the indisputable Catalan masters of the Golden Age, Bernat Martorell and Jaume Huguet. The highlight of the Thyssen collection is Fra Angelico's *Madonna of Humility* (c1430), while the Cambó bequest contains some wonderful Old Masters. Also unmissable is the Modernista collection, which includes Ramon Casas's mural of himself and Pere Romeu on a tandem which decorated Els Quatre Gats (*see p182*). The rich collection of decorative arts includes original furniture from Modernista houses.

Museu d'Arqueologia de Catalunya

Passeig de Santa Madrona 39-41 (93 423 21 49/ 93 423 65 77/www.mac.cat). Metro Poble Sec. **Open** 9.30am-7pm Tue-Sat; 10am-2.30pm Sun. **Admission** €3; €2.10 reductions; free under-16s. **Credit** (shop only) MC, V. **Map** p341 C10.

The time frame for this archaeology collection starts with the Palaeolithic period, and there are relics of Greek, Punic, Roman and Visigothic colonisers, up to the early Middle Ages. A massive Roman sarcophagus is carved with scenes of the rape of Persephone, and an immense statue of Aesculapius, the god of medicine, towers over one room. A few galleries are dedicated to the Mallorcan Talayotic cave culture, and there is an exemplary display on the Iberians, the pre-Hellenic, pre-Roman inhabitants of south-eastern Spain. An Iberian skull with a nail driven through it effectively demonstrates a typical method of execution from that time. The display ends with the marvellous, jewel-studded headpiece of a Visigoth king. One of the best-loved pieces, inevitably, is an alarmingly erect Priapus, found during building work in Sants in 1848 and kept under wraps 'for moral reasons' until 1986.

Museu Etnològic

Passeig de Santa Madrona s/n (93 424 68 07/ www.museuetnologic.bcn.cat). Metro Poble Sec. **Open** *June-Sept* 10am-6pm Tue-Sat; 11am-3pm Sun. *Oct-June* 10am-7pm Tue, Thur, Sat; 10am-2pm Wed, Fri-Sun. **Admission** €3.50; €1.70 reductions; free under-16s. Free 1st Sun of mth. **No credit cards**. **Map** p341 B10.

The Ethnology Museum houses a vast collection of items, from Australian Aboriginal boomerangs to rugs and jewellery from Afghanistan, although by far the most comprehensive collections are from Catalonia. Of the displays upstairs, most outstanding are the Moroccan, Japanese and Philippine exhibits, though there are also some interesting pre-Columbian finds. The attempts to arrange the pieces thematically, however, are not altogether successful: a potentially fascinating exhibition entitled 'Taboos', for instance, was a rather limp look at nudity in different cultures.

Museu Militar

Castell de Montjuïc, Ctra de Montjuïc 66 (93 329 86 13/www.museomilitarmontjuic.es). Metro Paral·lel then funicular & cable car. **Open** *Apr-Sept* 9.30am-7pm Tue-Sun. *Oct-Mar* 9.30am-5pm Tue-Sun. **Admission** €3; €1.50 reductions; free under-7s. **No credit cards**. **Map** p341 C12.

The Military Museum's days are numbered – in 2009, it's set to become an International Peace Centre, though the remit of this is still undecided. For now, however, the exhibits include armour, swords, lances, muskets (beautiful Moroccan *moukhala*), rifles and pistols. Other highlights include 23,000 lead soldiers representing a Spanish division of the 1920s.

Museu Olímpic i de l'Esport

Avda Estadi 60 (93 292 53 79/www.fundacio barcelonaolimpica.es). Bus 50, 55, 61. **Open** *Apr-Sept* 10am-8pm Mon, Wed-Sat; 10am-2.30pm Sun. *Oct-Mar* 10am-6pm Mon, Wed-Sat; 10am-2.30pm Sun. **Admission** €4; €2.50 reductions; free under-14s. **Credit** AmEx, MC, V. **Map** p341 B11.

Opened in 2007 in a new building across from the stadium, the Olympic and Sports Museum gives an overview of the Games (and, indeed, all games) from Ancient Greece onwards. As well as photos and film footage of great sporting moments and heroes, there

Jardí Botànic. *See p95.*

SIGHTS

are an array of objects (Ronaldinho's boots, Mika Häkkinen's Mercedes), along with a collection of opening ceremony costumes and Olympic torches. Perhaps more entertaining are the interactive displays, such as one that compares your effort at the long jump with that of the pros.

Pavelló Mies van der Rohe

Avda Marquès de Comillas (93 423 40 16/www. miesbcn.com). Metro Espanya. **Open** 10am-8pm daily. **Admission** €4; €2 reductions; free under-18s. **Credit** (shop only) MC, V. **Map** p341 B9.
Mies van der Rohe built the Pavelló Alemany (German Pavilion) for the 1929 Universal Exhibition not as a gallery but as a simple reception space, sparsely furnished by his trademark 'Barcelona Chair'. The pavilion was a founding monument of modern rationalist architecture, with its flowing floor plan and a revolutionary use of materials. Though the original pavilion was demolished after the exhibition, a fine replica was built on the same site in 1986, the simplicity of its design setting off the warm tones of the marble and expressive Georg Kolbe sculpture in the pond.

Poble Espanyol

Avda Marquès de Comillas (93 325 78 66/ www.poble-espanyol.com). Metro Espanya. **Open** *Village & restaurants* 9am-8pm Mon; 9am-2am Tue-Thur; 9am-4am Fri; 9am-5am Sat; 9am-midnight Sun. *Shops* Dec-May 10am-6pm daily. June-Aug 10am-8pm daily. Sept-Nov 10am-7pm daily. **Admission** €8; €5-€6 reductions; €20 family ticket; free under-4s. *Combined ticket with MNAC* €12. **Credit** AmEx, MC, V. **Map** p341 A9/B9.
Built for the 1929 Universal Exhibition and designed by the Modernista architect Puig i Cadafalch, this composite Spanish village is variously charming or kitsch depending on your taste, and features reproductions of traditional buildings and squares from every region in Spain. The cylindrical towers at the entrance are copied from the walled city of Ávila and lead on to a typical Castilian main square from which visitors can explore a tiny whitewashed street from Arcos de la Frontera in Andalucía, then on to the 16th-century House of Chains from Toledo, and so on. There are numerous bars and restaurants, a flamenco *tablao* and more than 60 shops selling Spanish crafts. Outside, street performers recreate bits of Catalan and Spanish folklore.
▶ *B-estival takes place here each year; see p255.*

Telefèric de Montjuïc (cable car)

Estació Funicular, Avda Miramar (93 318 70 74/www.tmb.net). Metro Paral·lel then Funicular. **Open** *Nov-Mar* 10am-6pm daily. *Apr-May, Oct* 10am-7pm daily. *June-Sept* 10am-9pm daily. **Tickets** €5.70 one way; €7.90 return; €4.50 one way reductions; €6 return reductions; free under-4s. **No credit cards. Map** p341 C11/D11.

The rebuilt system has eight-person cable cars that soar from the funicular up to the castle. In the summer months, the *Picnic al Cel* offers the chance to enjoy a vertiginous dining experience.

POBLE SEC & PARAL·LEL

Poble Sec, the name of the neighbourhood between Montjuïc and the Avda Paral·lel, actually means 'dry village'; it was 1894 before the thousands of poor workers who lived on the flanks of the hill celebrated the installation of the area's very first water fountain (which is still standing today in C/Margarit).

These days, Poble Sec is a friendly, working-class area of quiet, relaxed streets and leafy squares, with an increasingly Latin American flavour, reflecting the large immigrant population from Ecuador and elsewhere. Some 27 per cent of the 40,000 people in Poble Sec have arrived over the past five years.

Towards the Avda Paral·lel are some distinguished Modernista buildings, which local legend maintains were built for *artistas* from the nude cabarets by their rich sugar daddies. At C/Tapioles 12 is a beautiful, narrow wooden Modernista door with particularly lovely writhing ironwork, while at C/Elkano 4 is La Casa de les Rajoles, which is known for its peculiar mosaic façade.

The name Paral·lel derives from the fact that the avenue coincides exactly with 41° 44' latitude north, one of Ildefons Cerdà's more eccentric conceits. This was the prime centre of Barcelona nightlife in the first half of the 20th century, and was full of theatres, nightclubs and music halls. A statue on the corner with C/Nou de la Rambla commemorates Raquel Meller, a legendary star of the street who went on to equal celebrity around the world. She now stands outside Barcelona's notorious live-porn venue, the Bagdad. Apart from this, most of the area's cabarets have long since disappeared, although there are still some theatres and cinemas hereabouts.

Refugi 307

C/Nou de la Rambla 169 (93 256 21 22/ www.museuhistoria.bcn.cat). Metro Paral·lel. **Open** (guided tour & by appointment only) 11am, noon (Catalan), 1pm (Spanish) Sat, Sun. **Admission** €2. **No credit cards. Map** p341 D11.
About 1,500 Barcelona civilians were killed during the air bombings of the Civil War, a fact that the government long silenced. As Poble Sec particularly suffered the effects of bombing, a large air-raid shelter was built partially into the mountain at the top of C/Nou de la Rambla; this is one of some 1,200 in the entire city. Now converted into a museum, it is worth a visit. The tour takes about 90mins.

The Eixample

The city's most eye-catching neighbourhood is full of surprises.

The Barri Gòtic is the first stop for most visitors. But with its showstopping Modernista architecture, elegant boutiques and cutting-edge restaurants, it's the Eixample that forms the crucible for Barcelona's image as a city of design.

Zooming out to an aerial perspective, it is also the Eixample that gives Barcelona its distinctive appearance: the entire middle section of the city looks as if it has been stamped with a sizzling waffle iron. This extraordinary city plan, the expansion (*eixample* in Catalan, *ensanche* in Spanish) of Barcelona into an orthogonal grid of

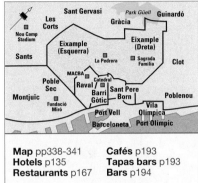

Map pp338-341	**Cafés** p193
Hotels p135	**Tapas bars** p193
Restaurants p167	**Bars** p194

identical blocks, was designed as an extendible matrix for future growth, gradually coming to connect Barcelona with the outlying villages of Gràcia, Sarrià, Les Corts, Sant Gervasi and Sant Martí de Provençals. It essentially unifies the city as we know it today.

INTO THE EIXAMPLE

The Eixample was Europe's first expansive work of urban planning, necessitated by the chronic overcrowding of old Barcelona which, by the 1850s, had become rife with cholera and crime, tightly corseted by its much-hated city walls. It was eventually decided the walls must come down, whereupon the Ajuntament held a competition to build an ambitious urban zone on the sloping fields outside the city's ramparts. The competition was won by municipal architect Antoni Rovira i Trias, whose popular fan-shaped design can be seen at the foot of the statue of him in the Gràcia plaça that bears his name. The Madrid government, however, vetoed the plan, choosing instead the work of social idealist Ildefons Cerdà, a military engineer.

Cerdà's plan, reflecting the rationalist mindset of the era, was for a grid of uniform blocks with chamfered corners (known as *illes* in Catalan, *manzanas* in Spanish) to stretch from Montjuïc to the Besòs river, criss-crossed by the diagonal highways of Avda Diagonal and Avda Meridiana, meeting at Plaça de les Glòries, which was to become the hub of the modernised city. The ideas were utopian: each block was to be built on only two sides and be no more than two or three storeys high; the remainder of the space was to contain gardens, their leafy extremes joining at the crossroads and forming a quarter of a bigger park. Predictably, however, developers made a travesty of Cerdà's plans and a concrete orchard of gardenless, fortress-like, six- or seven-storey blocks grew up instead.

Fortunately, the period of construction coincided with Barcelona's golden age of

INSIDE TRACK
COURTYARDS

In 1985, the ProEixample was set up to reclaim some 50 of the courtyards that were proposed in Ildefons Cerdà's original plans, so that everybody living in the area should be able to find an open space within 300 metres of their home. Two of the better examples are the fake beach around the **Torre de les Aigües water tower** (C/Llúria 56) and the patio at **Passatge Permanyer** (C/Pau Claris 120).

Streetwise Passeig de Gràcia

Boulevard of Modernista marvels.

A colossal sugar rush of grandiose Modernista masterpieces and ooh-la-la designer shops, the central boulevard of Passeig de Gràcia is one of the most fascinating streets in Europe for a stroll. It follows the line traced by the old rural lane known as the Camí de Jesus (Road of Jesus) through fields and gardens from Barcelona to the then separate village of Gràcia. In 1827, before the Eixample had grown up around it, the broad new avenue was lined with fairground attractions and embellished with gas lighting, a pedestrian central promenade and Italianate side gardens known as the Tívoli, a name which is preserved in the theatre on C/Casp. Where it was once a favourite spot for aristocrats to show off their fine clothes and carriages, it's now the place where they yak loudly into iPhones while double-parking Porsche Cayennes.

Naturally, no expense was spared with the architecture, and there are some 20 buildings that are real jewels of Modernisme. The culmination of the frenzy of swirling colours and ornate stone carving is the **Manzana de la Discòrdia** (*see p101*) but other world-class buildings include Enric Sagnier's neo-Gothic **Cases Pons i Pascual** (nos.2-4) and the gigantic **Cases Rocamora** (nos.6-14) with their mustard-tiled cupolas and Gothic stonework. Further up, the **Casa Vídua Marfà** (no.66) has one of the most breathtakingly sumptuous entrance halls in the Eixample, while semicircular **La Unió i el Fènix** (no.21) is decorated with classical sculptures by Frederic Marès. The **Casa Casas** (no.96) was once home to Ramon Casas, one of the city's greatest painters, and is now design emporium Vinçon – head upstairs for a look at the lush Modernista interior. Topping the boulevard is the stately **Casa Fuster** (no.132), once home to Catalan poet Salvador Espriu and now a hotel.

Being the swankiest street in town, Passeig de Gràcia also boasts its own special accessories; the magnificent wrought-iron lamp posts were designed by Pere Falqués, with curving benches of broken white tile beneath, while Gaudí's signature hexagonal pavement slabs, reminiscent of honeycomb, are decorated with intertwining nautilus shells and starfish. First designed in a smaller size for the patio of the **Casa Batlló** (*see p102*), they were repeated in his aquatic-looking apartment block **La Pedrera** (*see p108*) before covering the whole boulevard.

architecture: the city's bourgeoisie employed Gaudí, Puig i Cadafalch, Domènech i Montaner and the like to build them ever more daring townhouses in an orgy of avant-garde one-upmanship. The result is extraordinary but can be tricky to negotiate on foot; the lack of open spaces and similarity of many streets can cause confusion. The city council, meanwhile, is attempting to make the area more liveable by reclaiming pavement space for pedestrians, repaving roads with noise absorbant materials and reducing traffic.

The overland railway that ran down C/Balmes was the dividing line of the neighbourhood. Either side of this, the fashionable **Dreta** ('Right') contains the most distinguished Modernista architecture, the main museums and the shopping avenues. The **Esquerra** ('Left') was built slightly later; it contains some less well-known Modernista sights. Other subdivisions of the Eixample include the wealthy Sagrada Família area, and the scrappier residential neighbourhoods of Sant Antoni, near the Raval, and Fort Pienc, to the south of Glòries, which has been dubbed the city's new 'Chinatown', filled with Asian families and businesses.

In its entirety, the Eixample covers about nine square kilometres. However, most of the items of interest for visitors are within a few blocks of the grand central boulevard of **Passeig de Gràcia** which ascends directly from the city's central square of Plaça Catalunya. Incorporating some of Barcelona's finest Modernista buildings, it is the showpiece of the **Quadrat D'Or** (Golden District) – a square mile of open-air museum between C/Muntaner and C/Roger de Flor that contains 150 protected buildings, many of them Modernista gems.

THE DRETA

The central boulevard of Passeig de Gràcia has always been the Eixample's most desirable address and is where you'll find Modernisme's most flamboyant townhouses. The three most famous are Gaudí's humpbacked **Casa Batlló** (No. 43), Puig i Cadafalch's **Casa Amatller** (No.41) and Domènech i Montaner's **Casa Lleó Morera**, a decadently melting wedding cake of a building (partially defaced during the architecturally delinquent Franco era) on the corner of C/Consell de Cent at No.35. These are collectively known as the Manzana de Discòrdia.

As the area surrounding Passeig de Gràcia is one of the wealthiest parts of the city, it is not surprising that it's also extraordinarily rich in privately owned art collections and museums; these include the new **Fundación Alorda**

Derksen and **Fundació Suñol**, along with the **Museu Egipci de Barcelona**, the **Fundació Francisco Godia**, the **Fundació Vila Casas** (Espai VolART, C/Ausiàs Marc 22, 93 481 79 85) and the **Fundació Antoni Tàpies**. The area is equally rich in shopping with a mix of boutiques, international designers and high street brands jostling for space along the golden retail belts of Passeig de Gràcia, the parallel Rambla de Catalunya and the central section of the Avinguda Diagonal.

For most visitors, however, the crowning glory of the Eixample experience is the darkly beautiful **Sagrada Família**. Whether you love it or hate it (George Orwell called it 'one of the most hideous buildings in the world'), it has become the city's emblem and sine qua non of Barcelona tourist itineraries. A less famous masterpiece in the shape of Domènech i Montaner's **Hospital de la Santa Creu i Sant Pau** bookends the northerly extreme of the Avda Gaudí. A few blocks south, there's more welcome green space in the **Parc de l'Estació del Nord** and, on C/Marina, one of Barcelona's weirdest museums, the macabre **Museu de Carrosses Fúnebres**.

The streets above the Diagonal boast some striking Modernista buildings, such as Puig i Cadafalch's 1901 **Palau Macaya** at Passeig de Sant Joan 108. Other buildings of interest include the tiled **Mercat de la Concepció** on C/Aragó, designed by Rovira i Trias, and the turret-topped **Casa de les Punxes**, designed yet again by the prolific Puig i Cadafalch, and which combines elements of Nordic Gothic with Spanish plateresque. Moving down C/Roger de Llúria, you pass the **Casa Thomas** and the **Palau Montaner**, both designed by Lluís Domènech i Montaner, and on reaching C/Casp, you arrive at one of Gaudí's lesser-known

SIGHTS

INSIDE TRACK
MANZANA DE DISCORDIA

The three most famous Modernista buildings sit on the block known rather strangely as the **Manzana de Discòrdia**. It's a Catalan appropriation of the Spanish word *manzana* (rather than the usual Catalan word *illa*) which puns on the double meaning of 'block' and 'apple', and alludes to the fatal choice of Paris when judging which of a bevy of divine beauties would win the golden Apple of Discord. If the volume of camera-toting admirers is anything to go by, the fairest of these Modernista lovelies is undoubtedly Gaudí's Casa Batlló, permanently illuminated by flashbulbs.

works, the **Casa Calvet**. If you look right you'll see the egg-topped **Plaça de Braus Monumental**, but the city's last active bullring is now mainly frequented by tour buses from the Costa Brava; out of season, it hosts tatty travelling circuses. Not far from the bullring, at C/Lepant 150, is the ultra-modern concert hall of **L'Auditori de Barcelona**, which also houses the newly reopened **Museu de la Música**.

☐☐☐☐ Casa Àmatller

Passeig de Gràcia 41 (93 487 72 17/www. amatller.org). Metro Passeig de Gràcia. **Open** 10am-8.30pm daily. **Admission** free; guided tour €5; reductions €2.50. **Map** p338 G8.
Built for chocolate baron Antoni Àmatller, this playful building is one of Puig i Cadafalch's finest creations. Inspired by 17th-century Dutch townhouses, it has a distinctive stepped Flemish pediment covered in shiny ceramics, while the lower façade and doorway are decorated with lively sculptures by Eusebi Arnau. These include chocolatiers at work, almond trees and blossoms (in reference to the family name) and Sant Jordi slaying the dragon.

Besides chocolate, Àmatller's other great love was photography. His daughter later converted the family home into an art institute and archive for her father's vast archives, from which excellent selections are on display in the ground floor exhibition space. The guided tour of the house lasts around an hour and includes the ornate entrance hall, Antoni Àmatller's period photography studio and a tasting of Àmatller chocolate in the original kitchen. The façade of the building is currently undergoing restoration and it will be sheathed in particularly unphotogenic green netting for nearly all of 2009.
▶ *For more on Puig i Cadafalch, see p46.*

☐☐☐☐ Casa Àsia

Avda Diagonal 373 (93 238 73 37/www.casa asia.org). Metro Diagonal. **Open** *Exhibitions* 10am-8pm Mon-Sat; 10am-2pm Sun. *Library* 10am-8pm Mon-Fri; 10am-2pm Sat. *Café* 10am-9pm Mon-Fri* **Admission** free. **Map** p338 G6.
This cultural centre for Asia and the Asian Pacific is housed in the jaw-droppingly ornate Palau Baró

INSIDE TRACK
CASA COMALAT

The splendid Casa Comalat at Avda Diagonal 442 has the unusual distinction, in the Eixample, of two façades. The front has 12 voluptuously curvy stone balconies complete with ornate wrought-iron railings, while the more radical back façade (C/Còrsega 316) has a colourful harlequin effect with curiously bulging green-shuttered balconies.

---

de Quadras, designed by Puig i Cadafalch. If you can tear your eyes away from the lavish carvings and mosaics, there are a variety of excellent temporary exhibits covering anything from modern Chinese abstract art to Iranian graphics. The underlying function of this organisation, however, is the promotion of Asian culture in Barcelona with language courses, international conferences and cinema cycles (often subtitled in English). It also features an oriental café on the ground floor and an excellent multimedia library on the fourth floor, which allows visitors to hire CDs, DVDs and books on presentation of their passport or ID card.
▶ *The centre runs Festival Asia (see p229).*

★ Casa Batlló

Passeig de Gràcia 43 (93 216 03 06/www. casabatllo.cat). Metro Passeig de Gràcia. **Open** 8am-8pm daily. **Admission** €17.50; €14 reductions; free under-7s. **Credit** MC, V. **Map** p338 G8.
In one of the most extreme architectural makeovers ever seen, Gaudí and his long-time collaborator Josep Maria Jujol took an ordinary apartment block and remodelled it inside and out for textile tycoon Josep Batlló between 1902 and 1906. The result was one of the most impressive and admired of all Gaudí's creations, although opinions differ on what the building's remarkable façade represents, particularly its polychrome shimmering walls, its sinister skeletal balconies and its humpbacked scaly roof. Some say it's the spirit of carnival, others a Costa Brava cove. However, the most popular theory, which takes into account the architect's deeply patriotic feelings, is that it depicts Sant Jordi and the dragon: the idea being that the cross on top is the knight's lance, the roof is the back of the beast, and the balconies below are the skulls and bones of its hapless victims.

The chance to explore the interior (at a cost) offers the best opportunity of understanding how Gaudí, sometimes considered the lord of the bombastic and overblown, was really the master of tiny details, from the ingenious ventilation in the doors to the amazing natural light reflecting off the azure walls of the inner courtyard and the way the brass window handles are curved so as to fit precisely the shape of a hand. An apartment within is open to the public and access has been granted to the attic and roof terrace: the white-washed arched rooms of the top floor, originally used for laundering and hanging clothes, are among the master's most atmospheric spaces.

Fundación Alorda Derksen

C/Aragó 314 (93 272 62 50/www.fundacioad. com). Metro Girona or Passeig de Gràcia. **Open** 10am-1pm, 4-7pm Wed, Fri. 10am-2pm, 4-8pm Sat. Closed Aug. **Admission** €5; €3 reductions. **No credit cards. Map** p339 H8.
A garden furniture mogul might seem at first glance to be an unlikely art collector but Manuel Alorda and

SIGHTS

La Pedrera. *See p108.*

his wife Hanneke Derksen proved that there is no conflict between decking and painting when they opened this impressive gallery, dedicated to 21st-century art, in April 2008. Some pieces in the inaugural exhibition (running until April 2009) come from their own collection but as a patron of Tate Modern and the MACBA, Alorda's connections allowed him to borrow high-profile works of art that have never before been seen in Barcelona. The 24 large-scale pieces include part of Damien Hirst's *Butterfly* series, the *Spots* series and hyperrealist works themed on the birth of Hirst's son. Catalan conceptual artist Jaume Plensa's body sculpture of metal letter 'cells' also impresses as does Anselm Kiefer's colossal naval-themed piece, *Die Grosse Fracht*.

Fundació Antoni Tàpies

C/Aragó 255 (93 487 03 15/www.fundaciotapies. org). Metro Passeig de Gràcia. **Open** 10am-8pm Tue-Sun. **Admission** €6; €4 reductions; free under-16s. **Credit** (over €6) MC, V. **Map** p338 G8.
Antoni Tàpies exploded on to the art scene in the 1950s when he began to incorporate waste paper, mud and rags into his paintings, eventually moving on to whole pieces of furniture, running water and girders. Today, he is Barcelona's most celebrated living artist and his trademark scribbled and paint-daubed pieces are sought after for everything from wine bottle labels to theatre posters.

The artist set up the Tàpies Foundation in this, the former Montaner i Simon publishing house, in 1984, dedicating it to the study and appreciation of contemporary art. In a typically contentious act,

Tàpies crowned the building with a glorious tangle of aluminium piping and ragged metal netting (*Núvol i Cadira*, or Cloud and Chair). The building remains one of the earliest examples of Modernisme to combine exposed brick and iron and is now a cultural centre and museum dedicated to the work and life of the man himself, with exhibitions, symposiums, lectures and films. At the time of writing the foundation was closed for large-scale interior remodelling and unlikely to reopen until late 2009.
▶ *There may be works by Tàpies on display at MACBA; see p81.*

Fundació Francisco Godia

C/Diputació 250 (93 272 31 80/www. fundacionfgodia.org). Metro Passeig de Gràcia. **Open** 10am-8pm Mon, Wed-Sun. Closed Aug. **Admission** €4.50; €2.10 reductions; free under-5s. **Credit** (shop only) MC, V. **Map** p342 F8.
Newly transplanted in late 2008 from a first-floor flat to the Casa Garriga Nogués – a Modernista masterpiece in its own right – this vast private art collection now has enough room to breathe, with two floors of exhibition space. Godia was a Formula 1 driver for Maserati in the 1950s who funnelled his considerable fortune into an impressive selection of medieval religious art, historic Spanish ceramics, sculpture and modern painting. The permanent collection resides on the upper floor and largely consists of medieval sculptures and paintings, including Alejo de Vahia's *Pietà* and a Baroque masterpiece by Lucio Giordano, along with some outstanding Romanesque sculptures. The inaugu-

Profile Sagrada Família

Gaudí's unfinished masterpiece.

'Send Gaudí and the Sagrada Família to hell,' wrote Picasso, and while it is easy to see how some of the religious clichés of the building and the devotional fervour of its creator might annoy an angry young Cubist, Barcelona's iconic temple still manages to inspire delight in equal measure.

Gaudí dedicated more than 40 years to the project, the last 14 exclusively, and is buried beneath the nave. Many consider the crypt and the Nativity façade, which were completed in his lifetime, as the most beautiful elements of the church. The latter, facing C/Marina, looks at first glance as though some careless giant has poured candle wax over a Gothic cathedral, but closer inspection shows every protuberance to be an intricate sculpture of flora, fauna or human figure, combining to form an astonishingly moving stone tapestry depicting scenes from Christ's early years.

Providing a grim counterpoint to the excesses of the Nativity façade is the Passion façade on C/Sardenya, featuring bone-shaped columns and haunting, angular sculptures by Josep Maria Subirachs showing the 12 stations of the *via crucis*. The vast metal doors, set behind the sculpture of the flagellation of Jesus, are particularly arresting, covered in quotations from the Bible in various languages. The Glory façade on C/Mallorca, the final side to be built and the eventual main entrance to the temple, is currently shooting up behind the scaffolding and is devoted to the Resurrection, a mass of stone clouds and trumpets emblazoned with words from the Apostles' Creed.

The most amazing thing about the Sagrada Família project, however, is that it is happening at all. Setbacks have ranged from 1930s anarchists blowing up Gaudí's detailed plans and models to lack of funds. Ongoing work is a matter of conjecture and controversy, with the finishing date expected to be somewhere within the region of 25-30 years. It was hoped the masterpiece would be completed in 2026 to

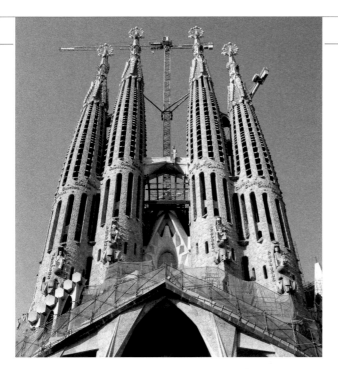

SIGHTS

coincide with the 100th anniversary of Gaudí's death, although this now seems unlikely. This is, however, somewhat of an improvement on the prognosis in the 1900s, when construction was expected to last several hundred years; advanced computer technology is now being used to shape each intricately designed block of stone offsite to speed up the process. The latest tribulation to the architects is the municipal approval of plans to build the AVE bullet train tunnel just a few feet away from the temple's foundations.

An estimated five million tourists visit the Sagrada Família each year, more than two-and-a-half million of them paying the entrance fee. (A combination of ticket revenues and charitable donations funds the continued construction of the project and spending currently runs at about €1 million a month.) A ticket allows you to wander through the interior of the church, a marvellous forest of columns laid out in the style of the great Gothic cathedrals, with a multi-aisled central nave crossed by a transept. The central columns are fashioned of porphyry, perhaps the only natural element capable of supporting the church's projected great dome; destined to rise 170m (558ft), this will make the Sagrada Família once again the highest building in the city. A range of tours are available.

An admission ticket also gives visitors access to the museum in the basement, offering insight into the history of the construction, original models for sculptural work and the chance to watch sculptors working at plaster-cast models through a large window.

TAKE THE TRIP UP
The highlight of any trip is a vertiginous hike up one of the towers (you can also take a lift), which affords amazing views through archers' windows.

ral temporary exhibition on the ground floor show-cases Godia's contemporary collection with pieces by Ramon Casas, Eduardo Chillida, Picasso, Antoni Tàpies and Joan Miró.

𝗙𝗥𝗘𝗘 Fundació Joan Brossa

C/Provença 318 (93 467 69 52/www.fundacio-joan-brossa.org). Metro Diagonal or Verdaguer. **Open** 10am-2pm, 3-7pm Mon-Fri. Closed Aug. **Admission** free. **Map** p338 G7.

This polymathic artist (1919-98) left his fingerprints all over his home city, not only in physical sculptures such as the letters spelling 'Barcino' by the cathedral or the *Illusory Clock* outside the Poliorama Theatre on La Rambla but also in his vast legacy of poems, theatre plays, tireless campaigning for the Catalan language, the Espai Escènic Joan Brossa theatrical space in the Born, and the founding of the Dau-al-Set avant-garde art movement in 1948. The permanent collection at the foundation fills three white rooms with some 35 of Brossa's visual and object poems along with posters, manuscripts, books and plays along with photographs and screenings of some of his short films.

Fundació Suñol

Passeig de Gràcia 98 (93 496 10 32/www.fundaciosunol.org). Metro Diagonal. **Open** 4-8pm Mon-Wed, Fri, Sat. **Admission** €5; €2.50 reductions. **No credit cards. Map** p338 G7.

Opened in 2007, the foundation's two floors house the contemporary art collection of businessman Josep Suñol. There are 100 pieces, including painting, sculpture and photography, on show at a time, shuffled every six months (Jan and July) from an archive of 1,200 pieces amassed over 35 years. The collection includes historic artists of the avant-garde, predominantly Catalan and Spanish: Picasso, Miró and Pablo Gargallo, with international input from Giacometti, Man Ray and Warhol.

With superfluities removed, including labels, and chronology abandoned, works are arranged in careful, coherent compositions, by style, colour or even mood, in serene interlinking rooms of varying sizes. Helpful English-speaking staff and a pamphlet aid visitors and an additional information booklet costs €2. Nivell Zero offers a large exhibition space to younger avant-garde artists, with shorter-term poetry cycles, installations and multimedia projects.

★ Hospital de la Santa Creu i Sant Pau

C/Sant Antoni María Claret 167 (93 291 90 00/www.santpau.cat). Metro Hospital de Sant Pau. **Map** p339 L5/L6.

When part of the roof of the gynaecology department collapsed in 2004, it was clear that restoration work was needed on the century-old Modernista 'garden city' hospital. By spring 2009 the last of the departments will have been transferred to the modern Nou Sant Pau building to the north of the

grounds and the old complex will cease to be a functioning hospital although there are tentative plans to turn part of it into a museum of Modernisme.

Scaffolding and builders will be on the grounds for the next decade or so but the renovations will be gradual and the complex still open to visitors who come to admire Domènech i Montaner's masterpiece. A UNESCO World Heritage Site, the hospital is a collection of 20 pavilions abundantly adorned with the colourful Byzantine, Gothic and Moorish flourishes that characterise the architect's style and set in peaceful gardens that spread over nine blocks in the north-east corner of the Eixample. It is set at a 45° angle from the rest of Ildefons Cerdà's grid system, so that it catches more sun: Domènech i Montaner built the hospital very much with its patients in mind, convinced that aesthetic harmony and pleasant surroundings were good for the health.

The public enjoy free access to the grounds, and guided tours (€5; €2.50 reductions) in English are held daily at 10.15am and 12.15pm.

𝗙𝗥𝗘𝗘 Museu de Carrosses Fúnebres

C/Sancho de Avila 2 (93 484 17 10). Metro Marina. **Open** 10am-1pm, 4-6pm Mon-Fri; 10am-1pm Sat, Sun (call in advance to check). **Admission** free. **Map** p343 K10.

Finding this, surely the most obscure and macabre museum in Barcelona, hasn't got any easier. You'll need to ask at the reception desk of the Ajuntament's funeral service and, eventually, a security guard will take you down to a perfectly silent and splendidly shuddersome basement housing the world's largest collection of funeral carriages and hearses dating from the 18th century through to the 1950s. There are ornate Baroque carriages and more functional Berlins and Landaus, and a wonderful '50s silver Buick. The white carriages were designed for children and virgins; there's a windowless black-velour mourning carriage for the forlorn mistress, ensuring both her presence and anonymity. The vehicles are manned by ghoulish dummies dressed in period gear whose eyes follow you around the room, making you glad of that security guard. The museum is supposed to be moving to the cemetery on Montjuïc some day, although progress is, naturally, funereal.

Museu de la Música

L'Auditori, C/Padilla 155 (93 256 36 50/ www.museumusica.bcn.cat). Metro Glòries. **Open** 11am-9pm Mon, Wed-Fri; 10am-7pm Sat, Sun. **Admission** €4; €3 reductions; free under-16s. **Credit** MC, V. **Map** p343 K9.

Finally rehoused in the Auditori concert hall in 2007 after six years in hibernation, the Music Museum comprises over 1,600 instruments displayed like precious jewels in red velvet and glass cases along with multimedia displays, interactive exhibits and musical paraphernalia. Spanning ancient civilisations to the modern day and including instruments from all

Hospital de la Santa Creu i Sant Pau.

corners of the world, the museum's high note is the world-class collection of guitars dating from the 17th century. Temporary exhibitions so far have concentrated on famous Catalan musicians, including the partnership between pianist and composer Enric Granados and cellist Pau Casals.

Museu Egipci de Barcelona
C/València 284 (93 488 01 88/www. museuegipci.com). Metro Passeig de Gràcia.
Open 10am-8pm Mon-Sat; 10am-2pm Sun.
Admission €11; €8 reductions; free under-5s.
Credit AmEx, MC, V. **Map** p338 G7.
One of the finest collections of Ancient Egyptian artefacts in Europe, this collection is owned by prominent Egyptologist Jordi Clos and spans 3,000 years of Nile-drenched culture. The exhibits include religious statuary, such as the massive baboon heads used to decorate temples, everyday copper mirrors and alabaster headrests, and some really rather moving infant sarcophagi. Outstanding pieces include some painstakingly matched fragments from the Sixth Dynasty Tomb of Iny, a bronze statuette of the goddess Isis breastfeeding her son Horus, and mummified cats, baby crocodiles and falcons. Another highlight is a 5,000-year-old bed, which still looks comfortable enough to sleep in. On Friday and Saturday nights, there are dramatic reconstructions of popular themes, such as the mummification ritual or the life of Cleopatra, for which reservations are essential. The museum entrance fee is waived for guests staying at the Hotel Claris, which is also owned by Clos.

Museu del Perfum
Passeig de Gràcia 39 (93 216 01 21/www. museudelperfum.com). Metro Passeig de Gràcia.
Open 10.30am-7.30 Mon-Fri; 10.30am-1.30 Sat.
Admission €5; €3 reductions. **No credit cards. Map** p338 G8.
In the back room of the Regia perfumery sits this collection of nearly 5,000 scent bottles, cosmetic flasks and related objects. The collection is divided in two. One shows all manner of unguent vases and essence jars in chronological order, from a tube of black eye make-up from pre-dynastic Egypt to Edwardian atomisers and a prized double-flask pouch that belonged to Marie Antoinette. The second section exhibits perfumery brands such as Guerlain and Dior; some are in rare bottles, among them a garish Dalí creation for Schiaparelli and a set of golliwog flasks by Vigny Paris. The museum's most recent addition includes a collection of 19th-century perfume powder bottles and boxes.

FREE Parc de l'Estació del Nord
C/Nàpols (no phone). Metro Arc de Triomf.
Open 10am-sunset daily. **Admission** free.
Map p343 J10/K10.
Otherwise known as Parc Sol i Ombra (meaning 'Sun and Shadow'), this small but well-used park is perked up by the three pieces of landscape art in glazed blue and white ceramic by New York sculptor Beverly Pepper. Along with a pair of incongruous white stone entrance walls, *Espiral Arbrat* (Tree Spiral) is a spiral bench set under the cool shade of lime-flower trees, while *Cel Caigut* (Fallen

SIGHTS

Sky) is a 7m-high (23ft) ridge rising from the grass. The colourful tilework recalls Gaudí's *trencadís* smashed-tile technique.

★ La Pedrera (Casa Milà)

Passeig de Gràcia 92-C/Provença 261-265 (93 484 59 00/www.caixacatalunya.cat/obrasocial). **Metro Diagonal. Open** *Jan, Dec* 9am-6.30pm daily. *Feb-Nov* 9am-8pm daily. **Admission** €8; €4.50 reductions; free under-12s. **Credit** MC, V. **Map** p338 G7.

Described variously as rising dough, molten lava and a stone lung, the last secular building designed by Antoni Gaudí, the Casa Milà (popularly known as La Pedrera, 'the stone quarry') has no straight lines and is a stupendous and daring feat of architecture, the culmination of the architect's experimental attempts to recreate natural forms with bricks and mortar (not to mention ceramics and even smashed-up cava bottles). Now a UNESCO World Heritage Site, it appears to have been washed up on shore, its marine feel complemented by Jujol's tangled balconies, doors of twisted kelp ribbon, seafoamy ceilings and interior patios as blue as a mermaid's cave. When it was completed in 1912, it was so far ahead of its time that the woman who financed it as her dream home, Roser Segimon, became the laughing stock of the city – hence the ugly 'stone quarry' tag. Its rippling façade led local painter Santiago Rusiñol to quip that a snake would be a better pet than a dog for the inhabitants of the building. But La Pedrera has become one of Barcelona's best-loved buildings, and is adored by architects for its extraordinary structure: it is supported entirely by pillars, without a single master wall, allowing the vast asymmetrical windows of the façade to invite in great swathes of natural light.

There are three exhibition spaces. The first-floor art gallery hosts free shows of eminent artists, while the upstairs is dedicated giving visitors a finer appreciation of Gaudí: accompanied by an audio guide (included in the admission price) you can visit a reconstructed Modernista flat on the fourth floor, with a sumptuous bedroom suite by Gaspar Homar, while the attic, framed by parabolic arches worthy of a Gothic cathedral, holds a museum offering an insightful overview of Gaudí's career. Best of all is the chance to stroll on the roof of the building amid its *trencadís*-covered ventilation shafts: their heads are shaped like the helmets of medieval knights, which led the poet Pere Gimferrer to dub the spot 'the garden of warriors'. *Photo p103.*

★ Sagrada Família

C/Mallorca 401 (93 207 30 31/www.sagrada familia.org). Metro Sagrada Família. **Open** *Mar-Sept* 9am-8pm daily. *Oct-Feb* 9am-6pm daily. **Admission** €8; €5 reductions; €3 8-10 years; free under-8s. *Lift to spires* €2. **Credit** (shop only) MC, V. **Map** p339 K7. *See pp104-105* **Profile.**

THE ESQUERRA

When Cerdà designed the Eixample he consciously tried to avoid creating any upper- or lower-class side of town, imagining each of his homogeneous blocks as a cross-section of society. This vision of equality did not come to pass, however, and the left side of the tracks was immediately less fashionable than the right; eventually it was to become the repository for the sort of city services the bourgeoisie didn't want ruining the upmarket tone of their new neighbourhood. A huge slaughterhouse was built at the eastern edge of the area (and was only knocked down in 1979, when it was replaced by the Parc Joan Miró). Also here is the busy Hospital Clínic, an ugly, functional building that covers two blocks between C/Corsega and C/Provença; on C/Entença, a little further out, was the grim, star-shaped La Model prison. It has been relocated out of town and replaced by subsidised houses and offices. The vast Escola Industrial on C/Comte d'Urgell, formerly a Can Batlló textile factory, was redesigned in 1909 as a centre to teach workers the methods used in the textile industry. Another building worth seeing is the central Universitat de Barcelona building on Plaça Universitat, completed in 1872. It is an elegant construction with a pleasant cloister-like garden. If you want to visit a market frequented by locals rather than tourists, try the Ninot, by Hospital Clínic.

The Esquerra also contains a number of Modernista jewels, such as the Casa Boada (C/Enric Granados 106) and the Casa Golferichs (Gran Via 191), built in 1901 by Joan Rubio i Bellver, one of Gaudí's main collaborators and now a civic centre. Beyond the hospital, the Esquerra leads to Plaça Francesc Macià, centre of the business district and a gateway to the Zona Alta. In recent years ProEixample has restored many of the interior patios in the Eixample and reduced the traffic lanes in several streets. In a turnaround of fortunes, the lower left side of the Eixample has also become home to the 'Gaixample', an affluent gay neighbourhood where the rainbow flag flies from many a restaurant, bar and hairdresser.

Parc Joan Miró (Parc de l'Escorxador)

C/Tarragona (no phone). Metro Espanya. **Open** 10am-sunset daily. **Map** p341 C8.

Covering an area the size of four city blocks, the old slaughterhouse (*escorxador*) was demolished in 1979 to provide much-needed parkland, although there's little greenery. The rows of palms and pines are dwarfed by Miró's sculpture *Dona i Ocell* (Woman and Bird) getting its feet wet in a rather grim cement lake; there's a good playground for small children.

SIGHTS

Gràcia & Other Districts

The city's outlying neighbourhoods hold treasures aplenty.

Cities have a way of devouring everything in their path, which is why it was inevitable that the town of **Gràcia** would disappear inside the urban maw when Barcelona's city walls were demolished. By 1897, the independent district had been swallowed up by the city, and Gràcia's nominal autonomy was rendered irrelevant. Still, it retains its character and continues to draw visitors – as do its neighbours on the city's outskirts, from football pilgrims heading to the Nou Camp to families seeking enlightenment at CosmoCaixa.

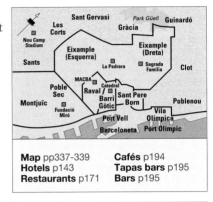

Map pp337-339	**Cafés** p194
Hotels p143	**Tapas bars** p195
Restaurants p171	**Bars** p195

GRACIA

Gràcia's reputation as a breeding ground for political insurgency came from the effects of industrial expansion. Centred around the 17th-century convent of Santa Maria de Gràcia, it was a village in 1821, with just 2,600 residents. But by the time it was annexed 78 years later, its population had risen to 61,935; it had become the ninth largest town in Spain and a hotbed of Catalanism, republicanism and anarchism.

Dissent has been a recurring feature in Gràcia's history: streets boast names such as Llibertat, Revolució and Fraternitat; and for the 64 years preceding the Civil War, there was a satirical political magazine called *La Campana de Gràcia*, named after the famous bell in Plaça Rius i Taulet. However, few vestiges of radicalism remain. Sure, the *okupa* squatter movement inhabits a relatively high number of buildings in the area, but the middle-class population has been waging an increasingly successful campaign to dislodge them.

Gràcia is both 'alternative' and upmarket, and anything bigger than a shoebox costs a fortune to rent or buy, but for many, it's the only place to be in Barcelona. As a consequence it radiates a sort of global chic of sleek bars, yoga centres, shiatsu, acupuncture and every form of holistic medicine, as well as piercing and tattoo parlours, dotted among the antique shops and *jamonerías*. The *barri* is a favourite hangout of the city's bohemians: there are numerous workshops and studios here, and the many small, unpretentious bars are often frequented by artists, designers and students.

The neighbourhood really comes into its own for a few days in mid August, when its famous *festa major* grips the entire city (*see p228*). Residents spend months preparing startlingly original home-made street decorations and there is fierce competition for the prize of best decorated street, and all Barcelona converges on the tiny *barri* to party. Open-air meals are laid on for the residents of Gràcia, bands are dotted on every street, films are screened in *plaças* and bars, while old-timers sing along to *habaneros* (shanties) and resident squatters pogo to punk bands.

Much of Gràcia was built in the heyday of Modernisme, something evident in the splendid main street, C/Gran de Gràcia. Many of the buildings are rich in nature-inspired curves and fancy façades, but the finest example is Lluís Domènech i Montaner's Casa Fuster at no.2, recently reopened as a luxury hotel (*see p143*). Gaudí's disciple Francesc Berenguer was responsible for much of the civic architecture,

Square Necessities

Sit back and relax in some of Gràcia's public spaces.

The sense of Gràcia being a place apart is enhanced by its many squares, giving it the feel of a town within a town. The grandest is the **Plaça Rius i Taulet**, named in honour of a former Barcelona mayor. On the seaward side stands Gràcia town hall, the work of the Modernista architect and Gaudí disciple, Francesc Berenguer, while on the other three sides you can sit at terrace bars in the shade of laburnum trees. The square is dominated by an outsized belltower (33 metres or 108 foot high), a symbol of rebellion ever since the so-called Revolta de les Quintes in 1870, when 300 women stormed the town hall in protest at plans to introduce military conscription. Throughout the revolt, which lasted a week before being suppressed, the belltower chimed, summoning people to join the resistance.

A little further north is the **Plaça del Diamant**, just around the corner from the much-loved Verdi cinema. The plaça is not as lively as Rius i Taulet, although there is a small playground for toddlers.

The square was made famous by the novel of the same name by Mercè Rodoreda, published in English as *The Time of the Doves*. Livelier though not lovelier is Plaça del Sol, noisy at night from its many bars, though by day you can sit peacefully in the shade of the magnolias at Café del Sol and watch the world stroll by.

Close by is the serene and elegant **Plaça de la Virreina**, dominated by the 19th-century church of Sant Joan de Gràcia. The church stands on the site of the former Palau de la Virreina, home to the wife of the elderly viceroy of Peru. She was widowed at an early age, dedicated her life to good works, and is now commemorated with a fountain and a small bronze statue of the Old Testament figure of Ruth carrying the sheaves of wheat she gleaned. Some of the interior of the church is the work of the same Berenguer who built the town hall in Plaça Rius I Taulet, as is the narrow, Modernista house, Casa Rubinat, on the east side of the square at C/Or 44.

most notably the Mercat de la Llibertat (Barcelona's oldest covered market and still proudly adorned with Gràcia's old coat of arms) and the old Casa de la Vila (Town Hall) in Plaça Rius i Taulet.

However, the district's most overwhelming Modernista gem is one of Gaudí's earliest and most fascinating works, the **Casa Vicens** of 1883-88, hidden away in C/Carolines. The building is a private residence and not open to visitors, but the castellated red brickwork and colourful tiled exterior with Indian and Mudéjar influences should not be missed; notice, too, the spiky wrought-iron leaves on the gates. And one of Gaudí's last works, the extraordinary **Park Güell**, is a walk away, across the busy Travessera de Dalt and up the hill. It's well worth the effort (there are even escalators at certain points): not only for the architecture, but for the magnificent view of Barcelona and the sea.

Photography buffs should also note the **Fundació Foto Colectània**. And, just off C/Sants is C/Sant Medir, the starting point for the *barri*'s **Festa de Sant Medir** (*see p224*), held in mid March every year, where local representatives canter around in horse-drawn carriages throwing caramel sweets to children.

FREE Fundació Foto Colectània

C/Julián Romea 6, D2 (93 217 16 26/www. colectania.es). FGC Gràcia. **Open** 11am-2pm, 5-8.30pm Mon-Sat. Closed Sat in Aug. **Admission** free-€3; depending on exhibition. **Map** p338 F5.

This private foundation is dedicated to the promotion of the photography of major Spanish and Portuguese photographers from the 1950s to the present. It also has an extensive library of Spanish and Portuguese photography books.

★ FREE Park Güell

C/Olot (Casa-Museu Gaudí 93 219 38 11). Metro Lesseps/bus 24, 25. **Open** *Park* 10am-sunset daily. *Museum* Apr-Sept 10am-7.45pm daily. Oct-Mar 10am-5.45pm daily. **Admission** *Park* free. *Museum* €4; €3 reductions; free under-9s. **Credit** (shop only) MC, V. **Map** p341 H2/H3/J2/J3. *See p112* **Profile**. *Photo p114*.
▶ *To understand Gaudí's vision, see pp50-53.*

SANTS

Sants, or at least the immediate environs of Estació de Sants, which is all that most visitors see of the area, stands as a monument to the worst of 1970s urban design. To coincide with the arrival in February 2008 of the overdue high-speed AVE train link with Madrid, the station has had a makeover. It is no longer shabby, but it's not a place you'd want to hang

around, and few people do. And when they step outside, most take one look at the forbidding Plaça dels Països Catalans, a snarl of traffic around a roundabout whose centrepiece looks like a post-Miró bus shelter, and make a hasty exit. However, for those with time to spare, Sants merits a few hours' investigation for historic, if not aesthetic, reasons. Mid August is one of the better times to visit as, immediately following the Festa Major de Gràcia, Sants launches its own, albeit lower-key, version, and the *barri* sheds its drab industrial coat in favour of street parties, decorations and music.

Sants was originally built to serve those who arrived after the town gates had shut at 9pm, with inns and blacksmiths to cater for latecomers. In the 19th century, though, it became the industrial motor of the city. Giant textile factories such as Vapor Vell (which is now a library), L'Espanya Industrial (now the **Parc de l'Espanya Industrial**) and **Can Batlló** (still a workplace) helped create the wealth that the likes of Eusebi Güell spent on the Modernista dream homes that still grace the more salubrious areas of the city. The inequality did not go unnoticed. The *barri* was a hotbed of industrial action: the first general strike in Catalonia broke out here in 1856, only to be violently put down by the infamous General Zapatero (known as the 'Tiger of Catalonia'). The left-wing nationalist ERC party, which now shares power in the Generalitat, was founded here in 1931, at C/Cros 9.

Most routes of interest start and end at the hub of the *barri*, Plaça de Sants, halfway up C/Sants high street, where Jorge Castillo's *Ciclista* statue is also to be found. Also worth checking out are the showy Modernista buildings at nos.12, 130, 145 and 151, all designed by local architect Modest Feu.

Returning to Plaça de Sants and taking C/Olzinelles, you'll find the quaint Plaça Bonet i Mixi and the Parroquia de Santa Maria del Sants church, from which it is believed the *barri* got its name. This is the focal point for locals around Easter, when Semana Santa (Holy Week) grips Spain. Following C/Sants in the direction of Montjuïc, the road name changes to C/Creu Coberta, an old Roman road once known as the Camí d'Espanya, 'the road to Spain'. Following

---

INSIDE TRACK
JOSE CARRERAS

Opera fans may be interested in visiting one of Sant's oldest streets, the tiny commercial thoroughfare of C/Galileu, where tenor José Carreras was born at no.1 in 1946.

Profile Park Güell

Gaudí's Utopian garden city that never was.

SIGHTS

Gaudí's brief was to emulate the English garden cities so admired by his patron Eusebi Güell (which is the reason for the unusual spelling of 'park'): to lay out a self-contained suburb for the wealthy, but also to design the public areas. The original plan was for the plots to be sold off and the properties themselves subsequently designed by other architects. The idea never took off – perhaps because it was too far from the city, perhaps because it was too radical – and

GETTING THERE
The best way to get to the park is on the 24 bus; if you go via Lesseps metro, be prepared for a steep uphill walk.

the Güell family donated the park to the city in 1922.

Park Güell (listings p111) is a real fairy-tale place; the fantastical exuberance of Gaudí's imagination is breathtaking. The visitor was previously welcomed by two life-sized mechanical gazelles – a typically bizarre religious reference by Gaudí to medieval Hebrew love poetry – although these were unfortunately destroyed in the Civil War. The two gatehouses that do still remain were based on

designs the architect made earlier for the opera *Hänsel and Gretel*, one of them featuring a red and white mushroom for a roof. From here, walk up a splendid staircase flanked by multicoloured battlements, past the iconic mosaic lizard sculpture, to what would have been the main marketplace. Here, 100 palm-shaped pillars hold up a roof, reminiscent of the hypostyle hall at Luxor. On top of this structure is the esplanade, a circular concourse surrounded by undulating benches in the form of a sea-serpent decorated with shattered tiles – a technique called 'trencadís', which was actually perfected by Gaudí's overshadowed but talented assistant Josep Maria Jujol.

The park itself, now a UNESCO World Heritage Site, is magical, with twisted stone columns supporting curving colonnades or merging with the natural structure of the hillside. The park's peak is marked by a large cross and offers an amazing panorama of Barcelona and the sea beyond. Gaudí lived for a time in one of the two houses built on the site (which was, in fact, designed by his student Berenguer). It has since become the Casa-Museu Gaudí; guided tours, of which some are in English, are available.

C/Creu Coberta further, you'll find the large, lively and colourful Mercat d'Hostafrancs, where there's also a stop for the tourist bus. Further along still is C/Sant Roc and the Modernista-inspired Església de l'Angel Custodi.

FREE Parc de l'Espanya Industrial

Passeig de Antoni (no phone). Metro Sants-Estació. **Open** 10am-sunset daily. **Admission** free. **Map** p341 B7.

In the 1970s, the owners of the old textile factory announced their intention to use the land to build blocks of apartments. The neighbourhood's residents, though, put their collective foot down and insisted on a park, which was eventually laid out in 1985. The result is a puzzling space, designed by Basque Luis Peña Ganchegui, with ten watchtowers overlooking a boating lake with a statue of Neptune in the middle, flanked by a stretch of mud used mainly by dog walkers, but little in the way of greenery. By the entrance children can climb over Andrés Nagel's *Drac*, a massive and sinister black dragon sculpture.

Les Corts

Another village engulfed by the expanding city in the 19th century, Les Corts ('cowsheds' or 'pigsties'), remains one of the most Catalan of the city's *barris*, but the rows and rows of unlovely apartment blocks have stamped out almost any trace of its bucolic past. Something has been retained, however, in the Plaça de la Concòrdia, a quiet square dominated by a 40-metre (131-foot) bell tower. This is an anachronistic oasis housing the civic centre Can Deu, formerly a farmhouse and now home to a great bar hosting jazz acts every other Thursday. The area is much better known, though, for what happens every other weekend, when tens of thousands pour in to watch FC Barcelona, whose Camp Nou takes up much of the west of the *barri*. Note that at night the area is the haunt of transvestite prostitutes and their kerb-crawling clients.

★ Nou Camp – FC Barcelona

Avda Arístides Maillol, access 9, Les Corts (93 496 36 00/08/www.fcbarcelona.com). Metro Collblanc, Les Corts or Maria Cristina. **Open** *Apr-mid Oct* 10am-8pm Mon-Sat; 10am-2.30pm Sun. *Mid Oct-Mar* 10am-6.30pm Mon-Sat; 10am-2.30pm Sun. **Admission** €8.50; €6.80 reductions; free under-5s. *Guided tour* €13; €10.40 reductions. **Credit** AmEx, DC, MC, V. **Map** p337 A3/4.

Nou Camp, where FC Barcelona has played since 1957, is one of football's great stadiums, a vast cauldron of a ground that holds 98,000 spectators. That's a lot of noise when the team is doing well, and an awful lot of silence when it isn't. If you can't get there on match day (and you can usually pick up tickets if you try) but love the team, it's worth visiting the club museum. The excellent guided tour of the stadium takes you through the players' tunnel to the dugouts and then, via the away team's changing room, on to the President's box, where there is a replica of the European Cup, which the team won at Wembley in 1992 and again in Paris in 2006. The club museum commemorates those glory years, making much of the days when the likes of Kubala, Cruyff, Maradona, Koeman and Lineker trod the hallowed turf, with pictures, video clips and souvenirs spanning the century that has passed since the Swiss business executive Johan Gamper and the Englishman Arthur Witty first founded the club. Last tour begins an hour before closing time.
► *For match tickets, see p278 Inside track.*

TIBIDABO & COLLSEROLA

Before car pollution blurred the horizon, it was said that you could see Mallorca from Tibidabo, which takes it name from the Devil's temptation of Christ, when he took Jesus to the top of a mountain and offered him all before him, with the words '*tibi dabo*' (Latin for 'To thee I will give'). This gave rise to the name of the dominant peak of the Collserola massif, with its sweeping views of, if not Mallorca, at least the whole of the Barcelona conurbation stretching out to the sea: quite a tempting offer, given the present-day price of the city's real estate. The neo-Gothic Sagrat Cor church crowning the peak has become one of the city's most recognisable landmarks; it's clearly visible for miles around. At weekends, thousands of people head to the top of the hill in order to whoop and scream at the funfair. Nowadays the only one in Barcelona, it's been running since 1921 and has changed little since: the rides are creaky and old-fashioned, but very quaint. The marionette show is also a survivor from the early days, but a more recent addition is the first freefall ride in Spain, where visitors are dropped 38 metres (125 feet) in 2.8 seconds. Within the funfair is also the Museu d'Autòmats, a fine collection of fairground coin-operated machines from the early 1900s.

Getting there on the **Tramvia Blau** (Blue Tram; *photo p116*) and then the **funicular railway** is part of the fun; between the two is Plaça Doctor Andreu, a great place for an alfresco drink. For the best view of the city, either take a lift up Norman Foster's tower, the **Torre de Collserola**, or up to the *mirador* at the feet of Christ atop the Sagrat Cor.

The vast **Parc de Collserola** is more a series of forested hills than a park; its shady paths through holm oak and pine opening out to spectacular views. It's most easily reached by FGC train on the Terrassa-Sabadell line from Plaça Catalunya or Passeig de Gràcia, getting off at Baixador de Vallvidrera station. A ten-minute walk from the station up into the woods (there's an information board just outside the station) will take you to the Vil·la Joana, an old *masia* covered in bougainvillea and containing the **Museu Verdaguer** (93 204 78 05, www.museuhistoria.bcn.cat, open 10am-1.30pm Sat, Sun, admission free) dedicated to 19th-century Catalan poet Jacint Verdaguer, who used this as his summer home. Just beyond the Vil·la Joana is the park's information centre (93 280 35 52, open 9.30am-3pm daily), which has free basic maps and more detailed maps for sale. Most of the information is in Catalan, but staff are helpful. There's also a snack bar.

Funicular de Tibidabo

Plaça Doctor Andreu to Plaça Tibidabo (93 211 79 42). FGC Avda Tibidabo then Tramvia Blau. **Open** As funfair (*see p234*), but starting 30mins earlier. **Tickets** *Single* €2. *Return* €3. Free under-3s. **No credit cards.**
This art deco vehicle offers occasional glimpses of the city below as it winds through the pine forests up to the summit. The service has been operating since 1901, but only according to a complicated timetable. If it's not running, take the FGC line from Plaça de Catalunya to Peu del Funicular, get the funicular up to Vallvidrera Superior, and then catch the 111 bus to Tibidabo (a process not half as complicated as it sounds). Alternatively, it's nearly an hour's (mostly pleasant) hike up from Plaça Doctor Andreu for those who are feeling energetic.

Torre de Collserola

Ctra de Vallvidrera al Tibidabo (93 211 79 42/ www.torredecollserola.com). FGC Peu Funicular then funicular. **Open** *Apr-June, Sept* 11am-2pm, 3.30-6pm Wed-Fri; 11am-2pm, 3.30-7pm Sat, Sun. *July, Aug* 11am-2pm, 3.30-7pm Wed-Fri; 11am-2pm, 3.30-8pm Sat, Sun. *Oct-Mar* 11am-2pm, 3.30-5pm Wed-Fri; 11am-2pm, 3.30-6pm Sat, Sun. **Admission** €5; reductions €4; free under-4s. **Credit** AmEx, MC, V.
Just five minutes' walk from the Sagrat Cor is its main rival and Barcelona's most visible landmark, Norman Foster's communications tower, built in 1992 to transmit images of the Olympics around the world. Those who don't suffer from vertigo attest to the wonderful views of Barcelona and the Mediterranean from the top.

ZONA ALTA

Zona Alta (the 'upper zone', or 'uptown') is the name given collectively to a series of smart neighbourhoods including Sant Gervasi, Sarrià, Pedralbes and Putxet that stretch out across the lower reaches of the Collserola hills. The handful of tourist sights found here include the Palau Reial de Pedralbes (not to be confused with the Palau Reial Major in the Barri Gòtic),

with its gardens and museums, the **Museu de les Arts Aplicades**, the **CosmoCaixa** science museum and the **Pedralbes Monastery**, which is still well worth a visit even though its selection of religious paintings from the Thyssen-Bornemisza collection has been moved to the revamped Museu Nacional d'Art de Catalunya (MNAC; *see p92*). The centre of Sarrià and the streets of old Pedralbes around the monastery retain a flavour of the sleepy country towns these once were.

For many downtown residents, the Zona Alta is a favourite place to relax in the parks and gardens that wind in to the hills. At the end of Avda Diagonal, next to the functional Zona Universitària (university district), is the Jardins de Cervantes, with its 11,000 rose bushes, the striking *Rombes Bessons* (Twin Rhombuses) sculpture by Andreu Alfaro and, during the week, legions of picnicking students, continuing in the scholastic traditions of the founder of Catalan literature, Ramon Llull. From the park, a turn back along the Diagonal towards Plaça Maria Cristina and Plaça Francesc Macià will take you to Barcelona's main business and shopping district. Here is the small Turó Parc, a semi-formal garden good for writing postcards amid inspirational plaques of poetry. The Jardins de la Tamarita, at the foot of Avda Tibidabo, is a pleasant dog-free oasis with a playground, while further up at the top of the tramline is the little-known Parc de la Font de Racó, full of shady pine and eucalyptus trees. A fair walk to the north-east, an old quarry has been converted into a swimming pool, the **Parc de la Creueta del Coll**.
Gaudí fans are rewarded by a trip up to the **Pavellons de la Finca Güell** at Avda Pedralbes 15; its extraordinary and rather frightening wrought-iron gate features a dragon into whose gaping mouth the foolhardy can fit their heads. Once inside the gardens, via the main gate on Avda Diagonal, look out for a delightful fountain designed by the master himself. Across near Putxet is Gaudí's relatively sober Col·legi de les Teresianes (C/Ganduxer 85-105), while up towards Tibidabo, just off Plaça Bonanova, rises his Gothic-influenced Torre Figueres or Bellesguard.

CosmoCaixa

C/Teodor Roviralta 47-51 (93 212 60 50/www. fundacio.lacaixa.es). Bus 60/FGC Avda Tibidabo then Tramvia Blau (see p113). **Open** 10am-8pm Tue-Sun. **Admission** €3; €2 reductions; free under-7s. *Planetarium* €2; €1.50 reductions; free under-7s. **Credit** AmEx, DC, MC, V.
Said to be the biggest science museum in Europe, CosmoCaixa doesn't, perhaps, make the best use of its space. A glass-enclosed spiral ramp runs down an impressive six floors, but actually represents

SIGHTS

quite a long walk to reach the main collection five floors down. Here you'll find the Flooded Forest, a reproduction of a corner of Amazonia complete with flora and fauna, and the Geological Wall, along with temporary exhibitions.

From here, it's on to the Matter Room, which covers 'inert', 'living', 'intelligent' and then 'civilised' matter: in other words, natural history. However, for all the fanfare made by the museum about taking exhibits out of glass cases and making scientific theories accessible, many of the displays still look very dated. Written explanations often tend towards the impenetrable, containing phrases such as 'time is macroscopically irreversible', and making complex those concepts that previously seemed simple.

On the plus side, the installations for children are excellent: the Planetarium pleases those aged five to eight, and the wonderful Clik (ages three to six) and Flash (seven to nine) introduce children to science through games. Toca Toca! ('Touch Touch') educates children on which animals and plants are safe and which to avoid. One of the real highlights, for both young and old, is the hugely entertaining sound telescope outside on the Plaça de la Ciència.

▶ *For more family attractions, see pp232-234.*

★ Monestir de Pedralbes

Baixada del Monestir 9 (93 256 21 22). FGC Reina Elisenda. **Open** *Apr-Sept* 10am-5pm Tue-Sat; 10am-3pm Sun. *Oct-Mar* 10am-2pm Mon-Sat; 10am-3pm Sun. **Admission** €6; €4 reductions; free under-16s. Free 1st Sun of mth. **Credit** (shop only) AmEx, DC, MC, V.

In 1326, the widowed Queen Elisenda of Montcada used her inheritance to buy this land and build a convent for the Poor Clare order of nuns, which she soon joined. The result is a jewel of Gothic architecture with an understated single-nave church with fine stained-glass windows and a beautiful three-storey 14th-century cloister. The place was out of bounds to the general public until 1983, when the nuns, a closed order, opened it up as a museum in the mornings (when they escape to a nearby annexe).

The site offers a fascinating insight into life in a medieval convent, taking you through its kitchens, pharmacy and refectory, with its huge vaulted ceiling. To one side is the tiny chapel of Sant Miquel, with murals dating from 1343 by Ferrer Bassa, a Catalan painter and student of Giotto. In the former dormitory next to the cloister is a selection of illuminated books, furniture and items reflecting the artistic and religious life of the community. The price includes an audio-guide.

▶ *Tickets are valid for Museu d'Història de la Ciutat (see p57) and the Refugi 307 (see p98).*

Museu de les Arts Aplicades

Palau Reial de Pedralbes, Avda Diagonal 686 (93 280 16 21/www.museuceramica.bcn.cat/www. museuartsdecoratives.bcn.cat/www.museutextil.bcn.cat). Metro Palau Reial. **Open** 10am-6pm Tue-

Tramvia Blau. *See p114.*

Sat; 10am-3pm Sun. **Admission** €3.50; €2 reductions. *Combined admission* with temporary exhibition €5; €3 reductions; free under-16s. Free 1st Sun of mth. **No credit cards. Map** p337 A2.

In 2008, the Museu Tèxtil, previously located in the Born, joined the ceramic and decorative arts museums in the Palau Reial de Pedralbes, built in the 1920s and briefly used as a royal palace. The Textile Museum provides a chronological tour of clothing and fashion, from its oldest piece, a man's Coptic tunic from a seventh-century tomb, through to Karl Lagerfeld. Among many curiosities, such as an 18th-century bridal gown in black figured silk and the world's largest collection of kidskin gloves, the real highlight is the fashion collection – from Baroque to 20th-century – one of the finest of its type anywhere.

The Museum of Decorative Arts is informative and fun, and looks at the different styles informing the design of artefacts in Europe since the Middle Ages, from Romanesque to art deco and beyond. A second section is devoted to post-war Catalan design of objects as diverse as urinals and man-sized inflatable pens.

The Ceramics Museum is equally fascinating, showing how Moorish ceramic techniques from the 13th century were developed after the Reconquista with the addition of colours (especially blue and yellow) in centres such as Manises (in Valencia) and Barcelona. Upstairs is a section dedicated to 20th-century ceramics, with a room devoted to Miró and Picasso. The three museums, along with several smaller collections, are to be merged into a Museu de Disseny (Design Museum).

SIGHTS

FREE Parc de la Creueta del Coll

C/Mare de Déu del Coll (no phone). Metro Penitents. **Open** 10am-sunset daily. **Admission** free.

Created from a quarry in 1987 by Josep Martorell and David Mackay, the team that went on to design the Vila Olímpica, this park boasts a sizeable swimming pool complete with a 'desert island' and a sculpture by Eduardo Chillida: a 50-ton lump of curly granite suspended on cables, called *In Praise of Water*.

Pavellons de la Finca Güell

Avda Pedralbes 15 (93 317 76 52/www. rutadelmodernisme.com). Metro Palau Reial. **Open** 10.50am-2pm Mon, Fri-Sun. *Tours* in English 10.15am, 12.15pm. **Admission** €5; €2.50 reductions. **No credit cards**. **Map** p337 A3.

Industrial textile businessman Eusebi Güell bought what is now Palau Reial in 1882 as a summer home, contracting Gaudí to remodel the entrance lodges and gardens for the estate. In 1883, they began to build what would be one of Gaudí's first projects in Barcelona for the Güell family.

The huge gardens were accessed by three entrances, of which only two remain today. The Porta del Drac (Dragon's Gate) is the most impressive and used to be the private entrance for the Güell family. This entrance was connected to the Güell home in Barcelona by a private, walled road exclusively for their use when the family travelled between the city and the country. Nowadays, the gatehouses belong to the University of Barcelona. Interestingly, the family of Güell's original groundsman still lives in the same small house on the site.

The Pavellons must be visited with a guide, and tours are offered in Spanish and English. Really though, it isn't much of a tour, lasting for about 25 minutes with a look at nothing more than the gate and the stables. This was the first project on which Gaudí used his signature 'trencadís' or mosaic motif.

► *For more on Gaudí, see pp50-53.*

Tramvia Blau

Avda Tibidabo (Plaça Kennedy) to Plaça Doctor Andreu (93 318 70 74/www.tramvia.org/ tramviablau). FGC Avda Tibidabo. **Open** *Mid June-mid Sept* 10am-8pm daily. *Mid Sept-mid June* 10am-6pm Sat. *Frequency* 20mins. **Tickets** €2.30 single; €3.50 return. **No credit cards**.

Barcelonins and tourists have been clanking 1,225m (4,000ft) up Avda Tibidabo in the 'blue trams' since 1902. In the winter months, when the tram only operates on weekends, a rather more prosaic bus (no.195) takes you up (or you can walk it in 15 minutes).

POBLENOU & BEYOND

In its industrial heyday, Poblenou was known as 'little Manchester' due to the concentration of cotton mills. Now, the old mills and other factories are being bulldozed or remodelled as the district is rebranded as a technology and business district, snappily tagged 22@, which will exist side by side with the innumerable garages, exhaust fitters, wheel balancers and car washes that are a feature of the *barrio*.

The main drag, the pedestrianised Rambla de Poblenou, dating from 1886, is a much better place for a relaxing stroll than its busy central counterpart, and gives this still-villagey area a heart. Meanwhile, a bone's throw away, the city's oldest and most atmospheric cemetery, the Cementiri de Poblenou, shows that most *barcelonins* spend their death as they did their life: cooped up in large high-rise blocks. Some were able to afford roomier tombs, many of which were built at the height of the romantic-Gothic craze at the end of the 19th century. A leaflet or larger guide (€15) sold at the entrance suggests a route around 30 of the more interesting monuments.

Nearby, Plaça de les Glòries finally seems ready to fulfil its destiny. The creator of the Eixample, Ildefons Cerdà, hoped that the square would become the new centre of the city, believing his grid-pattern blocks would spread much further north than they did and shift the emphasis of the city from west to east. Instead, it became little more than a glorified roundabout on the way out of town. Nowadays, it's best known for its huge commercial shopping complex and the bustling market Mercat Els Encants (www.encantsbcn.com, open Mon, Wed, Fri, Sat from 7.30am), which has everything from kitchen sinks to dodgy DVDs. From here, a wide and relatively quiet stretch of Diagonal is filled with joggers, cyclists and in-line skaters as it leads towards the sea.

Els Encants is already casting about for a new home – the Monumental bullring has been tipped as a possible site – as work is about to begin on remodelling the ghastly, traffic-choked Glòries, partly to open up the land around the hugely phallic **Torre Agbar**, and to form a gateway to Diagonal Mar and the new commercial and leisure area on the shoreline, known as the Fòrum, after the event in 2004 for which it was created. The tower, designed by French architect Jean Nouvel and owned by the Catalan water board, has been a bold and controversial project. A concrete skyscraper with a domed head and a glass façade, it's not unlike London's famed Gherkin. Nouvel says it's been designed to reflect the Catalan mentality: the concrete represents stability and severity; the glass, openness and transparency. At 144 metres (472 feet), it's Barcelona's third highest building (behind the two Olympic towers) and contains no fewer than 4,400 multiform windows. Remarkably, it has no air-conditioning: the windows let the breeze do the

SIGHTS

job. Nouvel claims Gaudí as the inspiration for the multicoloured skin – it has 4,000 LED lights that change colour at night – of a building that has already polarised public opinion and come to dominate the district. Ask any taxi driver to take you to *el supositori* (the suppository) and they'll know you mean the Torre Agbar.

The new, walled **Parc Central del Poblenou** opened in spring 2008, and was designed by the French architect Jean Nouvel. It's one of a number of highly designed gardens in Barcelona and features giant plants, an island, a cratered lunar landscape and a perfumed garden. It opened to decidedly mixed reviews from the locals: aesthetically pleasing though it is, only time will tell if the park takes on a life of its own and if the hundreds of weeping willows can survive the rigours of the Mediterranean climate.

Another breath of fresh air is the **Parc del Clot**. Just beyond it is the Plaça de Valentí Almirall, with the old town hall of Sant Martí and a 17th-century building that used to be the Hospital de Sant Joan de Malta somewhat at odds with the buildings that have mushroomed around them. Further north, up C/Sagrera, the entrance to a former giant truck factory now leads to the charming **Parc de la Pegaso**. The area also has a fine piece of recent architecture, the supremely elegant Pont de Calatrava bridge. Designed by Santiago Calatrava, it links to Poblenou via C/Bac de Roda.

Diagonal Mar

To many people, the Diagonal Mar development represents the worst hypocrisy of the Barcelona authorities: pure venality dressed up as philanthropy. The stalking horse for the five-star hotels and luxury apartments that were to come was the Fòrum, a six-month cultural symposium held in 2004. Its tangible legacy are the enormous conference halls and hotels that draw many wealthy business clients into the city, together with a scarcely believable increase in real-estate values. More recently, the Fòrum has benefited the city's youth, with its wide-open spaces providing an excellent venue for two of Barcelona's biggest music festivals, Primavera Sound (*see p255*) and Summercase (*see p255*).

If you're approaching from the city, the first sign of this resurgent *barri* is **Parc de Diagonal Mar**, containing an angular lake decorated with scores of curling aluminium tubes and vast Gaudian flowerpots. Designed by the late Enric Miralles (he of Scottish Parliament fame), the park may not be to most *barcelonins*' taste, but flocks of seagulls have found it an excellent roosting spot. Just over the road from here is the Diagonal Mar shopping

Parc Central del Poblenou.

centre, a still woefully undervisited three-storey mall of high-street chains, cinemas and the grand Hotel Princesa, a triangular skyscraper designed by architect, designer, artist and local hero Oscar Tusquets.

The **Edifici Fòrum**, a striking blue triangular construction by architects Herzog and de Meuron (responsible for London's Tate Modern), is the centrepiece of the €3-billion redevelopment. The remainder of the money was spent on the solar panels, marina, new beach and the Illa Pangea, an island 60 metres (197 feet) from the shore, accessible only by swimming. Soon the Fòrum will be joined by Zaha Hadid's nearby Spiralling Tower, an extraordinary construction, like a hastily stacked pack of cards, which will serve as a university building.

It's all a far cry from the local residential neighbourhood, Sant Adrià de Besòs, a poor district of tower blocks that includes La Mina, a neighbourhood rife with drug-related crime. It's hoped that the new development will help regenerate the area, best known for its Feria de Abril celebrations in April (*see p255*), the Andalucian community's version of the more famous annual celebrations in Seville.

HORTA & AROUND

Horta was once a picturesque little village that still remains aloof from the city that swallowed it in 1904. Originally a collection of farms (its name means 'market garden'), the *barrio* is still peppered with old farmhouses, such as Can Mariner on C/Horta, dating back to 1050, and the medieval Can Cortada at the end of C/Campoamor, which is now a huge restaurant located in beautiful grounds. An abundant water supply also made Horta the place where much of the city's laundry was done: a whole community of *bugaderes* (washerwomen) lived and worked in lovely C/Aiguafreda, where you can still see their wells and open-air stone washtubs.

To the south, joined to Gràcia by Avda Mare de Déu de Montserrat, the steep-sided neighbourhood of Guinardó, with its steps and escalators, consists mainly of two big parks. **Parc del Guinardó**, a huge space designed in 1917 (making it Barcelona's third oldest park) full of eucalyptus and cypress, is a relaxing place to escape.

The Vall d'Hebron is a leafy area located just above Horta in the Collserola foothills. Here, formerly private estates have been put to public use; among them are the chateau-like Palauet de les Heures, now a university building. The area was one of the city's four major venues for the Olympics and is rich in sporting facilities, including public football pitches, tennis courts, and cycling and archery facilities at the Velòdrom. It's also the home to one of Barcelona's major concert venues. Around these environs there are several striking examples of street sculpture, including Claes Oldenburg's *Matches* and Joan Brossa's *Visual Poem* (in the shape of the letter 'A'). The area also conceals the rationalist **Pavelló de la República**, built in 1992 as a facsimile of the emblematic rationalist pavilion of the Spanish Republic designed by Josep Lluís Sert for the Paris Exhibition in 1937 and later to hold Picasso's *Guernica*, and the **Parc del Laberint**, dating back to 1791 and surrounded by a modern park. More modern still is the Ciutat Sanitària, Catalonia's largest hospital; a good proportion of *barcelonins* first saw the light of day here.

Parc del Laberint

C/Germans Desvalls, Passeig Vall d'Hebron (010/www.bcn.cat/parcsijardins). Metro Mundet. **Open** 10am-sunset daily. **Admission** €2.05; €1.30 reductions; free under-5s, over-65s. Free Wed, Sun.

In 1791, the Desvalls family, owners of this marvellously leafy estate, hired Italian architect Domenico Bagutti to design scenic gardens set around a cypress maze, with a romantic stream and a waterfall. The mansion may be gone (replaced with a 19th-century Arabic-influenced building), but the gardens are remarkably intact, shaded in the summer by oaks, laurels and an ancient sequoia. Best of all, the maze, an ingenious puzzle that intrigues those brave enough to try it, is also still in use. Nearby stone tables provide a handy picnic site. On paying days, last entry is one hour before sunset.

THE OUTER LIMITS

L'Hospitalet de Llobregat lies beyond Sants, completely integrated within the city's transport system but nevertheless a distinct municipality, one with its own sense of separateness. It is the second biggest city in Catalunya and has one of the highest population densities in Europe. The area also boasts a rich cultural life, with good productions at the **Teatre Joventut** (C/Joventut 10, 93 448 12 10, www.l-h.es/webs/teatre Joventut) and excellent art exhibitions at the **Tecla Sala Centre Cultural**.

Sant Andreu is another vast residential district in the north-east of the city, and was once a major industrial zone. Apart from the Gaudí-designed floor mosaic in the Sant Pacià church on C/Monges, there's little reason to venture here, unless you have an historical interest in Josep Lluís Sert's rationalist Casa Bloc, which were originally workers' residences from the brief Republican era.

The name of Nou Barris, across the Avda Meridiana, translates as 'nine neighbourhoods', but the area is actually a collection of 11 former hamlets. The council has compensated for the area's poor housing (many tower blocks were built in the area in the 1950s and have fallen into disrepair) with the construction of public facilities such as the Can Dragó, a sports centre incorporating the biggest swimming pool in the city, and Parc Central. The district is centred on the roundabout at Plaça Llucmajor, which also holds Josep Viladomat's bold *La República*, a female nude holding aloft a sprig of laurel as a symbol of freedom. The renovation of the nearby Seu de Nou Barris town hall has brightened up an area in urgent need of a revamp, but it's not quite a tourist draw yet.

FREE Tecla Sala Centre Cultural

Avda Josep Tarradellas 44, Hospitalet de Llobregat (93 338 57 71/www.l-h.cat/ccteclasala). Metro La Torrassa. **Open** 11am-2pm, 5-8pm Tue-Sat; 11am-2pm Sun. **Admission** free. Tecla Sala is an old textile factory now housing a vast library and excellent gallery, which exhibits a varied mixture of national and international artists.

Consume

**Grand Hotel
Central**.
See p129.

Where to Stay

Barcelona offers boutique on a budget and luxury at a price.

The economic downturn, or '*la crisis*' as the Spanish would have it, has its flipside. Barcelona's popularity during the last decade and a half has seen it grow rather too big for its boots, with hotel prices reaching excruciating levels. But thanks to the slowdown, hoteliers have had to rethink drastically. Nowadays, the travelling masses want to see quality at a fair price: while there are still plenty of luxury options for those who can afford it, creativity in the mid-range is starting to boom with rooms ranging between €80 and €150 a night. And there are even some bargains at the top end.

STAYING IN THE CITY

The glut of top-end accommodation means that hotels are continually revising their rates and bargains are there for the taking. It's well worth doing a little extra research and not taking the brochure price at face value. At the budget end, many *hostales* are situated in fabulous old buildings with elaborate doorways and grand staircases, though the rooms aren't always so elegant. There's also been a rise in boutique B&Bs, bright places with en-suite bathrooms, internet access and other modern essentials.

With the city's growing niche as a conference capital, booking ahead is strongly advised. High season runs year round and finding somewhere to lay your head at short notice can be tough. Hotels generally require you to guarantee your booking with credit-card details or a deposit; it's always worth calling a few days before arrival to reconfirm the booking (get it in writing if you can; many readers have reported problems) and check the cancellation policy. Often you will lose at least the first night. *Hostales* are more laid-back and don't always ask for a deposit.

To be sure of a room with natural light or a view, ask for an outside room (*habitació/habitación exterior*), which will usually face the street. Many of Barcelona's buildings are built around a central patio or airshaft, and the inside

rooms (*habitació/habitación interior*) around them can be quite gloomy, albeit quieter. However, in some cases (especially in the Eixample), these inward-facing rooms look on to large, open-air patios or gardens, which benefit from being quiet and having a view.

Hotels listed under the expensive and moderate brackets all have air-conditioning as standard. Air-conditioning is increasingly common even in no-frills places, however, and around half the *hostales* in the budget listings are equipped with it.

The law now prohibits smoking in communal areas in hotels. As a result, some hotels have banned smoking altogether, and many have the majority of floors/rooms as non-smoking.

Theft can be a problem, especially in lower-end establishments. If you're sleeping cheap, you might want to travel with a padlock to lock your door, or at least lock up your bags. Check to see if youth-hostel rooms have lockers if you're sharing. Use hotel safes where possible.

Star ratings & prices

Accommodation in Catalonia is divided into two official categories: hotels (H) and *pensiones* (P). To be a hotel (star-rated one to five), a place must have en-suite bathrooms in every room. Ratings are based on physical attributes rather than levels of service; often the only difference between a three- and a four-star hotel is the presence of a meeting room. *Pensiones*, usually cheaper and often family-run, are star-rated one or two, and are not required to have en-suite bathrooms (though many do). *Pensiones* are

> ❶ Red numbers given in this chapter correspond to the location of each hotel on the street maps. *See pp337-345.*

also known as *hostales*, but, confusingly, are not youth hostels; those are known as *albergues*.

For a double room, expect to pay €50-€75 for a budget *pensión*, €80-€180 for a mid-range spot and €200 upwards for a top-of-the-range hotel. However, prices vary depending on the time of year; always check for special deals. All bills are subject to seven per cent IVA (value added tax) on top of the basic price; this is not normally included in the advertised rate, but we have factored it into the prices we have given. Breakfast is not included unless stated.

Booking Agencies

Barcelona Hotel Association

Via Laietana 47, 1º-2ª, Barri Gòtic (93 301 62 40/www.barcelonahotels.es). Metro Urquinaona or Jaume I. **Open** *Sept-June* 9am-6pm Mon-Fri; *July, Aug* 8.30am-2.30pm Mon-Fri. **Map** p344 D3.
The website of this hoteliers' organisation lists 264 hotels and apartments in all categories, with special offers and last-minute rates. Credit-card details must usually be given to secure a reservation online. Reservations cannot be made in the office, although information is available there.

Barcelona On-Line

Gran Via de les Corts Catalanes 662, Eixample (93 343 79 93/www.barcelona-on-line.es). Metro Passeig de Gràcia. **Open** 9am-7pm Mon-Fri; 9am-2pm Sat. **Map** p342 G8.
At this highly professional agency, you can book hostel, hotel rooms and private apartments online,

on the phone or at the office. Staff are multilingual and the service is free but there may be a fee if you cancel less than 48 hours before arrival. You'll need to make a prepayment for apartment reservations.

Viajes Iberia

Plaça de Sants 12, Eixample (93 431 90 00/www.viajesiberia.com). Metro Plaça de Sants. **Open** 9.30am-1.30pm, 4.30-8pm Mon-Fri; 10am-1.30pm Sat. **Credit** AmEx, DC, MC, V. **Map** p337 A7.
This agency can book a room at many of Barcelona's hotels and some *pensiones*. The reservation fee varies, and you will need to pay a deposit.
Other locations throughout the city.

Hotels

BARRI GOTIC & LA RAMBLA

La Rambla is flanked by hotels ranging from no-frills to luxury, but the totally touristy environment – not to mention the noise – may prove a bit much for some people. The medieval labyrinth of the Gòtic conceals some cheaper alternatives, but bear in mind that old buildings can often be grotty rather than charming.

Expensive

H10 Racó del Pi

C/Pi 7 (93 342 61 90/www.h10hotels.es). Metro Liceu or Jaume I. **Rates** €181-€230 double. **Rooms** 37. **Credit** AmEx, DC, MC, V. **Map** p344 C4 ➊

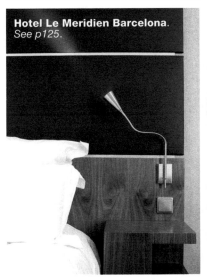

Hotel Le Meridien Barcelona. *See p125.*

THE BEST
HOTEL POOLS

For 360° rooftop views
H1898. *See below.*

For fashionable pool parties
Granados 83. *See p137.*

For moonlight swimming
AC Miramar. *See p134.*

Part of the H10 chain, the Racó del Pi gets top marks for location just next to the iconic Plaça del Pi, and also offers bright, spacious rooms with handsome terracotta-tiled bathrooms, unusual for this part of town. An elegant glass conservatory on the ground floor and a glass of cava on arrival are both nice touches, and occasional special offers can make it a good deal. Check the website for details.
Bar. Disabled-adapted room. Internet (free Wi-Fi). No-smoking floors (2). TV.
Other locations H10 Catalunya Plaza, Plaça Catalunya 7, Eixample (93 317 71 71); and throughout the city.

H1898
La Rambla 109 (93 552 95 52/www.nnhotels.com). Metro Catalunya or Liceu. **Rates** €181-€490 double. **Rooms** 169. **Credit** AmEx, DC, MC, V. **Map** p344 B3 ❷
A dapper luxury hotel in a 19th-century building – the former Philippine Tobacco Company headquarters. Rooms are candy-striped; one floor is all perky green and white, another is red and white, and so on. The more expensive rooms have wooden-decked terraces, while some of the suites have private plunge pools. For those of lighter wallets, the rooftop deck with its navy-tiled pool and luxurious four-poster day beds elevates the experience considerably.
Bar (2). Business centre. Disabled-adapted rooms (4). Gym. Internet (free Wi-Fi). No-smoking hotel. Parking (€24.60/day). Pool (outdoor/indoor). Restaurant. Room service. Spa. TV: pay movies.

Hotel Barcelona Catedral
C/Capellans 4 (93 304 22 55/www.barcelona catedral.com). Metro Jaume I. **Rates** €160-€283 double. **Rooms** 80. **Credit** AmEx, DC, MC, V. **Map** p344 B3 ❸
This newcomer to the heart of the city is sleek, modern and relaxed with a hip vibe. The Barcelona Catedral is the kind of place where Costes plays in a lobby that doubles as a funky lounge and cocktail bar. Rooms, while not particularly exciting, are bright and comfortable, with vast bathrooms and king-size beds. A garden terrace and a colourful rooftop deck with pool are added pluses.

Bar. Business centre. Disabled-adapted rooms (5), Gym. Internet (free Wi-Fi). No-smoking floors (3). Parking (€31.50/day). Pool (outdoor). Restaurant (closed Aug). Room service. TV: pay movies.

Hotel Le Meridien Barcelona
La Rambla 111 (93 318 62 00/www.barcelona. lemeridien.com). Metro Liceu. **Rates** €430-€480 double. **Rooms** 233. **Credit** AmEx, DC, MC, V. **Map** p344 B3 ❹
After a €23-million refurbishment Le Meridien is now arguably the poshest place on La Rambla, and it's fair to say that if you need to ask the price you probably can't afford it. In keeping with this, it has maintained its conservative look, opting for classy hardwood floors, polished marble and leather furnishings, along with Egyptian cotton bedlinen, rain showers and plasma-screen TVs. But at this price you'd expect a lot more facilities: a rooftop, perhaps, or at least a teak-decked terrace. Still, Jean George Vongerichten helped design the menu at gourmet restaurant Cent Onze. Children under 12 stay free. *Photo p123.*
Bar. Disabled-adapted rooms (4). Gym. Internet (free Wi-Fi). No-smoking floors (8). Parking (€20-€25/day). Restaurant. Room service. TV.

Hotel Neri
C/Sant Sever 5 (93 304 06 55/www.hotel neri.com). Metro Jaume I. **Rates** €275-€325 double. **Rooms** 22. **Credit** AmEx, DC, MC, V. **Map** p345 C5 ❺
Arguably the sexiest boutique in town, this is the perfect treat for a naughty weekend, located in a former 18th-century palace. The vampish lobby-cum-library teams flagstone floors with crushed red velvet chaises longues and lashings of gold leaf, though the rooms are slightly more understated. Neutral tones, natural materials and rustic finishes (untreated wood and unpolished marble) stand in stylish contrast to lavish satins, sharp design and high-tech perks (hi-fis, plasma-screen TVs). The mini bar stocks not only champagne, but candles and incense, and the lush rooftop garden provides plenty of private nooks for dangerous liaisons.
Bar. Disabled-adapted room. Internet (free Wi-Fi). No-smoking rooms (10). Restaurant. Room service. TV: pay movies.

Hotel Petit Palace Opera Garden
C/Boqueria 10 (93 302 00 92/www.hthoteles. com). Metro Liceu. **Rates** €140-€320 double. **Rooms** 61. **Credit** AmEx, DC, MC, V. **Map** p345 B5 ❻
A private mansion was completely gutted to create this minimalist hotel on a busy street just off La Rambla. The rooms are white and futuristic, with a different zingy colour on each floor and opera scores printed on the walls above the beds. Lamps and chairs lend a 1960s air, so pack your kinky boots and groovy flares to enjoy your stay to the full. Some bathrooms have massage showers, others jacuzzi

Grand Hotel Central. *See p129.*

baths. Only breakfast is served in the chic dining room. There's a little-known public garden at the back: a real luxury in this densely packed area. *Bar. Disabled-adapted rooms (3). Internet (free Wi-Fi). No-smoking floors (3). Room service. TV.*

Moderate

Bonic B&B

C/Josep Anselm Clavé 9, 1°-4ª (mobile 626 05 34 34/www.bonic-barcelona.com). Metro Drassanes. **Rates** €90-€95. **Rooms** 8. **No credit cards.** **Map** p345 B8 **7**

Bonic is painted in daisy-fresh colours with sunlight streaming through the windows and lots of meticulously restored original features, such as ornately tiled floors. Attention to detail is exceptional for the price, with the gregarious Fernando doing all he can to make you feel at home. Free newspapers and magazines, tea, coffee and water, and flowers in the three immaculate, communal bathrooms all add up to an experience that raises the budget bar considerably. *Internet (free Wi-Fi). No-smoking hotel. TV.*

Duc de la Victòria

C/Duc de la Victòria 15 (93 270 34 10/www.nh-hotels.com). Metro Catalunya. **Rates** €115-€190 double. **Rooms** 156. **Credit** AmEx, DC, MC, V. **Map** p344 C3/4 **8**

The trusty NH chain has high standards of comfort and service, and this good-value downtown branch is thankfully no exception to the rule. The rooms, with a blue-and-beige colour scheme, may not be very exciting, but the superior quality beds ensure a sound night's sleep. And note that it's just a stone's throw from La Rambla.

Disabled-adapted rooms (4). Internet (Wi-Fi €10/hr, €17/24hrs). No-smoking floors (5). Restaurant (lunch and dinner Mon-Fri only). Room service. TV: pay movies.

Hostal Jardí

Plaça Sant Josep Oriol 1 (93 301 59 00). Metro Liceu. **Rates** €86-€98 double. **Rooms** 44. **Credit** AmEx, DC, MC, V. **Map** p345 B5 **9**

Despite its considerable fame, the best thing about the Hostal Jardí remains its location on one of the city's loveliest squares. Inside, however, it's a bit of a plain Jane, with overly bright lighting and stark decor. If you stay, the best rooms are on the top floor, with a balcony. Otherwise, expect something small, and clinical, though all have en-suite bathrooms, and the place is sparkling clean.

No-smoking hotel. TV.

Hotel Duquesa de Cardona

Passeig Colom 12 (93 268 90 90/www. hduquesadecardona.com). Metro Drassanes or Jaume I. **Rates** €181-€300 double. **Rooms** 40. **Credit** AmEx, DC, MC, V. **Map** p345 C7 **10**

This elegantly restored 16th-century palace retains many original features and is furnished with natural materials – wood, leather, silk and stone – that are complemented by a soft colour scheme reflecting the paintwork. The cosy bedrooms make it the ideal hotel for a romantic stay, particularly the deluxe rooms and junior suites on the higher floors, which have views out across the harbour. Guests can sunbathe and linger over lunch on the decked roof terrace and then cool off in the mosaic-tiled plunge pool. The arcaded hotel restaurant serves a menu of modern Catalan dishes.

Business centre. Disabled-adapted room. Internet (free high-speed; Wi-Fi in rooms €9/hr, €15/day). No-smoking floors (1). Pool (outdoor). Restaurant. Room service. TV.

Hotel Medinaceli

Plaça del Duc de Medinaceli 8 (93 481 77 25/ www.gargallo-hotels.com). Metro Drassanes. **Rates** €155 double. **Rooms** 44. **Credit** AmEx, DC, MC, V. **Map** p345 B8 ⓫

The rooms in this restored palace near the harbour are done out in soothing rusty shades. Some of the bathrooms have jacuzzi baths, while others come with massage showers. Repro versions of the sofa Dalí created inspired by Mae West's lips decorate the lobby, to match the crimson velvet thrones in the first-floor courtyard. Staff are very helpful, but rooms overlooking the street can be noisy.

Bar. Disabled-adapted room. Internet (€12/day Wi-Fi). TV.

Marina View B&B

Passeig de Colom 22 (93 317 59 20/mobile 609 206 493/www.marinaviewbcn.com). Metro Drassanes. **Rates** (incl breakfast) €115.50-€139 double. **Rooms** 6. **Credit** MC, V. **Map** p345 C8 ⓬

Located in a 19th-century townhouse with views over the Port Vell, this simple little place is laid-back, friendly and fun, with nautically themed rooms such as 'Captain's Cabin' and 'Columbus' painted in sunshine colours. Marina View has got all the homely details just right, such as the breakfast trolley loaded with fresh juice, tea/coffee and croissants, as well as personalised service where staff give the impression that nothing is too much trouble.

Internet (free Wi-Fi). TV: cable.

Budget

Hostal Fontanella

Via Laietana 71, 2° (93 317 59 43/www.hostal fontanella.com). Metro Urquinaona. **Rates** €59-€80 double. **Rooms** 11. **Credit** AmEx, DC, MC, V. **Map** p344 D2 ⓭

The splendid Modernista lift lends a somewhat unjustified aura of grandeur to this 11-room *hostal*, where Laura Ashley devotees will feel totally at home amid the chintz, lace and dried flowers. The downside of the Fontanella's central location – on the thoroughfare bordering the Born, the Barri Gòtic and the Eixample – is that outward-facing rooms are abuzz with the sound of traffic. However, it's a clean and comfortable place, and the double-glazing makes the outdoors somewhat less present inside. *TV.*

Hostal Lausanne

Portal de l'Àngel 24, 1° 1ª (93 302 11 39/ www.hostalresidencialausanne.com). Metro Catalunya. **Rates** €50-€65 double. **Rooms** 17. **Credit** AmEx, DC, MC, V. Map p344 C3 ⓮

On one of downtown's busiest shopping streets, this *hostal* occupies the first floor of an impressive building. Unlike some *hostales*, the place feels spacious, with light pouring in from both ends of the building. Of the 17 basic rooms, four have en-suite bathrooms and some have balconies. It may be a bit dated, but it's friendly and safe, with a backpacker vibe. The street fills up during the day, but it's quiet at night. *Internet (free shared terminal). TV room.*

Other locations Hostal Europa, C/Boqueria 18, Barri Gòtic (93 318 76 20).

Hostal Rembrandt

C/Portaferrissa 23, pral (93 318 10 11/www. hostalrembrandt.com). Metro Liceu. **Rates** €50-€65 double. **Rooms** 27. **Credit** MC, V. **Map** p344 C4 ⓯

The Rembrandt is a charming 27-room *hostal* that is fairly stylish (for the price) with lots of wood panelling, soft lighting and a lift. A bonus is the pretty interior courtyard, which makes for a pleasant chillout zone/eating area. Rooms out front can be a little noisy, but the passing stream of humanity means you will never be bored. If the Rembrandt is fully booked, bear in mind that the same people also rent out apartments on nearby C/Canuda (€75-€150 for two people, minimum three-night stay).

Internet (€3/hr shared terminal). No-smoking hotel.

Hostal Sol y K

C/Cervantes 2, 2° (93 318 81 48/www.solyk.com). Metro Jaume I or Liceu. **Rates** €53.50-€80.25 double. **Rooms** 14. **Credit** AmEx, DC, MC, V. **Map** p345 C6 ⓰

Bright and cheerful with pleasing designer touches (slate bathrooms, groovy leather bedheads), this is a bargain for those who don't need frills. There's no breakfast, and not all rooms are en suite, but all have washbasins, and the traditional, patterned tiles and exposed wood beams give the Sol y K plenty of character. Light sleepers will benefit from bringing earplugs with them, as noise carries from the street, and towels are for the skinny.

Internet (free Wi-Fi).

Pensió Alamar

C/Comtessa de Sobradiel 1, 1°-2ª (93 302 50 12/ www.pensioalamar.com). Metro Jaume I or Liceu. **Rates** €36-€48 double. **Rooms** 12. **Credit** AmEx, DC, MC, V. **Map** p345 C6 ⓱

A basic, but tasteful family-run *hostal*. Beds are new and excellent quality, with crisp cotton sheets, and windows are double-glazed to keep noise to a minimum. The downside is that 12 rooms share two bathrooms. There are good discounts for longer stays, and larger rooms for families. Single travellers are made very welcome, with no supplement for occupying a double room, and guests can so their laundry and cook in a well-equipped kitchen. *TV room.*

CONSUME

THE BEST
HOTEL GARDENS

For reclining in a hammock
Hotel Arts. See p133.

For seeking shade on a rooftop
Hotel Neri. See p125.

For designer landscaping
ABaC Restaurant Hotel. See p145.

Pensión Hostal Mari-Luz
*C/Palau 4 (93 317 34 63/www.pensionmariluz.
com). Metro Jaume I or Liceu*. **Rates** €35-€52
double. **Rooms** 14. **Credit** AmEx, DC, MC, V.
Map p345 C6 ⑱
The entrance and staircase of this 18th-century
stone building are certainly imposing, but you then
have to climb several flights of stairs to reach the
Mari-Luz. The effort is well worth it – stripped wood
doors and old floor tiles add character to the otherwise plain but quiet rooms, some of which face a
plant-filled inner courtyard. There are dorms as well
as double and triple rooms.
Other locations Pensión Fernando, C/Ferran
31, Barri Gòtic (93 301 79 93).

BORN & SANT PERE

New hotels are cropping up in revamped old
buildings in these medieval areas. The Born
is an established cool zone, with many
restaurants, bars and boutiques.

Expensive

Grand Hotel Central
*Via Laietana 30 (93 295 79 00/www.grandhotel
central.com). Metro Jaume I*. **Rates** €187-€375
double. **Rooms** 147. **Credit** AmEx, DC, MC, V.
Map p345 D5 ⑲
Another of the recent wave of Barcelona hotels
to adhere to the unwritten design protocol that
grey is the new black. The Central's shadowy,
almost Hitchcockian corridors open up on to
sleekly appointed rooms that come with flat-screen
televisions, DVD players and Korres toiletries,
although some guests have complained that the
bathroom lighting is too dim. But the real charm of
the hotel lies up above your room, up on the roof.
Here you can sip a cocktail and admire the fabulous
views while floating in the vertiginous infinity pool.
Photo p126.
*Bar. Business centre. Disabled-adapted rooms
(3). Gym. Internet (free high-speed in rooms, free
Wi-Fi in communal areas). No-smoking floors (6).
Parking (€25/day). Pool (outdoor). Restaurant.
Room service. TV.*

Moderate

Banys Orientals
*C/Argenteria 37 (93 268 84 60/www.hotel
banysorientals.com). Metro Jaume I*. **Rates** €105
double. **Rooms** 56. **Credit** AmEx, DC, MC, V.
Map p345 D6 ⑳
Banys Orientals is one of the best deals to be found
in Barcelona. It exudes cool, from its location at the
heart of the Born to the stylish shades-of-grey min-
imalism of its rooms, and nice touches such as complimentary mineral water on the landings. The main
debit is the small size of some of the double rooms.
*Disabled-adapted room. Internet (free high-speed).
No-smoking floors (2). Restaurant. TV.*

Barceló Raval
*Rambla del Raval 17-21 (93 320 14 90/902 101
001/www.barcelo.com). Metro Drassanes*. **Rooms**
186. **Rates** €120-€160 double. **Credit** AmEx,
MC, DC, V. **Map** p342 E10 ㉑
This cylindrical building now dominates the
Rambla del Raval and promises to become something of an icon of the *barrio*. A hip cocktail lounge
designed by Jordi Gali and the avant-garde tapas bar
are upping the ante still more. The smart oval-
shaped roof terrace offers 360° views (with key
buildings usefully labelled from a viewing platform)
and a plunge pool. Bedrooms are fairly uniform but
airy and modern, with a technology port for all your
multimedia needs and a Nespresso machine for
those bleary mornings after. Note that the opening
offers are great value, but may change by 2009.
*Bar. Disabled-adapted rooms (20). Gym.
Internet (free Wi-Fi). No-smoking floors.
Parking. Pool (outdoor). Restaurants (2).
Room service. TV: cable.*

Chic&basic
*C/Princesa 50 (93 295 46 52/www.chicandbasic.
com). Metro Arc de Triomf or Jaume I*. **Rates**
€118-€193 double. **Rooms** 31. **Credit** AmEx,
DC, MC, V. **Map** p345 F5 ㉒
This first floor hostal takes white-on-white to
extremes, though not entirely unsuccessfully.
Rooms come in sizes XL, L and M with white cotton
sheets, white floors, white walls, mirrored cornicing
and glassed in wet rooms in the centre for hosing
yourself down. Elsewhere the playful vibe continues with a chill-out room furnished with fairytale
sofas and pouffes; it also has tea- and coffee-making
facilities, a fridge and a microwave. There are similarly designed apartments.
*Bar. Disabled-adapted room. Gym. Internet (free
Wi-Fi). No-smoking hotel. Restaurant. TV.*

Ciutat Barcelona
*C/Princesa 35 (93 269 74 75/www.ciutat
barcelona.com). Metro Jaume I*. **Rates** €107-
€170 double. **Rooms** 78. **Credit** AmEx, DC,
MC, V. **Map** p345 E5 ㉓

CONSUME

The Ciutat Barcelona is a jolly, primary-coloured affair, offering a refreshing contrast to the chocolate and charcoal shades of most of Barna's smart hotels. Retro shapes prevail in the furnishings and decoration, and rooms are very small but reasonably comfortable. The big draw, however, is a swanky wood-decked roof terrace complete with shaded tables and a decent-sized plunge pool.
Disabled-adapted rooms (4). Internet (free high-speed in rooms, free Wi-Fi in communal areas). No-smoking floors (4). Pool (outdoor). Restaurant. Room service. TV: cable.

Hotel Ciutat Vella.

Hotel Constanza
C/Bruc 33 (93 270 19 10/www.hotelconstanza. com). Metro Urquinaona. **Rates** (incl breakfast) €100-€120 double. **Rooms** 48. **Credit** AmEx, MC, V. **Map** p344 E1 ㉔
This quiet and pleasant boutique has been around for a few years now and continues to please. The theme is oriental, with Japanese silk screens, orchid and pebble prints and sleek teak furniture creating an atmosphere of Zen-like calm. The best rooms are at the back, some with smart walled-in terraces, and it has comfortable single rooms. The Constanza also does a good buffet breakfast.
Bar. Disabled-adapted room. Internet (free high-speed in rooms). No-smoking hotel. Restaurant. TV: cable.

Budget

Pensió 2000
C/Sant Pere Més Alt 6, 1º (93 310 74 66/ www.pensio2000.com). Metro Urquinaona. **Rates** €72-€80 double. **Rooms** 6. **Credit** AmEx, MC, V. **Map** p344 D3 ㉕
Pensió 2000 is a good-value *pension* located in a fine old building across from the Palau de la Música Catalana. Only two of the rooms are en suite, but the shared facilities are kept clean. The large rooms make it suitable for holidaying families.

RAVAL

The Raval is the edgy neighbour of the Barri Gòtic, but recent regeneration means it's also the trendiest *barrio* for bars and restaurants, with a lively multicultural atmosphere.

Expensive

Casa Camper
C/Elisabets 11 (93 342 62 80/www.casacamper. com). Metro Catalunya. **Rates** (incl breakfast & snack) €225-€264 double. **Rooms** 25. **Credit** AmEx, DC, MC, V. **Map** p344 A3 ㉖
Devised by the Mallorcan footwear giant, this is a holistic concept-fest of a hotel, designed by Ferran Amat of Vinçon fame. It's quirky, and has as one of its USPs a bedroom-living room arrangement so

CONSUME

that you get two spaces for the price of one. Less cleverly, the living rooms are situated across the corridor from the bedrooms, so in order to enjoy the cinema-sized TV screen and hammock you'll need to pack respectable pyjamas or risk the dash of shame. There are no minibars, but you can help yourself to free snacks and refreshments in the café whenever you fancy.
Bar. Business centre. Disabled-adapted room. Internet (free Wi-Fi). No-smoking hotel. Restaurant. TV: pay movies, DVD.

Moderate

Abba Rambla Hotel

C/Rambla del Raval 4 (93 505 54 00/www. abbaramblahotel.com). Metro Liceu or Sant Antoni. **Rates** €100-€257 double. **Rooms** 49. **Credit** AmEx, MC, V. **Map** p342 E10 ㉗
The Abba Rambla is a comfortable and friendly base, although the modern rooms have an inescapably chain-hotel feel to them. More stylish are the ground-floor lounge and breakfast bar, where you eat perched on high stools. Some good offers are available online, particularly in the winter, so it's a place worth checking before booking.
Bar. Disabled-adapted room. Internet (€6/hr; €9/day Wi-Fi). No-smoking floors (3).

Hostal Gat Xino

C/Hospital 155 (93 324 88 33/www.gat accommodation.com). Metro Sant Antoni. **Rates** (incl breakfast) €85-€100 double. **Rooms** 35. **Credit** AmEx, MC, V. **Map** p342 E10 ㉘
This is the second 'Gat' to open, and it has a similar cheap and chic vibe to the Gat Raval (*see p133*); a bright breakfast room complete with apple-green polka-dot walls, a patio and a roof terrace with black beanbags on which to chill out. There's more bright green to be found in the bedrooms (all of which are en suite), with good beds, crisp white linen, flat-screen TVs and backlit panels of Raval scenes. The best rooms have large balconies.
Bar. Internet (€6.50/hr shared terminal or Wi-Fi). No-smoking hostal. TV.

Hotel Ciutat Vella

C/Tallers 66 (93 481 37 99/www.hotelciutatvella. com). Metro Catalunya or Universitat. **Rates** €97-€207 double. **Rooms** 40. **Credit** AmEx, DC, MC, V. **Map** p344 A2 ㉙
More hostal-like than the sister branch (Ciutat de Barcelona, C/Princesa 33-35, 932 697 475) across town, this is a fun and funky option when the budget's tight. Rooms and decor are done simply in white with splashes of pillar-box red. There's Wi-Fi and a hearty breakfast served in a lounge downstairs, and best of all a fabulously kitsch Astroturf rooftop terrace with hot tub, which, unlike most of the aquatic fun available in Barcelona, is open late enough to bathe under the stars.

Bar. Disabled-adapted rooms (1). Internet (free shared terminal, free Wi-Fi in communal areas). No-smoking floors (4). TV: cable.

Hotel Curious

C/Carme 25 (93 301 44 84/www.hotelcurious. com). Metro Liceu. **Rates** (incl breakfast) €80-€105 double. **Rooms** 24. **Credit** AmEx, DC, MC, V. **Map** p344 A4 ㉚
Curious is an unusual new addition to the Raval with a more art-based approach to design. The rather funky mauve-hued lobby is in total contrast to more monotone bedrooms, which have giant black and white prints depicting Barcelona *barrios* and other landscapes. Other hotels include Hostal Marenostrum (C/Sant Pau 2, 93 318 53 40). *Photo p137.*
Bar. Internet (free shared terminal; free Wi-Fi). TV: cable.

Hotel España

C/Sant Pau 9-11 (93 318 17 58/www.hotel espanya.com). Metro Liceu. **Rates** (incl breakfast) €111 double. **Rooms** 83. **Credit** AmEx, DC, MC, V. **Map** p345 A5 ㉛
The lower floors at this Modernista landmark were designed by Domènech i Montaner in 1902. The main restaurant is decorated with floral tiling and elaborate woodwork, while the larger dining room is best seen rather than savoured. The food may be average but the mermaid murals by Ramon Casas are dreamy, and the bar boasts a sculpted marble fireplace. After all this grandeur, the bedrooms seem a bit understated, though some still have their original Modernista tiles, moulded ceilings and doors that open on to a bright interior patio.
Disabled-adapted rooms (2). Internet (€5/hr shared terminal). Restaurant. TV.

Hotel Mesón Castilla

C/Valldonzella 5 (93 318 21 82/www.meson castilla.com). Metro Universitat. **Rates** (incl breakfast) €150-€166 double. **Rooms** 57. **Credit** AmEx, DC, MC, V. **Map** p344 A2 ㉜
If you want a change from modern design, check into this chocolate-box hotel, which opened in 1952. Before then, it belonged to an aristocratic Catalan family. The communal areas are full of antiques and artworks, while all rooms have tiled floors and are decorated with hand-painted furniture from Olot in northern Catalonia. The best rooms have terraces, and there is also a delightful plant-filled terrace off the breakfast room.
Parking (€21.40/day). TV.

Hotel Sant Agustí

Plaça Sant Agustí 3 (93 318 16 58/www.hotelsa. com). Metro Liceu. **Rates** (incl breakfast) €110-€164 double. **Rooms** 82. **Credit** AmEx, DC, MC, V. **Map** p345 A5 ㉝
With its sandstone walls and huge, arched windows that look out on to the *plaça*, not to mention the

CONSUME

pink-marble lobby filled with forest-green furniture, this imposing hotel is the oldest in town. Previously the convent of St Augustine, it was converted into a hotel in 1840. Rooms are spacious and comfortable, but there's no soundproofing. Good buffet breakfast. *Bar. Disabled-adapted rooms (2). Internet (free shared terminal, free Wi-Fi in communal areas). Restaurant (dinner only). TV.*

Budget

Hostal Gat Raval

C/Joaquin Costa 44, 2º (93 481 66 70/www. gataccommodation.com). Metro Universitat. **Rates** €65-€82 double. **Rooms** 24. **Credit** AmEx, MC, V. **Map** p342 E9 ❸❹
Smart, clean and funky with bright rooms, each boasting a work by a local artist. Some rooms have balconies while others have views of the MACBA. The only downsides are that nearly all the bathrooms are communal (though very clean) and there is no lift. Laptops for hire at €6.50/hr. *Internet (€6.50/hr Wi-Fi). No-smoking hostal. TV.*

Hostal La Palmera

C/Jerusalem 30 (93 317 09 97/hostalla palmera@terra.es). Metro Liceu. **Rates** (incl breakfast) €54-€59 double. **Rooms** 20. **Credit** MC, V. **Map** p344 A4 ❸❺
With a great location behind La Boqueria, this well-run, basic *hostal* is a short stagger from some of Raval's funkiest bars, but is surprisingly quiet at night. The decor is unremarkable, but the rooms are light, airy and spotless, most have en-suite bathrooms and some have balconies overlooking the market. **Other locations** Hostal Bertolin, C/Carme 116, 1º, Raval (93 329 06 47/reservations 93 317 09 97).

Hosteria Grau

C/Ramelleres 27 (93 301 81 35/www.hostal grau.com). Metro Catalunya. **Rates** €58-€112 double. **Rooms** 19. **Credit** AmEx, DC, MC, V. **Map** p344 B2 ❸❻
This charming, family-run *hostal* oozes character, with a tiled spiral staircase and fabulous 1970s-style communal areas, including a funky café next door. The open fireplace is a luxury if you visit in the winter. Rooms are comfortable and fairly quiet; the cheaper ones share a bathroom. There are also six apartments on the top floor. A popular choice, so book well in advance. *Bar. Internet (free shared terminal, free Wi-Fi). No-smoking hotel. TV room.*

BARCELONETA & THE PORTS

Hotels are springing up along Barcelona's waterfront, particularly in the stretch between the Hotel Arts and the Fòrum, north of the city centre. These are mostly aimed at business travellers, so rates tend to fall at weekends and during holiday periods.

Expensive

Hotel AB Skipper

C/Litoral 10 (93 221 65 65/www.hotelabskipper. com). Metro Ciutadella. **Rates** €182-€385 double. **Rooms** 241. **Credit** AmEx, DC, MC, V. **Map** p343 J12 ❸❼
Situated near the Port Olimpic, the Skipper is a swish American-style five-star reeling in visiting long-weekenders with some good package deals. Think supersize rooms with slick touches like Egyptian cotton sheets and huge bathrooms. It's also good on outdoor space with a large heated pool for year round use, hammocks on the lawns, and a full-service spa. Additional treats include a lazy Sunday brunch, luxury rooftop pool and bar, and the AB Skipper yacht, which guests can charter for private use if they've left their boat at home. *Business centre. Disabled-adapted rooms (4). Gym. Internet (free Wi-Fi). No-smoking floors (4). Parking (€26.75/day) Pool (outdoor 2). Restaurants (2). Room service. TV: cable*

Hotel Arts

C/Marina 19-21 (93 221 10 00/www.ritzcarlton. com). Metro Ciutadella-Vila Olímpica. **Rates** €390-€813 double. **Credit** AmEx, DC, MC, V. **Map** p343 K12 ❸❽
The 44-storey, Ritz-Carlton-run Arts continues to score top marks for unfailingly exemplary service. Bang & Olufsen CD players, interactive TV, sea and city views and a 'Club' floor for VIPs are just some of the hedonistic perks that await guests. The avant-garde flower arrangements make the lobby a pleasant place to hang out rather than just pass through. Outdoors, the beachfront pool overlooks Frank Gehry's bronze fish sculpture, and a range of bars and restaurants cater to every taste. The spectacular duplex apartments have round-the-clock butlers and chef services, while the luxurious Six Senses Spa on floors 42 and 43 has fabulous views and is open to non-guests. In summer, a children's club will look after your offspring. *Photo p138.*
See also p146 **The Mile-High Club.**
Bar. Business centre. Disabled-adapted rooms (4). Gym. Internet (free high-speed, free Wi-Fi). No-smoking floors (37). Parking (€37.50/day). Pool (outdoor). Restaurants (4). Room service. Spa. TV: DVD.

Moderate

Hotel 54

Passeig Joan de Borbó 54 (93 225 00 54/www. hotel54barceloneta.com). Metro Barceloneta. **Rates** €150-€180 double. **Rooms** 27. **Credit** AmEx, MC, V. **Map** p342 G13 ❸❾

CONSUME

It's been a long time coming, but finally the beach gets an affordable hotel in the shape of the 54. There is neon mood lighting above the bed, while muted tones of dove grey and charcoal against steel, blond-wood and glass give it a contemporary feel. It has one of the best roof terraces in the city for cocktails while admiring the views of the port, and you can get tapas at Snack 54 or have a dance at diminutive club Suite Royale downstairs. It has been taken over by Best Western but little has changed.
Bar. Internet (free Wi-Fi). No-smoking floors (2). Parking (€20/day). TV.

MONTJUIC & POBLE SEC

Poble Sec is a quiet neighbourhood between Montjuïc mountain and the Avda Paral·lel.

Expensive

AC Miramar

Plaça Carlos Ibáñez 3, Passeig de Miramar (93 281 16 00/www.ac-hotels.com). Metro Paral·lel. **Rates** €215-€321 double. **Rooms** 75. **Credit** AmEx, DC, MC, V. **Map** p342 D12 ⓴

Designer Dreams

A new wave of hotels is set to revolutionise Barcelona's hotel scene.

Barcelona's visionary new hoteliers like to do things differently. Even the most basic of places these days comes with mood lighting and quirky interiors, and architects and interior designers are being briefed by owners to go wild with technology, materials and, yes, eco-design.

Ricardo Bofill's much anticipated sail-shaped **W Hotel** (www.starwood hotels.com/whotels), due to open in September 2009, seems to bob gently out at sea on the top of Passeig Joan de Borbó. Although the eye-popping design has been altered somewhat to adhere to town planning, it still promises great things. This is 'Wonderland', after all, and its spectacular location, combined with hip interiors and lots of designer eye candy within (including original modern artworks), will surely make it one of the city's most sought after destination hotels.

The **Barceló Raval** (*see p129*) is unlikely to be received quite so excitedly, though the inky coloured, cylindrical hotel does look set to become one of this up-and-coming *barrio*'s most emblematic projects. In keeping with the recent trend for buildings that glow, it too will be bathed in a muted diaphanous light at night.

ME Barcelona (*see p147*) is the most exciting skyscraper to pierce the city skyline since the Torre Agbar – 120 metres of steel and glass piercing the heavens like a giant, cubist knitting needle. Opened in August 2008, it has an interior that is just as spectacular, boasting colourful perspex walls and a giant ostrich egg chandelier above the bar.

Critics were so impressed with Enric Ruiz-Geli's plans for the **Prestige Forest** eco-hotel (www.prestigehotels.com), scheduled to open sometime in 2010,

that it appeared as part of the New Architecture in Spain exhibit at MoMA, New York in 2006. It's been a long time coming, but when it does this revolutionary project will be shrouded in a spectacular web of 5,000 LEDs or 'leaves' as they are known, that register sunlight and temperatures by day to cut energy costs and glow in pretty colours at night.

Finally, there's the **Suites Avenue** (www.derbyhotels.es) by Japanese great Toyo Ito, scheduled to open late in 2008. When it's complete, it will grace the Passeig de Gràcia sheathed in a double skin of steel. The apartments will be filled with collections of primitive art, to contrast with the up-to-the-minute decor.

Barceló Raval.

The AC chain's flagship hotel is perched on top of Montjuïc, where the air's just a little bit fresher than in the city below and the view is fabulous. True, it has a slightly corporate air, what with its champagne marble and cappuccino sofas, but there is lots to recommend the hotel nonetheless, notably the scented orange-tree patio for drinks, a 'healthy' Mediterranean restaurant, a pale turquoise pool lit by fibre-optics at night and English-style lawns. Bedrooms are fairly uniform, but it is worth opting for something smaller towards the top, which rewards with a hot tub on the terrace.
Bar. Disabled-adapted rooms (2). Gym. Internet (€12/day Wi-Fi). No-smoking hotel. Parking (€21.50/day). Pool (indoor/outdoor). Restaurant. Spa. TV: cable.

Moderate

Hotel Nuevo Triunfo
C/Cabanes 34 (93 442 59 33/www.hotel nuevotriunfo.net). Metro Paral·lel. **Rates** €107-€153 double. **Rooms** 40. **Credit** MC, V. **Map** p342 E11 ④①
With 40 fresh, bright and spotless rooms, the Hotel Nuevo Triunfo is located in a peaceful street at the foot of Montjuïc. Rooms are bland but comfortable enough, and the four most desirable – two of which are singles – counteract the austerity of the sparse, modern fittings with their charming plant-filled terraces. This is a worthwhile place to try should the other central hotels be full.
Disabled-adapted room. Internet (€3/hr shared terminal). No-smoking floors (3). TV.

Budget

Hostal BCN Port
Avda Paral·lel 15, entl (93 324 95 00/www. hostalbcnport.com). Metro Drassanes or Paral·lel. **Rates** €79-€90 double. **Rooms** 29. **Credit** MC, V. **Map** p342 E12 ④②
A smart *hostal* near the ferry port, the BCN Port has rooms that are furnished in a chic contemporary style with not a hint of the kitsch decor prevalent in more traditional budget places. All the rooms have en-suite bathrooms, as well as televisions and air-conditioning. Check the website for discounts.
Internet (shared terminal; free Wi-Fi in most rooms). No-smoking rooms (25). TV.

Melon District
Avda Paral·lel 101 (93 329 9667/www.melon district.com). Metro Poble Sec. **Rates** €65-€120 double. **Rooms** 18. **Credit** MC, V. **Map** p341 D10 ④③
Although Melon District is aimed at students staying for a few weeks, its good value has started pulling in more short-term guests too. Apart from price it offers a fresh, clean look, friendly service and cleverly thought out facilities. Single and double rooms

have access to a shared 'cooking lounge', but are also good on little details like providing two desks in the double. Studios have private kitchens. Cleaning, bed change and towels can be provided for €68 a month, along with bath packs and internet packages, plus there's a rooftop pool and chill-out space.
Disabled-adapted rooms (2). Internet (free Wi-Fi). Parking (€21/day).

EIXAMPLE

Uptown and upmarket, the broad avenues forming the vast grid of streets of the Eixample district contain some of Barcelona's most expensive and fashionable hotels, along with some great budget options hidden away in Modernista buildings.

Expensive

Casanova BCN Hotel
Gran Via de les Corts Catalanes 559 (93 396 48 00/www.casanovabcnhotel.com). Metro Universitat or Urgell. **Rates** €137-€360 double. **Rooms** 124. **Credit** AmEx, DC, MC, V. **Map** p342 E8 ④④
Casanova is a smart new hotel suitable for those looking to try something a shade different. The charcoal grey and black decor with streaks of lime green are par for the course, but, each room has its own Nespresso machine, suites have two bathrooms, giant candles are scattered through the lounge areas and there's a small spa. The rooftop pool was still a work in progress at the time of writing, but should be in place for the summer of 2009. A Mexican themed cocktail and ceviche bar lends freshness to the usual tapas offerings.
Bar. Disabled-adapted rooms (5). Internet (free high-speed in rooms). No-smoking floors (5). Parking (€25/day). Pool (outdoor). Restaurant. Spa. TV: cable.

Hotel Axel
C/Aribau 33 (93 323 93 93/www.axelhotels. com). Metro Universitat. **Rates** €188-€210 double. **Rooms** 66. **Credit** AmEx, DC, MC, V. **Map** p342 F8 ④⑤
Housed in a Modernista building, with multi-coloured tiles in the lobby and bright rooms with bleached floors, the Axel is a cornerstone of the 'Gaixample', as the area around the hotel is known. The good-looking staff sport T-shirts with the logo 'heterofriendly', and certainly everyone is made welcome. King-size beds come as standard, as does free mineral water and erotic artwork. The 'Superior' rooms have hydro-massage bathtubs and stained-glass gallery balconies. The Sky Bar on the rooftop is where it all happens, with a little pool, jacuzzi, sun deck, sauna and steam room. Non-guests are welcome to frequent the bar and roof terrace, where club nights are held, so there is always a bit of a buzz going on.

CONSUME

Bar. Business centre. Disabled-adapted rooms (2). Gym. Internet (free Wi-Fi). No-smoking floors (5). Pool (outdoor). Restaurant. Room service. TV.

Hotel Claris

C/Pau Claris 150 (93 487 62 62/www.derby hotels.com). Metro Passeig de Gràcia. **Rates** €161-€375 double. **Rooms** 120. **Credit** AmEx, DC, MC, V. **Map** p338 G7 ❹❻

Antiques and contemporary design merge behind the neo-classical exterior of the Claris, which contains the largest private collection of Egyptian art in Spain. Some bedrooms are on the small side, while others are duplex, but all have Chesterfield sofas and plenty of art. Warhol prints liven up the fashionable East 47 restaurant. The rooftop pool is just about big enough to swim in, with plenty of loungers, and a cocktail bar and DJ.

Business centre. Disabled-adapted rooms (2). Gym. Internet (free Wi-Fi). No-smoking floors (3). Parking (€22/day). Pool (outdoor). Restaurant. Room service. TV.
▶ *If the Claris is full, the Granados is run by the same people (see below).*

Hotel Granados 83

C/Enric Granados 83 (93 492 96 70/www. derbyhotels.com). Metro Diagonal. **Rates** €120-€435 double. **Rooms** 77. **Credit** AmEx, DC, MC, V. **Map** p338 F7 ❹❼

The original ironwork structure of this former hospital lends an unexpectedly industrial feel to the Granados 83. The bare-bricked rooms include duplex and triplex versions, some with their own terraces and plunge pools. For mortals in the standard rooms, there is a rooftop pool and sun deck.

Bar (2). Business centre. Disabled-adapted rooms (2). Internet (free high-speed). No-smoking hotel. Parking (€18.50/day). Pool (outdoor). Restaurant. Room service. TV.
▶ *Fully booked? Try the Claris, which is run by the same people (see left).*

Hotel Jazz

C/Pelai 3 (93 552 96 96/www.nnhotels.com). Metro Catalunya. **Rates** €172-€315 double. **Rooms** 108. **Credit** AmEx, DC, MC, V. **Map** p344 A1 ❹❽

Rooms at the Hotel Jazz are super-stylish, in calming tones of, naturally, grey, beige and black, softened with parquet floors and spiced up with dapper pinstripe cushions and splashes of funky colour. The beds are larger than usual for hotels, and the bathrooms feature cool, polished black tiles. A rooftop pool and sun deck top things off.

Bar. Business centre. Disabled-adapted rooms (4). Internet (free shared terminals, free Wi-Fi in rooms). No-smoking hotel. Pool (outdoor). TV.
Other locations Hotel Barcelona Universal, Avda Paral·lel 76-78, Poble Sec (93 567 74 47); and throughout the city.

Hotel Majestic

Passeig de Gràcia 68 (93 488 17 17/www. hotelmajestic.es). Metro Passeig de Gràcia. **Rates** €470-€740 double. **Rooms** 399. **Credit** AmEx, DC, MC, V. **Map** p338 G7 ❹❾

The Majestic has long been one of Barcelona's grandest hotels. Behind a neo-classical façade lies a panoply of perks, such as a service that allows you to print a selection of the day's newspapers from all over the world from the comfort of the lobby. Its

Hotel Curious. *See p131.*

CONSUME

crowning achievement is the ninth floor, which boasts an apartment and a sumptuous Sagrada Família Suite with a private, outdoor jacuzzi. Non-guests can enjoy the high life in the rooftop pool and gym, which offer wonderful views out over the city while you sweat or swim. Rooms are suitably opulent, decorated with classical flair. The Drolma restaurant is one of the finest, and priciest, in the city. *Bars (2). Business centre. Disabled-adapted rooms (4). Gym. Internet (€6/hr; €15/day Wi-Fi). No-smoking floors (7). Parking (€26.50/day). Pool (outdoor). Restaurant. Room service. TV: pay movies.*

Hotel Murmuri

Rambla Catalunya 104 (93 550 06 00/www.murmuri.com). Metro Diagonal. **Rates** €229-€450 double. **Rooms** 53. **Credit** AmEx, DC, MC, V. **Map** p338 F/G7 ⑩

A sophisticated cut above its sister hotel, the Majestic (*see p137*), round the corner, Murmuri has an effortless chic about it. Creamy tones with gilt trim and sculpted flower arrangements give the interior a cool, calm atmosphere, attracting a well-heeled, grown-up crowd, and there's a lively lobby for drinks and a slick Thai restaurant. Bedrooms are spacious and airy, and generously stocked with Molton Brown toiletries. For a sophisticated shopping weekend at the heart of the designer quarter, few places beat it. A victim of leaner times, it also offers good deals on the website. *Photo p143.*

Bar. Disabled-adapted rooms (2). Internet (€15/day Wi-Fi). No-smoking floors (2). Restaurant. TV: cable.

Hotel Omm

C/Rosselló 265 (93 445 40 00/www.hotelomm.es). Metro Diagonal. **Rates** €225-€315 double. **Rooms** 91. **Credit** AmEx, DC, MC, V. **Map** p338 G6 ⑤

It was the Omm that redefined the hotels of the Eixample, establishing a new breed of smart, sophisticated urban accommodation for discerning travellers. Bedrooms are light and bright, as opposed to black on black corridors, and enjoy what may well be the city's comfiest beds and double bathrooms. The restaurant, set up by the Roca brothers, now boasts one Michelin star, but there's also a healthy bistro alternative, as well as an extensive wine and cocktail bar. An ultra trendy club occupies the perfectly soundproofed basement, and a bar and pool area perches on the roof with views straight over the witchscarers of Gaudi's La Pedrera next door.

Bar. Disabled-adapted rooms (2). Gym. Internet (free high-speed, free Wi-Fi). No-smoking floors (4). Pool (outdoor). Restaurant. Room service. TV.

Hotel Pulitzer

C/Bergara 8 (93 481 67 67/www.hotelpulitzer.es). Metro Catalunya. **Rates** €171-€320 double. **Rooms** 91. **Credit** AmEx, DC, MC, V. **Map** p344 B2 ㊷

Situated just off Plaça de Catalunya, the Pulitzer has become a popular place to meet before a night out. A discreet façade reveals an impressive lobby that's stuffed with comfortable white leather sofas, a reading area overflowing with glossy picture books and a swanky bar and restaurant. The rooftop terrace is a fabulous spot for a cocktail, with squishy loungers, scented candles and tropical plants, and views across the city. The rooms themselves are not big, but they are sumptuously decorated and come complete with cool grey marble, fat fluffy pillows and kinky leather trim.
Bar. Disabled-adapted rooms (3). Internet (free Wi-Fi). No-smoking floors (4). Restaurant. Room service. TV.

Prestige Paseo de Gràcia
Passeig de Gràcia 62 (93 272 41 80/www. prestigehotels.com). Metro Passeig de Gràcia. **Rates** €220-€440 double. **Rooms** 45. **Credit** AmEx, DC, MC, V. **Map** p338 G7 ⑤③
Perfectly situated for just about everything, this sublime boutique hotel was created by architect Josep Juanpere, who took a 1930s building and revamped it with funky oriental-inspired minimalist design and Japanese gardens. The rooms are equipped with B&O TVs, intelligent lighting systems, free minibars and even umbrellas. Outside their rooms, the hotel's guests hang out in the cool Zeroom lounge-bar-library, where expert concierges (of the funky rather than fusty variety) are constantly on hand to help you get the most out of your stay in Barcelona. The free parking is a real boon in this part of town.
Bar. Disabled-adapted room. Internet (free Wi-Fi). Parking (free). No-smoking floors (5). Room service. TV.

Moderate

Hostal d'Uxelles
Gran Via de les Corts Catalanes 688, pral (93 265 25 60/www.hotelduxelles.com). Metro Tetuán. **Rates** €90-€104 double. **Rooms** 21. **Credit** AmEx, MC, V. **Map** p343 H8 ⑤④
A pretty, tastefully decorated *hostal*, with friendly staff, d'Uxelles is a delightful place to stay and a bargain to boot. The angels above reception are a hint of what's to come within: Modernista tiles, cream walls with gilt-framed mirrors, antique furnishings, canopies above the beds and bright, Andaluz-tiled bathrooms (all en suite). The best rooms have plant-filled balconies with tables and chairs, where you can have breakfast.
No-smoking rooms (16). Room service. TV.
Other locations Hostal d'Uxelles, 2 Gran Via de les Corts Catalanes 667, entl 2ª, Eixample (93 265 25 60).

Hostal Goya
C/Pau Claris 74, 1° (93 302 25 65/www. hostalgoya.com). Metro Urquinaona. **Rates** €90-€115 double. **Rooms** 19. **Credit** MC, V. **Map** p344 D1 ⑤⑤
Why can't all *hostales* be like this? Located in a typical Eixample building with fabulous tiled floors, the bedrooms are done out in chocolates and creams, with comfortable beds, chunky duvets and cushions; the bathrooms are equally luxurious. The best rooms either give on to the street or the terrace at the back. The Goya is excellent value and a real gem. What's more, guests leaving the city in the evening can still use a bathroom to shower and change before they go. That's service.
No-smoking hostal. TV room.

Hotel Advance
C/Sepulveda 180 (93 289 28 92/www.hotel advance.com). Metro Universitat. **Rates** €140-€300 double. **Rooms** 36. **Credit** AmEx, DC, MC, V. **Map** p342 E9 ⑤⑥
The Hotel Advance displays all the usual signs of coolness in the lobby (dark paintwork, deep sofas, a futuristic fireplace) but in reality it is a bit of a sleepy hollow, making it a great retreat from the madness of the town centre. Rooms are smart, comfortable and very peaceful, bathrooms are bigger than average and there's a roof terrace for catching a few rays. It doesn't have a bar, but friendly staff are happy to share their local knowledge. Prices fluctuate a fair amount, so keep an eye out for special offers.
Bar. Disabled-adapted room. Internet (free Wi-Fi). No-smoking hotel. Room service. TV: cable.

Hotel Arts.
See p133.

CONSUME

Hotel Soho

Gran Via de les Corts Catalanes 543-545 (93 552 96 10/www.nnhotels.com). Metro Urgell. **Rates** €140-€170 double. **Credit** AmEx, DC, MC, V. **Map** p342 E8 ⑰

The Soho lives up to its Manhattan namesake in that it has the feel of a New York village loft. A duplex-height lobby filled with the light of numerous glass art installations leads into a comfortable basement business space with library, desks, sofas, a small terrace and free internet. On the first floor there's a breakfast room, and a cocktail bar and plunge pool on the roof. Generously proportioned bedrooms have been done out in tasteful olive greens and wood, with gargantuan beds, plasma-screen TVs and glass bathrooms by Philippe Starck. The best have spacious terraces. It's trendy, but not achingly so and has earned itself a loyal following. Book well in advance. *Bar. Disabled-adapted rooms (2). Internet (free Wi-Fi). No-smoking hotels. Pool (outdoor). Restaurant. TV: cable.*

Market Hotel

Passatge Sant Antoni Abat 10 (93 325 12 05/www.markethotel.com.es). Metro Sant Antoni. **Rates** (incl breakfast) €99.50-€140 double. **Rooms** 46. **Credit** AmEx, MC, V. **Map** p342 D9 ⑱

The people who brought us the wildly successful Quinze Nits chain of restaurants have gone on to apply their low-budget, high-design approach to this hotel. The monochrome rooms, though not huge, are comfortable and stylish for the price and downstairs is a handsome and keenly priced restaurant, typical of the group. What's more, the nearby Mercat Sant Antoni is closed for two years, thus ensuring you won't be woken at dawn by shouting stallholders. *Disabled-adapted rooms (2). Internet (free Wi-Fi). Restaurant. TV.*

the5rooms

C/Pau Claris 72 (93 342 78 80/www.thefive rooms.com). Metro Catalunya or Urquinaona. **Rates** (incl breakfast) €155-€190 double. **Rooms** 5. **Credit** MC, V. **Map** p344 D1 ⑲

The5rooms is a chic and comfortable B&B in a handsome building, where the delightful Jessica Delgado makes every effort to encourage guests to feel at home. Books and magazines are dotted around the stylish sitting areas and bedrooms, and breakfast is served at any time of day. There are now two apartments in the neighbouring building and plans to add more rooms in 2009. Whether the name will reflect the new number remains to be seen. *Internet (free Wi-Fi). No-smoking hotel. Room service. TV.*

Villa Emilia

C/Calàbria 115-117 (93 252 52 85/www.hotel villaemilia.com). Metro Rocafort. **Rates** €130-€180 double. **Rooms** 53. **Credit** AmEx, DC, MC, V. **Map** p341 D8 ⑳

> ### INSIDE TRACK
> ### PACKAGE DEALS
>
> Many hotels are now offering extremely good-value packages that could include anything from room upgrades and gourmet meals to spa treatments and wine tastings. Being pushy pays off.

A great value hotel that makes being located a little away from the action well worth it. There's not much to discover in the immediate vicinity but Emilia compensates with the glam Zinc Bar in the lobby complete with black chandeliers and red velvet sofas, where you can snack on quality tapas washed down with local wine and vermouth. The pièce de résistance, however, is the open-air lounge on the rooftop, with plush sofas, candles, a well-stocked bar and a buzzer for service. The rooms are decent with large comfortable beds, and decor that aims for a good night's sleep rather than design awards. *Photo p145. Bar. Disabled-adapted rooms (2). Internet (free Wi-Fi). No-smoking hotel. Restaurant. TV: cable.*

Budget

Hostal L'Antic Espai

Gran Via de les Corts Catalanes 660, pral (93 304 19 45/www.anticespai.com). Metro Passeig de Gràcia or Urquinaona. **Rates** €65-€135 double. **Rooms** 10. **Credit** AmEx, DC, MC, V. **Map** p342 G8 ㉑

A real find for lovers of character places and fans of Almodóvar-style chintz. Each room is individually decorated and rammed with antiques, be it an ornately carved wooden bedhead, a teardrop chandelier, a faux Louis XV dresser or a silken throw. All have en suite bathrooms and a little 21st-century gadgetry such as plasma TVs and free Wi-Fi, some have balconies and there is also a patio out back somewhat bizarrely planted with silk flowers. *Internet (free Wi-Fi). No-smoking hostal. TV.*

Hostal Central Barcelona

C/Diputació 346, pral 2ª (93 245 19 81/www.hostalcentralbarcelona.com). Metro Tetuán. **Rates** €61-€83 double. **Rooms** 20. **Credit** DC, MC, V. **Map** p343 J8 ㉒

Lodging at the Central, spread across two floors of an old Modernista building, is like staying in a rambling flat rather than a *hostal*. Rooms have original tiling and high ceilings, but are kitted out with air-conditioning and double glazing. Most have en-suite facilities, but the modern glass-brick cubicles in some eat up bedroom space. Clean and friendly, this is a bargain for budget travellers and a metro ride away from most sights. *Internet (free Wi-Fi). No-smoking hostal.*

CONSUME

Hostal Eden

*C/Balmes 55, pral 1ª (93 452 66 20/www.hostal
eden.net). Metro Passeig de Gràcia.* **Rates** €57-
€75 double. **Rooms** 30. **Credit** AmEx, MC, V.
Map p338 F8
Located on three floors of a Modernista building, this
warm and relaxed *hostal* with friendly, helpful staff
offers free internet access and has a sunny patio with
a shower for you to cool off. The best rooms have
marble bathrooms with corner baths, and nos.114
and 115, at the rear, are quiet and have large windows overlooking the patio.
*Internet (free shared terminals). No-smoking
rooms (8). TV.*

Hostal Girona

*C/Girona 24, 1° 1ª (93 265 02 59/www.
hostalgirona.com). Metro Urquinaona.* **Rates**
€65-€83 double. **Rooms** 26. **Credit** DC, MC, V.
Map p344 F1
A gem of a *hostal,* filled with antiques, chandeliers
and oriental rugs. The rooms may be on the simple
side, but all have charm to spare, with tall windows,
pretty paintwork (gilt detail on the ceiling roses) and
tiled floors. It's worth splashing out on rooms in the
refurbished wing, with en-suite bathrooms, although
the rooms in the older wing are good too, and some
have en-suite showers. Brighter, outward-facing
rooms have small balconies overlooking C/Girona
or bigger balconies on to a huge and quiet patio.
Internet (free Wi-Fi). TV.

Hostal San Remo

*C/Ausiàs Marc 19, 1°-2ª (93 302 19 89/www.
hostalsanremo.com). Metro Urquinaona.* **Rates**
€64-€68 double. **Rooms** 7. **Credit** MC, V.
Map p344 E2
Staying in this bright, neat and peaceful apartment
feels a bit like staying with an amenable relative.
The friendly owner Rosa and her fluffy white dog
live on site and take good care of their guests. All
seven of the rooms have air-conditioning and shiny
bedspreads; five out of seven have en-suite bathrooms, and most of them have a little balcony and
double glazing. A good place to stay.
No-smoking hostal. TV.

Residencia Australia

*Ronda Universitat 11, 4° 1ª (93 317 41 77/
www.residenciaustralia.com). Metro Universitat.*
Rates €55-€79 double. **Rooms** 4. **Credit** MC, V.
Map p344 B1
Maria, the owner of Residencia Australia, quit Spain
for Oz in the 1950s and only returned after Franco's
death to carry on the family business and open this
small, friendly, home-from-home *pensión.* There are
just four cute rooms (one en suite); all are cosy, clean
and simply furnished. There's a minimum two-night
stay. The family also has two apartments nearby
that can be booked if rooms are full.
Internet (free Wi-Fi). No-smoking hotel. TV.

Hotel Murmuri. *See p138.*

GRACIA

Gràcia is off the beaten tourist track, which
only adds to its allure. Its narrow streets and
leafy squares have a villagey feel to them,
and there are more and more interesting
restaurants, shops and night-time activities
to test out, although hotels hard to come by.

Expensive

Casa Fuster

*Passeig de Gràcia 132 (93 255 30 00/www.
hotelcasafuster.com). Metro Diagonal.* **Rates**
€495-€680 double. **Rooms** 96. **Credit** AmEx,
DC, MC, V. **Map** p338 G6
There was a lot of talk about the Fuster when it first
opened. Many complained that this historic building should have been preserved as a public space.
The famed Café Viennese answers that demand
somewhat, though when a cup of tea costs €15 you
won't find many locals drinking it. What is so
appealing for the luxury end of the market, however, is the air of exclusivity that envelopes you on
arrival. Service is spot on, rooms – while rather small
– feel regal in their dove grey and purples, and there
are fresh flowers every day. The rooftop pool has a
jacuzzi area and truly spectacular views, while the
gourmet restaurant has a clubby, insider feel.
*Bar. Business centre. Disabled-adapted rooms
(5). Gym. Internet (free high-speed, free Wi-Fi).
No-smoking floors (3). Parking (€33/day). Pool.
Restaurant. Room service. TV: pay movies.*

CONSUME

Moderate

Hotel Confort

Travessera de Gràcia 72 (93 238 68 28/www.
mediumhoteles.com). Metro Diagonal or Fontana.
Rates €101-€192 double. **Rooms** 36. **Credit**
AmEx, DC, MC, V. **Map** p338 F5 ⑱
The Confort is light years ahead of other similar
establishments, with 36 simple but smart, modern
bedrooms with curvy, light wood furnishings and
gleaming marble bathrooms. All the rooms get lots
of light, thanks to several interior patios. There's a
bright dining room and lounge, with a large leafy
terrace that makes a lovely setting for a sunny summer breakfast or a cool drink on a balmy night.
Disabled-adapted room. Internet (free Wi-Fi). TV.
Other locations Hotel Monegal, C/Pelai 62,
Eixample (93 302 65 66); and throughout the city.

Budget

Hostal HMB

C/Bonavista 21, 1° (93 368 20 13/www.
hostalhmb.com). Metro Diagonal. **Rates** €76-
€84 double. **Rooms** 13. **Credit** MC, V.
Map p338 G6 ⑲
The spick and span HMB opened in 2006 and immediately proved a good addition to local budget hotels.
The hostal is on the first floor (there's a lift), and the
13 rooms have shiny tiled floors and furniture, flat-
screen TVs and good lighting. All rooms have private
bathrooms with decent showers. Bright contemporary artwork adorns the lobby and corridors.
Internet (free Wi-Fi). TV.

OTHER DISTRICTS

Sants is convenient if you have an early train
to catch, and it's pleasantly far from the crowds
that fill the rest of the city. Poblenou has the
added advantage of proximity to the beach.

Expensive

ABaC Restaurant Hotel

Avda Tibidabo 1, Tibidabo (93 319 66 00/
www.abacbarcelona.com). FCG Tibidabo. **Rates**
€220-265 double. **Rooms** 15. **Credit** AmEx,
DC, MC, V.
This swanky new uptown hotel combines a 19th-
century villa with a state-of-the-art glass pavilion
clad in teak lattices giving it a modern Japanese air.
The 15 bedrooms have luxuries like an Hermès wel-
come pack and jacuzzi with chromotherapy.
Combined with perfectly manicured lawns, a
Michelin-starred restaurant of the same name, and
a white-on-white cocktail lounge in the basement,
ABaC is now one of Barcelona's classiest addresses.
Bar. Internet (free Wi-Fi). No-smoking hotel.
Parking (€32.30/day). Restaurant. Room
service. Spa. TV: cable.

Gran Hotel La Florida

Carretera de Vallvidrera al Tibidabo 83-93,
Tibidabo (93 259 30 00/www.hotellaflorida.com).
FCG Peu del Funicular. **Rates** €234-€285 double.
Rooms 70. **Credit** AmEx, DC, MC, V.
From 1925 to the 1950s, this was Barcelona's grand-
est hotel, frequented by royalty and stars. It has lav-

Villa Emilia. *See p141.*

CONSUME

The Mile-High Club

Three local hotels accept no limitations as they tower above the town.

Barcelona's on the up, literally. In the highest rooms of the futuristic skyscrapers that have transformed Barcelona's skyline in the last five years, hedonism waits. They have it all: views, service and all those extra details to make you feel just fabulous, darling.

Nowhere is this more evident than in Poblenou and along the fringes of the Avda Diagonal. **ME Barcelona** (*see p147*) pierces the skyline here like a silver needle, and takes five-star luxury to the next level by offering a full 'lifestyle experience'. Designed by the French architect Dominique Perrault, urban thrill-seekers head straight for the top, where instead of settling for a suite, you can bag the whole 29th floor.

This 120 square metre (1,300 square foot) white 'playroom' offers multimedia systems (70 TV channels including 'alternative adult entertainment', iPods and a personal 'experience manager' on call 24/7 to answer your every whim. You can recline on a feather mattress, or swim in the monster tub while admiring views that take in the Torre Agbar, the swirling turrets of the Sagrada Família and the mountains. Compared to other millionaire's crash-pads, this is a snip at €2,500-€5,000 a night.

You can't get closer to the beach though, than the **Hotel Arts** (*see p133*), a beachfront skyscraper designed by Bruce Graham, with a distinctive scaffold exterior and fabulous flower arrangements by Donna Stain. It's more conservative than ME, but when it comes to service with style, nowhere beats it. The Arts is all about comfort – yours – and the top floor corner suites of steel and glass give 360° views of both sea and city. If you're out to impress, duplex suites with their sweeping staircases and fully equipped kitchens (which come with a butler and private chef) are the way to go. These two-storey suites start at around €1,800 a night.

When Richard Rogers' futuristic **Hesperia Tower** (*see p147*) opened in 2005, a troop of dancers abseiled down the front, but it wasn't enough to stop murmurs of discontent about the location by the side of a motorway. Fast-forward a few years, and the inside is so fabulous, nobody cares. It also boasts duplex suites – on the 25th floor – and each bedroom has a large jacuzzi from which to admire the landscape. Executive duplex suites here start at €476 a night, making them the cheapest of the lot. And the Hesperia also offers Pink Rooms, complete with glossy magazines and posh toiletries.

Hotel Arts.

ish suites, private terraces and gardens, a five-star restaurant, a summer outdoor nightclub, and a luxury spa. Perched as it is on Tibidabo, La Florida offers bracing walks in the hills and breathtaking 360° views, especially from the jaw-dropping infinity pool (with a heated indoor part for winter dips). It's a good choice if you want to relax in opulent style and spend most evenings in the hotel. Getting a cab from town at night can be tricky

Bar. Business centre. Disabled-adapted rooms (2). Gym. Internet (free Wi-Fi). No-smoking floors (5). Parking (€19.30/day). Pool (outdoor/indoor). Restaurants (2). Room service. TV: pay movies.

Hesperia Tower Hotel

Gran Via de les Corts Catalanes 144 (93 413 50 00/www.hesperia-tower.com). FGC Màgoria La Campana. Bus 9. **Rates** €230-€396 double. **Rooms** 280. **Credit** AmEx, DC, MC, V. *See p146* **The Mile-High Club.**
Bars (2). Disabled-adapted rooms (4). Gym. Internet (free wireless). No-smoking floors (13). Parking (€27.85/day). Pool (indoor). Restaurants (2). Room service. Spa. TV: cable.

ME Barcelona

C/Pere IV 272-286, Poblenou (93 367 20 50/ www.me-barcelona.com). Metro Poblenou. **Rates** €183-€190 double. **Rooms** 259. **Credit** AmEx, DC, MC, V.
See p146 **The Mile-High Club.**
Bar. Business centre. Disabled-adapted rooms (5). Internet (free Wi-Fi). Gym. No-smoking floors (15). Parking (€35.50/day). Pool (outdoor). Restaurant. Room service. Spa. TV: cable.

Moderate

Anita's B&B

C/August Font 24, Tibidabo (93 254 67 93/ www.anitasbarcelona.com) Metro Penitents then bus 124. **Rates** (incl breakfast) €85 double. **Rooms** 3. **No credit cards.**
A true retreat, this small and friendly bed and breakfast offers a home-style experience and is ideal if you're looking for a more peaceful city break. The centre is about 20 minutes away by taxi. But the advantages are that, being situated high up, the air is that little bit fresher than in the city and the views are fabulous (all rooms have a balcony and en suite bathrooms). Bedrooms are tasteful with cosy quilts and flowers, communal areas are well-stocked with guide books and magazines, and the breakfast is one of the best in Barcelona.
Internet (free Wi-Fi). Room service. TV: DVD.

Petit Hotel

C/Laforja 67, 1°-2ª, Sant Gervasi (93 202 36 63/www.petit-hotel.net). FGC Muntaner. **Rates** €88-€105 double. **Rooms** 4. **Credit** MC, V. **Map** p338 E5 ⑦

This charming and convivial B&B has four neat, fresh-feeling bedrooms set around the comfortable and softly lit lounge. Although only two of the rooms are en suite, the others have large, immaculate modern bathrooms located just outside. The owners, Rosa and Leo, are happy to chat to guests and provide information on the city. Breakfast, which is better than in many hotels, is served 8.30am-1.30pm. *Internet (€4/hr shared terminal). TV.*

Budget

Hostal Poblenou

C/Taulat 30, Poblenou (93 221 26 01/www. hostalpoblenou.com). Metro Poblenou. **Rates** (incl breakfast) €75 double. **Rooms** 9. **Credit** MC, V.
Poblenou is a delightful *hostal* in an elegant restored building. The rooms are light and airy with their own bathrooms, and breakfast is served on a sunny terrace. Guests can help themselves to tea, coffee and mineral water at no extra cost. The owner, Mercedes, is on hand to provide any information you might need. *Photo p149.*
Internet (free Wi-Fi). TV.

Hostal Sofía

Avda Roma 1-3 entl, Sants (93 419 50 40/ www.hostalsofia.es). Metro Sants Estaciò. **Rates** €50-€60 double. **Rooms** 17. **Credit** DC, MC, V. **Map** p341 C7 ⑦
The 17 basic rooms of Hostal Sofia, situated just across the busy roundabout from the city's main station, are a very sound budget option if an early train or quick stopover forces you to spend the night in the city. Some rooms have en-suite bathrooms. As the *hostal* is on the first floor and traffic is constant, outward-facing rooms are usually very noisy.
TV (some rooms).

Apartment Hotels

Barcelona Center Plaza

C/Ronda Sant Pere 38, 1° 1ª (93 315 07 42/ www.barcelonacenterplaza.com). Metro Urquinaona. **Rates** €75-€90 2 people. **Credit** AmEx, DC, MC, V. **Map** p344 E2 ⑦
All studios have a properly equipped kitchen and a dining area. Some of the decor is a bit nursery-school (fluffy clouds painted above the bed), but on the whole it's very comfortable and nicely done. There is another branch at C/Comtal 9 called Barcelona Center House. The rooms aren't quite so pretty, but some have private terraces.
Internet (free Wi-Fi in rooms). TV: cable.

Boria

C/Bòria 24-26 (93 295 58 93/www.boriabcn. com). Metro Jaume I. **Rates** €114-€174 2 persons (€50 extra adult). **Rooms** 9. **Credit** AmEx, DC, MC, V. **Map** p345 D5 ⑦

Located in an 18th-century palace, Boria is half hotel, half apartment, offering sophisticated loft-style rooms and suites that boast polished wood floors, plush rugs and designer fixtures and fittings, as well as cleverly incorporated kitchens, dining areas and office space. Communal zones include a smart and sleek library downstairs, and a wood-decked roof terrace. A restaurant and café are due to open soon. *Bar. Internet (free Wi-Fi). Restaurant. Room service. TV: cable.*

Hispanos Siete Suiza

C/Sicilia 255, Eixample (93 208 20 51/ www.hispanos7suiza.com). Metro Sagrada Família. **Rates** (apartments, incl breakfast) €175-€250 1-2 people; €205-€236 3 people; €230-€290 4 people; €390-€520 up to 6 people. **Apartments** 19. **Credit** AmEx, DC, MC, V. **Map** p339 J7 **⑩**
Lovers of vintage automobiles will get a real kick out of the Hispanos Siete Suiza, named after the seven lovingly restored pre-war motors that take up much of the lobby. The 19 elegant and spacious apartments each have a kitchen and sitting area decked out with parquet floors, a terrace and two bedrooms. Decor is classical with no designer trickery. All profits go to the cancer research foundation that runs the hotel. (Rates rise during holidays.) *Bar. Disabled-adapted room. Internet (free high-speed). Parking (€23.50/day). Restaurant. Room service. TV.*

Apartment & Room Rentals

Short-term room and apartment rental is a rapidly expanding market. People who have visited the city several times, or want to spend longer than a few days, are increasingly opting for self-catering accommodation. Some firms rent out their own apartments, while others act as intermediaries between apartment owners and visitors, taking a cut of the rents.

When renting, it pays to use a little common sense. Check the small print (payment methods, deposits, cancellation fees, etc) and exactly what is included (cleaning, towels and so on) before booking. Note that apartments offered for rental tend to be very small.

In addition to the firms listed below, check the following firms: www.rentthesun.com, www.inside-bcn.com, www.oh-barcelona.com, www.barcelona-home.com, www.destination bcn.com, www.rentaflatinbarcelona.com, www. friendlyrentals.com, www.1st-barcelona.com, www.apartmentsbcn.net, www.flatsbydays. com, and the gay-oriented www.outlet4spain. com. In addition, www.habitservei.com can help to find rooms in shared flats, and www.loquo. com functions as a sort of Iberian Craig's List.

Hostal Poblenou. See p147.

Barcelona-Home

C/Viladomat 89-95, Ent 3 (93 423 34 73/www. barcelona-home.com). **Open** 10am-2pm, 3-7pm Mon-Fri. **Rates** vary. **No credit cards**. **Map** p341 D9 **⑳**
A reputable company staffed by knowledgeable young people, Barcelona-Home aims to sort out accommodation problems and provides other services including guided tours, airport transfers, language courses and whatever else clients might need. Apartment rental prices are surprisingly reasonable considering the level of service, and the website is a great starting point for information on Barcelona.

Youth Hostels

Alberg Mare de Déu de Montserrat

Passeig de la Mare de Déu del Coll 41-51, Gràcia (93 210 51 51/93 483 83 63/www.tujuca.com). Metro Vallcarca. **Open** *Reception* 8am-3pm, 4.30-11pm daily. **Rates** (incl breakfast) €16.55-€21 under-25s; €22-€25 over-25s; €2/per person/stay sheets. **Credit** DC, MC, V.
Located in a magnificent building north of the centre, this 214-bed hostel boasts an architectural edge, with many original features, including Modernista tilework, whimsical plaster carvings and stained-glass windows, not to mention the beautiful gardens. IYHF cards are not obligatory (available here for €6), but beds cost €2 extra without one.

CONSUME

Disabled-adapted room. Internet (€3/hr shared terminals). No-smoking hostel. Parking (free). Restaurant. TV room.

Barcelona Mar Youth Hostel

C/Sant Pau 80, Raval (93 324 85 30/www. barcelonamar.com). Metro Paral·lel. **Open** 24hrs daily. **Rates** (incl breakfast) €18-€28; €2.50 per person/stay sheets. **Credit** AmEx, DC, MC, V. **Map** p342 E11 ⓲

With its pleasant communal areas, sparkling washrooms and handy on-site facilities, this is cheap as chips. There are no individual rooms, only dorms neatly stacked with bunk beds (150 in total), but there are areas that can be curtained off for privacy. *Disabled-adapted room. Internet (free shared terminal). Laundry. Lockers (free). No-smoking hostel. TV room.*

Other locations Alfonso XIII 28, Badalona (93 399 14 20/www.barcelonadream.net).

Center Ramblas Youth Hostel

C/Hospital 63, Raval (93 412 40 69/www.center-ramblas.com). Metro Liceu. **Open** 24hrs daily. **Rates** (incl breakfast) €17-€21.50 under-25s; €20.85-€25.55 over-25s; €2-€3 per person/ towels. **No credit cards. Map** p344 A4 ⓱

This super-friendly hostel has 201 beds in all, in dorms that sleep three to ten. Facilities include free internet access, a communal fridge, microwave, safes and individual lockers for each guest. It's a good place to make friends, but beds sell out fast, so reserve your space at least two weeks in advance. *Disabled-adapted room. Internet (free terminal). Lockers (free). No-smoking hostel. TV room.*

Centric Point

Passeig de Gràcia 33, Eixample (93 215 65 38/ www.centricpointhostel.com/www.equity-point. com). Metro Passeig de Gràcia. **Open** 24hrs daily. **Rates** (incl breakfast) €25-€31 per person dormitory; €40-€65 per person twins; single use €120. €2 per person/night sheets/blankets/ towels. **Credit** DC, MC, V. **Map** p338 G8 ⓲

The newest addition to the Equity Point group goes considerably upmarket, with more than 400 beds in an impressive Modernista building in one of the swankiest locations in the city. There are doubles and dorms, mostly with en-suite facilities. There is free internet access, satellite TV and breakfast. Lots of information on Barcelona is available. *Disabled-adapted rooms (2). Internet (free Wi-Fi). Lockers (free). No-smoking hostel. TV room.*

Gothic Point

C/Vigatans 5, Born (93 268 78 08/www. gothicpoint.com). Metro Jaume I. **Open** 24hrs daily. **Rates** (incl breakfast) €17.50-€23 per person; €65-€75 twins; single use €55. €2 per person/night sheets/blankets/towels. **Credit** DC, MC, V. **Map** p345 D6 ⓲

Belonging to the same group as Centric Point, this friendly 154-bed hostel has a faintly Asian feel. Dorms (six to 14 beds) are a bit cramped, and although an undersheet and pillowcase are provided, anything else must be rented. There are washing machines and dryers, a microwave and fridge. Beach bums might prefer to stay at Sea Point on the seafront. *Disabled-adapted room. Internet (free terminal). Lockers (€1.50). No-smoking hostel. TV room.*

Other locations Sea Point, Plaça del Mar 1-4, Barceloneta (93 224 70 75/www.seapoint hostel.com); La Ciutat Albergue Residencia, Alegre de Dalt 66, Zona Alta (93 213 03 00/http://laciutat.nnhotels.es).

Itaca Alberg-Hostel

C/Ripoll 21, Barri Gòtic (93 301 97 51/www.itaca hostel.com). Metro Catalunya or Urquinaona. **Open** *Reception* 7am-4am daily. **Rates** (incl sheets) €18-€26 dormitory; €55-€65 twin. **Credit** MC, V. **Map** p344 D4 ⓮

Although right in the centre of the city, this is a laid-back place where you can recharge your batteries in peace. It has a homely atmosphere highlighted by its swirling murals, squishy sofas and lobby music; there's also a communal kitchen, a breakfast room and shelves of books and games. Its 33 beds are in five cheerful and airy dorms, all with balconies. The bathrooms are clean. *Dining room. Internet (€1.60/hr shared terminal). Kitchen. Lockers (free). No-smoking hostel.*

Campsites

For more on local campsites, get the *Catalunya Campings* or the *Campsites Close to Barcelona* books, or see www.campingtotal.org and www.barcelonaturisme.com.

Camping Masnou

Carretera N2, km 633, El Masnou (93 555 15 03/www.campingmasnou.com). **Open** *Reception* Oct-May 9am-noon, 3-7pm daily. June-Sept 8am-10pm daily. *Campsite* 7am-11.30pm daily. **Rates** €7/person; €5.50 1-10s; free under-1s; €7 car/caravan; €5.50 electricity. **Credit** MC, V.

Alongside the tents there's space for camper vans, plus a swimming pool, restaurant and bar.

Tres Estrellas

Carretera C-31, km 186.2, Gavà (93 633 06 37/ www.camping3estrellas.com). **Open** *Reception* mid Mar-mid Oct 9am-9pm daily. *Campsite* 24hrs daily. Closed mid Oct-mid Mar. **Rates** €5.30-€7.13/person; €4.16-€4.73 3-10s; free under-3s; €6.73-€8.11 car/caravan; €5.05 electricity. **Credit** MC, V.

The campsite is by the beach, 12km from Barcelona. There's a regular bus service into town.

Restaurants

Tradition rubs shoulders with innovation in Barcelona's kitchens.

Spain's culinary revolution has been one of the world's most significant gastronomic shake-ups in recent years; stale old clichés of boil-in-the-bag paella and calamares 'n' chips are rarely employed even in jest these days. Barcelona has greeted this new dawn with open arms, and the city's chefs now give the Basques a run for their money when it comes to unrestrained creativity and the dogged pursuit of ever-more-superior produce. Mass immigration has also played its part, adding ethnic variety to a culinary scene that offers both tradition and adventure.

THE LOCAL SCENE

At the top end of the scale, the tendrils of influence unfurling from überchef Ferran Adrià (*see pp176-177* **Profile**) and his Costa Brava restaurant El Bulli cannot be overestimated. Many of the city's top chefs, such as Carles Abellan at Comerç 24 (*see p155*) or Jordi Ruiz (*see p153*) at Neri Restaurante, have done training stints in Adrià's kitchen, a fact often reflected in the experimental nature of their dishes, while Adrià's influence is equally evident in the menus of dozens of other eateries.

More traditional restaurants remain, of course, but they've been joined of late by a number of restaurants offering cuisine from around the world. It's become increasingly easy to find a plate of momo dumplings, hand-rolled maki, Peking duck or a masala dosa in the city. Hell: there's even a fish and chip shop.

What happens when

Lunch starts around 1.30 or 2pm and continues until roughly 3.30pm or 4pm; dinner is served from about 9pm until 11.30pm or midnight. Some restaurants open earlier in the evening, but arriving before 9.30pm or 10pm generally means you'll be dining alone or in the company of foreign tourists. Booking a table is generally

> ❶ Blue numbers given in this chapter correspond to the location of each restaurant as marked on the street maps. *See pp402-412.*

a good idea at weekends, and also on Monday lunchtimes, when few restaurants are open. Many also close for lengthy holidays, including about a week over Easter, two or three weeks in August or early September, and often the first week in January. We have listed closures of more than a week where possible.

Prices and payment

Eating out in Barcelona is not as cheap as it used to be, but low mark-ups on wines keep the costs reasonable for northern Europeans and Americans. All but the real high-end eateries normally provide an economical fixed-price *menú del dia* (*menú* is not to be confused with the menu, which is *la carta*) at lunchtime, usually a starter, a main, a dessert, bread and something to drink. The idea is to provide cheaper meals for workers: while it can be a bargain, it should not be considered a taster menu or a showcase for the chef's greatest hits.

Laws governing the issue of prices are routinely flouted, but, legally, menus must declare if the seven per cent IVA (VAT) is included in prices or not (it rarely is, but we have included it in the prices below), and also if there is a cover charge (such a thing is officially illegal, but is generally expressed as a charge for bread). Catalans, and the Spanish in general, tend to tip very little, but tourists will let their conscience decide.

We've used the € symbol to indicate not only where a restaurant's main courses are low-priced, but where the mark up on drinks is reasonably low, and where there is no (or a very small) cover charge.

CONSUME

Mercè Vins.

RESTAURANTS

Barri Gòtic

★ Cafè de l'Acadèmia

C/Lledó 1 (93 319 82 53). Metro Jaume I.
Open 9am-noon, 1.30-4.30pm, 8.45pm-11.30pm
Mon-Fri. Closed 3wks Aug. **Main courses** €13.
Set lunch €10.35-€14.45. **Credit** AmEx, DC,
MC, V. **Map** p345 D6 ❶ Catalan
An assured approach to the classics of Catalan cuisine, combined with the sunny terrace tables on the pretty Plaça Sant Just, make this one of the best-value restaurants around. The brick-walled dining room gets full and the tables are close together, so it doesn't really work for a romantic date, but it's an animated spot for a power breakfast among the suits from nearby City Hall. The set lunch changes daily, but eat à la carte for quail stuffed with duck's liver and *botifarra* with wild mushroom sauce, or duck confit with poached onion and orange sauce.

★ € Can Culleretes

C/Quintana 5 (93 317 30 22). Metro Liceu.
Open 1.30-4pm, 9-11pm Tue-Sat; 1.30-4pm Sun.
Closed 3wks July, 1wk Aug. **Main courses**
€9.50. **Set lunch** €12.50-€15.50 Mon-Fri.
Set dinner €22-€28 daily. **Credit** MC, V.
Map p345 B5 ❷ Catalan
The rambling dining rooms at the 'house of tea-spoons' have been packing 'em in since 1786. The secret to this restaurant's longevity is a straightforward one: honest, hearty cooking and decent wine served at the lowest possible prices. Under huge oil paintings and a thousand signed black-and-white photos, diners munch sticky boar stew, tender pork with prunes and dates, goose with apples, partridge escabeche and superbly fresh seafood.

El Gran Café

C/Avinyó 9 (93 318 79 86). Metro Liceu. **Open**
1-4.30pm, 7.30pm-midnight daily. **Main courses**
€15. **Set lunch** €13 Mon-Fri. **Credit** AmEx, DC,
MC, V. **Map** p345 C6 ❸ Mediterranean
The fluted columns, bronze nymphs, suspended globe lamps and wood panelling help El Gran replicate a classic Parisian vibe. The cornerstones of brasserie cuisine – onion soup, duck magret, tarte tatin and even crêpes suzette – are all present and correct. The imaginative Catalan dishes spliced into the menu also work, but the distinctly non-Gallic attitude towards the hastily assembled set lunch is less convincing.

€ Machiroku

*C/Moles 21 (93 412 60 82). Metro Catalunya
or Urquinaona.* **Open** 1.30-3.30pm, 8.30-11.30pm
Mon-Fri; 8.30-11.30pm Sat. Closed Aug. **Main
courses** €10. **Set lunch** €8.50 Mon-Fri. **No
credit cards.** **Map** p344 D3 ❹ Japanese
A cosy, modest space decorated with Japanese wall hangings and prints. Service is charming and friendly and the various set menus at lunchtime offer good value, featuring rice and miso soup and then a choice of sushi, teriyaki, yakinuku (chargrilled beef) or a bento box with vegetable and prawn tempura. A short wine list has some excellent options.

Matsuri

Plaça Regomir 1 (93 268 15 35). Metro Jaume I.
Open 8.30-midnight Sat. **Main courses** €12.
Credit MC, V. **Map** p345 C6 ❺ Asian
A welcoming space painted in tasteful shades of ochre and terracotta, with the obligatory trickling fountain, wooden carvings and wall-hung candles, but saved from eastern cliché by some thoroughly occidental jazz in the background. Reasonably

priced tom yam soup and pad Thai feature, while the less predictable choices include *pho bo* – a Vietnamese broth with meat and spices, and sake niku, a delicious beef dish with wok-fried broccoli and a lightly perfumed soy sauce.

▶ *For anyone wanting a quicker, lighter supper, the owners have recently opened the Matsuri Sushi Bar alongside.*

€ Mercè Vins

C/Amargós 1 (93 302 60 56). Metro Urquinaona. **Open** 8am-4pm Mon-Fri. **Set lunch** €10. Closed 2wks Aug. **Credit** V. **Map** p344 D3 ❻ **Catalan**
A cosy lunch restaurant in the heart of the Barri Gòtic. Aimed at office workers, it only serves a *menú del día*, which changes daily but might include a pumpkin soup or inventive salad, followed by *botifarra* with sautéed garlic potatoes. Dessert regulars are flat, sweet *coca* bread with a glass of muscatel, chocolate flan or figgy pudding. In the morning it opens for breakfast, which here tends to be *pa amb tomàquet* (bread rubbed with tomato) topped with cheese or ham. *Photo p152.*

€ Mesón Jesús

C/Cecs de la Boqueria 4 (93 317 46 98). Metro Jaume I or Liceu. **Open** 1-4pm, 8-11pm Mon-Fri. Closed Aug. **Main courses** €11. **Set lunch** €10.50 Mon-Fri. **Set dinner** €18 Mon-Fri. **Credit** MC, V. **Map** p345 B5 ❼ **Spanish**
Old-school Castilian is a surprisingly uncommon look among Barcelona's restaurants, and the gingham tablecloths, oak barrels and cartwheels hung at Mesón Jesús are something of a novelty. The menu is limited and never changes, but the dishes are reliably good and inexpensive to boot – try the sautéed green beans with ham to start, then the superb grilled prawns or a tasty *zarzuela* (fish stew). The waitresses are incessantly cheerful with a largely non-Spanish-speaking clientele, and especially obliging when it comes to dealing with children.

Neri Restaurante

C/Sant Sever 5 (93 304 06 55/www.hotel neri.com). Metro Jaume I. **Open** 1.30-4pm, 8.30-11pm daily. **Main courses** €28. **Set lunch** €20 Mon-Fri; €30 Sat, Sun. **Credit** AmEx, DC, MC, V. **Map** p345 C5 ❽ **Catalan**
These days, any Barcelona restaurant worth its *fleur de sel* has an alumnus of acclaimed chef Ferran Adrià heading up its kitchens, and the Neri is no exception. Jordi Ruiz has eschewed the wilder excesses of molecular gastronomy, however, and cooks with a quiet assurance in tune with the sombre Gothic arches, crushed velvet and earthy tones of his dining room, creating a perfect, tiny lamb Wellington to start; cannelloni formed with artichoke petals and stuffed with wild mushrooms, or a tender fillet of hake on a bed of creamed parsnip with apricots and haricot beans.

El Paraguayo

C/Parc 1 (93 302 14 41). Metro Drassanes. **Open** 1-4pm, 8pm-midnight Tue-Sun. **Main courses** €17. **Set lunch** €12 Tue-Fri. **Credit** AmEx, DC, MC, V. **Map** p345 B8 ❾ **Paraguayan**
The only way to go at El Paraguayo, as with most South American restaurants, is to order a fat juicy steak, a bottle of good cheap house Rioja and a bowl of piping hot yucca chips. The rest is menu filler. As to which steak, a helpful chart walks you through the various cuts, most of them unfamiliar to European butchers, but a *bife de chorizo* should satisfy the ravenous. The place itself is cosy and wood-panelled, brightened with Botero-esque oil paintings of buxom madams and their dapper admirers.

€ Peimong

C/Templers 6-10 (93 318 28 73). Metro Jaume I. **Open** 1-4pm, 8-11.30pm Tue-Sat; 1-4pm Sun. Closed 2wks Aug. **Main courses** €8.50. **Credit** DC, MC, V. **Map** p345 C6 ❿ **Peruvian**
Not, perhaps, the fanciest-looking restaurant around (think Peruvian gimcracks, strip lighting and tapestries of Macchu Pichu) or indeed the fanciest-looking food, but it sure is tasty. Start with a pisco sour and a dish of big fat yucca chips, or maybe some spicy corn tamales, and then move on to *cèviche* for an explosion of lime and coriander; or the satisfying *lomo saltado* – pork fried with onions, tomatoes and coriander. Service is particularly friendly, there are two types of Peruvian beer and even – for the very nostalgic or the hypoglycaemic – Inca Kola.

Els Quatre Gats

C/Montsió 3 (93 302 41 40/www.4gats. com). Metro Catalunya. **Open** 1pm-1am daily. **Main courses** €23. **Set lunch** €14.85 Mon-Fri; €24.60 Sat. **Credit** AmEx, DC, MC, V. **Map** p344 C3 ⓫ **Catalan**
Dazzling in its design, Els Quatre Gats is an unmissable stop for those interested in Modernista architecture and indeed the art of the period, being the former regular meeting place of Picasso and other luminaries of the period. Nowadays it chiefly caters to tourists, and is no crucible for Catalan gastronomy, nor is it cheap. There is, however, a more reasonably priced and generously portioned set lunch, and when it's all over you can buy the T-shirt.

▶ *To appreciate the building without forking out for dinner, visit its café; see p182.*

INSIDE TRACK
DRINKING THE WATER

Tap water is safe but heavily chlorinated in Barcelona, so you're better off with bottled. Spaniards often prefer their water served at room temperature; ask for it *fria* if you want it chilled.

CONSUME

An unforgettable location in the heart of Barcelona

el Jardí de l'Àngel
RESTAURANT & BAR

Mediterranean cuisine in a unique environment

Menus with seven first course options as well as seven second course options and a variety of desserts: 18 - euros (+ VAT)

This spectacular restaurant, located in the heart of Barcelona, opens its do to the public for business meals, romantic evenings, family reunions and those simply wishing to enjoy a pleasant gastronomic experience under its c outdoor canopy or on the peaceful terrace. Surrounded by a beautiful gard with palm trees and colourful vegetation, and original, artistically decorated wa El Jardi de l'Ángel offers guests a calm refuge away from the hustle and bus of the Gothic neighbourhood. Our esteemed chef prepares traditional cuisin with a touch of the modern in the presentation, cooking and preparation of t food, using only the freshest and most carefully selected ingredients.

We invite you to experiment a new world of sensations and flavors with t excelence service and client's treament.

www.eljardidelangel.es

Restaurante El Jardí de l'Àngel Portal de l'Àngel, 17 • 08002 Barcelona • 93 318 41 41
Located inside the Hotel Albinoni

barcelo
world ra

€ Les Quinze Nits

Plaça Reial 6 (93 317 30 75). Metro Liceu. **Open**
1-3.45pm, 8.30-11.30pm daily. **Main courses** €8.
Set lunch €8.70 Mon-Fri. **Credit** AmEx, MC, V.
Map p345 B6 ⑫ **Spanish**
The staggering success of the Quinze Nits enterprise (there are now countless branches here in
Barcelona and now in Madrid, along with a handful of hotels) is down to one simple concept: style
on a budget. All the restaurants have a certain
Manhattan chic, yet you'll struggle to pay much
more than €20 a head. The food plays second fiddle and is a hit-and-miss affair, but order simple
dishes and at these prices you can't go far wrong.
▶ *The queues tend to be shorter at the other*
branches, such as nearby La Fonda (C/Escudellers
10, 93 301 75 15) and La Dolça Herminia
(C/Magdalenes 27, 93 317 06 76) in the Born.

★ Shunka

C/Sagristans 5 (93 412 49 91). Metro Jaume
I. **Open** 1.30-3.30pm, 8.30-11.15pm Tue-Fri; 2-
3.30pm, 8.30-11.15pm Sat, Sun. Closed Aug & ten
days at Christmas. **Main courses** €17. **Credit**
AmEx, DC, MC, V. **Map** p344 D4 ⑬ **Japanese**
The speciality here, one of few really good Japanese
restaurants in the Old City, is prime-grade *toro*,
fatty and deliciously creamy tuna belly. It's wildly
expensive as a main, but you can sample it as
nigiri-zushi. The house salad with raw fish also
makes for a zingy starter, then you'll find all the
usual staples of the sushi menu, along with hearti-
er options such as the *udon kakiage*, a filling broth
of langoustine tempura, vegetables and noodles . It
can be hard to get a table, though a new branch is
rumoured to be opening just next door

Taxidermista

Plaça Reial 8 (93 412 45 36). Metro Liceu.
Open 1.30-4pm, 7.30pm-12.30am Tue-Sun.
Closed 3wks Jan. **Set lunch** €10.70 Tue-Fri. **Credit** AmEx, DC,
MC, V. **Map** p345 B6 ⑭ **Mediterranean**
When this was a taxidermist's, Dalí ordered 200,000
ants, a tiger, a lion and a rhinoceros – the latter was
wheeled into the Plaça Reial so that he could be photographed atop the beast. Those who leave here
stuffed nowadays are mostly tourists, but standards
remain reasonably high. À la carte offerings include
foie gras with quince jelly; langoustine ravioli with
seafood sauce; and some slightly misjudged fusion
elements (wok-fried spaghetti with vegetables).

Tokyo

C/Comtal 20 (93 317 61 80). Metro Catalunya.
Open 1.30-4pm, 8-11.30pm Mon-Sat. Closed Aug.
Main courses €15. **Set lunch** €13.91 Mon-
Thur. **Credit** MC, V. **Map** p344 D3 ⑮ **Japanese**
A small and simple space, where suspended beams,
plastic plants and slatted wooden partitions are
used to clever effect and the walls are lined with

photos and drawings from grateful clients. The
speciality is *edomae* (hand-rolled *nigiri-zushi*), but
the meat and vegetable sukiyaki, which is cooked
at your table, is also good, while the *menú* of sushi
and tempura is great value. The *daifuku* (red bean)
and *midori* (green tea) *mochi* rolls to finish are
something of an acquired taste.

Born & Sant Pere

★ El Atril

C/Carders 23 (93 310 12 20/www.atrilbarcelona.
com). Metro Jaume I. **Open** 1.30-4.30pm, 7.30-
12.30pm Tue-Sun. **Main courses** €12.50. **Set**
lunch €9.80-€10.50 Tue-Fri; €12.50 Sat, Sun.
Credit DC, MC, V. **Map** p345 E/F5 ⑯ **Global**
Opened in 2008, El Atril's handful of tables already
require a reservation on most nights of the week
thanks to some reliably good cooking traversing a
broad range of cuisines. On the tapas menu fried
green plantains with coriander and lime mayonnaise
sit alongside *botifarra* with caramelised onions,
while a catholic selection of main courses includes a
bowl of Belgian-style mussels and chips, a kangaroo burger and a green curry.

★ Cal Pep

Plaça de les Olles 8 (93 310 79 61/www.cal
pep.com). Metro Barceloneta. **Open** 8-11.45pm
Mon; 1.30-4pm, 8-11.45pm Tue-Fri; 1.30-4pm
Sat. Closed Aug and Easter week. **Main**
courses €15. **Credit** AmEx, DC, MC, V.
Map p345 E7 ⑰ **Seafood**
As much tapas bar as restaurant, Cal Pep is always
packed: get here early for the coveted seats at the
front. There is a cosy dining room at the back, but
it's a shame to miss the show. The affable Pep will
take the order steering the neophytes towards the
trifásico – a mélange of fried whitebait, squid rings
and shrimp. Other favourites are the exquisite little
tallarines (wedge clams), and *botifarra* sausage with
beans. Then, squeeze in four shot glasses of foam –
coconut with rum, coffee, crema catalana and lemon.

Comerç 24

C/Comerç 24 (93 319 21 02/www.comerc24.
com). Metro Arc de Triomf. **Open** 1.30-3.30pm,
8.30pm-11pm Tue-Sat. **Main courses** (tapas)
€12. **Credit** MC, V. **Map** p344 F4 ⑱ **Catalan**
Carles Abellan trained under Ferran Adrià (*see*
p179) but now ploughs his own, very successful, fur-
row in this urbane and sexy restaurant. A selection
of tiny playful dishes changes seasonally for the
most part, but normally includes the ever popular
'Kinder egg' (lined with truffle) and the tuna sashimi and seaweed on a wafer-thin pizza crust. Adrià's
latest discoveries continue to affect Abellan's menu,
so recently he's been embracing all things Eastern,
with tuna dashi soup and so on. *Photo p159*.
▶ *For details of Tapaç24, Carles Abellan's take on*
trad tapas, see p194.

CONSUME

Menu Glossary

How to get what you want in the restaurants of Barcelona.

CATALAN	SPANISH	ENGLISH	CATALAN	SPANISH	ENGLISH
Essential terminology			**llebre**	*liebre*	hare
una cullera	*una cuchara*	a spoon	**llengua**	*lengua*	tongue
una forquilla	*un tenedor*	a fork	**llom**	*lomo*	loin (usually
un ganivet	*un cuchillo*	a knife			pork)
una ampolla de	*una botella de*	a bottle of	**oca**	*oca*	goose
una altra	*otra*	another (one)	**ous**	*huevos*	eggs
més	*más*	more	**perdiu**	*perdiz*	partridge
pa	*pan*	bread	**pernil (serrà)**	*jamón serrano*	dry-cured ham
oli d'oliva	*aceite de oliva*	olive oil	**pernil dolç**	*jamón york*	cooked ham
sal i pebre	*sal y pimienta*	salt and pepper	**peus de porc**	*manos de cerdo*	pigs' trotters
amanida	*ensalada*	salad	**pintada**	*gallina de Guinea*	guinea fowl
truita	*tortilla*	omelette	**pollastre**	*pollo*	chicken
(note: **truita** can also mean 'trout')			**porc**	*cerdo*	pork
la nota	*la cuenta*	the bill	**porc senglar**	*jabalí*	wild boar
un cendrer	*un cenicero*	an ashtray	**vedella**	*ternera*	veal
vi negre/ rosat/blanc	*vino tinto/ rosado/blanco*	red/rosé/ white wine	**xai/be**	*cordero*	lamb
bon profit	*Aproveche*	Enjoy your meal	**Peix i marisc**	**Pescado y mariscos**	**Fish & seafood**
sóc...	*soy...*	I'm a...	**anxoves**	*anchoas*	anchovies
vegetarià/ ana	*vegetariano/ a*	vegetarian	**bacallà**	*bacalao*	salt cod
diabètic/a	*diabético/a*	diabetic	**besuc**	*besugo*	sea bream
			caballa	*verat*	mackerel
Cooking terms			**calamarsos**	*calamares*	squid
a la brasa	*a la brasa*	chargrilled	**cloïsses**	*almejas*	clams
a la graella/ planxa	*a la plancha*	cooked on a hot plate	**cranc**	*cangrejo*	crab
a la romana	*a la romana*	fried in batter	**escamarlans**	*cigalas*	crayfish
			escopinyes	*berberechos*	cockles
al forn	*al horno*	baked	**espardenyes**	*espardeñas*	sea cucumbers
al vapor	*al vapor*	steamed	**gambes**	*gambas*	prawns
fregit	*frito*	fried	**llagosta**	*langosta*	spiny lobster
rostit	*asado*	roast			
ben fet	*bien hecho*	well done	**llagostins**	*langostinos*	langoustines
a punt	*medio hecho*	medium	**llamàntol**	*bogavante*	lobster
poc fet	*poco hecho*	rare	**llenguado**	*lenguado*	sole
			llobarro	*lubina*	sea bass
Carn i aviram	**Carne y aves**	**Meat & poultry**	**lluç**	*merluza*	hake
ànec	*pato*	duck	**moll**	*salmonete*	red mullet
bou	*buey*	beef	**musclos**	*mejillones*	mussels
cabrit	*cabrito*	kid	**navalles**	*navajas*	razor clams
colomí	*pichón*	pigeon	**percebes**	*percebes*	barnacles
conill	*conejo*	rabbit	**pop**	*pulpo*	octopus
embotits	*embutidos*	cold cuts	**rap**	*rape*	monkfish
fetge	*higado*	liver	**rèmol**	*rodaballo*	turbot
gall dindi	*pavo*	turkey	**salmó**	*salmón*	salmon
garrí	*cochinillo*	suckling pig	**sardines**	*sardinas*	sardines
guatlla	*codorniz*	quail	**sípia**	*sepia*	squid
			tallarines	*tallarinas*	wedge clams

CONSUME

CATALAN	SPANISH	ENGLISH	CATALAN	SPANISH	ENGLISH
tonyina	*atún*	tuna	**porros**	*puerros*	leek
truita	*trucha*	trout	**tomàquets**	*tomates*	tomatoes
(note: **truita** can also mean 'omelette')			**xampinyons**	*champiñones*	mushrooms

CATALAN	SPANISH	ENGLISH	CATALAN	SPANISH	ENGLISH
Verdures	**Legumbres**	**Vegetables**	**Postres**	**Postres**	**Desserts**
albergínia	*berenjena*	aubergine	**flam**	*flan*	crème caramel
all	*ajo*	garlic			
alvocat	*aguacate*	avocado	**formatge**	*queso*	cheese
bolets	*setas*	wild mush-rooms	**gelat**	*helado*	ice-cream
			música	*música*	dried fruit and nuts, served with muscatel
carbassos	*calabacines*	courgettes			
carxofes	*alcahofas*	artichokes			
ceba	*cebolla*	onion			
cigrons	*garbanzos*	chickpeas	**pastís**	*pastel*	cake
col	*col*	cabbage	**tarta**	*tarta*	tart
enciam	*lechuga*	lettuce			
endivies	*endivias*	chicory	**Fruïta**	**Fruta**	**Fruit**
espinacs	*espinacas*	spinach	**figues**	*higos*	figs
mongetes blanques	*judías blancas*	haricot beans	**gerds**	*frambuesas*	raspberries
			maduixes	*fresas*	strawberries
mongetes verdes	*judías verdes*	French beans	**pera**	*pera*	pear
			pinya	*piña*	pineapple
pastanagues	*zanahorias*	carrot	**plàtan**	*plátano*	banana
patates	*patatas*	potatoes	**poma**	*manzana*	apple
pebrots	*pimientos*	peppers	**préssec**	*melocotón*	peach
pèsols	*guisantes*	peas	**prunes**	*ciruelas*	plums

CONSUME

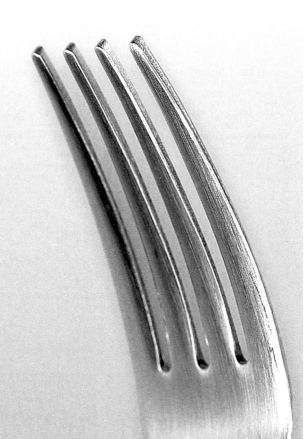

taxidermista...cafè restaurant
Plaça Reial 8   08002 Barcelona   tel. 93 412 45 36
www.taxidermistarestaurant.com   info@taxidermistarestaurant.com

Cuines Santa Caterina

Mercat Santa Caterina, Avda Francesc Cambó (93 268 99 18). Metro Jaume I. **Open** 1-4pm, 8-11.30pm daily. **Main courses** €11. **Credit** AmEx, DC, MC, V. **Map** p344 E4 ⑲ **Global**

It's not as dazzling as it was when it opened in 2005, with higher prices and a slightly more lax attitude to quality control, but CSC still has its charms. The menu holds a little of everything you fancy, from langoustine tempura to a baked spud with cheese and *sobrassada* sausage, with an excellent chocolate tart or red-fruit millefeuille to finish. The rice, flour, oil and crates of veg arrayed along the vast windows, coupled with the well-made olive wood furniture, lend everything an honest Mediterranean tone.

▶ *The same group owns Agua (see p164) and Bestial (see p164), among others.*

Diez

C/Mercaders 10 (93 310 21 79). Metro Jaume I. **Open** 9pm-1am daily. Closed 2wks Aug. **Main courses** €14. **Credit** AmEx, DC, MC, V. Map p345 D5 ⑳ **Global**

Low ceilings, Gothic arches, subtle lighting and handsome flower arrangements make eating in this former stables a cosy affair, perfect for a date. The menu is almost as enticing, with a creative edge that works in a roast fennel and orange salad but can verge on the fussy – as in the *escalivada* (roast veg) with fried filo and a goat's cheese foam. Tuna with mango and pak choi or duck magret with mangetout are tasty enough and lemon mousse with Space Dust makes for a zingy finish. *Photo p160.*

Habana Vieja

C/Banys Vells 2 (93 268 25 04). Metro Jaume I. **Open** 1.30-3.30pm, 8.30-11.30pm Mon-Sat. **Main courses** €15.50. **Credit** AmEx, DC, MC, V. **Map** p345 E6 ㉑ **Cuban**

Habana Vieja's most popular dishes are *ropa vieja* (shredded beef); *picadillo habanera* (minced meat with spices) and *tasajo* (shredded horsemeat with green peppers), optionally accompanied with some rather bland boiled yucca and the like, plus, more obligatorily, a good strong mojito. It's good fun, and terribly quaint, with prettily painted wooden fittings, but it's hard to shake off the feeling that this sort of traditional, carb-a-gogo cooking shouldn't come a bit cheaper, particularly once you've factored in €6.50 for a portion of rice.

€ Itztli

C/Mirallers 7 (93 319 68 75/www.itztli.es). Metro Barceloneta or Jaume I. **Open** noon-11pm Tue-Sun. **Main courses** €3.50. **Credit** AmEx, DC, MC, V. **Map** p345 E6 ㉒ **Mexican**

Fortify yourself in the interminable queue for entry to the Picasso Museum with a takeaway chicken burrito from this nearby Mexican snack bar. Keenly priced around the €3.50 mark, burritos also come with beef, chilli con carne or veg, as do tacos. Also

on offer are quesadillas, wraps, nachos and salads, and there's a good range of Mexican beers, tinned goods and fiery chilli sauces for sale.

Other locations C/Sant Miquel 60 (93 225 63 63).

★ Mosquito

C/Jaume Giralt 53 (93 315 17 44/www.mosquito tapas.com). Metro Arc de Triomf or Jaume I. **Open** 8pm-midnight Mon; 1pm-4pm, 8pm-midnight Tue-Thur, Sun; 1pm-4pm, 8-1am Fri, Sat. **Main courses** (tapas) €5. **Credit** MC, V. **Map** p344 F4 ㉓ **Asian**

Rehoused in a bigger, post-industrial space with an expanded menu to match, Mosquito continues to turn out affordable, shareable, Asian 'tapas', and has now added some excellent beers, some brewed especially for the restaurant; the *trigo* (wheat) is superb. Of the new dishes, the *xiaolong bao* (steamed pork dumplings) and crispy duck are more than toothsome, and regulars will be happy to see that the crunchy potato *chaat* still heads up the list.

Mundial Bar

Plaça Sant Agustí Vell 1 (93 319 90 56). Metro Arc de Triomf or Jaume I. **Open** 9pm-midnight Tue; 1-4pm, 9pm-midnight Wed-Sat; 1-4pm Sun. Closed 3wks Aug. **Main courses** €17. **Credit** MC, V. **Map** p344 F4 ㉔ **Seafood**

Comerç 24. *See p155.*

CONSUME

Diez. See p159.

Since 1925, this venerable family establishment has been dishing up no-frills platters of seafood, cheeses and the odd slice of cured meat. Colourful tiles add charm to the rather basic decor, but it's not as cheap as it looks. People come for the steaming piles of fresh razor clams, shrimp, oysters, fiddler crabs and the like, but there's also plenty of tinned produce, so check the bar displays to see exactly which is which.

★ € La Paradeta

C/Comercial 7 (93 268 19 39/www.laparadeta.com). Metro Arc de Triomf or Jaume I. **Open** 8-11.30pm Tue-Fri; 1-4pm, 8pm-midnight Sat; 1-4pm Sun. **Main courses** €10. **No credit cards. Map** p345 F6 **Seafood**
Superb seafood, served refectory-style. Choose from glistening mounds of clams, mussels, squid, spider crabs and other fresh treats, decide how you'd like it cooked (grilled, steamed or *a la marinera*), pick a sauce (Marie Rose, spicy local *romesco*, *all i oli* or onion), buy a drink and wait for your number to be called. A great and cheap experience for anyone not too grand to clear their own plate.
Other locations Ptge Simó 18, Eixample (93 450 01 91).

★ Re-Pla

C/Montcada 2 (93 268 30 03). Metro Jaume I. **Open** noon-11pm Tue-Sat. **Main courses** €16. **Credit** DC, MC, V. **Map** p345 E5 **Global**

INSIDE TRACK
CALÇOTS IN WINTER

In winter, look out for calçots, a spring onion-like Catalan speciality. They're fire-blackened and dipped in romesco sauce; eat them by tipping back your head and lowering them in. Bibs may be provided.

The stunning new look at this longtime favourite is halfway between a French bistro and tapas bar; the emphasis is now less on the tables and more on sitting up at the new marble bar. There's a *menú del dia* for €12.50; otherwise, it's tapas or *raciones* (divine pig's trotters with foie, outstanding *pa amb tomàquet*). Drinks include Mahou on tap (a fine beer, often ignored here because it's from Madrid), plus some good wines by the glass. One other very cool touch: there's a serving hatch out on to the street.
Other locations Pla, C/Bellafila 5, Barri Gòtic (93 412 65 52).

★ Wushu

Avda Marquès de l'Argentera 1 (93 310 73 13/ www.wushu-restaurant.com). Metro Jaume I. **Open** 1pm-midnight Tue-Sat; 1-4pm Sun. **Main courses** €13.50. **Set lunch** €9.90 Tue-Fri. **Credit** MC, V. **Map** p345 E5 **Asian**
Still in the Born, but now in bigger premises, Wushu has managed to maintain its quality while serving three times as many people. Brad Ainsworth learned his trade under Sydney superchef Neil Perry; his healthy Asian cooking ranges from good to delectable, as evinced by the superb laksa, pad Thai, kangaroo yakisoba and Vietnamese rice-paper rolls. Save space for pudding, however; Wushu's other secret weapon is a supremely talented pastry chef.

Raval

★ Biblioteca

C/Junta de Comerç 28 (93 412 62 21/www. bibliotecarestaurant.com). Metro Liceu. **Open** 8-11.30pm Mon-Fri; 1-4pm, 8-11.30pm Sat. Closed 2wks Aug. **Main courses** €13. **Credit** AmEx, MC, V. **Map** p345 A5 **Mediterranean**
A tranquil, elegant space with beige minimalist decor, and a display of cookbooks. From Bocuse to Bourdain, they are all for sale, and their various influences collide in the menu. Increasingly, though,

it draws from the Catalan culinary canon, with a good *esqueixada* (salt cod salad) or a reasonable onion *coca* (flat, crispy bread) with anchovies to start, followed by gamier mains that might include venison pie or pig's trotters stuffed with prunes.

Dos Trece

C/Carme 40 (93 301 73 06/www.dostrece.net). Metro Liceu. **Open** 9am-midnight Tue-Sun. **Main courses** €12. **Set lunch** €11 Tue-Thur; €12 Fri-Sun. **Credit** AmEx, DC, MC, V. **Map** p344 A4 ㉙ **Global**

Another to fall victim to the council's crackdown on late-night music, Dos Trece had to ditch its DJs and jam sessions, and instead has turned its cosy basement space into another dining room – this one with cushions and candles for post-prandial lounging. Apart from a little fusion confusion (ceviche with nachos, and all manner of things with yucca chips) the food's not half bad for the price, and includes one of the few decent burgers to be had in Barcelona.

€ Elisabets

C/Elisabets 2-4 (93 317 58 26). Metro Catalunya. **Open** 7am-11pm Mon-Sat. Closed 3wks Aug. **Set lunch** €9.75 Mon-Fri. **Set dinner** €13.75 Fri. **No credit cards. Map** p344 B3 ㉚ **Catalan**

Also open in the mornings for breakfast, and late night for drinking at the bar, Elisabets maintains a sociable local feel, despite the recent gentrification of its street. Dinner, served only on Fridays, is actually a selection of tapas, and otherwise only the set lunch or myriad *bocadillos* are served. The lunch deal is terrific value, however, with osso buco, vegetable

and chickpea stew, baked cod with garlic and parsley, and roast pork knuckle all making regular appearances on the menu. *Photo p161.*

€ Las Fernández

C/Carretas 11 (93 443 20 43). Metro Paral·lel. **Open** 9pm-1am Tue-Sun. Closed 2wks Aug. **Main courses** €7.50. **Credit** DC, MC, V. **Map** p342 E10 ㉛ **Spanish**

An inviting entrance, pillar-box red, is a beacon of cheer on one of Barcelona's less salubrious streets. Inside, the three Fernández sisters have created a bright and unpretentious bar/restaurant that specialises in wine and food from their native León. Alongside *cecina* (dried venison), gammon and sausages from the region are lighter, Mediterranean dishes and generous salads; smoked salmon with mustard and dill; pasta filled with wild mushrooms; and sardines with a citrus escabeche.

€ Juicy Jones

C/Hospital 74 (93 443 90 82). Metro Liceu. **Open** noon-11.30pm daily. **Main courses** €6. **Set lunch** €8.50 daily. **Credit** AmEx, MC, V. **Map** p342 F10 ㉜ **Vegetarian**

Alongside its two menus, one European and one Indian, this colourful vegan restaurant has an inventive list of juices and smoothies, salads and filled baguettes. While its heart is in the right place, it's mostly aimed at backpackers and staffed, it would seem, by somewhat clueless language-exchange students (don't expect a speedy lunch). Bring a book. **Other locations** C/Cardenas 7, Barri Gòtic (93 302 43 20).

Elisabets.

CONSUME

**CASUAL
FOOD
FOR
CASUA
PEOPL**

SANDWICH&FRIENDS®
CASUALFOOD

Chic and modern restaurants with the greatest sandwiches in Barcelona. They also serve fresh salads desserts and ice creams. The sophisticated interior of the restaurant is designed by Cesc Pons, and al the stores have a spectacular mural designed by the famous international artist, Jordi Labanda

**Opening hours: Sun-Wed 9:30am-1am, Thurs-Sat 9:30am-2:30am. Kitchen open all day.
Sandwich&Friends locations:**

CITY CENTRE
Rambla Catalunya 5
Tel. 93 342 73 76

RAVAL
C/Hospital 102-104
Tel. 93 329 82 77

BORN
Passeig del Born 27
Tel. 93 310 07 86

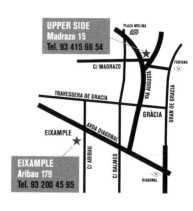

UPPER SIDE
Madrazo 15
Tel. 93 415 66 54

EIXAMPLE
Aribau 179
Tel. 93 200 45 95

www.sandwichandfriends.com

★ Mam i Teca

C/Lluna 4 (93 441 33 35). Metro Sant Antoni.
Open 1-4pm; 8.45pm-midnight Mon, Wed-Fri,
Sun; 8.45pm-midnight Sat. Closed 2wks Aug.
Credit AmEx, MC, V. **Map** p342 E10 ❸ **Catalan**
A bright little tapas restaurant with only three
tables, so it pays to reserve. All the usual tapas, from
anchovies to cured meats, are rigorously sourced,
and complemented by superb daily specials such as
organic *botifarra*, pork confit and asparagus with
shrimp. The bar (which is also open afternoons) is
worth mentioning for a superior vodka and tonic.

Organic

C/Junta de Comerç 11 (93 301 09 02/www.
antoniaorganickitchen.com). Metro Liceu. **Open**
12.30pm-midnight daily. **Main courses** €11. **Set
lunch** €10 Mon-Fri; €14 Sat, Sun. **Credit** AmEx,
DC, MC, V. **Map** p345 A5 ❷ **Vegetarian**
The last word in refectory chic, Organic is better
designed and lighter in spirit ('Don't panic, it's
organic!') than the majority of the city's vegetarian
spots. The friendly staff will usher you inside and
give you a rundown on options; an all-you-can-eat
salad bar, a combined salad bar and main course,
or the fully whammy – salad, soup, main course
and dessert. Beware the extras, drinks and so on,
which can hitch up the prices considerably.
Other locations Organic Take Away, C/Xuclà 15
(93 318 49 30); Organic Tapas Santa Rita, C/Hospital
45 (93 302 21 73).

€ Pla dels Àngels

C/Ferlandina 23 (93 329 40 47). Metro
Universitat. **Open** 1.30-4pm, 9-11.30pm
daily. **Main courses** €6.50. **Set lunch** €6.40
Mon-Fri. **Credit** DC, MC, V. **Map** p342 F9 ❺
Mediterranean
Appropriately, given its position opposite MACBA,
Pla dels Àngels is a riot of colour and chimera, something that also translates to its menu. The range of
salads on offer might include mango, yoghurt and
mint oil, or radicchio, serrano ham and roast peppers,
followed by a short list of pasta and gnocchi and a
couple of meat dishes. The cheap set lunch includes
two courses and a glass of wine. *Photo p164.*
► *For more on the MACBA, see p81.*

Ravalo

Plaça Emili Vendrell 1 (93 442 01 00). Metro Sant
Antoni. **Open** 8pm-1am Tue-Sun. **Main courses**
€9. **Credit** MC, V. **Map** p342 E10 ❻ **Pizza**
Perfect for fans of the thin and the crispy, Ravalo's
table-dwarfing pizzas take some beating, thanks to
flour (and a chef) imported from Naples. Most of the
pizzas come with the cornerstone toppings you'd
expect in any pizzeria; less familiar offerings include
the Pizza Soufflé, which comes filled with ham,
mushrooms and an eggy mousse (better than it
sounds, really). The restaurant's terrace overlooking a quiet square is open year-round.

Sésamo

C/Sant Antoni Abat 52 (93 441 64 11). Metro
Sant Antoni. **Open** 1-3.30pm, 8.30-11.30pm Mon,
Wed-Sat; 8.30-11.30pm Sun. **Main courses** €11.
Set lunch €9.50 Mon-Fri; €11 Sat. Closed Aug.
Credit MC, V. **Map** p342 E10 ❼ **Vegetarian**
Sésamo's head cook recently took up the reins of
management, and revamped the menu a little: the
front room now offers meaty Argentinan fare.
However, despite the change, the back space continues to concentrate on excellent vegetarian cooking. Sésamo has never taken itself too seriously,
and has always offered an interesting and creative
bunch of dishes – crunchy polenta with baked
pumpkin, gorgonzola and radicchio; spicy curry
with dahl and wild rice and a selection of Japanese
tapas – in a buzzing atmosphere.

Silenus

C/Àngels 8 (93 302 26 80). Metro Liceu. **Open**
1.30-4pm, 8.30-11.30pm Mon-Thur; 1.30-4pm,
8.30pm-midnight Fri, Sat. **Main courses** €16.50.
Set lunch €15 Mon-Sat. **Credit** AmEx, DC, MC,
V. **Map** p344 A3 ❽ **Mediterranean**
Named after one of the drunken followers of
Dionysus, Silenus is nonetheless all about restraint.
Its quiet dining room has an air of scuffed elegance,
with carefully chipped and stained walls whereon
the ghost of a clock is projected and the faded leaves
of a book float up on high. The food, too, is artistically presented. It's not especially cheap, but the set
lunch is generally a good bet, offering dishes from
Caesar salad to crunchy gnocchi with creamed
spinach or spicy *botifarra* with puréed potatoes.

La Verònica

C/Rambla de Raval 2-4 (93 329 33 03). Metro
Liceu. **Open** *Sept-July* 7pm-midnight Mon-Thur;
7pm-1am Fri; 1pm-1am Sat; noon-midnight Sun.
Aug 7pm-midnight daily. **Main courses** €11.
Credit MC, V. **Map** 342 E10 ❾ **Pizza**
La Verònica's shortcomings (its huge popularity with
young foreigners, the minuscule spacing between
tables) are all but hidden by night, when candles add
a cosy glow to the red, orange and yellow paintwork.
Its pizzas are crisp, thin and healthy, and come with
such toppings as smoked salmon, or apple, gorgonzola and mozzarella. Salads include the Nabocondensor,
a colourful tumble of parsnip, cucumber and apple,
and there is a short, reliable wine list.
► *Head across the road to the Café de les Delícies
(see p189) for a post-dinner drink.*

INSIDE TRACK
KEEP THE CUTLERY

In all but the smartest restaurants, don't
be surprised if you're asked to hang on to
the same cutlery for different courses.

CONSUME

Pla dels Àngels. See p163.

Barceloneta & the Ports

Agua
*Passeig Marítim 30 (93 225 12 72/www.agua
deltragaluz.com). Metro Barceloneta/bus 45, 57,
59, 157.* **Open** 1-3.45pm, 8-11.30pm Mon-Thur,
Sun; 1-4.30pm, 8pm-12.30am Fri, Sat. **Main
courses** €15. **Credit** AmEx, DC, MC, V. **Map**
p343 J13 **⑩ Mediterranean**
Agua's main draw is its large terrace overlooking the
beach, but the relaxed dining room is usually
buzzing. The menu rarely changes, but regulars
never tire of the competently executed monkfish tail
with *sofregit*, the risotto with partridge, and fresh
pasta with juicy prawns. Scrummy puddings include
marron glacé mousse and sour apple sorbet. Book
ahead, especially during summer and at weekends.

Bestial
*C/Ramón Trias Fargas 2-4 (93 224 04
07/www.grupotragaluz.com). Metro Barceloneta.*
Open 1-4pm, 8-11.30pm daily. **Main courses**
€16.50. **Set lunch** €18.50 Mon-Fri. **Credit**
AmEx, DC, MC, V. **Map** p343 K13 **⑪ Italian**
A peerless spot for alfresco seaside dining, with
tiered wooden decking and ancient olive trees.
Bestial's dining room is also a stylish affair, with
black-clad waiters sashaying along sleek runways,
their trays held high. The food is modern Italian:
dainty mini-pizzas, rocket salad with parma ham and
a lightly poached egg, tuna with black olive risotto

and all the puddings you'd hope to find – panna cotta,
tiramisu and limoncello sorbet. At weekends, a DJ
takes to the decks, and drinks are served until 2am.

★ Can Majó
*C/Almirall Aixada 23 (93 221 54 55). Metro
Barceloneta.* **Open** 1-4pm, 8-11.30pm Tue-Sat;
1-4pm Sun. **Main courses** €21. **Credit** AmEx,
MC, V. **Map** p343 H13 **㊷ Seafood**
Famous for its fresh-from-the-nets selection of oysters, scallops, Galician clams, whelks and just about
any other mollusc you care to mention. While the
menu reads much as you'd expect for a Barceloneta
seafood restaurant, with plates of shellfish or (exemplary) fish soup to start, followed by rich paellas and
exquisitely tasty *fideuà*, the quality is a cut above
the norm. Sit inside the dapper green and yellow dining room, or within the periwinkle blue picket fence,
overlooking the sea.

Can Ramonet
*C/Maquinista 17 (93 319 30 64). Metro
Barceloneta.* **Open** noon-midnight daily. Closed
2wks Jan. **Main courses** €20. **Credit** AmEx,
DC, MC, V. **Map** p343 H12 **㊸ Seafood**
Tucked away in the *barrio* of Barceloneta, this
quaint, rose-coloured space with two quiet terraces
is mostly overlooked by tourists, and consequently,
it suffers none of the drop in standards of some of
those paella joints on the seafront. Spectacular displays of fresh seafood show what's on offer that day,
but it's also worth sampling the velvety fish soup
and the generous paellas.
Other locations C/Carbonell 5 (93 268 33 13).

Can Solé
*C/Sant Carles 4 (93 221 50 12/www.cansole.
cat). Metro Barceloneta.* **Open** 1.30-4pm, 8-11pm
Tue-Sat; 1.30-4pm Sun. Closed 2wks Aug.
Main courses €20. **Credit** AmEx, DC, MC, V.
Map p342 H13 **㊹ Seafood**
Portly, jovial waiters have been charming moneyed
regulars for over a hundred years at Can Solé. Over
time, many of these diners have added to the framed
photos, sketches and paintings that line the sky-blue
walls. What continues to lure them is the freshest
shellfish (share a plate of *chipirones* in onion and garlic, Cantabrian anchovies or red shrimp to start) and
fillets of wild turbot, lobster stews and sticky paellas. Beware the steeply priced extras (coffee, cover).

★ Kaiku
*Plaça del Mar 1 (93 221 90 82). Metro
Barceloneta.* **Open** 1-3.30pm Tue-Sun. Closed
3wks Aug & 1wk Dec. **Main courses** €11.
Set lunch €10 Tue-Fri. **Credit** MC, V. **Map**
p342 G13 **㊺ Seafood**
With its simple look, missable façade and paper
tablecloths, Kaiku looks a world apart from the
upmarket seafood restaurants that pepper this *barrio*, but its dishes are in fact sophisticated takes on

CONSUME

the seaside classics. At Kaiku a salad starter comes with shavings of foie gras or red fruit vinaigrette, and paella is given a rich and earthy spin with wild mushrooms. Book ahead, particularly for a terrace table looking out across the beach.

Set Portes

Passeig Isabel II 14 (93 319 30 33/www.7 portes.com). Metro Barceloneta. **Open** 1pm-1am daily. **Main courses** €18. **Credit** AmEx, DC, MC, V. **Map** p345 E7  **Seafood**

The eponymous seven doors open on to as many dining salons, all kitted out in elegant 19th-century decor. Long-aproned waiters bring regional dishes, served in enormous portions, including a stewy fish *zarzuela* with half a lobster, a different paella daily (shellfish, for example, or rabbit and snails), and a wide array of fresh seafood or heavier dishes such as herbed black-bean stew with pork sausage, and *orujo* sorbet to finish. Reservations are available only for certain tables; without one, get there early or expect a long wait outside.

El Suquet de l'Almirall

Passeig Joan de Borbó 65 (93 221 62 33). Metro Barceloneta. **Open** 1-4pm, 8.30-11pm Tue-Sat; 1-4pm Sun. Closed 2wks Aug. **Main courses** €20. **Credit** MC, V. **Map** p342 G13 **Seafood**

One of the famous beachfront *xiringuitos* that was moved and refurbished in time for the 1992 Olympics, El Suquet remains a friendly family-run concern despite the smart decor and mid-scale business lunchers. The fishy favourites range from *xató* salad to *arròs negre* and include a variety of set menus, such as the 'blind' selection of tapas, a gargantuan taster menu and, most popular, the *pica-pica*, which includes roast red peppers with anchovies, a bowl of steamed cockles and clams, and a heap of *fideuà* with lobster.

Montjuïc & Poble Sec

La Bella Napoli

C/Margarit 12 (93 442 50 56). Metro Paral·lel. **Open** 8.30pm-midnight Tue; 1.30-3.45pm, 8.30pm-midnight Wed-Sun. **Main courses** €12. **Credit** DC, MC, V. **Map** p341 D10 **Italian**

La Bella Napoli's welcoming Neapolitan waiters can talk you through the long, long list of antipasti and pasta dishes, while you can't go wrong with the crispy baked pizzas – such as the Sofia Loren, complete with provolone, basil, bresaola, cherry tomatoes, rocket and parmesan. Beer is Moretti, the wine list all-Italian; in fact the only thing lacking authenticity is the catalogue of pre-made ice-cream desserts. There is own-made tiramisu, but you have to ask. *Photo p168.*

La Font del Gat

Passeig Santa Madrona 28 (93 289 04 04). Funicular Parc Montjuïc/bus 55. **Open** 1-4pm

Kaiku.

Tue-Sun. Closed 3 wks Aug. **Main courses** €17. **Set lunch** €11.50 Tue-Fri. **Credit** MC, V. **Map** p341 B11 **Catalan**

La Font del Gat is a welcome watering hole high on Montjuïc between the Miró and ethnological museums. The small, informal-looking restaurant has a surprisingly sophisticated menu: ravioli with truffles and wild mushrooms, for example, or foie gras with Modena caramel. However, most come for the set lunch: start with scrambled egg with Catalan sausage and peppers or a salad, follow it with baked cod or chicken with pine nuts and basil, and finish with fruit or a simple dessert. Tables outside have a surcharge.

▶ *For more on the Fundació Joan Miró, see p95.*

€ La Soleá

Plaça del Sortidor 14 (93 441 01 24). Metro Poble Sec. **Open** noon-midnight Tue-Sat; noon-4.30pm Sun. **Main courses** €9. **Set lunch** €7. **No credit cards. Map** p341 D11 **Global**

An unassuming but jolly neighbourhood joint, with a sunny terrace on the Plaça del Sortidor. There's barely a continent that isn't represented on the menu, which holds houmous, tabouleh and goat's-cheese salad plus juicy burgers served with roquefort or mushrooms, smoky tandoori chicken, Mexican tacos, vegetable samosas and slabs of Argentine beef. Between 4pm and 8.30pm, the kitchen is officially closed, but simple platters of cold hams, cheeses and so on are served.

CONSUME

★ Tapioles 53

C/Tapioles 53 (93 329 22 38/www.tapioles 53.com). Metro Paral·lel or Poble Sec. **Open** 9-11pm Tue-Sat. Closed Aug. **Set dinner** €38 or €58. **Credit** MC, V. **Map** p341 D11 **51 Mediterranean**

Tucked down a residential Poble Sec street, behind a doorbell and slatted blinds, Tapioles is both elegant and homely, with accomplished but unpretentious food. It changes daily but has included gnocchi with goat's cheese and sage butter; boeuf bourguignon; fresh pasta with baby broad beans and artichokes; rose-water rice pudding with pomegranate, or ginger and mascarpone cheesecake. The freshest produce is bought every day, and cooked according to demand, so booking is obligatory.

Eixample

Alkimia

C/Indústria 79 (93 207 61 15). Metro Joanic or Sagrada Família. **Open** 1.30-3.30pm, 8.30-11pm Mon-Fri. Closed 3wks Aug. **Main courses** €29.50. **Credit** DC, MC, V. **Map** p339 J6 **52 Catalan**

Even before Alkimia was awarded its Michelin star it was notoriously tricky to get a table. Chef Jordi Vilà is hugely respected, and turns out complex dishes that play with Spanish classics – for instance, liquid *pa amb tomàquet* with *fuet* sausage, wild rice with crayfish and strips of tuna on a bed of foamed mustard. There is also an enviably stocked wine cellar. What is lacking, however, is a great deal of warmth in either the minimalist dining room or from the occasionally tight-lipped waiting staff.

Casa Calvet

C/Casp 48 (93 412 40 12). Metro Urquinaona. **Open** 1-3.30pm, 8.30-11pm Mon-Sat. Closed 2wks Aug. **Main courses** €28.50. **Credit** AmEx, DC, MC, V. **Map** p344 E1 **53 Catalan**

Casa Calvet allows the time-strapped visitor to sample some excellent cooking and appreciate the master of Modernisme at the same time. One of Gaudí's more understated buildings from the outside, Casa Calvet has an interior full of glorious detail in the carpentry, stained glass and tiles. The food is up to par, with surprising combinations almost always hitting the mark: sole with pistachio sauce and sautéed aubergine; scallops with black olive tapenade with wild mushroom croquettes, and roast beef with apple sauce and truffled potatoes. The puddings are superb – try goat's cheese cream with pistachio and beetroot ice-cream.

▶ *Learn more about the life and work of Antoni Gaudí on pp50-53.*

★ Cinc Sentits

C/Aribau 58 (93 323 94 90/www.cincsentits. com). Metro Passeig de Gràcia or Universitat. **Open** 1.30-3.30pm Mon; 1.30-3.30pm, 8.30-11.15pm Tue-Sat. Closed 2wks Aug. **Main courses** €22.50. **Set lunch** €29-€59 Tue-Fri. **Credit** AmEx, MC, V. **Map** p338 F7 **54 Catalan**

Talented chef Jordi Artal shows respect for the classics (flat *coca* bread with foie gras and crispy leeks, duck magret with apple), while adding a personal touch in dishes such as a Palamós prawn in *ajoblanco* (garlic soup) with cherries and an ice-cream made from their stones. To finish, save room for the artisanal Catalan cheeses or the 'false egg' with white chocolate around a passionfruit yolk. Thus far overlooked by the Michelin men, this is one of the more affordable of the city's top-end dining destinations.

Fast Good

C/Balmes 127 (93 452 23 74/www.fast-good.com). Metro Diagonal/FGC Provença. **Open** 12.30pm-midnight daily. Closed Aug. **Main courses** €6. **Credit** AmEx, DC, MC, V. **Map** p337 F7 **55 Fast food**

Ferran Adrià's take on a fast-food restaurant is for people of taste in a hurry. There are great-quality burgers (garnished with mint and tarragon, say, or roquefort, rocket and sundried tomato), along with panini, various ethnic takes on roast chicken and a sublime fry-up – eggs with *jamón ibérico* and chips fried in olive oil. There's a good range of salads, while fresh fruit juices and yoghurt shakes are more in evidence than Diet Coke. Eat in or take away.

▶ *For more on Adrià, see pp176-177.*

Gresca

C/Provença 230 (93 451 61 93/www.gresca.net). Metro Diagonal/ FGC Provença. **Open** 1.30-3.30pm, 8.30-10.30pm Mon-Fri; 8.30-10.30pm Sat. Closed 2wks Aug. **Credit** MC, V. **Map** p338 F7 **56 Modern European**

A potentially great new restaurant let down by a dining room rendered clamorous by a steel floor. The lighting, too, is a bit spotty and unforgiving, but sympathetic, if harried, service and excellent food go some way towards smoothing what, with luck, are teething troubles. There is a classy wine list, sensibly organised by style, but the real highlights are dishes such as foamed egg on a bed of jamón ibérico, fennel and courgette, or puddings like the *coca* bread with roquefort and lychee and apple sorbet. One to watch. *Photo p172.*

Hanoi II

Avda Sarrià 37 (93 444 10 99). Metro Hospital Clínic. **Open** 12.30-4pm, 7.30pm-midnight Mon-Sat; 12.30-4pm Sun. **Main courses** €12. **Credit** AmEx, MC, V. **Map** p338 D5 **57 Vietnamese**

This little sister of the frenetic and slightly kitsch original branch of Hanoi on C/Enric Granados is a muted version, with low lighting, teak chairs, elevator music and prints of Miró paintings. It's also considerably easier to get a table, even at weekends. The Vietnamese menu is the same, however, with duck or prawn *nem* rolls, chicken *musi* (chopped with

CONSUME

La Bella Napoli. *See p165.*

water chestnuts and pine nuts, and which you then roll up in lettuce leaves) and beef *chempy* (with orange peel and vegetables, fried with honey).

Manairó

C/Diputació 424 (93 231 00 57/www. manairo.com). Metro Monumental. **Open** 1.30-4pm, 8.30-11pm Mon-Sat. **Main courses** €21. **Credit** AmEx, MC, V. **Map** p339 K8 ⑤ **Catalan**

If you're curious to try some of the more extreme experiences in postmodern haute cuisine (we're talking tripe and brains rather than the latest flights of fancy from the Blumenthal school), Manairó is the place to start. Its divine tasting menu takes in small portions of Catalan specialities such as *cap i pota* (a stew of calves' head and feet) and langoustine with botifarra sausage and cod tripe, and renders them so delicately that the most squeamish diner will be seduced. Other star turns include a 'false' anchovy – actually a long strip of marinated tuna dotted prettily with pearls of red vermouth.

Moo

C/Rosselló 265 (93 445 40 00/www.hotelomm.es). Metro Diagonal. **Open** 1.30-3.45pm, 8.30-10.45pm Mon-Sat. Closed Aug. **Main courses** (half portions) €18.50. **Set lunch** €45. **Set dinner** €70-€100. **Credit** AmEx, DC, MC, V. **Map** p338 G6 ⑤ **Catalan**

The tables at Moo are as desirable as the rooms in its parent, Hotel Omm. Inventive cooking, overlooked by the celebrated Roca brothers, is designed as half portions, the better to experience the full range, from sea bass with lemongrass to exquisite suckling pig with a sharp Granny Smith purée. Particular wines (from a list of 500) are suggested to go with every course, and many dishes are even built around them: finish, for example, with 'Sauternes', the wine's bouquet perfectly rendered in mango ice-cream, saffron custard and grapefruit jelly.

► *For more on the Hotel Omm, see p138. The Rocas also run a restaurant in Girona; see p293.*

Noti

C/Roger de Llúria 35 (93 342 66 73/ www.noti-universal.com). Metro Passeig de Gràcia or Urquinaona. **Open** 1.30-4pm, 8.30pm-midnight Mon-Fri; 8.30pm-midnight Sat. **Main courses** €25. **Set lunch** €23.55 Mon-Fri. **Credit** AmEx, DC, MC, V. **Map** p342 G8 ⑥ **Mediterranean**

Housed in the former offices of *El Noticiero* newspaper, which won awards for their design, Noti pulls in a glamorous selection of the great and the good for its globetrotting range of dishes. Centrally positioned tables surrounded by reflective glass and gold panelling make celebrity-spotting unavoidable, but other reasons for coming here include steak tartare, squid stuffed with pigs' trotters and a good selection of French cheeses.

Paninoteca D'E

C/Rosselló 242 (93 554 38 96/www.elpanino de.com). Metro Diagonal. **Open** *Sept-June* 9am-midnight Mon-Thur; 9am-1am Fri; 1pm-1am Sat; 1pm-midnight Sun. *July* 9am-1am Mon-Fri; 1pm-1am Sat. *Aug* 1-4pm, 8.30pm-12.30am Mon-Sat. **Main courses** €11. **Credit** DC, MC, V. **Map** p338 G6/7 ⑥ **Pizza**

The shtick at top chef Sergi Arola's new 'fast food' restaurant is the 'cocapizza' – a fusion of the Catalan *coca* (a flat, crispy, bread) and a traditional pizza. In

CONSUME

truth, what this amounts to is… well, a pizza. But oh, what a pizza! The toppings are beyond reproach, bringing together the best locally produced goods and the odd delicacy from afar. Along with the familiar options, try the smoked chicken (with egg and green tomatoes) or the roast beef (with mozzarella, gherkins, rocket, tomato and Kalamata oil).

★ Saüc

Ptge Lluís Pellicer 12 (93 321 01 89/www. *saucrestaurant.com). Metro Hospital-Clínic.* **Open** 1.30-3.30pm, 8.30-10.30pm Tue-Sat. Closed 3wks Aug & 1wk Jan. **Main courses** €29.50. **Credit** AmEx, MC, V. **Map** p338 E6 ⑫ **Catalan**

Top-notch but unstuffy, Saüc ('elderberry') is overlooked by the section of international media crazy for 'Spain is the new France' restaurant stories. This may be down to chef Xavier Franco's focus on precise, imaginative cooking, without the tricksy, experimental approach of some of his peers. There's the odd nod to fashion (cherry gazpacho, liquorice in the puddings); but otherwise a rigorous approach to sourcing and tradition is evident in dishes such as terrine of *cap i pota* with chickpea cream, a slow-poached egg and sturgeon caviar from the Vall d'Aran.

INSIDE TRACK
THE WINE LIST

Catalonia is nowadays turning out some excellent wines. Most come from the Penedès DO, but look out, too, for Priorat, Costers del Segre and Montsant.

Toc

C/Girona 59 (93 488 11 48/www.tocbcn.com). *Metro Girona.* **Open** 1.30-3.30pm, 8.30-10.45pm Mon-Fri; 8.30-11.30pm Sat. Closed 2wks Aug. **Main courses** €18.50. **Set lunch** €32. **Credit** AmEx, MC, V. **Map** p343 H8 ⑥ **Catalan**

Minimalist to the point of clinical, Toc nonetheless offers a menu that is all heart and colour. Old Catalan favourites such as *esqueixada* (salt cod salad) and *cap i pota* (calves' head stew) are revived with pzazz alongside squab and truffled pâté or chilled beetroot gazpacho. Look out for the green-tea fruitcake with pears in red wine to finish, and a well-thought-out wine list with some excellent local bottles.

Tragaluz

Ptge de la Concepció 5 (93 487 01 96/www. *grupotragaluz.com). Metro Diagonal.* **Open** *Sept-July* 1.30-4pm, 8.30pm-midnight daily. *Aug* 1.30-4pm, 8.30-midnight Mon-Fri; 8.30pm-midnight Sat. **Main courses** €17. **Set lunch** €24.60 Mon-Fri. **Credit** AmEx, DC, MC, V. **Map** p338 G7 ⑭ **Mediterranean**

The stylish flagship for this extraordinarily successful restaurant group has weathered the city's culinary revolution well and is still covering new ground in Mediterranean creativity. It doesn't come cheap, and the wine mark-up is particularly hard to take, but there's no faulting tuna tataki with a cardamom wafer and a dollop of ratatouille-like pisto; monkfish tail in a sweet tomato sofrito with black olive oil; or juicy braised oxtail with cabbage. Finish your meal with cherry consommé or a thin tart of white-and-dark chocolate.

▶ *For other restaurants in the Tragaluz group, see Agua (p164) and Bestial (p164).*

Situated in the heart of Barcelona in the Ribera neighbourhood, you'll find the restaurant Peps Buffet. Close to the emblematic church Santa Maria del Mar and neighbours with the Picasso Museum on Calle Gruñi number 5.

The architecture of the restaurant dates back to the 17th century, and the decor is in a typical Catalan style with a rustic ambience. You can appreciate the building's original features; the most splendid is an antique well with a spiral staircase that leads down to the bathrooms.

Home-made Catalan cuisine - just like grandma used to make.

CONTEMPORARY PASTRY, CREATIVE FOOD & COCKTAILS

Valencia 227 (Rambla Catalunya - Balmes)
Tel/Fax: 934 875 964
www.dolso.es

Next opening - Dolso Pastry Shop - May 2009
Duc de la Victoria 13 (Gothic)

Namaste

Namaste was the first Indian restaurant to open in Barcelona and is the place to go for fine, rich and authentic Indian cooking. Namaste's secret lies in carefully selected ingredients, which are cooked with great care by professional Indian chefs. It's a real treat to be able to enjoy an authentic Indian meal in an exotically-decorated restaurant, and that's what you get at Namaste. And every Saturday night, the restaurant hosts a show of live Bollywood music and dance.

C/Villarroel 70 (with Diputació) Urgell
Tel. 93 451 4027
C/Entença 137 (with Avda Roma) Entenca/Tarragona
Tel. 93 226 1919
www.restaurantehindunamaste.net
Tues-Sun, 1pm-3.45pm, 8.15pm-11.45pm. Closed Mon

€ Ty-Bihan

Ptge Lluís Pellicer 13 (93 410 90 02).
Metro Hospital Clínic. **Open** 1.30-3.30pm
Mon; 1.30-3.30pm, 8.30-11.30pm Tue-Fri; 8.30-
11.30pm Sat. Closed Aug. **Main courses**
€7.80. **Set lunch** €11.50 Mon-Fri. **Credit**
V. **Map** p338 E6 ⑮ **French**
A small restaurant and centre for all things Breton,
with live music on Wednesday nights. There's a
blend of specialities of the region with Spanish produce in starters such as *andouille* sausage and
membrillo (quince jelly), but from there on it's
French all the way, with a range of sweet and
savoury *galettes* (crêpes made with buckwheat
flour), some scrumptious little blinis (try them
smothered with strawberry jam and cream) or
crêpes suzettes served in a pool of flaming Grand
Marnier. The Petite menu will take care of *les
enfants*, while a bowl or two of Breton cider takes
care of the grown-ups.

La Verema

*C/Comte d'Urgell 88 (93 451 68 91). Metro
Urgell.* **Open** *June-Sept* 1.30-4pm Mon; 1.30-4pm,
8.30-11pm Tue-Thur; 1.30-4pm, 8.30pm-midnight
Fri, Sat. *July, Aug* 1.30-4pm Mon; 1.30-4pm, 8.30-
11pm Tue-Thur; 1.30-4pm, 8.30pm-midnight Fri.
Main courses €11.45 Mon-Fri; €20.35 Sat. **Set
lunch** €10.70. **Credit** AmEx, MC, V. **Map** p342
E8 ⑯ **Mediterranean**
An unexpected little neighbourhood find, La
Verema doesn't look much from the outside, but
takes its food very seriously. Sit up at the bar to
enjoy three oysters and a glass of cava (€7) or nib-
ble on some tapas while tasting some of the superb
wines on its list, or step down into a small dining
room for a great-value *menú del día*. From the
night-time à la carte menu, don't miss – among
other things – the artichoke hearts filled variously
with wild mushrooms and quail's egg, goat's
cheese and anchovy, or Iranian caviar.

★ Windsor

*C/Còrsega 286 (93 415 84 83/www.restaurant
windsor.com). Metro Diagonal.* **Open** 1-4pm,
8.30-11pm Mon-Fri; 8.30-11pm Sat. Closed Aug.
Main courses €25. **Credit** AmEx, DC, MC, V.
Map p337 F6 ⑰ **Catalan**
Let down slightly by a smart but drab dining room,
and a clientele formed, in great part, by English-
speaking business execs, Windsor nevertheless
serves some of the most creative and uplifting food
around. Most dishes riff on the cornerstones of
Catalan cuisine – pigs' trotters stuffed with *cap i
pota*, squab risotto and so on – while others have a
lighter, Mediterranean feel: turbot with orange
risotto and citrus powder, or salt cod with stewed
tomatoes and olives.
▶ *Dry Martini (see p194) is a few minutes' walk
away, and the perfect place for a cocktail before
or after dinner.*

Gràcia

Botafumeiro

*C/Gran de Gràcia 81 (93 218 42 30/www.bota
fumeiro.es). Metro Fontana.* **Open** 1pm-1am
daily. **Main courses** €26. **Credit** AmEx, DC,
MC, V. **Map** p337 G5 ⑱ **Seafood**
The speciality at this vast Galician restaurant is
seafood in every shape and form, served with military precision by a fleet of nautically clad waiters.
The sole cooked in cava with prawns is superb, as
are more humble dishes such as a cabbage and
pork broth typical of the region. The platter of
seafood (for two people) is an excellent introduction to the various molluscs of the Spanish coastline. It can be hard to get a table at peak times, but
the kitchen is open all day. *Photo p175.*

€ Cantina Machito

*C/Torrijos 47 (93 217 34 14). Metro Fontana
or Joanic.* **Open** 1-4pm, 7pm-1.30am daily.
Main courses €10. **Credit** MC, V. **Map**
p341 H5 ⑲ **Mexican**
Every day is Day of the Dead in this cheerily decked
out little Mexican joint, with its tissue paper bunting
and chaotic hubbub. The minuscule writing on the
menu and low lighting make for some guesswork
when placing your order, but the choices are standard enough – quesadillas, tacos, ceviche and enchi-
ladas – with a couple of surprises thrown in for good
measure, such as the tasting platter of insects.
Service can be slow and the kitchen a little heavy-
handed with the sauces, but the portions are huge
and prices reasonable.

Envalira

Plaça del Sol 13 (93 218 58 13). Metro Fontana.
Open 1.30-4pm, 9pm-midnight Tue-Sat; 1.30-5pm
Sun. Closed Aug. **Main courses** €12. **Credit**
MC, V. **Map** p337 G5 ⑳ **Spanish**
Most regions of Spain are represented on the menu
at this profoundly traditional restaurant. There is
a particular emphasis on Galicia (*caldeirada galle-
ga* is a hearty fish stew, *lacón con grelos* is gammon with turnip tops and *tarta de Santiago* is an
almond cake), but the Basque oxtail stew is also
tasty. The dining room could use a lick of paint and

THE BEST
VEGETARIAN EATS

For students
Juicy Jones. *See p161.*

For saving the planet
Organic. *See p163.*

For converting meat-eaters
Sésamo. *See p163.*

CONSUME

Gresca. See p167.

some subtlety in its lighting; arrive early for the more comfortable leather banquettes at the front, and book ahead at weekends.

★ € Himali

C/Milà i Fontanals 68 (93 285 15 68). Metro Joanic. **Open** noon-4pm, 8pm-midnight Tue-Sun. **Main courses** €9. **Set lunch** €8.25. **Credit** AmEx, MC, V. **Map** p341 H6 **71 Nepalese**

A comic metaphor for modern-day Barcelona, Himali moved into what was a local boozer, but has retained the silhouettes of famous Catalans – Dalí and Montserrat Caballé among them – on the windows, while inside there are Nepalese prayer flags and tourist posters of the Himalayas. The alien and impenetrable menu looks a bit daunting, but the waiters are useful with recommendations, or you could start with momo dumplings or Nepalese soup, followed by *mugliaco kukhura* (barbecued butter chicken in creamy tomato sauce) or *khasi masala tarkari* (baked spicy lamb). All dishes include rice and nan bread.

Mesopotamia

C/Verdi 65 (93 237 15 63). Metro Fontana. **Open** 8.30pm-midnight Tue-Sat. Closed 2 wks Dec. **Main courses** €12.75. **Set dinner** €30. **No credit cards. Map** p341 H4 **72 Iraqi**

The policy at Barcelona's only Iraqi restaurant is to have everything on the menu at the same price, so that the cost won't hold anybody back from ordering what they want. The menu is based on Arab 'staff of life' foods, such as yoghurt and rice. Best value is the enormous taster menu, which includes great Lebanese wines, a variety of dips for your *riqaq* bread, bulgur wheat with aromatic roast meats and vegetables, sticky baklava and Arabic teas. Also good are the potato croquettes stuffed with minced meat, almonds and dried fruit.

€ Octubre

C/Julián Romea 18 (93 218 25 18). Metro Diagonal/FGC Gràcia. **Open** 1.30-3.30pm, 9-11pm Mon-Fri; 9-11pm Sat. Closed Aug. **Main courses** €11. **Credit** MC, V. **Map** p338 F5 **73 Catalan**

Time stands still in this quiet little spot, with its quaint old-fashioned decor, swathes of lace and brown table linen. Time often stands still, in fact, between placing an order and receiving any food, but this is all part of Octubre's sleepy charm. Also contributing to its appeal is a roll-call of reasonably priced, mainly Catalan dishes: squid stuffed with meatballs on a bed of *samfaina (see p173)*; pig's trotter with fried cabbage and potato, and cod with a nut crust and pumpkin purée.

Restaurante Hofmann

C/Granada del Penedès 14-16 (93 218 71 65/www.hofmann-bcn.com). FCG Gràcia. **Open** 1.30-3pm, 9-11.15pm Mon-Fri. Closed Aug. **Main courses** €25. **Set lunch** €41.75. **Credit** AmEx, DC, MC, V. **Map** p337 F5 **74 Global**

Recently transplanted here from a space in its associated cookery school in the Born, Hofmann puts its pupils to good use in its top-class kitchens and dining room. The affordable lunch *menú* might start with a truffle salad, followed by bream in bacon or a rack of lamb with mustard sauce, but, as is the case with the à la carte menu, the puddings are really the high point. Artful constructions such as a jam jar and lid made of sugar and filled with red fruit, or a tarte tatin in a spun-sugar 'cage', are as delicious as they are clever.

San Kil

C/Legalitat 22 (93 284 41 79). Metro Fontana or Joanic. **Open** 1-4pm, 8.30pm-midnight Mon-Sat. Closed 2wks Aug. **Main courses** €11. **Credit** MC, V. **Map** p339 J4 **75 Korean**

Catalan Dishes

A primer of local cuisine.

Some dishes apparently from other cuisines – risotto, canelons, ravioli – are entrenched in the Catalan culinary tradition. Two names borrowed from the French are foie (as opposed to *fetge/higado* or foie gras), which has come to mean hare, duck or goose liver micuit with liqueur, salt and sugar; and *coulant*, rather like a small soufflé but melting in the centre.

For a menu glossary, *see pp156-157.*

a la llauna literally 'in the tin' – baked on a metal tray with garlic, tomato, paprika and wine

all i oli garlic crushed with olive oil to form a mayonnaise-like texture, similar to aïoli

amanida catalana/*ensalada catalana* mixed salad with a range of cold meats

arròs negre/*arroz negro* 'black rice', seafood rice cooked in squid ink

botifarra/*butifarra* Catalan sausage. Variants include *botifarra negre* (blood sausage) and *blanca* (mixed with egg)

botifarra amb mongetes/*butifarra con judías* sausage with haricot beans

calçots variety of large spring onion, only available from December to spring, and eaten chargrilled, with *romesco* sauce

carn d'olla traditional Christmas dish of various meats stewed with *escudella*, then served separately

conill amb cargols/*conejo con caracoles* rabbit with snails

crema catalana cold custardy dessert with burned sugar topping, similar to crème brûlée

escalivada grilled and peeled peppers, onions and aubergine

escudella winter stew of meat and vegetables

espinacs a la catalana/*espinacas a la catalana* spinach fried in olive oil with garlic, raisins and pine nuts

esqueixada summer salad of marinated salt cod with onions, olives and tomato

fideuà/*fideuá* paella made with vermicelli instead of rice

mar i muntanya a traditional Catalan combination of meat and seafood, such as lobster and chicken in the same dish

mel i mató curd cheese with honey

pa amb tomàquet/*pan con tomate* bread prepared with tomato, oil and salt

picada mix of nuts, garlic, parsley, bread, chicken liver and little chilli peppers, often used to enrich and thicken dishes

romesco a spicy sauce from the coast south of Barcelona, made with crushed almonds and hazelnuts, tomatoes, oil and a special type of red pepper (*nyora*)

samfaina a mix of onion, garlic, aubergine and red and green peppers (like ratatouille)

sarsuela/*zarzuela* fish and seafood stew

sípia amb mandonguilles/*sepia con albóndigas* cuttlefish with meatballs

suquet de peix/*suquet de pescado* fish and potato soup

torrades/*tostadas* toasted *pa amb tomàquet* (see above)

xató salad containing tuna, anchovies and cod, with a *romesco*-type sauce.

CONSUME

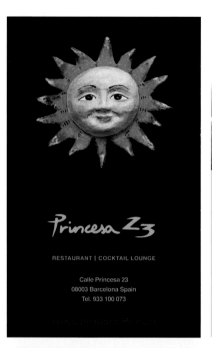

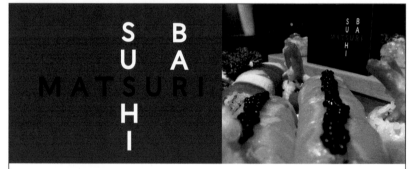

Botafumeiro. See p171.

If you've never eaten Korean food before, it pays to gen up a bit before you head to this bright and spartan restaurant. *Panch'an* is the ideal starter for the beginner in this cuisine: four little dishes containing vegetable appetisers, one of which will be tangy *kimch'i* (fermented cabbage with chilli). Then try mouth-watering *pulgogi* – beef served sizzling at the table and eaten rolled into lettuce leaves – and maybe *pibimbap* – rice with vegetables (and occasionally meat) topped with a fried egg. Finish up with a shot of soju rice wine.

★ Shojiro

C/Ros de Olano 11 (93 415 65 48). Metro Fontana. **Open** 1.30-3.30pm Mon, Tue; 1.30-3.30pm, 9-11.30pm Wed-Sat. Closed Aug. **Set lunch** €18.50 (all incl) Mon-Fri. **Set dinner** €35-€43 (only food). **Credit** MC, V. **Map** p338 G5 ⑰ **Japanese**

A curious but surprisingly successful mix of Catalan and Japanese applies to the decor as much as the food at Shojiro, with original mosaic flooring and dark-green paintwork setting off a clean feng-shuied look. There are only set meals on offer (water, wine, coffee and tax are all included in lunch). So, starting with an amuse-bouche, then might be foie steamed with *umeshu* (plum wine), mackerel cooked with miso and white aubergine, followed by venison with wild mushrooms and black basil. Two puddings are also included in the price.

La Singular

C/Francisco Giner 50 (93 237 50 98). Metro Diagonal or Fontana. **Open** 1.30-4pm, 9pm-midnight Mon-Thur; 1.30-4pm, 9pm-1am Fri;

9pm-1am Sat. Closed last wk Aug & 1st wk Sept. **Main courses** €12. **Set lunch** €10 Mon-Fri. **Credit** MC, V. **Map** p338 G6 ⑰ **Mediterranean**

While this is often described as a lesbian-friendly restaurant, in fact that's the least noteworthy thing about it, and all are made welcome. Most come here for the good-value set lunch (salads and light pasta dishes to start, followed by dishes such as roast beef carpaccio with red cabbage and onion) in snug surroundings of red walls with pale green woodwork and a tiny, leafy patio. It can get noisy when full; it's best to come early and beat the rush. Reservations are necessary for Friday and Saturday nights.

Other districts

Artkuisine

C/Madrazo 137, Sant Gervasi (93 202 31 46/ www.artkuisine.blogspot.com). FGC Sant Gervasi. **Open** *Sept-June* 1.30-3.45pm, 8.30-11.45pm Tue-Sat. *July* 1.30-3.45pm, 8.30-11.45pm Mon-Sat. Closed 3wks Aug. **Main courses** €24. **Set lunch** €20.70-€26 Mon-Fri. **Credit** AmEx, DC, MC, V. **Map** p338 E4 ⑱ **Mediterranean**

Artkuisine's French credentials do not leap out sporting berets and strings of onions. Instead, they make themselves known in other, more subtle ways: the buttermilk Regency furniture, the charming and soigné waiting staff, and the classical approach underpinning the chef's wilder flights of fancy. Who would have thought, for example, that cocoa and banana compôte would complement oxtail stew, or that tonka bean and vanilla ice-cream would work with tarte tatin? The French, apparently.

Profile Ferran Adrià

The pioneer of culinary surrealism.

CONSUME

Widely considered to be the world's greatest chef, Ferran Adrià has seen his restaurant **El Bulli** (*see p179*) win the San Pellegrino Best Restaurant in the World award four times. In his home country, 'Ferran' is such a big star that his surname is used as infrequently as Ronaldinho's, say, or Diana's. Everyone knows his favourite bars and favourite restaurants;

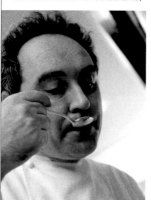

and, most appealingly, everyone has seen him in them. Frequently. For all his super-stardom, lofty gastronomic ideals and worldwide following, Ferran is nothing if not a man of the people.

What Willy Wonka was to chocolate, Adrià is to Catalan cuisine. His most fantastical, playful, irreverent creations fuse science with poetry to create a culinary voyage, taking the diner on a journey by mouthfuls. If that sounds far-fetched, how about a bed of algae foam supporting three tiny heaps: one containing an explosive combination of Thai flavours, the next Japanese and finally a spoonful of Mexico? Or 'Kellogg's paella', where featherlight grains of rice infused with prawn and squid

TRY YOUR LUCK
El Bulli is perpetually booked, but it's worth calling in the morning: there are surprisingly frequent cancellations.

flavours are served in a plastic sachet that is to be ripped open and the contents poured into the mouth?

These are the kind of dishes that propelled Adrià into the international spotlight almost a decade ago, and his ceaseless ingenuity has not let up since. After experimenting with hot jellies, edible clingfilm and paper dotted with flowers, soups that are both hot and cold, exploding ravioli, 'spherification' (extracting the essence of a foodstuff and presenting it in a quivering globule that resembles the original pea, oyster and so on), Adrià is currently on an Asian tip, and El Bulli diners can nowadays expect jellified dashi, nori crisps and sake martinis to feature.

Adrià started working at El Bulli at the tender age of 22, and within a few months had become head chef.

Now, 24 years later, he has three Michelin stars under his belt. Gourmet pilgrims travel from around the world to the remote culinary mecca of El Bulli, several kilometres from Roses up an almost inaccessible dirt track.

Even today, chefs continue to line up to work with the master. The most coveted positions are in Adrià's workshop in the Barri Gòtic, where he spends half the year (when the restaurant itself is closed) inventing new fantasies in foam and leafing through his vast library of recipe books looking for more dishes to deconstruct. There he and his team of alchemists play around with texture, temperature and, above all, smell, creating aerosols that evoke the mustiness of a forest, or perhaps the salty air and seaweed of the coast.

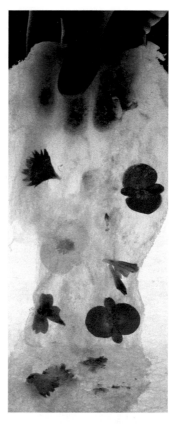

The gastronomic world holds its breath whenever Adrià announces his latest project, but more than a few toques were raised and heads were scratched when he recently declared a foray into the murky and often ugly world of fast food. The result, however, is the hugely successful (if woefully named) **Fast Good** (*see p167*), a stylish chain of restaurants decorated in hot pink and lime that aims to bring gourmet dining to people who are short of time, money or both.

THREE TO VISIT

Can't get into El Bulli? Here's a trio of Ferran's faves to visit instead.

Jamonísimo
Where Ferran takes Heston when he's in town. *See p214.*

Quimet i Quimet
Where he goes for cockles and clams. *See p192.*

Boadas
His favourite spot for an americano (Campari and vermouth). *See p189.*

CONSUME

Can Travi Nou

*C/Jorge Manrique s/n, Parc de la Vall de Hebron,
Horta (93 428 03 01/www.gruptravi.com). Metro
Horta or Montbau.* **Open** 1.30-4pm, 8.30-11pm
Mon-Sat; 1.30-4pm Sun. **Main courses** €16.50.
Credit AmEx, DC, MC, V. **Catalan**
An ancient rambling farmhouse clad in bougainvillea and perched high above the city, Can Travi Nou
offers wonderfully rustic dining rooms with roar-
ing log fires in winter, while in summer the action
moves out to a covered terrace in a bosky, candlelit
garden. The food is hearty, traditional Catalan cuisine though it's a little expensive for what it is, and
suffers from the sheer volume being churned out
of the kitchen. Puddings are better and served with
a *porrón* (a glass jug with a drinking spout) of muscatel. But Can Travi Nou is really all about location, location, location.

Hisop

*Passatge Marimon 9, Sant Gervasi (93 241
32 33/www.hisop.com). Metro Hospital Clínic or
Diagonal.* **Open** 1.30-3.30pm, 8.30-11pm Mon-Fri;
9-11pm Sat. Closed 3wks Aug. **Main courses**
€23. **Set lunch** €26.75. **Credit** AmEx, DC, MC,
V. **Map** p337 E5 ⑦ **Mediterranean**
Run by two young, enthusiastic and talented chefs,
Hisop aims to bring serious dining to the non-
expense-account masses by keeping its prices on
the low side and its service approachable. The €52
tasting menu is a popular choice among diners with
dishes that vary according to the season, but often
includes their rich 'monkfish royale' (served with
its liver, a cocoa-based sauce and tiny pearls of saffron) and a pistachio soufflé with Kaffir lime ice-
cream and rocket 'soup'.

Icho

*C/Deu i Mata 69-95, Les Corts (93 444 33 70/
www.ichobcnjapones.com). Metro Maria Cristina.*
Open 1.30-3.30pm, 9-11.30pm Tue-Sat. Closed
2 wks Aug. **Main courses** €20. **Set lunch** €30
Tue-Fri. **Credit** AmEx, MC, V. **Map** p337 C5 ⑧
Japanese/Spanish
In a coolly designed space under the NH Constanza,
Icho (in Japanese it means gingko tree – of which
three graceful examples sit outside) fuses Japanese
with Spanish cooking. This really shouldn't work,
but in fact it does, beautifully – perhaps because you
can offset the digestive demands of tender suckling
pig and pumpkin pureé with a platter of sushi, or
balance a starter of foie and eel with tuna tartare and
creamed tofu with wasabi. The portions aren't large,
so order several and share them around.

La Parra

*C/Joanot Martorell 3, Sants (93 332 51 34).
Metro Hostafrancs.* **Open** 8.30pm-12.30am Tue-
Fri; 1.30-4.30pm, 8.30pm-12.30am Sat; 1.30-
4.30pm Sun. Closed Aug. **Main courses** €14.50.
Credit MC, V. **Map** p341 B7 ⑧ **Catalan**

A charming converted 19th-century coaching inn
with a shady vine-covered terrace. The open wood
grill sizzles with various parts of goat, pig, rabbit
and cow, as well as a few more off-piste items such
as deer and even foal. Huge, oozing steaks are
slapped on to wooden boards and accompanied by
baked potatoes, calçots, grilled vegetables and *all i
oli*, with jugs of local wines from the giant barrels.

★ Els Pescadors

*Plaça Prim 1, Poblenou (93 225 20 18/www.
elspescadors.com). Metro Poblenou.* **Open** 1-
3.45pm, 8pm-midnight daily. **Main courses**
€25. **Credit** AmEx, DC, MC, V. **Seafood**
In a forgotten, almost rustic square of Poblenou lies
this first-rate fish restaurant, with tables under the
canopy formed by two huge and ancient *ombú* trees.
Suspend your disbelief with the crunchy sardine
skeletons that arrive as an aperitif (trust us, they're
delicious), and move on to tasty fried chipirones, followed by cod and pepper paella or creamy rice with
prawns and smoked cheese. Creative desserts
include the likes of strawberry gelatine 'spaghetti'
in a citric soup. The waiters are masters of their art.

La Venta

*Plaça Doctor Andreu, Tibidabo (93 212 64
55/www.restaurantelaventa.com). FGC Avda
Tibidabo, then Tramvia Blau.* **Open** 1.30-3.15pm,
9-11.15pm Mon-Sat. **Main courses** €15. **Credit**
AmEx, DC, MC, V. **Mediterranean**
La Venta's pretty Moorish-influenced interior plays
second fiddle to the terrace during every season:
shaded by day and uncovered by night in summer,
sealed and warmed with a wood-burning stove in
winter. Of the food, complex starters include lentil
and spider crab salad; sea urchins au gratin (a must);
and langoustine ravioli, filled with leek and foie
mousse. Simpler but high-quality mains run from
rack of lamb to delicate monkfish in filo pastry with
pesto. Friendly service is a bonus.

Out of town

★ El Bulli

Cala Montjoi (972 15 04 57/www.elbulli.com).
Open *Apr-June* 8-10pm Wed-Sat; 1-2.30pm, 8-10pm
Sun. *July-Sept* 7.30-10pm daily. Closed Oct-Mar.
Set dinner €230. **Credit** AmEx, DC, MC, V.
Darling of the Sunday papers, El Bulli is possibly
the most talked-about restaurant in the world today;
thus it merits a mention here, despite its location up
on the Costa Brava. There is only a *degustación*, and
diners must arrive by 8.30pm if they are to finish
the 30 or so courses by midnight. Dinner is an
extraordinary experience, occasionally exalted and
frequently frustrating: diners are cosseted like
guinea pigs, their reactions scanned by the maître
d' and the great Ferran Adrià himself.
▶ *For more information on Adrià,
see pp176-177.*

CONSUME

Cafés, Tapas & Bars

Fearsome coffee, informal eats and some cool, refreshing brews.

'Catalonia is not Spain' is a phrase you'll see emblazoned across walls and T-shirts all over Barcelona, and nowhere is it more true than in the matter of tapas bars. Catalans simply don't share the need to *tapear* – float from place to place with friends, eating a plate of anchovies here, a ramekin of kidneys in sherry there… Many visitors, blissfully unaware, are herded towards shameless tourist traps, in pursuit of a misguided ideal of 'Spanishness'. We advise you to stick to those we mention below.

Bars are another matter entirely, and Catalans have in common with all Spaniards a love of social drinking that supports the highest number of bars per capita in the world. Still, the emphasis is very much on the social: though it's considered perfectly normal to consume alcohol at breakfast, you'll rarely see a local drunk.

WHAT TO ORDER

If you ask for a *caña*, you'll be given a small draught beer; a *jarra* is closer to a pint. Ask for a *cerveza*, and you'll be given a bottle. Damm beer is ubiquitous: Estrella, a strong lager, is the most popular variety, though there's also a stronger lager (Voll Damm) and a dark one (Bock Damm). Moritz beer, also locally brewed and with a slightly fruitier flavour, has recently made a comeback. Shandy (*clara*) is popular, untainted by the stigma it has in the UK.

Among wines, Rioja is well known, but there are many excellent wines from other regions in the north of Spain, such as the Priorat in Catalonia, Navarra or Ribera del Duero. Most wine drunk here is red (*negre/tinto*), but Galicia produces good whites too, including a slightly sparkling and very refreshing wine called *vino turbio*. Of course, Catalonia has its many cavas, running from *semi-sec* (which is 'half-dry', but actually pretty sweet) to *brut nature* (very dry).

Spanish coffee is very strong and generally excellent. The three basic types are *café solo*

(*cafè sol* in Catalan, also known simply as 'café'), a small black coffee equivalent to an espresso; *cortado/tallat* is the same but with a little milk; and *café con leche/cafè amb llet*, the same with more milk. Cappuccino has yet to catch on. Then there's *café americano* (a tall black coffee diluted with more water), and spiked coffee (a *carajillo*, which is a short, black coffee with a liberal dash of brandy). If you want another type of liqueur, you must be specific: *carajillo de ron* (rum), say, or *carajillo de whisky*. A *trifásico* is a *carajillo* with a layer of milk. Decaffeinated coffee (*descafeinado*) is widely available and usually very good, but ask for it *de máquina* (from the machine) unless you want a sachet of Nescafé and a cup of milk.

Tea, on the other hand, is pretty poor. If you can't live without it, ask for cold milk on the side ('*leche fría aparte*') or run the risk of getting a glass of hot milk and a teabag. Basic herbal teas, such as chamomile (*manzanilla*), limeflower (*tila*) and mint (*menta*), are common. Except in busy bars, or when sitting outside, you won't usually be required to pay until you leave. If you have trouble attracting a waiter's attention, a loud but polite '*oiga*' or, in Catalan, '*escolti*' is acceptable. On the vexed question of throwing detritus on the floor (cigarette ends, paper napkins, olive pits and so on), it's safest to keep an eye on what the locals are doing and act accordingly.

❶ Green numbers given in this chapter correspond to the location of each café, bar and tapas bar on the street maps. See pp337-345.

BARRI GOTIC

Cafés

Ácoma

C/Boqueria 21 (93 301 75 97/www.acomacafe. com). Metro Liceu. **Open** 9.30am-12.30am daily. **Credit** AmEx, DC, MC, V. **Map** p345 B5 ❶

A regular enough looking bar from the street, Ácoma is almost unique in the Old City for its sheltered patio at the back. Here there are tables in the shade of an orange tree and the rear of the Santa Maria del Pi church, and a small pond from which bemused fish and turtles can observe singer-songwriters and small groups perform for a young and merry foreign crowd. Salads, burgers, burritos and the like are served from midday to 11.30pm.

★ Café de l'Opera

La Rambla 74 (93 317 75 85). Metro Liceu. **Open** 8am-2.30am Mon-Thur, Sun; 8am-3am Fri, Sat. **Credit** DC, MC, V. **Map** p345 B5 ❷

Cast-iron pillars, etched mirrors and bucolic murals create an air of fading grandeur at Café de l'Opera, which now seems incongruous among the fast-food joints and tawdry souvenir shops on La Rambla. Coffee, hot chocolate, pastries and a handful of tapas are served by attentive bow-tied waiters to a largely tourist clientele, but given the atmosphere (and the opposition), there's no better place for a coffee on the city's most celebrated boulevard.

Caj Chai

C/Sant Domènec del Call 12 (mobile 610 334 712). Metro Jaume I. **Open** 3-10pm daily. **No credit cards. Map** p345 C5 ❸

A cosy tearoom, where first flush Darjeeling is approached with the reverence afforded to a Château d'Yquem. A range of leaves comes with tasting notes describing not only the origins, but giving suggestions for maximum enjoyment – Waternymph (an aromatic Oolong), for example, is apparently the ideal tea for those moments 'when your thoughts have been interrupted'. In summer, iced teas are accompanied by a dollop of sorbet.

La Clandestina

Baixada Viladecols 2 (93 319 05 33). Metro Jaume I. **Open** 10am-10pm Mon-Thur; 10am-midnight Fri; 11am-midnight Sat; 11am-10pm Sun. Closed 1wk Aug. **No credit cards. Map** p345 D6 ❹

What used to be a slightly hippie tearoom in which dreadlocked students would sip masala chai and lassi while reminiscing about their trip to Rajasthan

> Bars more oriented towards late-night socialising and pre-clubbing drinks are listed in Music & Nightlife; *see pp253-267.*

is now a slightly hippie tearoom where young professionals take advantage of free Wi-Fi and ponder the decent art (all for sale). It's still a very relaxed vibe, however, especially when friends are sharing a hookah of apple, peach or strawberry tobacco.

La Granja

C/Banys Nous 4 (93 302 69 75). Metro Liceu. **Open** *June-Sept* 9.30am-1.30pm, 5-9pm Mon-Sat. *Oct-May* 9.30am-1.30pm, 5-9pm Mon-Sat; 5-9pm Sun. Closed Aug. **No credit cards. Map** p345 C5 ❺

La Granja is an old-fashioned café filled with yellowing photos and antiques, which has its very own section of Roman wall. You can stand your spoon in the tarry-thick hot chocolate, which won't be to all tastes; but the *xocolata amb café*, a mocha espresso, or the *xocolata picant*, chocolate with chilli, pack a mid-afternoon energy punch.

★ Milk

C/Gignas 21 (93 268 09 22/www.milkbarcelona. com). Metro Jaume I. **Open** *Aug* 7pm-3am Mon-Fri; 11am-3am Sat, Sun. *Sept-July* 6pm-3am Mon-Fri; 11am-3am Sat, Sun. **Credit** AmEx, DC, MC, V. **Map** p345 D7 6 ❻

Still unchallenged in the Old City in its provision of a decent brunch, Milk's fry-ups, pancakes and smoothies have been extended to Saturday as well as Sunday (until 4pm). Its candlelit, low-key baroque look, charming service and cheap prices make it a good bet at any time, with solid home-made bistro grub from Caesar salad to fish and chips.

Els Quatre Gats

C/Montsió 3 bis (93 302 41 40/www.4gats.com). Metro Catalunya. **Open** 10am-1am daily. **Credit** AmEx, DC, MC, V. **Map** p344 C3 ❼

The essence of fin-de-siècle Barcelona, the 'Four Cats' was designed by Modernista heavyweight Puig i Cadafalch and patronised by the cultural glitterati of the era, most notably Picasso, who hung out here with Modernista painters Santiago Rusiñol and Ramon Casas. These days it's mostly frequented by tourists, but is an essential stop nonetheless.

▶ *For the adjoining restaurant, see p153.*

Schilling

C/Ferran 23 (93 317 67 87). Metro Liceu. **Open** *Sept-July* 10am-3am Mon-Thur; 10am-3am Fri, Sat; noon-2.30am Sun. *Aug* 6.30pm-3am daily. **Credit** AmEx, DC, MC, V. **Map** p345 B5 ❽

Schilling's large windows on to the main thoroughfare connecting La Rambla with the Plaça Sant Jaume were once *the* spot to see and be seen, and although it's lost some of its cachet, it's still undeniably elegant, the high ceilings, bookshelves and traditional air contrasting with the fiercely modern young waiting staff. Weave through to the back for more intimate seating.

La Vinatería del Call. *See p184.*

CONSUME

Tapas

★ Bar Celta

C/Mercè 16 (93 315 00 06). Metro Drassanes.
Open noon-midnight Tue-Sun. **Credit** AmEx,
MC, V. **Map** p345 C7 ➒

Celta's unapologetically '60s interior is fiercely lit,
noisy and not recommended for anyone feeling a
bit rough. It is, however, one of the more authentic
experiences to be had in the Gòtic. A Galician tapas
bar, it specialises in food from the region, such as
lacón con grelos (boiled gammon with turnip tops)
and good seafood, accompanied by crisp Albariño
wine served in traditional white ceramic bowls. A
characterful place.

★ Bar Pinotxo

*La Boqueria 466-467, La Rambla 89 (93
317 17 31). Metro Liceu.* **Open** 6am-5pm
Mon-Sat. Closed 3wks Aug. **No credit cards.**
Map p344 B4 ➓

Just inside the entrance, on the right-hand side, of
the Boqueria, is this essential market bar, run by
Juanito, one of the city's best-loved figures. In the
early morning the place is popular with ravenous
night owls on their way home and, at lunchtime,
foodies in the know. Various tapas are available,
along with excellent daily specials such as tuna
casserole or scrambled eggs with clams.
▶ *The Boqueria is one of Europe's best food
markets; see p211.*

Cervecería Taller de Tapas

*C/Comtal 28 (93 481 62 33/www.taller
detapas.com). Metro Catalunya.* **Open** 9am-
midnight Mon-Thur; 9am-1am Fri, Sat; noon-
midnight Sun. **Credit** AmEx, DC, MC, V.
Map p344 D3 ⓫

Although strictly speaking a tapas bar, with a wide
range and a useful menu in English, the Cervecería
has tried to fill a gap in the market by providing a
reasonable selection of beers from around the world.
The list provides a refreshing alternative to the ubiquitous Estrella, with Argentine Quilmes, Brazilian
Brahma (this one, admittedly, via Luton), Bass Pale
Ale, Leffe and Hoegaarden, among others.
▶ *The same company runs two tapas bars with
tables outside in lively squares (see p185).*

Onofre

*C/Magdalenes 19 (93 317 69 37/www.onofre.
net). Metro Urquinaona.* **Open** 10am-5pm, 8pm-
12.30am Mon-Fri; 1pm-5pm, 8pm-1.30am Sat.
Closed Aug. **Credit** DC, MC, V. **Map** p344 D3 ⓬

It's tiny and not especially well known, but Onofre
has a merited following among local gourmands for
its impeccably sourced wines, cured meats, pâtés,
hams and artisanal cheeses sourced from around the
country. Increasingly, it provides more elaborate
dishes, too, such as a scallop gratin with caramelised
onion, or a pear tatin with melted goat's cheese
and sobrassada sausage. There's a simpler set lunch
menu that costs €9.50.

El Portalón.

CONSUME

El Portalón

C/Banys Nous 20 (93 302 11 87). Metro Liceu.
Open 9am-midnight Mon-Sat. Closed Aug.
Credit MC, V. **Map** p345 C5 ⑬

A rare pocket of authenticity in the increasingly touristy Barri Gòtic, this traditional tapas bar is located in what were once medieval stables, and it doesn't seem to worry too much about inheriting the ancient dust. The tapas list is long, but the *torrades* are also good: toasted bread topped with red peppers and anchovy, cheese, ham or whatever takes your fancy. House wine comes in terracotta jugs.

Taller de Tapas

Plaça Sant Josep Oriol 9 (93 301 80 20/www. tallerdetapas.com). Metro Liceu. **Open** 9am-midnight Mon-Fri; 10am-1am Sat; noon-midnight Sun. **Credit** AmEx, DC, MC, V. **Map** p345 B5 ⑭

At its best, Taller de Tapas is an easy, multilingual environment, with plentiful outdoor seating, in which to try tapas from razor clams to local wild mushrooms. At busy periods, however, the service can be hurried and unhelpful, with dishes prepared

---

INSIDE TRACK
LOCATION, LOCATION

Most bars and cafés charge a supplement for terrace tables. Some also operate a three-tier system depending on whether you're sitting down, standing at the bar, or outside.

---

in haste and orders confused, so it pays to avoid the lunchtime and evening rush hours.
Other locations C/Argenteria 51, Born (93 268 85 59).

★ La Vinateria del Call

C/Sant Domènec del Call 9 (93 302 60 92). Metro Jaume I or Liceu. **Open** 8.30pm-1am Mon-Sat; 8.30pm-midnight Sun. **Credit** AmEx, DC, MC, V. **Map** p345 C5 ⑮

An atmospheric little bar, with a high priority on the sourcing of its wine, hams and cheeses, and excellent home-made dishes, including a delicious fig ice-cream. Despite the antique fittings and dusty bottles, the staff – like the music they play – are young and lively, and some speak English. *Photo p183.*

Bars

Bar Bodega Teo

C/Ataulf 18 (93 315 11 59). Metro Drassanes or Jaume I. **Open** 9am-4pm, 5pm-2am Mon-Thur; 9am-4pm, 5pm-3am Fri, Sat. Closed Aug. **Credit** AmEx, MC, V. **Map** p345 C7 ⑯

Mornings see BBT filling with ancient locals who've been coming to this old *bodega* since 1951 to fill their jugs and bottles with wine from huge oak barrels. Night times are a different proposition altogether, with young foreigners and *barcelonins* sipping pomegranate cosmopolitans amid the changing decor – fairy lights, futuristic insect lamps, a back-lit panel of an expressive mandarin duck – and various extravagant floral displays on the bar.

★ Ginger

C/Palma de Sant Just 1 (93 310 53 09). Metro Jaume I. **Open** 7pm-2.30am Tue-Thur; 7pm-3am Fri, Sat. Closed 3wks Aug. **Credit** MC, V. **Map** p345 D6 ⑰

Ginger manages to be all things to all punters: a swish art deco cocktail bar with comfortable butter-cup yellow banquettes; purveyor of fine tapas and excellent wines, and, above all, a superbly relaxed place to chat and listen to music. Admittedly the foreigner quotient has risen in recent years but it would be short-sighted to dismiss this little gem of Barcelona nightlife for that.

Ice-cream

Gelaaati!

C/Llibreteria 7 (93 310 50 45). Metro Jaume I. **Open** 11am-midnight daily. Closed Jan.
No credit cards. Map p345 C/D5 ⑱

One of the more recent *gelateries*, Gelaaati! has built up a loyal following quickly, and with good reason. All its flavours are made on the premises every day, using natural ingredients – no colourings, no preservatives. Especially good are the hazelnut, pistachio and raspberry ice-creams; unusual flavours include soya bean, celery, and avocado.

BORN & SANT PERE

Cafés

Bar del Convent

Plaça de l'Acadèmia (no phone). Metro Arc de Triomf or Jaume I. **Open** 9am-10pm Mon-Thur; 10am-midnight Fri, Sat. **No credit cards. Map** p345 F5
The 14th-century Convent de Sant Agustí has had a new lease of life in recent years – first with James Turrell's fabulous 'light sculpture' surrounding the C/Comerç entrance, then with the opening of a dynamic civic centre, and now this secluded little café has opened in the cloister. There are croissants, pastries and light dishes available all day, and live music, DJs, storytellers and other performances on Friday and Saturday nights.

La Báscula

C/Flassaders 30 (93 319 98 66). Metro Jaume I. **Open** 7pm-midnight Wed-Fri; 1pm-midnight Sat. **No credit cards. Map** p345 E6
After a sustained campaign the threat of demolition has been lifted from this former chocolate factory turned café. Just as well, since it's a real find, with good vegetarian food and a large dining room situated out back. An impressive list of drinks runs from chai to Glühwein, taking in cocktails, milkshakes, smoothies and iced tea, and the pasta and cakes are as good as you'll find anywhere.

Drac Café

Parc de la Ciutadella, Passeig Lluís Companys entrance (93 310 76 06/www.draccafe.com). Metro Arc de Triomf. **Open** 9am-9pm Tue-Sun. **No credit cards. Map** p343 H10
With this alfresco terrace café the Parc de la Ciutadella finally has a healthy alternative to the *kioskos* serving overpriced beer and bags of rainbow popcorn. Not much more than a *kiosko* itself, the friendly 'Dragon Café' serves breakfast all day, along with salads, nachos, guacamole and houmus, served tapas-style. To guard against the perils of outdoor eating, the tables are warmed by gas heaters in winter and cooled with 'vaporisers' in summer.

★ Rococó

C/Gombau 5-7 (93 269 16 58). Metro Jaume I. **Open** *Sept-July* 9am-midnight Mon-Thur; 9am-1am Fri, Sat. *Aug* 10am-midnight Mon-Thur; 10am-1am Fri; 6pm-1am Sat. Closed 2wks Aug. **Credit** MC, V. **Map** p344 E4
On the ground floor of a nondescript block, Rococó manages to live up to its name thanks to red velvet seating, flock wallpaper and gilt-edged paintings. A wildly varied menu takes in a range of delicious *bocadillos* on home-made ciabatta, gnocchi with wild mushroom sauce, Vietnamese rice-paper rolls and apple crumble. It's one of the few oases left for smokers – there's a bit of a fug at busy times.

Tèxtil Cafè

C/Montcada 12 (93 268 25 98/www.textilcafe. com). Metro Jaume I. **Open** *Nov-Feb* 10am-8pm Tue, Wed; 10am-midnight Thur- Sun. *Mar-Oct* 10am-midnight Tue-Thur, Sun; 10am-1am Fri, Sat. **Credit** MC, V. **Map** p345 E6
The Textile Museum has moved up to the Museu de les Arts Aplicades in Pedralbes (*see p136*), but the café is to stay in the graceful 14th-century courtyard of what has become the Barcelona Design Centre. It's a good place for breakfast or lunch, and, for a €5 supplement, has a DJ on Wednesday nights and live jazz on Sundays.

Tapas

El Bitxo

C/Verdaguer i Callís 9 (93 268 17 08). Metro Urquinaona. **Open** 7pm-midnight Mon; 1pm-midnight Tue-Thur; 1pm-1am Fri, Sat. **No credit cards. Map** p344 D3
A small, lively tapas bar specialising in excellent cheese and charcuterie from the small Catalan village of Oix, along with more outré fare such as salmon sashimi with a coffee reduction. The wine list is steadily increasing and now has around 30 suggestions, all of them good. Being so close to the Palau de la Música, the bar can get packed in the early evening before concerts.

★ Euskal Etxea

Placeta Montcada 1-3 (93 310 21 85). Metro Barceloneta or Jaume I. **Open** *Bar* 7pm-midnight Mon; noon-5pm, 7pm-midnight Tue-Sat.

Mudanzas. *See p187.*

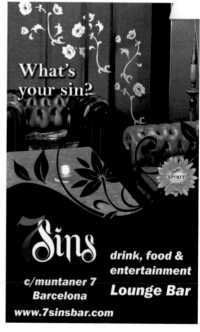

Counting Platelets

Good things come on cocktail sticks in many Barcelona hangouts.

The custom of giving a free tapa, or just a saucer of crisps or olives, is almost unheard of in Catalonia, and hopping from bar to bar is not as popular as it is in other regions, but what has caught on big-time in Barcelona are pintxo bars. A *pintxo* consists of some ingenious culinary combination on a small slice of bread – platters of them are generally brought out at particular times, often around 1pm and again at 8pm. *Pintxos* come impaled with toothpicks, which you keep on your plate, so that the barman can tally them at the end. The Brits and other tourists hold the worst reputation for abusing this eminently civilised system by 'forgetting' to hand over all their toothpicks.

Without a decent grasp of the language, tapas bars can be quite intimidating unless you know exactly what you want. Don't be afraid to seek guidance, but some of the more standard offerings will include tortilla (potato omelette), *patatas bravas* (fried potatoes in a spicy red sauce and garlic mayonnaise), *ensaladilla* (Russian salad), *pinchos morunos* (small pork skewers), *champiñones al ajillo* (mushrooms fried in garlic), *gambas al ajillo* (prawns and garlic), *mejillones a la marinera* (mussels cooked in a tomato and onion sauce), *chocos* (squid fried in batter), *almejas al vapor* (steamed clams with garlic and parsley), *pulpo* (octopus) and *pimientos del padrón* (little green peppers, one or two of which will kick like a mule).

Restaurant 8.30-11.30pm Mon; 1.30-4pm, 8.30-11.30pm Tue-Sat. Closed 1wk Dec-Jan. **Credit** AmEx, MC, V. **Map** p345 E6 ㉕
A Basque cultural centre and the best of the city's many *pintxo* bars. Help yourself to dainty *jamón serrano* croissants, chicken tempura with saffron mayonnaise, melted *provolone* with mango and crispy ham, or a mini-brochette of pork, but hang on to the toothpicks spearing each one: they'll be counted up and charged for at the end.

Bars

Casa Paco

C/Allada-Vermell 10 (no phone/www.casapaco. org). Metro Arc de Triomf or Jaume I. **Open** *Apr-Sept* 9am-2am Mon-Thur, Sun; 9am-3am Fri, Sat; *Oct-Mar* 6pm-2am Tue-Thur, Sun; 6pm-3am Fri, Sat. **No credit cards. Map** p345 E6 ㉖
Not much more than a hole-in-the-wall with a handful of zinc tables outside, Casa Paco is the improbable nerve centre for a young and thrusting scene that attracts DJs from the higher echelons of cool. Daytime, mind you, it's just a nice place for parents to sit on the terrace and have a cheeky beer while the children amuse themselves in the playground just in front.

Gimlet

C/Rec 24 (93 310 10 27). Metro Barceloneta or Jaume I. **Open** 10pm-3am daily. **No credit cards. Map** p345 F6 ㉗
On quiet nights this discreet little wood-panelled cocktail bar, its long mahogany counter burnished by the same well-clad elbows for years, has something of an Edward Hopper feel. Friday and Saturday nights are an altogether different proposition, however, and you'll need to make yourself noticed to get a drink from the unsmiling bar staff. Popular with a slightly older crowd.

Mudanzas

C/Vidrieria 15 (93 319 11 37/www.mudanzas. barceloca.com). Metro Barceloneta or Jaume I. **Open** *Sept-July* 10am-2.30am Mon-Thur, Sun; 10am-3am Fri, Sat. *Aug* 5.30pm-2.30am Mon-Thur, Sun; 5.30pm-3am Fri, Sat. **Credit** MC, V. **Map** p345 E6 ㉘
Eternally popular with all ages and nationalities, Mudanzas has a beguiling, old-fashioned look, with marble-topped tables, a black-and-white chequered floor and a rack of newspapers and magazines, many of them in English. Be warned: it can get very smoky in the winter months, though relief can be found at the tables on the mezzanine. *Photo p185.*

Bar Seco. *See p192.*

La Vinya del Senyor

Plaça Santa Maria 5 (93 310 33 79). Metro Barceloneta or Jaume I. **Open** noon-1am Mon-Thur; noon-2am Fri, Sat; noon-midnight Sun. **Credit** AmEx, DC, MC, V. **Map** p345 E7
Though many pull up a chair simply to appreciate the splendours of Santa Maria del Mar's Gothic façade, it's a crime to take up the tables of the 'Wine of the Lord' without sampling a few of the excellent vintages on its list, along with some top-quality cheeses, hams and other tapas.

El Xampanyet

C/Montcada 22 (93 319 70 03). Metro Jaume I. **Open** noon-4pm, 7-11.30pm Tue-Sat; noon-4pm Sun. Closed Aug. **Credit** MC, V. **Map** p345 E6 ③⓪
The eponymous bubbly is actually a pretty low-grade cava, if truth be told, but a drinkable enough accompaniment to the house tapa; a saucer of Cantabrian anchovies. Lined with coloured tiles, barrels and antique curios, the bar chiefly functions as a little slice of Barcelona history, and has been in the hands of the same family since the 1930s.

RAVAL

Cafés

Baraka

C/Valldonzella 25 (93 304 10 61). Metro Universitat. **Open** 2-11pm Tue-Fri; 5-11pm Sat. Closed Aug. **Credit** MC, V. **Map** p342 F9 ③①
At the back of a beautiful old building converted into a health-food shop is this cosy little bar, where everything from the wine and beer to the milk used in the fair-trade coffee, is organic and cheap – not a common combination. Should anything ail you, the amiable staff will make up an appropriate medicinal tea from the shop's stock of more than 100 herbs.

Bar Kasparo

Plaça Vicenç Martorell 4 (93 302 20 72). Metro Catalunya. **Open** *May-Aug* 9am-midnight Tue-Sat. *Sept-Apr* 9am-10pm Tue-Sat. Closed mid Dec-mid Jan. **No credit cards**. **Map** p344 B2 ③②
Still the best of the various café terraces now sitting on the edges of the quiet, traffic-free Plaça Vicenç Martorell, Kasparo serves tapas, *bocadillos*, salads and a varying selection of more substantial dishes, available all day. There is no indoor seating, so this is more of a warm weather proposition.

Bar Mendizábal

C/Junta de Comerç 2 (no phone). Metro Liceu. **Open** 10am-midnight daily. **No credit cards**. **Map** p344 A4 ③③
Considered something of a classic, Bar Mendizábal has been around for decades, its multicoloured tiles and serving hatch a feature in thousands of holiday snaps. Really it's little more than a hole in the wall, whence juices, sandwiches and soup are ordered, and carried to tables on the other side of the road.

Buenas Migas

Plaça Bonsuccés 6 (93 318 37 08). Metro Liceu. **Open** *June-Sept* 10am-midnight Mon-Thur, Sun; 10am-1am Fri, Sat. *Oct-May* 10am-11pm Mon-Thur, Sun; 10am-midnight Fri, Sat. **Credit** MC, V. **Map** p344 B3 ③④
A doggedly wholesome place, all red gingham and pine and chewy spinach tart. The speciality is tasty focaccia with various toppings, along with the usual

A favourite with traders from the vintage clothing shops on the pedestrianised C/Riera Baixa, Resolis blends a trad look and run-of-the-mill tapas (tortilla, Manchego cheese, prawns) with an immaculate selection of vinyl and some fanciful foodstuffs (ceviche with oriental sauce). In the summer months, its serving hatch to the alley alongside is thronged.

Els Tres Tombs

Ronda Sant Antoni 2 (93 443 41 11). Metro Sant Antoni. **Open** 6am-2am daily. **No credit cards. Map** p342 E10 ③⑧

Not, perhaps, the most inspired tapas bar in town, with its overcooked *patatas bravas*, sweaty Manchego and vile loos, but Els Tres Tombs is still a long-time favourite for its pavement terrace and proximity to the Sunday morning book market. The *tres tombs* in question are nothing more ghoulish than the 'three turns' of the area performed by a procession of men on horseback during the Festa dels Tres Tombs in January (*see p231*).

Bars

Bar Lobo

C/Pintor Fortuny 3 (93 481 53 46/www.grupo tragaluz.com). Metro Catalunya. **Open** 9am-midnight Mon-Wed, Sun; 9am-3am Thur-Sat. **Credit** MC, V. **Map** p344 B3 ③⑨

The watchword is moody (not least among the waiting staff) in this stark, monochrome space, with punky artwork from celebrated graffiti artists. It comes alive with DJs and studied lounging on the mezzanine at night, however, and by day its terrace is a peaceful, sunny space for coffee or breakfast.

★ Boadas

C/Tallers 1 (93 318 95 92). Metro Catalunya. **Open** *Sept-June* noon-2am Mon-Thur; noon-3am Fri, Sat. *July, Aug* noon-3pm, 6pm-2am Mon-Thur; noon-3pm, 6pm-3am Fri, Sat. **No credit cards. Map** p344 B3 ④⓪

Set up in 1933 by Miguel Boadas, born to Catalan parents in Havana (where he became the first barman at the legendary La Floridita), this classic cocktail bar has changed little since Hemingway used to come here. In a move to deter the hordes of rubbernecking tourists, they have instituted a dress code.

Cafè de les Delicies

Rambla del Raval 47 (93 441 57 14). Metro Liceu. **Open** 10am-2am Mon, Tue, Thur, Sun; 10am-3am Fri, Sat. Closed 3wks Aug. **No credit cards. Map** p342 E10 ④①

After an overhaul in the kitchen, the delightful Cafè de les Delicies is now serving breakfast, along with tapas and light dishes in its dining room at the back. Off the corridor there's a snug with armchairs, but otherwise the buzzing front bar is the place to be, with its theatre-set mezzanine, '70s jukebox, shelves of books and reams of club flyers.

high-fibre, low-fun cakes you expect to find in a vegetarian café. Its terrace sprawls across the wide pavement and continues across the street. **Other locations** Baixada de Santa Clara 2, off Plaça del Rei, Barri Gòtic (93 319 13 80).

★ Granja M Viader

C/Xuclà 4-6 (93 318 34 86/www.granja viader.cat). Metro Liceu. **Open** 5-8.45pm Mon; 9am-1.45pm, 5-8.45pm Tue-Sat. Closed Aug. **Credit** AmEx, MC, V. **Map** p344 B3 ③⑤

The chocolate milk drink Cacaolat was invented in this old *granja* in 1931, and it is still on offer, along with strawberry and banana milkshakes, *orxata* (tiger nut milk) and hot chocolate. It's an evocative, charming place with century-old fittings and enamel adverts, but the waiters refuse to be hurried.

El Jardí

C/Hospital 56 (93 329 15 50). Metro Liceu. **Open** 10am-11pm Mon-Fri; 10am-midnight Sat. **Credit** MC, V. **Map** p344 A4 ③⑥

The courtyard of the Gothic Antic Hospital is a tranquil, tree-lined spot a million miles from the hustle of C/Hospital. Terrace café El Jardí actually has two separate bars – go to the lesser known, further from the entrance, for more chance of a table. Breakfast pastries and all the usual tapas are present and correct, along with pasta dishes, quiches and salads.

Tapas

Resolis

C/Riera Baixa 22 (93 441 29 48). Metro Liceu. **Open** 1pm-2am Mon-Thur; 1pm-2.30am Fri, Sat. **Credit** MC, V. **Map** p342 E10 ③⑦

CONSUME

CONSUME

★ Las Guindas

C/Sant Pau 126 (mobile 670 437 709).
Metro Paral·lel. **Open** 7pm-2.30am Mon-Thur,
Sun; 7pm-3am Fri, Sat. **No credit cards**.
Map p342 E11 ㊷
Las Guindas is a long narrow bar with a crimson-
hued retro look, deeply funky mural and DJs fighting for turntable space to show off their acquisitions
of vinyl from the '50s to the '70s. Monday night is
rockabilly night, but the rest of the week you're as
likely to hear northern soul or boogaloo. For all this,
Las Guindas is refreshingly attitude free.

London Bar

C/Nou de la Rambla 34 (93 318 52 61).
Metro Liceu. **Open** *Aug* 10.30am-3am daily.
Sept-July 8am-3am daily. **Credit** AmEx, MC,
V. **Map** p345 A6 ㊸
Since it had its live music licence revoked, this
beloved classic, smoky old bar has had to rely on the
pool table or the occasional football match to enter-
tain its patrons. The TV screen is hidden at the back,
however, and easily avoided; there are plenty of
other things to feast your eyes on, from the period
posters to the graceful swirls of the nicotine-stained
turn-of-the-century woodwork.

★ Marsella

C/Sant Pau 65 (93 442 72 63). Metro Liceu.
Open 10pm-2.30am Mon-Thur; 10pm-3am Fri,
Sat. **No credit cards**. **Map** p342 E/F11 ㊹
Opened in 1820 by a native of Marseilles, who may
just have changed the course of Barcelona's artistic
history by introducing absinthe, still a mainstay of
the bar's delights. Untapped 100-year-old bottles of
the stuff sit in glass cabinets alongside old mirrors
and William Morris curtains, probably covered in
the same dust kicked up by Picasso and Gaudí.

★ The Quiet Man

*C/Marqués de Barberà 11 (93 412 12 19). Metro
Liceu.* **Open** 6pm-2am Mon-Thur, Sun; 6pm-3am
Fri, Sat. **Credit** MC, V. **Map** p345 A6 ㊺
One of the first and best of the city's many Oirish
pubs, the Quiet Man's a peaceful place with wooden
floors and stalls that mostly eschews the beautiful
game for occasional poetry readings and pool tournaments. There is Guinness (properly poured) and
Murphy's, and you're just as likely to see Catalans
as you are to see homesick expats or tourists.

BARCELONETA & THE PORTS

Cafés

La Miranda del Museu

*Plaça Pau Vila 3 (93 221 17 47). Metro
Barceloneta.* **Open** 10am-7pm Tue; 10am-8pm
Wed; 10am-7pm, 9-11pm Thur-Sat; 10am-5pm
Sun. **Credit** MC, V. **Map** p345 E8 ㊻

There's no need to buy a ticket to the Museu
d'Història de Catalunya to make the most of this little-known rooftop museum café with fabulous
views. The set lunches don't break any ground gas-
tronomically, but are reasonable enough, or you can
take coffee and a croissant to its vast terrace and
watch the boats bobbing in the harbour.
▶ *The statue rising from the skyline in the*
direction of Montjuïc is the Virgin de la Mercè,
atop the church named after her; see p61.

Tapas

Bar Colombo

C/Escar 4 (93 225 02 00). Metro Barceloneta.
Open noon-3am daily. Closed 2wks Jan-Feb.
No credit cards. **Map** p342 G13 ㊼
Deck-shod yachties and monied locals stroll by all
day, oblivious to this unassuming little bar and its
sunny terrace overlooking the port. In fact, nobody
seems to notice it; odd, given its fantastic location
and generous portions of *patatas bravas*. The only
drawback is the nerve-jangling techno that occasionally fetches up on the stereo.
▶ *If the food on offer seems a bit greasy, sneak*
in a topped focaccia from the branch of Buenas
Migas (see p188) on the corner of Passeig Joan
de Borbó opposite.

★ La Cova Fumada

C/Baluard 56 (93 221 40 61). Metro Barceloneta.
Open 9am-3pm Mon-Wed; 9am-3pm, 6-8.15pm
Thur, Fri; 9am-1pm Sat. Closed Aug. **No credit
cards**. **Map** p343 H13 ㊽
An authentic family-run *bodega*, hugely popular
with local workers, where you'll need to arrive early
for a cramped and possibly shared table. Said to be
the birthplace of the spicy potato *bomba*, La Cova
Fumada also turns out a great tomato and onion
salad, delicious chickpeas with *morcilla* (black pudding) and unbeatable marinated sardines.

El Vaso de Oro

C/Balboa 6 (93 319 30 98). Metro Barceloneta.
Open 9am-midnight daily. Closed Sept.
No credit cards. **Map** p343 H12 ㊾
The enormous popularity of this long, narrow cruise
ship style bar tells you everything you need to know
about the tapas, but it also means that he who hes-
itates is lost when it comes to ordering. Elbow out a
space and demand, loudly, *chorizitos, patatas bravas,*
solomillo (cubed steak) or *atún* (tuna, which here
comes spicy). The beer (its storage, handling and
pouring) is also a point of great pride.

Bars

The loud, tacky bars lining the Port Olímpic
draw a mixture of drunken stag parties staring
at the go-go girls and curious locals staring at
the drunken stag parties.

Tapaç24.

Taking on the Tapa

Barcelona's avant-garde chefs return to basics.

CONSUME

Carles Abellan caused quite a ripple in the city's dining scene a few years with the opening of übercool **Comerç 24** (*see p155*). Frequently described by a fawning international press as an 'avant-garde tapas restaurant', in fact it serves *platillos*, small dishes of which the diner can order several. These are inspired by Abellan's time spent in the kitchens of El Bulli, training under experimental chef Ferran Adrià, and bear little resemblance to the tortilla and fried squid that constitute most people's experience of tapas.

Which is not to say that he doesn't approve of these old favourites; in fact, with his latest venture he has become their unlikely standard bearer. **Tapaç24** (*see p194*) is an old-school bar, serving traditional tapas of excellent quality. Among the oxtail stews, fried prawns and cod croquettes, however, his fans will also find playful snacks more in keeping with his previous style. The McFoie Burger is an exercise in fast-food heaven, as is the Bikini – a small version of his signature take on the ham and cheese toastie, only this one comes with truffle.

The times they are a-changin', and Abellan is not the only El Bulli alumnus to be attempting a revival of trad tapas in the city. Brother (and pastry chef) to Ferran Adrià, Albert, opened **Inopia** (*see p194*) a couple of years ago, and it's been rammed ever since. As with Tapaç24, the emphasis has been on a revival of old techniques and recipes, using the best ingredients. Inopia's stark, overlit look and awkwardly L-shaped room, along with a determinedly straightforward approach was initially a disappointment for those expecting El Bulli-style culinary fireworks, but has since won over its public with a slavish devotion to finding the best-quality produce and meticulous care in its preparation.

Bar Mut.

★ Can Paixano

*C/Reina Cristina 7 (93 310 08 39/www.can
paixano.com). Metro Barceloneta.* **Open** 9am-
10.30pm Mon-Sat. Closed 3wks Aug-Sept.
No credit cards. Map p345 E8 ⑤⓪
The 'Champagne Bar' as it's invariably known, has
a huge following among young Catalans and legion-
foreigners who think they discovered it first. It can
be impossible to talk, get your order heard or move
your elbows, and yet it's always mobbed for its age-
old look and atmosphere, dirt-cheap bottles of house
cava and (literally) obligatory sausage butties.

MONTJUIC & POBLE SEC

Cafés

Bar Seco

*Passeig Montjuïc 74 (93 329 63 74). Metro
Paral·lel.* **Open** 9am-1am Tue-Thur; 9am-2.30am
Fri, Sat. Closed 2wks Aug. **No credit cards.**
Map p341 D11 ⑤①
The 'Dry Bar' is, in fact, anything but, and its ethi-
cally friendly choices range from local beers and
organic wines to fair-trade Brazilian *cachaça*.
Opened in late 2006 and despite a quiet location, it
has already gathered a following for the quality of
its Italian-Spanish vegetarian dishes and tapas, its
fresh milkshakes and a heavenly home-made chocolate and almond cake. Those who run it are keen
advocates of the Slow Food Movement. *Photo p188.*

Tapas

★ Quimet i Quimet

*C/Poeta Cabanyes 25 (93 442 31 42). Metro
Paral·lel.* **Open** noon-4pm, 7-10.30pm Mon-Fri;
noon-4pm Sat. Closed Aug. **Credit** MC, V.
Map p341 D11 ⑤②
Packed to the rafters with dusty bottles of wine, this
classic but minuscule bar makes up for in tapas
what it lacks in space. The specialities are *conservas* (shellfish preserved in tins), which aren't always
to non-Spanish tastes, but the *montaditos*, sculpted
tapas served on bread, are spectacular. Try salmon
sashimi with cream cheese, honey and soy, or cod,
passata and black olive pâté. Get there early for any
chance of a surface on which to put your drink.

Rosal 34

*C/Roser 34 (93 324 90 46/www.rosal34.com).
Metro Paral·lel.* **Open** *July* 8pm-midnight Mon;
1.30-4pm, 8pm-midnight Tue-Sat. *Aug* 1.30-4pm,
8pm-midnight Tue-Sat. *Sept-June* 1.30-4pm, 8pm-
midnight Tue-Sat; 1.30-4pm Sun. **Credit** MC, V.
Map p342 D11 ⑤③
A bright, upmarket tapas restaurant, where some
excellent dishes come at a price. Tuna tartare with
mustard, salmon roe and lamb's lettuce is tasty, as
is the foie micuit with fig jam, though a langoustine
tail coated in crushed peanuts and served with a
Parmesan cream leaves the overall mouth-feel of a
1970s party snack. Order conservatively.

Bars

★ La Caseta del Migdia

Mirador del Migdia, Passeig del Migdia (mobile 617 956 572). Bus 55 or funicular, then 10min walk. Follow signs to Mirador de Montjuïc. **Open** *June-Sept* 8pm-2.30am Thur-Sat; noon-1am Sun. *Oct-May* noon-7pm Sat, Sun. **No credit cards.** **Map** p341 A12 ❸

Completely alfresco, high up in a clearing among the pines, this is a magical space, scattered with deckchairs, hammocks and candlelit tables. DJs spinning funk, rare groove and lounge alternate surreally with a faltering string quartet; food is pizza and other munchies. To find it, follow the Camí del Mar footpath south around the castle, and be aware it's a lot cooler up here than in town.

Tinta Roja

C/Creu dels Molers 17 (93 443 32 43/www. tintaroja.net). Metro Poble Sec. **Open** *Bar* 8.30pm-2am Thur; 8pm-3am Fri, Sat; 7pm-1am Sun. Closed 2wks Aug. **Admission** *Bar* free. **No credit cards. Map** p341 D10 ❺

This smooth and mysterious bar was once a dairy farm, but these days it is an atmospheric spot for a late drink. Push through the depths of the bar to be transported to a Buenos Aires bordello/theatre/circus/cabaret by plush red velvet sofas, smoochy niches and an ancient ticket booth.

EIXAMPLE

Cafés

Bauma

C/Roger de Llúria 124 (93 459 05 66). Metro Diagonal. **Open** 8am-midnight Mon-Fri, Sun. Closed 3wks Aug. **Credit** AmEx, DC, MC, V. **Map** p338 G6 ❺

An old-style café-bar that's good for lazy Sunday mornings, with its battered leather seats, ceiling fans and shady tables outside, although staff can sometimes be less than friendly. There's a decent list of bocadillos and tapas, along with well-priced, substantial dishes such as baked cod and wild boar stew served from the adjoining restaurant.

Café del Centre

C/Girona 69 (93 488 11 01). Metro Girona. **Open** 8am-11.30pm Mon-Fri. Closed Aug. **Credit** MC, V. **Map** p343 H8 ❺

Possibly the only café of its type left in the Eixample, with a delightfully dusty air, Modernista wooden banquettes, walls stained with the nicotine of ages and marble tables sitting on a chipped chequered floor that almost certainly dates back to the bar's opening in 1873. It's still in the hands of the same family, whose youngest members' attempts to instigate change don't seem to have progressed much beyond a list of fruit teas.

Dolso

C/València 227 (93 487 59 64). Metro Passeig de Gràcia. **Open** 1pm-12.30am Mon-Sat. **Credit** AmEx, DC, MC, V. **Map** p338 F7 ❺

Heaven on earth for the sweet of tooth, Dolso is a 'pudding café', where even the fabulously on-trend retro baroque wallpaper is chocolate-coloured. Desserts run from light (a gin and tonic rendered in clear jelly, lemon sorbet, candied peel and juniper berries) to wickedly indulgent (chocolate fondant with sherry reduction and passion fruit sorbet). A short range of sandwiches and topped ciabatta keeps the spoilsports happy.

Tapas

★ Bar Mut

C/Pau Claris 192 (93 217 43 38). Metro Diagonal. **Open** 9am-midnight Mon-Fri; 11.30am-midnight Sat, Sun. **Credit** AmEx, DC, MC, V. **Map** p338 G6 ❺

Bar Mut has an ineffably Gallic feel, with its etched glass, bronze fittings, *chanteuses* on the sound system, and Paris prices. The tapas are undeniably superior, however: try everything from a carpaccio of scallops and sea urchin to fried eggs with foie. Come early in the morning for breakfast dishes such as haricot beans with wild mushrooms and *morcilla* or poached egg with chips and chorizo sauce. In a word? *Formidable.*

► *The same owner also operates Re-Pla (see p160), which promises to bring a similar idea to the Old City.*

La Bodegueta

Rambla de Catalunya 100 (93 215 48 94). Metro Diagonal. **Open** *Sept-July* 8am-2am Mon-Sat; 6.30pm-1am Sun. *Aug* 7pm-1am daily. **No credit cards. Map** p338 G7 ❻

This delightful old *bodega*, with a pretty tiled floor, is unreconstructed, dusty and welcoming, supplying students, businessmen and pretty much everyone in between with reasonably priced wine, vermouth on tap and prime-quality tapas. The emphasis is placed on locally sourced products (try Montserrat tomatoes with tuna), among old favourites such as *patatas bravas*. Expect smoking and shouting aplenty.

Cervesería Catalana

C/Mallorca 236 (93 216 03 68). Metro Passeig de Gràcia. **Open** 8am-1.30am Mon-Fri; 9am-1.30am Sat, Sun. **Credit** AmEx, DC, MC, V. **Map** p338 F7 ❻

The 'Catalan Beerhouse' lives up to its name with a winning selection of brews from around the world, but the real reason to come is the tapas. A vast array is yours for the pointing; only hot *montaditos*, such as bacon, cheese and dates, have to be ordered from the kitchen. Arrive early for a seat at the bar, and even earlier for a pavement table.

**THE BEST
TERRACES**

To watch the sunset
La Caseta del Migdia. *See p193.*

For letting kids off the leash
Bar Kasparo. *See p188.*

To listen to music
Ácoma. *See p182.*

To take in the view
La Miranda del Museu. *See p190.*

Inopia

C/Tamarit 104 (93 424 52 31/www.bar inopia.com). Metro Poble Sec. **Open** 7-11pm Mon-Fri; 1-3.30pm, 7-11pm Sat. Closed Aug. **Credit** MC, V. **Map** p341 D9 ⑫
See p191 **Taking on the Tapa**.

★ Tapaç24

C/Diputació 269 (93 488 09 77/www.carles abellan.com). Metro Passeig de Gràcia. **Open** 9am-midnight Mon-Sat. **Credit** AmEx, DC, MC, V. **Map** p342 G8 ⑬
See p191 **Taking on the Tapa**.

Bars

★ Dry Martini

C/Aribau 162-166 (93 217 50 72). FGC Provença. **Open** *Sept-July* 1pm-2.30am Mon-Thur; 1pm-3am Fri; 6.30pm-3am Sat; 6pm-2.30am Sun. *Aug* 6.30pm-2.30am Mon-Thur, Sun; 6.30pm-3am Fri, Sat. **Credit** AmEx, DC, MC, V. **Map** p338 F6 ⑭
A shrine to the famous cocktail, which is honoured in Martini-related artwork and served in a hundred forms. All the trappings of a trad cocktail bar are here (bow-tied staff, leather banquettes, drinking antiques and wooden cabinets displaying a century's worth of bottles) but there's a notable lack of stuffiness: the musical selection owes more to trip hop than middle-aged crowd-pleasers, and the barmen welcome all comers.

Xix Bar

C/Rocafort 19 (93 423 43 14/www.xixbar.com). Metro Poble Sec. **Open** 6.30pm-1.30am Mon-Thur; 6.30pm-3am Fri, Sat. **Credit** MC, V. **Map** p341 C/D9 ⑮
Xix (pronounced 'chicks', and a play on the street number, among other things) is a newish, unconventional cocktail bar in the candlelit surroundings of a prettily tiled former *granja* (milk bar). It's dead cosy and just a little bit scruffy, which makes the list of 20 brands of gin all the more unexpected.

Ice-cream

★ Cremeria Toscana

C/Muntaner 161 (93 539 38 25). Metro Hospital Clínic, FGC Provença. **Open** *Apr-Oct* 1pm-midnight Tue-Sun. *Nov-Mar* 1pm-9pm Tue-Sun. **No credit cards.** **Map** p338 E6 ⑯
In this charming little ice-cream parlour, with its antique-strewn mezzanine, around 20 authentically Italian flavours are made daily, ranging from zingy mandarin to impossibly creamy coconut. '*I dopocena*' ('after dinner') are miniature gourmet sundaes, mixing – among others – parmesan and pear flavours; mascarpone and tiramisu; chocolate and pistachio, or liquorice and mint.
Other locations C/Canvis Vells 2, Born (93 268 07 29).

GRACIA

Cafés

Bo

Plaça Rius i Taulet 11 (93 368 35 29). Metro Diagonal or Fontana. **Open** 10am-1am Mon-Thur; 10am-2.30am Fri-Sun. **Credit** MC, V. **Map** p338 G5 ⑰
It claims to serve the best *patatas bravas* in Barcelona, but really we love Bo for its terrace on one of Gràcia's most lively and emblematic squares. Its reasonably original sandwiches, little terracotta dishes of *gambas al ajillo* or octopus, and the generously portioned tapas are also a boon.
▶ *If Bo's tables are full, try those of Amelie in the adjoining space.*

Flash Flash

C/Granada del Penedès 25 (93 237 09 90). FGC Gràcia. **Open** 1.30pm-1.30am daily. **Credit** AmEx, DC, MC, V. **Map** p338 F5 ⑱
Opened back in 1970, this bar was a design sensation in its day, with its white leatherette banquettes and walls imprinted with silhouettes of a life-size frolicking, Twiggy-like model. They describe it as a *tortilleria*, with 60 or so tortilla variations available, alongside a list of child-friendly dishes and adult-friendly cocktails.

La Nena

C/Ramón y Cajal 36 (93 285 14 76). Metro Fontana or Joanic. **Open** *Oct-July* 9am-10pm daily. *Aug, Sept* 9am-2pm, 4-10pm daily. Closed 3wks Aug. **No credit cards.** **Map** p339 H5 ⑲
With whitewashed stone walls, piles of books and games, and a gaily painted table-and-chair set for children, La Nena is wonderfully cosy, or would be if the staff would only lighten up. The speciality is sugar and spice and all things nice; waffles, crêpes, hot chocolate, fresh juices and ice-cream. Savoury delights include sandwiches and toasted bread with various toppings. Note there is no alcohol.

Tapas

Bodega Manolo
C/Torrent de les Flors 101 (93 284 43 77).
Metro Joanic. **Open** 10am-5.30pm Tue, Wed;
10am-5.30pm, 9-11pm Thur, Fri; noon-5.30pm,
9-11pm Sat; noon-3pm Sun. Closed Aug. **No**
credit cards. Map p339 H4 ⑩
A smoky but likeable old family *bodega* with a
faded, peeling charm, barrels on the wall and rows
of dusty bottles. Manolo specialises not only in reasonably priced wine, but in easy food: try the foie
gras with port and apple, or a fresh anchovy salad
with Greek yoghurt and tomato confit. Push through
the bar to the dining room at the back.

★ Sureny
Plaça de la Revolució 17 (93 213 75 56). Metro
Fontana or Joanic. **Open** 8.30pm-midnight Tue-
Thur, Sun; 8.30pm-1am Fri, Sat. Closed 2 wks
Apr, 2 wks Dec. **Credit** MC, V. **Map** p339 H5 ⑪
A well-kept gastronomic secret, Sureny boasts
superb gourmet tapas and waiters who know what
they're about. In addition to the usual run-of-the-mill
tortilla 'n' calamares fare, look out for dishes such
as tuna marinated in ginger and soy sauce, partridge, venison and other game when in season, and
a sublime duck foie with redcurrant sauce.
▶ *To round off an evening of tapas with some*
spectacular ice-cream, cross the square to the
Gelateria Caffetteria Italiana (see below).

Bars

Noise i Art
C/Topazi 26 (93 217 50 01). Metro Fontana.
Open 6pm-2.30am Tue-Thur, Sun; 7pm-3am Fri,
Sat. Closed 2wks end Aug, 1st wk Sept. **Credit**
AmEx, MC, V. **Map** p338 H4 ⑫
Colourful, pop art decor coupled with a chilled and
convivial atmosphere makes this the perfect bar to
sit and shoot the breeze. It's occasionally livened up
with a flamenco session, and all the usual Gràcia
food staples, such as houmous and tabbouleh, are
served. We could live without the Madonna and
Depeche Mode videos looping on a giant screen, but
the large spirit measures do help.

Ice-cream

★ Gelateria Caffetteria Italiana
Plaça Revolució 2 (93 210 23 39). Metro Fontana
or Joanic. **Open** 5pm-12.30am daily. Closed *mid*
Dec-mid Jan. **No credit cards. Map** p339 H5 ⑬
Run by an Italian mother and daughter, the
Caffetteria Italiana is famous for its own-recipe dark
chocolate ice-cream – of which it runs out every
night. The freshly made, additive-free flavours
include fig, strawberry, peach: basically, whatever
fruit happens to be in season. Prepare to queue on
balmy summer evenings.

OTHER DISTRICTS

Cafés

Café Berlin
C/Muntaner 240-242, Sant Gervasi (93 200 65
42). Metro Diagonal. **Open** *Sept-July* 10am-2am
Mon-Wed; 10am-3am Thur-Sat. *Aug* 6pm-2am
Mon-Wed; 7pm-3am Thur-Sat. **Credit** MC, V.
Map p338 E5 ⑭
Downstairs in the basement, the low sofas fill up
with amorous couples, while upstairs everything is
sleek and light, with brushed steel, dark leather and
a Klimt-like mural. A rack of newspapers and plentiful sunlight make Berlin popular for coffee or
snacks all day; as well as tapas, there are also pasta
dishes, *bocadillos* and cheesecake, but be aware of
the 20% surcharge for pavement tables.

★ Fragments Café
Plaça de la Concòrdia 12, Les Corts (93 419 96
13/www.fragmentscafe.com). Metro Les Corts or
Maria Cristina. **Open** 10am-1am Tue, Wed, Sun;
10am-3am Thur-Sat. Closed 2wks Aug. **Credit**
MC, V. **Map** p337 B4/5 ⑮
A superb new tapas bar, with a smart, classy look
in the one remaining pocket of charm left in the
neighbourhood of Les Corts. Sit on the tables in the
square or the bar's own garden at the back (candlelit
at night), and order some *vermut* (which here is on
tap) and *gildas* (anchovies with chilli) before you so
much as begin to peruse the menu. Later there are
scrambled eggs with foie, juicy steaks, home-made
pasta and cherry crumble to finish.

Tapas

L'Esquinica
Passeig Fabra i Puig 296, Horta (93 358 25
19). Metro Virrei Amat or Vilapicina. **Open**
8am-midnight Tue-Sat; 8am-4pm Sun. Closed
last 2wks Aug. **No credit cards.**
Think of it not as a trek, but as a quest; queues outside are testament to the great value of the tapas. On
especially busy nights you'll be asked to take a number, supermarket-style. Waiters will advise first-
timers to start with *chocos* (creamy squid rings),
patatas bravas with *all i oli*, llonganissa sausage and
tigres (stuffed mussels). After which the world is
your oyster, cockle or clam.

Quimet d'Horta
Plaça Eivissa 10, Horta (93 358 19 16). Metro
Horta. **Open** 9am-midnight Mon, Tue-Sun.
Closed Aug. **Credit** AmEx, MC, V.
Sadly, Juanito the house parrot has gone to the great
perch in the sky (though his image remains on
the menu), but the same regulars have been coming
to Quimet for decades, to chew the fat over a beer in
the sunshine. Ciabatta sandwiches are a speciality
and come with every filling imaginable.

CONSUME

Shops & Services

From mainstream malls to backstreet boutiques.

The centre of Barcelona is so crammed with retail outlets that it can feel like one enormous open-air department store. Such is the city's wholehearted dedication to commerce that, a couple of Christmases back, the Ajuntament stopped beating about the bush and decorated the streets not with reindeers or shiny baubles but with strings of red plastic shopping bags. The city is a shopper's delight, packed with stores both big and small: there's a reason why one of the city's many promotional slogans is '*Barcelona, la millor botiga del món*' ('Barcelona, the best shop in the world').

SHOPPING PRACTICALITIES

As with most other major cities, the call of the mall grows ever stronger. However, although the credit crunch has picked off many small start-ups, there are still plenty of alternatives. Barcelona is known for its old specialist shops – there's nowhere better to browse for just the right kind of pork sausage or votive candle.

One-off street fashion is another strong suit in Barcelona. A walk around the Born, Raval and Gràcia reveals an ever-changing line-up of local designers selling from hole-in-the-wall shops. More off-grid options include the recent arrival of 'pop-up shops', or 'guerrilla shops' as they're known here. These include everything from tiny set-ups in private flats – such as **El Vestidor** (C/Portaferrissa 25, Barri Gòtic, open 11am-8pm Sat, Sun) which shows clothes by 12 emerging local designers – to the annual architect-designed installation **Fashion Pop-Up**, held every May at Maremàgnum centre *(see p198)* with more established names such as Txell Miras and El Delgado Buil.

Most shops don't open until 10am and then close for lunch from 2pm; after lunch, they're usually open from 5pm until about 8pm. Many small shops also close on Saturday afternoons and all day on Monday.

The rate of sales tax (IVA) depends on the type of product: it's currently seven per cent on food and 16 per cent on most other items. In any of the 700 or so shops that display a Tax-Free Shopping sticker on their door, non-EU residents can request a Tax-Free Cheque on purchases of more than €90.16 (call Tax-Free Shopping, 902 435 482, for further information).

Before leaving the EU, these must be stamped at customs (at Barcelona airport, it's located in Terminal A by the Arrivals gate) and can immediately be reclaimed in cash at the adjacent branch of La Caixa bank.

Note that if you're paying by credit card, you usually have to show photographic ID, such as a passport or driving licence. Bargain-hunters should note that sales (*rebaixes/rebajas*) begin after the retail orgy of Christmas and Epiphany, running from 7 January to mid February, and again during July and August.

Returning goods, even when they are faulty, can be difficult. *See p313* for consumer rights.

General

DEPARTMENT STORES

El Corte Inglés
Plaça Catalunya 14, Eixample (93 306 38 00/ www.elcorteingles.es). Metro Catalunya. **Open** 10am-10pm Mon-Sat. **Credit** AmEx, DC, MC, V. **Map** p344 C2.

The mother ship of Spanish retail, this giant white monolith sits on Plaça Catalunya and stocks all the major international brand names, along with plenty of Spanish labels. This branch is the place for toiletries and cosmetics, clothes and accessories and homewares. It also houses a well-stocked but pricey supermarket and a gourmet food store in the basement, plus services ranging from key cutting to currency exchange; on the top floor, there's a restaurant with great views (but service station-style food). The Portal de l'Àngel branch stocks CDs, DVDs, books, electronic equipment, stationery and sports gear, from trainers to training bikes.

Where to Shop

Barcelona's best shopping neighbourhoods in brief.

BARRI GOTIC

The Saturday-afternoon hordes head to the big-name chain stores that line **Avda Portal de l'Àngel** and **C/Portaferrissa**, but there are plenty of less mainstream retail options. It's possible to spend hours browsing antiques on **C/Banys Nous**, where tiny shops specialise in furniture, posters or textiles. The streets around **Plaça Sant Jaume** house some lovely, old-fashioned stores selling hats, candles, traditional toys and stationery. For something more modern, try the independent boutiques on **C/Avinyó**, which offer affordable, streetwise fashion and household items with a twist.

BORN & SANT PERE

The streets leading off the **Passeig del Born** are a rabbit warren of stylish little boutiques offering quality, rather than quantity. Hip music, intimidating sales assistants and heartbreaking prices are part of the shopping experience, but so are gorgeous clothing, shoes and accessories from a clique of fast-rising local and international designers. Nearby **C/Argenteria** was named after its denizen silversmiths, and a handful of shops there follow the tradition, selling affordable, if mainstream, trinkets.

RAVAL

Raval's shopping, concentrated on the streets between the Boqueria market and Plaça dels Àngels, has a youthful bent: head to **C/Riera Baixa** and **C/Tallers** for second-hand clothing and streetwear, and **C/Bonsuccès** for specialist record shops. **C/Doctor Dou** and **C/Elisabets** feature some trendy boutiques and shoe shops; the latter also has a couple of design stores. **C/Pelai**, along Raval's top edge, has an impressive number of shoe stores.

BARCELONETA & THE PORTS

Barcelona's seafront shopping is concentrated in the shopping centre of **Maremàgnum**, which houses a large, if sterile, confection of high-street fashion stores that are at least open late.

EIXAMPLE

Passeig de Gràcia is home to enough high fashion and statement jewellery to satisfy even a footballer's wife. Chanel, Dior, Cartier and friends are present and correct, as are Spanish luxury brands Tous, Loewe and, on adjacent Consell de Cent, Catalan fashion hero Antoni Miró. A stone's throw away, the tree-lined **Rambla de Catalunya** is a pleasant place for browsing high-street fashion.

GRACIA & OTHER DISTRICTS

Independent shops rule in bohemian Gràcia: head to the bottom end of **C/Verdi** or the streets around **Plaça Rius i Taulet** for quirky little boutiques selling clothing, accessories and gifts. Local design collective Ruta Gràcia (www.rutagracia.com) lists dozens of independent retailers on its website.

CONSUME

Other locations Avda Diagonal 471-473, Eixample (93 493 48 00); Avda Diagonal 617, Eixample (93 366 71 00); L'Illa (sports clothing only), Avda Diagonal 545, Eixample (93 363 80 90); Avda Portal de l'Àngel 19-21, Plaça Catalunya, Eixample (93 306 38 00).

MALLS

★ Barcelona Glòries

Avda Diagonal 208, Eixample (93 486 04 04/ www.lesglories.com). Metro Glòries. **Open** *Shops* 10am-10pm Mon-Sat. **Map** p343 L8.
Since opening in 1995, this mall, office and leisure centre has become a focus of local life. There's a seven-screen cinema (foreign films are mostly dubbed into Spanish) and more than 220 shops,

including a Carrefour supermarket, an H&M, a Mango and a Disney Store, facing on to a large, café-filled square decorated with jets of coloured water. Family-friendly attractions include a free pram-lending service, play areas and entertainment such as bouncy castles and trampolines.

Diagonal Mar

Avda Diagonal 3, Poblenou (93 567 76 37/ www.diagonalmar.com). Metro El Maresme-Forum. **Open** *Shops* 10am-10pm Mon-Sat. *Food court & entertainment* 10am-midnight Mon-Thur; 10am-2am Fri, Sat; 11am-midnight Sun.
This three-level mall at the sea end of Avda Diagonal has an airy marine theme and a sea-facing roof terrace filled with cafés and restaurants of the fast-food variety. As well as major anchors, such as

an Alcampo supermarket, Zara and FNAC, there's a particular emphasis on children's clothes and toy shops, plus plenty of smaller global brands (Miss Sixty to Swarovski). Extras include a wheelchair-lending service and golf carts in which to drive your purchases to your car; for the kids, there's a crèche, a play area and miniature cars for hourly rental.

▶ *After shopping, let off steam in Enric Miralles' nearby Parc de Diagonal Mar; see p118.*

L'Illa

Avda Diagonal 545-557, Eixample (93 444 00 00/www.lilla.com). Metro Maria Cristina. **Open** 10am-9.30pm Mon-Sat. *Supermarket* 9.30am-9.30pm Mon-Sat. **Map** p337 C4.
This monolithic mall is designed to look like the Rockefeller Center fallen on its side, stretching 334m (1,100ft) along Avda Diagonal. It features all the usual fashion favourites but also has a good range of Catalan brands such as Camper, Custo and Antonio Miró. L'Illa has been gaining a good reputation for its food offerings, with specialist gourmet food stalls and interesting eateries such as sushi and oyster bars.

Maremàgnum

Moll d'Espanya, Port Vell (93 225 81 00/www.maremagnum.es). Metro Drassanes. **Open** 10am-10pm daily. **Map** p342 F12/13.
When Viaplana and Piñon's black-mirrored shopping and leisure centre opened in 1995, it was *the* place to hang out. After years of declining popularity, it's ditched most of the bars and discos and taken a step upmarket: residents now include the likes of chocolate shop Xocoa, Calvin Klein and boudoirish Lollipops, which deals in Parisian accessories. All the high-street staples are present (Mango, H&M, Women's Secret) and the ground floor focuses on the family market, with sweets, children's clothes and a Barça shop. There's also a Starbucks and a handful of tapas restaurants.

Pedralbes Centre

Avda Diagonal 609-615, Pedralbes (93 410 68 21/www.pedralbescentre.com). Metro Maria Cristina. **Open** 10.30am-9pm Mon-Sat. **Map** p337 B4.
When this black Rubik's Cube of a building opened in the early '90s, it caused such excitement that it even inspired a short-lived TV soap of the same

name. The mall's focus is on upmarket clothes, accessories and homewares, with plenty of local names such as Elena Miró, Majoral jewellers and Luis Guirau in among the likes of Hello Kitty and Timberland. The cafés and restaurants appeal to ladies who lunch, with salad buffets and gourmet tapas along with a crèche, regular catwalk shows and art exhibitions. In winter, the mall's plaza is transformed into an ice rink.

MARKETS

In 2009, the **Modernista Sant Antoni** market will close for refurbishment and the stalls move to a temporary site on Ronda Sant Antoni where C/Villarroel meets C/Riera Alta. Its Sunday book market will be held around the area where C/Comte Borrell meets C/Tamarit.

Other general markets include **Del Ninot** (C/Mallorca 133, Eixample, 93 453 65 12, closed Sun) and **La Barceloneta** (Plaça Font 1, Barceloneta, 93 221 64 71, closed Sun). Also look out for the **book and coin market** (*see p199*), food markets (*see p211*) and the **Fira de Santa Llúcia** Christmas market (*see p230*). See also www.bcn.cat/mercats municipals for details of the 40 permanent neighbourhood markets.

Specialist

BOOKS & MAGAZINES

A glut of shops specialising in comics, film and other visual arts can be found on Passeig de Sant Joan in the Arc de Triomf area. Elsewhere, **Kowasa** (C/Mallorca 235, Eixample, 93 215 80 58, www.kowasa.com) runs fine exhibitions in addition to its extensive stock of books about photography. For books on Catalonia, head to the **Palau Robert** shop (*see p320*). **FNAC** (El Triangle, Plaça Catalunya 4, 93 344 18 00, 902 10 06 32, www.fnac.es) has a large selection of English-language books on the second floor.

English language

BCN Books

C/Roger de Llúria 118, Eixample (93 457 76 92/www.bcnbooks.com). Metro Passeig de Gràcia. **Open** *July, Aug* 10am-8pm Mon-Fri. *Sept-June* 10am-8pm Mon-Fri; 10am-2pm Sat. **Credit** MC, V. **Map** p338 G/H7.
This well-stocked English-language bookstore has a wide range of learning and teaching materials for all ages. There's also a decent selection of contemporary and classic fiction, a good kids' section, some travel guides and plenty of dictionaries.
Other locations C/Amigó 81, Eixample (93 200 79 53).

INSIDE TRACK
MUSEUM BOOKSTORES

Some of the best places in which to find books on art, design and architecture are museum gift stores. In particular, try the **MACBA** (*see p81*), **CaixaForum** (*see p95*) and the **Museu d'Història de la Ciutat** (*see p63*).

Casa del Llibre

*C/Passeig de Gràcia 62, Eixample (93 272 34 80/
www.casadellibro.com). Metro Passeig de Gràcia.*
Open 9.30am-9.30pm Mon-Sat. **Credit** AmEx,
DC, MC, V. **Map** p338 G7.
Part of a well-established Spanish chain, this bookstore offers a diverse assortment of titles that
includes some English-language fiction. Glossy,
Barcelona-themed coffee-table tomes with good gift
potential sit by the front right-hand entrance.

Hibernian Books

*C/Montseny 17, Gràcia (93 217 47 96/www.
hibernian-books.com). Metro Fontana.* **Open**
4-8.30pm Mon; 10.30am-8.30pm Tue-Sat. Closed
1wk Aug. **No credit cards. Map** p338 G5.
With its air of pleasantly dusty intellectualism,
Hibernian feels like a proper British second-hand
bookshop,. There are books here for all tastes, from
beautifully bound early editions to classic Penguin
paperbacks, biographies, cookbooks, poetry and
plays – in all more than 30,000 titles. Part-exchange
is possible here.

Specialist

★ Altaïr

*Gran Via de les Corts Catalanes 616, Eixample
(93 342 71 71/www.altair.es). Metro Universitat.*
Open 10am-2pm, 4.30-8.30pm Mon-Fri; 10am-
3pm, 4-8.30pm Sat. **Credit** AmEx, DC, MC, V.
Map p342 F8.
Every aspect of travel is covered in this, the largest
travel bookshop in Europe. You can pick up guides
to free eating in Barcelona, academic tomes on
geolinguistics, handbooks on successful outdoor
sex, and CDs of tribal music. Of course, all the less
arcane publications are also here: maps for hikers,
travel guidebooks, multilingual dictionaries, travel
diaries and equipment such as mosquito nets.
▶ *For more travel-related shops and services,
see pp220-221.*

Book & Coin Market

*C/Comte Borrell with C/Tamarit, Eixample (93
423 42 87). Metro Sant Antoni.* **Open** 8am-2pm
(approx) Sun. **No credit cards. Map** p342 D9.
This temporary set-up, in operation only while the
Sant Antoni market is being refurbished (it's due to
reopen in 2012), houses tables packed with every
manner of reading material from arcane old tomes
to well-pawed bodice-rippers and yellowing comics.
There are also stacks of coins and more contemporary ware such as music, software and posters.
Arrive early to beat the crowds.

Continuarà

*Via Laietana 29, Barri Gòtic (93 310 43 52/
www.continuara.org). Metro Jaume I.* **Open**
10.30am-2.30pm, 4-9pm Mon-Sat. **Credit** DC,
MC, V. **Map** p345 D5.

Joguines Monforte. *See p201.*

The comic scene is big in Spain, and this two-storey
shop has been serving Barcelona's substantial
geek community since 1980. The ground floor has
both national and imported comics and comix, prin-
cipally in English and French, along with plenty of
posters, DVDs, CDs and figurines. The first floor is
a temple to manga and Amerimanga, with a huge
selection of Japanese merchandising.

CHILDREN

General

The third floor of the Plaça Catalunya branch
of **El Corte Inglés** has a large selection
of clothes, toys and baby equipment, while
Galeries Maldà (C/Portaferrissa 22, no phone,
Barri Gòtic) is a small shopping centre with
plenty of kids' shops.

Chicco

*Ronda Sant Pere 5, Eixample (93 301 49 76/
www.chicco.es). Metro Catalunya.* **Open** 10am-
8.30pm Mon-Fri; 10am-9pm Sat. **Credit** AmEx,
DC, MC, V. **Map** p344 D2.
The market leader in Spain, this colourful store has
every conceivable babycare item, from dummies and
high chairs to bottle-warmers and travel cots. Its
clothes and shoes are practical and well-designed,
and made for children up to eight years old.
Other locations Diagonal Mar, Avda Diagonal
3, Poblenou (93 356 03 74).

Fashion

Larger branches of **Zara** have decent clothes sections. **Kiddy's Class**, which has branches all over town, sells exclusively Zara's children's clothing. For cheapo kids' shoes and casual clothes, head to **Decathlon** (*see p220*).

Mujer

C/Carders 28, Sant Pere (93 315 15 31). Metro Jaume I. **Open** 10am-3pm, 5-8pm Mon-Fri; 11am-9pm Sat. Closed last 2wks Aug. **Credit** AmEx, DC, MC, V. **Map** p345 F5.

Run by the energetic Lulu, Mujer is the local nerve centre for expat parents. It stocks imported funky baby gear from the likes of Cath Kidston or Twisted Twee and is the perfect place to pick up a tiny Metallica T-Shirt or an AC/DC one-size. There's also a range of maternity wear, baby accessories, books, toys and a chill-out space for playing and breastfeeding in comfort. Lulu also runs regular sessions of happy clapping, baby massage and the like.

★ Du Pareil au Même

Rambla Catalunya 95, Eixample (93 487 14 49/ www.dupareilaumeme.com). Metro Diagonal/ FGC Provença. **Open** 10am-8.30pm Mon-Sat. **Credit** AmEx, DC, MC. V. **Map** p338 F/G7.

This French chain stocks everything a pint-sized fashionista might need, though the girls do a bit better than the boys. Newborns to 14-year-olds are served with a covetable range of funky, bright and well-designed clothes at great prices.

Toys

Imaginarium

Passeig de Gràcia 103, Eixample (902 21 42 15/ www.imaginarium.es). Metro Diagonal. **Open** 9am-9pm Mon-Sat. **Credit** MC, V. **Map** p338 G6.

As well as the endless racks of excellent toys that made Imaginarium famous, the new three-floor flagship store for Spain's biggest toy chain has a hairdresser's, shoe department, computer zone, a multilingual book department (including a solid English-language selection) and a play area and reading corner. The friendly assistants run regular craft activities, balloon-bending sessions and puppet shows, while the top floor Saborea restaurant has organic food in appropriately small portions. **Other locations** throughout the city.

★ El Ingenio

C/Rauric 6, Barri Gòtic (93 317 71 38/www.el-ingenio.com). Metro Liceu. **Open** 10am-1.30pm, 4.15-8pm Mon-Fri; 11am-2pm, 5-8.30pm Sat. **Credit** (purchases over €6) MC, V. **Map** p345 B5.

At once enchanting and disturbing, El Ingenio's handcrafted toys, tricks and costumes are reminders of a pre-digital world where people made their own entertainment. Its cabinets are full of practical jokes and curious toys; its fascinating workshop produces the oversized heads and garish costumes used in Barcelona's traditional festivities.

Joguines Monforte

Plaça Sant Josep Oriol 3, Barri Gòtic (93 318 22 85/www.joguinesmonforte.com). Metro Liceu. **Open** 9.30am-1.30pm, 4-8pm Mon-Fri; 10am-2pm, 4.30-8.30pm Sat. **Credit** MC, V. **Map** p345 B5.

This venerable toy shop has been selling traditional toys, board games and everything you need for a game of billiards since 1840. Try the Spanish version of snakes and ladders (*el juego de la oca*, or the 'goose game') and ludo (*parchís*) along with chess , jigsaws, painted tin toys and outdoor games such as croquet and skittles. *Photo p199.*

ELECTRONICS & PHOTOGRAPHY

The area around Ronda Sant Antoni is the best place to go if you're looking for hardware for your PC. **Life Informática** (C/Sepúlveda 173, Sant Antoni, 93 390 02 30, www.lifeinformatica. com) is good for parts; **PC City** (C/Casanova 2, Eixample, 902 10 03 02, www.pccity.es) is a reliable option for hardware. For photography, if Casanova Foto doesn't have what you need, try **ARPI** (La Rambla 38-40, Barri Gòtic, 93 301 74 04), which has a wide range but poor service.

BCN Computers

C/Mozart 26, Gràcia (93 217 61 66/615 090 073). Metro Fontana. **Open** 10am-2pm, 4-8pm Mon-Fri. **No credit cards. Map** p338 G6.

Everything for Macs and PCs: software in English, hardware and software installations, repairs for personal computers and laptops and ADSL support. There's English-speaking customer service; unlike many local shops, staff offer a free evaluation of your computer's problems when you take it for repair.

Casanova Foto

C/Pelai 18, Raval (93 302 73 63/www.casanova foto.com). Metro Universitat. **Open** 10am-2pm, 4.30-8.30pm Mon-Fri; 10am-2pm, 5-8.30pm Sat. **Credit** MC, V. **Map** p344 B1.

An extensive stock of new and second-hand digital and film equipment: camera bodies, lenses, tripods, darkroom gear, bags and more. There's also a slow but thorough repair lab, and they offer the full range of processing services for film and digital photos. **Other locations** Casanova Professional, C/Tallers 68, Raval (93 301 61 12).

CTA Serveis

C/Consell de Cent 382, Eixample (93 244 03 50/ www.cta.es). Metro Girona. **Open** 9am-2pm, 4-7pm Mon-Fri. Closed 3wks Aug. **Credit** MC, V. **Map** p343 H8.

Computer installation and repairs, including Macs.

FASHION
Designer

Antonio Miró
C/Consell de Cent 349, Eixample (93 487 06 70/
www.antoniomiro.es). Metro Passeig de Gràcia.
Open 10.30am-8.30pm Mon-Sat. **Credit** AmEx,
DC, MC, V. **Map** p338 G8.
Miró famously likes to cause a stir on the catwalk,
using illegal immigrants and even local prisoners to
model his wares. His clothes, however, for men and
women, couldn't be less controversial, with sober,
almost uniform-like designs in muted tones. His dif-
fusion line, Miró jeans, is more relaxed and playful.
Other locations C/Consell de Cent 349-351,
Eixample (93 487 06 70).

Como Agua de Mayo
C/Argenteria 43, Born (93 310 64 41/www.comoa
guademayo.es). Metro Jaume I. **Open** 10am-
8.30pm. **Credit** AmEx, DC, MC, V. **Map** p345 E6.
A temple for coquettish Carrie Bradshaw style on a
mid-range budget. Think lots of mixing and matching of patterns with plenty of candy-bright shoes.
Labels include Amaya Arzuaga, Antik Batik, Lydia
Delgado and Miriam Ocáriz; footwear comes courtesy of Otto et Moi, Pedro Garcia and Chie Mihara.
If the door is shut, you'll need to buzz to get in.

★ Custo Barcelona
Plaça de les Olles 7, Born (93 268 78 93/
www.custo-barcelona.com). Metro Jaume I.
Open 10am-10pm Mon-Sat. **Credit** AmEx,
DC, MC, V. **Map** p345 E7.
The Custo look is synonymous with Barcelona style,
and the loud, cut-and-paste print T-shirts have
spawned a thousand imitations. Custodio Dalmau's
signature prints can now be found on everything
from coats to jeans to swimwear for both men and
women, but a T-shirt is still the most highly prized
(and highly priced) souvenir for visiting fashionistas.
There's also a Custo Vintage (Plaça del Pi 2, Barri
Gòtic, 93 304 27 53), with clothes from past seasons.

THE BEST
LOCAL FASHIONS

For the club
A T-shirt from **Custo Barcelona**.
See above.

For the catwalk
A dress from **MTX Barcelona**.
See p205.

For the beach
Espadrilles from **La Manual**
Alpargatera. See p209.

Other locations C/Ferran 36, Barri Gòtic (93
342 66 98); La Rambla 109, Barri Gòtic (93 481 39
30); L'Illa, Avda Diagonal 545-557, Eixample (93
322 26 62).

Jean-Pierre Bua
Avda Diagonal 469, Eixample (93 439 71 00/
www.jeanpierrebua.com). Bus 6, 7, 15, 33, 34,
67, 68/tram T1, T2, T3. **Open** 10am-2pm,
4.30-8.30pm Mon-Sat. **Credit** AmEx, DC, MC, V.
Map p338 E5.
The clothes are the highest of high-end fashion, the
assistants are model-beautiful, and the shop itself
has the air of a runway at a Paris catwalk show. No
inferiority complexes are allowed: if you have the
money, the figure and the label knowledge (and *only*
if), come to worship at the altar of Miu Miu, Dries
van Noten, Alexander McQueen and many more.

Jordi Labanda
C/Rosselló 232, Eixample (93 496 14 03/www.
jordilabanda.com). Metro Diagonal. **Open**
10am-8.30pm Mon-Sat. **Credit** AmEx, DC, MC,
V. **Map** p338 G6.
After years of drawing beautiful people in beautiful
outfits, it was a logical step for Barcelona's most successful illustrator to design his own fashion line.
Labanda's shop is a monochrome arrangement of
blinding white and glossy black with off-kilter mirrors that form a seamless continuity with a collection of '60s-inspired, slim-line, monochrome clothes.
Naturally, the most popular items are the bright car-
toon T-shirts that made him famous.

★ Josep Font
C/Provença 304, Eixample (93 487 21 10/www.
josepfont.com). Metro Diagonal. **Open** Sept-July
10am-8.30pm Mon-Sat. *Aug* 10am-2pm, 4.30-
8.30pm Mon-Sat. **Credit** AmEx, DC, MC, V.
Map p338 G7.
Tomboys should turn away now: Font's romantic
and feminine designs are dripping with ribbons and
ruffles yet never stray into Barbara Cartland territory. Look for cute '50s-inspired shorts suits, floral
maxi dresses and sumptuous materials, from shim-
mery silks to millefeuille chiffon, all temptingly displayed in a quirked-up art nouveau space.

Miriam Ponsa
C/Princesa 14, Born (93 295 55 62/www.miriam
ponsa.com). Metro Jaume I. **Open** 3.30-8.30pm
Mon; 11am-8.30pm Tue-Sat. **Credit** AmEx, DC,
MC, V. **Map** p345 E5.
Miriam Ponsa's designs are squarely aimed at affluent young urbanites with a taste for stripped-down,
quasi-Japanese style. The clothes are generally loose
fitting and with a strong vertical silhouette while
materials can get pretty quirky; you might find
yourself wondering how a T-shirt splattered in
dripped latex or a hole-punched grey leather waist-
coat could ever look so good.

Get All Dolled Up

I'm a celebrity, get me… a Lolita?

The brainchildren of Barcelona-based designer María del Mar González, quirky and colourful Lolitas are the ultimate in voodoo chic. These personalised male or female rag dolls are made to look exactly like real people and come in all ages, in singles, couples or groups, and are created with bendy arms and legs, so that they may hug, clutch, pose, perch or slump on the sofa in the style of their human equivalent. Soft and forever smiling, they're quiet, attentive and don't raid the fridge.

González began making Lolitas five years ago as family gifts. Soon, though, her friends were putting in orders. Since these early days, the Lolitas empire has spread, with up to 50 of the little fellows racing out of the workshop every week. Lolitas are handmade with care and enthusiasm in a busy workshop at the back of shop **Novedades** (C/Peu de la Creu 24, 93 329 16 36). Each is unique and based on a real person's physical features, style and character traits.

González is up for a challenge and happy to whip up anyone you like in any outfit, be it a frilly dress, jeans and sneakers or leather pants. Her Lolitas come complete with fashionable hair-dos, meticulously styled. They even come with distinguishing props: be it a duffel coat, skateboard, parasol or pet. Personalised puppies are part of the new Animalolis range and ready-made accessories include Lolitas brooches, bags, and T-shirts. You can even order a celebrity dolly just as Spanish *Marie Claire* did with their request for a mini Christina Ricci.

To order one, simply fill in details of your friend's physical features, favourite clothes and shoes, jobs, interests and mannerisms on the website and provide a good photo. The more details the better. You can also do it in person at Novedades or various shops around town (see website for details). It takes about six weeks for your Lolita to arrive; an 18-20cm doll costs around €105. For more on the little beauties, see www.lolitasbcn.com.

CONSUME

MTX Barcelona

C/Rec 32, Born (93 319 13 98/www.mertxe-hernandez.com). Metro Barceloneta. **Open** 11am-9pm Mon-Sat. **Credit** AmEx, DC, MC, V. **Map** p345 F6.

Right now, nobody in Barcelona is hipper than local designer Mertxe Hernández. Her clothes have the distinction of being utterly different but immediately recognisable: colourful, multi-layered textiles, slashed and restructured to make a kind of soft and feminine body armour.

▶ *Mertxe has also made the tourist T-shirt sexy: you can also find her sharp designs in the shops at La Pedrera (see p108), the Liceu opera house (see p271) and the Museu Picasso (see p73).*

★ Santa Eulalia

Passeig de Gràcia 93, Eixample (93 215 06 74/ www.santaeulalia.com). Metro Diagonal. **Open** 10am-8.30pm Mon-Sat. **Credit** AmEx, DC, MC, V. **Map** p338 G6.

Barcelona's oldest design house and a pioneer in the local catwalk scene, Santa Eulalia was founded in 1843 and remains a seriously upmarket proposition. The prêt-à-porter collection is fresh and up-to-the minute and carries labels such as Balenciaga, Jimmy Choo, Stella McCartney and Ann Demeulemeester. Services include bespoke tailoring and wedding wear for grooms. The C/Pau Casals branch is for men only. **Other locations** C/Pau Casals 8, Eixample (93 201 70 51).

Lailo.

Discount

One of Barcelona's hotspots for bargain clothes shopping is C/Girona. In particular, the two blocks between C/Ausiàs Marc and Gran Via de les Corts Catalanes are lined with remainder stores and factory outlets of fluctuating quality. **Mango Outlet**, crammed with last season's unsold stock, far outshines the competition: the C/Girona branch (No.37, 93 412 29 35) is larger and more frantic, while the uptown branch (C/Pau Casals 12, 93 209 07 73) offers a more select choice of clothing.

Elsewhere, **Lefties** (Plaça Universitat 11, 93 317 50 70) is a remainder store crammed with discounted items for men, women and children from the Inditex stable (which includes Zara, Pull & Bear and Bershka, among others). The El Corte Inglés outlet store is known as the **Centre d'Oportunitats** (Travessera de les Corts 268, 93 366 71 00).

Stockland

C/Comtal 22, Barri Gòtic (93 318 03 31).
Metro Urquinaona. **Open** 10am-8.30pm Mon-Sat.
Credit AmEx, DC, MC, V. **Map** p344 D3.
A far cry from the elbow-deep frenzy of many remainder stores, this elegant boutique specialises in end-of-line clothing for women designed by respected Spanish names such as Josep Font, Jesús del Pozo and Purificación García at discount prices. Smart styles predominate; eveningwear is upstairs.

General

Adolfo Domínguez

C/Ribera 16, Born (93 319 21 59/www.adolfo dominguez.com). Metro Barceloneta. **Open** 11am-9pm Mon-Sat. **Credit** AmEx, DC, MC, V. **Map** p345 F7.
The women's department has finally caught up with the men's tailoring that for many years was Domínguez's forte, particularly his elegantly cut suits and shirts. Expect to find sharp, flattering jackets along with surprisingly adventurous separates in luxurious materials along with well-made shoes and bags. The more casual U de Adolfo Domínguez line courts well-to-do youths, but doesn't quite attain the effortless panache of its grown-up precursor. This under-visited two-storey flagship store is supplemented by several others around the city.
Other locations Passeig de Gràcia 32, Eixample (93 487 41 70); Passeig de Gràcia 89, Eixample (93 215 13 39); Avda Diagonal 490, Gràcia (93 416 17 16); and throughout the city.

Cortefiel

Avda Portal de l'Àngel 38, Barri Gòtic (93 301 07 00/www.cortefiel.com). Metro Catalunya.
Open 10am-8.30pm Mon-Sat. **Credit** AmEx, DC, MC, V. **Map** p344 C3.
Cortefiel is a popular chain that casts a wider net than Mango or Zara, and its fine tailored jackets and elegant, mature renditions of current trends appeal to a variety of women (from conservative students

to fashion-conscious fiftysomethings). If you like a bit of glitz, take a peek at the swankier Pedro del Hierro collection downstairs. Both labels have less prominent, but successful, menswear lines.
Other locations L'Illa, Avda Diagonal 545-557, Eixample (93 405 35 44); and throughout the city.

Free
C/Ramelleres 5, Raval (93 301 61 15). Metro Catalunya. **Open** 11am-8.30pm Mon-Sat. **Credit** V. **Map** p344 B3.
A skate emporium that has grown exponentially to cater for Barcelona's expanding population of enthusiasts. For boys, there's casualwear from Stüssy, Carhartt et al; girls get plenty of Compobella and Loreak Mendian. The requisite chunky or retro footwear comes courtesy of Vans, Vision and Etnies.
Other locations C/Rec 16, Born (93 295 50 36); C/Viladomat 319, Eixample (93 321 72 90); Passeig Bonanova 63, Sarrià (93 212 30 57).

Lobby
C/Ribera 5, Born (93 319 38 55/www.lobby-bcn. com). Metro Barceloneta. **Open** 11am-8.30pm Mon-Sat. **Credit** AmEx, DC, MC, V. **Map** p345 F7.
One of the new breed of multifunctional spaces devoted to a clued-up lifestyle concept, with designs from emerging talents and the newest offerings from larger brands. Although there are perfumes, homewares and magazines, Lobby's strongest suit is clothing: for the girls, there's Jaume Roca, Lilith and Pleats Please (by Issey Miyake), while the boys can choose from the likes of Final Home and Unity.

On Land
C/Princesa 25, Born (93 310 02 11/www.on-land.com). Metro Jaume I. **Open** 5-8.30pm Mon; 11am-2pm, 5-8.30pm Tue-Fri; 11am-8.30pm Sat. Closed 2wks Aug. **Credit** AmEx, DC, MC, V. **Map** p345 E5.
This little oasis of urban cool has all you need to hold your head up high against the Barcelona hip squad: bags and wallets by Becksöndergaard and Can't Go Naked; cute dresses by Boba; elegant pencil skirts from Conni Kaminski; loose cotton trousers by IKKS and covetable T-shirts by Fresh From the Lab.
Other locations C/València 273, Eixample (93 215 56 25).
▶ *Just down the street is the similarly fashionable Miriam Ponsa; see p202.*

Used & vintage

The narrow C/Riera Baixa in the Raval is where most of Barcelona's second-hand clothes retailers cluster. It's a great place to hunt for unique items, although prices aren't as low as you might expect. **Holala! Ibiza** at No.11 (93 441 99 94) has thrift-store staples; at No.7, **Smart and Clean's** 1960s and '70s second-hand gear is largely made up of mod essentials,

with a decent range of leather jackets and vintage trainers as well (93 441 87 64, www. smartandclean.com). On the corner, **GI Joe** has military surplus gear (C/Hospital 82, 93 329 96 52, www.gijoebcn.com).

Lailo
C/Riera Baixa 20, Raval (93 441 37 49). Metro Liceu or Sant Antoni. **Open** 11am-2pm, 5-8pm Mon-Sat. Closed 1wk end Aug. **Credit** AmEx, DC, MC, V. **Map** p342 E10.
Lailo stands out from the second-hand crowd by the quality of its stock. If you want something for a one-off occasion, you can hire everything from the tuxedos to the coming-out gowns.
▶ *Lailo also has a 'museum' of old costumes, some dating back to the 18th century, from the Liceu theatre. For the theatre itself, see p271.*

Produit National Brut
C/Avinyó 29, Barri Gòtic (93 268 27 55). Metro Jaume I or Liceu. **Open** 11am-9pm Mon-Sat. **Credit** MC, V. **Map** p345 C7.
Mixed in with bright and cutesy new clothes from the likes of Cheap Monday and Pepa Karnero is a good supply of second-hand fashions and vintage pieces with an emphasis on the late '70s and early '80s. Expect plenty of loud nylon shirts, US high-school ties and smock dresses, along with a lot of denim, corduroy and leather.
Other locations C/Ramalleres 16-20, Raval (93 301 99 09).

Le Swing
C/Riera Baixa 13, Raval (93 324 84 02). Metro Liceu or Sant Antoni. **Open** 10.30am-2.30pm, 4.30-8.30pm Mon-Sat. **Credit** AmEx, DC, MC, V. **Map** p342 E10.
Today's second-hand is known as vintage, and thrift is not on the agenda. Fervent worshippers of Pierre Cardin, YSL, Dior, Kenzo and other fashion deities scour all corners of the sartorial stratosphere and deliver their booty back to this little powder puff of a boutique. The odd Zara number and other mere mortal brands creep in as well.
Other locations C/Doctor Dou 11, Raval (93 302 36 98); C/Notariat 3, Raval (93 301 98 70).

> ### INSIDE TRACK
> ### LA ROCA VILLAGE
>
> If you're a dedicated designer bargain-hunter, make the 30-minute pilgrimage just outside the city to **La Roca Village** (93 842 39 39, www.larocavillage.com). More than 50 discount outlets will tempt you with designer apparel from popular brands such as Antonio Miró, Versace, Diesel and Camper.

CONSUME

Go
Shopping
Go
Diagonal
Mar

Fashion & Accessories

Lifestyle

Electronics

Restaurants

Cinemas & Leisure

Valid during 2009

Diagonal Mar®
centre comercial

Bring this advertisement to Starbucks Coffee Diagonal Mar and enjoy complimentary tall cup exclusive beverage on us

www.diagonalmarcentre.es   Tel. 902 530 300   Open: 10am to 10pm

 Fòrum Route "Fòrum" Stop   Ronda Litoral. Exit 24   El Maresme/Fòrum   El Maresme   7

FASHION ACCESSORIES & SERVICES

Cleaning & repairs

Any shop marked '*rapid*' or '*rápido*' does shoe repairs and key cutting; **El Corte Inglés** (*see p196*) has both in the basement.

La Hermosa
C/Formatgeria 3, Born (93 319 97 26).
Metro Jaume I. **Open** 10am-9pm Mon-Sat.
No credit cards. Map p345 E6.
A washing and dry-cleaning facility. Opt for self-service washing and drying (€5.50 to wash 8kg, not including drying or soap) or go for the drop-off service (€13 for 8kg, €20 for 14kg). Dry-cleaning takes two to three days.

LavaXpres
C/Ferlandina 34, Raval (no phone). Metro Sant Antoni or Universitat. **Open** 8am-11pm daily.
No credit cards. Map p342 E9.
This self-service, American-owned launderette is open 365 days a year. There are machines that take 18kg of washing – plenty big enough for a rucksack-full of dirty clothes. Smaller 9kg loads cost €3.50.
Other locations C/Nou de Sant Francesc 5, Barri Gòtic; C/Carders 29, Born; Passeig Elisabets 3, Raval; Avda Paral·lel 101, Poble Sec.

Tintorería Ferran
C/Ferran 11, Barri Gòtic (93 301 87 30).
Metro Liceu. **Open** 9am-2pm, 4.30-8pm Mon-Fri.
Credit V. **Map** p345 B5.
Services at this reliable cleaners include the cleaning of large items such as duvets and rugs, mending (which can be pricey), service washes and delivery. Look out for offers.

Hats

Hatquarters
Plaça de la Llana 6, Born (93 310 18 02/www. hatquarters.com). Metro Jaume I. **Open** 11am-8.30pm Mon-Sat. **Credit** AmEx, DC, MC, V.
Map p345 E5.
You won't find anything as vulgar as a tourist sombrero at Chad Weidmar's tiny temple to the titfer. From raffia and tweed cadet caps, leather bucket hats to felt fedoras – by Goorin Bros, Cassel Goorin and Sant Cassel – the simple application of any piece of headwear in this shop will get you past the toughest nightclub bouncer in town.

Sombreria Obach
C/Call 2, Barri Gòtic (93 318 40 94). Metro Jaume I or Liceu. **Open** *Oct-July* 9.30am-1.30pm, 4-8pm Mon-Fri; 10am-2pm, 4.30-8.30pm Sat. *Aug, Sept* 9.30am-1.30pm, 4-8pm Mon-Fri; 10am-2pm Sat. **Credit** MC, V. **Map** p345 C5.

Sombreria Obach's old-fashioned display windows are worth seeing for themselves: Kangol's mohair berets share space with fedoras, while monteras (matador's caps with Mickey Mouse ears) face off with *barrets* (traditional red Catalan beanies).

Jewellery

The Born's C/Argenteria takes its name from the numerous silversmiths who established themselves here in the 15th century. Even today, the street and the surrounding area are home to a number of shops selling silver jewellery, such as **Joid'art** (Plaça Santa Maria 7, Born, 93 310 10 87, www.joidart.com), which is part of a successful chain that has pretty, affordable pieces in its shops throughout Barcelona. Nearby, boutiques such as **Ad Láter** (C/Ases 1, no phone) or **Alea Majoral Galería de Joyas** (C/Argenteria 66, 93 310 13 73,www.aleagaleria.com) exhibit pieces by innovative local jewellery designers.

Upmarket jewellers naturally gravitate towards the glamorous shopping districts, such as Passeig de Gràcia and Avda Diagonal.

Bagués
Passeig de Gràcia 41, Eixample (93 216 01 73/ www.bagues.com). Metro Passeig de Gràcia.
Open *Sept-July* 10am-8.30pm Mon-Fri; 10am-1.30pm, 5-8.30pm Sat. *Aug* 10am-1.30pm, 4.30-8.30pm Mon-Fri; 10am-1.30pm Sat.
Credit AmEx, DC, MC, V. **Map** p338 G8.
Bagués is perhaps the city's most prestigious jeweller. Lluis Masriera, the original master jeweller of the house, created revolutionary pieces using a 'translucid enamel' technique at the start of the 20th century. His signature motifs, the art nouveau favourites of flowers, insects and birds, are reflected in today's designs.
▶ *Bagués is housed in the Modernista palace Casa Amatller, now open for tours; see p102.*

Helena Rohner
C/Espaseria 13, Born (93 319 88 79/www. helenarohner.com). Metro Barceloneta. **Open** 5-8.30pm Mon; 11am-2.30pm, 5-8.30pm Tue-Fri; noon-3pm, 5-9pm Sat. Closed 2wks Aug.
Credit AmEx, DC, MC, V. **Map** p345 E7.
The style is *Barbarella*-at-the-boardroom in the boutique of one of Spain's most successful jewellery designers. Spare clean lines in gold or silver wrap around big, smooth chunks of ebony, coral, porcelain or even wood to create a look that's sleek but funky. Big rings are a speciality.

Lingerie & underwear

Rambla de Catalunya is a mecca for underwear shoppers, with boutiques such as **La Perla** (No.88, 93 467 71 49). There's inexpensive

CONSUME

Capricho de Muñeca.

swimwear and underwear at high-street chains such as **Oysho** (No.77, 93 488 36 01, www.oysho.com), from the same stable as Zara. **Vanity Fair** (No.11, 93 317 65 45) strikes a happy medium with reasonably priced Spanish labels and its own range. **El Corte Inglés** (*see p196*) has men's and women's underwear.

★ Le Boudoir
C/Canuda 21, Barri Gòtic (93 302 52 81/ www.leboudoir.net). Metro Catalunya. **Open** *Sept-July* 10am-8.30pm Mon-Fri; 10.30am-9pm Sat. *Aug* 11am-9pm Mon-Sat. **Credit** AmEx, DC, MC, V. **Map** p344 C3.
Think Dita Von Teese in an 18th-century French boudoir: feather boas, stockings, masks, gloves and, of course, racks of sexy bras, knickers, basques and suspender belts. To show you how to use it all, the shop runs monthly striptease classes.
Other locations Pedralbes Centre (*see p198*).

Janina
Rambla de Catalunya 94, Eixample (93 215 04 84). Metro Diagonal/FGC Provença. **Open** *Sept-July* 10am-8.30pm Mon-Sat. *Aug* 10am-2pm, 5-8.30pm Mon-Sat. **Credit** AmEx, MC, V. **Map** p338 G7.
Good-quality women's underwear and nightwear by Calvin Klein, Christian Dior, La Perla and others. Some larger sizes are stocked; alternatively, bras can be sent to a seamstress to be altered overnight.
Other locations Avda Pau Casals 8, Eixample (93 202 06 93).

Women's Secret
C/Portaferrissa 7-9, Barri Gòtic (93 318 92 42/ www.womensecret.com). Metro Liceu. **Open** 10am-9pm Mon-Sat. **Credit** AmEx, DC, MC, V. **Map** p344 B4.
There are some sexy pieces at Women's Secret, but the stock is mostly versatile strap bras, brightly printed cotton PJs and a funky line of under-/ outerwear in cartoonish stylings: skimpy shorts, miniskirts and vest tops.
Other locations Avda Portal de l'Àngel, Barri Gòtic (93 318 70 55); and throughout the city.
▶ *Mykini, mix-and-match combinations of bikini bottoms and tops, has decorations designed by jeweller Helena Rohner (see p207).*

Luggage

Capricho de Muñeca
C/Brosoli 1, Born (93 319 58 91/www.capricho demuneca.com). Metro Jaume I. **Open** 5-9.30pm Tue-Fri, 1-9.30pm Sat. **Credit** MC, V. **Map** p345 E6.
Soft leather handbags in cherry reds, chocolate browns and parma violet made by hand just upstairs by designer Lisa Lempp. Sizes range from the cute and petit to the luxuriously large. Belts and wallets complement the handbags.

Casa Antich
C/Consolat del Mar 27-31, Born (93 310 43 91/ www.casaantich.com). Metro Jaume I. **Open** 9am-8.30pm Mon-Fri; 9.30am-8.30pm Sat. **Credit** AmEx, DC, MC, V. **Map** p345 D7.

A luggage shop that, in levels of service and size of stock, recalls the golden age of travel. Here you can still purchase trunks for a steam across the Atlantic, and ladies' vanity cases that would be perfect for a sojourn on the Orient Express. But you'll also find computer cases, backpacks and shoulder bags from the likes of Kipling and Mandarina Duck.

Scarves & textiles

Textiles were once one of Barcelona's main industries. It's a legacy visible in many of the street names of the Born, where you'll find the highest concentration of textile shops and workshops in the city.

Almacenes del Pilar

C/Boqueria 43, Barri Gòtic (93 317 79 84/ www.almacenesdelpilar.com). Metro Liceu. **Open** 10am-2pm, 4-8pm Mon-Sat. Closed 2wks Aug. **Credit** AmEx, DC, MC, V. **Map** p345 B5.
An array of fabrics and accessories for traditional Spanish costumes is on display in this colourful, shambolic interior, dating all the way back to 1886. Making your way through bolts of material, you'll find the richly hued brocades used for Valencian *fallera* outfits and other rudiments of folkloric dress from various parts of the country. Lace *mantillas*, and the high combs over which they are worn, are stocked, along with fringed, hand-embroidered pure silk mantones de manila (shawls) and colourful wooden fans.

Alonso

C/Santa Anna 27, Barri Gòtic (93 317 60 85/ www.tiendacenter.com). Metro Liceu. **Open** 10am-8pm Mon-Sat. Closed 1wk Aug. **Credit** AmEx, DC, MC, V. **Map** p344 C3.
Elegant Catalan ladies have come to Alonso for those important finishing touches for their outfit for more than a century. Behind the Modernista façade lie soft gloves in leather and lace, intricate fans, both traditional and modern, and scarves made from mohair and silk.

Shoes

Footwear outlets line the main shopping strips, such as Avda Portal de l'Àngel or C/Pelai; chains include **Casas Sabaters** (along

with their U-Casas shops aimed at younger fashionistas and Casas International for top-line names) **Royalty**, **Querol**, **Tascón** and **Vogue**, which have huge but similar collections.

Camper

C/Pelai 13-37, Eixample (93 302 41 24/www. camper.com). Metro Catalunya. **Open** 10am-10pm Mon-Sat. **Credit** AmEx, DC, MC, V. **Map** p344 B2.
Mallorca-based eco shoe company Camper has sexed up its ladies' line in recent years. Each year, the label seems to flirt more with high heels (albeit rubbery wedgy ones) and girly straps. Of course, it still has its classic round-toed and clod-heeled classics, and the guys still have their iconic bowling shoes. But Camper is still definitely worth another look if you've previously dismissed them.
Other locations Plaça del Àngels 6, Raval (93 342 41 41); Passeig de Gràcia 30, Eixample (93 481 61 75); and throughout the city.

Czar

Passeig del Born 20, Born (93 310 72 22). Metro Jaume I. **Open** 5-10pm Mon; noon-10pm Tue-Sat. **Credit** MC, V. **Map** p345 E6.
The hippest trainers are presented here as if they're valuable pieces in a museum. You should be able to find an Adidas Originals or Vision Streetwear pair to suit even the most demanding of street feet. The collection is aimed chiefly at men, but girls have a small and sassy range at the back.

Kwatra

C/Gran de Gràcia 262, Gràcia (93 237 66 37). Metro Lesseps. **Open** 11am-2.30pm, 4-8.30pm Mon-Sat. **Credit** AmEx, DC, MC, V. **Map** p338 G4.
This is urban trainer heaven, with the latest models and limited editions from Nike, 555DSL, Vans, Adidas, Converse, Onitsuka Tiger, Diesel, Puma, Quicksilver and Roxy. There's also a small but very covetable selection of bags and T-shirts from the same labels.
Other locations C/Antic de Sant Joan 1, Born (93 268 08 04).

La Manual Alpargatera

C/Avinyó 7, Barri Gòtic (93 301 01 72/ www.lamanual.net). Metro Liceu. **Open** *Jan-Sept, Dec* 9.30am-1.30pm, 4.30-8pm Mon-Fri; 10am-1.30pm, 4.30-8pm Sat. *Oct, Nov* 9.30am-1.30pm, 4.30-8.30pm Mon-Fri; 10am-1.30pm Sat. **Credit** AmEx, DC, MC, V. **Map** p345 C6.
La Manual Alpargatera opened in 1910, stocking handmade espadrilles. The store has shod such luminaries as Pope John Paul II and Jack Nicholson during its years of service – be warned, however, that these names are good indications of the kind of styles you'll find on sale. However, for a basic beach shoe, the prices are astoundingly low.

CONSUME

★ Muxart
C/Rosselló 230, Eixample (93 488 10 64/www. muxart.com). Metro Diagonal. **Open** 10am-2pm, 4.30-8.30pm Mon-Fri; 10am-2pm, 5-8.30pm Sat. **Credit** AmEx, DC, MC, V. **Map** p338 G6/7.
Muxart sells shoes around which to build an outfit. The materials are refined, and the styles are sharp, avant-garde and blatantly not designed to be hidden under a pair of baggy beige slacks. Lines for men and women are complemented by equally creative and attractive bags and accessories.
Other locations Rambla de Catalunya 47, Eixample (93 467 74 23).

Le Shoe
C/Tenor Viñas 4-6, Sant Gervasi (93 200 54 20/www.leshoe.com). FGC Muntaner/bus 6, 7, 15, 33, 34, 67, 68. **Open** 10.30am-2.30pm, 5-8.30pm Mon-Fri. Closed 2wks Aug. **Credit** AmEx, DC. MC, V. **Map** p338 E4.
It's a little off the beaten shopping track, but Le Shoe is well worth the trip for any dedicated footwear fanatic willing to blow a month's salary on the latest killer heels from the likes of Marc Jacobs, Alessando dell'Acqua, Robert Clergerie, Nebuloni or Sonia Rykiel. For a cheaper designer fix, there's an outlet store on Rambla de Catalunya 77.

Muxart.

FOOD & DRINK

Drinks

Lavinia
Avda Diagonal 605, Eixample (93 363 44 45/ www.lavinia.es). Metro Maria Cristina. **Open** 10am-9pm Mon-Sat. **Credit** AmEx, DC, MC, V. **Map** p338 D5.
This ultra-slick store houses the largest selection of wines in Europe. Knowledgeable, polyglot staff happily talk customers through the store's rows of horizontally displayed Spanish and international wines, including exceptional vintages and special editions at good prices. They'll also help you put together cases to send home and let you try before you buy.
▶ *For more on Catalonian wine country, see pxxx.*

Torres
C/Nou de la Rambla 25, Raval (93 317 32 34/ www.vinosencasa.com). Metro Drassanes or Liceu. **Open** 9am-2pm, 4-9pm Mon-Sat. **Credit** MC, V. **Map** p345 A6.
Torres's shiny shop is a bit out of place in the rundown end of the Raval, but it's worth a visit. There's a good range of Spanish wines (with a particularly fine cava section) along with interesting beers and spirits from elsewhere, including black Mallorcan absinthe. Prices are competitive.

★ Vila Viniteca
C/Agullers 7, Born (902 32 77 77/www. vilaviniteca.es). Metro Jaume I. **Open** *Sept-June* 8.30am-8.30pm Mon-Sat. *July, Aug* 8.30am-8.30pm Mon-Fri; 8.30am-2pm Sat. **Credit** DC, MC, V. **Map** p345 D7.
This family-run business has built up a stock of more than 6,000 wines and spirits since 1932. Whether you want to blow €1,245 on a magnum of 2003 L'Ermita or just snag a €5 bottle of table wine, you'll find something to drink. The selection here is mostly Spanish and Catalan, but does cover international favourites. The new food shop next door at No.9 stocks fine cheeses, cured meats and oils.
Other locations Vinacoteca, València 595, Eixample (93 232 58 35).

General

The supermarket in the basement of **El Corte Inglés** (*see p196*) in Plaça Catalunya has a gourmet section of local and foreign specialities.

Carrefour Express
La Rambla 113, Barri Gòtic (93 302 48 24). Metro Catalunya. **Open** 10am-10pm Mon-Sat. **Credit** MC, V. **Map** p344 B3.
The opening hours, the chemist and the unbeatable location make up for the slight shabbiness, the confusing layout and the agonising checkout queues.

CONSUME

La Boqueria.

Colmado Quilez
Rambla Catalunya 63, Eixample (93 215 23 56).
Metro Passeig de Gràcia. **Open** *Jan-mid Oct*
9am-2pm, 4.30-8.30pm Mon-Fri; 9am-2pm Sat.
Mid Oct-Dec 9am-2pm, 4.30-8.30pm Mon-Sat.
Credit MC, V. **Map** p338 F/G8.
Colmados – old-school grocery stores – are relics of
the old way of shopping before the invasion of the
supermarkets. This is one of the few surviving
examples in the Modernista Eixample, with floor-to-
ceiling shelves stacked full of gourmet treats: local
preserved funghi in cute mushroom-shaped bottles
(Delicias del Bosque), and the store's own-label
caviar, cava, saffron and anchovies.

Markets

For more on markets, *see p198.* **Mercat
Santa Caterina** (Avda Francesc Cambó, 93
319 57 40, www.mercatsantacaterina.net), in a
remarkable Gaudiesque building designed by
the late Enric Miralles, is also worthy of note.

★ La Boqueria
La Rambla 89, Raval (93 318 25 84/www.
boqueria.info). Metro Liceu. **Open** 8am-8.30pm
Mon-Sat. **Map** p344 B4.
Thronged with tourists searching for a little bit of
Barcelona's gastro magic, and usually ending up
with a pre-sliced quarter of overpriced pineapple,
Europe's biggest food market is still an essential
stop. Admire the orderly stacks of ridged Montserrat
tomatoes, the wet sacks of snails and the oozing
razor clams on the fish stalls. If you can't or don't

want to cook it all yourself, you can eat instead at
several market tapas bars.
    If you visit in the morning, you'll see the best pro-
duce, including the smallholders' fruit and vegetable
stalls in the little square attached to the C/Carme side
of the market, where prices tend to be cheaper. But
if you come only to ogle, remember that this is where
locals come to shop. Don't touch what you don't
want to buy, ask before taking photos and watch out
for vicious old ladies with ankle-destroying wheeled
shopping bags.

Specialist

La Botifarreria de Santa Maria
C/Santa Maria 4, Born (93 319 97 84). Metro
Barceloneta or Jaume I. **Open** 8.30am-2.30pm,
5-8.30pm Mon-Fri; 8.30am-3pm Sat. Closed Aug.
Credit MC, V. **Map** p345 E7.
In this charming old shop, metres and metres of the
typical Catalan botifarra sausage are made anew
every day, along with unusual variations (cider,

INSIDE TRACK
ARTISAN FOOD FAIRS

The city is home to a number of artisan
food fairs, similar in spirit to farmers'
markets in the UK. The most central is at
picturesque **Plaça del Pi**, held on the first
and third weekends of the month (Friday
to Sunday) and during local fiestas.

squid, Cabrales cheese, even chocolate). Before Lent, look out for the traditional yellowy egg botifarras. Other porky treats on offer include farmhouse pâtés, top quality acorn-fed ham and some of the more unusual types of local cured sausages such as *xolís*.

★ Caelum

C/Palla 8, Barri Gòtic (93 302 69 93). Metro Liceu. **Open** 5-8.30pm Mon; 10.30am-8.30pm Tue-Thur; 10.30am-11pm Fri, Sat; 11.30am-9pm Sun. Closed 1wk Aug. **Credit** AmEx, DC, MC, V. **Map** p344 C4.

Spain's monks and nuns have a naughty sideline in traditional sweets including 'pets de monja' (little chocolate biscuits known as 'nuns' farts') candied saints' bones, and drinkable goodies such as eucalyptus and orange liqueur, all beautifully packaged. If you'd like to sample before committing to a whole box of Santa Teresa's sugared egg yolks, there's a café downstairs on the site of the medieval Jewish thermal baths.

La Campana

C/Princesa 36, Born (93 319 72 96). Metro Jaume I. **Open** 10am-9pm daily. **Credit** MC, V. **Map** p345 E5.

Founded in 1922, this lovely old shop sells *turrons*, blocks of nougat traditionally eaten at Christmas. They come in two types: soft (Xixona) or hard and brittle (Alicant). In the summer, there's *orxata*, an ice-cold drink made from tiger nuts; there are also wide ranges of ice-creams and pralines.
Other locations C/Flassaders 15, Born (93 319 72 96).

▶ *Those with a sweet tooth may like the wares at nearby ice-cream parlour Gelaaati!; see p184.*

★ Casa Gispert

C/Sombrerers 23, Born (93 319 75 35/www. casagispert.com). Metro Jaume I. **Open** *Jan-Sept* 9.30am-2pm, 4-7.30pm Tue-Fri; 10am-2pm, 5-8pm Sat. *Oct-Dec* 9.30am-2pm, 4-7.30pm Mon-Fri; 10am-2pm, 5-8pm Sat. **Credit** MC, V. **Map** p345 E6.

Casa Gispert radiates a warmth that has something to do with more than just its original wood-fired nut and coffee roaster. Like a stage-set version of an olde school shoppe, its wooden cabinets and shelves groan with the finest and most fragrant nuts, herbs, spices, preserves, sauces, oils and seasonings. The pre-packed kits for making local specialities such as *panellets* (Halloween bonbons) make great gifts.

Escribà

Gran Via de les Corts Catalanes 546, Eixample (93 454 75 35/www.escriba.es). Metro Urgell. **Open** 8am-3pm, 5-9pm Mon-Fri; 8am-9pm Sat, 8am-3pm Sun. **Credit** DC, MC, V. **Map** p342 E8.

Antoni Escribà, the 'Mozart of Chocolate', died in 2004, but his legacy lives on. His team produces jaw-dropping creations for Easter, from a chocolate

Caelum.

Grand Canyon to a life-size model of Michelangelo's *David*. The smaller miracles include cherry liqueur encased in red chocolate lips. The Rambla branch is situated in a pretty Modernista building.
Other locations La Rambla 83, Raval (93 301 60 27).

▶ *To see more of Escribà's chocolate sculptures, visit the Museu de la Xocolata; see p233.*

★ Formatgeria La Seu

C/Daqueria 16, Barri Gòtic (93 412 65 48/ www.formatgerialaseu.com). Metro Jaume I. **Open** 10am-2pm, 5-8pm Tue-Thur; 10am-3.30pm, 5-8pm Fri, Sat. Closed Aug. **No credit cards**. **Map** p345 D6.

Spain has long neglected its cheese heritage – this is the only shop in the country to specialise in Spanish-only farmhouse cheeses. Scottish owner Katherine McLaughlin hand-picks her wares, such as a manchego that knocks the socks off anything you'll find in the market or the truly strange Catalan tupí. She also stocks six varieties of cheese ice-cream and some excellent value olive oils. Her taster plate of three cheeses and a glass of wine for just a few euros is a great way to explore what's on offer.

★ Jamonísimo

C/Provença 85, Eixample (93 439 08 47/ www.jamonisimo.com). Metro Hospital Clínic. **Open** *Sept-July* 5-9pm Mon; 9.30am-2.30pm, 5-9pm Tue-Fri; 9.30am-2.30pm, 5.30-9pm Sat.

CONSUME

Herboristeria del Rei.

Aug 9.30am-2.30pm, 5-9pm Mon-Fri; 9.30am-2.30pm Sat. **Credit** AmEx, DC, MC, V.
Map p338 D7.
This is where Alain Ducasse, Joël Robuchon and Ferran Adrià buy their ham: simply the best available acorn-fed Iberian hams, made by artisans who control the entire process from breeding to curing. The dedicated and passionate salesmen are also happy to talk you through the purchase of jamón paraphernalia such as leg holders and knives, and there are tables where you can try a 'plate of three textures' or divine ham croquettes matched with great Spanish wines.

Olive

Plaça de les Olles 2, Born (93 310 58 83). Metro Barceloneta. **Open** 10.30am-9pm Mon-Sat.
Credit DC, MC, V. **Map** p345 E7.
Buying from small-scale producers of olive oil-based delicacies in Provence, Tuscany and Spain, this French chain has ventured below the Pyrenees. As well as oils, fruit vinegars, compotes and a cornucopia of other mouthwatering delights, it has gorgeously packaged soap, candles and cosmetics.

Papabubble

C/Ample 28, Barri Gòtic (93 268 86 25/ www.papabubble.com). Metro Barceloneta or Drassanes. **Open** 10am-2pm, 4-8.30pm Tue-Fri; 10am-8.30pm Sat; 11am-7.30pm Sun. Closed 2wks Aug. **Credit** AmEx, MC, V. **Map** p345 C7.
Push through the crowds to watch the Australian owners stretch, roll and chop their kaleidoscopic rock candy into lollies, sticks, humbugs and novelty sculptures. The goodies come in any flavour from strawberry to lavender or passion fruit.

Gifts & souvenirs

Arlequí Mascares

C/Princesa 7, Born (93 268 27 52/www. arlequimask.com). Metro Jaume I. **Open** 10.30am-8.30pm Mon-Sat; 10.30am-4.30pm Sun.
Credit MC, V. **Map** p345 D5.
The walls here are dripping with masks, crafted from papier mâché and leather. Whether gilt-laden or in feathered commedia dell'arte style, simple Greek tragicomedy styles or traditional Japanese or Catalan varieties, they make striking fancy dress or decorative staples. Other trinkets and toys include finger puppets, mirrors and ornamental boxes.
Other locations Plaça Sant Josep Oriol 8, Barri Gòtic (93 317 24 29); C/Caballeros 10, Poble Espanyol (93 426 21 69).

Cereria Subirà

Baixada de Llibreteria 7, Barri Gotic (93 315 26 06). Metro Jaume I. **Open** 9am-1.30pm, 4-7.30pm Mon-Fri; 9am-1.30pm Sat. **Credit** AmEx, DC, MC, V. **Map** p345 D5.
With a staircase fit for a full swish from Scarlett O'Hara, this exquisite candle shop dates back to the pre-electric days of 1716 when candles were an everyday necessity at home and in church. These days, the votive candles sit next to novelties such as After Eight-scented candles and candles in the shape of the Sagrada Família, alongside related goods such as garden torches and oil burners.

Dos i Una

C/Rosselló 275, Eixample (93 217 70 32). Metro Diagonal. **Open** 10.30am-2pm, 5-8.30pm Mon-Sat. **Credit** AmEx, DC, MC, V.
Map p338 G6/7.
The first ever design shop in Barcelona (est. 1977) and an early patron of celebrated designer Javier Mariscal, Dos i Una stocks good quality designer frippery such as retro, round-cornered postcards in glorious Technicolor, cheese graters in the shape of flamenco dancers, flower-shaped tea cups, chrome cuckoo clocks, colourful prints and jewellery.

Flora Albaicín

C/Canuda 3, Barri Gòtic (93 302 10 35). Metro Catalunya. **Open** 10.30am-1pm, 5-8pm Mon-Sat.
Credit AmEx, MC, V. **Map** p344 B3.

This tiny boutique is bursting at the seams with brightly coloured flamenco frocks, polka-dotted shoes, head combs, bangles, shawls and everything else you need to dance the *sevillanas* in style.
▶ *Shop here before going to the nearby Feria de Abril de Catalunya (see p225).*

★ Herboristeria del Rei
C/Vidre 1, Barri Gòtic (93 318 05 12).
Metro Liceu. **Open** 4-8pm Tue-Fri; 10am-8pm Sat. Closed 1-2wks Aug. **Credit** MC, V.
Map p345 B6.
Designed by a theatre set designer in the 1860s, this atmospheric shop hides myriad herbs, infusions, ointments and unguents for health and beauty. More up-to-date stock includes vegetarian foods, organic olive oils and organic mueslis; it's also a good place to buy saffron.

★ El Rei de la Màgia
C/Princesa 11, Born (93 319 39 20/www.
elreidelamagia.com). Metro Jaume I. **Open**
Sept-June 10am-2pm, 5-8pm Mon-Fri; 11am-2pm Sat. *July, Aug* 11am-2pm, 5-8pm Mon-Fri.
Credit MC, V. **Map** p345 E5.
Cut someone in half, make a rabbit disappear or try out any number of other professional-quality stage illusions at the beautiful old 'King of Magic.' Less ambitious tricksters can practise their sleight of hand with the huge range of whoopee cushions, squirty flowers and itching powder.
▶ *The same people run the Museu de la Màgia; see p233.*

Xilografies
C/Freneria 1, Barri Gòtic (93 315 07 58). Metro Jaume I. **Open** 10am-2pm Mon-Sat. Closed Aug.
No credit cards. **Map** p345 D5.
Using painstakingly detailed 18th-century carved boxwood blocks that have been passed down in her family for generations (some of which are displayed in a glass cabinet in this tiny shop), Maria creates *ex libris* stickers for books, bookmarks, notepaper, address books and prints. She also sells

Flors Navarro.

pens, birthday cards, prints of 18th-century maps and reproduction pocket sundials.

Flowers

The 18 flower stalls dotting the Rambla de les Flors originated from the old custom of Boqueria market traders giving a free flower to their customers. There are also stands at the **Mercat de la Concepció** (C/Aragó 311, Eixample, 93 457 53 29, www.laconcepcio.com), on the corner of C/València and C/Bruc (map p339 H7), some of which are open all night. Many local florists also offer the Interflora delivery service.

Flors Navarro
C/València 320, Eixample (93 457 40 99/www.
floresnavarro.com). Metro Verdaguer. **Open**
24hrs daily. **Credit** AmEx, MC, V. **Map** p338 H7.
At Flors Navarro, fresh-cut blooms, pretty house plants and stunning bouquets are available to buy 24 hours a day. A dozen red roses can be delivered anywhere in the city, until 10pm, for €36.

HEALTH & BEAUTY

Hairdressers

Llongueras

Passeig de Gràcia 78, Eixample (93 215 41 75/www.llongueras.com). Metro Passeig de Gràcia. **Open** *Sept-June* 9am-7pm Mon-Sat. *July, Aug* 9am-6pm Mon-Fri; 9am-1pm Sat. **Credit** AmEx, DC, MC, V. **Map** p338 G7.

A safe bet for all ages, this pricey Catalan chain has well-trained stylists who take the time to give a proper consultation, wash and massage. The cuts are up-to-the-minute but as natural as possible. **Other locations** throughout the city.

Raffel Pagès

C/Canuda 22-24, Barri Gòtic (93 301 25 99/ www.raffelpages.com). Metro Catalunya. **Open** 9am-8pm Mon-Fri; 9am-2pm Sat. **Credit** MC, V. **Map** p344 C3.

The huge advantage of this chain is that they don't take appointments: whenever you feel the spontaneous need for a change of style, you can simply wander right in. With a whole army of stylists waiting to pounce, there's never a queue; although service won't be particularly personalised or lingering, it will be professional, competent and well priced. **Other locations** throughout the city.

Rock & Roll

C/Palma de Sant Just 12, Barri Gòtic (93 268 74 75). Metro Jaume I. **Open** 10.30am-8pm Tue-Fri; 10am-4pm Sat. Closed 3wks Aug. **Credit** AmEx, MC, V. **Map** p345 C6.

Blinding white decor and bleeping electronica usually indicate tyrannical stylists, but those that work here don't insist on the latest fashion foibles: if you want a tiny trim, that's what you'll get. A basic cut and blow-dry is €35 for women and €23 for men.

Opticians

Grand Optical

El Triangle, Plaça Catalunya 4, Eixample (93 304 16 40/www.grandoptical.com). Metro Catalunya. **Open** 10am-10pm Mon-Sat. **Credit** AmEx, DC, MC, V. **Map** p344 B2.

There are some English-speaking staff at this handy optical superstore in the centre of town. Efficient service means that you should be able to have your prescription sunglasses or standard specs ready in as little as an hour. All products come with a year's guarantee, which is redeemable in any Grand Optical outlet worldwide.

Pharmacies

Pharmacies (*farmàcies/farmàcias*) are signalled by large green and red neon crosses. About a dozen operate around the clock, while more have late opening hours; some of the most central are listed below. The full list of pharmacies that stay open late and/or all night is posted outside every pharmacy door and in the local papers. You can also call two helplines, 010 and 098, for information. Late-night pharmacies may appear closed, but you'll get help by knocking on the shutters.

Farmàcia Alvarez

Passeig de Gràcia 26, Eixample (93 302 11 24). Metro Passeig de Gràcia. **Open** 8am-10.30pm Mon-Thur; 8am-midnight Fri; 9am-midnight Sat. **Credit** MC, V. **Map** p342 G8.

Farmàcia Cervera

C/Muntaner 254, Eixample (93 200 09 96). Metro Diagonal/FGC Gràcia. **Open** 24hrs daily. **Credit** AmEx, MC, V. **Map** p338 E5.

Farmàcia Clapés

La Rambla 98, Barri Gòtic (93 301 28 43). Metro Liceu. **Open** 24hrs daily. **Credit** AmEx, MC, V. **Map** p344 B4.

Farmàcia Vilar

Vestibule, Estació de Sants, Sants (93 490 92 07). Metro Sants Estació. **Open** 7am-10.30pm Mon-Fri; 8am-10.30pm Sat, Sun. **Credit** AmEx, MC, V. **Map** p341 B7.

Shops

The ground floor of **El Corte Inglés** (*see p196*) also has a good range of toiletries.

Sephora

El Triangle, C/Pelai 13-37, Eixample (93 306 39 00/www.sephora.es). Metro Catalunya. **Open** 10am-10pm Mon-Sat. **Credit** AmEx, DC, MC, V. **Map** p344 B2.

Sephora is your best bet for unfettered playing around with scents and make-up. Make-up and toiletries include most of the usual mid- to high-end brands; there are also handy beauty tools, such as eyebrow tweezers and pencil sharpeners. **Other locations** Diagonal Mar, Avda Diagonal 3, Poblenou (93 356 23 19); La Maquinista, C/Potosí s/n, Sant Andreu (93 360 87 21).

INSIDE TRACK
NO PRESCRIPTION NEEDED

The Spanish attitude to dispensing drugs is relaxed. You can legally obtain many drugs that are more tightly regulated in other countries, including contraceptive pills and some antibiotics, without a prescription.

CONSUME

Spas & salons

★ Aire de Barcelona

Passeig Picasso 22, Born (902 555 789/www. airedebarcelona.com). Metro Arc de Triomf or Jaume I. **Open** 10am-midnight daily. *Baths* (90 mins) €24; (incl 15-min massage) €35. **Credit** MC, V. **Map** p343 H11.

Opened in 2008, these subterranean, bare-bricked Arab baths are superbly relaxing, and offer a range of extra massages in addition to the basic package of hot and cold pools, jacuzzi, salt-water pool, hammam and relaxation zone. Entrance is offered every two hours from 10am and reservations are advisable. If you've left your swimsuit at home, you can borrow one, or buy one for a mere €10.

Instituto Francis

Ronda de Sant Pere 18, Eixample (93 317 78 08/www.institutofrancis.com). Metro Catalunya. **Open** 9.30am-8pm Mon-Fri; 9am-4pm Sat. **Credit** DC, MC, V. **Map** p344 D2.

Europe's largest beauty centre has seven floors and more than 50 staff all dedicated to making you beautiful – inside and out. As well as offering all the usual facials, massages, anti-cellulite treatments and manicures, the institute specialises in depilation, homeopathic therapies and non-surgical procedures such as teeth whitening and micropigmentation.

HOUSE & HOME

Antiques

If you don't mind haggling, dealers set up stands at Port Vell at weekends. C/Palla is the main focus for antiques in the Barri Gòtic; however, they're of variable quality. Dazzlingly expensive antiques can be found on C/Consell de Cent in the Eixample; there are more affordable goodies around C/Dos de Maig, near Els Encants fleamarket (*see p219*). Other worthwhile markets include the **stamp and coin market** on Plaça Reial (9am-2.30pm Sun), and the weekly **book and coin market** (*see p199*).

Antiques Market

Plaça Nova, Barri Gòtic (93 302 70 45). Metro Jaume I. **Open** 10am-9pm Thur. Closed 3wks Aug. **No credit cards**. **Map** p344 C4.

Thanks in part to its location in front of the cathedral, this market charges prices that are targeted at tourists – be prepared to haggle. The set-up dates from the Middle Ages, but antiques generally consist of smaller and more modern items: sepia postcards, *manila* shawls, pocket watches, typewriters, lace, cameras and jewellery, among bibelots and bric-a-brac. In the first week of August, and from 27 November to 20 December, the market is held at Avda Portal de l'Àngel.

L'Arca de l'Àvia.

L'Arca de l'Àvia

C/Banys Nous 20, Barri Gòtic (93 302 15 98/ www.larcadelavia.com). Metro Liceu. **Open** 5-8pm Mon; 10.30am-2pm, 5-8pm Tue-Fri; 11am-2pm Sat. Closed 2wks Aug. **Credit** AmEx, DC, MC, V. **Map** p345 C5.

Specialising in antique textiles, the 'Grandmother's Ark' smells wonderfully of cloves and freshly ironed linen and is bursting with both antique and reproduction curtains, bed linen, table cloths, clothes and a snowstorm of handmade lace. It's particularly popular with brides seeking original lace veils, and is also the perfect place to go in search of a jaw-dropping lace *mantilla* (lace headdress) or lavishly embroidered *mantones* (fringed silk shawls).

Bulevard dels Antiquaris

Passeig de Gràcia 55, Eixample (93 215 44 99/ www.bulevarddelsantiquaris.com). Metro Passeig de Gràcia. **Open** 10.30am-1.30pm, 4.30-8.30pm Mon-Sat. **Credit** AmEx, MC, V. **Map** p338 G7.

This small antiques 'mall' is one of the most convenient and safest places to shop for antiques in Barcelona (experts inspect every object for authenticity). Miró and Tapies fans can buy limited-edition prints of works by these local artists at March (No.42). Check out the style of ethnic art that influenced the likes of Miró at Raquel Montagut (No.11), where you can pick up a Nigerian funeral urn if that's just what your hallway is missing. Collectors will love the antique playthings at Tric Trac (No.43) and Govary's (No.54).

Queviures Murria.

Farmàcia Nordbeck.

Preservation Orders

The backstory behind Barcelona's fabulous frontage.

Barcelona's loyalty to the old ways of retail is reflected in more than just quaintly long-winded service. Just as many shops have stayed in the same familial hands for generations, they have also maintained their original façades and fittings. All this means that time-strapped tourists can shop and sightsee all at once.

Starting in the Born, **Casa Gispert** (*see p213*) has kept its 150-year-old elegant mirror, glass and wood frontage, dark wood fittings and ancient roasting oven. Crossing the Via Laietana into the Barri Gòtic, the slightly younger **Herboristeria del Rei** (*see p215*) conserves a stunning interior of marble, mahogany and painted glass dating from 1860.

Although there are some Modernista jewels worth seeking out among the tacky souvenir shops of La Rambla, the Antigua Casa Figueras, now home to the **Escribà** pâtisserie (*see p213*), is the product of a whole team of Modernista artists, from sculptor Lambert Escaler to mosaic artist Mario Maragliano. This is just down the street from the **Boqueria** (*see p211*), which has recently renovated some of its Modernista wrought iron and stained glass in a bid to boost its landmark status even further. Pop through the market up to C/Carme and you'll find one of the Raval's few Modernista treasures – the **El Indio** textile store (no.24), with a stunning flourish-laden theatrical frontage of marble and Modernista motifs.

But the Eixample, as the cradle of Modernista architecture, is where you'll find the most preened and preserved frontages. **Forn Sarret**'s (C/Girona 73) extravagantly crafted, graceful wooden door frames seem to herald the entrance to a fairy world rather than the place to buy your daily loaf. And **Queviures Murria**'s (C/Roger de Llúria 85, 93 215 57 89) shopfront is a veritable art gallery, featuring original hand-painted adverts for local booze Anis del Mono by Modernista artist Ramon Casas.

Pharmacies, however, are the cream of the crop when it comes to retaining original Modernista splendours. One of the most stunning is **Farmàcia Nordbeck** (C/Ausias Marc 31), which dates from around 1905. Its façade is divided by three wood-panelled pillars carved with ornate floral motifs – patterns that are repeated in the stained–glass doors and original wooden interior. But there are plenty more with intriguing interiors: look for the stained-glass orange tree welcoming you to **Farmàcia Bolos** (Rambla de Catalunya 77), the painted bandstand on the ceiling of **Farmàcia Ferrer Argelaguet** (C/Roger de Lluria 74) and **Farmàcia Puigoriol**'s (C/Mallorca 312) pretty, stone-encrusted glass doors.

Els Encants

C/Dos de Maig 177-187, Plaça de les Glòries,
Eixample (93 246 30 30/www.encantsbcn.com).
Metro Glòries. **Open** 9am-6pm Mon, Wed, Fri,
Sat. *Auctions* 7-9am Mon, Wed, Fri. **No credit
cards. Map** p343 L8.

The new location of this open-air flea market has
been up in the air for years, but the Ajuntament has
finally decided to put it in the central plaza of the
remodelled Sant Antoni market. It should open in
2012; but for now, the market remains a crazy and
chaotic antidote to the Glòries shopping mall next
door with its stew of shouts, musty smells and tee-
tering piles of everything from old horseshoes and
Barça memorabilia to cheap electrical gadgets, religious relics and ancient Spanish schoolbooks.

  If you want to buy furniture at a decent price, join
the commercial buyers at the auctions from 7am, or
arrive at noon, when unsold stuff drops in price.
Don't forget to check out the vast warehouses on the
market's outskirts, where you may find a bargain –
even if you have to dig your way through a pile of
junk to find it. Avoid Saturdays, when prices shoot
up and the crowds move in, and be on your guard
for pickpockets and short-changing.

General

Recdi8

C/Espaseria 7, Born (93 268 02 57/www.recdi8.
com). Metro Jaume I. **Open** 11.30am-2.30pm,
5-8.30pm Mon-Thur; 11.30am-2pm, 5-9pm Fri,
Sat. Closed 2wks Aug. **Credit** AmEx, DC, MC, V.
Map p345 E7.

Chrome goat horn coat hooks, flowery bicycle bas-
kets and novelty piggy banks are just some of the
fripperous goodies on display. However, while
Recdi8 scores high on the quirkometer, it also has a
fairly healthy showing in taste tests. All the products are made by top style houses such as Tom
Dixon or Muuto, and have some serious design
thought behind them.

  The store's nearby furniture showroom (C/Flor de
Lliri 4, 93 310 69 39) has similarly bright and happy
gear from turquoise bubble chairs to yellow felt rugs
cut like paper snowflakes.

▶ *There are a few more designer goodies mixed
with the fashions at nearby Lobby; see p205.*

★ Vinçon

Passeig de Gràcia 96, Eixample (93 215 60 50/
www.vincon.com). Metro Diagonal. **Open** 10am-
8.30pm Mon-Sat. **Credit** AmEx, DC, MC, V.
Map p338 D4.

This is one of the vital organs that keeps Barcelona's
reputation as a city of cutting-edge design alive. The
building itself is a monument to the history of local
design: the upstairs furniture showroom is surrounded by Modernista glory (and you get a peek at
Gaudí's La Pedrera); downstairs in the kitchen, bathroom, garden and other departments, everything is

black, minimalist and hip. Although not cheap,
almost everything you buy here is, or will be, a
design classic, whether it's a Bonet armchair or the
so-called 'perfect' corkscrew.
Other locations TincÇon, C/Rosselló 246,
Eixample (93 215 60 50).

MUSIC & ENTERTAINMENT

C/Tallers, C/Valldonzella, C/Bonsuccès and
C/Riera Baixa in the Raval are dotted with
music shops catering to all tastes and formats,
with plenty of sheet music and instruments.
Mainstream music selections are found in
the huge Avda Portal de l'Àngel branch of
El Corte Inglés (*see p196*) and, more cheaply,
at **FNAC** (El Triangle, Plaça Catalunya 4, 93
344 18 00, www.fnac.es), which also has world
music and acres of classical.

CDs & records

Casa Beethoven

La Rambla 97, Raval (93 301 48 26/www.casa
beethoven.com). Metro Liceu. **Open** 9am-2pm,
4-8pm Mon-Fri; 9am-1.30pm, 5-8pm Sat. Closed
3wks Aug. **Credit** MC, V. **Map** p344 B4.

The sheet music and songbooks on sale in this old
shop in the Raval cover the gamut from Wagner to
the White Stripes, with a concentration on opera.
Books cover music history and theory, while CDs
are particularly strong on both modern and classical Spanish music.

Discos Castelló

C/Tallers 3, 7, 9 & 79, Raval (93 302 59 46/
www.discoscastello.es). Metro Catalunya. **Open**
10am-8.30pm Mon-Sat. **Credit** AmEx, DC, MC,
V. **Map** p344 B2.

Discos Castelló is a home-grown cluster of small
shops, each with a different speciality in music: No.3
is devoted to classical; the largest shop, at No.7, covers pretty much everything; No.9 does hip hop, rock
and alternative pop plus T-shirts and accessories;
and No.79 is best for jazz, '70s pop, electronica and
ethnic music.
Other locations throughout the city.

Gong

C/Consell de Cent 343, Eixample (93 215 34 31/
www.gongdiscos.com). Metro Passeig de Gràcia.
Open 10am-9pm Mon-Sat. **Credit** AmEx, MC,
V. **Map** p338 G8.

An unglamorous but serious record shop chain with
a wide range of stock, which also stretches to DVDs,
books and video games. The poor can flick through
the always extensive bargain rack (and a big box of
old vinyl records). Gong is a reliable source of concert tickets and information.
Other locations Barcelona Glòries, Avda
Diagonal 208, Eixample (93 486 00 28).

CONSUME

CONSUME

Instruments

Guitar Shop

C/Tallers 27, 46 & 61, Raval (93 93 412 19 19/93 317 50 50/93 412 66 22/www.theguitar shop.es). Metro Catalunya. **Open** 10am-2pm, 4.30-8.30pm Mon-Fri. **Credit** AmEx, DC, MC, V. **Map** p344 B2.

A mecca for fretheads, this trio of shops has all the goodies: cedarwood Antonio Aparicio classical guitars, Prudencio Saez flamenco guitars, and cheap Admiras to strum on the beach. At No.27, there's a whole host of vintage Fenders, '80s Marshall amps and the like; bargain-hunters can browse the second-hand equipment at No.61.

New Phono

C/Ample 35-37, Barri Gòtic (93 315 13 61/www.newphono.com). Metro Jaume I. **Open** 10am-2pm, 4.30-8pm Mon-Fri; 10am-2pm Sat. Closed 2wks Aug. **Credit** AmEx, DC, MC, V. **Map** p345 C7.

New Phono's cluster of display rooms holds a range of wind, string and percussion instruments and accessories, while keyboards and recording equipment reside over the road (nos.39-40). Ask about their range of cheaper second-hand instruments and check the noticeboard for musical contacts.

SPORTS & FITNESS

The tourist shops on La Rambla stock a huge range of football strips.

La Botiga del Barça

Maremàgnum, Moll d'Espanya, Port Vell (93 225 80 45). Metro Drassanes. **Open** 10am-10pm daily. **Credit** AmEx, DC, MC, V. **Map** p342 F12/13.

Everything for the well-dressed Barça fan, from the standard blue and burgundy strips to scarves, hats, crested ties, aftershave and even underpants, plus calendars, shirts printed with your name, shield-embossed ashtrays, beach towels and so on. **Other locations** C/Jaume I, Barri Gòtic (93 269 15 32); Ronda Universitat 24, Barri Gòtic (93 318 64 77); Museu del FC Barcelona, Nou Camp (93 409 02 71).

INSIDE TRACK
PHONES FROM FNAC

For a mobile or a Spanish SIM card to use for cheaper calls, head to **FNAC** (El Triangle, Plaça Catalunya 4, 93 344 18 00, 902 10 06 32, www.fnac.es). Make sure your mobile handset is unlocked first. The cards work on a pay-as-you-go basis; top-ups can be easily purchased in tobacconists and ATMs.

Decathlon

C/Canuda 20, Barri Gòtic (93 342 61 61/www. decathlon.es). Metro Catalunya. **Open** 9.30am-9.30pm Mon-Sat. **Credit** AmEx, DC, MC, V. **Map** p344 C3.

Whether you need boxing gloves or a bivouac, a beach volleyball or a bicycle lock, this multi-storey French chain will probably be able to see you right. Additional services include bike repair and hire, and team kit stamping.

Other locations L'Illa, Avda Diagonal 545-557, Eixample (93 444 01 65); Gran Via 2, Gran Via de les Corts Catalanes 75-97, L'Hospitalet de Llobregat (93 259 15 92).

TICKETS

FNAC (El Triangle, Plaça Catalunya 4, 93 344 18 00, www.fnac.es) has a very efficient ticket desk situated on its ground floor, covering everything from theme parks to gigs. Concert tickets for smaller venues are often sold in record shops and at the venues themselves; check street posters around the city for further details.

For Barça tickets, *see below and p277.*

Servi-Caixa – La Caixa

902 332 211/www.servicaixa.com. **Credit** AmEx, DC, MC, V.

Use the special Servi-Caixa cashpoints (you'll find them in most larger branches of La Caixa), dial the phone number or check the website to buy tickets for cinemas, concerts, plays, museums, amusement parks and Barça games. You'll need to show the card with which you made the payment when you collect the tickets; check the pick-up deadline.

Tel-entrada – Caixa Catalunya

902 101 212/www.telentrada.com. **Credit** MC, V.

Tickets for theatre performances, cinemas (including shows at the IMAX), concerts, museums and sights over the phone, online from the website above, or even over the counter at any branch of the Caixa Catalunya savings bank. Tickets can be collected from either Caixa Catalunya cashpoints or the tourist office at Plaça Catalunya (*see p320*).

TRAVELLERS' NEEDS

FNAC (El Triangle, Plaça Catalunya 4, 93 344 18 00, 902 10 06 32, www.fnac.es) and **El Corte Inglés** (*see p196*) both have travel agencies, and www.rumbo.es is also worth checking if you're planning a trip abroad. If you're in the market for new luggage, try **Casa Antich** (*see p208*).

If you have items to send overseas, post offices will send anything weighing up to 30 kilos. For shipping larger boxes and items,

Smelling the Coffee

We reveal the real cost of living in Barcelona.

Prime Minister Zapatero caused a mild furore in 2007 when he claimed that a coffee in a bar only cost 80¢. As anyone living in the real world of massive price inflation would know, the actual cost of is about 50 per cent higher at around €1.20. Maybe the PM is a tea-drinker.

But it's not just the bars that have hoicked their prices. From handbags to haircuts, the euro doesn't stretch as far as it used to in Barcelona. So what can you get for your money these days?

UNDER €5
Stamp for a postcard to the UK **60¢**
Fresh white baguette **90¢**
Training football at Decathlon (*see p220*) **€3**
Litre of Borges extra virgin olive oil **€3.60**
Taxi ride from Plaça Catalunya to Parc Ciutadella **€3.80**

UNDER €10
Cinema ticket at Yelmo Icària (*see p238*) **€7**
One-zone ten-ride card for the metro/bus/train **€7.20**
Pair of basic espadrilles from La Manual Alpargatera (*see p209*) **€7.80**

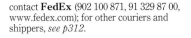

Bottle of Llopart nature cava **€8.95**
Bottle of Torres 10 brandy **€9.49**

UNDER €20
Kilo of top-quality botifarra sausage from Botifarrería Santa María (*see p211*) **€10.20**
Barça scarf from La Botiga del Barça (*see p220*) **€12**
DVD of *The Orphanage* **€17.95**
Ticket to the Zoo (*see p234*) **€15.40**
72 mid-size nappies **€16**

UNDER €50
Two-day travelcard for the Bus Turístic (*see p311*) **€26**
Dozen red roses from Flors Navarro (*see p215*) **€30**
Wash, cut and blow-dry at Raffel Pagès (*see p216*) **€33**
Battery-operated salt mill from Vinçon (*see p219*) **€37.70**
Penélope Cruz jeans at Mango **€39.90**

€50 PLUS
Silicone vibrator at Le Boudoir (*see p208*) **€70-€100**
High-heeled Catalina leather sandals from Camper (*see p209*) **€90**
Basic Admira guitar (La Paloma model) from New Phono (*see p220*) **€109**
Custo Barcelona T-shirt (*see p202*) **€110**
Leg of top-quality, acorn-fed jamón **€400-€500**

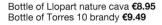

CONSUME

contact **FedEx** (902 100 871, 91 329 87 00, www.fedex.com); for other couriers and shippers, *see p312*.

Halcón Viajes
C/Aribau 34, Eixample (93 454 59 95/902 300 600/www.halconviajes.com). Metro Universitat. **Open** 9.30am-1.30pm, 4.30-8pm Mon-Fri; 10am-1pm Sat. **Credit** AmEx, DC, MC, V. **Map** p338 F8.
This mammoth chain has exclusive deals with Air Europa and Globalia, among others, and can offer highly competitive rates in most areas. Service tends to be quite brisk but efficient.
Other locations throughout the city.

Orixà Viatges
Altaïr, Gran Via de les Corts Catalanes 616, Eixample (93 342 66 26/www.orixa.com). Metro Universitat. **Open** *Mid July-mid May* 10am-2pm, 4.30-7.30pm Mon-Fri. *Mid May-mid July* 10am-2pm, 4.30-7.30pm Mon-Fri; 10am-1pm Sat. **Credit** MC, V. **Map** p342 F8.
Located within the Altaïr travel bookshop, this agency specialises in group and adventure tours in exotic locations, although it also provides all the standard travel services you would expect. English-speaking agents are available.
Other location C/Aragó 227, Eixample (93 487 00 22).

The city's monthly magazine in English

Arts & Entertainment

Montjuïc de Nit.
See p228.

Calendar

Fancy a date?

There are times, in Barcelona, when it can be hard to step out for coffee without bumping into a giant, tripping over a dwarf or sharing the pavement with a dragon. While visitors gasp and fumble for their cameras, Catalans sidestep these strange creatures without so much as a backward glance. This isn't to say that *barcelonins* don't throw themselves into the folkloric festivities with admirable zeal – it's just that there are more city festivals than there are weeks of the year.

The array of religious events and old-fashioned pageants, all of which spotlight what makes Catalonia unique, are supplemented by a wide variety of more modern celebrations. You're just as likely to stumble across a festival of rock documentaries, graffiti art, hip hop or cyber sculpture as you are to see a traditional parade: Sónar alone attracts 80,000 people each year (*see p255*).

LOCAL TRADITION

The key events in the Barcelona year are September's **Festes de la Mercè**, the main city celebrations that offer a wild variety of events. The Mercè and the other 30 or so neighbourhood festes share many traditional ingredients: dwarfs, *castellers* (human castles), and *gegants* (huge papier-mâché/fibreglass giants dressed as princesses, fishermen, sultans and even topless chorus girls), and two unique exercises: the *correfoc* and the *sardana*.

The **correfoc** ('fire run') is a frenzy of pyromania. Groups of horned devils dance through the streets, brandishing tridents that spout fireworks and generally flouting every safety rule in the book. Protected by cotton caps and long sleeves, the more daring onlookers try to stop the devils and touch the fire-breathing dragons being dragged along in their wake.

The orderly antidote to this pandemonium is the **sardana**, Catalonia's folk dance. Watching the dancers executing their fussy little hops and steps in a large circle, it's hard to believe that *sardanes* were once banned as a vestige of pagan witchcraft. The music is similarly restrained, a reedy noise played by an 11-piece *cobla* band. The *sardana* is much harder than it looks, and the joy lies in taking part rather than watching. To try your luck, check out the *sardanes populars* held in front of the cathedral (noon-2pm Sun Jan-Aug & Dec; 6-8pm Sat, noon-2pm Sun Sept-Nov) and in the Plaça Sant Jaume (6pm Sun Oct-July), or see www.fed.sardanista.cat for monthly displays around the city (*see also p60* **It's a fair hop**).

INFORMATION

Organisers are prone to change dates. For more information, try tourist offices, the city's information line (010) and the cultural agenda section at www.bcn.cat. Newspapers also carry details, especially in their Friday or Saturday supplements. Events listed below that include public holidays, when most of the city's shops, bars and restaurants close, are marked *.

EVENTS

Spring

For music festivals, *see p254*; for art festivals, *see p241*; for film festivals, *see p240*.

Festes de Sant Medir de Gràcia

Gràcia to Sant Cugat & back (www.santmedir. org). Starting point Metro Fontana. **Date** 3 Mar. **Map** p340 G4/5 & p339 H4/5.

On or around the feast day of St Emeterius (Sant Medir in Catalan), for almost 200 years colourfully decorated horse-drawn carts have gathered around the Plaça Trilla to ride up to his hermitage in the Collserola hills. The most popular element are the carts that circle the streets of Gràcia and shower the crowd with 100 tons of blessed boiled sweets.

El Feile
Various venues (93 423 76 68/www.elfeile.com). **Date** Week of 17 Mar.
This Saint Patrick's celebration of all things Gaelic has become an established part of the Barcelona calendar in its short life. It embraces music, dance and stand-up comedy, as well as sports such as Gaelic football, rugby and hurling.
▶ *The celebrations are enjoyed with particular enthusiasm at the Quiet Man pub; see p190.*

Setmana Santa* (Holy Week)
Date 21-27 Mar 2009.
Easter for Catalans is a relatively sober affair, with none of the pageantry embraced by their southern cousins. The main event is the blessing of the palms on *diumenge de rams* (Palm Sunday). Crowds surge into the cathedral clutching bleached palm fronds bought from stalls around the city; these are then used to bring luck to households. On Good Friday, a series of small processions and blessings takes place in front of the cathedral. On Easter Sunday, godparents dole out the *mones*: chocolate confections, more elaborate than humble Easter eggs.

Fira de la Terra
Parc de la Ciutadella and Passeig Lluís Companys, Born (www.diadelaterra.org). Metro Arc de Triomf. **Date** late Apr. **Map** p343 H/J 10/11.
The Fira de la Terra is a two-day eco-festival to celebrate Earth Day (22 April), although it's normally held on the nearest weekend to the actual day. There are handicrafts, food stalls and performances, along with talks on environmental issues, though most of the activities are aimed at children.

Sant Jordi
La Rambla & all over Barcelona (www.bcn.cat/stjordi). **Date** 23 Apr.
See p227 **Profile**.

★ Feria de Abril de Catalunya
Fòrum area (www.fecac.com). Metro El Maresme-Fòrum. **Date** end Apr/May.
A pale imitation of Seville's grand Feria de Abril, this week-long, sprawling and joyously tacky event is still a whole heap of fun, especially for fans of fried squid and candy floss. The rows of decorated marquees are a sea of polka dots, as young and old twirl on and off the stages, and onlookers glug manzanilla sherry and scarf some of the greasiest food imaginable. It's great for children, and there's a funfair.

Festival del Grec. *See p226.*

Dia del Treball* (May Day)
Various venues. **Date** 1 May.
A day of demonstrations and marches led by trade unionists representing various left-wing organisations. The main routes cover Plaça da la Universitat, Via Laietana, Passeig de Gràcia, Passeig Sant Joan and Plaça Sant Jaume.

Sant Ponç
C/Hospital. Metro Liceu. **Date** 11 May.
Map p344 A4.
A street market held in honour of the patron saint of beekeepers and herbalists, and ablaze with candied fruit, fresh herbs, natural infusions, honey and honeycomb, most of it straight off the farmer's cart.
▶ *The beautiful Antic Hospital de la Santa Creu is nearby; see p79.*

Barcelona Poesia & Festival Internacional de Poesia
All over Barcelona (93 316 10 00/ www.bcn.cat/barcelonapoesia). **Date** mid May.
This poetry festival started in 1393 as the courtly Jocs Florals (Floral Games), named after the prizes: a silver violet for third prize; a golden rose as second; and, naturally, a real flower for the winner. The games died out in the 15th century but were resuscitated in 1859 as a vehicle for the promotion of the Catalan language. Prizes went to the most suitably florid paeans

For the full listings of venues mentioned here, see their entries in the guide.

ARTS & ENTERTAINMENT

to the motherland; these days, Spanish is permitted, as are Basque and Galician. Many languages can be heard at the International Poetry Festival.

Festa Major de Nou Barris

All over Nou Barris (www.bcn.cat). Metro Virrei Amat. **Date** mid May.

What the humble neighbourhood of Nou Barris lacks in landmark architecture, it makes up for with vim, and along with some great cultural programming, it has a very lively *festa major*, attracting top-notch local bands, along with the usual parades and street fairs. The Nou Barris flamenco festival runs concomitantly, and also brings in some big names.
▶ *There's more flamenco at the annual Festival Guitarra; see p254.*

Dia Internacional dels Museus

All over Barcelona (http://icom.museum/imd.html & www.lanitdelsmuseus). **Date** around 18 May.

Proposed by the International Council of Museums, this worldwide day of free museum entrance has an annual theme with related activites; in 2009 this will be 'Museums and Tourism'. Note that the recommended date is 18 May, but this can vary from year to year. La Nit dels Museus is a new initiative where 21 museums offer free entry on the previous night from 7pm to 1am.

La Tamborinada

Parc de la Ciutadella, Born (93 414 72 01/ www.fundaciolaroda.net). Metro Ciutadella-Vila Olímpica. **Date** late May.

A one-day festival aimed at children, which fills the Ciutadella park with concerts, workshops and circus performances, along with games from snakes and ladders to a towering wall for rock-climbing.

Festa dels Cors de la Barceloneta

Barceloneta. **Date** Weekend of Whitsun (31 May 2009). **Map** p343 H12/13.

In a Pentecostal tradition dating back 150 years, more than 20 choirs of workers parade through the streets of the *barrio* in elaborate costumes garlanded with objects typical of their profession – nets and oars for a fisherman, cereal boxes and sausages for a grocer – on the Saturday morning before Whitsun. They then pile into coaches and take off on a weekend jolly, returning for more parading, fireworks and revelry on Monday evening.

★ L'Ou Com Balla

Ateneu Barcelonès, C/Canuda 6; Casa de l'Ardiaca, C/Santa Llúcia 1; Cathedral cloisters; Museu Frederic Marès; all in Barri Gòtic (information Institut de Cultura 93 301 77 75/www.bcn.cat/icub). **Date** 12-15 June 2009.

L'Ou Com Balla (the 'dancing egg') is a local Corpus Christi tradition dating from 1637: a hollowed-out eggshell is set spinning and bobbing in apparent *perpetuum mobile* on the spout of various fountains

garlanded for the occasion with flowers. The Sunday Corpus Christi procession leaves from the cathedral in the early evening; on the Saturday, there's free entry to the Ajuntament, the Palau Centelles behind it and the Museu d'Història de la Ciutat, along with *sardanes* at 7pm outside the cathedral.

Summer

★ Sant Joan*

All over Barcelona. **Date** night of 23 June.

In the weeks leading up to the feast of St John, the streets become a terrifying war zone of firecrackers and cowering dogs. This is mere limbering up for the main event – on the night of 23 June there are bonfires and firework displays all over the city, but especially the beach, running until dawn. Cava is the traditional tipple, and piles of *coca* – flat, crispy bread topped with candied fruit – are consumed. Special metro and FGC trains run all night and the 24th is a much-needed holiday.

Festa de la Música

All over Barcelona (93 316 10 00/www.bcn.cat/ festadelamusica). **Date** late June.

Started in France in 1982 and now celebrated in more than 100 countries, the three-day Festival of Music sees amateur musicians from 100 countries take to the streets. All events are free, and you're as likely to see a child slapping a bongo as a first-rate blues band, symphony orchestra or choir.

Gran Trobada d'Havaneres

Passeig Joan de Borbó, Barceloneta (93 316 10 00/www.amicshavaneres.com). Metro Barceloneta. **Date** last Sat in June. **Map** p345 E7/8.

The barnacled legacy of Catalonia's old trade links with Cuba, *havaneres* are melancholy 19th-century shanties accompanied by accordion and guitar. The main event is at the port town of Calella de Palafrugells, but the Barcelona satellite is no less fun. Performances by groups dressed in stripy shirts, with salty sea-dog names such as Peix Fregit (fried fish) and Xarxa (fishing net), are followed by *cremat* (flaming spiced rum) and fireworks.

★ Festival del Grec

Various venues (93 316 10 00/www.bcn.cat/grec). **Tickets** €5-€45. **Date** late June-early Aug.

Named after the Greek amphitheatre (Teatre Grec) that forms such an integral part of its programming, this is the major cultural festival of the year. It brings together dozens of shows from around the world, encompassing dance, music, theatre and circus. Increasingly there are performances in English, with Catalan surtitles. *Photo p225.*

★ Música als Parcs

93 413 24 00/www.bcn.cat/parcsijardins. **Date** June-Aug.

Profile Sant Jordi

Cry Déu for Jaume, Catalunya and Sant Jordi.

The fact that Shakespeare, Cervantes and Sant Jordi (St George) all died on 23 April gave rise to the Day of the Book, with Catalonia hitching its patron saint's feast day to the celebratory wagon. A delicious coincidence? Hardly. Though Cervantes' tombstone states 23 April, the date almost certainly refers to his burial and not his death. Shakespeare died while England was using the Julian calendar, and thus actually died on 3 May. And as for St George, they say *he killed a dragon*. Anyone got a pinch of salt?

George has come a long way from the Cappadocian town in which he was supposedly born. There's no historical source for his origins, nor for the idea that he was a Roman soldier, and not even that he was martyred. But then there aren't that many historical sources at all for obscure third-century soldiers. All we have are traces of a man whose mark in history has been obscured by later legends.

The oldest traditions state that George was a soldier who refused to abjure his religion despite the orders of the Emperor Diocletian, and was thus beheaded. However, his sufferings soon underwent inflation, taking in poison drinks, molten lead and being sawn in two. Miraculously, he was even restored to life three times before expiring. While accepting George's sanctity, canonising him in 494 as one of those 'whose names are reverenced among men, but whose acts are known only to God', Pope Gelasius I was sceptical about his invulnerability and forbade the promulgation of such tales.

The cult of St George really took off with the Crusades. Those knights that survived brought the Cappadocian home with them; and then, in the 13th

century Jacobus de Voragine's *Golden Legend* featured a new twist: dragon-killing. George became the emblem of the chivalric culture of medieval Europe, a hero to the peasantry who took every advantage of clerically sanctioned days off.

Later, because St George offered protection to seafarers, port cities such as Barcelona duly adopted him as patron. The saint reciprocated: according to Jaume I, George helped the Catalans conquer the city of Mallorca, and the saint played his part in the Reconquista.

On **April 23**, nearly every building bears the red and gold Catalan flag, bakeries sell Sant Jordi bread streaked with red pâté, and red roses decorate the city's many paintings of George in his dragon-slaying glory. Men traditionally give woman a rose tied to an ear of wheat; women reciprocate with a book. And all for a humble soldier about whom much is believed but little is known.

ONE TO SEE
The city is full of images of its patron saint, but the best is the one carved by Pere Johan in 1418 on the **Palau de la Generalitat** (*see p65*).

This series of free, alfresco concerts runs throughout the summer months in some of Barcelona's loveliest parks. It comprises two cycles; jazz from June to August on Wednesdays and Fridays at 10pm in Ciutadella park in front of the fountain and, in July, young musicians perform a varied classical concert programme from Thursday to Saturday in various parks. A new introduction in 2008 was the municipal band, who boost the programme on occasional Thursdays with shows of crowd pleasers from Gershwin, *West Side Story* and the like.

★ Montjuïc de Nit
Montjuïc (www.bcn.cat/cultura/montjuicnit).
Date early July.
In line with other 'White Night' or 'Nuit Blanche' events across Europe, Barcelona has laid on its own night of dusk-to-dawn entertainment, all of it free. While Rome, Paris, Brussels and others hold theirs in early October, the date was felt to be uncomfortably close to the Mercè celebrations. Instead, a quiet weekend in July was picked for a vibrant selection of music, theatre, dance, cinema and art, with Montjuïc's museums staying open until 3am or so. One of the highlights of 2008, the inaugural year, was a mesmerising midnight performance by La Fura dels Baus in the Olympic Stadium.

Festa Major del Raval
www.bcn.cat/cultura. Metro Drassanes or Liceu.
Date mid to late July
Over three days, events include giants, a fleamarket, children's workshops and free concerts on the Rambla del Raval. This particular *festa major* prides itself on multiculturalism, with music from around the world and ethnic food stalls.

Nits d'Estiu CaixaForum
CaixaForum (93 476 86 00/www.fundacio. lacaixa.es). **Date** every Wed in July, Aug
Many museums hold Nits de Estiu (Summer Nights) programmes in July and August, but CaixaForum has one of the best. All its exhibitions are open until midnight, and there are concerts of varying stripes, films (€2) and other activities.

Festa de Sant Roc
Various venues around Plaça Nova, Barri Gòtic (010/www.bcn.cat). Metro Jaume I. **Date** 12-16 Aug. **Map** p344 C4.
The Festa de Sant Roc, celebrated every year since 1589, is the Barri Gòtic's street party. It's hard to beat for lovers of Catalan traditions: there are parades with the giants and fat heads, *sardana* dancing and 19th-century street games. The festivities, which centre around the Plaça Nova in front of the cathedral, conclude with a *correfoc* and fireworks.

★ Festa Major de Gràcia
All over Gràcia (93 459 30 80/www.festamajorde gracia.cat). Metro Fontana. **Date** 3rd wk in Aug. **Map** p338 G4/5 & p339 H4/5.
The main event at Gràcia's extravagant *festa major* is its street competition, where residents transform some 25 streets into pirate ships, rainforests and Jurassic landscapes. The festival opens with giants

Montjuïc de Nit.

and castles in Plaça Rius i Taulet, and climaxes with a *correfoc* and a *castell de focs* (castle of fireworks). In between, there are some 600 activities, from concerts to *sardanes* and bouncy castles. Recent years have been marred by vandalism and late-night scuffles with the police.

Festa Major de Sants
All over Sants (93 490 62 14/www.bcn.cat). *Metro Plaça de Sants or Sants Estació.* **Date** last wk in Aug.

One of the lesser-known *festes majors*, Sants has a traditional flavour, with floral offerings to images of St Bartholomew at the local church and the market. Major events, such as the *correfoc* on the night of the 24th, can be found in the Parc de l'Espanya Industrial; others are held at Plaça del Centre, C/Sant Antoni, Plaça de la Farga and Plaça Joan Peiro, behind Sants station.

Autumn

Diada Nacional de Catalunya*
All over Barcelona. **Date** 11 Sept.

Catalan National Day commemorates Barcelona's capitulation to the Bourbon army in the 1714 War of the Spanish Succession, a bitter defeat that led to the repression of many Catalan institutions. It's lost some of its vigour but is still a day for national re-affirmation, with the Catalan flag flying on buses and balconies. There are several marches throughout the city, the centre being the statue of Rafael Casanova (who directed the resistance) on the Ronda Sant Pere.

▶ *Many make a pilgrimage to the monastery at Montserrat, Catalonia's spiritual heart; see p290.*

★ Festival Asia
Various venues (www.casaasia.es/festival). **Tickets** free-€15. **Date** late Sept.

This week of twirling saris, Chinese acrobats, music, workshops and stalls from 17 Asian countries, has expanded from its base at the Mercat de les Flors to take in a number of venues, but mostly in the Parc de la Ciutadella. The festival now runs with the Festes de la Mercè; *see below*.

★ Festes de la Mercè*
All over Barcelona (www.bcn.cat/merce). **Date** week of 24 Sept.

This immense, week-long event in honour of the patron saint of the city, Our Lady of Mercy, opens with giants, dragons and *capgrosses* in the Plaça Sant Jaume. It's followed by more than 600 events including *sardanes* and *correfocs* (a tamer version for children, followed by the biggest and wildest of the year on the Saturday night). Other highlights include dazzling fireworks displays from the beaches, free concerts, a seafront air show, sporting events including a swim across the port and a regatta, and a heap of activities for children. The pressure on the

centre has been eased since 2008, when many events were staged up at Montjuïc castle or in the former textile factory, Fabra i Coats, in Sant Andreu. Even so, 100,000 people descended on the Barri Gòtic to watch the final parade.

Mostra de Vins i Caves de Catalunya
Moll de la Fusta, Port Vell (93 552 48 00). Metro Drassanes. **Date** during Festes de la Mercè, Sept. **Map** p342 F12.

This outdoor wine and cava fair has been running since 1980 and now showcases more than 400 labels from around 50 Catalan *bodegas*. Big names include Torres, Freixenet, Codorniu, Pinord and Mont Marçal; also on show are fine cheeses and charcuterie. Ten wine or cava tastings with a free glass cost €6; four food tastings cost €5.

▶ *For wine country in Catalonia, see p289.*

Festa Major de la Barceloneta
All over Barceloneta (93 221 72 44/www. *cascantic.net). Metro Barceloneta.* **Date** late Sept, early Oct. **Map** p343 H12/13.

This tightly knit maritime community throws itself into the local *festes* with incredible gusto. The fun kicks off with fireworks on the beach, a 24-hour football tournament, *falcons* (acrobatic groups), *sardana* dancing and a free tasting of traditional crispy *coca* bread washed down with muscatel, and ends with more of the same ten days later. In between, expect parades, music, fire-breathing dragons, open-air cinema and bouncy castles. Look out, too, for a character called General Bum Bum, who parades with a wooden cannon but stops periodically to fire sweets into crowds of scrabbling children.

La Castanyada*
All over Barcelona. **Date** 31 Oct-1 Nov.

All Saints' Day and the evening before are known as the Castanyada after the traditional treats of *castanyes* (roast chestnuts) along with *moniatos* (roast sweet potatoes) and *panellets* (small almond balls covered in pine nuts). The imported tradition of Halloween has grown in popularity of late, and there are now several celebrations around town. Tots Sants (All Saints') is also known as the Dia dels

Difunts (Day of the Dead); the snacks switch to white, bone-shaped *ossos de sant* cakes. Thousands visit local cemeteries over the weekend to sprinkle the graves with holy water, leave flowers, hold vigils, and honour and pray for the dead.

Winter

Fira de Sant Eloi

C/Argenteria, Born (93 319 84 51/ www.acar.cat). **Date** 1-24 Dec.
Neither as sprawling nor as lively as the Fira de Santa Llúcia (*see below*), this Christmas street fair nonetheless has some pretty handmade gifts, from leather bags and hand-painted ceramics to wooden puppets, and there is live music from 6-8pm.

★ Fira de Santa Llúcia

Pla de la Seu & Avda de la Catedral (93 402 70 00/www.bcn.cat/nadal). Metro Jaume I. **Dates** 2-23 Dec. **Map** p344-345 D4/5.
Dating from 1786, this traditional Christmas fair has expanded to more than 300 stalls selling all manner of handcrafted Christmas decorations and gifts, along with mistletoe, poinsettias and Christmas trees. The most popular figure on sale for Nativity scenes is the curious Catalan figure of the *caganer* (crapper), a small figure crouching over a steaming turd with his trousers around his ankles. Kids line up for a go on the giant *caga tió*, a huge, smiley-faced 'shitting log' that poops out pressies upon being beaten viciously by a stick; smaller versions are on sale in the stalls. There's also a Nativity scene contest, musical parades and exhibitions, including the popular life-size Nativity scene in Plaça Sant Jaume.

Nadal* & Sant Esteve* (Christmas Day & Boxing Day)

Dates 25 & 26 Dec.
The Catalan equivalent of the Christmas midnight Mass is the *missa del gall* (cockerel's mass), held at dawn. Later, the whole family enjoys a traditional Christmas feast of *escudella i carn d'olla* (a meaty stew), seafood and roast truffled turkey, finishing off with great ingots of *turrón*. The *caga tió* (*see above* Fira de Santa Llúcia) gives small gifts but the real booty doesn't arrive until the night of 5 January.

INSIDE TRACK
FREE ADMISSION

In addition to International Museum Day on 18 May, more and more museums are waiving admission on public holidays – particularly **Santa Eulàlia** (12 Feb), **Sant Jordi** (23 Apr), **Corpus Cristi** (*see p226* L'Ou Com Balla), the **Diada** (11 Sept) and the **Mercè** (24 Sept). Look out for 'Portes Obertes' ('open doors').

El Dia dels Sants Innocents

Date 28 Dec.
The name is an incongruous reference to King Herod's Massacre of the Innocents, but in fact this is a cheerful local version of April Fool's Day, with cut-out newspaper figures attached to the backs of unsuspecting victims. The media also introduces fake stories into the day's coverage.

Cap d'Any* (New Year's Eve)

Date 31 Dec & 1 Jan.
In Spain, New Year's Eve tends to be a time for family dinners, with most people emerging to party after midnight, but there is always a group of revellers to be found in Plaça Catalunya. The drill is to wear red underwear for luck in the coming year, and to eat 12 grapes, one for each chime of the clock, at midnight. It's harder than you'd think, and tinned, pre-peeled versions are available. During the day, look out for L'Home dels Nassos, the man who has as many noses as days the year has left (it being the last day, the sly old fox has only one) who parades and throws sweets to the children.

★ Cavalcada dels Reis

www.bcn.es/nadal. **Date** 5 Jan, 5-9pm.
Epiphany is the big Christmas event here, and is marked by the Kings' Parade. Melchior, Gaspar and Balthasar arrive aboard the Santa Eulàlia boat at the bottom of La Rambla before beginning a grand parade around town with a retinue of acrobats, circus clowns and child elfs. The route is published in the newspapers, but normally starts at the lower

Festa del Tres Tombs.

entrance of Ciutadella, running up C/Marquès de l'Argentera and Via Laietana. Later that night, children leave their shoes out on the balcony stuffed with hay for the kings' camels; in the morning, they're either full of presents or edible sugar coal depending on their behaviour the previous year. The following day is a holiday.

★ Festa dels Tres Tombs
Sant Antoni. Metro Sant Antoni. **Date** 17 Jan. **Map** p342 E10.
St Anthony's day naturally enough also marks the *festa major* of the district; all the usual ingredients of music, and *gegants* here include a monstrous, symbolic fire-breathing pig – the form the devil took when tempting the saint. Anthony is patron saint of animals and on his feast day it's still the custom to bring pets to the church of St Anthony to be blessed. Afterwards, horsemen ride three circuits (*tres tombs*) in a formal procession from Ronda Sant Antoni, through Plaça Catalunya, down La Rambla and along C/Nou de la Rambla.

Sa Pobla a Gràcia
Gràcia, around Plaça del Diamant (www.bcn.cat). *Metro Fontana.* **Date** around 17 Jan. **Map** p338 G4/5.
Another celebration in honour of St Anthony, who is one of the world's most venerated saints, this one imported from Mallorca. Two days of Balearic folk festivities see street bonfires, parades of dragons and giants, and candlelit singing (in *mallorquín*) in the Plaça del Diamant.

★ Santa Eulàlia
All over Barcelona. **Date** wk of 12 Feb.
The city's blowout winter festival is in honour of Santa Eulàlia (Laia), who met her end at the hands of the Romans after revolting tortures, Barcelona's co-patron saint and a special favourite of children. Her feast day on 12 February kicks off with a ceremony in Plaça Sant Jaume, followed by music, *sardanes* and parades, with Masses and children's choral concerts held in the churches and cathedral. In the evening, the female giants gather in Plaça Sant Josep Oriol, then go to throw flowers on the Baixada de Santa Eulàlia before a final boogie in the Plaça Sant Jaume. The Ajuntament and the cathedral crypt (where she's buried) are free and open to the public, as are more than 30 museums. The festival closes on Sunday evening with *correfocs* (for adults and children) centred around the cathedral.

Carnaval (Carnival)
All over Barcelona (www.bcn.cat/carnaval). **Date** Shrove Tuesday & Ash Wednesday (24 Feb & 25 Feb 2009).
The city drops everything for a last hurrah of overeating, overdrinking and underdressing prior to Lent. The celebrations begin on Dijous Gras (Mardi Gras) with the appearance of potbellied King Carnestoltes – the masked personification of the carnival spirit – followed by the grand weekend parade, masked balls, *fartaneres* (neighbourhood feasts, typically with lots of pork), food fights and a giant *botifarrada* (sausage barbecue) on La Rambla, with most of the kids and market traders in fancy dress.

ARTS & ENTERTAINMENT

Children

An awfully big adventure.

Children are absorbed into Mediterranean life to an extent that can both delight and shock parents from other parts of the world. Still, if you and they can adapt to later bedtimes, eating in restaurants without worrying about mess or noise, and having strangers start conversations with your little ones, you'll all have a better time for it. Because kids are expected to rub along with adults, you won't find a dazzling range of child-oriented attractions. But Barcelona is a natural playground, and small children are as delighted by its spooky medieval alleys after dark as they are with its sandy beaches by day.

PRACTICALITIES

Public transport is only free for under-fours. An increasing number of metro stations have lifts; see the maps on pp350-52. Officially, pushchairs are supposed to be folded up on the metro, but most people just grapple with the obstacle course and the guards don't interfere. All buses are low enough to wheel buggies straight on.

To see what's on for kids, www.timeout.cat and www.toc-toc.cat carry listings (though you'll need a basic knowledge of Catalan), and www.kidsinbarcelona.com is a reliable source for all kinds of information. Lulu at **Mujer** (*see p201*) has also become a de facto information service for English-speaking mums.

ENTERTAINMENT

Attractions

The two most obviously child-friendly attractions are the excellent **Zoo** and the marginally less exciting **Aquarium**. The **Magic Fountain** (Font Mágica, *see p92*) is also a huge hit; and a simple stroll down **La Rambla**, past the living statues, entertainers, artists and general hubbub, can be a good bet. Fun transport options include the two cable car systems (*see p87 and p98*), the **Blue Tram** (*see p114*) and the **rickshaws** (*see p311*).

There isn't a multitude of museums aimed at kids; one of the better ones is **CosmoCaixa**, the science museum. A must-see for junior footy fiends is the **Museu del FC Barcelona** (*see*

p114), where kids can walk from the dressing rooms through the tunnel and take a few steps on the pitch. The fake Spanish village of **Poble Espanyol** (*see p91*) also has a certain appeal.

★ L'Aquàrium

Moll d'Espanya, Port Vell (93 221 74 74/ www.aquariumbcn.com). Metro Barceloneta or Drassanes. **Open** *Oct-May* 9.30am-9pm Mon-Fri; 9.30am-9.30pm Sat, Sun. *June, Sept* 9.30am-9.30pm daily. *July, Aug* 9.30am-11pm daily. **Admission** €16.50; €11-€13 reductions; free under-4s. **Credit** AmEx, DC, MC, V. **Map** p342 G13.

The main draw here is the Oceanari, a giant shark-infested tank traversed via a glass tunnel on a slow-moving conveyor belt, but naturally other aquaria house shoals of kaleidoscopic fish where kids can play 'hunt Nemo'. The upstairs section is devoted to children: for pre-schoolers, Explora! has 50 knobs-and-whistles style activities, such as turning a crank to see how ducks' feet move underwater or climbing inside a mini-submarine, though much of the equipment is looking a bit the worse for wear. Older children should head to Planet Aqua – an extraordinary, split-level circular space with Humboldt penguins.

★ CosmoCaixa

C/Teodor Roviralta 47-51, Zona Alta (93 212 60 50/www.cosmocaixa.com). Bus 17, 22, 58/ FGC Avda Tibidabo then Tramvia Blau (see p114). **Open** *July-mid Sept* 10am-8pm daily. *Mid Sept-June* 10am-8pm Tue-Sun. **Admission** €3; €2 reductions; free under-3s. *Planetarium* €2; €1.50 reductions; free under-3s. **Credit** AmEx, DC, MC, V.

Child-specific attractions at the science museum include the Bubble Planetarium (a digital 3D simulation of the universe); the Toca Toca! space where supervisors guide the exploration of natural phenomena such as tarantulas and snakes, and the candy-bright Javier Mariscal-designed spaces of Clik (for three- to six-year-olds) and Flash (for seven- to nine-year-olds), where children learn how to generate electricity and how a kaleidoscope works.

Museu de Cera

Ptge de la Banca 7, Barri Gòtic (93 317 26 49/ www.museocerabcn.com). Metro Drassanes. **Open** *Mid July-mid Sept* 10am-10pm daily. *Mid Sept-mid July* 10am-1.30pm, 4-7.30pm Mon-Fri; 11am-2pm, 4.30-8.30pm Sat, Sun. **Admission** €10; €6 reductions; free under-5s. **Credit** MC, V. **Map** p345 B7.

A fun but somewhat shabby wax museum, featuring all the usual characters: Frankenstein, Luke Skywalker, Princess Diana (here holding hands with Mother Teresa while Charles and Camilla look smug). Children who've been to Madame Tussauds are unlikely to be impressed. *Photo p234.*

▶ *Want more kitsch? Visit the adjacent 'enchanted forest' café, El Bosc de les Fades.*

Museu de la Màgia

C/Oli 6, Born (93 319 73 93/www.elreydela magia.com). Metro Jaume I. **Open** *Show* 6pm Sat; noon Sun. Closed July-Sept. **Admission** €8. **No credit cards. Map** p345 B3.

This collector's gallery of 19th- and 20th-century tricks and posters from the magic shop El Rei de la Màgia will enchant any budding magicians. To see some live sleight of hand, book for the shows; places are limited. They're not in English, but they are fairly accessible regardless.

Museu de la Xocolata

C/Comerç 36, Born (93 268 78 78/www.museu delaxocolata.cat). Metro Arc de Triomf or Jaume I. **Open** 10am-7pm Mon, Wed-Sat; 10am-3pm Sun. **Admission** €4.30; €3.75 reductions; free under-7s. **Credit** MC, V. **Map** p345 F5.

The best-smelling museum in town draws chocoholics of all ages to its collection of chocolate sculptures made by Barcelona's master *pastissers* for the Easter competition. These range from multicoloured models of Gaudí's Casa Batlló to characters from *Chicken Run*, while audio-visual shows and touch-screen computers help children make their way through what would otherwise be the rather dry history of the cocoa bean. Reserve in advance for weekend chocolate figurine-making courses and lessons in cooking desserts.

Platja de l'Eixample

C/Roger de Llúria 56 interior, Eixample (93 291 62 60/637 40 28 66). Metro Girona. **Open** *End June-July* 10am-8pm Mon-Sat; 10am-3pm Sun. *Aug* 10am-8pm Mon-Fri; 10am-3pm Sat, Sun. **Admission** €1.40; free under-1s. **No credit cards. Map** p338 G8.

Zoo. *See p234.*

In the summer, this leafy inner patio becomes the 'Eixample Beach', an oasis for the under-sevens. There's a knee-high wading pool, plenty of sand with buckets and spades provided, trees for shade and a water tower in the centre, along with outdoor showers, changing tents and toilets.

Tibidabo Funfair

Plaça del Tibidabo, Tibidabo (93 211 79 42/ www.tibidabo.es). FGC Avda Tibidabo. **Open** *Nov-mid Dec, mid Jan-Feb* 11am-6pm Sat, Sun. *Mar, Apr* 11am-7pm Sat, Sun. *May, June* 11am-8pm Sat, Sun. *July* 11am-8pm Wed-Fri; 11am-11pm Sat; 11am-10pm Sun. *Aug* 11am-10pm Wed-Sun. *1st 2wks Sept* 11am-8pm Wed-Fri; 11am-9pm Sat, Sun. *2nd 2wks Sept* 11am-9pm Sat, Sun. *Oct* 11am-8pm Sat, Sun. Closed mid Dec-mid Jan. **Admission** *individual rides* €11-€14. *Unlimited rides* €24; €19 reductions; €7-€14 children under 1.2m (3ft 11in); free children under 90cm (2ft 11in). **Credit** MC, V.

This hilltop fairground, dating from 1889, is investing millions in getting itself bang up to date, with the terrifying freefall Pendulum and a hot-air balloon style ride for smaller children. Adrenalin freaks are waiting for the rollercoaster currently under construction. The many other attractions include a house of horrors, bumper cars and the emblematic Avió, the world's first popular flight simulator when it was built in 1928. Don't miss the antique mechanical puppets and contraptions at the Museu d'Autòmats, and there are hourly puppet shows at the Marionetàrium (from 1pm). At the weekends, there are circus parades at the end of the day and, in summer, *correfocs* (fire runs) and street theatre.

★ Zoo

Parc de la Ciutadella, Born (93 225 67 80/ www.zoobarcelona.com). Metro Barceloneta or Ciutadella-Vila Olímpica. **Open** *Mar, Oct* 10am-6pm daily. *Apr-Sept* 10am-7pm daily. *Nov-Feb* 10am-5pm daily. **Admission** €15.40; €9.30 3-12s. Free under-3s. **Credit** MC, V. **Map** p343 J11/12.

The dolphin shows are the big draw, but the decently sized zoo has plenty of other animals, all of whom look happy enough in reasonably spacious enclosures and the city's comfortable climate. Favourites include giant hippos, the prehistoric-looking rhino, sea lions, elephants, giraffes, lions and tigers. Child-friendly features include a farmyard zoo, pony rides, picnic areas and two excellent playgrounds. If all that walking is too much, there's a zoo 'train'. Bear in mind that on hot days many of the animals are sleeping and out of sight, and when the temperature drops below 13° many are kept inside. *Photo p233.*

Festivals

The **Festes de Santa Eulàlia** in February are specially geared towards children, with hands-on activities and even a mini *correfoc*. **La Mercè** and the local *festes majors* of each area also have plenty of parades and music; the

Museu de Cera. See p233.

decorated streets of **Festa Major de Gràcia** are especially popular with younger children, and there's a raft of bouncy castles, circus performers and story telling in many of the district's squares. More hits include the carnival parades of **Carnestoltes** or gathering sweets from the streets at the **Festes de Sant Medir de Gràcia**. Christmas traditions are also very child-centred, with racks of pooping *caganers* and pooping logs at the Santa Llúcia market. The Three Kings' procession on 5 January is also a guaranteed hit. For all, *see pp224-231*.

Music, film & theatre

The **Auditori** (*see p270*) and the **Palau de la Música** (*see p271*) often run cycles of family concerts, normally on Sundays. English-language children's theatre is rare, with the exception of the Christmas pantomime, but **La Puntual** (C/Allada Vermell 15, Born, mobile 639 30 53 53, www.lapuntual.info) is a little puppet theatre that often has language-free shows. To catch a film in English, the best bet is the huge **Yelmo Icària Cineplex** (*see p238*) for mainstream blockbusters, while the **FilmoTeca de la Generalitat** (*see p238*) shows original-language children's films on occasional Sundays at 5pm. On a rainy or cold day, the **IMAX Port Vell** (*see p238*) is a good if pricey standby, although the films are only shown in Spanish and Catalan.

PARKS

The **Parc de la Ciutadella** (*see p69*) has shady gardens, a giant mammoth sculpture, play parks, picnic areas, rowing boats and a zoo, which provide a packed day out. Gaudí's quirky **Park Güell** (*see p111*) makes up for its lack of grass with bright gingerbread houses and winding coloured benches. High above the city, the **Parc de la Creueta del Coll** (*see p115*) has a large playground, table-tennis tables, a picnic area and great views, and the large artificial lake is filled up in summer for use as an outdoor public swimming pool. The delightful **Parc del Laberint** (*see p119*) has hidden benches and elfin tables, picnic areas and a deceptively difficult maze, while the **Jardins de la Tamarita** (*see p115*) form a tranquil dog-free enclave of swings and slides hidden away next to the stop for the Tramvia Blau. The lovely **Parc del Castell de l'Oreneta** (Camí de Can Caralleu & Ptge Blada, Zona Alta, 93 413 24 80) has great views, picnic areas, pony rides for three- to 12-year-olds at weekends (11am-2pm, €6) and a miniature train on Sundays. The largest of them all is the **Parc de Collserola** (*see p114*), perfect for young nature lovers. The beachfront esplanades are ideal places for bicycle riding.

EATING & DRINKING

It's rare to find a children's menu in Barcelona, but many restaurants will provide smaller portions on request. That said, there's little need to do so when children and tapas were so clearly made for each other. Basque *pintxo* bars such as **Euskal Etxea** (*see p185*) are an even better option, as children can simply serve themselves from the food that is laid out, waiting for hungry young mouths, on the bar. An important point to remember for families with early-eating children is that most restaurants in Barcelona don't serve lunch before 1.30pm or dinner before 9pm, so play it like the locals and encourage a siesta followed by tea at 5pm so the children can hold out for a late dinner. However, if the children need a snack, there are plenty of options available: **Bar Mendizábal** (*see p188*) is good for fresh

ARTS & ENTERTAINMENT

juices and healthy sandwiches, and there's all-day pizza at **Al Passatore** (Pla del Palau 8, Born, 93 319 78 51). For relaxing in the sun (near a playground), you could try the outdoor terraces at **Bar Kasparo** (*see p188*), Casa Paco (*see p187*) or **Filferro** (C/Sant Carles 29, Barceloneta, 93 221 98 36). **La Miranda del Museu** (*see p190*), at the Catalan history museum, has fantastic views and plenty of terrace space on which to play. There's also lots of safe open space around the beachfront terraces. Ferran Adrià's 'fast-food' restaurant **Fast Good** (*see p167*) has a good kids' menu.

OUT OF TOWN
Catalunya en Miniatura
Can Balasch de Baix, Torrelles de Llobregat (93 689 09 60/www.catalunyaenminiatura.com). By car A2 south to Sant Vicens dels Horts then left to Torrelles de Llobregat (5km/3 miles)/by bus 62 Soler i Sauret (info 93 632 51 33) from Travessera de les Corts. **Open** *July, Aug* 10am-8pm daily. *Sept-June* 10am-6pm Tue-Sun. **Admission** €10; €7.50 4-12s; free under-4s. **Credit** MC, V.

Highlights of these tiny renderings of 170 of Catalonia's most emblematic buildings and sights include a miniature Montserrat, Girona cathedral and everything Gaudí ever laid a finger on. An appropriately munchkin-sized train circles part of the complex, and clowns perform at 1pm on Sundays in the amphitheatre.

Illa de Fantasia
Finca Mas Brassó, Vilassar de Dalt (93 751 45 53/www.illafantasia.com). By car NII north to Premià de Mar then left (24km/15 miles). **Open** *June-mid Sept* 10am-7pm daily. **Admission** €17; €13 under 1.40m; free under-1m. **Credit** AmEx, DC, MC, V.

A large water park with foam slides, kamikaze-style rides and rubber-dinghy chutes, along with pools, a restaurant, supermarket and a range of activities. There's also a picnic/barbecue area in a pine grove.

Port Aventura
977 77 90 90/www.portaventura.es. Train from Passeig de Gràcia (1hr 15mins). **Open** *Mid Mar-mid June, mid Sept-Oct* 10am-7pm daily. *Mid June-mid Sept* 10am-midnight daily. *Nov, Dec* 10am-6pm Fri; 10am-7pm Sat, Sun. **Admission** €39; €31 reductions. *Night ticket* (7pm-midnight) €25; €20.50 reductions. Free under-4s. **Credit** AmEx, DC, MC, V.

A theme park with some 90 rides spread across five internationally themed areas (Mexico, the Far West, China, Polynesia and the Mediterranean), while Popeye and the Pink Panther roam the time-space continuum and hug your kids. The truly stomach-curdling Dragon Khan rollercoaster is one of the highlights; for the little ones, there's the usual slew of carousels and spinning teacups. There are also 100 daily live shows and a spectacular lakeside Fiesta Aventura with lights, music and fireworks.

BABYSITTING & CHILDCARE
Canguro Gigante
Passeig de Sant Gervasi 16-20, Sant Gervasi (93 211 69 61). FGC Avda Tibidabo. **Open** 9am-8pm Mon-Fri. Closed Aug. **Rates** from €6/hr. **No credit cards**.

A daycare centre for children aged one to ten. Meals are available. Some English is spoken.

Cinc Serveis
C/Pelai 50, 3º, 1ª, Eixample (93 412 56 76/24hr mobile 639 361 111/609 803 080/www.5serveis. com). Metro Catalunya. **Open** 9.30am-1.30pm, 4.30-8.30pm Mon-Fri. **No credit cards**. **Map** p344 B2.

The basic rate after 8pm is €11 per hour, plus the cost of the sitter's taxi home. Long-term rates are cheaper and vary according to the age of the child.

Happy Parc
C/Pau Claris 97, Eixample (93 317 86 60/ www.happyparc.com). Metro Passeig de Gràcia. **Open** *July, Aug* 5-9pm daily. *Sept-June* 5-9pm Mon-Fri; 11am-9pm Sat, Sun. Closed last 2wks Aug. **Rates** €4/hr; €1 each subsequent 15mins. **No credit cards**. **Map** p342 G8.

Ball pools, twister slides and more are on offer at this giant indoor fun park and drop-in daycare centre for children up to 11 years old (maximum height 1.45m/4ft 7in). Note that kids have to bring socks.

Tender Loving Canguros
Information Mobile 647 605 989/www. tlcanguros.com. **Open** 9am-9pm Mon-Sat. **No credit cards**.

English resident Lucie Bloor provides short- and long-term nannies and babysitters. All speak fluent English. Prices start at €8 an hour; the agency fee is €15 per session.

INSIDE TRACK
NURSING MATTERS

Nappy-changing rooms and special breastfeeding areas are not widely provided. There are mother-and-baby facilities in El Corte Inglés (*see p197*), the airport, the large shopping malls and Poble Espanyol, but be warned that most nappy changes occur in the car or the pram; breastfeeding is totally accepted in public as long as you are discreet.

Film

The re-emergence of the arthouse and the slow death of dubbing

Offering a love triangle between Penélope Cruz, Javier Bardem and Scarlett Johansson, *Vicky Cristina Barcelona* had the gossip mags buzzing and filmgoers' hearts a-flutter long before its 2008 release. The lesbian scene alone generated enough advance publicity to justify the Ajuntament's vast subsidy to Woody Allen, the movie's director.

It didn't hurt, of course, that Bardem had scooped the 2008 Oscar for best supporting actor, and that Cruz had recently been nominated for best actress. But in the end, despite smouldering turns from the pair, the real showstealer was the city itself, which is just what the Ajuntament had hoped. And the high profile granted to the city by the movie came on the back of yet another great year for Spanish film, with the success of Isabel Coixet's *Elegy* (starring Cruz and Ben Kingsley) joined by unexpected international hits for Juan Antonio Bayona's *The Orphanage* and Jaume Balagueró's *Rec*, chillers both.

LOCAL MOVIEMAKERS

The paramount figure of Spanish cinema, both at home and abroad, continues to be Pedro Almodóvar, whose films invariably shoot to the top of the charts. However, Barcelona-born Isabel Coixet has also found success with her mainstream films, many of which have featured Hollywood-friendly actors and an English script (*My Life Without Me*, *The Secret Life of Words*). Alejandro Amenábar (*The Others*, *The Sea Inside*) is another Spanish director who's found global recognition through English-language movies. And even genre-hopping wild child Álex de la Iglesia (*Perdita Durango*, *Ferpect Crime*) returned to the language of Shakespeare for his most recent film, *Oxford Murders*.

From the next generation of film-makers, Fernando León de Aranoa (*Barrio*, *Mondays in the Sun*, *Princesas*) has built an impressive body of work as a Loach-esque social realis, though with greater doses of well-observed naturalist comedy. Equally distinctive are the many ethereal dreamscapes created by director Julio Medem, including *Cows*, *Lovers of the Arctic Circle*, *Sex and Lucia* and *Chaotic Ana*.

SEEING FILMS

Release dates vary widely. Blockbusters are usually released more or less simultaneously worldwide, but smaller productions can sometimes take up to three years to arrive at cinemas, long after they're available on DVD. The dubbing of films into Catalan can often play a part in any delay.

Newspapers carry full details of all cinema screenings, as does the weekly *Time Out Barcelona* magazine and its online version at www.timeout.cat. Subtitled (as opposed to dubbed) films are marked VO or VOSE (for '*versió original subtitulada en espanyol*'). Some larger cinemas open at 11am, but most have their first screenings around 4pm. Evening showings start around 7.30-8.30pm; later screenings begin usually at 10.15-10.45pm. On Fridays and Saturdays, many cinemas have a late-night session starting around 1am. Weekend evenings can be very crowded, especially for recent releases, so turn up early.

You can buy tickets for a number of cinemas online, via their website or at www.entradas. com or ServiCaixa (*see p220*).

ORIGINAL-LANGUAGE CINEMAS

Boliche

Avda Diagonal 508 (93 218 17 88). Metro Diagonal/FGC Provença. **Tickets** *Mon, Tue, Thur €6.70; Wed €5.50; Fri-Sun €7.* **No credit cards.** **Map** p338 F6.

This comfortable four-screen cinema has recently made the move from dubbed films and now shows crowd-pleasers in their original languages.

Casablanca-Gràcia

C/Girona 173-175, Eixample (93 459 03 26). Metro Verdaguer. **Tickets** *Mon, Tue, Thur-Sun €6.50. Wed €4.80.* **No credit cards.** **Map** p339 H6.

Three screens show independent Spanish and European films; if none appeals, its sister cinema, the Kaplan, is just a few blocks away and also VO. **Other locations** Casablanca-Kaplan, Passeig de Gràcia 115, Eixample (93 218 43 45).

Cinemes Méliès

C/Villarroel 102, Eixample (93 451 00 51/ www.cinesmelies.net). Metro Urgell. **Tickets** *Mon €3. Tue-Sun €4.50.* **No credit cards.** **Map** p338 E8.

Cinemes Méliès is a small, two-screen cinema that is the nearest that Barcelona comes to an art house theatre, with an idiosyncratic roster of accessible classics alongside more recent films that aren't quite commercial enough for general release. This is the place to bone up on your Billy Wilder, Antonioni, Hitchcock and others, with up to eight films per week and a ten-classics-for-€20 offer.

Renoir-Floridablanca

C/Floridablanca 135, Eixample (93 228 93 93/ www.cinesrenoir.com). Metro Sant Antoni. **Tickets** *Mon €4.80. Tue-Fri €6.50. Sat, Sun €6.80. Late show Fri, Sat €4.80.* **Credit** MC, V. **Map** p342 E9.

This, the more central of the Renoir cinemas, screens up to eight independent, offbeat American, British and Spanish films per day, though note that programming tends towards the worthy. **Other locations** Renoir-Les Corts, C/Eugeni d'Ors 12, Les Corts (93 490 43 05).

Verdi

C/Verdi 32, Gràcia (93 238 79 90/www. cines-verdi.com). Metro Fontana. **Tickets** *1st screening daily €5. Mon €5. Tue-Sun €7.* **Credit** MC, V. **Map** p339 H5.

The five-screen Verdi and its four-screen annexe Verdi Park on the next street have transformed this corner of Gràcia, bringing with them vibrant bars and cheap eats for the crowds that flock to their diverse programme of independent, mainly European and Asian cinema. At peak times, chaos reigns; arrive early and make sure you don't mistake the line to enter for the ticket queue, which can stretch to Madrid on rainy Sundays. **Other locations** Verdi Park, C/Torrijos 49, Gràcia (93 238 79 90).

Yelmo Icària Cineplex

C/Salvador Espriú 61, Vila Olímpica (information 93 221 75 85/tickets 902 22 09 22/www.yelmocineplex.es). Metro Ciutadella-Vila Olímpica. **Tickets** *Mon €5.50. Tue-Sun €7; €5.50 before 3pm & reductions.* **Credit** AmEx, MC, V. **Map** p343 K12.

The Icària is a vast multiplex, which has all the atmosphere of the near permanently empty shopping mall that surrounds it, but what it lacks in charm, it makes up for in choice, with 15 screens offering Hollywood blockbusters and mainstream foreign and Spanish releases. Weekends are seat-specific, so queues tend to be slow-moving; it's worth booking your seat online before you go.

SPECIALIST CINEMAS

Some bars serve films with the drinks. **Planeta Rai** (C/Carders 12, principal, 93 268 13 21, Born, www.pangea.org/rai, closed mid July-Aug) shows European *cine d'auteur* twice a week on Tuesdays and Thursdays (€2).

FilmoTeca de la Generalitat

Cinema Aquitania, Avda Sarrià 31-33, Eixample (93 410 75 90/http://cultura.gencat.net/filmo). Metro Hospital Clínic. **Shows** 3 screenings daily. Closed Aug. **Tickets** €2.70; €2 reductions; €18 for 10 films. **Credit** (block tickets only) AmEx, MC, V. **Map** p338 D5.

Funded by the Catalan government, the Filmoteca is a little dry for some tastes, offering comprehensive seasons of cinema's more recondite auteurs, alongside better-known classics, plus screenings each spring of all films nominated for the Goya Awards. Overlapping cycles last two or three weeks, with each film screened at least twice at different times. Books of 20 and 100 tickets bring down the price per film to a negligible amount. The 'Filmo' also runs an excellent library of film-related books, videos and magazines at Portal Santa Madrona 6-8 (93 316 27 80), just off La Rambla.

IMAX Port Vell

Moll d'Espanya, Port Vell (93 225 11 11/ www.imaxportvell.com). Metro Barceloneta or Drassanes. **Tickets** €8-€12. **Credit** MC, V. **Map** p342 G12.

The predictable programming lets down the IMAX experience, and only if you're very lucky will you catch anything that's not about sharks, dinosaurs or adventure sports. If these rock your boat, however, you're in for a treat. Note that not all films are 3-D; check the website to see which is which.

Maldà Arts Forum

C/Pi 5, Barri Gòtic (93 481 37 04/www.cine malda.es). Metro Catalunya or Liceu. **Tickets** *Mon* €5. *Tue, Wed* €6. *Thur* €6.50. *Fri-Sun* €6.80. **No credit cards. Map** p344 C4.
In its latest incarnation the well-loved Cine Maldà is now showing indie and arthouse films. On Tuesday nights, Maldà plays host to Cine Ambigú, showing little-known films from around Europe. See www.retinas.org for details.

Sessió Continua

Sala de Cinema Auditori, Estació de França, Born (93 265 64 62/www.sessiocontinua.com). Metro Barceloneta. **Open** 8.30pm Thur. **Admission** free. **Map** p343 H12.
Indie and cult films are shown free every Thursday in this university auditorium at the side of the Estació de França. Add your name on the Catalan-only website (click on 'Forum' and fill in your name and how many people) to be put on a list at the door.

On Locations

Sometimes, the biggest star of a movie is the city in which it's shot.

'I have discovered,' announced Pedro Almodóvar a while ago, 'that Barcelona is also Marseille, Havana and Naples'. Film and commercials directors across the world agree, lining its streets with dolly tracks and generally messing up residents' lives to such an extent that the Ajuntament has had to put a limit on the amount of filming in the Old City.

Still, despite the disruption, it hasn't escaped the locals' notice that this is all good publicity. A joint enterprise between the council, the tourist board and the local film commission has brought about a great website, www.barcelonamovie.com, which flags some of the highlights of Barcelona's filmic career and collates them into a series of routes. The site is still in its fledgling stages, and the golden goose that was *Vicky Cristina Barcelona* is still

being dissected, but readers can already track the locations of such movies as Almodóvar's *All About My Mother* (1999) and Tom Tykwer's *Perfume* (2006).

As well as synopses, awards details and 'Did you know?' sections about the films, there are interactive maps that give interesting historical and cultural information about the locations, along with many relevant film stills. *Perfume* may have performed feebly at the box office, but the intruiging facts detailed here might boost a few DVD sales. Apparently, two and a half tons of fish and one ton of meat were used in converting the Plaça de la Mercè to authentically filthy 18th-century marketplace, while Catalan *enfants terribles* La Fura dels Baus were enlisted to choreograph the mass orgy in the final scene, shot in the Poble Espanyol.

ARTS & ENTERTAINMENT

FESTIVALS

Barcelona is home to an increasing number of film festivals. Though none is as big or brash as **Sitges'** (*see below*), they all show interesting work unlikely to feature elsewhere. New events pop up every year, but regular festivals, in addition to these below, include the following: Women's (June), Animation (June), Jewish (July), Gay and Lesbian (July and October), Open Air Shorts (September), Documentaries (February and October), Human Rights (October), and African (November). OVNI, a well-established alternative video festival, takes place every 18 months, in early spring and late autumn; the next is scheduled for spring 2010.

Gandules
Information (93 306 41 00/www.cccb.org). CCCB (see p79). Date Aug 10pm Tue-Thur. Admission free.
A series of outdoor films are screened in the deckchair-strewn patio of the CCCB. It gets extremely crowded, so arrive early for any chance of a seat.

In-Edit Beefeater Festival
Cine Rex, Gran Via 463 & Aribau Club, Gran Via 565-567 (www.in-edit.beefeater.es). **Tickets** €5 (one film); €30 (6 films). **Date** Last week Oct.
A well-regarded cinema festival of musical documentaries, which range from jazz to flamenco.

Barcelona Visual Sound
Various venues (www.barcelonavisualsound.org). **Date** Late Feb.
Ten-day showcase for untried film talent covering shorts, documentaries, animation and web design.

Barcelona Asian Film Festival
Various venues (www.baff-bcn.org). **Date** Late Apr-early May. **Tickets** free-€6.
The BAFF has grown to include some of the sharpest and most broad-ranging programming of any of the city's film festivals.

Sala Montjuïc
Castell de Montjuïc (www.salamontjuic.com). **Date** July. **Admission** €4.
A blend of classics and recent independent cinema shown three times a week throughout July, transforms the grassy moat of the castle into an outdoor cinema. Bring a picnic and and turn up early for the jazz band. A free bus service runs from Espanya metro from 8.30-9.30pm and after the film.

L'Alternativa
CCCB (see p79). www.alternativa.cccb.org. **Tickets** free-€5. **Date** Late Sept.
A festival of independent, mostly European cinema.

Sitges Festival Internacional de Cinema de Catalunya
Auditori Melia Sitges, C/Joan Salvat Papasseit 38 (93 894 99 90/www.cinema sitges.com.) **Advance tickets** available from Tel-entrada (902 101 212/www.telentrada.com). **Date** Oct.
Sitges' Film Festival is widely recognised as the leading European festival for gore, horror, sci-fi and fantasy, offering dozens of screenings, as well as a host of conferences, retrospectives, premieres and appearances from the leading figures in the rarefied world of genre film-making. During the festival, a special late-night train service returns to Barcelona after the final screening of the evening.

Verdi. See p238.

Galleries

Miró's many successors make hay beneath the Mediterranean sun.

Drawn by the dazzling Mediterranean light and the physical beauty of the city, artists have long flocked to Barcelona. Yet although contemporary art is supported here, young artists arriving in Barcelona today sometimes suffer from a lack of resources. Demand outstrips supply for the city's expensive studio spaces, while public funding is generally directed at big institutions and – understandably enough – locally born artists.

There's mediocrity on the local scene, but there's also a good deal of excellent art. The galleries in this chapter are all reliable sources of the latter.

THE LOCAL SCENE

The art scene has lightened up since the 1980s and '90s, when any gallery serious about selling had to elbow its way on to a small section of C/Consell de Cent in the Eixample and show someone famous. These days, the scene is more relaxed, keen to experiment with what it sells and where it sells it. In the spruced-up Raval, **Àngels Barcelona** and **NoguerasBlanchard** host lively, contemporary shows and the occasional performance. Local artists and the city's many street artists are given support by **ADN**, while **Loft** and **Tasneem** are refreshingly non-Eurocentric. And of the locally based artists, look out in particular for Catalan artists Alicia Framis, Frederic Amat and Ester Partegàs, Scottish artist Jo Milne, Briton Hannah Collins and Dutchman Bert van Zelm.

Gallery listings appear in the *Guia del Ocio* and *Time Out Barcelona* magazines. Note that public exhibition spaces and galleries are covered in this guide under 'Sightseeing', while commercial galleries are listed below.

Festivals

Entrepreneurial individuals are always prepared to invest in the art scene and there's a keen public that swarm to springtime events, such as May's video art fair **Loop** (www.loop-barcelona.com, www.loop-videoart.com),

emerging art fair **Swab** (www.swab.es). In July, **Interfèrencia** grapples with the relationship between art and the public space (www.marato.com).

Later in the year, the last weekend in October offers the chance to check out the latest progeny of the union between mind and machine at pioneer cyber-art festival **Art Futura** (www.artfutura.org). In December, along with contempor, there's **Drap Art** (93 268 48 89, www.drapart.org): held at CCCB market (*see p79*) and FAD exhibition space, it's an international creative recycling festival, with concerts, performances, workshops and a Christmas market.

COMMERCIAL GALLERIES

Barri Gòtic

Local dealer **Artur Ramón** (C/Palla 10, 23 & 25, 93 302 59 70, www.arturamon.com) has various outlets on C/Palla, near the cathedral, including lithographs by Picasso, Mariano Fortuny and Joan Serrà at No.23.

Galería Trama

C/Petritxol 8 (93 317 48 77/www.galeriatrama. com). Metro Liceu. **Open** 10.30am-2pm, 4-8pm Tue-Sat. Closed Aug. **Credit** AmEx, MC, V. **Map** p344 B4.

About the author
Alex Phillips has lived in Barcelona for a decade. She writes on cultural themes for the local English-language press.

> Barcelona's art museums and non-commercial galleries are covered in the Sightseeing section; *see pp55-119.*

THE BEST
ARTISTIC SPECIALISTS

For contemporary art
Galería NoguerasBlanchard. *See below.*

For classical art
Sala Parés. *See below.*

For photography
Kowasa Gallery. *See p243.*

For emerging artists
Galeria ADN. *See p243.*

For world art
Loft Barcelona. *See below.*

For digital art
NIU. *See p244.*

The Galería Trama is an unassuming space, but it is the contemporary arm of Sala Parés opposite, and quietly displays some fabulous painting, photography and media work. Aziz & Cucher, Jo Milne and Julio Vaquero are among the featured artists.

★ Loft Barcelona
C/Ample 5 (93 301 11 12/www.espace-ample. com). Metro Drassanes or Jaume I. **Open** 11am-2pm, 5-8.30pm Tue-Sat. Closed 3wks Aug. **Credit** AmEx, MC, V. **Map** p345 B7.
When Loft opened in 2003, the local scene didn't know what to make of French collector Bertrand Cheuvreux's quirky space, dedicated solely to contemporary Chinese art. Since then, local (and commercial) interest in China, and in international art in general, has shot up; this wonderful haven, with a lovely patio out back, has come into its own, lending intriguing, ingenious and often hilarious works to big shows. Inaugurations are recommended as the nearby Off*Ample space (Passatge de la Pau 10) often hosts performances by Chinese exhibitors. Dart gallery downstairs shows French art.

★ Sala Parés
C/Petritxol 5 (93 318 70 20/www.salapares. com). Metro Liceu. **Open** *July-Sept* 4-8pm Mon; 10.30am-2pm, 4.30-8.30pm Tue-Sat. *Oct-June* 4-8pm Mon; 10.30am-2pm, 4.30-8.30pm Tue-Sat; 11.30am-2pm Sun. Closed 3wks Aug. **Credit** AmEx, MC, V. **Map** p344 B4.
Elegant Sala Parés, founded in 1840, is a grand, two-tier space that smells deliciously of wood varnish and oil paint. Conservative figurative and historical paintings are the main staple, although it was also here that a young Picasso had his very first solo show in 1905. In September, Sala Parés hosts the Young Painters' Prize.

Born

Galería Maeght
C/Montcada 25 (93 310 42 45/www.maeght. com). Metro Jaume I. **Open** 10am-2pm, 4-7pm Tue-Fri; 10am-3pm Sat. Closed 3wks Aug. **Credit** AmEx, DC, MC, V. **Map** p345 E6.
The sistership of the prestigious French gallery, Galeria Maeght occupies what was a Renaissance palace. The exterior grandeur fades inside, although the taupe paintwork and worn carpets seem appropriate for the sombre Spanish greats such as Antoni Tàpies, Eduardo Arroyo and Pablo Palazuelo.

Iguapop Gallery
C/Comerç 15 (93 310 07 35/www.iguapop.net). Metro Barceloneta or Jaume I. **Open** 5-9pm Mon; 11am-2.30pm, 5-9pm Tue-Sat. **Credit** MC, V. **Map** p345 F5.
Unpretentious Iguapop is the antithesis of the snooty art gallery that calls itself commercial but shuns the label shop. The same company sells clothes and fashion accessories and produces music. A nice 200sq-m space and a liberal exhibitions policy, featuring many artists with something interesting to say, make for a refreshing visit.

Raval

Art/design bookshop **Ras** (C/Doctor Dou 10, 93 412 71 99, www.actar.es) is good for a browse. Check out the gallery at the back (*photo p244*).

Àngels Barcelona
C/Pintor Fortuny 27 (93 412 54 00/www.galeria delsangels.com). Metro Catalunya. **Open** noon-2pm, 5-8.30pm Tue-Sat. Closed Aug. **No credit cards. Map** p344 A3.
Hurrah to local gallery owner and entrepreneur Emilio Álvarez for keeping the Barcelona contemporary art world alive and its various factions talking to one another. This smart space shows photography, video and hosts the occasional performance. A space nearby is dedicated to furniture design and called Room Service (C/Àngels 16, 93 302 10 16), while Álvarez's restaurant Carmelitas shows lo-fi video art at mealtimes (C/Doctor Dou 1, 93 412 46 84, www.carmelitasgallery.com).

Galería NoguerasBlanchard
C/Xuclà 7 (93 342 57 21/www.nogueras blanchard.com). Metro Liceu. **Open** *Sept-June* 10.30am-7pm Tue-Sat. Closed Aug. **No credit cards. Map** p342 B3.
Occupying a sociable slot on C/Xucla, and famed locally for the prowling kitty-cats painted on the wall outside, Àlex Nogueras and Rebecca Blanchard have proven themselves adept at talent-spotting. Artists Marine Hugonnier and Ignacio Uriarte regularly feature; Cuban artist Wilfredo Prieto is their *nom célèbre*, having won the Cartier Award in 2008.

Eixample

Established galleries reside on C/Consell de Cent, between Rambla de Catalunya and Balmes. **Galeria Carles Taché** (C/Consell de Cent 290, 93 487 88 36, www.carlestache.com) is where you can get and lug home that Tony Cragg sculpture you've always wanted. The two branches of **Galeria Joan Prats** (Rambla Catalunya 54, 93 216 02 84 and C/Balmes 54, 93 488 13 98, www.galeriajoanprats.com) are also top-notch. Further along, towards the university, new gallery/showroom **A34** (C/Aribau 34, 93 451 55 79) hosts a few impressive shows a year: Picasso sketches and the photography of Karl Blossfeldt and Hiroshi Sugimoto included. For innovative shows, look further up on C/Mercaders.

Galeria ADN

C/Enric Granados 49 (93 451 00 64/www. adngaleria.com). Metro Passeig de Gràcia. **Open** *Sept-May* 10am-2pm, 4pm Tue-Sat. Closed Aug. **Credit** AmEx, MC, V. **Map** p338 F7.
ADN (DNA in English) favours less-established contemporary artists, half of whom are locally based. Collective shows are on the hit and miss side so far as quality is concerned, but good to check out if you're hungry for raw talent. (They once showed the video work of Alejandro Vidal, later swiped by posher gallery Joan Prats.) ADN support the worthy social projects of young architect Sergio Cirugeda who creates ingenious foldable homes that clamp to buildings or nestle in trees.

Galeria Estrany · De La Mota

Ptge Mercader 18 (93 215 70 51/www.estrany delamota.com). FGC Provença. **Open** *Sept-June* 10.30am-1.30pm, 4.30-8.30pm Tue-Sat. *July* 10.30am-1.30pm, 4.30-8.30pm Mon-Fri. Closed Aug. **No credit cards**. **Map** p338 F7.
This cavernous basement is one of the most intriguing art spaces in the city: outstanding contemporary exhibitions, particularly in photography and film from the likes of Finnish artist Esko Männikkö and Scottish film buff Douglas Gordon.

Galeria Joan Gaspar

Plaça Doctor Letamendi 1 (93 323 08 48/ www.galeriajoangaspar.com). Metro Universitat or Passeig de Gràcia. **Open** *Oct-May* 10.30am-1.30pm, 5-8pm Tue-Sat; *June-Sept* 10.30am-1.30pm, 5-8pm Tue-Fri. **Credit** AmEx, DC, MC, V. **Map** p338 F8.
This is the present location of the celebrated Sala Gaspar, which in 1960, in the throes of the Franco era, mounted a solo show of the paintings of the exiled Pablo Picasso for which queues stretched down the block and all the celebrities of Barcelona rebelliously attended. Nowadays, Joan Miró and Antoni Clavé are on display, among others.

Galeria Toni Tàpies

C/Consell de Cent 282 (93 487 64 02/www. tonitapies.com). Metro Passeig de Gràcia. **Open** *July, Sept* 10am-2pm, 5-8.30pm Tue-Fri. *Oct-June* 10am-2pm, 5-8.30pm Tue-Fri; 11am-2pm; 5-8.30pm Sat. Closed Aug. **Credit** DC, MC, V. **Map** p342 F8.
Owned by the son of the famous painter, Tàpies hosts a classy mix of locals and internationals: the excellent video work of Portuguese artist João Onofre and local artist Tere Recarens included.
▶ *On a related note, visit the Fundació Antoni Tàpies; see p101.*

Kowasa Gallery

C/Mallorca 235 (93 487 35 88/www.kowasa. com/gallery). Metro Passeig de Gràcia. **Open** 11am-2pm, 5-8.30pm Mon-Sat. Closed Aug. **Credit** AmEx, DC, MC, V. **Map** p338 F7.
A must for fans of photography, Kowasa Gallery, located above a bookshop, exhibits historical and contemporary photography. Agustí Centelles, Joan Colom and Eugeni Forcano set the standards for contemporary Catalans, such as Toni Catany.

ProjecteSD

Ptge Mercader 8 (93 488 13 60/www.projectesd. com). FGC Provença. **Open** *Sept-June* 11.30am-8.30pm Tue-Sat. *July* 11.30am-8.30pm Tue-Fri. Closed Aug. **No credit cards**. **Map** p338 F7.
Silvia Dauder's penchant for new photography and film is sculpted into subtle, provocative and highly original shows. Limited-edition artists' texts,

Galería Maeght.

ARTS & ENTERTAINMENT

detailed explanations in English and Silvia's own bilingual talents complement the exhibitions. You'll enter intrigued, but emerge informed. Look out for Patricia Dauder and Pieter Vermeersch.

Gràcia & Zona Alta

Galería Alejandro Sales

C/Julián Romea 16, Gràcia (93 415 20 54/www. alejandrosales.com). FGC Gràcia. **Open** *Oct-June* 11am-2pm, 5-8.30pm Tue-Sat. *July, Sept* 11am-2pm, 5-8.30pm Tue-Fri. Closed Aug. **No credit cards**. **Map** p338 F5.

Alejandro Sales's contemplative, sophisticated exhibitions are given the space and tranquillity they deserve. High-profile painters José Cobo, Mark Cohen and Pep Duran are regulars.

▶ *The excellent Fundació Foto Colectània is on the same street (see p111).*

Galeria H₂O

C/Verdi 152, Gràcia (93 415 18 01/www.h2o.es). Metro Lesseps. **Open** 4-8pm Tue-Fri; 11am-1pm Sat. Closed Aug. **Credit** V. **Map** p339 H4.

Local architect Joaquim Ruiz Millet and writer Ana Planella founded this friendly Gràcia gallery in 1989. Design and photography shows and book publications feature on the agenda.

Tasneem Gallery

C/Castellnou 51, Zona Alta (93 252 35 78/www. tasneemgallery.com). FGC Tres Torres. **Open** 11am-2pm Tue; 11am-2pm, 4-8pm Wed-Fri; 10am-2pm Sat. Closed Aug. **Credit** MC, V.

Ras. *See p242.*

International development consultant Tasneem Salam has opened this welcome addition to the gallery scene in the leafy barrio of Sarrià. It displays all kinds of contemporary African and Asian art, be it photography, paintings or furniture. Tasneem looks to the Philippines and Indonesia for shows in 2009.

THE FRINGE

Active artists' collectives include Art Liv (www.artliv.org), **Gràcia Arts Project** (www.graciaartsproject.com) and **La Xina ART** (www.laxinaart.org). Barri Gòtic's **Tallers Oberts** (www.tallersoberts.org) sees artists opening their studios to the public for two weekends in late May. **Barcelona Creativa** (www.barcelonacreativa.info) offers an electronic classified ads page aimed at promoting creative projects. Civic centres can be supportive, Poblenou's **Centre Civic Can Felipa** (C/Pallars 277, 93 266 44 4) particularly so. Established production centre **Hangar** (Passatge del Marqués de Santa Isabel 40, Poblenou, 93 308 40 41, www.hangar. org), has a limited number of studios, offers workshops, exchanges and is a good place to get information.

NIU

C/Almogàvers 208, Poblenou (93 356 88 11/ www.niubcn.com). Metro Glòries or Llacuna/bus 40, 42. **Open** 4-10pm Mon-Sat. Closed 2wks Aug. **Credit** MC, V. **Map** p343 off L10.

NIU is a buzzing centre for media and audio-visual art, incorporating a small exhibition space, live music, conferences, workshops and information on a kaleidoscopic array of musical and art events.

CLASSES

For those inspired to create, **Masia Can Serrat** (93 771 00 37, www.canserrat.org) in Montserrat Natural Park, offers board, lodging and studio space. For courses in life drawing, painting or sculpture in the city centre, try **Cercle Artístic de Sant Lluc** (93 302 45 79, www.santlluc.com), although you must register with the group to attend.

Gay & Lesbian

We're here, we're queer... now, where can we get a beer?

Is Barcelona the new Amsterdam? The city thrusts its credentials into the faces of visitors with bars, clubs, hotels and festivals... and that's before you reach the beautiful beach town of Sitges, probably the gayest village in Europe and just a short train ride down the coast. The sea change since Franco's death (homosexuality was illegal until 1978) has brought about gay marriage and adoption, gay hotels, the staging of the 2008 gay and lesbian EuroGames, and even a gay circus (www.gaycircus.net). Queer Catalonia has never had it so good.

ARTS & ENTERTAINMENT

THE LOCAL SCENE

The scene – *el ambiente* in Spanish – is mostly limited to a small and otherwise unnoteworthy area in the Eixample. Bordered by the streets Diputació, Villarroel, Aragó and Balmes, it's delightfully if somewhat dizzily nicknamed the **Gaixample**. But there are also shops and bars dotted throughout the Old City, along with alfresco cruising behind Plaça d'Espanya in the leafy shadows of Montjuïc. There's also the aesthetically challenged 'Chernobyl beach' – take the train or tram to **Sant Adrià de Besòs** and wander about in front of the three huge cooling towers.

That said, most of the city's nightlife is pretty mixed, and there's a lot of fun to be had off the official scene – a keen ear to the ground and the occasional flyer will often deliver an embarrassment of riches when it comes to partying in Barcelona. Don't worry about dress codes: you can wear anything or almost nothing. The summer's fiestas at shacks on gay-friendly Marbella beach are a particularly fine example of minimum advertising, maximum raving. For more about life after dark, *see pp253-67*.

For more information, pick up free copies of gay rag *Shanguide* in bars and gay shops around town, or have a look on the handy www.shangay.com, www.barcelonagay.com and www.catalunya-lgbt.cat.

About the authors

Roberto Rama and Dylan Simanowitz have lived, worked and partied in Barcelona for the last four years.

Festivals

The place to head for **carnival** (*see p231*), in February, is Sitges, but Barcelona takes over in summer. At the end of June, **Gay Pride** usually centres on the Plaça Universitat, with parades and concerts; in July, **Loveball** (www.loveball.info) includes parties, cinema and cultural offerings from flamenco to gay art. The **Mostra Internacional de Cinema Gai i Lesbià** film festival (www.cinemalambda.com) is also held in July; August 2008, meanwhile, saw the arrival of the gay and lesbian **Circuit Festival** (www.circuitfestival.net), mixing clubbing, cinema, art and a water park.

BARS

Gaixample

The bars mentioned below have proved more durable than most, given the fickle nature of the local scene. However, we advise you to ask around about a venue – is it still worth visiting, is it still open – before shelling out on a cab fare and making a special journey.

El Cangrejo

C/Villarroel 86 (no phone). Metro Universitat or Urgell. **Open** 10.30pm-3am Thur-Sat; 10.30pm-2.30am Sun. **No credit cards.** **Map** p342 E8.

If you can ignore first impressions based on the decor (which looks as if Gaudí sneezed violently), you'll find a lively and friendly bar attracting a younger crowd similar to that of the original Cangrejo in the Raval.

ARTS & ENTERTAINMENT

Col·lectiu Gai de Barcelona

Ptge Valeri Serra 23 (93 453 41 25/www. colectiugai.org). Metro Universitat or Urgell. **Open** 7-9.30pm Mon-Thur; 7-9.30pm, 11pm-3am Fri; 11pm-3am Sat. **No credit cards.** **Map** p342 E8.

A good place to come for information, the headquarters of this local gay association is home to an easygoing, quiet and unpretentious bar, with cheap drinks and few tourists.

Dietrich

C/Consell de Cent 255 (93 451 77 07). Metro Universitat. **Open** 10.30pm-2.30am Mon-Thur, Sun; 10.30pm-3am Fri, Sat. **Credit** MC, V. **Map** p342 E8.

Dietrich is a classic club, although now somewhat careworn, that generally attracts a mixed and lively crowd. Acrobats and drag artists perform on the dancefloor, and the friendly international bar crew speak English.

People Lounge

C/Villarroel 71 (93 532 75 27/www.peoplebcn. com). Metro Universitat or Urgell . **Open** 8.30pm-3am daily. **Credit** MC, V. **Map** p342 E8.

People Lounge offers a good alternative if you are tired of trekking around from bar to bar listening to non-stop Europop. Decked out as a facsimile of an English pub it attracts a more mature crowd and has plenty of space to sit, have a drink and chat.

Plata Bar

C/Consell de Cent 233 (93 452 46 36). Metro Universitat. **Open** 6pm-2.30am Mon-Thur, Sun; 6pm-3am Fri, Sat. **Credit** MC, V. **Map** p342 E8.

Tucked into one of the corners of the Gaixample this lively cocktail bar spills out into the street on warm evenings. Take your pick from the standard cocktail menu, grab a seat and watch the world pass by.

Punto BCN

C/Muntaner 63-65 (93 453 61 23/www.arena disco.com). Metro Universitat. **Open** 6pm-2.30am Mon-Thur, Sun; 6pm-3am Fri, Sat. **No credit cards.** **Map** p342 E8.

Punto BCN is a Gaixample staple but it's still a bit on the sterile side, though it's one of the few places where you'll find anybody early on. Tables on the mezzanine give a good view of the crowd so you can take your pick before the object of your affections heads off in to the night.

► *Free passes to the Arena clubs (see p247) are available behind the bar.*

★ Sweet BCN

C/Casanova 75 (no phone). Metro Universitat. **Open** 8pm-2.30am Tue-Thur, Sun; 8pm-3am Fri, Sat. **Credit** MC, V. **Map** p345 E8.

Seamlessly subsumed into the ever-expanding Matinee empire (D-Boy, Space, L'Atlantida in Sitges,

among others), Sweet has subtle lighting, ultra cool design and a young trendy crowd to rival anywhere in the Born. But be warned: prices are high.

Z:eltas Club

C/Casanova 75 (93 451 84 69/www.zeltas.net). Metro Universitat. **Open** 11pm-3am daily.
Z:eltas is one of the more stylish of the Gaixample's bars. Although open every day, it only really comes into its own later on in the week, when the trendy young *guapos* show their appreciation for the DJs' tunes (mainly funky house) by squashing each other on the mini dancefloor.

The rest of the city

Schilling (*see p182*), **La Concha** (*see p259*) and **Zelig** (C/Carme 116, no phone), though not exclusively gay, are all worth taking a look at. During the long summer months, the action moves to the shore and the *xiringuitos* on the Marbella beach are the place to be, especially the first on this stretch (with the sea to your right) – **El Dulce Deseo de Lorenzo** (www.lorenzo.chiringuitogay.com).

Kiut. *See p251.*

La Bata de Boatiné

C/Robadors 23, Raval (no phone). Metro Liceu.
Open 11.30pm-3am Wed-Sat; 11.30pm-2.30am
Sun. **No credit cards. Map** p345 A5.
The rapid redevelopment and gentrification of the
area makes one wonder how long this grungy, semi-
underground bar can survive, but for now La Bata
still holds pride of place on the alternative BCN gay
scene. Cheap drinks mean it can get packed, so fight
your way down the long narrow bar to where the
action is – if you dare.

Burdel 74

*C/Carme 74, Raval (mobile 678 464 515). Metro
Liceu.* **Open** 8pm-3am Tue-Sun. **No credit
cards. Map** p342 E10.
A bit of a Raval staple, Burdel's louche, intimate
interior has more than a touch of Almodóvar's high-
camp chic about it. Deep reds and hallowed divas
on the walls make it ideal for taking a date, or swing
by for the bingo on Sunday nights.

New Chaps

*Avda Diagonal 365, Eixample (93 215 53
65/www.newchaps.com). Metro Diagonal or
Verdaguer.* **Open** 9pm-3am Mon-Sat; 7pm-3am
Sun. **No credit cards. Map** p338 G6.
The more mature clientele that frequents this sex
bar avoids studying the rather bizarre collection of
objects hung around the place and instead heads for
the busy darkroom downstairs. If you're tempted,
make sure you check in your valuables first.

La Penúltima

*C/Riera Alta 40 (mobile 675 246 262). Metro
Sant Antoni, Raval.* **Open** 7pm-3am Tue-Sun.
No credit cards. Map p342 E9.
This slightly kitsch former *bodega*, where ancient
barrels of wine contrast with glass-fronted displays
of Barbie dolls, makes a comforting change from the
muscle-bound posing bars of the Gaixample. A
mixed and friendly place, it's one of the few places
populated before midnight.

CLUBS

Spain's recent anti-smoking laws have resulted
in many clubs having a tiny, packed smokers'
dancefloor and a larger non-smoking area
which is pretty empty.

Gaixample

Arena

Classic & Madre *C/Diputació 233*
VIP & Dandy *Gran Via de les Corts Catalanes
593 (93 487 83 42/www.arenadisco.com).
Metro Universitat.* **Open** 12.30am-6am Mon-Sat;
7.30pm-5am Sun. **Admission** (incl 1 drink) €6
Mon-Thur; €7 Fri; €12 Sat. **No credit cards.
Map** p338 F8/p342 F8.

The four Arena clubs are still packing them in every
week with a huge variety of punters. The USP is that
you pay once, get your hand stamped and can then
switch between all four clubs. Madre is the biggest
and most full-on, with thumping house and a darkroom; there are shows and strippers at the beginning
of the week, but Wednesday's semi-riotous foam
party is where it's really at. VIP doesn't take itself
too seriously and is popular with just about everyone, from mixed gangs of Erasmus students to parties of thirtysomethings down from Sabadell, all
getting busy to Snoop Dogg and vintage Mariah
Carey. Classic is similarly mixed, if even cheesier,
playing mostly handbag, and, finally, Dandy bangs
away with vintage chart hits.
▶ *Admission is also good for lesbian club Aire;
see p249.*

Bear Factory

*Ptge Domingo 3 (no phone/www.bearfactory
barcelona.com). Metro Passeig de Gràcia.* **Open**
11pm-5am Fri, Sat. **Admission** €5 Fri; (incl 1
drink) €6 Sat. **No credit cards. Map** p338 G7.
Still number one with the hirsute – despite the fairly stiff competition in the city – this late-opening,
spacious and well-designed bar has a good-sized
dancefloor with unsurprising dance music and a
small but busy darkroom.

Martins

*Passeig de Gràcia 130 (93 218 71 67/www.
martins-disco.com). Metro Diagonal.* **Open**
midnight-6am Wed-Sun. **Admission** (incl
1 drink) €12. **Credit** MC, V. **Map** p338 G6.
Catching up with Metro, with three bars, porno
lounge and decent dancefloor, Martins can be
packed at the weekends (especially Saturdays). The
first Saturday of every month is men only.

★ Metro

*C/Sepúlveda 185 (93 323 52 27/metrodisco.bcn).
Metro Universitat.* **Open** 1-5am Mon; midnight-
6am Tue-Sun. **Admission** (incl 1 drink) €15.
Credit MC, V. **Map** p342 C5.
Metro is a fixture on the Barcelona gay scene and its
popularity seldom wanes. It's particularly packed at
weekends, making the smaller of the two dancefloors, specialising in Latin beats, something of a
challenge for the flamboyant. The larger one has
more traditional house. The corridor-like darkroom
is where the real action takes place.

INSIDE TRACK
HOME SWEET HOME

Spaniards often live with their parents
well past the first flush of youth, so don't
be surprised if that Latin lover sweeps
you off to the back of a car.

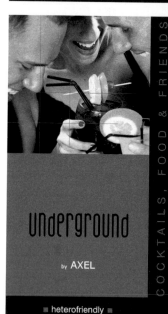

The rest of the city

Ácido Óxido

*C/Joaquin Costa 61, Eixample (93 268 10 19).
Metro Universitat.* **Open** 6am-9.30am daily.
Admission (incl 1 drink) €10. **No credit
cards**. **Map** p342 C5.

If you're having one of those nights when you just
have to keep going (or you haven't picked up yet),
stagger to this recently reopened 'after-hours'. It
claims to have the darkest darkroom in town.

★ D-Boy

*Ronda Sant Pere 19-21, Eixample (93 318 06
86/www.matineegroup.com). Metro Urquinaona.*
Open midnight-6am Thur-Sat. **Admission** (incl
1 drink) €18. **No credit cards**. **Map** p342 E2.

The much-loved Salvation recently reopened, after
a €2m makeover and much fanfare, as D-Boy. With
two spaces, one for house and another for deep
house, and a huge darkroom, it's kept its megatron
and go-gos, but you can be the judge of whether
adding a few pink lasers gives a club the right to
have an attitude and pricing policy that might
exceed its actual charms.

LESBIAN BARS & NIGHTCLUBS

Barcelona's lesbian scene doesn't seem to
have much consistency, with bars struggling to
survive amid constant changes of ownership.

On the other hand, there are several thriving
groups that organise regular parties, including
Nextown Ladys (www.nextownladys.com),
Silk (http://silkbcn.spaces.live.com) and
Outside the Closet (www.outsidethe
closet.com). Check online for details of the
activities and events they arrange. You'll also
find lesbians in some of the spots that are
favoured by gay men, such as **Arena** (*see
p247*) or **La Bata de Boatiné** (*see p245*).
The second *xiringuito* on Marbella beach
functions as a lesbian meeting place, which
is liveliest on Sunday evenings, when it
becomes **El Misterioso Secreto de
Amparo** (www.amparo.chiringuito
lesbico.com). Admission to the bars listed
below is free unless otherwise stated.

Aire

*C/València 236, Eixample (93 454 63 94/
www.arenadisco.com). Metro Passeig de Gràcia.*
Open 11pm-3am Thur-Sat. **Admission** (incl
1 drink) €5 Fri; €6 Sat. **No credit cards**.
Map p338 F7.

The girly outpost of the Arena group is the city's
largest lesbian club and as such sees a decent variety of girls (and their male friends, by invitation)
head down to shoot pool and dance to pop, house
and 1980s classics. On the first Sunday of the month,
there's a women-only strip show.

► *The admission price to gay megaclub Arena
(see p247) also allows for entry here.*

Antinous Libreria Café. *See p251.*

★ Can Fly

Baixada de Viladecols 6, Barri Gòtic (mobile 675 618 473). Metro Jaume I. **Open** 5pm-2am Mon-Thur; 5pm-3am Fri, Sat. **Admission** free. **Credit** MC, V. **Map** p345 D6.

Patchwork graffiti meets rustic in this tranquil café/bar. If you don't want to wait until midnight to get your evening started, this is a cosy spot to start with a drink, a tapa and a flirt. A warm atmosphere is generated by friendly staff, who welcome all comers, femme or butch, local or foreign. There are also tables outside in a pretty square.

Free Girls

C/Marià Cubí 4, Gràcia (no phone). Metro Fontana/FGC Gràcia. **Open** 11.30pm-3am Thur-Sat; 7pm-2am Sun. **No credit cards**. **Map** p338 F5.

Free Girls was previously known as Via, when it was one of the longest-running lesbian haunts in Barcelona. Its new guise sees it staying faithful to its girlie origins and the friendly atmosphere for which it was known. The small dancefloor fills with a mixed crowd early in the evening, which becomes increasingly female as the night wears on.

Marriage à la Mode

With this ring…

Since 2005, Spain has enjoyed the most liberal laws in Europe governing homosexual rights. Same-sex couples are not only allowed to marry (rather than just form a 'civil partnership'), but also to adopt children. Even two non-Spaniards may marry on Spanish territory if they are legally resident. As such, because the paperwork is relatively uncomplicated, Barcelona is becoming something of a Las Vegas for gay couples. The number of foreign gays and lesbians registered in the Barcelona census in order to get married is steadily increasing, and there's an average of one foreign gay wedding a week at the Register Office.

After an initial rush of weddings – more than 4,500 gay couples tied the knot in the first year after the law was passed – the Ministry of Justice estimates that around 2,000 gay couples marry each year in Spain. However, the actual figure may be much higher: this does not include data from the 7,000 Spanish Peace Court or the Basque Country. On Valentine's Day 2008, Spain even held its first religious gay wedding, when two men were married by an Anglican priest in Gran Canaria.

The law has gradually given rise to a whole satellite industry with everything from lesbian and gay wedding planners such as **Les n' Gay** (www.les-and-gay.com) or **Bodas Lesgay** (www.bodaslesgay.com) to luxury honeymoon packages at gay **Hotel Axel** (*see p135*). The latest addition is a couture wedding outfitters for gay grooms.

The first shop of its kind in Europe, **BY** (C/Muntaner 22, Eixample, 93 451 89 83, www.bybcn.es) opened in May 2007 and is already attracting clients from all over Spain and further abroad with its suave yet quirky outfits. BY's bespoke couture is squarely aimed at the slim of hip and the fat of wallet and suits cost from around €2,500 to more than €15,000. To make the outfits extra special, staff can personalise the linings with initials, poems or even photos.

Even the problem of what to serve for a truly over-the-rainbow dessert on the Big Day has been resolved: local ice-cream company **Bodn** (93 497 61 12) now produces an artisan sorbet in the six striped colours of the gay flag.

★ Kiut

C/Consell de Cent 280, Eixample (no phone).
Metro Passeig de Gràcia. **Open** midnight-
5.30am Thur-Sat. **Admission** Free (women);
€10 (men). **Credit** (Bar only) AmEx, MC, V.
Map p342 F8.
Possibly Barcelona's only reliable girl bar for a little weekend glam. Early on, the music is beach
house; as the crowd starts to roll in, pop and commercial house take over. The dimly lit, chic space
has a mirrored dancefloor with video screens dividing smoking and non-smoking bars, and is frequented by all ages. Be warned that Thursday is drum 'n'
bass night with a straight crowd. *Photo p246.*

RESTAURANTS

In addition to the establishments listed below,
plenty of mixed restaurants in Barcelona have
large and enthusiastic gay followings. Among
the most popular are the Barri Gòtic's **La
Verònica** (Rambla de Raval 2-4, 93 329 33 03)
and **Venus Delicatessen** (C/Avinyó 25, 93
301 15 85). **La Singular** (C/Francisco Giner
50, 93 237 50 98) in Gràcia is popular with
lesbians, while **Zoologic** (C/Casanova 30,
Eixample, 93 453 52 49, www.zoologic
restaurant.com) is popular with all sorts
for its over-the-top drag cabarets.

El Bierzo a Tope

C/Diputacion 159, Eixample (93 453 70 45/
www.castrorestaurant.com). Metro Universitat.
Open 7am-midnight Mon-Sat. **Main courses**
€10. **Set menu** €8 Mon-Fri: €12 Sat. **Credit**
MC, V. **Map** p342 C5.
Serving traditional Spanish fare from Leon in large
portions and at reasonable prices, this restaurant is
understandably popular with bears and their admirers. There are good-value set menus served all day.

Castro

C/Casanova 85, Eixample (93 323 67 84/
www.castrorestaurant.com). Metro Universitat.
Open 1-4pm, 9pm-midnight Mon-Fri; 9pm-
midnight Sat. **Main courses** €12. **Set lunch**
€9 Mon-Fri. **Credit** MC, V. **Map** p342 C5.
Still ahead of the crowd as far as gay restaurants go,
Castro continues to provide imaginative dishes such
as duck breast with wild strawberries or deer in bal-
samic vinegar, all served by the cutest of staff.

Iurantia

C/Casanova 42, Eixample (93 454 78 87/
www.iurantia.com). Metro Universitat. **Open**
1.30-4pm, 9pm-midnight Mon-Fri; 9pm-midnight
Sat. **Main courses** €10. **Set lunch** €10. **Credit**
MC, V. **Map** p342 E8.
Though not a gay restaurant as such, Iurantia's
Gaixample location assures it's frequented by a styl-
ish crowd keen on the slick red paint job, downbeat

tunes and the menu, which varies from imaginative
fusion – octopus carpaccio – to popular and fairly
priced pasta and pizzas. Leave room for the home-
made bitter chocolate truffles with a touch of mint.

SHOPS & SERVICES
General shops

★ Antinous Libreria Café

C/Josep Anselm Clavé 6, Barri Gòtic (93 301 90
70/www.antinouslibros.com). Metro Drassanes.
Open 10.30am-2pm, 5-8.30pm Mon-Fri; noon-
2pm, 5-8.30pm Sat. **Credit** AmEx, DC, MC, V.
Map p345 B7.
This large, bright bookshop has an appealing café
at the back, an ideal spot in which to check out your
purchases (DVDs to postcards, poetry to magazines,
art to comics). The shop also has a great selection of
nude photobooks. *Photo p249.*

Complices

C/Cervantes 2, Barri Gòtic (93 412 72 83/
www.libreriacomplices.com). Metro Jaume I.
Open 10.30am-8pm Mon-Fri; noon-8pm Sat.
Credit AmEx, MC, V. **Map** p345 C6.
Barcelona's oldest gay bookshop is run by a helpful
lesbian duo who stock a variety of literature and
films – from highbrow paperback classics (some
available in English) and *Queer as Folk* box sets to
porn mags and DVDs.

D'Arness

C/Villarroel 43, Eixample (www.d-arness.com).
Metro Urgell. **Open** 5-9pm Mon-Sat. **Credit**
MC, V. **Map** p342 E8.
This small specialist leather shop has all the gear
you could need. From 10.30pm, Wednesday to
Sunday, the back room becomes a members-only sex
bar (join at the door).

Ovlas

Via Laietana 33, Barri Gòtic (93 268 76 91).
Metro Jaume I. **Open** 10.15am-8.30pm Mon-Fri;
10.15am-9pm Sat. **Credit** AmEx, MC, V.
Map p345 D4.
This large space keeps Barcelona's boys in lurid
briefs, singlets and revealing garments, making it a
perfect one-stop shop for a weekend in Sitges.

Hairdressers

Fashion Chaning

C/Diputació 159, Eixample (93 454 24 10).
Metro Urgell. **Open** 4-8pm Mon; 11am-8.30pm
Tue-Sat. **Credit** MC, V. **Map** p342 E8.
A gay hairdressing salon for boys and girls, where
men can ask for manicures, pedicures and facials
without getting odd looks. You can get your eye-
brows, eyelashes and even your body hair dyed.
▶ *For more hairdressers, see p216.*

ARTS & ENTERTAINMENT

Saunas

At both the establishments listed below,
you'll find plenty of showers, steam rooms and
dry saunas, along with bars and colourful porn
lounges. On arrival, you'll be supplied with
locker key, towel and flip-flops.

Corinto

*C/Pelai 62, Eixample (93 318 64 22). Metro
Catalunya.* **Open** noon-5am Mon-Thur; 24hrs
Fri-Sun. **Admission** €14.50. **Credit** MC, V.
Map p342 B2.
Nothing really changes at the Corinto, smack in the
centre, and it still remains the most popular place
for tourists to go get busy, aided by some fine vis-
tas of Plaça Catalunya and La Rambla.

Sauna Casanova

*C/Casanova 57, Eixample (93 323 78 60). Metro
Urgell.* **Open** 24hrs daily. **Admission** €14.50.
Credit MC, V. **Map** p342 E8.
Casanova still attracts plenty of well-muscled eye
candy for the visitor. It's at its busiest on Tuesday
and Thursday evenings, every night after the clubs
close and all day Sunday.

Sex shops

The following gay-oriented sex shops have
viewing cabins for DVDs.

Nostromo

*C/Diputació 208, Eixample (93 451 33 23).
Metro Universitat.* **Open** 11am-11pm Mon-Fri; 3-
11pm Sat, Sun. **No credit cards. Map** p342 E8.

Zeus

*C/Riera Alta 20, Raval (93 442 97 95).
Metro Sant Antoni.* **Open** 10am-9pm Mon-Sat.
Credit MC, V. **Map** p342 E10.

SITGES

To the surprise of many, Sitges is charmingly
pretty and quite family-oriented during the day.
But its Jekyll and Hyde character is revealed
during hot summer nights, when the town
literally bursts at the seams. The small gay
beach in the centre is where to preen and be
seen. But if you'd rather not have to stare
directly into your neighbour's armpit, hit
the seafront and walk right for an hour or
so to the nudist beach (with corresponding
cruising ground behind).

Accommodation

August can be a nightmare, so booking three
months in advance is advisable for anything
decent. This goes in particular for **El Xalet**

and its sister **Hotel Noucentista** (for both,
C/Illa de Cuba 35, 93 894 55 79, www.elxalet.
com, rates €80-€128 incl breakfast) both of
which occupy Modernista palaces and are
furnished with period furniture. Almost next
door is **Hotel Liberty** (C/Illa de Cuba 45, 93
811 08 72, www.libertyhotelsitges.com, rates
€72-€125 incl breakfast), with spacious rooms,
a lush garden and, if you feel like splashing
out, a luxury penthouse with two terraces
overlooking the town. The owners also have 41
apartments for rent – see www.staysitges.com.
The romantics' choice, naturally, is the **Hotel
Romàntic**, a beautifully restored 19th-century
house with a secluded palm-filled garden
(C/Sant Isidre 33, 93 894 83 75, www.hotel
romantic.com, rates €93-€110 incl breakfast,
closed Nov-Mar). In a quieter residential area is
the friendly French-run **Hotel Los Globos**
(Avda Nuestra Señora de Montserrat s/n, 93 894
93 74, www.hotellosglobos.com, rates €63-€100
incl breakfast), in need of slight redecoration
but with a balcony or private garden for each
room. Peter and Rico at **RAS** (mobile 607 14 94
51, www.raservice.com) may be able to help
you out if you're stuck.

Bars & nightclubs

Sitges has a definite circuit, which begins
around midnight with a drink at one of the
many pavement cafés on C/Primer de Maig,
aka Sin Street, or for the girls at **Mari Pili**
(C/Joan Tarrida Ferratges 14, mobile 653 771
071). The next move is to one of the earlier bars
(they start filling up around 1.30am), the best
of which is probably **Privilege** (C/Bonaire 24,
no phone); it even has a small dancefloor. From
here, move on to **Mediterraneo** (C/Sant
Bonaventura 6, no phone), which is spacious
but gets packed later on. For those who want to
dance, both **Organic** (C/Bonaire 15, no phone)
and **Trailer** (C/Angel Vidal 36, 93 894 04 01)
are in the centre of town. Otherwise, head out
to **L'Atlantida** at (Platja les Coves, 93 811 22
89, www.clubatlantida.com) on foot (20 mins),
by taxi or the free bus from the Calipolis hotel.
For other night-time activities, just head for
the beach.

Restaurants

For such a popular town, Sitges lacks
good restaurants. Still, if you're looking for
a particularly gay experience and aren't
too bothered about the food try **Parrots
Restaurant** (C/Joan Tarrida Ferratges 18,
93 811 12 19, mains €16, closed Nov-Dec).
Also worth a mention is **Monroe's** (C/Sant
Pau 36, 93 894 16 12, mains €14), which serves
a range of international cuisine.

ARTS & ENTERTAINMENT

Music & Nightlife

Beach parties to bhangra – Barcelona's clubbing starts here.

If tourism in Barcelona were to cater to one niche market, it would be that of the nightlife tourist. The city's reputation as a party town is secure – hen parties, Euro-club heads and Boys' Night Out groups head here from all over the continent. There isn't the 24-hour, seven-days-a-week party vibe that you'll find in Ibiza, but there's an energy and creativity in the local nightlife that isn't found anywhere else. It's a mood that's made and fostered by a population who party well, know when to go for it and when to call it quits, when to buy you a beer and when to leave you  alone, when to clap and when to soft-shoe... but who most of all understand that going out is a necessary part of life that should be done right.

ARTS & ENTERTAINMENT

THE LOCAL SCENE

Millions of words have been spent lamenting the clubs and bars that have fallen victim to the municipal government's recent anti-noise campaign, but visitors don't lack opportunities for after-dark indulgence. There are superclubs hosting superstar DJs and tiny venues playing the latest electro. There are lounge clubs and gilded ballrooms, *salsatecas* and Brazilian samba bars, seductive tango emporiums and alternative nights offering anything from northern soul to Bollywood bhangra.

Going out happens late here, with people rarely meeting for a drink much before 11pm – if they do, it's a pre-dinner thing. Bars tend to close around 2am, or 3am at weekends, and it's only after this that the clubs get going, so many offer reduced entrance fees or free drinks to those willing to be seen inside before 1am. And if you're still raring to go at 6am, just ask around – more often than not there'll be an after-party party catering to the truly brave.

Traditionally, you had to head uptown to hit the posh clubs, but the Port Olímpic is putting on some serious competition with places such as **Club Catwalk** and **CDLC** luring the *pijos* (well-groomed uptowners) downtown. There are also nightly beach parties running up and down the coast from Bogatell to Mataró through

the summer. Meanwhile, you'll find smaller venues pulsating with life in the Barri Gòtic, particularly around the Plaça Reial and C/Escudellers. Across La Rambla, in the Raval, you can skulk in the grittier, grungier places, though even the neighbourhood hasn't proven impervious to gentrification, and a number of upmarket nightspots have lately sprung up on C/Joaquín Costa and between the kebab joints of the Rambla del Raval. If street beers, dogs and vintage sweaters are your thing, Gràcia is heaven – though in truth it's better for drinking than it is for dancing.

Live music

While the licensing battles between club owners and the town hall continue to inspire apocalyptic images in the local media, the rumours of the death of the city's music scene are gradually fading away. In a long-awaited move, officials have simplified convoluted licensing laws and offered financial support to

---

About the author
Katie Addleman *is a writer and former deputy editor of* Barcelona Metropolitan *magazine.*

**INSIDE TRACK
ADVANCE INFORMATION**

You can get information and tickets from **Tel-entrada**, **Servi-Caixa** and **FNAC** (*see p220*). Specialist record shops, such as those on **C/Tallers** in the Raval, are good for information and club flyers.

---

those owners willing to go some way towards meeting the objections of local residents by soundproofing their spaces.

There's further evidence that all is not as bad as it seems: local acts continue to pop up, their success and profligacy attesting to Barcelona's tenacious relevancy on the wider Spanish music scene. Electro group Love of Lesbian, recently rebounded trip-hop pioneers Najwajean, hipster-folk favourites Fisheart, Cineplexx & the Odeons, and Catalan pop legend Miqui Puig are some names to look out for. There are also more active metal-core bands than you can shake a death rattle at, if that's your thing, and a slew of internationally-minded musicians drawing from a blend of rock, flamenco, rai, hip hop and various South American, Asian and African styles – the best known among them are Ojos de Brujo, Raval's 08001 and CaboSanRoque, who played to an enamoured audience at last year's Sónar festival.

Some of the main music venues for seeing international names (as well as hotly tipped unknowns and locals) are the multi-faceted **Razzmatazz** and the old dancehalls **La Paloma** and **Sala Apolo**; the first hosts both cutting-edge live and electronic music, while the latter specialises in feel-happy DJs and special theme nights. In July, there are concerts on the roof of **La Pedrera**. It's hardly avant-garde (tickets come with cava so you can sip wine and gaze out over the city to the accompaniment of soft jazz) but the location is unique.

Advance information

For concert information, see *Time Out Barcelona* or the Friday papers, which usually include listings supplements. Look in bars and music shops for free magazines such as *Go*, *AB*, *Mondo Sonoro* (all mostly independent pop/rock/electronica) and *Batonga!* (which covers world music). *Punto H* and *Suite* are good for keeping abreast of the club scene.

For more, see www.infoconcerts.cat, www.atiza.com, www.salirenbarcelona.com, www.barcelonarocks.com, and www.clubbingspain.com. For more about the city's many music festivals, try www.festivales.com and www.whatsonwhen.com.

FESTIVALS

Other festivals to look out for include **Flamenco Ciutat Vella** (*see p276*), **Festa de la Música** (*see p226*), **Festival del Grec** (*see p226*) and **Festival Asia** (*see p229*).

Festival Guitarra

Various venues (93 481 70 40/www.theproject. cat). **Tickets** €22-€42. **Date** Mar-June.
This prestigious festival of guitars and, indeed, all stringed instruments, is a classic on the Barcelona music scene and has the ability to attract world-class players, from Jackson Browne to John Williams. Styles span everything from flamenco to Latin sounds, classical guitar and gypsy jazz.

ARTS & ENTERTAINMENT

Diobar. See p258.

Primavera Sound

Parc del Fòrum (www.primaverasound.com).
Metro El Maresme-Fòrum. **Tickets** 3 days
€95. **Date** 28-30 May 2009.
Fast stealing Sónar's thunder, this three-day, six-stage music festival is one of the best in Spain. Credit for its success is due to its range of genres. There are rafts of electronica acts, DJs and local bands, plus a record fair and the Soundtrack Film Festival.

Festival de Música Creativa i Jazz de Ciutat Vella

All over Old City (www.bcn.cat/cultura).
Metro Catalunya. **Date** May-June
The Old City Festival of Creative Music and Jazz hosts a range of performances at intimate venues particularly suited to these sort of sounds.

★ Sónar

www.sonar.es. **Tickets** €30-€170. **Date**
mid June.
The three-day International Festival of Advanced Music and Multimedia Art (or Sónar, as it's more snappily known) remains a must for anyone into electronic music, contemporary urban art and media technologies. The event is divided into two distinct parts. SónarDay comprises multimedia art, record fairs, conferences, exhibitions and sound labs around the CCCB, while DJs play. Later, SónarNight means a scramble for the desperately overcrowded shuttle bus from the bottom of La Rambla out to the vast hangars of the site in Hospitalet (tip: share a cab between four – it'll cost you the same), where concerts and DJs are spread over SónarClub, SónarPark and SónarPub.

B-estival

Poble Espanyol (see p92) & Espacio Movistar (see p266) (93 481 70 40/www.b-estival.com).
Metro Espanya. **Tickets** €20-€45. **Date** July.
Defining itself as Barcelona's 'festival of rhythms', B-estival was born in 2006, and the impressive programming covers blues, soul, R&B and Brazilian music, with flamenco and rai to fill the gaps. In 2008, memorable acts included Macy Gray and Erykah Badu, along with an incongruous but energetic show from the B52s.

★ Summercase

Parc del Fòrum (www.summercase.com). Metro
El Maresme-Fòrum. **Tickets** €75 (day)-€150.
Date two days mid July.
Summercase is the two-day partner to Wintercase (*see p257*), with a healthy line-up of indie rock and some big-name dance acts. Recent performers have included Primal Scream, Daft Punk, Massive Attack, the Verve and Blondie.

Mas i Mas Festival

Various venues (93 319 17 89/www.masimas.
com). **Tickets** €6-€45. **Date** late July-early Sept.

This tasteful music festival stretches over the summer months and has gone from concentrating on Latin sounds to providing a little bit of everything.
▶ *Some concerts take place at the Palau de la Música Catalana; see p271.*

Festival L'Hora del Jazz

Various venues (www.amjm.org). **Date** Sept.
A three-week festival of local jazz acts, with free daytime concerts in public spaces such as Gràcia's Plaça Rius i Taulet (normally on Sunday lunchtimes). Some night-time concerts are also free.

Hipnotik

CCCB (see p79) www.hipnotikfestival.com.
Tickets €10-€35. **Date** mid Sept.
A two-day festival that celebrates everything hip hop, with competitions, workshops and a break-dancing championship to complement the concerts.

Weekend Dance

Parc del Fòrum, Poblenou (www.weekendance.es).
Tickets €55. **Date** mid Sept.
This one-day electronic dance festival floundered slightly in 2008 when the venue fell through (and the Prodigy and Groove Armada pulled out), but Fatboy Slim kept the crowds pleased. It's hoped the event will return to the Fòrum in 2009.

Barcelona Acció Musical (BAM)

Various venues (93 427 42 49/www.bam.es).
Date during the Festes de la Mercè, Sept.
BAM stages free concerts, mostly of jazz and singer-songwriters, on Plaça del Rei; more famous names perform outside the cathedral, with dance acts at the Fòrum and rumba at Portal de la Pau (near the Museu Marítim). The prime mover of what's known as *so Barcelona* (Barcelona Sound), BAM largely promotes leftfield *mestissa* (vaguely, ethnic fusion) in its mission to provide 'music without frontiers'.

LEM Festival

Various venues, Gràcia (93 237 37 37/www.
gracia-territori.com). **Tickets** free-€6. **Date** Oct.
A month-long, well-organised festival of multimedia art and experimental music. It mostly covers electronica, but also includes jazz and rock. Concerts are mostly free.

ARTS & ENTERTAINMENT

Festival de Músiques del Món

L'Auditori (see p270). Metro Marina. **Tickets**
€15-€25. **Date** Oct.
Staged every October, this world music festival features around 20 concerts, along with related exhibitions, films and workshops. Concerts might include anything from Mongolian throat-singing to Turkish whirling dervishes alongside such home-grown talent as flamenco singer Miguel Poveda, a regular at this event.

Festival de Tardor Ribermúsica

*Various venues, Born (93 319 3089/www.
ribermusica.org). Metro Barceloneta or Jaume
I.* **Date** late Oct.
A lively autumn music festival that boasts more than 100 free performances around the Born, and fills the squares, bars, galleries, shops, churches and clubs with concerts of all stripes.

Wintercase

*Razzmatazz (see p267) (www.wintercase.com).
Metro Marina.* **Tickets** €20-€40. **Date** Nov.
This festival showcases some of the finest indie bands over four nights every November. The Barcelona leg takes place in Razzmatazz, with past players including the likes of Ian Brown, Mercury Rev and Teenage Fanclub.

Festival Internacional de Jazz de Barcelona

93 481 70 40/www.theproject.cat. **Tickets**
€18-€75. **Date** late Oct-late Nov.
One of Europe's most well-respected jazz festivals has grown to embrace everything from bebop to gospel to tribute bands around a core of mainstream performers that have recently included Chick Corea, Bebo Valdés, Al Green, Herbie Hancock, Caetano Veloso and even Katie Melua. Venues included in the festival's programme range from the Palau de la Música, Luz de Gas and Razzmatazz to L'Auditori; there are also big-band concerts and swing dancing in the Ciutadella park.

Els Grans del Gospel

*Various venues (93 481 70 40/www.the
project.cat).* **Tickets** €15-€45. **Date** Dec.
A three-week festival of international gospel music, born of the gospel section of the International Jazz Festival (*see above*), which eventually became popular enough to stand alone.

Festival Internacional de Percussió

L'Auditori (see p270) (www.auditori.cat).
Tickets €15. **Date** Feb.
The festival name may be a slight misnomer, since at least half the acts of the International Percussion Festival are actually Catalan, but it's none the worse for that. At the end of the festival, CDs are made featuring the artists who performed during it.

VENUES

Barri Gòtic

Barcelona Pipa Club

*Plaça Reial 3, pral (93 302 47 32/www.bpipa
club.com). Metro Liceu.* **Open** 11pm-3am
daily. **Admission** free. **No credit cards**.
Map p345 B6.
A converted flat on Plaça Reial, decorated with oak, velvet, Sherlock Holmes-style memorabilia and a bar that's often impossible to get anywhere near, despite the prices. For all its genteel decor, it has a semi-underground quality and is rammed with young Americans and their Catalan friends. Ring the bell downstairs to get in.

★ Harlem Jazz Club

*C/Comtessa de Sobradiel 8 (93 310 07 55).
Metro Jaume I.* **Open** *July-Sept* 8pm-4am Tue-Thur; 8pm-5am Fri, Sat. *Oct-June* 8pm-4am Tue-Thur, Sun; 8pm-5am Fri, Sat. **Gigs** 10.30pm, midnight Tue-Thur, Sun; 11.30pm, 1am Fri, Sat. Closed 2wks Aug. **Admission** free Tue-Thur; (incl 1 drink) €7.50 Fri-Sun. **No credit cards**.
Map p345 C6.
Despite the DJ booth, live music is what the Harlem Jazz Club does best, so it's no surprise that it's a regular hangout for not-so-cashed-up musicians, buffs and students alike. A lot of local musical history's gone down at Harlem, and some of the city's greatest talents have emerged from here. Jazz, klezmer, funk and flamenco get a run in a venue that holds no musical prejudices.

★ Jamboree/Los Tarantos

*Plaça Reial 17 (93 319 17 89/www.masimas.
com). Metro Liceu.* **Open** 8pm-11am daily.
Shows *Jamboree* 9pm, 11pm daily. *Tarantos*
8.30pm, 9.30pm, 10.30pm daily. **Open** 1-5am
Mon-Thur, Sun; 1-6am Fri, Sat. **Admission**
Shows €6-12. *Club* €10. **Credit** DC, MC, V.
Map p345 B6.
Every night, the cave-like Jamboree hosts jazz, Latin or blues gigs by mainly Spanish groups – on Mondays, in particular, the outrageously popular What the Fuck (WTF) jazz jam session is crammed with a young local crowd. Upstairs, slicker sister venue Los Tarantos stages flamenco performances, then joins forces with Jamboree to become one fun, cheesy club later on in the evening. You'll need to leave the venue and pay again, but admission serves for both spaces.

La Macarena

*C/Nou de Sant Francesc 5 (no phone/www.
macarenaclub.com). Metro Drassanes.* **Open**
11.30pm-4.30am Mon-Thur, Sun; 11.30pm-5.30am
Fri, Sat. **Admission** free before 1.30am; €5
afterwards (but can vary). **No credit cards**.
Map p345 B7.

KGB. See p266.

La Macarena is smaller than your apartment but has big-club pretensions in the best sense: the music is excellent – minimal electro selected by resident DJs and the occasional big-name guest (who usually appear the day before or after a bigger gig elsewhere) – and complemented by a kicking sound system. Watch your bag and your drink.

Sidecar Factory Club

Plaça Reial 7 (93 302 15 86/www.sidecar factoryclub.com). Metro Liceu. **Open** 6pm-4.30am Mon-Thur; 6pm-5am Fri, Sat. **Admission** (incl 1 drink) €5 before 2am; €7 after 2am Mon-Thur; €7 Fri, Sat. *Gigs* €5-€15. **No credit cards**. **Map** p345 B6.

Sidecar still has all the ballsy attitude of the spit 'n' sawdust rock club that it once was and programming that includes breakbeat, indie, electro and live shows continues to pack in the local indie kids and Interrailers. Don't miss the insane spectacle of top-hatted, feather boa-ed audience participants singing karaoke to Slayer every Monday before midnight.

Born & Sant Pere

Club Mix

C/Comerç 21 (93 319 46 96/www.clubmixbcn. com). Metro Jaume I. **Open** 9pm-3am Tue-Sun. **Admission** free. **Credit** MC, V. **Map** p345 F5.

With an interior designed by local tastemaker Silvia Prada, a fashionable postcode and a menu of delicate finger foods, Mix attracts a professional, stylish crowd who enjoy both an after-work cocktail and an after-dinner piss-up. DJs play funk, soul and world beat on Thursdays, and safe and sophisticated rare groove the rest of the time. There's live bossa nova and jazz on Tuesdays.

★ Diobar

C/Marquès de l'Argentera 27 (93 319 56 19). Metro Barceloneta. **Open** 11pm-3am Thur-Sat. **Admission** free. **Credit** MC, V. **Map** p345 F7.

The basement of a Greek restaurant is the unlikely setting for this cosy and wildly popular club. There's no plate-throwing but instead, from Thursday through Saturday nights, it becomes a stone-walled temple of funk, soul and Latin beats as DJ Fred Spider hits the decks. *Photo p254.*

▶ *Other ex-Café Royale DJs play at the Red Lounge Bar; see p260.*

Dr Astin

C/Abaixadors 9 (no phone). Metro Jaume I. **Open** 11pm-2.30am Mon-Thur; 11pm-3am Fri, Sat. **Admission** free. **No credit cards**. **Map** p345 D6.

Small, grungy and loud, Dr Astin has been hammering out the house and techno beats for years. Its no-pretension, watering-hole-plus-dancefloor formula attracts neighbourhood hipsters and freaks alike, who come to tie one on before a big night out.

Raval

23 Robador

C/Robador 23 (no phone). Metro Liceu.
Open 8pm-2am Tue-Thur, Sun; 8pm-3am
Fri, Sat. **Admission** free. **No credit cards**.
Map p345 A5.
Inside this stone-walled and smoke-filled lounge,
Raval denizens dig the jazz jam on Wednesdays, the
flamenco on Sundays and, in between times, DJs
playing a genre-defying range of music (Joy Division
and DJ Shadow on the same night). A manga-style
mural on the back wall, by one of Barna's many graffiti artists, adds to the underground appeal. You'll
need to ring the bell by the door to get in.

Aurora

*C/Aurora 7 (mobile 680 518 250). Metro
Paral·lel.* **Open** *Aug, Sept* 9pm-2.30am Mon-Thur;
9.30pm-3am Fri, Sat. *Oct-July* 9pm-2.30am Mon-
Thur, Sun; 9.30pm-3am Fri, Sat. **Admission** free.
No credit cards. Map p342 E10.
DIY-stylish, low-lit and cheap. Aurora's regulars
chat over *cañas* during the week and bounce around
the wee dancefloor downstairs at weekends. The
smiling, chatty bar staff tune the stereo to 'reggae'
and 'T-Rex' and keep your cocktail topped up until
you wander out to the Rambla de Raval, looking to
satisfy your craving for late-night kebab.
▶ *Ease into the evening, and pick up club flyers,*
at nearby Cafè de les Delicies; see p188.

Bar Pastis

*C/Santa Mònica 4 (93 318 79 80/www.barpastis.
com). Metro Drassanes.* **Open** 7.30pm-2am Tue-
Thur, Sun; 7.30pm-3am Fri, Sat. **Admission**
free. **Credit** AmEx, MC, V. **Map** p345 A7.
This quintessentially Gallic bar once served pastis
to visiting sailors and denizens of the Barrio Chino
underworld. It still has a louche feel: floor-to-ceiling
clippings and oil paintings, Piaf on the stereo, paper
cranes swaying from the ceiling. But Ajuntament
crackdowns have put an end to live shows, and the
owner of 28 years has put it up for sale. Interested?

Big Bang

*C/Botella 7 (93 443 28 13/www.bigbangbcn.net).
Metro Liceu or Sant Antoni.* **Open** *Bar* 9.30pm-
2.30am Tue-Thur, Sun; 10.15pm-3am Fri, Sat.
Gigs around 10pm-1am Fri, Sat. *Jam session*
10.30pm-1am Sun. **Admission** *Bar & jam
sessions* free. *Gigs* prices vary. **No credit
cards. Map** p342 E10.
Big Bang is decked out like a New York jazz club,
circa 1930, with the low-lit smokiness and bar stool
seating that implies. The diner-style tiled floor leads
from the bar to the tiny stage, where groups of talented musicians play swing, rock 'n' roll, bebop and
every other vintage genre that should never have
gone out of style. Bring your Stetson and just a few
euros for beer; shows are almost always free.

★ La Concha

C/Guàrdia 14 (no phone). Metro Drassanes.
Open 5pm-2.30am Mon-Thur, Sun; 5pm-3am
Fri, Sat. **Admission** free. **No credit cards**.
Map p345 A6.
Papered with posters of vintage Spanish sexpot
Sara Montiel and filled with hookah smoke and the
sounds of Bollywood balladry, La Concha is a gem
of dusty fabulousness that stands in direct contrast
to all the slick and pretentious glamour of most of
the newer late-night bars. It's under Moroccan ownership and there are plans to introduce tea and
baklava in the afternoon.

Fellini

*La Rambla 27 (93 272 49 80/www.clubfellini.
com). Metro Liceu.* **Open** *July-mid Sept* 12.30am-
5am Mon-Thur; 12.30am-6am Fri, Sat. *Mid Sept-
June* 12.30am-5am Mon, Thur; 12.30-6am Sat.
Admission free before 1.30am Mon-Sat; €9
(with flyer), €12 Mon-Wed; €12 (with flyer),
€15 Thur-Sat. **No credit cards. Map** p345 A6.
For a club on La Rambla, Fellini draws a remarkably mixed and local crowd to its two floors of
tech-house and the Red Room, where you might find
rock, '80s or hip hop. The space is great (huge, well
divided and remarkably devoid of typical
nightclub tack), the barstaff efficient and the guest
DJs some of the world's best. Shame about the
meat-market vibe and the quick-to-anger, truck-
shaped bouncers.

Guru

*C/Nou de la Rambla 22 (93 318 08 40/www.
gurubarcelona.com). Metro Liceu.* **Open** 9pm-
2.30am Tue, Wed, Sun; 7pm-3am Thur-Sat.
Admission free. **No credit cards**.
Map p345 A6.
Guru has its eyes set on becoming the latest addition to the Raval bar scene's sleekification, but –
palm trees and mood lighting aside – you can't help
thinking that, with its white padded walls, it looks
rather like a rest room for the suicidal. But as a newcomer in tourist central, it hasn't yet achieved the
exclusive status it's aiming for and, as such, cosmo-
sipping, black-clad Parisians are still having to deal
with gangs of tipsy Scousers hopping about madly
to live salsa. Fusion tapas are served early evenings
from Thursday to Saturday.

Jazz Sí Club

*C/Requesens 2 (93 329 00 20/www.tallerde
musics.com). Metro Sant Antoni.* **Open** 7.45-
10.30pm Tue; 8.30-11pm Mon, Wed-Sat; 6.30-
10pm Sun. **Admission** (incl 1 drink) €4-€7.
No credit cards. Map p342 E10.
Tucked into a Raval side street, with cheap shows
every night and cheap bar grub, this truly authentic place is well worth seeking out. Since it functions
as both a venue for known-in-the-scene locals and
an auditorium for students of the music school

across the street, it's packed to the brim with students, teachers, music lovers and players. Nights vary between jazz, flamenco and Cuban, and there are jam sessions on Tuesdays and Saturdays.

Moog

C/Arc del Teatre 3 (93 301 72 82/www. masimas.com). Metro Drassanes. **Open** midnight-5am Mon-Thur, Sun; midnight-6am Fri, Sat. **Admission** €10. **Credit** DC, MC, V. **Map** p345 A7.

Moog's an odd club: long, narrow and enclosed, with the air conditioner pumping, it's a bit like partying on an aeroplane. The two floors are rather hilariously divided along gender lines: girls shake to pop and '80s upstairs, while there's non-stop hard house and techno downstairs for the boys. It's packed seven days a week, and Angel Molina, Laurent Garnier and Jeff Mills have all played here.

★ La Paloma

C/Tigre 27 (93 301 68 97/93 317 79 94/ www.lapaloma-bcn.com). Metro Universitat. **Open** 6-9.30pm, 11.30pm-5am Thur; 6-9.30pm, 11.30pm-2am Fri, Sat; 5.45-9.45pm Sun. **Admission** (incl 1 drink) €3-€8. **Credit** (bar only) MC, V. **Map** p342 E9.

This extraordinary dancehall is currently closed as it fights noise complaints, but the owners hope to reopen the doors some time in 2009. Arrive early and you'll see older *barcelonins* in full eveningwear elegantly circling the dancefloor. Take a seat in one of the plush balconies to admire the chandeliers and belle époque fittings. Once the foxtrot and tango have finished, DJs mix funk and Latin on Thursdays, with everything from electro to acid at the weekend. But phone first: no one knows when or how the battle over noise levels will end.

Barceloneta & the Ports

Around the quayside of the Port Olímpic, you'll find dance bars interspersed with seafood restaurants and mock-Irish pubs, with video screens and go-gos in abundance. It makes little difference which you choose.

CDLC

Passeig Marítim 32 (93 224 04 70/www.cdlc barcelona.com). Metro Ciutadella-Vila Olímpica. **Open** noon-2.30am daily. **Admission** free. **Credit** AmEx, MC, V. **Map** p343 J13.

Carpe Diem Lounge Club, to give the venue its full name, remains at the forefront of Barcelona's splash-the-cash, see-and-be-seen celeb circuit – the white beds flanking the dancefloor, guarded by a clip-boarded hostess, are perfect for showing everyone who's the daddy. Alternatively, for those not celebrating recently signed, six-figure record deals, funky house and a busy terrace provide an opportunity for mere mortals (and models) to mingle and

discuss who's going to finance their next drink and, secondly, how to get chatting to whichever member of the Barça team has just walked in.

Club Catwalk

C/Ramón Trias Fargas s/n (93 221 61 61/www. clubcatwalk.net). Metro Ciutadella-Vila Olímpica. **Open** midnight-6am Thur-Sun. **Admission** (incl 1 drink) €15-€18. **Credit** DC, MC, V. **Map** p343 K12.

Maybe it's the name or maybe it's the location, but most of the Catwalk queue seems to think they're headed straight for the VIP room – that's crisp white collars and gold for the boys and short, short skirts for the girls. Inside it's suitably snazzy; upstairs there's R&B and hip hop, but the main house room is where most of the action is, with everything from electro-house to minimal beats.

▶ *The club is located directly under the Hotel Arts; see p133.*

Le Kasbah

Plaça Pau Vilà (Palau del Mar) (93 238 07 22/ www.ottozutz.com). Metro Barceloneta. **Open** 11pm-3am daily. **Admission** free. **Credit** AmEx, MC, V. **Map** p345 E8.

A white awning over terrace tables heralds the entrance to this decidedly louche bar behind the Palau de Mar. Inside, a North African harem look seduces a young and up-for-it mix of tourists and students on to its plush cushions for a cocktail or two before they depart for other venues. But as the night progresses, so does the music, from chill-out early in the night to full-on boogie after midnight, when it gets packed.

Mondo

Edifici IMAX, Moll d'Espanya (93 221 39 11/ www.mondobcn.com). Metro Barceloneta or Drassanes. **Open** 11.30pm-3.30am Wed-Sat. **Credit** AmEx, DC, MC, V. **Map** p342 G12.

Arrive by yacht or Jaguar – anything less might not get you past the door. Upscale dining alongside amazing views of the port precede late-night caviar and champagne house parties with DJs from Hed Kandi and Hotel Costes. Multiple intimate VIP rooms provide privacy, pleasure and prestige.

Red Lounge Bar

Passeig Joan de Borbó 78 (mobile 626 561 309/ www.redloungebcn.com). Metro Barceloneta. **Open** 8pm-3am daily. **Admission** free. **Map** p342 G13.

More good news for those missing the legendary Café Royale: DJ Fred Guzzo is the man in charge at this stylish bar, blending funk, latin and rare groove for a mix of music aficionados and glossy-haired uptown kids drawn to the high-class harem look. Nurse Saturday's hangover at their Sunday evening lounge party: nothing like tapas, beers and beach views to help calm the regrets of the night before.

Going Underground

Tech-house rules the roost in Barcelona, but it's not the only sound on offer.

If the sounds blasting from car windows are any indication, the people of Barcelona have varied taste in music. But while bars and snack joints will complement their food and drink with just about anything – who knew Amy Winehouse could mix so well into Bob Seger? – there's segregation in clubland. Flamenco is played at flamenco clubs; Latin beats are limited to Latin clubs; and '80s music is spun upstairs or in back rooms (presumably to keep patrons' shame to a minimum). But everywhere else is dominated clubland's power couple: techno and house.

The reason is simple. In this heyday of the anti-noise crusaders, the industry is a house of cards. The eccentric, iconic **La Paloma** (*see p260*) has been closed indefinitely; concerts at artists' haunt **Vinilo** (*see p266*) have been given the axe; the life of near-centenarian **Bar Pastis** (*see p259*) depends upon eliciting the buried sentiment of the bureaucrats working to shut it down; and foreign DJs are leaving town in droves. Faced with such potential trouble, Barcelona's club owners aren't willing to take any musical risks. Most are coping with the problems by shooting for mainstream appeal, which explains the aural monotony.

Still, there's hope for clubgoers hungry for variety. Down in the clubbing underground, a handful of local promoters have recognised that a little spice makes for a far better dish. You'll need to time your visit carefully, but there are alternatives to tech-house hegemony…

On the second Thursday of every month, the Nuggets party in **La [2]** (*see p262*) hosts concerts by rockabilly guitar heroes, Japanese funk orchestras or hip hop groups. On the second Saturday of every other month, the Boiler Club brings international DJs to **Jazzroom** (C/Vallmajor 33, 93 319 17 89, www.masimas.com) to play vintage soul and rare funk records to a twisting, shouting crowd until dawn. Every now and then (check their MySpace page for updates) the aptly named **Contraflow** party spreads the Ninja Tune gospel through performances by label DJs and live acts, and locals with a ton of vinyl. And every Sunday, the recently transplanted Sunday Joint takes over **Born's Local Bar** (C/Ases 1, 93 310 13 57), where DJ Roger C digs into reggae, afrobeat, blues and funk, and comes up with all the records you've never heard before and can now no longer live without.

Local Bar.

ARTS & ENTERTAINMENT

★ Sala Monasterio

Passeig Isabel II 4 (mobile 609 780 405/
www.salamonasterio.com). Metro Barceloneta.
Open 9.30pm-2.30am Mon-Thur, Sun; 9.30pm-
3am Fri, Sat. **Admission** free-€6. **No credit
cards. Map** p345 E7.

Its entrance is easily missed; go in through the bar
at street level and descend to this low-ceilinged,
bare-brick cavern to hear all nature of jamming and
live music on a great sound system. On Monday
there are singer-songwriters, rock jams on Tuesday,
Wednesday sees Brazilian music, Thursday blues
jams, and weekends vary.

Montjuïc & Poble Sec

Barcelona Rouge

*C/Poeta Cabanyes 21 (93 442 49 85). Metro
Paral·lel.* **Open** 7pm-1am Tue, Wed, Sun; 7pm-
3am Thur-Sat. **Admission** free. **No credit
cards. Map** p342 D11.

Ah – comfy. This is a pretty place done up with
throw rugs, vintage lamps that don't do a whole lot
(the lighting concept is the uncomplicated 'dark')
and dusty sofas. Later in the night it gets packed
with singing, decked-out thirtysomethings who
don't mind getting tipsy in a place where it costs
quite a bit of coin to do so. There are occasional live
shows (normally Sundays).

La [2]

*C/Nou de la Rambla 111-113 (93 441 40 01/
www.sala-apolo.com). Metro Paral·lel.* **Open**
Concerts 9.30pm daily. *Club* 12.30am-6am Fri, Sat.
Admission *Concerts* €10-€25. *Club* (incl 1 drink)
€13. **Credit** AmEx, MC, V. **Map** p342 E11.

La [2] has excellent sound, an intimate layout and
the only hip flamenco night in the city (Mondays
from May to September). The music is reliably good,
with performances by more cultish artists than those
that play next door. Punters can stay on for indie-
rock club Nitsa.

▶ *Can't get in here? Sala Apolo is next door;
see below.*

Maumau

*C/Fontrodona 33 (93 441 80 15/www.
maumaunderground.com). Metro Paral·lel.*
Open 11pm-2.30am Thur; 11pm-3am Fri, Sat;
7pm-midnight Sun. **Admission** (membership)
€12. **No credit cards. Map** p342 D11.

Ring the bell by the anonymous grey door. In practice, out-of-towners are rarely charged membership,
but the card gets some good discounts for cinemas,
clubs and so on. Inside, a large warehouse space is
humanised with colourful projections, Ikea-style
sofas and scatter cushions, and a friendly, laid-back
crowd. DJ Wakanda schools us in the finer points of
deep house, jazz, funk or whatever other musical
development has currently taken his fancy.

Sala Apolo

*C/Nou de la Rambla 111-113 (93 441 40 01/
www.sala-apolo.com). Metro Paral·lel.* **Open**
Concerts 9.30pm daily. *Club* 12.30am-6am Wed-
Sat. **Admission** *Concerts* €10-€25. *Club* (incl 1
drink) €10 Wed; €12 Thur; €13 Fri, Sat. **Credit**
AmEx, MC, V. **Map** p342 E11.

Sala Monasterio.

Sala Apolo, one of Barcelona's most popular clubs, is a 1940s dancehall, with all that implies for atmosphere (good) and acoustics (bad). Live acts range from Toots & the Maytals to Killing Joke, but note that buying tickets for the band doesn't provide admission to the club night: you'll need to re-enter for that, and pay an extra charge. On Wednesdays, the DJs offer African and Latin rhythms; on Thursdays, it's funk, Brazilian, hip hop and reggae; and Fridays and Saturdays are an extravaganza of bleeping electronica.

Sala Instinto
C/México 7 (93 424 83 31/www.salainstinto. com). Metro Espanya. **Open** midnight-6am Wed-Sat; 9pm-4am Sun. **Admission** (incl 1 drink) €10. **No credit cards. Map** p341 B9.
Sessions in this packed, eclectic club run from soul and funk to world and house music, and the crowd varies according to the music: Thursday's is young and beer-swilling (checking out hip hop on a work night); Friday's is dreadlocked (taking in reggae and jungle sounds); and Saturday's is changeable (check the website, as the DJ schedule varies). It's not for glamour queens – the shoes are as low-key as the vibe – but if it's the music that makes the party, then it's worth the trip.

Sóló Bar
C/Margarit 18 (93 329 76 18). Metro Paral·lel or Poble Sec. **Open** 7.30pm-2.30am Mon, Tue, Thur, Sun; 7.30pm-3am Fri, Sat. **Concerts** 9pm Mon-Sat; 8pm Sun. **Admission** free. **No credit cards. Map** p341 D10.

Remember university? Lazy conversations, mindless tooling around on someone's guitar… Relive the glory at this sprawling but oddly cosy bar near the buzzing C/Blai, where stacked up board games and seemingly half-finished art projects comprise the student-living decor. Nightly shows run from blues spectaculars to didgeridoo trios, and there's a big screen for live football and rugby.

★ La Terrrazza
Poble Espanyol, Avda Marquès de Comillas s/n (93 272 49 80/www.laterrrazza.com). Metro Espanya. **Open** May-mid Oct midnight-6am Thur-Sat. **Admission** (incl 1 drink) €18 without flyer, €15 with flyer. **No credit cards. Map** p341 A9/B9.
Gorgeous, glamorous, popular (with the young, hair-gel-and-heels brigade), La Terrrazza is a nightclub that Hollywood might dream of. Wander through the night-time silence of Poble Espanyol to the starry patio that is the dancefloor for one of the more surreal experiences that it's possible to have with an highly priced G&T in your hand. Gazebos, lookouts and erotic paintings add to the magic, and if the music is mostly crowd-pleasing house tunes (the occasional big-name DJ, but no one truly fabulous), so what? That's not really what you came for.

Eixample

Antilla BCN Latin Club
C/Aragó 141 (93 451 45 64/www.antillasalsa. com). Metro Urgell. **Open** 11.30pm-3.30am Tue-Wed; 11.30pm-4.30am Fri, Sat; 9pm-3.30am Sun. *Gigs* around 12.30am Thur. **Admission** (incl 1 drink) €10. **No credit cards. Map** p338 E8.
This Caribbean cultural centre hosts exhibitions, publishes its own magazine (*Antilla News*) and offers classes to Latin dance enthusiasts. But when the sun goes down all cultural pretensions go out the window – it's a hedonistic jungle in there. Live salsa shows by entire orchestras and DJs playing rumba, merengue and *son* until six in the morning will spin your head and parch your throat until the only word you can croak is 'mojito'.

Bucaro
C/Aribau 195 (93 209 65 62/www.grupo costaeste.com/bucaro). FGC Provença. **Open** 11.30pm-4.30am Mon-Thur; 11pm-5.50am Fri, Sat. **Admission** free before 1am; (incl 1 drink) €10 after. **Credit** AmEx, MC, V. **Map** p338 F5.
Looking a tad jaded, Bucaro's white leather sofas and pouffes still manage to pull a crowd of glamour pusses, who stalk their prey from the mezzanine. There's chill-out and jazz in the bar at the front and house for the dancefloor at the back. Drinks are a couple of euros more expensive if you're sitting at a table. Dress code is smart.
▶ *If you like it here, try Opium, which is run by the same people; see p265.*

Eight Days a Week

Barcelona's clubbing scene isn't limited to Fridays and Saturdays.

What is it about Barcelona that keeps clubs performing at weekend-level every night of the week? Maybe it's the number of freelance graphic designers living here – when you're your own boss, who's to say that Sunday isn't the most logical night to debut those new wingtips? Maybe it's the constant stream of visitors seeking to be entertained and intoxicated on whatever day of the week happens to coincide with an easyJet sale. Or maybe it's the simple fact that in Spain, the right to party is as inalienable as that one about voting.

Still, let's be fair. Although many clubs are open five, six or seven days a week, not all school-night offerings were created equal – some are bigger and better than others. Take the summer-only Sunday-nighter at **Liquid** (*see p267*), for instance. The venue is actually a sports centre six days a week, but it's a den of ass-shaking iniquity on the seventh, with two DJ booths, a swimming pool and a never-fail line-up of international artists (with promoters' preferences leaning heavily towards Berliners) making the Monday-morning headache more than worth it.

If, by Monday night, you find yourself recovered, you're in luck. Formerly the unsexiest of all week nights, Mondays have come into their own in Barcelona

recently, with several clubs hosting specialised parties: Flamenco OB Sessions at **La [2]** (*see p262*) and the WTF jam night at **Jamboree** (*see p257*) draw people back week after week. But the best of the best Monday-night sessions is at **Sidecar** (*see p258*). One of the strangest spectacles you'll ever see, Anti-Karaoke involves costumed diehards earnestly lip-synching to Alice in Chains and Slayer while a capacity crowd screams, pumps their fists and rushes the stage. Seriously.

Tuesday's pick can't compete for weirdness, but it's still a school-night gem: Get Funkd, the weekly residency of local collective Barcelona Underground at **City Hall** (*see p265*), brings the best of the city's breakbeat, electro, dub, and raw funk DJs together. Meanwhile, Wednesdays at **Jazz Sí Club** (*see p259*) promise something altogether more refined – Ciclo Hot Jazz fills up early, with the city's most discerning buffs checking the best Dixieland jazz and swing groups this side of the Mason-Dixon Line. The best part? It's generally over by midnight, so when the weekend finally starts on Thursday, there's no excuse for videos and microwave popcorn. This is Barcelona: steel yourself.

Flamenco OB Sessions.

Buda Restaurante

C/Pau Claris 92 (93 318 42 52/www.buda restaurante.com). Metro Catalunya. **Open** 9pm-3am daily. **Admission** free. **Credit** MC, V. **Map** p344 D1.

The centre of Barcelona is strangely devoid of glamorous nightspots, or at least it was until Buda came along. The place has plenty of throne-style furniture and gilded wallpaper, topped off with a colossal chandelier. The laid-back staff (dancing on the bar seems completely acceptable) and upbeat house music make it excellent for drinks and an ogle.

City Hall

Rambla Catalunya 2-4 (93 317 21 77/www. grupo-ottozutz.com). Metro Catalunya. **Open** 10.30-6am daily. **Admission** (incl 1 drink) €12. Free before 2.30am with flyer. **Credit** (door only) MC, V. **Map** p344 C1.

City Hall ain't big, but it is popular. The music is mixed, from deep house to electro rock, and there's an older post-(pre-?) work crowd joining the young, tanned and skinny to show the dancefloors some love. Outside, the terrace is a melting pot of tourists and locals, who rub shoulders under the watchful (and anti-pot-smoking) eye of the bouncer. Flyers are easy to find, and often available outside during the week.

Danzarama

Gran Via de les Corts Catalanes 604 (93 301 97 43/reservations 93 342 52 70/www.danzarama. com). Metro Universitat. **Open** 7am-3am daily. **Admission** free. **Credit** AmEx, DC, MC, V. **Map** p342 F8.

Make your way past the flash restaurant upstairs – we're talking white sofas swinging from the ceiling – and down on to the brick-walled, loud dancefloor. With no entry charge and lots of tables, Danzarama has become a popular pre-party venue and thumping tunes make up for the club-priced drinks.
► *The gay-friendly Arena clubs are close at hand; see p247.*

Discothèque

C/Tarragona 141-147 (93 426 84 44/www. discotheque.info). Metro Tarragona. **Open** midnight-6am Thur-Sat; 7pm-12.30am Sun. **Admission** (incl 1 drink) €15 without flyer; €12 with flyer. **No credit cards. Map** p341 C7.

Phenomenally successful in the early noughties, big D is back. The club has adopted a purse-friendly, all-inclusive policy, with student night on Thursdays and special deals on drinks. Ibizan-style 'tea dance' Café Olé attracts a munificent crowd on Sundays.

Distrito Diagonal

Avda Diagonal 442 (mobile 607 11 36 02/ www.distritodiagonal.com). Metro Diagonal. **Open** midnight-6am Fri, Sat. **Admission** free before 3am; (incl 1 drink) €15 after. **No credit cards. Map** p338 G6.

Distrito Diagonal attracts a slightly older crowd with an easygoing atmosphere. The venue's bathed in red light, there are sounds from nu jazz to deep house and plenty of chairs to sink into. It's become a sought-after place for small promoters and one-off parties, which means the music can veer anywhere from Bollywood to hip hop.

Lotus Theatre

C/Bailen 22 (902 627 987/mobile 692 043 191/ www.lotustheatre.info). Metro Arc de Triomf or Tetuan. **Open** midnight-5am Thur-Sun. **Admission** (incl 1 drink) €12. **No credit cards. Map** p343 H9.

Formerly a strip club, this place was recently reborn as the city's hottest, biggest, newest, most over-hyped nightspot. Its former incarnation hasn't been forgotten – the decor is dark glass, marble, mirrors and poles, the barstaff appear to be Playboy bunnies on a working holiday and dancers in full burlesque occasionally adorn the tabletops. Live salsa and funk shows on weekends are followed by DJs playing funk, hip hop, house and R&B.

Luz de Gas

C/Muntaner 246 (93 209 77 11/www.luzdegas. com). FGC Muntaner. **Open** *Club* 1-5.30am daily. *Gigs* 11.30am daily. **Admission** (incl 1 drink) €18. **Credit** AmEx, DC, MC, V. **Map** p338 E5.

This lovingly renovated old music hall, garnished with chandeliers and classical friezes, is a mainstay on the live music scene and one classy joint. In between visits from international artists and benefit concerts for local causes, you'll find nightly residencies: blues on Mondays, Dixieland jazz on Tuesdays, disco on Wednesdays, pop-rock on Thursdays, soul on Fridays and vintage and Spanish rock on weekends.

Opium

C/París 193-197 (93 414 63 62/www.opium cinema.com). Metro Diagonal. **Open** 11.30pm-2.30am Tue-Thur, Sun; 11.30pm-3.30am Fri, Sat. Closed Aug. **Admission** free. **Credit** AmEx, MC, V. **Map** p338 F6.

Opium offers a break from the norm. For a start, the club is housed in a converted 1950s cinema, which means the projections are actually watchable. There are three bars, plenty of comfortable seating along with a small dancefloor; and if you're very wonderful, you may get to sit on a heart-shaped cushion in the tiny VIP area. With all this going for it, Opium has inevitably become the domain of Barcelona's monied classes. Drinks are dearer upstairs.

La Pedrera de Nit

C/Provença 261-265 (93 484 59 00/www. caixacatalunya.es/obrasocial). Metro Diagonal. **Open** *July* 9-11.30pm Fri, Sat. Closed Aug-June. **Admission** (incl 1 drink) €13.10 **Credit** MC, V. **Map** 340 G7.

ARTS & ENTERTAINMENT

In July, the gorgeous and hallucinatory roof terrace of Gaudí's La Pedrera becomes a jazz club with a view. Spend a fine Friday or Saturday evening engaged in the apex of civilised revelry: sip some cava, sway to live music and contemplate city life from several stories above it. Concerts are at 10pm; book well in advance as tickets sell fast.

Gràcia

★ Bar Elèctric
Travessera de Gràcia 233 (no phone/ www.myspace.com/barelectricbcn). Metro Joanic. **Open** 8pm-2am Tue-Thur, Sun; 8pm-3am Fri, Sat. Closed last wk July, 1st wk Aug. **No credit cards. Admission** free-€4. **Map** p339 H5
Elèctric was the first bar in Gràcia to be connected to the mains (as local legend has it), yet this former bastion of modernity seems not to have changed since. An innocuous entry opens into a sprawling bohemian den that has an agenda as colourful as its clientele: theatre, puppetry and storytelling on weekdays, live music (Brazilian jazz to cabaret) at night.

Gusto
C/Francisco Giner 24 (no phone). Metro Diagonal. **Open** 10pm-2.30am Tue-Thur; 10pm-3am Fri, Sat. **Admission** free. **No credit cards. Map** p338 G6.
Gusto doesn't fall in line with the neighbourhood's favoured shabby-chic aesthetic – it opts instead for a minimalist look, with sleek furnishings and a high-design interior that draws a quirky-hot clientele and DJs with crates of electro records. But it does have one bizarre feature to lure the alternative arts crowd that rules Gràcia: a back room with a floor that is, strangely, covered in sand.

Heliogabal
Ramón y Cajal 80 (no phone/www.heliogabal. com). Metro Joanic. **Open** 9pm-2.30am Mon-Thur, Sun; 9pm-3am Fri, Sat. *Concerts* 10pm. **Admission** free-€5. **No credit cards. Map** p339 H5.
Loved by habitués of the Gràcia arts scene, this low-key bar and performance venue is filled to bursting with neighbourhood cutie pies in cool T-shirts who just really adore live poetry. Events change nightly, running from live music to film screenings, art openings and readings, and programming focuses mostly on local talents. On concert nights arrive early for an 'at-least-I'm-not-standing' folding chair.

KGB
C/Alegre de Dalt 55 (93 210 59 06/www. salakgb.net). Metro Joanic. **Open** 1-6am Thur-Sat. **Admission** free before 3am with flyer; €12 (incl 1 drink) after 3am or without flyer. *Gigs* varies. **No credit cards. Map** p339 J4.
KGB is a cavern-like space that was, in its heyday, the rock 'n' roll disco barn capital of the city and 'un *after'* where Sidecar heads would bolt at 6am on the weekend. It still remains loud, whether featuring concerts or DJ sessions. Thursday's concerts tend towards pop rock, which then continues for the DJ sessions, while the occasional weekend gigs vary but are followed by tech-house. *Photo p258.*

Vinilo
C/Matilde 2 (mobile 626 464 759/http://vinilus. blogspot.com). Metro Fontana. **Open** 8pm-2.30am Mon-Thur, Sun; 7pm-3am Fri, Sat. **Admission** free. **No credit cards. Map** p338 G5.
Run by an affably hip family, Vinilo seems like an artist's den masquerading as a neighbourhood bar. The walls are papered with original prints and concert posters; a silent TV plays '80s cartoons on loop; the sandwiches are big and delicious and the beer selection nothing to scoff at. But it's the music that makes it: Sufjan Stevens, Coco Rosie, Leonard Cohen… You'll wish you lived here.

Other areas

Bikini
C/Déu i Mata 105, Les Corts (93 322 08 00/ www.bikinibcn.com). Metro Les Corts or Maria Cristina. **Open** *Club* midnight-5am Wed-Sun. **Admission** (incl 1 drink) €15. **Credit** MC, V. **Map** p337 C5.
Bikini lost some muscle in recent years, with the big-name stars it once booked replaced by little-knowns and ageing rockers. However, it showed a few signs of new life in 2008, offering shows from the likes of Martha Wainwright and the Ting Tings. Gigs are staged with the professional vigour of gold-ticket shows, and the club nights that follow are legendary. Divide your time between the rooms playing hip hop, pop, lounge or Latin sounds.

Elephant
Passeig dels Til·lers 1, Pedralbes (93 334 02 58/ www.elephantbcn.com). Metro Palau Reial. **Open** 11.30pm-5am Thur-Sat. **Admission** (incl 1 drink) €12. **Credit** MC, V. **Map** 338 A2.
If you have a Porsche and a model girlfriend, this is where you meet your peers. Housed in a converted mansion, Elephant is as elegant and hi-design as its customers. The big attraction is the outdoor bar and terrace dancefloor – though the low-key, low-volume (due to the neighbours' complaints) house music doesn't inspire much hands-in-the-air action.

Espacio Movistar
C/Martí i Franquès, Parc de Bederrida, Zona Universitària (93 490 77 31/www.espacio. movistar.es). Metro Palau Reial. **Open** times vary. **Admission** prices vary. **Credit** AmEx, DC, MC, V.
Up in the vicinity of Nou Camp, the main attraction of this mammoth two-tier white tent is a 1,000sq m (10,800sq ft) concert space that plays host to nation-

al and international money-spinning acts such as Alejandro Sanz, Arctic Monkeys and Scissor Sisters, plus music festivals and sporadic cinema and audiovisual events. There's also an exhibition space, a restaurant, a cybercafé and a chill-out zone, where you can almost escape the feeling of being digested by a giant publicity machine.

★ Liquid
Centre Poliesportiu L'Hospitalet Nord, Avda Manuel Azaña 21-23, L'Hospitalet (no phone/ www.liquidbcn.com). Metro Zona Universitària. **Open** *mid June-Aug* midnight-5.30am Sun. **Admission** (incl 1 drink) €15. **Credit** MC, V.
In an almost-criminal strike against the morale of the working population (or the sobriety of Monday mornings), this summer-only clubbing classic hosts the best of the best in European electronica – on Sundays. Miss Kitten, DJ Hell, Sascha Funke and the Hacker all passed through last year to 'party in the pool'. Yes, that's right, it's a swimming pool.

Mirablau
Plaça Doctor Andreu 1, Tibidabo (93 418 58 79). FGC Avda Tibidabo then Tramvia Blau. **Open** 11am-4am Mon-Thur; 11am-5.30am Fri-Sun. **Admission** free. **Credit** MC, V.
It doesn't get any more uptown than this, geographically and socially. Located at the top of Tibidabo, this small bar is packed with the high rollers of Barcelona, from local footballers living on the hill to international businessmen on the company card. Watch out for the the view and the artificial wind that sweeps through the tropical shrubbery outside.

Otto Zutz
C/Lincoln 15 (93 238 07 22/www.grupoottozutz.com). FGC Gràcia. **Open** midnight-4.30am Tue; midnight-5am Wed; midnight-6am Thur-Sat. **Admission** (incl 1 drink) €15. Free before 2.30am with flyer. **Credit** AmEx, DC, MC, V. **Map** p338 F4.
Otto Zutz should have been great. Located away from the maddening crowds of the old quarter in a three-floor former textile factory that oozes character, the potential was there in abundance but it got lost somewhere between the pretentious staff, mediocre house and bad R&B. The crowd doesn't seem to notice, though – this place sure can pack 'em in, especially when it comes to the young and dolled-up. Flyers are ubiquitous.

★ Razzmatazz
C/Almogàvers 122 (93 320 82 00/www. salarazzmatazz.com). Metro Bogatell or Marina. **Concerts** 9.30pm Mon-Sun. **Admission** varies. **Club** 1-5am Fri, Sat. **Admission** (incl 1 drink) €15. **Credit** AmEx, MC, V. **Map** p343 L10.
This monstrous club's five distinct spaces form the night-time playground of seemingly all young Barcelona. There's indie rock in Razz Club, techhouse in The Loft, techno pop in Lolita, electro pop in the Pop Bar and electro rock in the Rex Room. Live music runs from Arctic Monkeys to Banarama. The price of admission will usually get you into all five rooms (no matter what's on in each), though the gigs are normally ticketed separately.

Sala BeCool
Plaça Joan Llongueras (93 362 04 13/www. salabecool.com). Metro Hospital Clínic. **Open** *Gigs* 10pm Thur-Sat. *Club* midnight-5am Fri, Sat. **Admission** *Gigs* varies. *Club* (incl 1 drink) €12. **Credit** AmEx, DC, MC, V. **Map** p338 D5.
The latest from Berlin's minimal electro scene reaches Barcelona via this uptown concert hall. After the live shows by local rock stars or international indie success stories, a packed and music-loving crowd throbs to sophisticated electronica and its bizarre attendant visuals. Upstairs, in the Red Room, DJs playing indie pop rock provide an alternative to the pounding beats of the main room.

Sala Salamandra
Avda Carrilet 301, L'Hospitalet (93 337 06 02/ www.salamandra.cat). Metro Avda Carrilet. **Open** *Concerts* 9.30pm daily. **Club** midnight-5am Fri, Sat. **Admission** *Gigs* Prices vary. *Club* (incl 1 drink) €8 after 2am. **No credit cards.**
If you're willing to travel 30 minutes on the metro to L'Hospitalet, do it for a night at this 500-person, venue-cum-nightclub, which regularly hosts the best local artists, including Macaco, Muchachito Bombo Infierno and Kinky Beat. Local and visiting DJs take over after the shows, and it's worth sticking around; the music stays fun, the crowd local, the atmosphere unpretentious and the drinks fairly cheap.

Universal
C/Marià Cubí 182 bis-184 (93 201 35 96/ www.grupocostaeste.com/universal). FGC Muntaner. **Open** 11pm-3.30am Mon-Thur; 11pm-5am Fri, Sat. **Admission** free Mon-Thur; free before 1am, (incl 1 drink) €7 after 1am Fri, Sat. **Credit** AmEx, MC, V. **Map** p338 E5.
One of the few clubs in the city that caters to an older, well-dressed crowd, Universal doesn't charge admission, but the drink prices are steep. Upstairs is a chill-out area, complete with aquatic slide projections, while downstairs sports a sharper look. Later, the music moves from downtempo to soft house, which works the crowd up to a gentle shimmy.

ARTS & ENTERTAINMENT

Performing Arts

Get to know Barcelona one stage at a time.

Barcelona has a remarkable musical heritage and now, finally, it has suitable venues in which to hear it. Add to that theatre and dance troupes that honed their talent for physical spectacle through the Franco years when the Catalan language was banned and you have rich pickings indeed for the visiting culture vulture.

Three of the city's most venerable institutions for the performing arts have something to celebrate in 2009. It has been a decade since the Liceu opera house rose from the ashes after the devastating 1994 fire. L'Auditori was inaugurated in the same year. The extraordinary Palau de la Música Catalana reached its centenary in 2008, and a series of special concerts continue throughout the year.

Classical Music & Opera

The best news about the local music scene is that confidence is high and programmes are increasingly well rounded. Although the canon still reigns at Liceu, contemporary productions, local works and some adventurous formats add a bit of risk to its classical repertoire. A spanking new **Conservatori** – part of the Liceu – opened at the end of 2008, offering its own programme of chamber operas, recitals and contemporary compositions in a subterranean auditorium. Smaller venues such as **Auditori Axa** host less regular concerts, although generally of a high quality.

The main musical season runs September to June. During this time the city orchestra, the **OBC**, plays weekly at the Auditori, which also regularly hosts resident contemporary orchestra **BCN 216**. The Liceu stages a different opera every three or four weeks. Both the Auditori and the Palau de la Música hold several concert cycles of various genres, either programmed by the venues or by independent promoters (Ibercamera, Euroconcert or Promoconcert are the most high-profile). From June to August, concerts are taken outdoors. **Música als Parcs** is a programme of some 50 evening concerts held in a number of city parks (www.parcsijardins.cat). Additionally, various museums, among them the Fundació Miró (*see p91*), the CaixaForum (*see p91*) also hold small outdoor concerts. More serious musical activity, though, follows its audience out of the city and heads on up the coast, to festivals in the towns of Vilabertrán, Perelada, Cadaqués and Torroella de Montgrí.

INFORMATION AND TICKETS

The monthly *Informatiu Musical*, published by Amics de la Música (93 268 01 22, www.amicsmusica.org), lists concerts in all genres. Pick up a copy at tourist offices and record shops. Weekly entertainment guide *Guia del Ocio* has a music section, as does the weekly *Time Out Barcelona* (www.timeout.cat); both *El País* and *La Vanguardia* list forthcoming concerts. For children's events try www.toc-toc.cat. The council website, www.bcn.cat/cultura, also has details of many forthcoming events. Tickets for most major venues can be bought by phone or online from venues, or from Tel-entrada or ServiCaixa (*see p220*).

FESTIVALS

For more festivals, see also **Festa de la Música** *see p226*; **Festival del Grec** *see p226*; and **Música als Parcs** *see p226*.

Nous Sons – Músiques Contemporànies

L'Auditori (see p270). **Tickets** €10-€15.
Date Mid Mar-early Apr.
New Sounds is a burst of new music that continues to evolve yearly, and features national and international ensembles. The 12 or so concerts range from symphonic and chamber music to experimental,

improvisation and free jazz. Works by Arvo Pärt, John Adams and local composer Ramon Humet, winner of the prestigious Olivier Messiaen Prize in 2007, feature in the 2009 programme.

Festival de Música Antiga
L'Auditori (see p270). **Tickets** €12-€20. **Date** 30 Apr-30 May.
Go for Baroque at the Festival of Early Music, which features well-known performers from around the world. The accompanying free concerts of El Fringe festival is held over three days in outdoor spaces around the Barri Gòtic and offer young performers an opportunity to perform alongside more established musicians.

Tradicionàrius
Travessia de Sant Antoni 6-8 & various venues in Gràcia (93 218 44 85/www.tradicionarius.cat). **Metro Fontana. Date** Apr-June. **Tickets** free-€10. **No credit cards. Map** p338 G5.
Traditional concerts are held in a recently renovated auditorium in the district of Gràcia and groups venture into public squares and marketplaces to offer free concerts at weekends, and holds this spirited showcase of folk music and dance between April and June.

Nits de Mùsica
Fundació Joan Miró (see p91). **Tickets** €10; €40 for 6 concerts. **Date** Mid June-July.
When the rest of the city gets too hot, head up to the Fundació Miró for its annual Nits de Música series of jazz, improv and other musical performances. Some concerts take place on the roof terrace.

LEM
Various venues in Gràcia (93 237 37 37/ www.gracia-territori.com). **Date** Oct.
The main focus of the dynamic Gràcia Territori Sonor collective is the month-long LEM festival in autumn: held in various venues in Gràcia, it's a rambling series of musical happenings, many experimental, improvised and electronic, and most of them free. The larger-scale events are held at MACBA, La Pedrera and CaixaForum.

Festival d'Òpera de Butxaca i Noves Creacions
Various venues (93 301 84 85/mobile 659 454 879/www.fobnc.org/www.festivalopera butxaca.org). **Date** Oct-Nov.
A successful series of innovative and entertaining small-scale chamber operas (the name means the Festival of New and Pocket Operas) performed in various unlikely but atmospheric venues, including the former anatomy theatre of the Royal Academy of Medicine, as well as the more usual spaces.

AvuiMúsica
Associació Catalana de Compositors, Passeig Colom 6, space 4, Barri Gòtic (93 268 37 19/ www.accompositors.com). **Metro Jaume I.** **Tickets** €10; €5 reductions. **Date** Dec-June. **No credit cards. Map** p345 D7.
Not so much a festival as a season of small-scale contemporary concerts run by the Association of Catalan Composers and held at various venues around the city. Members of the association are well represented and include local composer Joan Albert Amargós, who was nominated for a Grammy in 2008.

ARTS & ENTERTAINMENT

Palau de la Música Catalana. *See p271.*

VENUES

In addition to the venues listed over the next few pages, several churches also hold concerts. Not only will the acoustics (usually) be excellent, but the spaces suit sacred music. The most popular is Santa Maria del Mar (*see p71*) in the Born, where Handel's *Messiah* draws the crowds at Christmas, but the more atmospheric are smaller chapels Santa Maria del Pi (*see p59*), Sant Felip Neri (*see p59*), Santa Anna (*see p59*) or the gorgeous Gothic convent in Pedralbes (*see p115*). Concerts run from Renaissance music to gospel, with everything in between.

★ L'Auditori

C/Lepant 150, Eixample (93 247 93 00/www. auditori.cat). Metro Marina. **Open** *Information* 8am-10pm daily. **Box office** noon-9pm Mon-Sat; 1hr before performance Sun. Closed Aug. **Tickets** vary. **Credit** MC, V. **Map** p343 K9.

Designed by architect Rafael Moneo and directed by the affable Joan Oller, L'Auditori tries to offer something to everyone. The 2,400-seat Pau Casals hall, dedicated to the Catalan cellist, provides a stable home for city orchestra OBC, now under the baton of conductor Eiji Oue (although it frequently performs with guest conductors). It is also a place for the revered Jordi Savall to straddle his viola da gamba in an excellent series of early music concerts

Laughter in the Dark

British and American comics transcend the language barrier in Barcelona.

Barcelona can be a cheap place to catch big-name stand-up comics from the UK, US and Australia, especially when they come over to try out their Edinburgh material away from the critics' acid tongues. As there is no strong tradition of stand-up in Spain, heckling is virtually unheard of.

Irish cultural festival El Feile first introduced professional English-language stand-up comedy to Spain in 2004 with such success that organiser Stephen Garland promptly formed the **Giggling Guiri** Comedy Club (mobile 610 317 656, www.comedyinspain.com) – *guiri* being rather unflattering slang for foreigner. Garland puts on regular evening shows at the **Cafè-Teatre Llantiol** (C/Riereta 7, Raval, 93 329 90 09, www.llantiol.com) starring practically the entire fringe line-up, from the likes of Jason Byrne and Paul Sinha to Mark Watson and Brendon Burns; likewise, Steve Barry's **Guinness Laughter Lounge** (mobile 627 185 038, www.gloungebcn.com) books established names like Ian Moore or Ben Norris at **La Riereta** theatre (C/Reina Amàlia 3, Raval, 93 442 98 44, www.lariereta.es).

Seeing award-winning headliners of this calibre perform at such intimate venues is a rare treat, and the snug surroundings often inspire the comics to greater heights of improv and experimentation than you might get at Edinburgh's Assembly Hall.

For those who understand a little Spanish, American hellion Rachel Arieff (*photo*) performs a raucous monthly stand-up show *Como ser feliz todo el tiempo* ('How To Be Happy All the Time') at the Cafè-Teatre Llantiol; the show is full of the observations of a foreigner in Spain. Transcending language barriers completely, Arieff's cult Anti-Karaoke sessions have made Monday night the new Saturday down at Sidecar club (*see p258*). The wardrobe is vaudevillian Rocky Horror, the songs might be anything from Barbra Streisand to AC/DC and the spirit is 'extreme cabaret'. Expect plenty of waggish compèring and lung-busting musical numbers from La Arieff while the rest of the material is belted out by anyone from drag queens to crowd-surfing cab drivers. Go. Take your feather boa.

ARTS & ENTERTAINMENT

called *El So Original* and running from October to April. A more intimate 600-seat chamber space, dedicated to choir leader Oriol Martorell, has a more diverse programme incorporating contemporary and world music, while experimental and children's work is staged in a 400-seat space named after jazz pianist Tete Montoliu. A late-night bus service connects the Auditori with Plaça Catalunya after evening performances.

Auditori Axa
L'Illa, Avda Diagonal 547, Les Corts (93 290 11 02/info.auditori@axa.es). Metro Maria Cristina. **Open** *Information* 8.30am-1.30pm, 3-5.30pm Mon-Fri. Closed Aug. **Tickets** vary. **Credit** varies. **Map** p337 C4.
This small venue in the unlikely setting of L'Illa, a monolithic shopping centre, hosts concerts about once a month. The Schubert cycle (93 290 11 02, www.schubertiada.com) and series of song recitals performed by Cor Vivaldi shared with L'Auditori (93 319 17 89, www.fundaciomasimas.org) are both annual events and are well worth catching.

Fundació Mas i Mas
C/Marià Cubí 199, Zona Alta (93 319 17 89/ www.fundaciomasimas). FGC Muntaner. **Open** Mon, Thur-Sun. **Concerts** 6pm, 7pm, 8pm. **Tickets** €6; €4 reductions. Closed Aug. **Map** p338 E5/F5.
A small 50-seater space offers short classical concerts by young performers, except on Fridays, which is tango night. In August, musicians switch venue to La Pedrera for 30 Minuts de Música sessions.

★ Gran Teatre del Liceu
La Rambla 51-59, Barri Gòtic (93 485 99 13/ tickets 902 53 33 53/www.liceubarcelona.com). Metro Liceu. **Open** *Information* 11am-2pm, 3-8pm Mon-Fri. **Box office** 2-8pm Mon-Fri; 1hr before performance Sat, Sun. Closed 2wks Aug. **Tickets** vary. **Credit** AmEx, MC, V. **Map** p345 A/B5.
Since it opened in 1847 two fires, a bombing and financial crisis have failed to quash the spirit and splendour of the Liceu, one of the most prestigious venues in the world and a huge success with the public. A restrained façade opens into an elegant 2,292-seat auditorium of red plush, gold leaf and ornate carvings. The latest mod cons include seat-back subtitles in various languages that complement the Catalan surtitles above the stage. Under the stewardship of artistic director Joan Matabosch and musical director Sebastian Weigle, the Liceu has consolidated its programming policy, mixing co-productions with leading international opera houses with its own in-house productions. Classical, full-length opera is the staple, although small format opera and contemporary classics feature. A new Catalan work is commissioned every four years and in April 2009 composer Enric Palomar premieres his one-act opera

La Cabeza del Bautista. A large basement bar hosts pre-performance talks, recitals plus children's shows and other musical events; the Espai Liceu is a 50-seat auditorium with a regular programme of screenings of past operas. Opened at the end of 2008, the swish 6-floor Conservatori (C/Nou de la Rambla 82-88, 93 304 11 13, www.conservatori-liceu.es), which is part of the Liceu, lends its 400-seater basement auditorium to classical and contemporary concerts, small-scale operas and even jazz.

★ Palau de la Música Catalana
C/Sant Francesc de Paula 2, Sant Pere (93 295 72 00/www.palaumusica.org). Metro Urquinaona. **Box office** 10am-9pm Mon-Sat; 1hr before performance Sun. Closed Aug for concerts. **Tickets** vary. **Credit** MC, V. **Map** p344 D/E3.
This extraordinary visual explosion of Modernista architectural flights of fancy is a UNESCO World Heritage site. Built in 1908 by Lluís Domènech i Montaner, it is certainly one of the most spectacular music venues anywhere on the planet and much work has been done to improve its acoustics. A 21st-century extension has added a terrace, a restaurant and a subterranean hall. The Palau has seen some of the best international performers over the years, including the likes of Leonard Bernstein and Daniel Barenboim. Its centenary celebrations go on throughout 2009, with a season of orchestral music called Palau 100 bringing in guest orchestras such as the Montreal Symphonic in April. Renowned mezzo-soprano Cecilia Bartoli is in town in the same month and virtuoso Frank Peter Zimmermann takes up his violin in May. *Photo p269.*
▶ *For more on this extraordinary building, refer to the Architecture chapter; see p46 and p73.*

ORCHESTRAS & ENSEMBLES

Barcelona 216
93 487 87 81/www.auditori.cat.
This small but prolific ensemble is led by David Albet, who also does the programming for the chamber space in L'Auditori. The group has a strong commitment to contemporary music of all types, featuring regularly in the Nous Sons programme in March and producing a series of experimental works, Digressions, also at L'Auditori, in April.

La Capella Reial de Catalunya, Le Concert des Nations & Hespèrion XXI
93 580 60 69/www.alia-vox.com.
The popularity of Catalonia's rich heritage in early music is due in large part to the efforts of the indefatigable Jordi Savall, the driving force behind these three interlinked musical groups which, between them, play around 300 concerts a year worldwide. La Capella Reial specialises in Catalan and Spanish Renaissance and Baroque music; Le Concert des

Nations is a period-instrument ensemble playing orchestral and symphonic work from 1600 to 1850; and Hespèrion XXI plays pre-1800 European music.

Diapasón
60 508 10 60/telungc@hotmail.com.
Diapasón is a septet specialising in Erik Satie and the more playful works of contemporary classical music. The group is led by composer/performer Domènec González de la Rubia.

Grup XXI
93 285 14 87/www.peterbacchus.com.
A contemporary music ensemble led by American flautist Peter Bacchus. A series of concerts dedicated to contemporary Catalan composers is held in the auditorium of La Pedrera in November.

Orfeó Català
93 295 72 00/www.palaumusica.org.
The Orfeó Català began life as one of 150 choral groups that sprang up as part of the patriotic and social renewal movements at the end of the 19th century and, due to its success, was banned by Franco after the Civil Was as a possible focus of Catalan nationalism. While it's no longer as pre-eminent on the musical scene as it once was, the group still stages around 25 performances a year, giving a cappella concerts, as well as providing a choir for the Orquestra Simfònica and other Catalan orchestras. The largely amateur group also includes a small professional nucleus, the Cor de Cambra del Palau de la Música, which gives 50 performances a year.

Orquestra Simfònica de Barcelona Nacional de Catalunya (OBC)
93 247 93 00/www.obc.cat.
The Orquestra Simfònica de Barcelona is the busiest orchestra in the city, performing at the Auditori almost every weekend of the season. Guest conductors in 2009 include Hans Graf and Yakov Kreizberg in the spring. The orchestra provides a fairly standard gallop through the symphonic repertoire, though Japanese director Eiji Oue has brought in a more adventurous programme. The orchestra is also committed to new Catalan composers, commissioning two works a year.

Orquestra Simfònica del Vallès
93 727 03 00/www.osvalles.com.
This provincial orchestra, based in the nearby town of Sabadell, performs regularly in Barcelona, often at the Palau de la Música Catalana, where it plays a dozen symphonic concerts each season.

Orquestra Simfònica i Cor del Gran Teatre del Liceu
93 485 99 13/www.liceubarcelona.com.
Upcoming operatic productions for the 2009 season include Richard Strauss's *Salome* in June and Giacomo Puccini's *Turandot* in July, both co-produced with major international opera companies. There's also a programme of concerts and recitals, and half a dozen colourful mini operas aimed at children (or their bigger brethren) including *The Superbarber of Seville*.

Teatre Lliure. See p274.

ARTS & ENTERTAINMENT

Trio Kandinsky
93 301 98 97/www.triokandinsky.com.
Formed in 1999, the Trio Kandinsky has an excellent reputation, performing contemporary repertoire as well as the classical canon.

Theatre & Dance

Catalan theatre was banned under Franco. After his death, troupes surged on to the streets, luring audiences with the spectacular and the daring. However, the excitement of the 1980s fizzled in the '90s, when groups became tired of the nomadic life and despondent with the lack of funding and dearth of performance spaces. The survivors were those companies such as **Els Comediants** and **La Fura dels Baus**, who stuck to the attention-seeking style of street theatre.

Finally though, a whiff of change is in the air. In 2004, a new municipal government put culture as a process and not just a product back on the agenda. This led to the availability of public cash for organisations that support creation, such as theatre groups **AreaTangent** (www.areatangent.com) and **Conservas** (http://conservas.tk), and dance groups **L'Estruch** (www.sabadell.cat) and **La Caldera** (www.lacaldera.info) in dance. The funding system is notoriously complicated, however, with groups or projects having to piece together minimal grants from an array of sources: municipal and city, public and private. It is hoped that the recent establishment of an independent funding body, Consell de les Arts, with an 11-strong board of artistic directors, can bring some coherence.

Most theatre is in Catalan although Spanish works tour and **Teatre Lliure** offers surtitles in English for major productions.

In the world of dance, performers such as Pina Bausch and the Compañia Nacional de Danza (directed by the revered Nacho Duato) fill grand venues such as the **Teatre Nacional** and the Liceu. Companies such as **Sol Picó** and **Erre que Erre** usually run a new show every year, as do **Metros**, **Mudances** and **Gelabert-Azzopardi**. There are a number of promising contemporary dancers that have established themselves abroad and are back in town: look out for Rafael Bonachela and Pere Faura in particular.

TICKETS AND TIMES
Main shows start around 9-10pm. On Sundays there are morning matinées aimed at family audiences and earlier evening shows at around 5-6.30pm; most theatres are dark on Monday. Advance bookings are best made through Servi-Caixa or Tel-entrada (*see p220*). The best places to find information are *Guía del Ocio*, *Time Out Barcelona* magazine and the *cartelera* (listings) pages of the newspapers. Online, check www.teatral.net and www.teatrebcn.com; for dance, try www.dansacat.org. You can also visit Canal Cultura at www.bcn.cat/cultura.

FESTIVALS
The **Grec Festival** (*see p226*) brings in major international acts in theatre and dance, some of which appear in an open-air amphitheatre on Montjuïc. The performing arts festival **Escena Poblenou** merits a trip to the beachside *barrio* in mid October (www.escenapoblenou.com) while in summer, **Dies de Dansa** (*see below*) is three days of free, open-air national and international dance in public sites such as the CCCB or the MACBA patios. **Complicitats** is a festival focusing on emerging dance held in February (93 318 87 87, www.lamekanica.com).

In addition to those below, new companies can launch their work at the **Mostra de Teatre** (93 436 32 62, www.mostradeteatre debarcelona.com) in October and November, when they're assigned two nights apiece and judged by a panel of directors.

★ Dies de Dansa
Various venues. Information Associació Marató de l'Espectacle (93 268 18 68/www.marato.com). **Date** Early July.
Under the GREC umbrella, this four-day Festival of Dance is free, with shows on the terraces of the CCCB, MACBA, CaixaForum, Museu Picasso and Fundació Miró, including popular events such as the Spanish-Portuguese breakdancing championships.

La Mercè Arts de Carrer
Various venues (www.bcn.cat/cultura/ artsdecarrer). **Date** late Sept.
Free three-day street performance festival.

MAJOR VENUES
Large-scale commercial productions are shown in **Teatre Condal** (Avda Paral·lel 91, Poble Sec, 93 442 31 32, www.teatrecondal.com), the **Borràs** (Plaça Urquinaona 9, Eixample, 93 412 15 82), and the **Tívoli** (C/Casp 10-12, Eixample, 93 412 20 63). For more information on these two latter venues, see www.grupbalana.com. The **Monumental** bullring (*see p102*) and the **Barcelona Teatre Musical** (C/Guàrdia Urbana s/n, Montjuïc, 93 423 64 63) are used for mega-shows and musicals.

★ Mercat de les Flors
Plaça Margarida Xirgú, C/Lleida 59, Poble Sec (93 426 18 75/www.mercatflors.org). Metro Poble Sec. **Box office** 1hr before

show. Advance tickets also available from Palau de la Virreina. **Tickets** vary. **No credit cards.** **Map** p341 C10.

British theatre director Peter Brook is credited with transforming this former flower market into a venue for the performing arts in 1985, when he was looking for a place to stage his legendary production of the *Mahabharata*. After decades of diffuse programming, the Mercat has finally focused in on national and international contemporary dance, and offers a strong programme that experiments with unusual formats and mixes in new technologies and live music. It also supports emerging dancers, producing the BCSTX cycle in April.

Teatre Lliure

Plaça Margarida Xirgú, Poble Sec (93 289 27 70/www.teatrelliure.com). Metro Poble Sec. **Box office** 11am-3pm, 4.30-8pm Mon-Fri; 2hrs before show Sat, Sun. **Tickets** €12-€16 Tue, Wed; €16-€22 Thur-Sun; reductions 25% discount. **Credit** MC, V. **Map** p341 C10.

Under its young and dynamic director, Àlex Rigola, the Teatre Lliure's main and mini stage host an adventurous array of theatre and dance that occasionally spills on to the square outside. The 2009 programme promises works by prolific local playwright Lluïsa Cunillé and the wildly imaginative pianist Carles Santos. Resident dance company Gelabert-Azzopardi perform in 2009, as do Mal Pelo, in a collaborative piece with writer John Berger. Bigger theatre shows are surtitled in English on Thursdays and Saturdays. *Photo p272.*

Teatre Nacional de Catalunya (TNC)

Plaça de les Arts 1, Eixample (93 306 57 00/ www.tnc.cat). Metro Glòries. **Box office** 3-9pm Tue-Sun. **Tickets** €15-€25; €10-€15 reductions. **Credit** AmEx, DC, MC, V. **Map** p343 K9.

The Generalitat-funded theatre designed by Ricardo Bofill boasts a vast airy lobby and three fabulous performance spaces. Director Sergi Belbel has opted for a good mix of contemporary and classical pieces and incorporated a fine contemporary dance programme, divided between a main stage and smaller stage. Works by new writers are normally performed in the more experimental Sala Tallers.

Teatre Poliorama

La Rambla 115, Barri Gòtic (93 317 75 99/ www.teatrepoliorama.com). Metro Catalunya. **Box office** 5-8pm Tue; 5-8.30pm Wed-Sat; 5-7pm Sun. **Open** till 9.30pm Wed-Sat for same day purchase. Closed 2wks Aug.

Tickets varies. **Credit** MC, V. **Map** p344 B3.

Run by private producers 3xtr3s, this once adventurous theatre now puts on predominantly mainstream comedies and musicals such as Monty Python's *Spamalot*, plus the odd piece of serious theatre. It also stages shows for children.

Teatre Romea

C/Hospital 51, Raval (information 93 301 55 04/tickets 902 10 12 12/www.teatreromea.com). Metro Liceu. **Box office** 5-8pm Tue-Sat. *Performances* 9pm Tue-Fri; 6.30pm, 10pm Sat; 6.30pm Sun. **Tickets** €16-€24. **Credit** (phone bookings only) AmEx, DC, MC, V. **Map** p344 A4.

The fertile imagination of artistic director Calixto Bieito runs rampant at Romea, although his theatre of the senses can prove wearisome. Bieito looks to contemporary European theatre for inspiration, although most works are in Catalan.

ALTERNATIVE THEATRES

There are many smaller theatres in Barcelona struggling for funding and audiences. Survivors are **Nou Tantarantana** (C/Flors 22, Raval, 93 441 70 22, www.tantarantana.com), the tiny **Espai Escènic Joan Brossa** (C/Allada-Vermell 13, Born, 93 310 13 64, www.espai brossa.com) and the unusual **L'Antic Teatre** (C/Verdaguer i Callis 12, Barri Gòtic, 93 315 23 54, www.lanticteatre.com). Additionally, **Versus Teatre** (C/Castillejos 179, Eixample, 93 232 31 84, www.versusteatre.com) and **Sala Muntaner** (C/Muntaner 4, Eixample, 93 451 57 52, www.salamuntaner.com) often produce interesting work.

The **Teatre de la R, Riereta** (C/Reina Amalia 3, Raval, 93 442 98 44, www.lariereta. es) hosts a few English works as does **Cafè-Teatre Llantiol** (C/Riereta 7, Raval, 93 329 90 09, www.llantiol.com), which holds monthly Giggling Guiri comedy nights (*see p270* **Laughter in the Dark**).

Sala Beckett

C/Alegre de Dalt 55 bis, Gràcia (93 284 53 12/ www.salabeckett.com). Metro Joanic. **Box office** from 8pm Wed-Sat; from 5pm Sun. Closed Aug. **Tickets** €6-€16; €4-€12 reductions. **No credit cards.** **Map** p339 J4.

This small but important venue was founded by the Samuel Beckett-inspired Teatro Fronterizo group, run by playwright José Sanchis Sinisterra. He's no longer based at the theatre, but his influence prevails. High rental costs and bigger ambitions may mean, however, that Sala Beckett is on the move. Check the website for updates.

THEATRE COMPANIES

As well as those reviewed below, companies to watch out for include the colourful satirical troupe **Les Chanclettes** and **Dagoll Dagom** (www.dagolldagom.com). Longstanding troupe **Els Joglars** (www.elsjoglars.com) was founded 40 years ago by Albert Boadella, who was imprisoned by Franco for his political stance but is currently in self-imposed exile from Catalonia after some high-profile spats regarding the regional government's linguistic policy.

For English-language theatre, look for the **Jocular** company (www.joculartheatre.com) who normally stage plays in June and November.

Els Comediants
www.comediants.com.
Els Comediants has its roots in commedia dell'arte and street performance; its mix of mime, circus, music, storytelling and fireworks is as likely to appear on the street to celebrate a national holiday as at any major theatre festival.

La Cubana
www.lacubana.es.
La Cubana's shows have a popular appeal and cartoonish quality, using multimedia effects, camp music and audience participation.

La Fura dels Baus
www.lafura.com.
This ostentatious troupe that started out on the streets of Barcelona in the early '80s with a donkey, a cart and some nihilistic ideas, now tours the world with hi-tech, polemical shows. Former founder member and ex-abattoir employee Marcel.li Antúnez Roca follows a similar vein in his solo shows.

Tricicle
93 317 4747/www.tricicle.com.
Local boys Carles Sans, Paco Mir and Joan Gràcia founded this mime trio 30 years ago. The goofy, clean-

cut humour appeals to the Spanish taste for slapstick; and children love it too. They're regulars in El Petit Liceu and have, among other feats, brought Monty Python's *Spamalot* to a local audience.

DANCE COMPANIES

In addition to those listed below, groups worth seeing include **Group Búbulus** (www.bubulus.net) and Toni Mira's company **Nats Nus** (www.natsnus.com). Its highly successful offshoot **Nats Nens** produces contemporary dance shows for children. For a comprehensive list check www.companyiesdansa.info.

Compañia Metros
www.metrosdansa.com.
Under local choreographer Ramón Oller, Metros mount entertaining productions such as *Madame Butterfly* and Lorca's *Bernarda Alba*. They usually bring a show to town for three weeks in the summer.

Compañia Mar Gómez
www.danzamargomez.com.
Compañia Mar Gómez provides a mix of contemporary dance and theatre with a wicked sense of humour and good music.

Erre que Erre
www.errequeerredanza.net.
This excellent collective of younger dancers turn complex ideas into contemplative performances, with well-measured doses of theatre and original music.

Compañia Mar Gómez.

Gelabert-Azzopardi

www.gelabertazzopardi.com.
Expect fluid, poetic performances from Barcelona's
Cesc Gelabert and Londoner Lydia Azzopardi.

Mal Pelo

www.malpelo.com.
Maria Muñoz and Pep Ramis incorporate images
and text in their shows. They perform a review of
their work at Mercat de les Flors in April 2009.

Marta Carrasco

www.martacarrasco.com.
Veteran dancer Marta Carrasco has choreographed
many plays and musicals. Lavish costumes and
extravagant set designs define her work.

Mudances

www.margarit-mudances.com.
Director Àngels Margarit produces melodic contemporary work that draws on world music and dance.
The company also produces works for family audiences, including *flexelf* at Mercat de les Flors in
spring 2009.

Raravis-Andrés Corchero-Rosa Muñoz

http://raravisdanza.com.
Quirky Raravis is the dancers' dance company –
minimalist and delightfully inventive.

Sol Picó

www.solpico.com.
Charismatic Sol Picó performs a rock 'n' roll inspired
piece at Mercat de les Flors in March 2009.

FLAMENCO

Local *cantaors*, such as Miguel Poveda, play
to sell-out crowds at the Palau de la Música or
smaller venues such as **Luz de Gas** (*see p265*),
as do singers from the south Paco de Lucía, Diego
de Cigala or Vicente Amigo. Dancers, including
Rafael Amargo, appear at the Liceu.

El Tablao de Carmen

*Poble Espanyol, Avda Marquès de Comillas,
Montjuïc (93 325 68 95/www.tablaodecarmen.
com). Metro Espanya.* **Open** 7pm-midnight

Tue-Sun. **Shows** 7.45pm, 10pm Tue-Sun.
Admission show & 1 drink €35; show &
dinner €69. **Credit** AmEx, DC, MC, V.
Map p341 A/B9.
This rather sanitised version of the flamenco *tablao*
sits in faux-Andalucian surroundings in the Poble
Espanyol. You'll find both stars and new young talent, displaying the various styles of flamenco singing,
dancing and music. It's advisable to book (up to a
week ahead in summer). The admission charge
includes entry to the Poble Espanyol after 7pm.

Los Tarantos

*Plaça Reial 17, Barri Gòtic (93 319 17 89/
www.masimas.com/tarantos). Metro Liceu.* **Open**
Flamenco show 8.30pm, 9.30pm, 10.30pm daily.
Admission €6. **Credit** MC, V. **Map** p342 B6.
This flamenco *tablao* has presented many top stars
over the years, as well as offering some *rumba catalana*. It now caters mainly to the tourist trade.

Festivals

De Cajón!

Various venues (www.theproject.cat). **Tickets**
€22-€42. **Date** June-July.
This high-quality new mini festival has snagged
some of Barcelona's top venues to showcase spectacular flamenco talents such as cantaor Antonio
Vargas 'Potito', flamenco pianist Diego Amador and
the world-famous guitarist Paco de Lucía.

Flamenco Ciutat Vella

*CCCB (see p79). Information (93 443 43 46/
www.flamencociutatvella.com). Metro Catalunya.*
Tickets €10-€20. **Date** May. **Map** p344 A2.
Although there are plenty of traditional performers
for the fan of flamenco, hard-line flamenco purists
should be warned that this festival also includes DJs
fusing the Andalucian music with anything from
electronica to jazz and rock.

Venues

Bar-restaurant **TiriTiTran** (C/Buenos Aires
28, Eixample, 93 410 86 77, www.tirititran.com)
is a favourite with flamenco aficionados;
impromptu performances often happen at
weekends, with concerts every Wednesday.
The Friday night flamenco shows at the
restaurant **Nervion** (C/Princesa 2, Born, 93
315 21 03, closed end Aug, 1st wk Sept) seem
to be aimed at tourists, but it is a lot cheaper
than the established *tablaos*: if you don't eat,
entry is €12 and includes a drink. **Flamenco
Barcelona** (C/Marquès de Barberà 6, Raval,
93 443 66 80, www.flamencobarcelona.com) is
a shop specialising in flamenco paraphernalia
and music, with exhibitions and occasional
concerts. It also offers flamenco guitar,
singing and dance courses.

Sport & Fitness

They're football crazy, football mad…

Listen in to any animated conversation in a local bar, and it's likely that the subject will be politics or sport – or often both. Catalans are famously obsessed with football and proud of the status of their biggest football team: rather than being the plaything of a rich oligarch, Barça literally belongs to the fans. The team has more than 163,000 members, which means that better than one in ten *barcelonins* has a say in the running of the club. The bestselling newspaper in town is called *Sport*, mostly dedicated to gossip surrounding Barça; players formed at the club's youth team now fill the world's top leagues and the Spanish national side.

BEYOND BARÇA

However, sport in the city is not only all about the beautiful game. Barcelona took advantage of the 1992 Olympics to equip itself with sports facilities, stadiums and inexpensive public gyms that put many larger cities to shame. As a result, other big events – the World Swimming Championships, the recent EuroGames (by and for gay and lesbian sportspeople) – have passed through town with great success.

Tickets for big games can often be bought by credit card with Servi-Caixa or Tel-entrada (*see p220*). Check www.agendabcn.com or see newspapers such as *El Mundo Deportivo* for event details. But you'll see the passion for sport all over town throughout the year, from lycra-clad granddads reliving the latest Tour de France to ambitious young racket-toting lads dreaming of becoming the next Rafael Nadal.

SPECTATOR SPORTS

Basketball

The ACB, Europe's most competitive league, runs from September to early June; league matches are on weekend evenings, with European matches played midweek.

AXA FC Barcelona

Palau Blaugrana, Travessera de les Corts 63-71, Les Corts (93 496 36 00/www.fcbarcelona.com). Metro Collblanc or Palau Reial. **Ticket office** *Sept-June* 9am-1.30pm, 3.30-6pm Mon-Thur;

9am-2.30pm Fri. *Aug* 8.30am-2.30pm Mon-Fri; also 2hrs before a game. Advance tickets available from day before match; if match is Sun, tickets available from Fri. **Tickets** €11-€58. **Credit** AmEx, MC, V.

From their heyday in the 1980s, when the stars of Barça's basketball team were as famous as the footballers and matches were played at the massive Sant Jordi stadium, Barcelona basketball has slipped in status. The team's triumph in the 2003 Euroleague, the basketball equivalent of the Champions League, was expected to herald a renaissance. But as the fortunes of Barça football soared with the arrival of president Joan Laporta, the basketball team managed to lose all its best players and its brilliant Serbian manager, Svetislav Pešić. Last year, despite clinching the Copa del Rey, the team contrived to change its coach and brought in many new faces. Xavi Pascual is building a new team around Juan Carlos 'The Bomb' Navarro and Australian forward David Anderson; it remains to be seen if this will help the team to more success both at home and in Europe. *See also p279* **Hoop and glory**.

Bullfighting

Plaza de Toros Monumental

Gran Via de les Corts Catalanes 749, Eixample (93 245 58 04/93 215 95 70). Metro Monumental. **Open** *Bullfights* Apr-Sept 6-7pm Sun. *Museum* Apr-Sept 11am-2pm, 4-8pm Mon-Sat; 10.30am-1pm Sun. **Admission** *Bullfights* €22-€120. Advance tickets available from Servi-Caixa. *Museum* €5; €4 reductions. **No credit cards**. **Map** p343 K8.

INSIDE TRACK
TICKETS PLEASE

Getting tickets for a Barça match can be a lottery: around 4,000 tickets usually go on sale on the day of the match – phone to find out when, and join the queue an hour or so beforehand at the intersection of Travessera de les Corts and Avda Arístides Maillol. 'Rented out' seats go on sale from these offices and can also be bought through Servi-Caixa. If there are none left, buy a *reventa* ticket from the touts at the gates.

Bullfighting in Barcelona can be a sorry affair. The impressive Modernista Monumental bullring has seen better days, and *anti-taurino* protesters can often outnumber the spectators on quiet days. However, there are occasional *corridas* worth seeing; they take place on Sundays in summer.

Football

While FC Barcelona fight it out for the *Primera Liga* title every year, usually with arch rivals Real Madrid, RCD Espanyol have managed to establish themselves as a reliable mid-table team with regular finishes in the top half of the league. The season runs from the last weekend in August to May, with games played late on Saturday evening or Sunday afternoon; check the press for details, and keep checking as kick-off times can change. Europa (based in Gràcia) and Júpiter (in Poblenou) are worthwhile semi-pro teams.

FC Barcelona

Nou Camp, Travessera de les Corts 63-71, Les Corts (93 496 36 00/www.fcbarcelona.com). Metro Collblanc or Palau Reial. **Ticket office** *Sept-June* 9am-1.30pm, 3.30-6pm Mon-Thur; 9am-2.30pm Fri. *Aug* 8.30am-2.30pm Mon-Fri; from 11am match days. Tickets available from 2wks before each match. **Tickets** €18-€170. Advance tickets for league games available from Servi-Caixa. **Credit** AmEx, DC, MC, V. **Map** p337 A4.

From hero to zero, the popularity of president Joan Laporta has nosedived spectacularly since the club achieved a historic double in 2006. After two very disappointing seasons, the winds of change have blown out Frank Rijkaard and wafted in a new manager, the ex-Dream Team midfielder Pep Guardiola, and a host of new signings. With the departure of Ronaldinho to AC Milan, the 'Fantastic Four' are now down to three, but an attacking line-up of Henry, Eto'o and Messi is still capable of intimidating any defence in the world.

RCD Espanyol

Estadi Olímpic de Montjuïc, Passeig Olímpic 17-19, Montjuïc (93 292 77 00/www.rcdespanyol. com). Metro Espanya then free bus or Paral·lel then Funicular de Montjuïc. **Ticket office** times vary, check website. **Tickets** €30-€55. **Credit** V. **Map** p341 A/B11.

After a great start last year, Espanyol managed to mess up a promising season and lose their successful manager in the process. New manager, Bartolomé 'Tintín' Márquez, is famous for his tough temperament and it's hoped that through a mixture of discipline, the influence of veterans such as Raúl Tamudo and Ivan de la Peña, and the blossoming of future stars such as Luis García, the team will be able to improve on its 12th place last year. The club is scheduled to move to its new 40,000-capacity, ground in Cornellà in 2009, but last minute hitches could keep them at Montjuïc until the end of the season. Tickets are available up to four days before the game, via Servi-Caixa or the ticket office.

Special events

Marató Barcelona

902 43 11 763/www.maratobarcelona.com. **Date** 1 Mar. **Fee** €45-€65. The city marathon starts and ends at Plaça Espanya.

Tennis

Reial Club de Tennis Barcelona-1899, C/Bosch i Gimpera 5, Les Corts (93 203 78 52/www. rctb1899.es). FGC Reina Elisenda/bus 63, 78. **Ticket office** *During competitions* 8.30am-1.30pm, 3.30-6.30pm Mon-Fri; 9am-1pm Sat. **Tickets** €20-€64; available from Servi-Caixa. **Credit** AmEx, MC, V. **Map** p337 B2.

The annual Open Seat Comte de Godó tournament in Pedralbes is considered one of the ATP circuit's most important clay-court tournaments. Many of the top players usually attend, including Rafael Nadal, who has already won the competition three times in a row. The 2009 tournament is scheduled to take place at the end of April.

La Cursa del Corte Inglés

93 270 17 30/www.cursaelcorteingles.net. **Date** May. Barcelona's seven-mile fun run in May is free to enter, and attracts over 50,000 participants.

Motorsports

Circuit de Catalunya, Ctra de Parets del Vallès a Granollers, Montmeló (93 571 97 00/www. circuitcat.com). By car C17 north to Parets del Vallès exit (20km/13 miles). **Times & tickets** vary by competition; available from Servi-Caixa. **Credit** MC, V. Barcelona boasts one of the world's best racing circuits at Montmeló. The Spanish Grand Prix is now a huge event and tickets can be hard to come by, so

Hoop and Glory

FC Barcelona's second sport.

Prevailing wisdom runs that basketball is a game involving ten hormonally challenged giants in shiny shorts, and only popular in the USA. Not quite. The current world champions are Spain and the NBA, the world's best and most glittery basketball competition, features a number of Spanish names. Chief among them is Pau Gasol, the Los Angeles Lakers forward who started out dribbling balls in the public courts of Barcelona and is now one of the key members of Jack Nicholson's favourite glamour team.

With football having such a big presence, it's easy to miss the the fact that the city's second most popular sport is, by a wide margin, basketball. After all, FC Barcelona isn't just a football team: it's a sporting institution with teams for hockey, basketball, handball, hockey and five-a-side, all of whom pull on Barça's famous *blaugrana* colours to defend the pride of the city on different sporting fronts. FC Barcelona (founded in 1926) is one of Europe's most successful

basketball teams, winner of the Euro League in 2003 and the Spanish league 21 times, second only to that inevitable Castilian rival: Real Madrid. Visitors may be surprised to see that Barcelona's important victories (especially those against Madrid) are celebrated with the same fervour as their football counterparts, with La Rambla heaving with flags and honking horns, although the profile of the people doing the celebrating may be noticeably younger, more earnest and more middle-class than the footy fans.

Going to a game at Barcelona's Palau Blaugrana, built to house the 'other' sports next to the football stadium, can be fun (for details, *see p277*). Although not up there with the Nou Camp for grandeur, the Palau holds a decent 8,000 spectators and the atmosphere can be surprisingly good. The protocol follows a similar template to the NBA, with clap-along standards booming through the PA, cheerleaders with pom-poms at each time-out (for the dads) and much Mexican waving.

ARTS & ENTERTAINMENT

book well in advance. Barcelona is also crazy about motorbikes, with local boys Dani Pedrosa and Toni Elías competing for the Moto GP, which also stops off at the Montmeló circuit.

Caminada Internacional de Barcelona

934 02 30 00/010/www.euro-senders.com/ internacional. **Date** 11-12 Oct.
The International Walk is conducted along several different routes of a variety of lengths.

ACTIVE SPORTS & FITNESS

The 237 municipally run facilities include an excellent network of *poliesportius* (sports centres). One-day entry tickets are usually available, but should the great outdoors prove irresistible, you can always just head to the beach: there's a free outdoor gym and table-tennis table at Barceloneta, and the sea is warm enough for swimming between May and October. All beaches have wheelchair ramps, and most of the city's pools are also fully equipped for disabled people. See Servei d'Informació Esportiva below for details.

Servei d'Informació Esportiva

Avda de l'Estadi 30-40, Montjuïc (93 402 30 00). Metro Espanya then escalators or Paral·lel then Funicular de Montjuïc/bus 50. **Open** *Oct-June* 8am-2pm, 4-8pm Mon-Thur; 8am-2.30pm Fri. *July-Sept* 8am-2.30pm Mon-Fri. **Map** p341 B10/11.
The Ajuntament's sports' information service is based at the Piscina Bernat Picornell. Call for information (note, though, that not all the staff speak English). Alternatively, you can consult the Ajuntament's very thorough listings on the Esports section of its website: www.bcn.cat.

Bowling

Bowling Pedralbes

Avda Dr Marañón 11, Les Corts (93 333 03 52/www.bowlingpedralbes.com). Metro Collblanc or Zona Universitaria. **Open** 10am-2am Mon-Thur; 10am-4am Fri, Sat; 10am-midnight Sun. *Aug* open only from 5pm daily. **Rates** €2.50-€4.75/person. **Credit** MC, V.
There are 14 lanes to try for that perfect 300, in an alley that hosts international tournaments. Early afternoons are quiet; otherwise, sit at the bar and wait to be paged. Shoe hire is available (€1), as are pool, snooker and *futbolín* (table football).

Cycling

The city council has been encouraging cycling as an environmentally conscious solution to Barcelona's traffic congestion problems – not

least through the introduction of the successful Bicing scheme (www.bicing.com), where bikes can be picked up and dropped off around town. In theory, membership of the scheme is restricted to residents, but many tourists have got round that by 'borrowing' addresses in town for registration.

The city has an efficient and ever-expanding network of cycle lanes, while the seafront is a good bet for leisure cycling; otherwise, try the spectacular Carretera de les Aigües, a flat gravel road that skirts along the side of Collserola mountain. To avoid a killer climb, take your bike on the FGC to Peu del Funicular station, then take the Funicular de Vallvidreira to the midway stop. For serious mountain biking, check http://amicsbici.pangea.org, which also has information on when you can take your bike on public transport.

Probike

C/Villarroel 184, Eixample (93 419 78 89/ www.probike.es). Metro Hospital Clínic. **Open** 10am-8.30pm Mon-Sat. **Credit** AmEx, MC, V. Closed 1wk Aug. **Map** p338 E6.
The Probike club organises regular excursions, from day trips to a more challenging summertime cross-Pyrenees run. Its centre, which has a broad range of equipment plus maps and information on all manner of routes, is a magnet for local mountain bikers.

Football

Barcelona International Football League

www.bifl.info/nicksimonsbcn@yahoo.co.uk. Matches, of Sunday League standard, are generally played at weekends from September to June among teams of expats and locals. New players are welcome (especially if they know how to kick a ball).

Golf

Catalonia has been a popular golfing-holiday destination for years. Visitors to Barcelona hoping to swing a club or two should book in advance; courses can often be full at weekends.

Club de Golf Sant Cugat

C/Villa, Sant Cugat del Vallès (93 674 39 08/ www.golfsantcugat.com). By train FGC from Plaça Catalunya to Sant Cugat/by car Túnel de

---

INSIDE TRACK
LOCK AND GO

A really good bicycle lock is a must; bike theft is big business, with thieves stealing even bells.

Vallvidrera (C16) to Valldoreix. **Open** 8am-8pm Mon; 7.30am-8.30pm Tue-Fri; 7am-9pm Sat, Sun. **Rates** *Non-members* €65 Mon-Thur; €150 Fri-Sun. **Club hire** €40. **Credit** MC, V.

Designed by Harry S Colt back in 1917 and built by British railway workers, the oldest golf course in Catalonia is a tight, varied 18-hole set-up, making the most of natural obstacles, that's challenging enough to host the Ladies' World Matchplay Tour. There's a restaurant and swimming pool on site. You may be asked to pay a membership fee depending on the time of year: call ahead.

Gyms & fitness centres

Sports centres run by the city council are cheaper and generally more user-friendly than most private clubs in the city. Phone the council's sport information service, Servei d'Informació Esportiva (*see p279*), for prices and locations.

Centres de Fitness DiR

C/Casp 34, Eixample (93 301 62 09/902 10 19 79/www.dir.es). Metro Urquinaona. **Open** 7am-10.45pm Mon-Fri; 9am-3pm Sat, Sun. **Rates** vary. **Credit** MC, V. **Map** p344 D1.

This plush, well-organised, private chain has 12 fitness centres. Additional installations vary from a huge outdoor pool (at DiR Diagonal) to a squash centre (DiR Campus).
Other locations DiR Campus, Avda Dr Marañón 17, Les Corts (93 448 41 41); DiR Diagonal, C/Ganduxer 25-27, Eixample (93 202 22 02); and throughout the city.

Europolis

Travessera de les Corts 252-254, Les Corts (93 363 29 92/www.europolis.es). Metro Les Corts. **Open** 7am-11pm Mon-Fri; 8am-8pm Sat; 9am-3pm Sun. **Rates** *Non-members* €10.40/day. *Membership* approx €49.30/mth, plus €79 joining fee. **Credit** MC, V. **Map** p337 B5.

As large and well equipped as any private gym in town, Europolis centres are municipally owned but run by the British chain Holmes Place. They provide exercise machines, as well as pools, classes, trainers and weight-lifting gear.
Other locations C/Sardenya 549-553, Gràcia (93 210 07 66).

Ice skating

FC Barcelona Pista de Gel

Nou Camp, entrance 7 or 9, Avda Joan III, Les Corts (93 496 36 30/www.fcbarcelona.com). Metro Collblanc or Maria Cristina. **Open** 10am-2pm, 4-6pm Mon-Thur; 10am-2pm, 4-8pm Fri; 10.30am-2pm, 5-8pm Sat, Sun. Closed Aug. **Rates** (incl skates) €11. **No credit cards.** **Map** p337 A4.

This functional rink is situated right next to the Nou Camp complex, which makes it a perfect place for the non-football fans in the family to spend 90 minutes or more. Gloves are obligatory, and on sale at €2 a pair. The rink is also used for ice-hockey matches.

Skating Roger de Flor

C/Roger de Flor 168, Eixample (93 245 28 00 /www.skatingclub.cat). Metro Tetuan. **Open** *July-mid Sept* 10.30am-1.30pm, 5-9pm Mon-Fri, Sun; 10.30am-2pm, 4.30-9.30pm Sat. *Mid Sept-June* 10.30am-1.30pm, 5-9pm daily. **Rates** (incl skates) €13.70. **Credit** MC, V. **Map** p339 J8.

A family-oriented ice rink off Avda Diagonal in the Eixample. Gloves (€3) are compulsory. Any non-skaters in a group can get in for €1 and then have use of the café.

In-line skating

The APB (Asociacion de Patinadores de Barcelona, www.patinar-bcn.com) organises skating convoys: beginners meet at the Fòrum at 10.15pm on Fridays. Pro skaters hook up at Plaça Catalunya at 10.30pm on Thursday and follow an 'unofficial' route. See www. sat.org.es/bcnskates for details. RODATS (635 629 948, www.rodats.com/tours) organises skating convoys and classes at four levels of difficulty (€10 per 90-minute class, and monthly courses for €30 or €55, depending on how many classes you do, €8 for equipment) on

Monday on the beachfront at Platja de Mar Bella, on Friday at the Fòrum (both days 7.30pm) and on Wednesday (10pm) in Parc Clot.

Going it alone, you're not officially allowed on roads or cycle paths, and the speed limit is ten kilometres/hour. The pedestrian broadways of Rambla de Catalunya, Avda Diagonal and Passeig Marítim are popular haunts.

Jogging & running

The seafront and the Parc de la Ciutadella are good locations. If you can handle the climb, or use other transport for the ascent, there are scenic runs on Montjuïc – especially around the castle and Olympic stadium – or try Park Güell/Carmel hills and Collserola.

Sailing

Base Nàutica de la Mar Bella

Avda Litoral, between Platja Bogatell & Platja de Mar Bella, Poblenou (93 221 04 32/www. basenautica.org). Metro Poblenou. **Open** *Apr-Aug* 10am-8pm daily. *Sept-Oct* 10am-7pm daily. *Nov-Dec* 10am-6pm daily. *Jan-Mar* 10am-5.30pm daily.* **Rates** *Windsurfing* €176.30/10hr course; €21.65/hr equipment hire. *Catamaran* €206.20/ 16hr course. *Kayak* €118.55/10hr course; €13.60-€16.50/hr equipment hire. **Credit** MC, V.

The Base Nàutica hires out catamarans and wind-surf gear to those with experience. There's a proficiency test for windsurfing held on Fridays at 4 or 5pm (€20 fee). You can hire a kayak without a test. There are also different options available for intensive or longer-term sailing proficiency courses.

Skiing

If you get tired of the urban bustle, the Pyrenees are only two-and-a half hours away. The best bet for a skiing day trip is the resort of La Molina (972 89 20 31, www.lamolina.cat). A RENFE train from Plaça Catalunya at 7.05am or 9.22am (€7.50 single, €15 return) takes you to the train station (get off at La Molina), then catch a bus up to the resort. A day's *forfait* will set you back around €38, or you can buy combined return train ticket and *forfait* for around €45. Trains return at 4.55pm and 7.15pm (check the timetable in the station or www.renfe.es). There are runs to suit all. More information is available at the La Molina office in El Triangle (C/Pelai, 93 205 15 15).

Swimming

The city has many municipal swimming pools, many of which are open air. It also has more than three miles of beach, which are patrolled by lifeguards in summer. For a list of pools,

contact the Servei d'Informació Esportiva (*see p279*). Flip-flops and swimming caps are generally obligatory.

Club de Natació Atlètic Barceloneta

Plaça del Mar, Barceloneta (93 221 00 10/ www.cnab.org). Metro Barceloneta then bus 17, 39, 64. **Open** *Oct-Apr* 6.30am-11pm Mon-Fri; 7am-11pm Sat; 8am-5pm Sun. *May-Sept* 6.30am-11pm Mon-Fri; 7am-11pm Sat; 8am-8pm Sun. **Admission** *Non-members* €10.10/day. **Membership** €34/mth, plus €69 joining fee. **Credit** AmEx, DC, MC, V. **Map** p342 G13.

This historic beachside centre has an indoor pool and two outdoor pools (one heated), as well as sauna (which costs extra) and gym facilities. There's a *frontón* (Spanish ball sports court), if you fancy a go at the world's fastest sport: *jai alai*, a fierce Basque game somewhere between squash and handball.

Poliesportiu Marítim

Passeig Marítim 33-35, Barceloneta (93 224 04 40/www.claror.cat). Metro Ciutadella-Vila Olímpica. **Open** *Sept-July* 7am-midnight Mon-Fri; 8am-9pm Sat; 8am-4pm Sun. *Aug* 7am-10pm Mon-Fri; 8am-9pm Sat; 8am-9pm Sun. **Admission** *Non-members* €14.40 Mon-Fri; €17 Sat, Sun; 5-visit pass €59; 10-visit pass €104. **Credit** AmEx, DC, MC, V. **Map** p343 K12.

This spa centre specialises in thalassotherapy; there are seven saltwater pools of differing temperatures, including one with waterfalls to massage shoulders, and an icy plunge-pool. There's also a sauna, a steam room and a slab of hot marble on which to rest weary bones that have been over exerted in the jacuzzi. Other services include a freshwater pool, a gym, bicycle hire and classes.

Tennis

Club Tennis Pompeia

C/Foixarda, Montjuic (93 325 13 48). Bus 13, 50. **Open** 8am-9pm daily. **Rates** *Non-members* €14/hr; €4.80 floodlights. €151.10/pass for July-Sept. **No credit cards**.

There are good rates for non-members at this pleasant club above the Poble Espanyol, with its seven clay courts and free racket hire.

Yoga

Yoga Studio

Plaça Universitat 4, 1º, 2ª, Eixample (93 451 29 28/www.yogastudio.es). Metro Universitat. **Open** 10.30am-10pm Mon-Fri. **Credit** MC, V. **Map** p342 F9.

Xavi and Pilar, founders of the popular Yoga Studio, offer a wide variety of different yoga styles from hatha to ashtanga. The centre runs one-off classes for €6, alongside its week or month-long courses.

Escapes & Excursions

Costa Brava.
See p301.

Getting Started

Vineyards and churches, villages and beaches await beyond Barcelona.

Just two hours separate sand from snow in this part of the world. But that's not all: a strong gastronomic heritage, pretty villages, fine wines and amazing festivals only add to the appeal of Catalonia.

The **Palau Robert** tourist centre (*see p320*) is a hub of useful information about the region. Catalunya Turisme (www.catalunyaturisme.com) is another thorough guide. And for details of Catalonia's network of *casa de pagès* (country houses or old farmhouses for rent), see the *Generalitat's Residències – Casa de pagès*.

GETTING AROUND

Public transport is good, but you'll need a car for far-flung destinations. For more on getting around, see the Generalitat's www.mobilitat.org.

By bus

The **Estació d'Autobusos Barcelona-Nord** (C/Alí Bei 80, map p343 J9) is the principal bus station for services around Catalonia. General information and timetables for all companies are on 902 26 06 06, www.barcelonanord.com.

By road

Over the last few years, Spain's roads have undergone a gradual process of renaming, and many locally available maps are still out of date. Road signs generally post both the new and the old name, but signage often doesn't make itself clear. Plan your route in advance.

Roads beginning C1 run north–south; C2 run east–west; C3 run parallel to the coast. Driving in or out of Barcelona, you'll come across either the **Ronda de Dalt**, running along the edge of Tibidabo, or the **Ronda Litoral** along the coast, meeting north and south of the city. They intersect with several motorways (*autopistes*): the C31 (heading up the coast from Mataró); the C33/AP7 (to Girona and France) and the C58 (Sabadell, Manresa), which run into Avda Meridiana; the AP2 (Lleida, Madrid), a continuation of Avda Diagonal that connects with the AP7 south (Tarragona, Valencia); and the C32 to Sitges, reached from the Gran Via.

All are toll roads, and are often expensive; when possible, we've given toll-free alternatives. Avoid the automatic ticket dispensers if on a motorbike: you'll pay less in the 'Manual' lanes. The **Túnel de Vallvidrera**, the continuation of Via Augusta that leads out of the city under Collserola to Sant Cugat, also has a high toll, as does the **Túnel de Cadí**, through the mountains just south of Puigcerdà. For more on tolls, call 902 20 03 20 or see www.autopistas.com.

By train

All **RENFE** trains (902 24 02 02, www.renfe.es) stop at **Sants** station, and some at **Passeig de Gràcia** (Girona, Figueres, south coast), **Estació de França** (south coast) or **Plaça Catalunya** (Vic, Puigcerdà). RENFE's local and suburban trains (*rodalies/cercanías*) are integrated into the metro and bus fares system (*see p309*); tickets for them are sold at separate windows.

Catalan Government Railways (**FGC**) serves destinations from **Plaça d'Espanya** and **Plaça Catalunya**. FGC information is available on 93 205 15 15 and at www.fgc.net.

On foot

Catalonia's hills and low mountain ranges are great for hiking and biking. In many places, it's made easier by GR (*gran recorregut*) long-distance footpaths, indicated with red-and-white signs; they may have inns, campsites or basic refuges en route. Good places for walking within reach of the city include the **Parc de Collserola** (*see p114*), **Montserrat** (*see p290*) and **La Garrotxa** (*see p298*). Another useful Generalitat website, www.gencat.net (click on 'Catalonia', then 'Touring routes in Catalonia'), has particularly good information on walks. For detailed walking maps, try **Altaïr** (*see p199*) or **Llibreria Quera** (C/Petritxol 2, 93 318 07 43).

Excursions

Delightful day-trips to coast, country and city.

Just a short ride from Barcelona, a very different atmosphere awaits – a world of monasteries, vineyards and market towns. You'll also find attractive and manageable cities such as **Girona** and **Tarragona**, better beaches such as those at **Sitges** or **Castelldefels** and, at **Colònia Güell**, more of Gaudí's fantastical creations. Hire a car and you'll have even more freedom to explore some of Catalonia's honey-coloured villages. But in many cases, the transport is part of the fun: take the cog-wheel train or cable car that ascends the mountain of **Montserrat** to its famous abbey.

Sandy Shores

ALONG THE COAST TO SITGES

The sands in Barcelona have become cleaner in recent years, but they can still seem pretty grubby in comparison to those found a short train ride away. Either side of the city, up and down the coast, lie a number of beautiful beaches that make a welcome and relatively isolated break from the hurly-burly of the city itself. Add the cluster of small, handsome towns that adjoin the beaches, and you have plenty of reasons to make your escape for an afternoon or more.

About half an hour south from Passeig de Gràcia station, the **Castelldefels** is a broad strand of sand. The backdrop of urban sprawl is particularly unlovely, but there's plenty of towel space to compensate. The beach is also something of a mecca for kite-surfers, as well as other watersports. Try the **Escola Náutica Garbí** (Passeig Marítim 271-275, mobile 609 752 175, www.escolagarbi.com) for equipment.

Two stops beyond the Castelldefels lies the tiny and relatively undiscovered port of **Garraf**. Its small curved beach is backed by green-and-white striped bathing huts, and the steep-sided mountains that surround it mean that development is not a worry. At the northern tip of the bay sits the **Celler de Garraf**, a magical Modernista creation built by Gaudí for the Güell family in 1895 but now home to a restaurant. Behind the village stretches the **Parc del Garraf** nature reserve, with hiking and biking trails (marked out on maps available from the tourist office in Sitges).

Further south along the coast, the pretty, whitewashed streets of **Sitges** do double-duty. In summer, they're packed with party-goers – since the 1960s, this has been Spain's principal gay resort, served by a hotchpotch of bars and discos (*see p252*). In winter, though, it's a different story: the scene is far more relaxed, and it's a mellow place for a getaway.

In the 19th century, the town was a fashionable retirement spot for local merchants who had made their fortunes in the Caribbean. More than 100 of the palaces owned by '*los americanos*', as they were known, are dotted around the centre of town. Pick up an excellent booklet from the tourist office, or take a tour of these houses with **Agis Sitges** (C/Lope de Vega 9, 2º-2ª, mobile 619 793 199, www.sitges.com/agis, €8) on the first and the third Sundays of the month.

Sitges's highest building, topping a rocky promontory, is the pretty 17th-century church of **Sant Bartomeu i Santa Tecla**, offering wonderful views of the sea. Behind the church is the extraordinary **Museu Cau Ferrat** (*see p286* **Profile**); over the road is the **Palau Maricel** (C/Fonollar, 93 894 03 64, tours €10, booking essential, closed Oct-June), an old hospital that's been converted into a Modernista palace and is now used as a concert hall in summer. The building contains medieval and Baroque paintings and sensuous marble sculptures. Also worth a look is the Museu Romàntic in the handsome **Casa Llopis** (C/Sant Gaudenci 1, 93 894 29 69,

ESCAPES & EXCURSIONS

Profile Cau Ferrat

Visit Santiago Rusiñol's studio in Sitges, once a hotbed of misbehaviour.

Transport Andy Warhol's Factory to Catalonia in the 1890s and you have Santiago Rusiñol's **Cau Ferrat** (C/Fonollar, Sitges, 93 894 03 64, www.diba.es, closed Mon, €3.50, reductions €1.75). The famous artist's home and studio in Sitges was once a crucible of Modernista art and culture, with celebrities and drug-fuelled parties debauched enough to match any pop art antics.

Rusiñol (1861-1931) was born in Barcelona to a dynasty of textile industrialists, but he left the family business at 28 for a bohemian life in Paris. While there, he developed his skills as a painter, a novelist and a playwright, and became a passionate collector of art and wrought iron. On his return, he shunned bourgeois Barcelona and decamped to Sitges, where he built his home and studio.

Family money allowed him to create a small but lavish shrine to Modernisme, including Gothic windows salvaged from the demolished Sitges castle, ornately carved wooden ceilings and 15th-century floor tiles. Rusiñol called it the Cau Ferrat meaning 'closed refuge', but the name also alludes to his enormous collection of *ferro forjat* (wrought iron) on display on the first floor.

Rusiñol filled the building with his art collection and populated it with like-minded friends, such as Picasso, Dalí, García Lorca, Manuel de Falla and Ramon Casas. A precursor of the infamous Els Quatre Gats café in Barcelona, Cau Ferrat swiftly became a safe haven for exiles from bourgeois society as well as a workshop where Rusiñol and his fellow artists developed their musical, literary and artistic projects.

Naturally, a certain amount of fin-de-siècle hellraising ensued,

but it was Rusiñol's more formal Festes Modernistes that really put Cau Ferrat on the art map. These extravagant annual festivals were dedicated to Catalan painting, theatre, poetry and literature and shot tiny, provincial Sitges to international fame. However, celebrity was brief: Rusiñol's urgent treatment for morphine addiction put an end to the revels after just five years.

Cau Ferrat remains much as it was then. The beamed upstairs hall is crammed with Rusiñol's unrivalled collection of 15th- and 16th-century wrought iron – everything from candelabra to giant keys – along with a stunning pair of paintings by El Greco, casually hung among the woodcarvings and cabinets of glassware. The ground floor is more modest in scale: a bedroom, a blue-painted kitchen decorated with ceramics and two airy studio rooms overlooking the sea and sky. Only the walls betray the building's past, crammed with works by Picasso, Casas and plenty of pieces by Rusiñol himself, including his famous painting of a woman delirious on morphine – a condition with which Rusiñol himself became all too familiar.

closed Mon), which portrays the lifestyle of the aristocratic 19th-century family that once lived there.

Those who prefer messing about in boats are served well at the Port Esportiu Aiguadolç. The **Centro Náutico Aiguadolç-Vela** (93 811 31 05, www.advela.net, closed Jan) rents out sailing boats and organises sailing excursions; a private hour-long session costs €40. To escape the crowds on Platja de Sant Sebastià or those south of the town centre, head just beyond the Port of Aiguadolç to **Platja de Balmins**, a hidden oasis with an excellent restaurant (La Caleta, *see below*).

Eating & drinking

In Garraf, commandeer a terrace table at **Chiringuito del Garraf** (Avda Llorach 3, 93 632 00 16, www.restaurantlacupulagarraf. com, times vary in winter, mains €12) for a long, lazy lunch. The food is average but the location is unbeatable.

The restaurants in Sitges can be expensive (there's better value just down the coast in the working port of Vilanova i la Geltrú), but there are good options here. A fisherman's lunch of steamed mussels, clams, razor clams, and *arròs negre* doesn't come better than from friendly **El Tambucho** (Port Alegre 49, Platja Sant Sebastià, 93 894 79 12, closed Nov & 2wks Dec, mains €18).

There's more seafood in the form of a tasting menu at **El Velero** (Passeig de la Ribera 38, 938 94 20 51, closed Mon, lunch Tue and 2wks Dec, mains €18), a real Sitges classic,

and **La Caleta** (Platja del Balmins, 93 811 20 38, closed Mon & Nov-Feb, mains €15), which offers great views and a more intimate vibe. **Restaurant Maricel** (Passeig de la Ribera 6, 93 894 20 54, www.maricel.es, closed dinner Tue & all day Wed Oct-Mar, mains €22) gives local produce an elegant twist. And be sure to leave time for a cava cocktail on the terrace at the delightful **Hotel Romàntic** (C/Sant Isidre 33, 93 894 83 75, www.hotelromantic.com, closed Nov-Mar).

Tourist information

Castelldefels *C/Pintor Serrasanta 4 (93 635 27 27/www.castelldefelsturismo.info).* **Open** *June-Sept* 10am-2pm; 4-8pm daily. *Oct-May* 9am-1pm, 3-5pm Mon-Fri. **Sitges** *C/Sinia Morera 1 (93 894 42 51/www. sitgestur.com).* **Open** *Mid June-mid Sept* 9am-8pm Mon-Sat. *Mid Sept-mid June* 9am-2pm, 4-6.30pm Mon-Sat.

Getting there

By bus Mon-Bus (93 893 70 60) runs a frequent service from 7.20am to 10.20pm to Sitges, and an hourly night service between 12.10am and 3.10am to Ronda Universitat 33 in Barcelona. **By train** Frequent trains leave from Passeig de Gràcia for Platja de Castelldefels (20mins) and Sitges (30mins), though not all stop at Castelldefels and Garraf.

From Ancient to Modern

TARRAGONA

Tárraco, as Tarragona was known to the Romans, was once Catalonia's biggest powerhouse. Dating back to 218 BC, it was the first Roman city to be built outside Italy; it was constructed with a flourish that ticked all the Roman boxes for hedonism, while also serving as a more sensible centre for commerce. The town is gradually being restored: modern-day Tarragona rather nattily integrates its crumbling ruins with modern town planning and an increasingly hip dining and wining scene. It's all far more appealing than the area's other main attraction: the ghastly but immensely popular **Port Aventura** theme park (977 77 90 90, www.portaventura.es), just a short drive from the town.

The **Passeig Arqueològic** (Avda Catalunya, 977 24 57 96), the path along the Roman walls that once ringed the city, has its entrance at **Portal del Roser**, one of three remaining towers. In the old part of town, Roman remains include the ancient Pretori –

INSIDE TRACK
CYCLE UP THE COAST

While you will find lovely sand by heading south towards Sitges, there are more opportunities for seaside lounging to the north. The beaches of the **Maresme fringe**, the coast immediately north of Barcelona, are all far better options than any of the city beaches. And while you can reach them by train from Plaça Catalunya, massively improved cycle paths mean that it's now possible to cycle all the way from Barcelona to Blanes along the seafront. The sand at **Montgat Nord** is pretty; although the railway separating land from littoral can dampen the atmosphere, the beaches further afield at **Caldes d'Estrac** (popularly known as Caldetes, and lined with a string of Modernista mansions), **Sant Pol de Mar** and touristy **Calella** are even better.

Catedral de Santa Maria.

praetorium (977 22 17 36), used as both palace and government office, and reputed to have been the birthplace of Pontius Pilate. Nearby, the ruined **Circ Romans** (977 23 01 71) was where the chariot races were held, while the **Museu Nacional Arqueològic** (Plaça del Rei 5, 977 23 62 09, www.mnat.es, closed Mon, €2.40) is home to an important collection of Roman artefacts and mosaics.

To see all of the **Catedral de Santa Maria**, not to mention an impressive collection of religious art and archaeological finds, you'll need a ticket for the **Museu Diocesà** (Pla de la Seu, 977 21 10 80, closed Sun). The cathedral was built on the site of a Roman temple to Jupiter, and is Catalonia's largest. The glorious cloister was built in the 12th and 13th centuries; the carvings alone are worth the trip.

Leading from the Old Town towards the sea, the **Passeig de las Palmeres** runs to the **Balcó del Mediterrani** and overlooks the Roman **amphitheatre** (Parc del Miracle, 977 24 25 79). The same street also leads to the pedestrianised, shop-addled **Rambla Nova**, from where you can follow C/Canyelles to the **Fòrum** (C/Lleida, 977 24 25 01) and the remains of the juridical basilica and Roman houses.

But while the town's history remains dominant, the biggest news in Tarragona in recent years has been the recent gentrification

of **El Serrallo**. This old port area now boasts fountains and slick promenades, upmarket fish restaurants and, in one of the old warehouses, the new **Museu del Port** (Moll de Costa 2, 977 25 94 42, closed Mon, €1.80, free under-16s), displaying the usual maritime accoutrements.

(Note: an all-in ticket for Tarragona's five main museums is €9, or €4.50 reductions. All are closed on Mondays.)

Eating & drinking

In the old city, **Les Coques** (C/Sant Llorenc 15, 977 22 83 00, closed Sun, mains €16) serves traditional roast kid and cod dishes, but

---

INSIDE TRACK
FALSET WINE FESTIVAL

While many old-fashioned wineries remain in Catalonia, the region has now begun to attract trendier winemakers, less concerned with following DO rules than just making tasty tipples. For drinkers keen on sampling some of these newer wines, it's worth timing a visit for the **Falset wine festival** (www.falset.org) at the start of May.

ESCAPES & EXCURSIONS

L'Anap (C/Comte 14, 977 25 3 8 25, www.
anap-restaurant.es, closed Sun, dinner Mon,
2wks Aug & 1st 2wks Jan, mains €18) is the
latest hot ticket, with dishes such as foie with
candy floss and monkfish in a sesame crust.
For snacks, **Le Vin** (C/Méndez Núñez 10,
977 23 00 20, www.devins.es, closed Sun) is a
new-wave tapas and wine bar showcasing the
best of local produce in an upmarket setting.

In El Serrallo, the excellent **Restaurant
Manolo** (C/Gravina 61-63, 977 22 34 84,
closed Mon, mains €25) does superb fresh
fish and seafood, but the terrace at swanky
designer **Estació Marítima** (Moll de Costa
4, 977 23 2 1 00, closed Sun, mains €25) puts
you right at the water's edge. Alternatively,
head out of the centre to the west to **Sol-Ric**
(Via Augusta 227, 977 23 20 32, closed Mon,
dinner Sun & all Jan, mains €15) for sturdy
post-hangover fodder.

Tourist information

Tarragona *C/Fortuny 4 (977 23 34 15/
www.tarragonaturisme.es).* **Open** 9am-2pm,
4-6.30pm Mon-Fri; 9am-2pm Sat.

Getting there

By bus Alsa (902 42 22 42, www.alsa.es) runs
12 buses daily from Barcelona Nord station.
By train RENFE trains run from Sants or
Passeig de Gràcia to Tarragona. Trains depart
hourly (journey time 1hr 6mins).

Drink in the Scenery
WINE COUNTRY

An easy day trip south-west from Barcelona lie
Catalonia's best-known wine regions, with a
range of *denominaciones de origen* from the
workaday **Penedès** to the prestigious **Priorat**.
With numerous companies offering guided
tours, and the wineries themselves now opening
their doors to visitors, Spain is becoming
serious destination for oenophiles.

The **Penedès** comprises gently undulating
hills and ancient Roman routes. It's the most
accessible destination if you're limited to
public transport – you can reach it in about
an hour by train. At its heart is **Vilafranca**,
a handsome medieval town with a lively
Saturday market and the elegant 14th-century
Basílica de Santa Maria. The town's
wine museum, **Vinseum** (Plaça Jaume I 1-3,
93 890 05 82, www.vinseum.cat, closed Mon),
has displays covering the usual ancient
winemaking tools as well as a train for taking
visitors out to the vineyards.

The two main wineries in the area are
both owned by the Torres family and offer
entertaining tours, but you'll need your own
transport, or a taxi, to take you there. **Torres**
(Finca El Maset, Pacs del Penedès, 93 817 74 87,
www.torres.es) is Penedès's largest winemaker;
but for serious wine-lovers, the more cutting-
edge **Jean León** (Pago Jean León, 93 899 55 12,
www.jeanleon.com, admission €6, under-16s
free) holds a sleek tasting room that looks on
to a sea of vines. Nearby **Albet i Noya** (Can
Vendrell de la Codina, Sant Pau d'Ordal, 93 899
48 12, www.albetinoya.com, tours €5.50) was
Spain's first organic winery and now leads the
way in restoring traditional, pre-phylloxera
varietals to the area. And there's also **Can
Ràfols dels Caus** (Avinyonet del Penedès,
93 897 00 13, www.canrafolsdelscaus.com),
which produces superb pinot noir and
delightful pink bubbles and is shortly due
to open a cool new designer *bodega*.

North of here is **Sant Sadurní d'Anoia**, the
capital of the Penedès cava industry: 90 per cent
of Spain's cava is made here, a fact celebrated
during Cava Week (www.cavatast.cat) every
October. It's not a pretty town, but its wine
producers are easily accessible on public
transport. **Codorníu** (Avda Codorníu, 93 818
32 32, www.grupocodorniu.com, admission
€2, booking necessary), one of the largest
producers, offers a theme-park style tour of its
Modernista headquarters, designed by Puig i
Cadafalch – a train takes visitors through parts
of the 26 kilometres (16 miles) of underground
cellars, finishing, of course, with a tasting.
Elsewhere, **Freixenet** (C/Joan Sala 2, 93 891 70
96, www.freixenet.es, admission €5, booking
necessary) is opposite Sant Sadurní station and
offers free tours and tastings. You can combine
a few of the wineries through **El Molí Tours**
(www.elmolitours.com), which offers boozy
sip-and-cycle day trips of the area.

The **Priorat** area is renowned for its full-
bodied (and full-priced) red wines. Monks
were producing wine here as long ago as the
11th century, but the area had been all but
abandoned as a centre of viticulture when
young winemaker **Alvaro Palacios** set up a
tiny vineyard here in the late 1980s. He battled
steep hills and a sceptical wine industry, but
within a few years he won global acclaim; the
region is now one of Spain's most exclusive.

The small **Alella** district, east of Barcelona,
is best known for light, dry whites, but more
important is **Terra Alta**: near the Priorat in
Tarragona, with Gandesa as its capital, the
area is famous for its heavy reds. **Montsant**,
a newly created DO, is also growing in
popularity; **Celler Capçanes**, located in the
region, makes one of the world's top kosher
wines and is also visitor-friendly.

Eating, drinking & sleeping

If you'd like to try terrific local wines in
Vilafranca, head to the **Inzolia** wine bar and
store (C/Palma 21, 93 818 19 38, www.inzolia.
com, closed Sun). **El Purgatori** (Plaça
Campanar 5, 93 892 12 63, closed lunch daily
& Wed Sept-July, mains €9.50) serves *pa amb
tomàquet* (bread with tomato) with charcuterie
and cheese. One of the best places to eat in the
Penedès is at **Cal Xim** (Plaça Subirats, 5 Sant
Pau d'Ordal, 93 899 30 92, www.calxim.com,
closed dinner Mon-Thur, Sat, all day Sun,
2wks Aug & 1wk Sept, mains €15), a cheery,
atmospheric spot popular with winemakers
for its upmarket grilled meats. **Cal Blay**
(C/Josep Rovira 27, Sant Sadurni, 93 891
00 32, www.calblay.com, mains €13.50) is
also excellent, serving new-wave dishes and
a good value fixed lunch.

If you're here for an extended stay, the range
of accommodation is broad. In the Penedès, the
Can Bonastre Wine Resort (Masquefa, 93
772 87 67, www.canbonastre.com, €214-€270)
stands testament to the boom in wine tourism,
and even has a vinotherapy spa. At the other
end of the spectrum, Torrelavit offers **Masia
Can Cardús** (93 899 50 18, www.masiasdel
penedes.com, €47), a more basic farm and
vineyard with rooms to rent.

In the Priorat, **Hostal Sport** (C/Miquel
Barceló 4-6, Falset, 977 83 00 78, www.hostal
sport.com, closed mid Jan-mid Feb, €91-€98.50)
is a good town-based option. **Cal Llop** (C/Dalt
21, Gratallops, 977 87 80 01, www.cal-llop.com,
€101-€130) offers boutique style, a modern mix
of stone, wood and iron, cobalt walls and exotic
flowers. Alternatively, **Mas Ardèvol** (Ctra
Falset a Porrera km 5.3, mobile 630 324 578,
www.masardevol.net, €91-€139, dinner €28)
is more rustic, with cheerful decor and mature
gardens. Both have good home cooking;
alternatively, there's top-flight cuisine at
Irreductibles (C/Font 38, Gratallops, 977
26 23 73, www.irreductibles.org, closed dinner
Wed, Thur, all Mon, Tue & Jan, menu €40.66),
the creation of acclaimed winemaker René
Barbier Jr.

Tourist information

Falset *C/Sant Marcel 2 (977 83 10 23/www.
turismepriorat.org).* **Open** 10am-2pm, 4-7pm
Mon-Fri; 10am-2pm Sat, 1-2pm Sun.
Sant Sadurní d'Anoia *C/Hospital 26 (93 891
31 88/www.cavatast.cat).* **Open** *Sept-July* 10am-
2pm, 4.30-6.30pm Tue-Fri; 10am-2pm Sat, Sun.
Aug 10am-2pm Sun.
Vilafranca del Penedès *C/Cort 14 (93 818
12 54/www.turismevilafranca.com).* **Open** 4-7pm
Mon; 9am-1pm, 4-7pm Tue-Sat.

Getting there

By bus **Alella** Sagales Barcelona Bus (902 13
00 14, www.sagales.es) from Plaça Urquinaona.
Alt Penedès Hispano Igualadina (93 804 44 51)
provides 15 buses daily from Sants.
Falset & Gandesa Hispano Igualadina (93 804
44 51). There are two buses daily from Sants.
By train **Alt Penedès** RENFE from Sants
or Plaça Catalunya; trains hourly 6am-10pm
(journey time 45mins), then taxi for Torres,
Jean León and Codorníu.
Falset & Gandesa RENFE from Sants or
Passeig de Gràcia to Marcà-Falset. Six trains
daily (2hrs). For Gandesa, go to Mora d'Ebre
(20mins) and catch a bus.

Heaven and Hell
MONTSERRAT

In many ways, it's unsurprising that
Montserrat is seen as the spiritual heart of
Catalonia. The vast bulbous-peaked sandstone
mass, whose name literally means 'jagged
mountain', dominates the landscape to the
west of Barcelona, its other-worldly appearance
lending it a mystical aura that's made it a centre
of worship and veneration for centuries. These
days, it's something of a tourist trap and gets
unbearably crowded in the summer. But it's still
a worthwhile excursion, if only for the views.

In the Middle Ages, Monserrat was an
important pilgrimage destination, as the
Benedictine monastery that sits near the top
became the jewel in the crown of a politically
independent fiefdom. Surrounded by a number

INSIDE TRACK
COLONIA GUELL

Just near Barcelona, on the western
outskirts of Santa Coloma de Cervelló,
stands the unusual **Colònia Güell**
(C/Claudi Güell 11, 93 630 58 70,
www.historiaviva.net, €4, reductions
€2.80). Textile baron Eusebi Güell
commissioned Antoni Gaudí to build a
garden city for the textile workers around
the factory where they worked. Like so
many of the great architect's projects,
it was never completed – but Gaudí
did finish the crypt of the church, an
extraordinary achievement with a ribbed
ceiling and twisted pillars. It's sometimes
closed for private events so call ahead.
With a sly detour, you can access it as
part of a day-trip to Montserrat.

Vilafranca.

of tiny chapels and hermitages, the monastery is still venerated by locals, who queue in the 16th-century basilica to say a prayer while kissing the orb held by **La Moreneta** (the Black Virgin). Open 7.30am-8.30pm daily, the basilica is at its most crowded around 1pm, when the celebrated boys' choir sings mass. Elsewhere in the monastery, there's a museum stocked with fine art by the likes of Picasso, Dalí, El Greco, Monet and Caravaggio, as well as collections of liturgical gold and silverware, archaeological finds and gifts for the Virgin.

If all this piety isn't to your taste, it's still worth the trip up the mountain by road, cable car or rack railway. The tourist office gives details of walks to the various caves; among them is **Santa Cova** where the statue was discovered, reachable via the funicular or a 20-minute hike from the monastery. The most accessible hermitage is **Sant Joan**, also 20 minutes or a funicular ride away. But the most rewarding trek is the lengthy one to the 1,235-metre (4,053-foot) peak of **Sant Jeroni**, which offers 360-degree views from a vertigo-inducing platform.

Eating & drinking

Eat before you leave or bring something with you: the characterless, pricey restaurants on Monserrat are best avoided.

Tourist information

Oficina de Turisme de Montserrat
Plaça de la Creu, Montserrat (93 877 77 77/ www.montserratvisita.com). **Open** *June-Sept* 9am-8pm daily. *Oct-May* 9am-6pm daily.

Getting there

By bus A bus run by Julià-Via (93 490 40 00) leaves at 9.15am from Sants bus station and returns at 5pm (6pm July-Sept); journey time is approx 80mins.
By train FGC trains from Plaça d'Espanya run hourly from 8.36am to Montserrat-Aeri (1hr) for the cable car (every 15mins); or to Monistrol de Montserrat for the rack train (hourly) to the monastery. The last cable car and rack train is at 6pm.

Country Life

VIC & AROUND

Vic.

ESCAPES & EXCURSIONS

Just 45 minutes away by train from the centre of Barcelona, Vic provides a handy taste of Catalan rural life. The beech forests, medieval villages, steep gorges and Romanesque hermitages make this area rewarding to explore by car, on foot or by bicycle, but it's also a centre of both paragliding and hot air ballooning (for which see Osona Globus, mobile 609 832 974, www.aircat.cat).

At the town's heart is the impressive arcaded **Plaça Major**, home to a famous market (Tuesday and Saturday mornings) that's nearly as old as the town itself. It's good for picking up local basketware, terracotta pots and, of course, the town's famous *embotits* (cured sausages), which are among the best in Spain. The **Museu Episcopal** (Plaça del Bisbe Oliva 3, 93 886 93 60, www.museuepisco palvic.com, closed Mon, admission €5, reductions €2.50, free under 10s) is worth a visit for its magnificent 12th-century murals and a superb collection of Romanesque and Gothic art.

There are also other architectural gems. In one corner of the market square is the Modernista Casa Comella; sgraffiti depicts the four seasons and was designed by Gaietà Buïgas, who was also responsible for the Monument a Colom in Barcelona. Vic also has many interesting churches, and the **Catedral de Sant Pere** contains Romanesque, Gothic and neo-classical elements, along with a set of dramatic 20th-century murals by Josep Lluís Sert, who is buried here. The **Temple Roma**, rediscovered in 1882 when the 12th-century walls that surrounded it were knocked down, now houses a gallery that shows Sert's work.

There's more of note outside the town. Following the C153 road towards Olot, **Rupit** is a lovely ancient village, built on the side of a medieval castle, its fairytale air enhanced by a precarious hanging bridge across the Ter gorge. Later building has been done so sympathetically to the style that it's difficult to tell the old from the new. Almost as lovely, and not quite as touristy, is nearby **Tavertet**.

Eating & drinking

The hotels in **Vic** are uninspiring, to say the least; if you're here for a longer stay, you're better off staying north around **Ripoll** (*see p300*). However, it does have several good restaurants, and some of the best charcuterie this side of France. **Restaurant Melba** (C/Sant Miquel dels Sants 1, 93 886 40 33, www.restaurantmelba.com, closed dinner Mon & Tue, mains €22) is a member of the Slow Food association and specialises in the *cuina volcànica* (volcanic cuisine) of the Osona region, using only local and seasonal products such as truffled sausages, wild asparagus and river trout. **Cardona 7** (C/Cardona 7, 93 886 38 15, tapas €6.50, closed lunch Tue-Fri, dinner Sun & all day Mon) serves new-wave tapas such as pig's trotter salad and salt cod in rosemary. **La Taula** (C/Sant Marius 8, 93 417 28 48, closed lunch Sat, all day Sun & Aug, mains €14.50, set lunch €15 Mon-Fri) offers a range of excellent value set menus.

Tourist information

Vic *C/Ciutat 4 (93 886 20 91/www.victurisme. cat)*. **Open** 10am-2pm, 4-8pm Mon-Fri; 10am-2pm, 4-7pm Sat; 10.30am-1.30pm Sun.

Getting there

By bus Empresa Sagalès (902 13 00 14) runs 6 buses from the Fabra i Puig bus station (near the metro of the same name) to Vic, and 5 buses from C/Casp 30. For Rupit, you should take a local bus from Vic.
By train RENFE from Sants or Plaça Catalunya to Vic. Trains leave about every 90mins. Journey time is 1hr 20mins.

ESCAPES & EXCURSIONS

An Urban Getaway

GIRONA

For travellers in search of big-city facilities without big-city stress, Girona i¶s a classy compromise. The city combines a healthy dose of culture with more hedonistic pursuits: within the city's beautifully restored medieval heart sits an imposing cathedral and some interesting museums. In addition, some of the region's best restaurants can be found here, along with a handful of smart bars.

The **River Onyar** divides the Old City from the new, and connects one to the other by the impressive Eiffel-designed bridge, the **Pont de les Peixateries**. A walk up the lively riverside **Rambla de la Llibertat** takes you towards the city's core and its one major landmark, the magnificent **cathedral**. The building's 1680 Baroque façade conceals a graceful Romanesque cloister and understated Gothic interior, which boasts the widest nave in Christendom. In the cathedral museum is the stunning 12th-century **Tapestry of Creation** and the **Beatus**, an illuminated set of tenth-century manuscripts.

Before their expulsion in 1492, the city's many Jews had their own district: the **Call**, whose labyrinthine streets running off and

around the C/Força are among the most beautifully preserved in Europe. The story of the community is told in the Jewish museum in the **Centre Bonastruc ça Porta** (C/Força 8, 972 21 67 61, www.ajgirona.org/call), built on the site of a 15th-century synagogue.

Heading north from here, the **Mudéjar Banys Àrabs** (C/Ferran el Catòlic, 972 19 07 97) is actually a Christian creation, a 12th-century bathhouse blending Romanesque and Moorish architecture. The nearby monastery of **Sant Pere de Galligants** is a fine example of Romanesque architecture, its beautiful 12th-century cloister rich with intricate carvings. The monastery also houses the **Museu Arqueològic** (Plaça Santa Llúcia 1, 972 20 26 32, www.mac.es, closed Mon), which shows day-to-day objects from the Paleolithic to the Visigothic periods. Continuing from here, the **Passeig Arqueològic** runs along what's left of the old city walls, intact until 1892.

Eating & drinking

The best restaurant in town, and one of the best in Spain, is the **Celler de Can Roca** (C/Sunyer 46, 972 22 21 57, www.cellerde canroca.com, closed Mon & Sun, last wk Aug, 2wks Dec & 2wks Jan, mains €40). Located in a quiet suburb, it's been cited by *Restaurant*

INSIDE TRACK
MAKING HISTORY

For all Girona's handsome charm, it also boasts a couple of unusual museums that take very different approaches to the past. At the **Museu D'Història de la Ciutat** (C/Força 27, 972 22 22 29, www.ajgirona.org/museu_ciutat, closed Mon), housed in an 18th-century monastery, look out for the alcoves with ventilated seating on the ground floor: this is where the deceased monks were placed to dry out for two years, before their mummified corpses were put on display. And over at eccentric **Museu del Cinema** (C/Sequia 1, 972 41 27 77, www.museudelcinema. org, closed Mon), meanwhile, you'll find a fascinating collection of early animation techniques right through to those of the present day.

magazine as one of the world's best 100 restaurants for its innovative dishes. Booking is essential.

For more low-key dining, **Massana** (C/Bonastruc de Porta 10, 972 21 38 20, closed dinner Tue, all day Sun & 2wks Jan, 2wks Aug & 2wks Dec, tasting menu €64.75) offers a more affordable alternative. Halfway up a medieval flight of steps, **Le Bistrot** (Pujada Sant Domènec 4, 972 21 88 03, mains €7), offers a cheap, tasty set lunch in a pretty setting.

The **Enoteca Gastaldi** (Plaça de Sant Pere 5, 972 00 35 38, tapas €6) has a pleasant walled terrace, and serves sophisticated tapas such as baked artichoke hearts and spoonfuls of foie. **Mimolet** (C/Pou Rodó 12, 972 20 21 24, www.mimolet.net, mains €19) is one of the city's most talked-about newcomers, serving excellent creative cooking and superb desserts.

The city's oldest restaurant is **Casa Marieta** (Plaça de la Independència 5-6, 972 20 10 16, www.casamarieta.com, closed Mon, mains €12), over the river from the old town. Also in the new town, an old Modernista flour factory houses **La Farinera** (Ptge Farinera Teixidor 4, 972 22 02 20, menu €9), which has good tapas.

Tourist information

Girona *Rambla de la Llibertat 1 (972 22 65 75/www.ajgirona.cat/turisme).* **Open** 8am-8pm Mon-Fri; 8am-2pm, 4-8pm Sat; 9am-2pm Sun.

Getting there

By bus Sagales Barcelona Bus (902 26 06 06, www.sagales.com) runs approximately five buses daily from Estació del Nord.
By train RENFE from Sants or Passeig de Gràcia (1hr 15mins). Trains leave hourly from 6am-9.15pm.

Girona.

ESCAPES & EXCURSIONS

Escapes

Into the hills or along the coast…

In this section, we look at some of the farther-flung parts of Catalonia, places that reward a stay of a couple of days or more. There's skiing to be had at **Puigcerdà**, hiking through the beech forest of **La Garrotxa** or along the route of Cistercian monasteries, birdwatching at the **Ebre Delta** and cycling along the region's disused railway tracks. Hedonists will make straight for the **Costa Brava**: some to the frenetic resorts of the south, others to the quieter villages of its upper reaches, a landscape loved by Dalí and peppered with spaces dedicated to his work.

The Delta Blues

TORTOSA & THE EBRE DELTA

Southern Catalonia has an entirely different flavour to the North, and is still little visited by outsiders. An appealing way to investigate its untapped charms is by starting at the town of **Tortosa**, the capital of the Baix Ebre, and using it as a base from which to explore the surrounding delta.

The town itself is an attractive place in its own right. Built on the site of a Roman temple, the town's magnificent Gothic cathedral is ringed by medieval alleyways; traces of the town's Jewish and Arab quarters can still be seen here (they're clearly signposted). There are also plenty of interesting Modernista buildings around the town. Among them are the colourful, Mudéjar-inspired pavilions of the former slaughterhouse (Escorxador), on the banks of the Ebre river.

Further inland, **Miravet** hangs suspended above the mighty Ebre, which you can still cross by car ferry. Within, the castle was rebuilt by the Knights Templar and is considered one of the best examples of their architectural prowess in Spain. Combined with its sleepy potters' quarter (eight workshops still operate) and its curiously Islamic flavour, it makes for an agreeable side trip.

Tortosa sits inland from the ecologically remarkable **Parc Natural del Delta de l'Ebre**. The towns of the delta are themselves nothing special, but the immense, flat, green expanses of wetlands, channels, dunes and still-productive rice fields are eerily beautiful. It's this variety of habitat that makes the area such a popular birdwatching destination. Birdwatchers can hope to tick off nearly half the 600 bird species found in Europe at the site. The flocks of flamingos make a spectacular sight as they shuffle around filter-feeding; elsewhere, the wetlands are full of herons, great crested grebes, spoonbills and marsh harriers.

The town of **Deltebre** is the base for most park services; from here, it's easy to embark on day trips to the bird sanctuaries, especially the remote headland of **Punta de la Banya**. The delta's flatness also makes it an ideal place for walking or cycling; for bicycle hire, check at the tourist office in Deltebre. Small boats offer trips along the river from the north bank about eight kilometres east of Deltebre.

Eating, drinking & sleeping

Tortosa itself has a wonderful parador, **Castell de la Suda** (977 44 44 50, €127-€171.50), built on the site of a Moorish fortress with panoramic views of the countryside. See www.paradors.es for occasional offers. On a very different level, the southern edge of the Ebre delta holds Platja dels Eucaliptus, a wide, sweeping beach where you'll find the **Camping Eucaliptus** (977 47 90 46, www.campinge ucaliptus.com, closed Oct-mid Mar, €4.40-€5.95/person; €6.25-€7.20/tent; €3.90-€5/car). Other options include **Hotel Rull** in Deltebre (Avda Esportiva 155, 977 48 77 28, www. hotelrull.com, €68-€95, mains €18), which organises occasional 'safaris', and the ecologically friendly **Delta Hotel** (Avda

ESCAPES & EXCURSIONS

INSIDE TRACK
CAJUN FOOD IN TORTOSA

Tortosa was recently twinned with the Mississippi – both, after all, have deltas. As a result, it's now the proud host of a successful and immensely enjoyable Cajun food and jazz festival, held every June.

---

del Canal, Camí de la Illeta, 977 48 00 46, www. deltahotel.es, €74-€95); both have restaurants.

Local culinary specialities include dishes made with delta rice, duck, frogs' legs and the curious *chapadillo* (sun-dried eels). You can try them all at **Galatxo** (Desembocadura Riu Ebre, 977 26 75 03, mains €15), at the mouth of the river. **L'Estany-Casa de Fusta** (l'Encanyissada s/n, 977 26 10 26, www. restaurantestany.com, mains €10) offers dishes such as stewed eel and wild duck in a traditional wood cabin.

Tourist information

Delta de l'Ebre *C/Doctor Martí Buera 22, Deltebre (977 48 96 79/www.parcsde catalunya.net).* **Open** *Oct-Apr* 10am-2pm, 3-6pm Mon-Sat; 10am-2pm Sun. *May-Sept* 10am-2pm, 3-7pm Mon-Sat; 10am-2pm Sun.
Tortosa *Plaça Carrilet 1 (977 44 96 48/ www.turismetortosa.com).* **Open** *Oct-Mar* 10am-1.30pm, 3.30-6.30pm Tue-Sat; 11am-1.30pm Sun. *Apr-Sept* 10am-1.30pm, 4.30-7.30pm Tue-Sat; 10am-1.30pm Sun.

Getting there

By train & bus RENFE from Sants or Passeig de Gràcia every 2hrs to Tortosa (journey time 2hrs) or L'Aldea (journey time 2hrs 30mins), then three buses daily (run by HIFE; 977 44 03 00) to Deltebre.

A Monk's Life

FOLLOWING THE CISTERCIAN ROUTE

The coast around Barcelona is hugely popular; as, of course, is the city itself. As a result, much of the non-coastal countryside in the area consists of roads less travelled by the tourist hordes, and they make a lovely change from the crowded norms along the beaches and ports.

There's no better example of this than **La Ruta del Cister** (the Cisterian Route; www.larutadelcister.info). Connecting the wonderful Cistercian monasteries of Poblet,

Santes Creus and Vallbona de les Monges, all of which can be visited on a single €9 ticket, the GR175 runs to more than 100 kilometres (62 miles), and offers a peaceful idyll for cyclists or ramblers. It may be located near Tarragona, but the route gives a completely different flavour of the region.

All three monasteries are easily accessible by car from **Montblanc**, 112 kilometres (70 miles) west of Barcelona and a beautiful town in its own right. In the Middle Ages, it was one of Catalonia's most powerful centres, with an important Jewish community. Its past is today reflected in its narrow medieval streets, magnificent 13th-century town walls, and its churches, the **Palau Reial** and the **Palau del Castlà** (Chamberlain's Palace).

Poblet, to the west, was founded in 1151 as a royal residence and monastery. The remarkable complex includes a 14th-century **Gothic royal palace**, the 15th-century chapel of **Sant Jordi** and the main **church**, which houses the tombs of most of the count-kings of Barcelona.

Santes Creus, founded in 1158, grew into a small village when families moved into the old monks' residences in the 1800s. Fortified walls shelter the **Palau de l'Abat** (Abbot's Palace), a monumental fountain, a 12th-century church and a superb Gothic cloister and chapterhouse.

Santa Maria de Vallbona, the third of these Cistercian houses, was, unlike the others, a convent for nuns. It has a fine part-Romanesque cloister but is less grand than the other two. Like them, it still houses a religious community.

Monestir de Poblet *977 87 02 54/www. poblet.cat.* **Open** *Mar-Sept* 10am-12.45pm, 3-6pm daily. *Oct-Feb* 10am-12.30pm, 3-5.30pm daily. **Admission** €5; €3 reductions; free under-12s. **No credit cards**.
Monestir de Santa Maria de Vallbona *973 33 02 66/www.vallbona.com.* **Open** *Mar-Oct* 10.30am-1.30pm, 4.30-6.30pm Mon-Sat; noon-1.30pm, 4.30-6.30pm Sun. *Nov-Feb* 10.30am-1.30pm, 4.30-5.30pm Mon-Sat; noon-1.30pm, 4.30-5.30pm Sun. **Admission** €3.50; €2.50 reductions; free under-12s. **No credit cards**.
Monestir de Santes Creus *977 63 83 29.* **Open** *Mid Mar-mid Sept* 10am-1pm, 3-6.30pm Tue-Sun. *Mid Sept-mid Jan* 10am-1pm, 3-5pm Tue-Sun. *Mid Jan-mid Mar* 10am-1pm, 3-5.30pm Tue-Sun. **Admission** €4.50; €3 reductions; free under-7s. Free Tue. **No credit cards**.

Eating, drinking & sleeping

In Montblanc, you'll need to book in advance in order to secure a room at the popular **Fonda dels Àngels** (Plaça dels Àngels 1, 977 86 01

73, closed Sun & 3wks Sept, €42.80, set menu €16 & €21), which also has a great restaurant. The **Fonda Colom** (C/Civaderia 5, 977 86 01 53, closed dinner Sun, Mon, 2wks Sept & 2wks Dec, mains €13.50) is a friendly old restaurant located behind the Plaça Major.

In L'Espluga de Francolí, en route to Poblet, the **Hostal del Senglar** (Plaça Montserrat Canals 1, 977 87 01 21, www.hostaldel senglar.com, €64-€72) is a great-value country hotel with lovely gardens, a swimming pool and an atmospheric if slightly pricey restaurant (mains €13). In Santes Creus the **Hotel La Plana del Molí** (Avda Plana del Molí 21, 977 63 83 09, closed 1wk Dec, €48) is set in extensive gardens. Try the delicious partridge broth or wild-boar stew at its restaurant (mains €10). The **Hostal Grau** (C/Pere El Gran 3, 977 63 83 11, closed mid Oct-June, €48, restaurant closed Mon & mid Dec-mid Jan, mains €13) is a reasonable option, with good Catalan food, as is the **Restaurant Catalunya** (C/Arbreda 2, 977 63 84 32, closed Wed, mains €14).

Tourist information

Montblanc *Antiga Església de Sant Francesc (977 86 17 33/www.montblancmedieval.cat).* **Open** 10am-1.30pm, 3-6.30pm Mon-Sat; 10am-2pm Sun.

Getting there

By bus Hispano Igualadina (93 804 44 51) runs a service to Montblanc from Sants station leaving at 3.30pm Mon-Fri. More buses run from Valls and Tarragona.
By train RENFE trains leave from Sants or Passeig de Gràcia to Montblanc. There are five trains a day. The journey takes about 2hrs.

Low-Key Catalonia
BESALU & OLOT

Besalú is one of Catalonia's loveliest towns, accessed by an impressive 12th-century fortified bridge spanning the Fluvià river. The town has, in the gentlest way, sold some of its soul to tourism, and these days piped music echoes through the cobbled streets.

Once home to a sizeable Jewish community, the town boasts the only remaining Jewish baths (*mikveh*) in Spain, dating back to the 13th century but only discovered in the 1960s. Charmingly, if the doors are locked when you arrive, the tourist office will give you a key so that you can let yourself in. Also worth a visit are the Romanesque church of Sant Pere and the arcaded Plaça de la Llibertat. The peculiar

Besalú.

Museu de Miniatures i Microminiatures (Plaça Prat de Sant Pere 15, 972 59 18 42, www.museuminiaturesbesalu.com, €3.50, reductions €2.50) houses such curios as the Eiffel Tower atop a poppy seed.

West from here the N260 runs to **Olot**, past a spectacular view of **Castellfollit de la Roca**, a village perched on the edge of a precipitous crag. Olot is the capital of the Garrotxa region and is surrounded by 38 inactive volcanoes. An earthquake in 1427 destroyed most of its oldest architecture, but it does have impressive 18th-century and Modernista buildings. In the last century, it was home to a school of landscape painters: the local **Museu de la Garrotxa** (C/Hospice 8, 972 27 91 30, closed Mon) has works by them, along with Ramon Casas, Santiago Rusiñol and other Modernista artists.

Off the G1524 toward Banyoles, which boasts a magnificent lake and is a popular destination for rowers in training, you'll see a vast beech forest, the **Fageda d'en Jordà**, immortalised by Catalan poet Joan Maragall, and the pretty, if touristy, village **Santa Pau**, with an impressive castle and arcaded squares.

Eating & drinking

Besalú is overflowing with good places to eat. The most famous is **Pont Vell** (C/Pont Vell 24, 972 59 10 27, www.restaurantpontvell.com, closed dinner Mon, all day Tue & mid Dec-mid Jan, €16), which offers a fine view of the bridge and a superb menu including scallops with truffles, cassoulet of white beans and clams, and sweet and sour rabbit. The terrace of the **Cúria Reial** (Plaça de la Llibertat 8-9, 972 59 02 63, closed dinner Mon, all day Tue & all Feb, mains €14) is more welcoming, however, with hearty traditional cooking such as Garrotxa lamb stewed with dates.

Located on the edge of Olot, surrounded by woodland, **Font Moixina** (Paratge de la Moixina s/n, 972 26 10 00, www.fontmoixina. com, closed Tue & all Feb, mains €14) is

The Green Way

Drop the car – instead, go hiking and biking across the tracks.

Former Socialist prime minister Felipe González is something of a fallen idol in Spain, but one of his government's better ideas was the repurposing of the country's 1,600 kilometres of disused railway tracks as hiking and cycle paths, known as the **Vías Verdes** (www.viasverdes.com).

Two interlinking *vías* run 135 kilometres from **Ripoll** in the foothills of the Pyrenees (*see p300*) all the way to **Sant Feliu de Guíxols** (*see p301*) on the Costa Brava. En route they pass through some spectacular scenery, such as the **Núria** gorge (*see p300*), romantic medieval villages such as **Besalú** (*see p297*) and pretty coves including **Cala Giverola** just north of Sant Feliu. In addition, it's easy cycling country, particularly if you start at Olot and head downhill to the coast.

Ripoll to **Sant Joan de les Abadesses** (*see p300*) is known as the 'Iron and Coal route' because at once formed part of a railroad carrying coal from the mountains to Barcelona. It closed for good in 1985 and is the toughest section of the route, rising up just after Sant Joan de Abadesses to nearly 1,000 metres. After that it's pretty much downhill all the way once you get to Olot.

From **Olot** (*see p298*) to **Girona** (*see p293*) and on to Sant Feliu is the 'Carrilet route', a network of narrow-gauge railway

tracks that connected the small towns and villages of the region at the end of the 19th century. Think Hobbits' Shire, with smooth grit paths framed by mountains, deep green forest, rolling pasture, fields of maize and babbling brooks.

There are plenty of picnic spots and handily located bars and restaurants, as well as various possibilities for staying over en route – from smart country hotels and boutique townhouses to more basic campsites – if you want to spread it over a few days. Bike rentals are available from firms such as **AMTA** (Antiga Estació, Les Preses, 972 69 20 23, http://atma. garrotxa.net); the English-speaking and very helpful **Cicloturisme i Medi Ambient** (C/Impressors Oliva 4, Girona (972 22 10 47, www.cicloturisme.com); and **Cicles Tarrés** (Avda Girona 29, Olot, 972 26 99 78, closed 2wks July and 1 wk Sept); Tornasol Aventura (C/Progrés 14, Ripoll, 972 70 27 47, www.tornasol. com) offers packages including bikes, hotel and tours.

The **Greenway Guide** is available at tourist offices anywhere en route. It includes maps, accommodation and camping tips, and services such as bike hire and trailer-taxis for you and your bike if you feel yourself running out of steam.

owned by the same people as Cúria Reial in Besalú and specialises in local cuisine. **La Deu** (Ctra de la Deu, 972 26 10 04, closed dinner Sun, mains €12) specialises in *cuina volcànica*, which includes beef stewed in onions and beer.

North of the town is the **Restaurant Les Cols** (Crta de la Canya, 972 26 92 09, closed Sun, Mon, dinner Tue & 2 wks Aug, mains €23), which is famed as much for its fabulous design as its food. The structure is a work of architectural brilliance that seamlessly combines a Modernist steel-and-glass dining room with an 18th-century farmhouse. It has a handful of swanky rooms for those who want to eat and sleep.

Sleeping

In Besalú, the 19th-century **Fonda Siqués** (Avda Lluís Companys 6-8, 972 59 01 10, www.grupcalparent.com, €56-€73.50), offers clean, basic rooms and is located above a charming restaurant (set meal €10). More upmarket is **Els Jardins de la Martana** (C/Pont 2, 972 59 00 09, www.lamartana.com, €94-€110), an eccentric and somewhat jaded stately home with a magnificent wood-panelled library and maze-like terraces and gardens. For a proper treat, **Sant Ferriol Hotel and Spa** (Jardins de Sant Ferriol, 972 59 05 32/972 59 03 31, www.santferriol. com, €200) is a lovingly restored Catalan farmhouse with 12 spacious rooms, most with their own terrace, and surrounded by idyllic countryside.

In Olot, **La Perla** (Avda Santa Coloma 97, 972 26 23 26, www.laperlahotels.com, €68-€76) is a large hotel with a good restaurant. Otherwise, on the corner of Plaça Major, try **Pensió La Vila** (C/Sant Roc 1, 972 26 98 07, www.pensiolavila.com, €48-€56), a modern and central place in which to stay.

South of Olot, in La Pinya, is **Mas Garganta** (972 27 12 89, www.masgarganta.com, closed Jan & Feb, €70), an 18th-century *masia* with magnificent views that has walking tours in conjunction with two *masies* nearby.

Tourist information

Olot *C/Hospici 8 (972 26 01 41/www.olot.cat).* **Open** *Mid Sept-June* 9am-2pm, 5-7pm Mon-Sat; 11am-2pm Sun. *July-mid Sept* 10am-8pm Mon-Sat; 11am-2pm Sun.

Getting there

By bus TEISA (93 215 35 66) to Besalú and Olot from the corner of C/Pau Claris and C/Consell de Cent.

Parc Nacional d'Aigüestortes. *See p300.*

Nearing the Pyrenees

BERGA, PUIGCERDA, RIPOLL & AROUND

The popular approach to the Pyrenees from Barcelona is via **Berga**, famous for the frenzied festival of La Patum at Corpus Christi. Further north, the giant cliffs of the **Serra del Cadí**, one of the ranges of the Pyrenees foothills, loom above the town, but the blight of endless holiday apartment blocks has taken its toll on the charm of its old centre.

Far prettier is the little town of **Bagà**, north of here on the C17. With its partially preserved medieval walls around an atmospheric old quarter, Bagà marks the beginning of the **Parc Natural del Cadí-Moixeró**, a mountain park containing wildlife and forest reserves, and some 20 or so ancient villages. All retain some medieval architecture, and many offer stunning views. Picasso stayed and painted in the village of **Gósol** in 1906. Rising above this are the twin peaks of **Pedraforça**, practically a pilgrimage for hiking enthusiasts and well worth the effort (allow a full day to get up there and back).

Above Bagà, the C16 road enters the Túnel del Cadí to emerge into the wide, fertile plateau of the **Cerdanya**. The area has a clear geographical unity, but the French/Spanish border runs through its middle. **Puigcerdà**, the capital of the area (on the Spanish side), is a popular ski-resort town but not wildly exciting. The best thing about it is the little yellow train that gets you here from Barcelona. From here there are many gentle hiking routes, which take in thermal spas and bald-headed peaks.

From here, you can head left after the Cadí tunnel to **La Seu d'Urgell**, **Sort** and on to the breathtaking highlands of the **Parc Nacional d'Aigüestortes**. A favourite for hikers in the spring and cross-country skiers in the winter the steep wooded slopes give way to deep, jade green lakes, giant waterfalls and glorious snowy peaks.

Alternatively, head south-east from Puigcerdà towards **Ribes de Freser**. This is the starting point for the narrow-gauge cog railway that runs via the pretty, if slightly gentrified, village of **Queralbs** along the Freser river up to the sanctuary of **Núria**, affording incredible views. Many choose to walk back to Queralbs (around two hours), following the path through dramatic rock formations, crumbling scree, pine-wooded slopes and dramatic, crashing waterfalls.

Núria itself nestles by a lake on a plateau at over 2,000 metres (6,500 feet), and was the first ski resort on this side of the border. Home to the second most famous of Catalonia's patron virgins, and a 12th-century wooden statue of the Madonna, it was a refuge and a place of pilgrimage long before then. The mostly 19th-century monastery that surrounds the shrine is nothing special, but its location is spectacular.

There's more monastic history south of Ribes de Freser in **Ripoll**. The extraordinary **Santa Maria de Ripoll** was founded in 879 by Wilfred 'the Hairy', who's buried here. The church has a superb 12th-century stone portal, its carvings among the finest examples of Romanesque art in Catalonia. Wilfred also founded the monastery and town of **Sant Joan de les Abadesses**, ten kilometres east up the C26, worth a visit for its Gothic bridge as well as the 12th-century monastery buildings. Neither town holds much charm outside its monastery.

Eating, drinking & sleeping

On the C26 outside Berga, the tiny village of Les Llosses has a couple of rustic *cases rurales* tucked away in the pine forests. **Domus de Maçanós** (972 70 45 75, mobile 689 68 79 92, www.elripolles.com/masmacanos, €108

half-board) is open year-round and has pretty stone arches, beams, log fires and fabulous views. In Bagà, the **Hotel Ca L'Amagat** (C/Clota 4, 93 824 41 60, www.hotelcalamagat. com, closed 1wk Dec & 1wk Jan, €55-€65) has rooms with large balconies, and a restaurant (closed Mon mid Sept-May, mains €15).

Puigcerdà has plenty of hotels in the town centre, including the small and charming **Avet Blau** (Plaça Santa Maria 14, 972 88 25 52, €80-€110) and the lovely **Villa Paulita** (Avda Pons i Gasch 15, 972 88 46 22, www.hospes.es, €130-€160), right by the lake. The **Hotel Rita-Belvedere** (C/Carmelites 6-8, 972 88 03 56, mobile 608 088 085, closed May-mid July, €45-€55) has a small garden and terrace. For French-influenced cuisine, try **La Col d'Hivern** (C/Baronia 7, 972 14 12 04, closed Mon-Wed, mains €17).

A little further out in Bolvir, the sumptuous **Torre del Remei** (C/Camí Reial s/n, 972 14 01 82, www.torredelremei.com, €251-€727, mains €25) also has one of the best (and pricier) restaurants in the area. In Bellver, the **Fonda Bianya** (C/Sant Roc 11, 973 51 04 75, €60-€80) is charming, with its sweet cornflower-blue woodwork, a sunny bar and a lively feel.

Towards Aigüestortes, the best bet for accommodation is Espot, which acts as a gateway to the park. **Els Avets** (Puerto de la Bonaigua, Alt Aneu, 973 62 63 55, www. elsavets.com, closed Oct, €50-€73) is a pleasant place in which to combine the great outdoors with a little modern comfort. The hotel offers lots of adventure sport-based package deals.

East in Ribes de Freser, the family-run **Hotel Els Caçadors** (C/Balandrau 24-26, 972 72 77 22, www.hotelsderibes.com, closed Nov, €89-€100) is the first eco-hotel in the Pyrenees and has decent food and comfortable rooms. If it's full, try **Hostal Porta de Núria** (C/Nostra Senyora de Gràcia 3, 972 72 71 37, €62-€51). **La Perdiu Blanca** (C/Puigcerdà 5, 972 72 71 50, closed Wed, mains €9) is a village classic.

In Queralbs, there's **Calamari Hostal l'Avet** (C/Major 17-19, 972 72 73 77, closed Mon-Thur from Oct-May, €80 half-board). The one good place to eat in Queralbs is **La Plaça** (Plaça de la Vila 2, 972 72 70 37, closed Tue, closed 2wks July & 2wks Oct, mains €8.50), which serves regional specialities.

East of here in Camprodon, the **Hotel Maristany** (Avda Maristany 20, 972 13 00 78, www.hotelmaristany.com, closed mid Dec-Jan, €125.50) is unexpectedly smart, with extravagantly formal gardens filled with topiary and roses, and a decent pool. It's a great treat after hiking, especially combined with dinner at **Can Po** (Ctra Beget s/n, 972 74 10 45, closed Mon-Thur Sept-July, mains €15); creative dishes in a romantic old farmhouse.

Tossa del Mar.

Tourist information

Berga *C/Angels 7 (93 821 13 84/wwwturisme berga.cat)*. **Open** 10am-2pm, 6-8pm Mon-Sat; 11am-2pm, 6-8pm Sun.
Puigcerdà *C/Querol 1 (972 88 05 42/www. puigcerda.com)*. **Open** 9am-1pm, 4-7pm Mon-Fri; 10am-1pm, 4.30-7pm Sat; 10am-1pm Sun.
Núria *Estació de Montanya del Vall de Núria (972 73 20 20/www.valldenuria.cat)*. **Open** *Mid July-mid Sept* 8.30am-6.45pm daily. *Mid Sept-mid July* 8.30am-5.45pm daily.
Ribes de Freser *Plaça del Ajuntament 3 (972 72 77 28/www.vallderibes.cat)*. **Open** 10am-2pm, 5-8pm Mon-Sat; 10am-1pm Sun.

Getting there

By bus Alsina-Graëlls (93 265 68 66) runs five buses daily to Berga from the corner of C/Balmes and Ronda de Universitat 11-13; journey time is about 2hrs. The same company runs buses to Puigcerdà from Estació del Nord; journey time is 3hrs. Otherwise, TEISA (93 215 35 66) runs one bus a day from the corner of C/Pau Claris and C/Consell de Cent to Ripoll, Sant Joan de les Abadesses and Camprodon.
By train Take RENFE from Sants or Plaça Catalunya. The journey time to Ripoll is 2hrs; to Puigcerdà, it's about 3hrs. For Queralbs and Núria, change to the *cremallera* train in Ribes de Freser.

Beauty and the Beasts

THE SOUTHERN COSTA BRAVA

In its heyday, the Costa Brava was the most exclusive resort area in Spain, attracting film stars, artists and writers to its sandy beaches. By the 1970s, though, things had changed. Encouraged by the local authorities, package tours from the UK descended on the area, and all manner of tacky restaurants and ugly apartment blocks soon followed. The area, which covers the stretch of coast between Blanes and the French border, is blighted by its reputation as the playground of unimaginative British holidaymakers. However, there's plenty to enjoy if you know where to stop.

Most of the good stuff is further north. Ruined by holiday-home high-rises, the towns of **Blane** and **Lloret del Mar** boast enviable locations but are really best avoided. Continue, instead, to **Tossa del Mar**, the southern entry to the Costa Brava proper and by far the loveliest town on this stretch. The painter Marc Chagall once described it as a 'blue paradise'; Ava Gardner spent so much time here with lover Frank Sinatra that they erected a statue in her honour. The new town has been constructed with little thought, but Tossa has retained one of Spain's most handsome medieval quarters.

Aiguablava.

The twisting 20-kilometre (12-mile) drive through coastal pine forests from here to **Sant Feliu de Guíxols** offers brief but unforgettable views of the sea. And when you arrive, Sant Feliu itself has superb Modernista buildings along the Passeig Marítim. Other sights include the **Benedictine monastery** (Plaça Monestir, 972 82 15 75, closed Mon, admission free) that incorporates the celebrated Porta Ferrada, a tenth-century portico, and the town museum, which will house the Carmen Thyssen-Bornemisza Catalan art collection in 2010. Sant Feliu also pulls in big names for an excellent music festival every summer. **Sant Pol** beach is three kilometres north of the crowded town sands, and offers more towel room.

Just north of Sant Pol, the GR92 path, or 'Camino de Ronda', starts out from below the Hostal de la Gavina in S'Agaró where Ava and Frank spent much of their time, and continues on along many secluded coves and rocky outlets for swimming. The sandy bay of **Sa**

Conca, considered to be one of the most beautiful beaches on the Costa Brava, has a couple of good *xiringuitos* for a sardine lunch. From here, there's a tedious stretch through the ugly **Platja d'Aro** that then picks up all the way to **Torre Valentina**, from where you can catch a bus back. The walk is ten kilometres.

Palamós has never really recovered from an attack by the infamous pirate Barba Roja (Redbeard) in 1543; the most exciting thing about the town is its famous and terrifyingly expensive giant red prawns. Continue, instead, to the area around **Palafrugell**, which has pretty villages built into its rocky coves. All of them make great bases for a little leisurely beach-hopping. The **Fundació Vila Casas** (Plaça Can Mario 7, 972 30 62 46, www. fundaciovilacasas.com, closed Tue) in Palafrugell itself houses a good collection of works by local artists and sculptors, and gives an idea of the kind of creativity the environment inspires.

Calella de Palafrugell, not to be confused with its ugly near-namesake down the coast, is a lively and attractive town sitting around a clear water bay. The cliff-top botanical gardens at **Cap Roig** (972 61 45 82, www.caproig.cat) host a wonderful music and arts festival every July and August, attracting names such as Caetano Veloso and London's Royal Ballet. Nearby **Llafranc** is not quite as pretty but has a long curved beach where you can swim between fishing boats in the bay.

Tamariu, known for its good seafood, is the perfect base for scuba-diving and fishing. Giro Nàutic (www.gironautic.com) is a useful portal for all things aquatic in the area. Next up is **Aiguablava**, with its modern parador and white sandy beach, and **Fornells** – the town that inspired Norman Lewis' *Voices of the Old Sea*, now much changed. Both are accessible from **Begur**, as is the small **Aiguafreda**, a cove that's sheltered by pines.

Beyond the Ter estuary and the Montgrí hills, which divide the Baix and Alt Empordà, is **L'Estartit**. This small resort town caters for tourists interested in exploring the **Illes Medes**, a group of rocky limestone outcrops. The biggest housed a British prison in the 19th century, but Les Illes are now home only to a unique ecosystem, an underwater paradise where divers can contemplate colourful coral and hundreds of different species of sea life. For a view of the islands, it's worth the climb up to the 12th-century **Castell de Montgrí**.

Eating & drinking

In Tossa, **Santa Marta** (C/Francesc Aromir 2, 972 34 04 72, www.restaurantsantamarta.com, closed Nov-Feb, mains €18) has a pretty terrace in the old town and specialises in Catalan cuisine. Upmarket **La Cuina de Can Simón** (C/Portal 24, 972 34 12 69, www.lacuinadecan simon.es, closed Tue Sept-July & 2wks Feb, 2wks Nov, mains €25-€36) is more eccentric, but serves excellent fish dishes, as does **Can Pini** (C/Portal 14, 972 34 02 97, closed Mon Sept-June, mains €15).

In Sant Feliu de Guíxols, try the **Nàutic** (Port Esportiu, 972 32 06 63, closed Mon, set lunch €14.70, set dinner €36) in the Club Nàutic sailing club, for great views and superb seafood. Also with a sea view, **El Dorada Mar** (Passeig Presidente Irla 15, 972 32 62 86, closed Wed Sept-July, mains €18) has a more traditional take on rice and fish dishes.

Calella has the fashionable **Tragamar** (Platja de Canadell, 972 61 43 36, www.grupo tragaluz.com, mains €14.50), while in Llafranc, **El Simpson** (Passeig Cipsela 10, 972 30 11 57, closed Nov-Feb; Mon-Fri Mar-May & Oct; Wed June & Sept, mains €14) is the haunt of well-heeled Catalans, and justifiably famous for excellent seafood. In Tamariu, there's good seafood at the **Royal** on the beachfront (Passeig de Mar 9, 972 62 00 41, closed mid Dec-Feb; Mon-Fri Nov, Dec & Mar, mains €18), or succulent roast lamb at **El Mossec** (C/Pescadors 8, 972 62 03 27, closed Jan; Wed June & Sept; Mon-Fri Oct-May, mains €12). In Aiguablava, the **Hotel Aiguablava** (Platja de Fornells, 972 62 20 58, www.aiguablava.com, closed Nov-Feb, mains €24.50, set lunch/dinner €39) has an excellent beachfront restaurant.

Sleeping

In Tossa, the **Hotel Diana** (Plaça España 6, 972 34 18 86, www.hotelesdante.com, closed Dec-Feb, €80-€135) is situated in a Modernista building with a beautifully preserved marble staircase and tiled floors, though the interior decor is somewhat wanting. Bargain rooms are available at **Fonda Lluna** (C/Roqueta 20, 972 34 03 65, www.fondalluna.com, €42-€64).

In Sant Feliu de Guixols, try the friendly **Hotel Plaça** (Plaça Mercat 22, 972 32 51 55, www.hotelplaza.org, €82-€120), close to the beach. North of Sant Feliu, in S'Agaró, the **Hostal de la Gavina** (Plaça de la Rosaleda, 972 32 11 00, www.lagavina.com, closed Nov-Easter, €215-€465) is a five-star in the European grand hotel tradition. Near the Platja d'Aro, **Mas Torrellas** (Ctra de Santa Cristina a Castell d'Aro km2, 972 83 75 26, closed Oct-Feb, €64-€95) is an 18th-century farmhouse with bags of charm.

On the road to Palamós, the **Hostal del Sol** (Ctra de Palamós, 972 32 01 93, www.hostaldelsol.es, closed Oct-Mar, €65-€115), is located in a Modernista mansion with a swimming pool and live music on the terrace through the summer. You'll also find fashionable **La Malcontenta** (Platja de Castell 12, 972 31 23 30, www.lamalcontentahotel.com, €155-255), which has a fabulous pool, plush beds and linen, and a designer air.

Llafranc has the famous **Hotel Llafranch** (Passeig de Cipsela 16, 972 30 02 08, www. hllafranch.com, closed Nov & Dec, €100-€158),

On the Beach

Coastal towns make the most of their locations with seaside festivals.

If there's one thing above all others at which the Spanish are world leaders, it's celebrating. The Barcelona calendar is full of fabulous festivals; *see pp224-231* for the best of them. And there are plenty more terrific events outside the city, especially up the coast towards France.

Some of the best coastal events are traditional. Held in Calella de Palafrugell on the first Saturday in July, **Cantata de las Habaneras** celebrates the return of native fishermen from the New World by singing shanties on the beach while sipping *cremat* (rum and sugar flambéed with coffee beans). And while the **Blanes Fireworks Festival** began in an official capacity 45 years ago, it dates back considerably longer. The spectacular event is held at the end of July; for information, call 972 33 03 48.

Others, though, are cultural. Between Calella and Blanes, the beachside town of Santa Susanna offers the unlikely prospect of a **Shakespeare Festival** (www.festivalshakespeare.com). Launched in 2003 in collaboration with the Teatre Lliure in Barcelona, the festival runs over ten days in late July and early August; some performances are staged in English.

There's more culture further up the coast in Sant Feliu de Guíxols at **La Porta Ferrada** (www.portaferrada.com), held in July and August. One of the oldest arts festivals in Catalonia, it includes everything from flamenco to Herbie Hancock. And up in Palafrugell (also in July and August), the clifftop **Jardins de Cap Roig** (botanic gardens) hosts dance, opera, jazz and classical music in a spectacular location.

ESCAPES & EXCURSIONS

which was a favourite haunt of Salvador Dalí and his cronies back in the 1960s. The **El Far de Sant Sebastià** (Platja de Llafranc s/n, 972 30 16 39, www.elfar.net, closed Jan, €220-€315), is a swanky address situated on the cliff tops. Alternatively, the friendly **Hotel Casamar** (C/Nero 3-11, 972 30 01 04, www.hotelcasamar. net, closed Jan-mid Mar, €55-€130) is a good budget option.

Tamariu offers the chilled-out **Hotel Tamariu** (Passeig de Mar 2, 972 62 00 31, www.tamariu.com, closed Nov-mid Feb, €99-€143), and the **Hotel Hostalillo** (972 62 02 28, www.hotelhostalillo.com, closed Oct-mid Mar, €52-€88), located above the beach in the middle of pine forest. Aiguablava's modern parador is **Platja d'Aiguablava** (972 62 21 62, www. parador.es, €145-€171).

Tourist information

L'Estartit *Passeig Marítim (972 75 19 10/www.visitestartit.com).* **Open** *June, Sept 9.30am-2pm, 4-8pm daily. July, Aug 9.30am-2pm, 4-9pm daily. Oct-May 9am-1pm, 3-6pm daily.*
Palafrugell *C/Carrilet 2 (972 30 02 28/www. visitpalafrugell.cat).* **Open** *May-June, Sept*

10am-1pm, 5-8pm Mon-Sat; 10am-1pm Sun. *July, Aug 9am-9pm Mon-Sat; 10am-1pm Sun. Oct-Apr 10am-1pm, 4-7pm Mon-Sat; 10am-1pm Sun.*
Sant Feliu de Guíxols *Plaça del Mercat 28 (972 82 00 51/www.guixols.cat).* **Open** *Mid June-mid Sept 10am-2pm, 4-8pm daily. Mid Sept-mid June 10am-1pm, 4-7pm Mon-Sat; 10am-2pm Sun.*

Getting there

By bus Sarfa (902 30 20 25, www.sarfa.com) runs 13 buses daily to Sant Feliu from Estació del Nord (journey time 1hr 20mins), and nine to Palafrugell (2hrs); some continue to Begur. Change in Palafrugell or Torroella for L'Estartit.

The French Connection

THE NORTHERN COSTA BRAVA

By comparison to the coastal stretch further south, the northern end of the Costa Brava is quieter, more isolated and less developed. Sure, there are large tourists resorts here, and some fairly unseemly architectural development.

Surreal Life

In artistic terms, the north-eastern corner of Spain belongs to Dalí.

Pablo be damned. Sure, the artist has his admirers; and, in Barcelona, he's celebrated by a fine museum. But north-east of the city, close to the French border, another very different artist dominates: Salvador Dalí, who lived and worked in this corner of Catalonia. Several Dalí-related landmarks remain intact, open to the public today.

Start just east of Girona at the 12th-century **Castell de Púbol**, bought by Dalí to house his wife-muse Gala (who's buried here) in her later years. Relations were strained by the time she moved in: Dalí had to book appointments to see her, and the tomb that he prepared for himself lies empty (he changed his mind), guarded by a stuffed giraffe and two oversized chess knights.

Due north lies Figueres, the capital of the Alt Empordà region and Dalí's birthplace. The artist donated many of his works to the **Teatre-Museu Dalí** (Plaça Gala-Salvador Dalí 5, 972 67 75 00, www.dali-estate.org, closed Mon Oct-June, €11, €8 reductions), housed in the town's old theatre, and also redesigned

the place, putting thousands of yellow loaves on the external walls and huge eggs on its towers. The highlight is the three-dimensional room-sized Mae West face, a collection of furniture arranged to look like the star when viewed from a certain angle; a plump red sofa takes the place of her famous pout. And if you're wondering what happened to Dalí's body after seeing the empty tomb at the Castell de Púbol, wonder no more: he's buried here.

East of here, on the coast, lies the relatively isolated Cadaqués, another former Dalí haunt. The artist spent his childhood summers here, then brought his surrealist circle along and eventually built his home – now a museum – in nearby Port Lligat. The **Casa-Museu de Port Lligat** (972 25 10 15, www.dali-estate.org, closed Mon mid Mar-mid June, closed Jan-mid Mar, €10, €8 reductions) is filled with zany furniture, peculiar fittings and stuffed animals, offering an extraordinary insight into the eccentric genius's lifestyle. Book in advance, as only eight people are allowed in at a time.

Calella de Palafrugell. *See p302.*

But there's also plenty of well-preserved history, numerous beautiful landscapes and a wealth of opportunities to get away from it all.

One of the main sites of interest on this stretch is **Empúries**. Here, you'll find the remains of an ancient city dating back to 600 BC, when it was founded by the Phoenicians and before it was recolonised by the Greeks and finally the Romans. Today, ruins from all three periods – including a stunning mosaic of Medusa, as well as the layout of the original Greek harbour – are visible. It's quite a contrast with the overcrowded tourist resort of **Roses**, on the other side of the huge Golf de Roses, which has little to recommend it apart from a 16th-century citadel and the nearby legendary restaurant **El Bulli** (*see p179*) in Cala Montjoi.

From Roses, the road coils over the hills that form the **Cap de Creus** nature reserve, before dropping spectacularly down to **Cadaqués**,

which has retained its charm thanks to a ban on the high-rise buildings that have blighted so much of the Spanish coastline. Dalí really put the place on the map; *see left* **Surreal Life**.

On the north side of the cape, up in the windswept hills you'll find the remarkable **Sant Pere de Rodes** fortified abbey (972 38 75 59, closed Mon, admission €4.50, reductions €3, free Tue), the area's most accomplished example of Romanesque architecture. A further climb takes you up to the **Castell de Sant Salvador**, an imposing tenth-century castle that seems to grow out of the rock, with unparalleled views out over the Pyrenees to France, and back into Catalonia.

Heading back inland, the capital of the Alt Empordà region is **Figueres**, where Dalí was born and is buried in his own museum in the city's old theatre, the **Teatre-Museu Dalí** (*see left* **Surreal Life**). It somewhat overshadows the city's other two fine museums: the **Museu de l'Empordà** (Rambla 2, 972 50 23 05, www. museuemporda.org, closed Mon, admission €2, reductions €1), which gives an overview of the area's history, and the **Museu del Joguet** (C/Sant Pere 1, 972 50 45 85, www.mjc.cat, closed Mon Oct-May, admission €5, reductions €4, or free with ticket to Teatre-Museu Dali), full of 19th- and early 20th-century toys, some of which belonged to Dali and Miró.

Between Figueres and the sea sits the **Parc Natural dels Aiguamolls de l'Empordà**, a haven for rare birds that flock to the marshy lowlands at the mouth of the Fluvia river in spring and autumn. As well as flamingos and moustached warblers, this nature reserve is home to turtles, salamanders and otters.

Eating, drinking & sleeping

Next to the ruins in Empúries, the **Hostal Empúries** (Platja Portitxol, 972 77 02 07, www. hostalempuries.com, €135-€160, set menu €34) offers starchy white rooms in a fantastic setting in front of the rocky beach. It serves good Mediterranean food all year round and arranges cookery courses. Near the beach in Sant Pere Pescador, **Ca la Caputxeta** (C/Disseminat 60, 972 25 03 10, www.caputxeta.com, €55-€65) has a lovely rustic feel and a laid-back vibe. Over the bay, a twisting drive from Roses, is the extraordinary and world-famous **El Bulli** (*see p179*). Reasonably nearby, sitting in a bay between Roses and Cadaqués, the **Hotel Cala Jóncols** (Ctra Vella de Roses a Cadaqués, 972 25 39 70, www.calajoncols.com, closed Nov-Mar, €110-€220 full board per person) is isolated and no-frills. It's a blissful hideaway for those who can do without luxuries, though it does have a pool.

Cadaqués has few hotels, and most are closed in winter – call ahead. The **Hotel Rocamar** (C/Virgen del Carmen s/n 972 25 81 50, www. rocamar.com, €77-€185) is the finest hotel in Cadaqués and set away from the rest of the town, looking back over the bay. Alternatively, **Playa Sol** (Platja Pianc 3, 972 25 81 00, www. playasol.com, closed Jan-mid Feb & Dec, €54-€110) also overlooks the sea, but has more of a business feel. Smaller and more basic is **Hotel Llané Petit** (C/Dr Bartomeus 37, 972 25 10 20, www.llanepetit.com, closed Jan, €72-€150). It has a pretty terrace overlooking the bay, and simply decorated rooms.

Over the hill in Port Lligat, the two-star **Hotel Port Lligat** (972 25 81 62, closed Nov; Mon-Thur Jan-Mar, Oct, Dec, €69-€130) is right next door to the Dali museum and has a boutiquey feel to it, while the **Hotel Calina** (Avda Salvador Dali, 33, 972 25 88 51, www. hotelcalina.com, €73-€140) is more modern

and more comfortable, and has a decent-sized swimming pool overlooking the beach. **Restaurant Casa Nun** (Plaça Portitxó 6, 972 25 88 56, closed Tue, Wed & lunch Thur Nov-May; lunch Tue-Thur June, July, Sept & Oct, mains €18) has a sea-facing terrace, lots of charm and good value set menus featuring boat-fresh fish. **Restaurant Can Rafa** (C/Passeig Marítim 7, 972 15 94 01, www. restaurantcanrafa.com, closed Dec; Wed Sept-June, mains €22) specialises in local lobster, while the pretty **Es Balconet** (C/Sant Antoni 2, 972 25 88 14, closed Tue and Jan, Feb & Nov, mains €15), up a winding street back from the bay, is good for paella. **Casa Anita** (C/Miguel Rosen, 972 25 84 71, www.casa-anita.com, closed Mon and Nov, mains €18) is fiercely popular (Dali used to eat here) and serves excellent seafood.

In Figueres, the **Hotel Duran** (C/Lasauca 5, 972 50 12 50, www.hotelduran.com, €86-€118, set menu €17) was an old haunt of Dali and exudes comfortable, battered elegance. The restaurant offers fine game and seafood. For clean and simple rooms, head for **La Barretina** (C/Lasauca 13, 972 67 34 25, www.hostalla barretina.com, closed Nov, €45-€48). **President** (Avda Salvador Dali 82, 972 50 17 00, www. hotelpresident.info, set lunch €16.50) offers solid Catalan fare and excellent seafood. C/Jonquera is the main drag for cheap *menús del dia*, which you can sample at alfresco tables. A couple of kilometres west, **Mas Pau** (Ctra de Figueres a Besalú, Avinyonet de Puigventós, 972 54 61 54, www.maspau.com, closed all Mon, lunch Tue, dinner Sun & all Jan-mid Mar, mains €25) is an excellent and creative restaurant.

Tourist information

Cadaqués *C/Cotxe 2A (972 25 83 15/www. cadaques.cat).* **Open** *June-Sept* 9am-9pm Mon-Sat; 10am-1pm Sun. *Oct-May* 9am-1pm, 3-6pm Mon-Sat; 10am-1pm Sun.
L'Escala *Plaça de les Escoles 1 (972 77 06 03/ www.lescala.cat).* **Open** *Mid June-mid Sept* 9am-8.30pm daily. *Mid Sept-mid June* 10am-1pm, 4-7pm Mon-Sat; 10am-1pm Sun.
Figueres *Plaça del Sol (972 50 31 55).* **Open** *July-Sept* 9am-8pm Mon-Sat; 10am-3pm Sun. *Oct-June* 10am-2pm Mon-Fri.

Getting there

By bus Sagales (902 26 06 06, www.sagales. com) runs several buses daily to Figueres from Estació del Nord (2hrs 30mins). Sarfa (902 30 20 25) runs two buses daily to Roses and Cadaqués (2hrs 15mins).
By train RENFE from Sants or Passeig de Gràcia to Figueres (2hrs). Trains leave every hour.

Directory

Getting Around

Barcelona's centre is compact and easily explored on foot. Bicycles are good for the Old City and port: there is a decent network of bike lanes across the city. The metro and bus systems are best for longer journeys. Cars can be a hindrance: there's little parking, and most of the city is subject to one-way systems. For transport outside Barcelona, *see p284*.

ARRIVING & LEAVING

By air

Aeroport de Barcelona

91 393 60 00/www.aena.es.
Barcelona's airport is at El Prat, south-west of the city. There are three main terminals (A, B and C), with a fourth (T-Sur) scheduled for completion in autumn 2009. Tourist information desks and currency exchanges are in terminals A and B. Website www.barcelona-airport.com also lists departures and arrivals.

Aerobús
The airport bus (93 415 60 20) runs from each terminal to Plaça Catalunya, with stops at Plaça d'Espanya, C/Urgell and Plaça Universitat. Buses to the airport go from Plaça Catalunya (in front of El Corte Inglés), stopping at Sants station and Plaça d'Espanya. Buses run every 8-10mins, leaving the airport 6am-1am Mon-Fri and 6.30am-1am at weekends, returning from Plaça Catalunya 5.30am-12.15am Mon-Fri and 6am-12.15am at weekends. The trip takes 35-45mins; a single is €4.05, a return (valid six days) €7.

City buses
Bus 46 runs between Plaça Espanya and the airport every half hour. The first leaves from Plaça Espanya between 5am-12.15am Mon-Fri and then between 9am-8pm at weekends. From the airport the first is at 5.30am and the last at 12.24am. Journey time is about 45mins.
At night the N17 runs every 20 minutes between the airport (from 10pm) and Plaça Catalunya (from 11pm), with several stops on the way, including Plaça d'Espanya and Plaça Universitat. Last departures are at 5am. Journey time is 45mins.

Airport trains
By train: the long overhead walkway between terminals A and B leads to the train station. The Cercanías train (C10) leaves the airport at 29 and 59 mins past the hour, 6.29am-10.59pm, with an extra train at 11.44pm daily, stopping at Barcelona Sants, Passeig de Gràcia and Estació de França. Trains to the airport leave Barcelona Sants at 25 and 55 mins past the hour, 5.25am-10.55pm daily (13mins earlier from Estació de França, 5mins earlier from Passeig de Gràcia). The journey takes 20-30mins and costs €2.60 one way (no return tickets). Tickets are valid only for 2hrs after purchase (902 24 02 02, www.renfe.es/cercanias; www.spanish-rail.co.uk, 020 7725 7063). The T-10 Zone 1 metro pass (*see p309*) is also valid.

Taxis
The basic taxi fare to town should be €15-€26, including a €3.10 airport supplement. Fares are about 15 per cent higher after 8pm and at weekends. There is a €1 supplement for each large piece of luggage placed in the car boot. All licensed cab drivers use the ranks outside the terminals.

Airlines
Terminals are shown in brackets. Numbers to dial from the UK are listed second.

Air Berlin (B) *93 478 7594/0870 738 8880/www.airberlin.com*
Aer Lingus (B) *902 50 27 37/ www.aerlingus.com*
Air Europa (B) *902 40 15 01/ www.air-europa.com*
bmi (B) *+44 (0)133 264 8181/ 0870 607 0555/www.flybmi.com*
bmibaby (B) *902 100 737/0870 126 6726/www.bmibaby.com*
British Airways (B) *902 11 13 33/0870 850 9850/www.ba.com*
easyJet (A) *807 260 026/0871 244 2366/www.easyjet.com*
Iberia (B or C) *902 400 500/0870 609 0500/www.iberia.com*
Jet2 (A) *902 88 12 69/0871 226 1737/www.jet2.com*
Monarch Airlines (A) *902 50 27 37/0870 040 5040/ www.flymonarch.com*
Ryanair (from Girona or Reus) *807 22 02 20/0871 246 0000/ www.ryanair.com*
Spanair (B) *97 191 60 47/902 13 14 15/www.spanair.com*

Thomsonfly (B) *91 414 1481/ 0870 190 0737/ www.thomsonfly.com*
Vueling (B) *93 378 78 78/902 33 39 33/www.vueling.com*

By bus

Most long-distance coaches (national and international) stop or terminate at Estació d'Autobusos Barcelona-Nord (C/Ali Bei 80, 902 26 06 06, www.barcelonanord.com, map p343 J9). The Estació d'Autobusos Barcelona-Sants at C/Viriat is only a secondary stop for many coaches, though some international Eurolines services (information 93 490 40 00, www.eurolines.es) both begin and end their journeys at Sants.

By car

The easiest way to central Barcelona from almost all directions is the Ronda Litoral, the coastal half of the ring road. Take exit 21 (Paral·lel) if you're coming from the south, or exit 22 (Via Laietana) from the north. Motorways also feed into Avda Diagonal, Avda Meridiana and Gran Via, which all lead to the city centre. Tolls are charged on most of the main approach routes, payable in cash (the lane marked 'manual'; motorbikes are charged half) or by credit card ('automatic'). For more on driving in Barcelona, *see p310*.

By rail

Most long-distance services run by the Spanish state railway company RENFE leave from Barcelona-Sants station, easily reached by metro. A few services from the French border or south to Tarragona stop at the Estació de França in the Born, which is otherwise sparsely served. Many trains stop at Passeig de Gràcia, which can be the handiest for the city centre and also has a metro stop.
RENFE operate the high-speed service AVE (Alta Velocidad) between Barcelona Sants and Madrid, via Zaragoza and Lleida. Travelling at speeds averaging 300km per hour, AVE whisks travellers to the Spanish capital in about 2hrs 45mins. A

single ticket to Madrid starts from €106.10 but there are special deals if you book online and in advance.

RENFE *National 902 24 02 02/ inter-national 902 24 34 02/www. renfe.es.* **Open** *National* 5am-10pm daily. *International* 7am-midnight daily. **Credit** AmEx, DC, MC, V. Some English-speaking operators. RENFE tickets can be bought online, at stations and travel agents, or reserved over the phone, and delivered for a small fee.

By sea

Balearic Islands ferries dock at the Moll de Barcelona quay, at the bottom of Avda Paral·lel; Trasmediterránea (902 45 46 45, 91 663 2850, www.trasmediterranea. es) is the main operator.

Grimaldi Lines runs a ferry a day, except Sundays, between Barcelona and Civitavecchia (near Rome) from the Moll Sant Bertran (93 508 88 50, www.grimaldi-ferries.com); or to Genoa three times a week from the Moll de Ponent, a few hundred metres south (902 40 12 00).

Cruise ships use several berths around the harbour. The PortBus shuttle service (93 415 60 20) runs between them and the bottom of La Rambla when ships are in port.

MAPS

For street, local train and metro maps, *see pp336-352.* Tourist offices provide a reasonable street map, or a better-quality map for €1. Metro maps (ask for *un plano/un plànol de metro*) are available free at all metro stations; bus maps can be obtained from the main Oficines d'Informació Turística (*see p320*). There is an excellent interactive street map at www.bcn.cat/guia.

PUBLIC TRANSPORT

Although it's run by different organisations, Barcelona's public transport is now highly integrated, with units on multi-journey tickets valid for up to four changes of transport (within 75 minutes) on bus, tram, local train and metro lines. The metro is generally the quickest and easiest way of getting around the city. All metro lines operate from 5am to midnight Monday to Thursday, Sunday and public holidays; 5am to 2am Friday and non-stop on Saturday. Buses run all night, to areas not covered by the metro system. Local buses

and the metro are run by the city transport authority (TMB). Two underground lines connect with the metro, run by Catalan government railways, the FGC. One runs north from Plaça Catalunya; the other west from Plaça d'Espanya to Cornellà. There are six tramlines following two main routes, though they are of limited use to visitors.

FGC information *Vestibule, Plaça Catalunya FGC station (93 205 15 15/www.fgc.net).* **Open** 7am-9pm Mon-Fri. **Map** p344 C1. **Other locations** FGC Provença; FGC Plaça d'Espanya.
TMB information *Main vestibule, Metro Universitat, Eixample (93 318 70 74/ www.tmb.net).* **Open** 8am-8pm Mon-Fri. **Map** p344 A1.
Other locations vestibule, Metro Sants Estació and Sagrada Família; vestibule, Metro Diagonal.

Fares & tickets

Journeys in the Barcelona urban area have a flat fare of €1.30, but multi-journey tickets (*tarjetas/ targetes*) are better value. The basic ten-trip targeta is the T-10 (*Te-Deu* in Catalan, *Te-Diez* in Spanish), which can be shared by any number of people travelling simultaneously; the ticket is validated in the machines on the metro, train or bus once per person per journey.

Along with the other integrated *targetes* listed below, the T-10 offers access to all five of the city's main transport systems (local RENFE and FGC trains within the main metropolitan area, the metro, the tram and buses). To transfer, insert your card into a machine a second time; unless 75mins have elapsed since your last journey, no other unit will be deducted. Single tickets do not allow free transfers.

You can buy T-10s in newsagents and Servi-Caixa cashpoints, as well as on the metro and train systems (from machines or the ticket office), but not on buses. More expensive versions of all *targetes* take you to the outer zones of the metropolitan region, but the prices listed below will get you anywhere in central Barcelona, and to the key sights on the outskirts of the city itself.

Integrated targetes
T-10 Valid for ten trips; each strip can be shared by two or more people. €7.20.
T-Familiar Gives 70 trips in any 30-day period; can be shared. €43.80.

T-50/30 Gives 50 trips in any 30-day period; but can only be used by one person. €29.80.
T-Dia A one-day travelcard. €5.50.
T-Mes Valid for any 30-day period. €46.25.
T-Trimestre Valid for three months. €127.
T-Jove Valid for three months; for under-21s only. €108.

Other targetes
2, 3, 4 & 5 Dies Two-, three-, four- and five-day travelcards on the metro, buses and FGC trains. Also sold at tourist offices. €10, €14.30, €18.30 and €21.70.
Barcelona Card A tourist scheme offering unlimited use of public transport for up to five days.

Buses

Many bus routes originate in or pass through Plaça Catalunya, Plaça Universitat and Plaça Urquinaona. However, they often run along parallel streets, due to the city's one-way system. Not all stops are labelled, and street signs are not always easy to locate.

Most routes run 6am-10.30pm daily except Sundays. There's usually a bus every 10-15mins, but they're less frequent before 8am, after 9pm and on Saturdays. On Sundays, buses are less frequent still; a few do not run at all. Only single tickets can be bought from the driver; if you have a *targeta*, insert it into the machine behind the driver as you board.

Night buses There are 16 urban night bus (*Nitbus*) routes (902 02 33 93, or TMB, *see p303*), most running from around 10.30-11.30pm to 4.30-6am nightly, with buses every 20-30mins, plus an hourly bus to the airport; *see p308*. Most pass through Plaça Catalunya. Fares and *targetes* are as for daytime buses. Plaça Catalunya is also the terminus for all-night bus services linking Barcelona with more distant parts of its metropolitan area.

Local trains

Regional trains to Sabadell, Terrassa and other towns beyond Tibidabo depart from FGC Plaça Catalunya, those for Montserrat from FGC Plaça d'Espanya.

All trains on the RENFE local network ('Rodalies/Cercanías') stop at Sants but can also be caught at either Plaça Catalunya and Arc de Triomf (for Vic and the Pyrenees, Manresa, the Penedès and Costa del

DIRECTORY

Maresme) or Passeig de Gràcia (for the southern coastal line to Sitges and the Girona-Figueres line north).

Metro

The metro is the easiest way to get around Barcelona. There are six lines, each colour coded: L1 (red), L2 (purple), L3 (light green), L4 (yellow), L5 (blue), L11 (dark green). For tickets and running times, *see p309*; for a map, *see pp350-351*.

Trams

Lines T1, T2 and T3 go from Plaça Francesc Macià, Zona Alta, to the outskirts of the city. The fourth line is more useful to visitors and runs from Ciutadella-Vila Olímpica (also a metro stop), via Glòries and the Fòrum, on to Sant Adrià (also a RENFE train station) the fifth line follows the same route, splitting off at Glòries to go on to Badalona.

All trams are fully accessible for wheelchair-users and are part of the integrated TMB *targeta* system. You can buy integrated tickets and single tickets from the machines at tram stops.

Tram information *Trambaix (902 19 32 75/www.trambcn.com)*. **Open** 9am-2pm, 4-7pm Mon-Thur; 9am-2pm Fri.

TAXIS

It's usually easy to find one of the 10,500 black-and-yellow taxis. There are ranks at railway and bus stations, in main squares and throughout the city, but taxis can also be hailed on the street when they show a green light on the roof and a sign saying *lliure/libre* ('free') behind the windscreen. Information on taxi fares, ranks and regulations can be found at www.emt-amb.com/links/cat/cimtaxi.htm.

Fares

Current rates and supplements are shown inside cabs on a sticker on the rear side window (in English). The basic fare for a taxi hailed in the street is €1.80 (€1.90 at nights, weekends and holidays), which is what the meter should register when you set off. The basic rates (82¢/km) apply 8am-8pm Mon-Fri; at other times, including public holidays, the rate is €1.04/km.

There are supplements for luggage (€1), for the airport (€3.10) and the port (€2.10), and for nights such as New Year's Eve (€3.10), as

well as a waiting charge. Taxi drivers are not required to carry more than €20 in change; few accept credit cards. There is a €2.10 supplement from midnight to 6am on Friday, Saturday and Sunday. And if a public holiday falls on one of these days there is an additional €3.10 supplement.

Radio cabs

These companies take bookings 24 hours daily. Phone cabs start the meter when a call is answered but, by the time it picks you up, it should not display more than €3.22 (€3.99 at night, weekends or public holidays). Supplements are added at the end of the journey.

Barnataxi 93 357 77 55.
Fono-Taxi 93 300 11 00.
Ràdio Taxi '033' 93 303 30 33.
Servi-Taxi 93 330 03 00.
Taxi Groc 93 322 22 22.
Taxi Miramar 93 433 10 20.

Receipts & complaints

To get a receipt, ask for *un rebut/un recibo*. It should include the fare, the taxi number, the driver's NIF (tax) number, the licence plate, the driver's signature and the date; if you have a complaint insist on all these, and the more details (time, route) the better. Complaints must be filed in writing to the Institut Metropolità del Taxi (93 223 51 51 ext 2168, www.taxibarcelona.info).

DRIVING

For information (only in Catalan or Spanish) on driving in Catalonia, call the Servei Català de Trànsit (93 567 40 00); the local government's information line (012), which has English speakers; or see www.gencat.net/transit. Driving in the city can be intimidating and time-consuming. If you do drive:

● Keep your driving licence, vehicle registration and insurance documents with you at all times.
● Do not leave anything of value, including car radios, in your car. Foreign plates can attract thieves.
● Be on your guard at motorway service areas, and take care to avoid thieves in the city who may try to make you stop, perhaps by indicating you have a flat tyre.

Breakdown services

If you're planning to take a car, join a motoring organisation such as the AA (www.theaa.com) or the RAC

(www.rac.co.uk) in the UK, which usually have reciprocal agreements.
RACE (Real Automóvil Club de España)
91 593 33 33/902 40 45 45/24hr help 902 30 05 05/www.race.es.

Car & motorbike hire

Car hire is relatively pricey, but it's a competitive market, so shop around. Ideally, you want unlimited mileage, 16% VAT (IVA) included and full insurance cover (*seguro todo riesgo*) rather than the third-party minimum (*seguro obligatorio*). You'll need a credit card as a guarantee. Most companies require you to have had a licence for at least a year; many also enforce a minimum age limit.

Europcar *Plaça dels Països Catalans, Sants (93 491 48 22/reservations 902 10 50 30/www.europcar.com). Metro Sants Estació.* **Open** 7am-11pm Mon-Fri; 8am-8pm Sat; 8am-10pm Sun. **Credit** AmEx, DC, MC, V. **Map** p341 B7. **Other locations** Airport, terminals B & C (93 298 33 00); C/Viladomat 214, Eixample (93 439 84 01); Gran Via de les Corts Catalanes 680, Eixample (93 302 05 43).
Motíssimo *C/Comandante Benítez 25, Sants (93 490 84 01/www.motissimo.es). Metro Badal.* **Open** *Oct-June* 8am-1.30pm, 4-8pm Mon-Fri; 10am-1pm Sat. *July-Sept* 9am-1.30pm, 4-8pm Mon-Fri. **Credit** AmEx, DC, MC, V. **Map** p337 A5.
Pepecar *C/Rivadeneyra, underground car park (807 41 42 43/902 36 05 35/www.pepecar.com). Metro Catalunya.* **Open** 8am-8pm Mon-Thur, Sat; 8am-8pm Fri, Sun. **Credit** AmEx, MC, V. **Map** p344 C2.
Vanguard *C/Viladomat 297, Eixample (93 439 38 80/www.vanguardrent.com). Metro Hospital Clínic.* **Open** 8am-1.30pm, 4-7.30pm Mon-Fri; 9am-1pm Sat, Sun. **Credit** AmEx, DC, MC, V. **Map** p337 D6.

Legal requirements

For driving laws and regulations (in Spanish), see the Ministry of Interior's website (www.dgt.es).

Parking

Parking is fiendishly complicated and municipal police are quick to hand out tickets or tow cars. In some parts of the Old City, access is limited to residents for much of the day. In some Old City streets, time-controlled bollards pop up, meaning your car may get stuck. Never park in front of doors marked 'Gual Permanent', indicating an entry with 24-hour right of access.

Pay & display areas The Àrea Verda contains zones only for use of residents (most of the Old City). In 'partial zones' (in Barceloneta, Gràcia and the Eixample), non-residents pay €2.80/hr with a 1hr or 2hr maximum stay (check the meter).

If you overstay by no more than an hour, you can cancel the fine by paying an extra €6; to do so, press *Anul·lar denùncia* on the machine, insert €6, then press Ticket. Some machines accept cards (AmEx, MC, V); none accepts notes or gives change. For information, check www.bcn.es/areaverda or call 010. There's a drop-in centre for queries on the ground floor of the Ajuntament building on Plaça Carles Pi i Sunyer 8-10, open 8.30am-5.30pm Mon-Fri.

Car parks Car parks (*parkings*) are signalled by a white 'P' on a blue sign. Those run by SABA (Plaça Catalunya, Plaça Urquinaona, Rambla de Catalunya, Avda Catedral, airport and elsewhere; 93 230 56 00, 902 28 30 80, www.saba.es) cost around €2.60/hr. Discount and long-stay passes (from 6-12hrs) are available in packs of 10 units. SMASSA car parks (Plaça Catalunya 23, C/Hospital 25-29, Avda Francesc Cambó 10, Passeig de Gràcia 60 and elsewhere; 93 409 20 21, www.bsmsa.es/mobilitat) cost €2.30-€2.70/hr.

Towed vehicles If police tow your car, they should leave a triangular sticker on the pavement where it was. The sticker should let you know to which pound it's been taken. If not, call 901 513 151; staff generally don't speak English. Recovering your vehicle within 4hrs costs €146.30, with each extra hour costing €1.60, or €19/day. You'll also have to pay a fine. You'll need your passport and documentation, or rental contract, to prove ownership. www.bsmsa.es has information in Catalan and Spanish.

CYCLING

There's a network of bike lanes (*carrils bici*) along major avenues and alongside the seafront; local authorities are very keen to promote cycling. Be warned that bike theft is rife: always carry a good lock. For information see www.bcn.cat/bicicleta. There are bike hire shops all over the city.

Bicicleta Barcelona
C/Esparteria 3, Born (93 268 21 05/www.bicicletabarcelona.com). Metro Barceloneta or Jaume I. **Open** 10am-7pm Mon-Sat; 10am-2pm Sun.

TOURS

Another way to get around (and to head to the beach) is to hire a Trixi rickshaw (www.trixi.com). Running 11am-8pm, March to November, and costing €10 per half-hour, they can be hailed on the street, or by calling 93 310 13 79.

By bike

Barcelona by Bicycle
Un Cotxe Menys, C/Esparteria 3, Born (93 268 21 05/www.bicicleta barcelona.com). Metro Barceloneta. **Open** 10am-7pm daily. **Tours** 11am daily. *Apr-Sept* 11am, 4.30pm Mon, Fri-Sun. **Rates** *Tours* €22. **Hire** €5 1hr; €11 half-day; €15 1 day; €65 1wk. **No credit cards. Map** p345 E7.
Meet in Plaça Sant Jaume and then head to the nearby shop for bikes and helmets followed by a three-hour English-speaking tour.

Fat Tire Bike Tours
C/Escudellers 48 (93 301 36 12/ www.fattirebiketoursbarcelona.com). Metro Drassanes. **Tours** *Feb-mid Apr, Nov-mid Dec* 11am daily. *Mid Apr-Oct* 11am, 4pm daily. **Rates** *Tours* €22. **Hire** €8 5hrs; €15 1 day. **No credit cards. Map** p345 C6.
Tours meet in Plaça Sant Jaume and last over four hours, taking in the Old City, Sagrada Família, Ciutadella park and the beach.

By bus

Barcelona Tours *93 261 56 79/www.barcelonatours.es.* **Tours** *Nov-May* 9am-8pm daily; every 15-20mins; *June-Oct* 9am-8pm daily; every 8-10mins. **Tickets** *1 day* €21; €13 reductions. *2 days* €25; €16 reductions. Free under-4s. Available on bus. **Credit** MC, V.
Though more frequent, off-season, than rival Bus Turístic, there are no discounts offered to attractions. It takes around three hours to cover the large tour circuit which includes La Pedrera, Sagrada Família, Park Güell and Nou Camp.

Bus Turístic
93 285 38 32/www.tmb.net. **Tours** *Apr-Oct* 9am-8pm daily; approx every 6-10mins. *Nov-Mar* 9am-7pm daily; approx every 30mins. **Tickets** *1 day* €20; €12 reductions. *2 days* €26; €16 reductions. Free

under-4s. Available from tourist office (credit MC, V) or on bus (no credit cards).
Bus Turístic (white and blue, with colourful images of the sights) runs three circular routes. Tickets are valid for all routes and ticket-holders get discount vouchers for a range of attractions.

Bus Turístic de Nit
93 285 38 32/www.tmb.net. **Tours** *May-Sept* 9.30pm (boarding from 9.10pm) Fri-Sun. **Tickets** €16; €10 reductions. Available from tourist offices or on bus. **No credit cards.**
The night tour bus (with guided commentary) is designed to show off the illuminations of the city.

On foot

Barcelona Walking Tours
93 285 38 32/www.barcelona turisme.com. **Tours** (in English) *Gothic* 10am daily. *Picasso* 10.30am Tue-Sun. *Modernisme* 4pm Fri, Sat. *Gourmet* 11am Fri, Sat. **Tickets** *Gothic, Modernisme* €11; €4.50 reductions. *Picasso, Gourmet* (reservations are essential) €15; €6.50 reductions. **No credit cards. Map** p344 C2.
Tours take 90mins to 2hrs, excluding the museum trip. All tours start in the underground tourist office in Plaça Catalunya.

My Favourite Things
Mobile 637 265 406/www.myft.net. Unusual outings (€26-€32) that include walking tours for families with children, urban design tours, and salsa or flamenco lessons.

Ruta del Modernisme
93 317 76 52/www.rutadel modernisme.com. **Rates** €12.
Not so much a route as a guidebook to 115 Modernista buildings, giving discounts on entry. It's available at the Plaça Catalunya tourist office (*see p320*), the Hospital Sant Pau and the Pavellons Güell.

By scooter

Barcelona Scooter Tours
Cooltra Motos, Passeig Joan de Borbó 80-84, Barceloneta (93 221 40 70/www.cooltra.com). Metro Barceloneta. **Tours** 10.30am, 5pm Sat. **Rates** €45 4hr tour; €25 2hr tour. **Hire** €15/day plus €10 ins. **Credit** AmEx, DC, MC, V. **Map** p342 G13.
There's a four-hour tour, a shorter express tour, a tour on a Harley-Davidson and a full-day *Shadow of the Wind* tour. Note that you must have at least three years' driving experience. Book 24hrs ahead.

DIRECTORY

Resources A-Z

ADDRESSES

Most apartment addresses consist of a street name followed by a street number, floor level and flat number, in that order. So, to go to C/València 246, 2º 3ª, find No.246, go to the second floor and find the door marked 3 or 3ª. Ground-floor flats are usually called *baixos* or *bajos* (often abbreviated *bxs/bjos*); one floor up, the *entresol/entresuelo* (*entl*), and the next is often the *principal* (*pral*). Confusingly, numbered floors start here: first, second, up to the *àtic/ático* at the top. Addresses occasionally point out whether a property number is on the left- or right-hand side of the street; 'right' is *dreta/derecha* (*dta/dcha*) and 'left' is *esquerra/izquierda* (*esq/izq*).

AGE RESTRICTIONS

Buying/drinking alcohol 18.
Driving 18.
Smoking 18.
Sex (hetero- and homosexual) 13.

ATTITUDE & ETIQUETTE

The Catalans are generally less guarded about personal space than people in Britain or the US. The common greeting between members of the opposite sex and between two women, even the first time that the two parties have met, is a kiss on both cheeks. Men usually greet each other by shaking hands. Don't be surprised if people bump into you on the street, or crowd or push past you on the bus or metro without apologising: it's not seen as rude.

Contrary to appearances, Catalans have an advanced queuing culture. They may not stand in an orderly line, but they're normally very aware of when it's their turn, particularly at market stalls. The standard drill is to ask when you arrive, *¿Qui es l'últim/la última?* ('Who's last?'), and say *jo* ('me') to the next person who asks.

BUSINESS

Admin services

The *gestoria*, a Spanish institution is designed to lighten the weight of local bureaucracy by dealing with it for you. A combination of bookkeeper, lawyer and business adviser, a good *gestor* can be helpful in handling paperwork.

CMB Assessors *C/Aribau 226, pral 2ª, Eixample (93 209 67 88). Metro Diagonal/FGC Gràcia.* **Open** *Oct-June* 9am-2pm, 4-7pm Mon-Fri; *July-Sept* 9am-2pm, 4-7pm Mon-Thur; 9pm-2pm Fri. Closed 2wks Aug. **Map** p338 F5.
Lawyers, economists and a *gestoria*.

Martin Howard Associates *C/Aribau 177, entl 1ª, Eixample (93 202 25 34/www.mhasoc.com).* **Open** *Sept-July* 9am-6pm Mon-Thur; 9am-8pm Fri. *Aug* 8am-3pm Mon-Fri. **Map** p338 F5.
Tax and accounts from British accountant Alex Martin.

Conventions & conferences

Barcelona Convention Bureau *Rambla Catalunya 123, pral, Eixample (93 368 97 00/www.barcelonaturisme.com). Metro Diagonal.* **Open** *Sept-mid June* 9am-2.30pm, 3.30-6.30pm Mon-Thur; 9am-3pm Fri. *Mid June-Aug* 8am-3pm Mon-Fri. **Map** p338 F6.

Fira de Barcelona *Avda Reina Maria Cristina, Montjuïc (93 233 20 00/www.firabcn.es). Metro Espanya.* **Open** *Mid Sept-mid June* 9am-1.30pm, 3.30-5.30pm Mon-Fri. *Mid June-mid Sept* 9am-2pm Mon-Fri. **Map** p341 B9.
One of Europe's largest exhibition complexes.

World Trade Center *Moll de Barcelona, Port Vell (93 508 88 88/www.wtcbarcelona.com). Metro Drassanes.* **Open** *Sept-June* 9am-2pm, 4-7pm Mon-Thur; 9am-3pm Fri. *July, Aug* 9am-3pm Mon-Fri. **Map** p342 F13. 130,000sq m (72,624sq ft) of office space in a modern complex.

Courier services

Estació d'Autobusos Barcelona-Nord *C/Ali Bei 80, Eixample (93 232 43 29). Metro Arc de Triomf.* **Open** 7.30am-2.30pm, 4-7.30pm Mon-Fri. **No credit cards. Map** p343 J9.

Missatgers Trèvol *C/Antonio Ricardos 14, La Sagrera (93 498 80 70/www.trevol.com). Metro Sagrera.* **Open** *Sept-July* 8am-7.30pm Mon-Fri. *Aug* 8am-3pm Mon-Fri. **No credit cards.**

Seur *902 10 10 10/www.seur.es.* **Open** 8am-8pm Mon-Fri; 9am-2pm Sat. **No credit cards.**

UPS *902 88 88 20/www.ups.com.* **Open** 8am-8pm Mon-Fri. **Credit** AmEx, MC, V.

Office & computer services

See p201 for computer shops.

Centro de Negocios *C/Pau Claris 97, 4º 1ª, Eixample (93 304 38 58/www.centro-negocios.com). Metro Passeig de Gràcia.* **Open** *Sept-July* 8am-9pm Mon-Fri. *Aug* 9am-2pm Mon-Fri. **No credit cards. Map** p342 G8.

Desks in shared offices, mailboxes, meeting rooms, secretarial services and administrative services.

Microrent C/Rosselló 35, Eixample (93 363 32 50/www. microrent.es). Metro Entença. **Open** Sept-June 9am-6pm Mon-Fri. July, Aug 8am-3pm Mon-Fri. **No credit cards. Map** p341 C6. Computer equipment for rent.

Translators

For more, see www.act.es.

DUUAL C/Ciutat 7, 2º 4ª, Barri Gòtic (93 302 29 85/www.duual. com). Metro Jaume I or Liceu. **Open** Sept-June 9am-2pm, 4-7pm Mon-Thur; 9am-2pm Fri. July 8.30am-3pm Mon-Fri. Closed 3wks Aug. **No credit cards. Map** p345 C6. **Traduit** C/Ribeira 6, 1º 2ª, Born (93 268 74 95/www.traduit.com). Metro Jaume I. **Open** 9am-2pm, 4-6.30pm Mon-Fri. **Credit** MC, V. **Map** p345 F7.

Useful organisations

Ajuntament de Barcelona Plaça Sant Miquel 4-5, Barri Gòtic (Information 010/93 402 70 00/ www.bcn.cat). Metro Jaume I. **Open** Sept-June 8.30am-5.30pm Mon-Fri. July, Aug 8.15am-2.15pm Mon-Fri. **Map** p345 C6. The city council. **Borsa de Valors de Barcelona** Passeig de Gràcia 19, Eixample (93 401 35 55/www. borsabcn.es). Metro Passeig de Gràcia. **Open** Reception 9am-5.30pm Mon-Fri. Library 9am-noon Mon-Fri. **Map** p344 C1. The stock exchange. **Generalitat de Catalunya** Information 012/new businesses 902 20 15 20/www.gencat.net. The Catalan government.

CONSULATES

Australian Consulate Plaça Gal.la Placidia 1, Gràcia (93 490 90 13/www.spain.embassy.gov.au). FCG Gràcia. **Open** 10am-noon Mon-Fri. Closed Aug. **Map** p338 F5. **British Consulate** Avda Diagonal 477, 13º, Eixample (93 366 62 00/www.ukinspain.com). Metro Hospital Clínic. **Open** Mid Sept-mid June 9.30am-2pm Mon-Fri. Mid June-mid Sept 8.30am-1.30pm Mon-Fri. **Map** p338 E5. **Canadian Consulate** C/Elisenda de Pinós 10, Sarrià (93 204 27 00/www.canada-es.org). FCG Reina Elisenda. **Open** 10am-1pm Mon-Fri.

Irish Consulate Gran Via Carles III 94, 10º, Les Corts (93 491 50 21). Metro Maria Cristina. **Open** 10am-1pm Mon-Fri. **Map** p337 B4. **New Zealand Consulate** Travessera de Gràcia 64, 2º, Gràcia (93 209 03 99). Metro Diagonal. **Open** 9am-2pm, 4-7pm Mon-Fri. **Map** p338 F5. **US Consulate** Passeig Reina Elisenda 23, Sarrià (93 280 22 27/www.embusa.es). FGC Reina Elisenda. **Open** 9am-1pm Mon-Fri. **Map** p337 B1.

CONSUMER

Ask for a complaint form (full de reclamació/hoja de reclamación), which many businesses and all shops, bars and restaurants are required to keep. Leave one copy with the business. Take the other forms to the consumer office.

Oficina Municipal d'Informació al Consumidor Ronda de Sant Pau 43-45, Barri Gòtic (93 402 78 41/ www.omic.bcn.es). Metro Paral·lel or Sant Antoni. **Open** 9am-2pm Mon-Fri. **Map** p342 E10. The official centre for consumer advice and complaints follow-up. **Telèfon de Consulta del Consumidor** 012. **Open** 9am-6pm Mon-Fri. Consumer advice.

CUSTOMS

Custom declarations are not usually necessary if you arrive from another EU country and are carrying legal goods for personal use. The amounts given below are guidelines only: if you come close to the maximums in several categories, you may still have to explain your personal habits to an interested but sceptical customs officer.

● 800 cigarettes, 400 small cigars, 200 cigars or 1kg loose tobacco.
● 10 litres of spirits (more than 22% alcohol), 90 litres of wine (less than 22% alcohol) or 110 litres of beer.
Coming from a non-EU country or the Canary Islands, you can bring:
● 200 cigarettes, 100 small cigars, 50 regular cigars or 250g (8.82oz) of tobacco.
● 1 litre of spirits (more than 22% alcohol) or 2 litres of wine or beer (more than 22% alcohol).
● 50g (1.76oz) of perfume.
● 500g coffee; 100g tea.
Visitors can also carry up to €6,000 in cash without having to declare it. Non-EU residents can

reclaim VAT (IVA) on some large purchases when they leave. For details, see p317.

DISABLED

www.accessiblebarcelona.com, run by a British expat wheelchair-user living in Barcelona, is a useful resource. Although many sights claim to be accessible, you may still need assistance. Phoning ahead to check is always a good idea.

Institut Municipal de Persones amb Disminució Avda Diagonal 233, Eixample (93 413 27 75/www.bcn.cat/ accessible). Metro Glòries or Monumental/bus 56, 62. **Open** 9am-2pm Mon-Fri. **Map** p343 K8. The official city organisation for the disabled has information on access to venues and transport, and can provide a map with wheelchair-friendly itineraries. It's best to call in advance to make an appointment, rather than just turning up. There are some English speakers available.

Transport

Access for disabled people to local transport is improving but still leaves much to be desired. For wheelchair-users, buses and taxis are usually the best bet. For transport information, call TMB (93 318 70 74) or 010. Transport maps, which can be picked up from transport information offices and some metro stations, indicate wheelchair access points and adapted bus routes. For a list of accessible metro stations and bus lines, check www.tmb.net and click on Transport for Everyone, or see the maps on pp350-352. However, even those stations with lifts can sometimes prove inaccessible, so wheelchair-users are advised to avoid the metro altogether.

Buses All the Aerobús airport buses, night buses and the open-topped tourist buses are fully accessible, though you may need assistance with the steep ramps. Adapted buses also alternate with standard buses on many daytime routes. Press the blue button with the wheelchair symbol to alert the driver before your stop.
Metro & FGC Only L2 has lifts and ramps at all stations. On L1 and L3, some stations have lifts. There is usually a step on to the train, the size of which varies; some assistance may be required. The

DIRECTORY

Montjuïc funicular railway is fully wheelchair-adapted. Accessible FGC stations include Provença, Muntaner and Avda Tibidabo. The FGC infrastructures at Catalunya and Espanya stations are accessible, but interchanges with metro lines are not.

RENFE trains Sants and Plaça Catalunya stations are wheelchair-accessible, but the trains are not. If you go to the Atenció al Viajero office ahead of time, help on the platform can be arranged.

Taxis All taxi drivers are officially required to transport wheelchairs and guide dogs for no extra charge, but cars can be small, and the willingness of drivers to co-operate varies widely. Special minibus taxis adapted for wheelchairs can be ordered from the Taxi Amic service, as well as from some general taxi services such as Servi-Taxi (93 330 03 00). You need to book at least 24-48hrs ahead.

Taxi Amic *93 420 80 88/ www.taxi-amic-adaptat.com.* **Open** 7am-11pm Mon-Fri; 9am-10pm Sat, Sun. Fares are the same as for regular cabs, but there is a minimum fare of €12 for Barcelona city (€13.75 at weekends), and more for the surrounding areas.

Trams All tram lines throughout Barcelona are fully accessible for wheelchair-users, with ramps that can access all platforms. Watch out for the symbol on each platform that indicates where the wheelchair-accessible doors will be situated.

Wheelchair-friendly museums & galleries

All of the below should be accessible to wheelchair users. CCCB; Espai Gaudí – La Pedrera; Fundació Joan Miró; Fundacio Antoni Tàpies; MNAC; Museu Barbier-Mueller d'Art Precolombi; Museu d'Arqueologia de Catalunya; Museu de les Arts Decoratives; Museu del Calçat; Museu de Cera de Barcelona; Museu del Temple Expiatori de la Sagrada Família; Museu d'Història de Catalunya; Museu d'Història de la Ciutat; Museu de la Ciència – Cosmo Caixa; Museu de la Xocolata; Museu Frederic Marès; Museu Picasso; Museu Tèxtil i d'Indumentaria; Palau de la Música; Palau de la Virreina.

DRUGS

Many people smoke cannabis openly in Spain, but possession or consumption in public is illegal. In private, the law is contradictory: smoking is OK, but you can be nabbed for possession or distribution. Enforcement is often not the highest of police priorities, but you could theoretically receive a fine. Larger amounts entail a fine and, in extreme cases, prison. Smoking in bars is also prohibited. Cocaine is also common in Spain, but if you are caught in possession of this or any other Class A drug, you are looking at a hefty fine, and possibly a long prison sentence.

ELECTRICITY

The standard voltage in Spain is 220V. Plugs are of the two-round-pin type. You'll need a plug adaptor to use British-bought electrical devices. If you have US (110V) equipment, you will need a current transformer as well as an adaptor.

EMERGENCIES

Emergency services *112.* Police, fire or ambulance.
Ambulance/Ambulància *061.* For hospitals and other health services, *see pp314-15.*
Fire/Bombers/Bomberos *080.*
Mossos d'Esquadra *088.* Catalan police force.

GAY & LESBIAN

Casal Lambda *C/Verdaguer i Callís 10, Barri Gòtic (93 319 55 50/www.lambdaweb.org). Metro Urquinaona.* **Open** 5-9pm Mon-Fri. Closed Aug. **Map** p344 D4.
Gay cultural organisation.

Coordinadora Gai-Lesbiana *C/Violant d'Hongria Reina d'Aragó 156, Sants (93 298 00 29/ www.cogailes.org). Metro Plaça de Sants.* **Open** 7-9pm Mon-Fri. Closed Aug. **Map** p341 A7.
This gay umbrella group works with the Ajuntament on concerns for the gay, bisexual and transsexual communities. Its Telèfon Rosa service (900 601 601, open 6-10pm daily) gives help or advice and is open all year round.

Front d'Alliberament Gai de Catalunya *C/Verdi 88, Gràcia (93 217 26 69/www.fagc.org). Metro Fontana.* **Open** 6-9pm Mon-Thur. **Map** p339 H4.
A vocal group that produces the *Debat Gai* information bulletin.

HEALTH

Visitors can obtain emergency care through the public health service, Servei Català de la Salut. EU nationals are entitled to free basic medical attention if they have the European Emergency Health Card (Tarjeta Sanitaria Europea), also known as the Health Insurance Card. This replaced the E111 form and is valid for one year. Contact the health service in your country of residence for details. If you don't have one but can get one sent or faxed within a few days, you will be exempt from charges. Citizens of certain other countries that have a special agreement with Spain, among them several Latin American states, can also have access to free care. For general details, check the website www.gencat.net/temes/eng/salut.ht m, or call the Catalan government's 24-hour health information line on 902 11 14 44 (press 2 for information) or the Instituto Nacional de Seguridad Social on 901 50 20 50 (press 3 for information), www.seg-social.es.

For non-emergencies, it's usually quicker to use private travel insurance rather than the state system. Similarly, non-EU nationals with private medical insurance can also make use of state health services on a paying basis, but private clinics are simpler.

Accident & emergency

In an emergency, go to the casualty department (*Urgències*) of any of the main public hospitals in the city. All are open 24 hours daily. The most central are the Clínic, which also has a first-aid centre for less serious emergencies two blocks away (C/València 184, 93 227 93 00, open 8.30am-10pm Mon-Fri) and Perecamps. Call 061 for an ambulance.

Centre d'Urgències Perecamps *Avda Drassanes 13-15, Raval (93 441 06 00). Metro Drassanes or Paral·lel.* **Map** p342 E11.
Hospital Clínic *C/Villarroel 170, Eixample (93 227 54 00). Metro Hospital Clínic.* **Map** p338 E6.
Hospital Dos de Maig *C/Dos de Maig 301, Eixample (93 507 27 00). Metro Hospital de Sant Pau or Cartagena.* **Map** p339 L6.
Hospital del Mar *Passeig Marítim 25-29, Barceloneta (93 248 30 00). Metro Ciutadella-Vila Olímpica.* **Map** p343 J12.
Hospital de Sant Pau *C/Sant Antoni Maria Claret 167, Eixample (93 291 90 00). Metro Hospital de Sant Pau.* **Map** p339 L5.

Complementary medicine

Integral: Centre Mèdic i de Salut *C/Diputació 321, 1º 1ª, Eixample (93 467 74 20/www. integralcentremedic.com). Metro Girona.* **Open** (by appointment only) 9am-9pm Mon-Fri. Closed Aug. **Map** p339 H8.

Contraception

All pharmacies sell condoms (*condoms/preservativos*) and other forms of contraception including pills (*la píndola/la píldora*), which can be bought without a prescription. You'll generally need a prescription to get the morning-after pill (*la píndola del dia seguent/la píldora del dia siguiente*) but some CAP health centres (*see below*) will dispense it free themselves. Many bars and clubs have condom vending machines.

Centre Jove d'Anticoncepció i Sexualitat *C/La Granja 19-21, Gràcia (93 415 10 00/www.centre jove.org). Metro Lesseps.* **Open** *Sept-mid June* noon-7pm Mon-Thur; 10am-2pm Fri. *Mid June-July* 10am-5pm Mon-Thur; 10am-2pm Fri. *Aug* 10am-2pm Mon-Fri. Closed 2wks Aug. **Map** p339 H4. A family-planning centre aimed at young people (under-25s).

Dentists

Most dentistry is not covered by the Spanish public health service (to which EU citizens have access). Check the classified ads in *Metropolitan* (*see p317*) for English-speaking dentists.

Institut Odontològic Calàbria *Avda Madrid 141-145, Eixample (93 439 45 00/www.ioa.es). Metro Entença.* **Open** 9am-1pm, 3-8pm Mon-Fri. Closed 1wk Aug. **Credit** DC, MC, V. **Map** p341 C6. These well-equipped clinics provide a complete range of dental services. Some staff speak English. **Other locations** Institut Odontològic Sagrada Familia, C/Sardenya 319, Eixample (93 457 04 53); Institut Odontològic, C/Diputació 238, Eixample (93 342 64 00).

Doctors

A **Centre d'Assistència Primària** (CAP) is a local health centre (aka *ambulatorio*), where you should be seen fairly quickly by a doctor, but you may need an appointment. There are around 40 in Barcelona; see www.bcn.cat for a full list of locations.

CAP Casc Antic *C/Rec Comtal 24, Sant Pere (93 310 14 21). Metro Arc de Triomf.* **Open** 8am-8pm Mon-Fri; (emergencies only) 9am-5pm Sat. **Map** p344 F4.

CAP Doctor Lluís Sayé *C/Torres i Amat 8, Raval (93 301 27 05). Metro Universitat.* **Open** 8am-8pm Mon-Fri; (emergencies only) 9am-5pm Sat. **Map** p344 A1.

CAP Drassanes *Avda Drassanes 17-21, Raval (93 329 44 95). Metro Drassanes.* **Open** 8am-8pm Mon-Fri; (emergencies only) 9am-5pm Sat. **Map** p342 E11.

CAP Vila Olímpica *C/Joan Miró 17, Vila Olímpica (93 221 37 85). Metro Ciutadella-Vila Olímpica or Marina.* **Open** 8am-8.30pm Mon-Fri. **Map** p343 K11.

Googol Medical Centre *Gran Via Carles III 37-39, Eixample (93 330 24 12/mobile 627 669 524/www.googolmedicacentre.com). Metro Les Corts.* **Open** 10am-6pm Mon-Fri. **Map** p337 A5. An English-speaking clinic.

Dr Mary McCarthy *C/Aribau 215, pral 1ª, Eixample (93 200 29 24/mobile 607 220 040). FGC Gràcia/bus 14, 58, 64.* **Open** by appointment. **Map** p338 F5. Dr McCarthy is an internal medicine specialist from the US.

Hospitals

See p314 **Accident & emergency**.

Opticians

See p216.

Pharmacies

See p216.

STDs, HIV & AIDS

Free, anonymous blood tests for HIV and other STDs are given at the Unidad de Infección de Transmisión Sexual (93 441 46 12) at CAP Drassanes (*see below*). HIV tests are also available at the Coordinadora Gai-Lesbiana (*see p314*), at the Asociació Ciutadana Antisida de Catalunya (C/Lluna 11, Raval, 93 317 05 05, www. acasc.info) and at Projecte dels Noms (C/Comte Borrell 164-166, 93 318 20 56, www.bcncheck point.com, closed Aug).

Actua *C/Gomis 38, Zona Alta (93 418 50 00/www.actua.org.es). Metro Vallcarca/bus 22, 27, 28, 73.* **Open** (appointment only) *Sept-June* 9am-2pm, 4-7pm Mon-Thur; 9am-2pm Fri. *July* 9am-3pm. Closed Aug. Support group for people with HIV.

AIDS Information Line *Freephone 900 21 22 22.* **Open** *Mid Sept-May* 8am-5.30pm Mon-Thur; 8am-3pm Fri. *June-mid Sept* 8am-3pm Mon-Fri.

HELPLINES

Alcoholics Anonymous *93 317 77 77/www.alcoholicos-anonimos.org.* **Open** 10am-1pm, 5-8pm Mon-Fri.

Narcotics Anonymous *902 11 41 47/www.na-esp.org.* **Open** hours vary.

Telèfon de l'Esperança *93 414 48 48/www.telefono esperanza.com.* **Open** 24hrs daily. Counselling and specialist help groups, from psychiatric to legal.

ID

From the age of 14, Spaniards are legally obliged to carry their DNI (identity card). Foreigners are also meant to carry an ID card or passport, and are in theory subject to a fine – in practice, you're more likely to get a warning. If you don't want to carry it around with you (wisely, given the prevalence of petty crime), it's a good idea to carry a photocopy or a driver's licence instead: technically, it's not legal, but usually acceptable. ID is needed to check into a hotel, hire a car, pay with a card in shops and exchange or pay with travellers' cheques.

INSURANCE

For health care and EU nationals, *see p314*. Some non-EU countries have reciprocal health-care agreements with Spain, but for most travellers, it's usually more convenient to have private travel insurance, which will also, of course, cover you in case of theft and flight problems.

INTERNET

Despite relatively high costs, Spain boasts a high concentration of internet users, and there are internet centres all over Barcelona. Most libraries (*see below*) have free internet points and wireless access for public use, although you may have to join the library first. The

DIRECTORY

city council has undertaken to bring free wi-fi access to 500 public spaces by 2010.

Bornet Internet Cafè *C/Barra de Ferro 3, Born (93 268 15 07/ www.bornet-bcn.com). Metro Jaume I.* **Open** 10am-11pm Mon-Fri; noon-11pm Sat, Sun. **Rates** €2.80/hr. **Credit** (for payments over €5) AmEx, MC, V. **Map** p345 E6.
easyEverything *La Rambla 31, Barri Gòtic (93 301 75 07/www. easyeverything.com). Metro Drassanes or Liceu.* **Open** 8am-2am daily. **No credit cards.** **Map** p345 A6.

LANGUAGE

See pp323-24 for vocabulary; see p319 for classes.

LEFT LUGGAGE

Look for signs to the *consigna*.

Aeroport del Prat Terminal B **Open** 24hrs daily. **Rates** €4/day.
Estació d'Autobusos Barcelona-Nord *C/Ali Bei 80, Eixample. Metro Arc de Triomf.* **Open** 24hrs daily. **Rates** €3-€4.50/day. **Map** p343 E5.
Train stations Sants-Estació & Estació de França, Born **Open** 6am-11.45pm daily. **Rates** €3-€4.50/ day. **Map** p341 A4 & p343 E6. Some smaller railway stations also have left-luggage lockers.

LEGAL HELP

Consulates (*see p313*) help tourists in emergencies, and recommend lawyers.

Marti & Associats *Avda Diagonal 584, pral 1ª, Eixample (93 201 62 66/www.martilawyers. com). Bus 6, 7, 15, 33, 34.* **Open** *Sept-July* 9am-8pm Mon-Thur; 9am-7pm Fri. *Aug* 9am-2pm, 4-7pm Mon-Thur, 9am-2pm Fri. **Map** p338 E5.

LIBRARIES

There is a network of public libraries around the city that offers free internet access, some English novels and information on cultural activities. Membership is free. Opening times are generally 10am-2pm, 3.30-8.30pm Monday-Saturday and 10am-2pm Sunday. See www.bcn.cat/icub/biblioteques/ or call 93 316 10 00 for details.

Private libraries (*see below*) are better stocked but generally require paid membership to use their facilities.

Ateneu Barcelonès *C/Canuda 6, Barri Gòtic (93 343 61 21/www.ateneubcn.org). Metro Catalunya.* **Open** 9am-11pm daily. **Map** p344 C3. The city's best private library, plus a wonderfully peaceful interior garden patio and a quiet bar. Membership is €22.36 a month.
Biblioteca de Catalunya *C/Hospital 56, Raval (93 270 23 00/www.bnc.cat). Metro Liceu.* **Open** 9am-8pm Mon-Fri; 9am-2pm Sat. **Map** p344 A4. The Catalan national collection is housed in the medieval Hospital de la Santa Creu. Readers' cards are required, but free one-day research visits are allowed for over-18s (take your passport with you to prove your identity).
British Council/Institut Britànic *C/Amigó 83, Zona Alta (93 241 97 11/www.britishcouncil. es). FGC Muntaner.* **Open** *Oct-mid June* 9.30am-12.30pm, 3.30-9pm Mon-Fri; 10.30am-2pm Sat. *Mid June-July, Sept* 9.30am-12.30pm, 4-8.30pm Mon-Fri. *Aug* 9.30-12.30pm Mon-Fri. **Map** p338 E4. Membership is obligatory for use of the library and borrowing materials. The charge is €62 a year.
Mediateca *CaixaForum, Avda Marquès de Comillas 6-8, Montjuïc (902 22 30 40/93 476 86 51/ www.mediatecaonline.net). Metro Espanya.* **Open** *Sept-June* 10am-8pm Mon-Fri; 10am-10pm Sat. *July, Aug* 10am-8pm Mon, Thur, Fri; 10am-10pm Tue, Sat; 10am-11pm Wed. **Map** p341 B9. You can borrow books, magazines, CDs, etc. Membership is €6 (€3 reductions). The lending desk is open 10am-7.30pm Mon-Fri.

LOST PROPERTY

If you lose something at the airport, report it to the lost property centre (Oficina d'objectes perduts/Oficina de objetos perdidos, Bloque Técnico building, between terminals B and C, 93 298 33 49). If you have mislaid anything on a train, look for the Atenció al Passatger/Atención al Viajero desk or Cap d'Estació office at the nearest station to where your property went astray. Call ahead to the destination station, or call station information and ask for *objetos perdidos*.

Municipal Lost Property Office *Oficina de Troballes, Plaça Carles Pi i Sunyer 8-10, Barri Gòtic (93 402 70 00/010). Metro Catalunya or Jaume I.* **Open** 9am-2pm Mon-Fri. **Map** p344 C4. All documentation or valuables found on city public transport and taxis, or picked up by the police in the street, should eventually find their way to this Ajuntament office, just off Avda Portal de l'Àngel.
TMB Lost Property Office *Diagonal metro station, L5 entrance (93 318 70 74/www. tmb.net).* **Open** 8am-8pm Mon-Fri. **Map** p338 G6. Items found on most public transport services are sent to this office, where they are stored for seven working days. After that, they are sent to the municipal office (*see below*). If the item was lost on a tram, call 902 193 275; on FGC trains, 93 205 15 15; for taxis, call 93 400 50 26.

MEDIA

Spanish and Catalan newspapers tend to favour serious and distinctly lengthy political commentary. There are no sensationalist tabloids in Spain: for scandal, the *prensa rosa* ('pink press', or gossip magazines) is the place to look. Television channels, though, go straight for the mass market, with junk television (*telebasura*) prevalent. Catalan is the dominant language on both radio and TV, less so in print.

Daily newspapers

Free daily papers of reasonable quality, such as *20 Minutes* and *Metro*, are handed out in the city centre every morning. The dailies tend to the high brow. Spanish readers can try *ABC*, *El Mundo*, *El País* and *La Vanguardia*; those conversant in Catalan have *Avui* and one of the editions of *El Periódico*.

English language

Foreign newspapers are available at most kiosks on La Rambla and Passeig de Gràcia, along with FNAC (*see p198*).
Barcelona Connect
A small free magazine with tips for travellers to the city (www.barcelonaconnect.com).
Catalonia Today
English-language weekly with a round up of local news and cultural events (www.cataloniatoday.cat).

Metropolitan
A free monthly magazine for English-speaking locals, distributed in bars and other anglophone hangouts (www.barcelona-metropolitan.com).

Listings & classifieds

The main papers have daily 'what's on' listings, with entertainment supplements on Fridays (most run TV schedules on Saturdays). For monthly listings, see *Metropolitan* or the handy *Butxaca*, which can be picked up in cultural information centres, such as Palau de la Virreina on La Rambla; and freebies such as *Mondo Sonoro* (www.mondo-sonoro.com) or *GO* (www.go-mag.com), which can be found in bars and music shops. Of the dailies, *La Vanguardia* has the best classifieds; you can also consult it at www.clasificados.es. www.infojobs.net is a popular resource for job vacancies.
Guia del Ocio
A weekly listings magazine, published Fridays, in Spanish (www.guiadelociobcn.com).
Primeramà
The largest classified-ad publication (www.anuntis.es).
Time Out Barcelona
A comprehensive weekly listings magazine in Catalan. There are plans to add a monthly pull-out section in English (www.timeout.cat).

Radio

There are vast numbers of local, regional and national stations, with the Catalan language having a high profile. Catalunya Música (101.5 FM) is mainly classical and jazz, while Flaix FM (105.7 FM) provides news and music. For something a little more alternative, try Radio Bronka (99 FM) or Radio 3 (98.7 FM), which has a wonderfully varied music policy. You can listen to the BBC World Service on shortwave on 15485, 9410, 12095 and 6195 KHz, depending on the time of day.

Television

The emphasis of Spanish television is on mass entertainment, with Catalan channels only marginally better. Films are mainly dubbed and advertising is interminable. The best of the bunch may be Barcelona TV, which produces the city's most groundbreaking viewing. Also worth a look is La2

('La Dos'), which is often compared to BBC2, with good late-night movies and documentaries.

MONEY

Spain's currency is the euro. Each euro (€) is divided into 100 cents (¢), known as *céntims/céntimos*. Notes come in denominations of €500, €200, €100, €50, €20, €10 and €5. Due to the increasing circulation of counterfeit notes, smaller businesses may be reluctant to accept anything larger than €50.

Banks & currency exchanges

Banks (*bancos*) and savings banks (*caixes d'estalvis/cajas de ahorros*) usually accept euro travellers' cheques for a commission, but they tend to refuse any kind of personal cheque except one issued by that bank. Some bureaux de change (*cambios*) don't charge commission, but rates are worse. Obtaining money through ATMs (which are everywhere) with a debit or credit card is the easiest option, despite the fees often charged.

Bank hours Banks are normally open between 8.30am and 2pm Mon-Fri. From October to April, most branches also open between 8.30am and 1pm on Saturdays. From October to May many savings banks (normally beginning 'Caixa' or 'Caja') are also open late on Thursdays, 4.30-7.45pm.
Out-of-hours banking Foreign exchange offices at the airport (terminals A and B) are open 7am-11pm daily. Others in the centre open late: some on La Rambla open until midnight, later between July and September. At Sants, change money at La Caixa (8am-8pm daily), there's another change point at Plaça Cataluñya 7. At the airport and outside some banks are automatic exchange machines that accept notes in major currencies.

Credit & debit cards

Major credit cards are accepted in hotels, shops, restaurants and other places (metro ticket machines and pay-and-display parking machines, for instance). American Express and Diners Club cards are less accepted than MasterCard and Visa. Many debit cards from other European countries mayu also be accepted. You can withdraw cash with major cards from ATMs, and banks will also advance cash against a credit card.

Note: you need photographic ID (a passport, driving licence or something similar) when using a credit or debit card in a shop, but that is usually not required in a restaurant.

Lost/stolen cards All lines have English-speaking staff and are open 24 hours daily. Maestro do not have a Spanish helpline.
American Express 902 11 11 35.
Diners Club 901 10 10 11.
MasterCard 900 97 12 31.
Visa 900 99 11 24.

Tax

The standard rate for sales tax (IVA) is 16 per cent; this drops to seven per cent in hotels and restaurants, and four per cent on some books. IVA may or may not be included in listed prices at restaurants, and it usually isn't included in rates quoted at hotels. If it's not, the expression *IVA no inclòs/incluido* (sales tax not included) should appear after the price. Beware of this when getting quotes on expensive items. In shops displaying a 'Tax-Free Shopping' sticker, non-EU residents can reclaim tax on large purchases when leaving the country.

OPENING TIMES

Most shops open from 9/10am to 1/2pm, and then 4/5pm to 8/9pm, Monday to Saturday. Many smaller businesses don't reopen on Saturday afternoons. All-day opening (10am to 8pm or 9pm) is becoming more common, especially for larger and more central establishments.
   Markets open at 7/8am; most stalls are shut by 2pm, although many open on Fridays and Saturdays until 8pm.
   Note that in summer, many of Barcelona's shops and restaurants shut for all or part of August (we have noted this where possible in our listings). Some businesses work a shortened day from June to September, from 8am or 9am until 3pm. Many museums close one day each week, usually Mondays.

POLICE

Barcelona has several police forces: the Mossos d'Esquadra (in a uniform of navy and light blue with red trim), the Guàrdia Urbana (municipal police – navy and pale blue), the Policia Nacional (national police – darker blue uniforms and white shirts, or blue, combat-style gear). The Mossos are the Catalan government's police force and are taking over from the other two police forces but the GU and the PN will keep control of certain matters, like immigration and terrorism, which are dealt with by central government.

The Guàrdia Civil is a paramilitary force with green uniforms, policing highways, customs posts, government buildings and rural areas.

Reporting a crime

If you're robbed or attacked, report the incident as soon as possible at the nearest police station (*comisaría*), or dial 112. In the centre, the most convenient is the 24-hour Guàrdia Urbana station (La Rambla 43, Barri Gòtic, 092/93 256 24 30), which often has English-speaking officers on duty; they may transfer you to the Mossos d'Esquadra (C/Nou de la Rambla 76-80, Raval, 088/93 306 23 00) to report the crime formally. To do this, you'll need to make an official statement (*denuncia*). It's highly improbable that you will recover your property, but you need the *denuncia* to make an insurance claim. You can also make this statement over the phone or online (902 10 21 12, www.policia.es); except for crimes involving physical violence, or if the author has been identified. You'll still have to go to the *comisaría* within 72 hours to sign the *denuncia*, but you'll be able to skip some queues.

POSTAL SERVICES

Letters and postcards weighing up to 20g cost 31¢ within Spain; 60¢ to the rest of Europe; 78¢ to the rest of the world – though prices normally rise on 1 January. It's usually easiest to buy stamps at *estancs* (*see below*). Mail sent abroad is slow: five to six working days in Europe, eight to ten to the USA. Postboxes in the street are yellow, sometimes with a white or blue horn insignia. For postal information ring 902 19 71 97 or go to www.correos.es.

Correu Central *Plaça Antonio López, Barri Gòtic (93 486 80 50). Metro Barceloneta or Jaume I.* **Open** 8.30am-9.30pm Mon-Fri; 8.30am-2pm Sat. **Map** p345 D7. Take a ticket from the machine as you enter and wait for your turn. Apart from the typical postal

services, fax-sending and receiving is offered (with the option of courier delivery in Spain, using the Burofax option). To send something express delivery, ask for *urgente*.
Other locations Ronda Universitat 23 and C/Aragó 282, Eixample (both open 8.30am-8.30pm Mon-Fri, 9.30am-1pm Sat); and throughout the city.
Estancs/estancos Government-run tobacco shops, which are known as *estancs/estancos* (at times, just *tabac*) and identified by a brown-and-yellow sign, are important institutions in Spain. As well as tobacco – still popular in the country – they supply postage stamps, public transport *targetes* and phonecards.
Post boxes A PO box (*apartado postal*) address costs €59.50 annually.
Postal Transfer *C/Ausiàs Marc 13-17, Eixample (93 301 27 32). Metro Urquinaona.* **Open** 8.30am-8.30pm Mon-Fri; 9.30am-1pm Sat. Apart from postal services, there's Western Union money transfer, internet access, cheap international calls, fax, photocopying and banking.
Poste restante Poste restante letters should be sent to Lista de Correos, 08080 Barcelona, Spain. Pick-up is from the main post office (*see above*); you'll need your passport when coming to claim your mail.

RELIGION

Anglican:
St George's Church
C/Horaci 38, Zona Alta (93 417 88 67/www.st-georges-church. com). FGC Avda Tibidabo. **Main service** 11am Sun. An Anglican/Episcopalian church with a mixed congregation. Activities include the Alpha course (directed at faith-seekers), a women's club, bridge and Sunday school. See website for details.
Roman Catholic:
Parròquia Maria Rein *Ctra d'Esplugues 103, Zona Alta (93 203 41 15). Metro Maria Cristina/bus 22, 63, 75.* **Mass** 10.30pm Sun. **Map** p337 A1. Mass is said in English at the above time on Sunday.
Jewish Orthodox:
Sinagoga de Barcelona & Comunitat Israelita de Barcelona *C/Avenir 24, Zona Alta (93 209 31 47/ www.cibonline.org). FGC Gràcia.* **Prayers** call for times. **Map** p338 F5.

Muslim: Mosque Islamic Cultural Council of Catalunya *C/Tallers 55, entl, 1, 2, Raval (93 301 08 31). Metro Catalunya.* **Prayers** 2pm daily. Phone for other times. **Map** p342 F10.

SAFETY & SECURITY

Pickpocketing and bagsnatching are epidemic in Barcelona, with tourists a prime target. Be especially careful around the Old City, particularly La Rambla, as well as at stations and on public transport, the airport train being a favourite. However, thieves go anywhere tourists go, including parks, beaches and internet cafés. Most street crime is aimed at the inattentive, and can be avoided by taking precautions:
● Avoid giving invitations: don't keep wallets in accessible pockets, keep your bags closed and in front of you. When you stop, put bags down beside you (or hold them on your lap), where you can see them.
● Don't flash wads of cash or fancy cameras.
● In busy streets or crowded places, keep an eye on what is happening around you. If you're suspicious of someone, move somewhere else.
● As a rule, Barcelona street thieves tend to use stealth and surprise rather than violence. However, muggings and knife threats do sometimes occur. Avoid deserted streets in the city centre if you're on your own at night, and offer no resistance when threatened.
● Don't carry more money and valuables than you need: use your hotel's safe deposit facilities, and take out travel insurance.

SMOKING

One effect of the recent tightening of the tobacco law is that there are as many signs telling you that you can smoke, as there are telling you that you can't.

Smoking is banned in banks, shops and offices; while in hotels, bars and restaurants larger than 100sq m (1,076sq ft), non-smoking zones are required by law. Those smaller than 100sq m must decide and indicate whether they are smoking or non-smoking. An increasing amount are opting for non-smoking, but with tobacco still relatively cheap and socially acceptable, it's common to see small crowds of employees or customers puffing away on the pavement.

Most hotels have non-smoking rooms or floors; although if you ask for a non-smoking room, some hotels may just give you a room that has had the ashtray removed. Some restaurants and a few, but growing, number of hotels, however, are completely smoke-free. Smoking bans in such places as cinemas, theatres and on public transport are widely respected.

STUDY

Catalonia is generally well disposed towards the European Union, and the vast majority of foreign students who come to Spain under the EU's Erasmus scheme are studying at Catalan universities or colleges. Catalan is usually the language spoken in these universities, although some lecturers are more relaxed than others about the use of Castilian in class for the first few months.

Secretaria General de Joventut – Punt d'Informació Juvenil *C/Calabria 147-C/Rocafort 116, Eixample (reception 93 483 83 83/ information 93 483 83 84/ www.gencat.net/joventut).* Metro *Rocafort.* **Open** *Oct-May* 10am-2pm, 4-8pm Mon-Fri. *June-July, Sept* 10am-2pm, 4.30-8.30pm Mon-Thur, 10am-2pm Fri. *Aug* 9am-3pm. Closed 1wk Aug. **Map** p341 D8.
Generalitat-run centre with a number of services: information for young people on travel, work and study.

Language classes

If you plan to stay in bilingual Barcelona for a while, you may want (or need) to learn some Catalan. The city is also a popular location for those coming to the country to study Spanish. See http://centrosasociados.cervantes.es for schools recommended by Spain's official language institute, the Instituto Cervantes.

Babylon Idiomas *C/Bruc 65, pral 1ª, Eixample (93 467 36 36/ www.babylon-idiomas.com).* Metro *Girona.* **Open** 9am-8pm Mon-Fri. **Credit** MC, V. **Map** p344 H8.
Small groups (up to eight people) run at all levels of Spanish.
Consorci per a la Normalització Lingüística *C/Quintana 11, 1° 1ª, Barri Gòtic (93 412 72 24/www.cpnl.cat).* Metro *Liceu.* **Open** *Mid Sept-mid*

June 9am-2pm Mon-Fri. *Mid June-mid Sept* 9am-1pm, 4-5.30pm Mon-Thur; 9am-2pm Fri. **No credit cards. Map** p345 B5.
The Generalitat organisation for the promotion of the Catalan language has centres around the city offering Catalan courses for non-Spanish speakers at very low prices or even for free (level one).
Other locations C/Mallorca 115, entl 1ª, Eixample (93 451 24 45); and throughout the city.
Escola Oficial d'Idiomes de Barcelona – Drassanes *Avda Drassanes, Raval (93 324 93 30/www.eoibd.es).* Metro *Drassanes.* **Open** *Sept-June* 8.30am-9pm Mon-Fri. **Map** p342 E11.
This state-run school has semi-intensive four-month courses, starting in October and February (enrolment tends to be in either September or January; check the website for details), at all levels in Spanish.
Other locations Escola Oficial, Avda del Jordà 18, Vall d'Hebrón (93 418 74 85/93 418 68 33); and throughout the city.
Estudios Hispánicos de la Universitat de Barcelona *Gran Via de les Corts Catalanes 585, Eixample (information 93 403 55 19/www.eh.ub.es).* Metro *Universitat.* **Open** Information (Pati de Ciències entrance) *mid June-Aug* 9am-2pm Mon-Fri. *Sept-mid June* 9am-2pm, 4-5.30pm Mon-Thur; 9am-2pm Fri. **Credit** AmEx, DC, MC, V. **Map** p342 F8.
Intensive, fortnight, three-month and year-long Spanish language and culture courses.
International House *C/Trafalgar 14, Eixample (93 268 45 11/www.ihes.com/bcn).* Metro *Urquinaona.* **Open** 8am-9pm Mon-Fri; 10am-1.30pm Sat. **Map** p344 E3.
Intensive Spanish courses running all year round.

TELEPHONES

Phonecards and phone centres give cheaper call rates, especially for international calls.

Dialling & codes

Normal Spanish phone numbers have nine digits; the area code (93 in the province of Barcelona) must be dialled with all calls, both local and long-distance. Spanish mobile numbers always begin with 6. Numbers starting 900 are freephone lines, while other 90 numbers are special-rate services. Those starting

with 80 are high-rate lines and can only be called from within Spain.

International & long-distance calls

To make an international call, dial 00 and then the country code, followed by the area code (omitting the first zero in UK numbers), and then the number. Country codes are as follows:
Australia 61.
Canada 1.
Irish Republic 353.
New Zealand 64.
South Africa 27.
United Kingdom 44.
USA 1.
To phone Spain from abroad, dial 00, followed by 34, followed by the number.

Mobile phones

The mobile phone, or *móvil*, is omnipresent in Spain. Calls are paid for either through direct debit or by using prepaid phones, topped up with vouchers. Most mobiles from other European countries can be used in Spain, but you may need to set this up before you leave. You may be charged international roaming rates even when making a local call, and you will be charged for incoming calls. Not all US handsets are GSM-compatible; check with your service provider before you leave.
If you're staying more than a few weeks, it may work out cheaper to buy a pay-as-you-go package when you arrive, from places such as FNAC (*see p198*), or buy a local SIM card for your own phone. These usually include a little credit, which you can then top up (from newsagents, cash machines and *estancs*).

Operator services & useful phone numbers

Operators normally speak Catalan and Spanish only, except for international operators, most of whom speak English.

General information (Barcelona) 010 (8am-10pm Mon-Sat). From outside Catalonia, but within Spain, call 807 117 700.
International directory enquiries 11825.
International operator for reverse charge calls Europe 1008; rest of world 1005.
National directory enquiries 11818 (Telefónica, the cheapest) or

DIRECTORY

DIRECTORY

11888 (*Yellow Pages*, which is more expensive, or free on www.pagina samarillas.com), among others.

National operator for reverse charge calls 1009. After the recorded message, press the asterisk key twice, and then 4.

Pharmacies, postcodes, lottery 098.

Telephone faults service (Telefónica) 1002.

Time 093.

Wake-up calls 096. After the message, key in the time at which you wish to be woken, in the 24hr clock, in four figures: for example, 0830 for 8.30am, 2030 for 8.30pm.

Weather 807 170 365.

Phone centres

Phone centres (*locutorios*) are full of small booths where you can sit down and pay at the end. They offer cheap calls and avoid the need for change. Concentrated particularly in streets such as C/Sant Pau and C/Hospital in the Raval, and along C/Carders-C/Corders in Sant Pere, they generally offer other services too, including international money transfer, currency exchange and internet access.

Locutorio *C/Hospital 17, Raval (93 318 97 39). Metro Liceu.* **Open** 10am-10pm daily. **No credit cards. Map** p344 A2.

Oftelcom *C/Canuda 7, Barri Gòtic (93 342 73 71). Metro Catalunya.* **Open** 9am-midnight daily. **No credit cards. Map** p344 B2.

Public phones

The most common type of payphone in Barcelona accepts coins (5¢ and up), phonecards and credit cards. There is a multilingual digital display (press 'L' to change language) and written instructions in English and other languages. Take plenty of small coins with you. For the first minute of a daytime local call, you'll be charged around 8¢; to a mobile phone around 13¢; and to a 902 number around 20¢. Calls to directory enquiries on 11818 are free from payphones, but you'll usually have to insert a coin to make the call (it will be returned when you hang up). If you're still in credit at the end of your call, you can make further calls by pushing the 'R' button and dialling again. Bars and cafés often have payphones, but these can be more expensive than street booths.

Telefónica phonecards (*targetes telefónica/tarjetas telefónica*) are sold at newsstands and *estancs* (*see p318*). Other cards sold at phone centres, shops and newsstands give cheaper rates on all but local calls. This latter type of card contains a toll-free number to call from any phone.

TIME

The local time is one hour ahead of Greenwich Mean Time, six hours ahead of US Eastern Standard Time and nine hours ahead of Pacific Standard Time. Daylight saving time runs concurrently with the United Kingdom: clocks go back in October and forward in March.

TIPPING

There are no rules for tipping in Barcelona, but locals don't tip much. It's fair to leave five to ten per cent in restaurants, unless the service has been bad. People sometimes leave a little change in bars. In taxis, tipping is not standard, but many people round up to the nearest 50¢. It's usual to tip hotel porters.

TOILETS

The problem of people urinating in the streets of the Old City has pressed the Ajuntament into introducing more public toilets. There are 24-hour public toilets in Plaça del Teatre, just off La Rambla, and more at the top of C/dels Àngels, opposite the MACBA. Most of the main railway stations have clean toilets. Parks such as Ciutadella and Güell have a few dotted about, but you need a 20¢ coin to use them. The beach at Barceloneta has six (heavily in demand) Portaloos; there are five further up at the beach at Sant Sebastià, and in season there are also toilets open under the boardwalk, along the beach towards the Port Olímpic. Most bar and café owners do not mind if you use their toilets (you may have to ask for the key), although some in the centre and at the beach are less amenable. Fast-food restaurants are good standbys.

Toilets are known as *serveis*, *banys* or *lavabos* (in Catalan) or *servicios*, *aseos*, *baños* or *lavabos* (in Spanish).

In bars or restaurants, the ladies' is generally denoted by a D (*dones/damas*), and occasionally by

an M (*mujeres*) or S (*señoras*) on the door; while the men's mostly say H (*homes/hombres*) or C (*caballeros*).

TOURIST INFORMATION

010 phoneline

Open 8am-10pm Mon-Sat. This city-run information line is aimed mainly at locals, but it does an impeccable job of answering all kinds of queries. There are sometimes English-speaking operators available. Call 807 117 700 from outside Catalonia but within Spain.

Centre d'Informació de la Virreina *Palau de la Virreina, La Rambla 99, Barri Gòtic (93 316 10 00/www.bcn.cat/cultura). Metro Liceu.* **Open** 10am-8pm Mon-Sat; 11am-3pm Sun. **Ticket sales** Virreina exhibitions 11am-8pm Tue-Sat; 11am-3pm Sun; timetable varies for other events, generally 10am-7pm Tue-Sat. **Map** p344 B4. The information office of the city's culture department has details of shows, exhibitions and special events.

Oficines d'Informació Turística *Plaça Catalunya, Eixample (information 93 285 38 34/93 285 38 32/www.bcn.cat/ www.barcelonaturisme.com). Metro Catalunya.* **Open** *Office* 9am-9pm daily. *Call centre* 9am-8pm Mon-Fri. **Map** p344 C2.

The main office of the city tourist board is underground on the El Corte Inglés/south side of the square: look for the big red signs with 'i' superimposed in white. It has information, money exchange, a shop and a hotel booking service, and sells phonecards and public transport for shows, sights and public transport. **Other locations** C/Ciutat 2 (ground floor of Ajuntament), Barri Gòtic; C/Sardenya (opposite the Sagrada Familia), Eixample; Plaça Portal Pau (opposite Monument a Colom), Port Vell; Sants station; La Rambla 115, Barri Gòtic; corner of Plaça d'Espanya and Avda Maria Cristina, Eixample; airport.

Palau Robert *Passeig de Gràcia 107, Eixample (93 238 80 91/www. gencat.net/probert). Metro Diagonal.* **Open** 10am-7pm Mon-Sat; 10am-2.30pm Sun. **Map** p338 G7. The Generalitat's centre for tourists is at the junction of Passeig de Gràcia and Avda Diagonal. It has maps and other essentials for Barcelona, but its speciality is a huge range of information in different media for attractions to be found elsewhere in Catalonia.

It also sometimes hosts interesting exhibitions on local art, culture, gastronomy and nature and has a pleasant garden out back.
Other locations Airport terminals A (93 478 47 04) and B (93 478 05 65), open 9am-9pm daily.

VISAS & IMMIGRATION

Spain is one of the European Union countries that's covered by the Schengen Agreement, which led to common visa regulations and limited border controls among member states that were signatories in the agreement. However, neither the UK nor the Republic of Ireland are signatories in this agreement; nationals of those countries will need their passports. Most European Union citizens, as well as Norwegian and Icelandic nationals, only need a national identity card.

Visas are not required for citizens of the United States, Canada, Australia and New Zealand who are arriving for stays of up to 90 days and not for work or study. Citizens of South Africa and other countries need visas to enter Spain; approach Spanish consulates and embassies in other countries for information. Visa regulations do change, so check before leaving home.

WATER

Tap water is drinkable in Barcelona, but it tastes of chlorine. Bottled water is what you will be served if you ask for *un aigua/agua* in a bar or restaurant; *fresca* is cold, *natural* is at room temperature. *Sin gas* is still water, *con gas* sparkling.

WHEN TO GO

Barcelona is usually agreeable year-round, though the humidity

in summer can be debilitating, particularly when it's overcast. Many shops, bars and restaurants close (especially during August). Public transport and cinemas can overcompensate for the summer heat with bracing air-conditioning.

Climate

Spring is unpredictable: warm, sunny days can alternate with winds and showers. Temperatures in May and June are pretty much perfect; the city is especially lively around 23 June, when locals celebrate the beginning of summer with all kinds of fireworks and fiestas. July and August can be decidedly unpleasant, as the summer heat and humidity kick in and make many locals leave town. Autumn weather is generally warm and fresh, with heavy downpours common around October. Crisp, cool sunshine is normal from December to February. Snow is very rare.

Public holidays

Most shops, banks and offices, and many bars and restaurants, close on public holidays (*festius/festivos*), and public transport is limited. Many take long weekends whenever a major holiday comes along. If the holiday coincides with, say, a Tuesday or a Thursday, many people will take the Monday or Friday off: this is what is known as a *pont/puente*.

New Year's Day/Any Nou 1 Jan
Three Kings/Reis Mags 6 Jan
Good Friday/Divendres Sant
Easter Monday/Dilluns de Pasqua
May (Labour) Day/Festa del Treball 1 May

Mon after Whitsun/Segona Pascua 1 June
Sant Joan 24 June
Verge de l'Assumpció 15 Aug
Diada de Catalunya 11 Sept
La Mercè 24 Sept
Dia de la Hispanitat 12 Oct
All Saints' Day/Tots Sants 1 Nov
Constitution Day/Día de la Constitución 6 Dec
La Immaculada 8 Dec
Christmas Day/Nadal 25 Dec
Boxing Day/Sant Esteve 26 Dec

WORKING & LIVING

Common recourses for English speakers in Barcelona are to find work in the tourist sector (often seasonal and outside the city), in a downtown bar or teaching English in the numerous language schools. For the latter, it helps to have the TEFL (Teaching English as a Foreign Language) qualifications; these can be gained in reputable institutions in the city as well as in your home country. Bear in mind that teaching work dries up in June until the end of summer, usually September, although it's possible to find intensive teaching courses during July. The amount of jobs in call centres for English speakers and other foreigners has also rocketed of late.

Queries regarding residency and legal requirements for foreigners who are working in Spain can be addressed to the Ministry of Interior's helpline 060 (where there are English-speaking operators). The Ministerio de Administraciones Públicas website www.map.es then click on extranjeria lays out the regulations. You can also download the forms you need.

EU citizens

EU citizens living in Spain for more three months are no longer issued with a resident's card (*tarjeta de residencia*) but need to have ID or passport from their own country.

Non-EU citizens

While in Spain on a tourist visa, you are not legally allowed to work. Those wanting a work permit officially need to be made a job offer while still in their home country. The process is lengthy and not all applications are successful. If you do get lucky, you can then apply for residency at a Spanish consulate in your home country.

THE LOCAL CLIMATE

Average temperatures and monthly rainfall in Barcelona.

	High (°C/°F)	Low (°C/°F)	Rainfall (mm/in)
Jan	13 / 56	6 / 43	44 / 1.7
Feb	15 / 59	7 / 45	36 / 1.4
Mar	16 / 61	8 / 47	48 / 1.9
Apr	18 / 64	10 / 50	51 / 2.0
May	21 / 70	14 / 57	57 / 2.2
June	24 / 76	17 / 63	38 / 1.5
July	27 / 81	20 / 67	22 / 0.9
Aug	29 / 84	20 / 67	66 / 2.6
Sept	25 / 78	18 / 64	79 / 3.1
Oct	22 / 71	14 / 57	94 / 3.7
Nov	17 / 63	9 / 49	74 / 2.9
Dec	15 / 59	7 / 45	50 / 2.5

DIRECTORY

Airline flights are one of the biggest producers of the global warming gas CO_2. But with **The CarbonNeutral Company** you can make your travel a little greener.

Go to **www.carbonneutral.com** to calculate your flight emissions then 'neutralise' them through international projects which save exactly the same amount of carbon dioxide.

Contact us at **shop@carbonneutral.com** or call into the office on **0870 199 99 88** for more details.

CarbonNeutral®flights

Spanish Vocabulary

Spanish is generally referred to as *castellano* (Castilian) rather than *español*. Many locals prefer to speak Catalan, but everyone in the city can also speak Spanish, and will switch to it if visitors show signs of linguistic jitters. The Spanish familiar form for 'you' – *tú* – is used very freely, but it's safer to use the more formal *usted* with older people and strangers (verbs below are given in the *usted* form). For menu terms, *see p156*.

PRONUNCIATION

● c before an **i** or an **e** and **z** are like **th** in **th**in
● c in all other cases is as in cat
● g before an **i** or an **e** and **j** are pronounced with a guttural **h**-sound that doesn't exist in English – like **ch** in Scottish 'lo**ch**', but much harder
● g in all other cases is as in **g**et
● h at the beginning of a word is normally silent
● ll is pronounced almost like a **y**
● ñ is like **ny** in can**y**on
● a single **r** at the beginning of a word and **rr** elsewhere are heavily rolled
● v is more like an English **b**
● In words ending with a vowel, **n** or **s**, the penultimate syllable is stressed: eg *barato, viven, habitaciones.*
● In words ending with any other consonant, the last syllable is stressed: eg *exterior, universidad.*
● An accent marks the stressed syllable in words that depart from these rules: eg *estación, tónica.*

BASICS

● **please** *por favor*; **thank you** (very much) *(muchas) gracias*; **you're welcome** *de nada*
● **hello** *hola*; **hello** (when answering the phone) *hola, diga*
● **goodbye/see you later** *adiós/ hasta luego*
● **excuse me/sorry** *perdón*;
● **excuse me, please** *oiga* (the standard way to attract attention, politely; literally, 'hear me')
● **OK/fine**/(to a waiter) **that's enough** *vale*
● **open** *abierto*; **closed** *cerrado*
● **entrance** *entrada*; **exit** *salida*
● **very** *muy*; **and** *y*; **or** *o*; **with** *con*; **without** *sin*; **enough** *bastante*

MORE EXPRESSIONS

● **good morning/good day** *buenos días*; **good afternoon/ good evening** *buenas tardes*; **good evening** (after dark)/**good night** *buenas noches*
● **do you speak English?** *¿habla inglés?*; **I'm sorry, I don't speak Spanish** *lo siento, no hablo castellano*; **I don't understand** *no lo entiendo*; **speak more slowly, please** *hable más despacio, por favor*; **wait a moment** *espere un momento*; **can you say that in Catalan?** *¿Cómo se dice eso en catalán?*
● **what's your name?** *¿cómo se llama?* **my name is…** *me llamo…*
● **Sir/Mr** *señor* (sr); **Madam/Mrs** *señora* (sra); **Miss** *señorita* (srta)
● **where is…?** *¿dónde está…?*; **why?** *¿porqué?*; **who?** *¿quién?*; **when?** *¿cuándo?*; **what?** *¿qué?*; **where?** *¿dónde?*; **how?** *¿cómo?*; **who is it?** *¿quién es?*; **is/are there any…?** *¿hay…?*
● **what time does it open/ close?** *¿a qué hora abre/cierra?*
● **pull** (on signs) *tirar*; **push** *empujar*
● **I would like** *quiero*; **how many would you like?** *¿cuántos quiere?*; **how much is it?** *¿cuánto vale?*
● **price** *precio*; **free** *gratis*; **discount** *descuento*; **do you have any change?** *¿tiene cambio?*
● **I don't want** *no quiero*; **I like** *me gusta*; **I don't like** *no me gusta*
● **good** *bueno/a*; **bad** *malo/a*; **well/ badly** *bien/mal*; **small** *pequeño/a*; **big** *gran, grande*; **expensive** *caro/a*; **cheap** *barato/a*; **hot** (food, drink) *caliente*; **cold** *frío/a*;
● **bank** *banco*; **to rent** *alquilar*; (for) **rent, rental** (en) *alquiler*; **post office** *correos*; **stamp** *sello*; **postcard** *postal*; **toilet** *el baño, el servicio, el lavabo*
● **airport** *aeropuerto*; **rail station** *estación de ferrocarril/ estación de RENFE* (Spanish railways); **metro station** *estación de metro*; **car** *coche*; **bus** *autobús*; **train** *tren*; **bus stop** *parada de autobus*; **the next stop** *la próxima parada*; **a ticket** *un billete*; **return** *de ida y vuelta*
● **excuse me, do you know the way to…?** *¿oiga, señor/ señora, sabe cómo llegar a…?*
● **left** *izquierda*; **right** *derecha*

● **here** *aquí*; **there** *allí*; **straight on** *recto*; **near** *cerca*; **far** *lejos*; **it is far?** *¿está lejos?*

ACCOMMODATION

● **do you have a double/single room for tonight?** *¿tiene una habitación doble/para una persona/para esta noche?*
● **we have a booking** *tenemos reserva*; **an inside/outside room** *una habitación interior/exterior*
● **with/without bathroom** *con/sin baño*; **shower** *ducha*; **double bed** *cama de matrimonio*; **with twin beds** *con dos camas*; **breakfast included** *desayuno incluido*; **air-conditioning** *aire acondicionado*

TIME

● **now** *ahora*; **later** *más tarde*
● **yesterday** *ayer*; **today** *hoy*; **tomorrow** *mañana*; **tomorrow morning** *mañana por la mañana*
● **morning** *la mañana*; **midday** *mediodía*; **afternoon/evening** *la tarde*; **night** *la noche*
● **at what time…?** *¿a qué hora…?*

NUMBERS

● **0** *cero*; **1** *un, uno, una*; **2** *dos*; **3** *tres*; **4** *cuatro*; **5** *cinco*; **6** *seis*; **7** *siete*; **8** *ocho*; **9** *nueve*; **10** *diez*; **11** *once*; **12** *doce*; **13** *trece*; **14** *catorce*; **15** *quince*; **16** *dieciséis*; **17** *diecisiete*; **18** *dieciocho*; **19** *diecinueve*; **20** *veinte*; **21** *veintiuno*; **22** *veintidós*; **30** *treinta*; **40** *cuarenta*; **50** *cincuenta*; **60** *sesenta*; **70** *setenta*; **80** *ochenta*; **90** *noventa*; **100** *cien*; **200** *doscientos*; **1,000** *mil*; **1,000,000** *un millón*

DATES & SEASONS

● **Monday** *lunes*; **Tuesday** *martes*; **Wednesday** *miércoles*; **Thursday** *jueves*; **Friday** *viernes*; **Saturday** *sábado*; **Sunday** *domingo*
● **January** *enero*; **February** *febrero*; **March** *marzo*; **April** *abril*; **May** *mayo*; **June** *junio*; **July** *julio*; **August** *agosto*; **September** *septiembre*; **October** *octubre*; **November** *noviembre*; **December** *diciembre*
● **spring** *primavera*; **summer** *verano*; **autumn** *otoño*; **winter** *invierno*

Catalan Vocabuary

Over a third of Barcelona residents use Catalan as their everyday language, around 70 per cent speak it fluently, and more than 90 per cent understand it. If you take an interest and learn a few phrases, it is likely to be appreciated.

Catalan phonetics are different from those of Spanish, with a wider range of vowel sounds and soft consonants. Catalans use the familiar (*tu*) rather than the polite (*vostè*) forms of the second person very freely, but for convenience, verbs are given here in the polite form. For menu terms, *see p173*.

PRONUNCIATION

● In Catalan, words are run together, so *si us plau* (please) is more like *sees-plow*.
● ç, and c before an i or an e, are like a soft s, as in sit; c in all other cases is as in cat
● e, when unstressed as in *cerveses* (beers), or Jaume I, is a weak sound, like centre or comfortable
● g before i or e and j are pronounced like s in pleasure; tg and tj are similar to dg in badge
● g after an i at the end of a word (Puig) is a hard ch sound, as in watch; otherwise, g is as in get
● h is silent
● ll is somewhere between the y in yes and the lli in million
● l·l has a slightly stronger stress on a single l sound; paral·lel sounds similar to the English parallel
● o at the end of a word is like the u sound in flu; ó is like the o in a word is similar to the o in tomato; ò is like the o in hot
● r beginning a word and rr are heavily rolled; but at the end of many words is almost silent, so *carrer* (street) sounds like carr-ay
● s at the beginning and end of words and ss between vowels are soft, as in sit; a single s between two vowels is a z sound, as in lazy
● t after l or n at the end of a word is almost silent
● v is more like an English b
● x at the beginning of a word, or after a consonant or the letter i, is like the sh in shoe, at other times like the English expert
● y after an n at the end of a word or in nys is not a vowel but adds a nasal stress and a y-sound to the n

BASICS

● please *si us plau*; thank you (very much) *(moltes) gràcies*; very good/great/OK *molt bé*; you're welcome *de res*
● hello *hola*; hello (when answering the phone) *hola, digui'm*
● goodbye/see you later *adéu/ fins després*
● excuse me/sorry *perdoni/disculpi*; excuse me, please *escolti* (literally, 'listen to me'); OK/fine *val/d'acord*
● open *obert*; closed *tancat* entrance *entrada*; exit *sortida* very *molt*; and *i*; or *o*; with *amb*; without *sense*; enough *prou*

MORE EXPRESSIONS

● good morning, good day *bon dia*; good afternoon/evening *bona tarda*; good evening (after dark), good night *bona nit*
● do you speak English? *parla anglés?*; I'm sorry, I don't speak Catalan *ho sento, no parlo català*; I don't understand *no ho entenc*; speak more slowly, please *parli més a poc a poc, si us plau*; can you say that in Spanish, please? *m'ho pot dir en castellà, si us plau?*; how do you say that in Catalan? *com es diu això en català?*
● what's your name? *com es diu?*; my name is... *em dic...*
● Sir/Mr *senyor (sr)*; Madam/ Mrs *senyora (sra)*; Miss *senyoreta (srta)*
● where is...? *on és...?*; why? *perquè?*; who? *qui?*; when? *quan?*; what? *qué?*; where? *on?*; how? *com?*; who is it? *qui és?*; is/are there any...? *hi ha...?/n'hi ha de...?*
● I would like...? *vull...* (literally, 'I want'); how many would you like? *quants en vol?*; how much is it? *quant val?*
● price *preu*; free *gratuit/de franc*; change, exchange *canvi*
● I don't want *no vull*; I like *m'agrada*; I don't like *no m'agrada*
● good *bo/bona*; bad *dolent/a*; well/badly *bé/malament*; small *petit/a*; big *gran*; expensive *car/a*; cheap *barat/a*; hot (food, drink) *calent/a*; cold *fred/a*
● toilet *el bany/el servei/el lavabo*
● airport *aeroport*; rail station *estació de tren/estació de RENFE*

(Spanish railways); metro station *estació de metro*
● car *cotxe*; bus *autobús*; train *tren*; bus stop *parada d'autobús*; the next stop *la propera parada*
● a ticket *un bitllet*; return *d'anada i tornada*
● left *esquerra*; right *dreta*
● here *aquí*; there *allà*; straight on *tot recte*; near *a prop*; far *lluny*; at the corner *a la cantonada*; as far as *fins a*; towards *cap a*; is it far? *és lluny?*

TIME

● now *ara*; later *més tard*
● yesterday *ahir*; today *avui*; tomorrow *demà*; tomorrow morning *demà pel matí*
● morning *el matí*; midday *migdia*; afternoon *la tarda*; evening *el vespre*; night *la nit*; late night (roughly, 1-6am) *la matinada*
● at what time...? *a quina hora...?*; in an hour *en una hora*; at 2 *a les dues*

NUMBERS

● 0 *zero*; 1 *u, un, una*; 2 *dos, dues*; 3 *tres*; 4 *quatre*; 5 *cinc*; 6 *sis*; 7 *set*; 8 *vuit*; 9 *nou*; 10 *deu*; 11 *onze*; 12 *dotze*; 13 *tretze*; 14 *catorze*; 15 *quinze*; 16 *setze*; 17 *disset*; 18 *divuit*; 19 *dinou*; 20 *vint*; 21 *vint-i-u*; 22 *vint-i-dos*, *vint-i-dues*; 30 *trenta*; 40 *quaranta*; 50 *cinquanta*; 60 *seixanta*; 70 *setanta*; 80 *vuitanta*; 90 *noranta*; 100 *cent*; 200 *dos-cents*, *dues-centes*; 1,000 *mil*; 1,000,000 *un milló*

DATES & SEASONS

● Monday *dilluns*; Tuesday *dimarts*; Wednesday *dimecres*; Thursday *dijous*; Friday *divendres*; Saturday *dissabte*; Sunday *diumenge*
● January *gener*; February *febrer*; March *març*; April *abril*; May *maig*; June *juny*; July *juliol*; August *agost*; September *setembre*; October *octubre*; November *novembre*; December *desembre*
● spring *primavera*; summer *estiu*; autumn *tardor*; winter *hivern*

Further Reference

BOOKS

Food & drink

Colman Andrews *Catalan Cuisine* A mine of information on food and more (with usable recipes).
Anya von Bremzen *New Spanish Table* A guide to Spanish staples with some entertaining anecdotes.
Alan Davidson *Tio Pepe Guide to the Seafood of Spain and Portugal* An excellent pocket-sized guide tof Spain's fishy delights.

Guides & walks

J Amelang, X Gil & GW McDonogh *Twelve Walks through Barcelona's Past* Well-thought-out walks by historical theme. Original and better informed than many walking guides.
Xavier Güell *Gaudí Guide* A handy guide, with good background on the architect's work.
Juliet Pomés Leiz & Ricardo Feriche *Barcelona Design Guide* Engaging listing of everything ever considered 'designer' in BCN.

History, architecture, art & culture

Jimmy Burns *Barça: A People's Passion* The first full-scale history in English of one of the world's most overblown football clubs.
JH Elliott *The Revolt of the Catalans* Fascinating, detailed account of the Guerra dels Segadors and the Catalan revolt of the 1640s.
Felipe Fernández Armesto *Barcelona: A Thousand Years of the City's Past* A solid history.
Ronald Fraser *Blood of Spain* A vivid oral history of the Spanish Civil War.
Gijs van Hensbergen *Gaudí* A thorough account of his life.
John Hooper *The New Spaniards* An incisive and very readable survey of the changes in Spanish society since the death of Franco.
Robert Hughes *Barcelona* The most comprehensive single book about Barcelona.
Temma Kaplan *Red City, Blue Period: Social Movements in Picasso's Barcelona* An interesting book, tracing the interplay of avant-garde art and avant-garde politics in the 1900s.

George Orwell *Homage to Catalonia* The classic account of Barcelona in revolution.
Abel Paz *Durruti, The People Armed* A biography of the legendary Barcelona anarchist.
Ignasi Solà-Morales *Fin de Siècle Architecture in Barcelona* Wide-ranging description of the city's Modernista heritage.
Colm Tóibín *Homage to Barcelona* Evocative and perceptive journey around the city: good on the booming Barcelona of the 1980s.
Manuel Vázquez Montalbán *Barcelonas* Idiosyncratic but insightful reflections by one of the city's most prominent writers.
Rainer Zerbst *Antoni Gaudí* Lavishly illustrated survey.

Literature

Pere Calders *The Virgin of the Railway and Other Stories* Ironic, engaging, quirky stories by a Catalan writer who spent many years in exile in Mexico.
Victor Català *Solitude* This masterpiece by female novelist Caterina Albert shocked readers in 1905 with its open, modern treatment of female sexuality.
Ildefonso Falcones *Cathedral of the Sea* Hugely popular historical novel, centred on the basilica of Santa Maria del Mar in the Born.
Juan Marsé *The Fallen* Classic novel of survival in Barcelona during the long *posguerra*.
Joanot Martorell & Joan Martí de Gualba *Tirant lo Blanc* The first European prose novel, from 1490: a rambling, bawdy, shaggy-dog story of travels, romances and chivalric adventures.
Eduardo Mendoza *City of Marvels; Year of the Flood* A sweeping saga of the city between its great Exhibitions in 1888 and 1929; and a more recent novel of passions in the city of the 1950s.
Maria-Antònia Oliver *Antipodes; Study in Lilac* Two adventures of Barcelona's first feminist detective.
Mercè Rodoreda *The Time of the Doves; My Cristina and Other Stories* A translation of Plaça del Diamant, the most widely read of all Catalan novels; plus a collection of similarly bittersweet short tales.

Carlos Ruiz Zafón *Shadow of the Wind* Enjoyable neo-Gothic melodrama set in post-war Barcelona.
Manuel Vázquez Montalbán *The Angst-Ridden Executive; An Olympic Death; Southern Seas* Three thrillers starring detective and gourmet Pepe Carvalho.

MUSIC

Barcelona Raval Sessions Dance/funk compilation of local artists, famous and unknown.
Lluís Llach An icon of the 1960s and '70s protest against the Franco regime. Brilliant musicianship.
Maria del Mar Bonet Though from Mallorca, del Mar Bonet sings in Catalan and specialises in her own compositions, North African music and Mallorcan music.
Mayte Martín Virtuoso flamenco and bolero singer.
Angel Molina Leading Barcelona DJ with an international reputation and various remix albums released.
Ojos de Brujo Leading proponents of *rumba catalana*.
The Pinker Tones Chirpy Barcelona-based duo spanning lounge, electro, funk and pop.
Pep Sala Excellent musician and survivor of the extremely successful Catalan group Sau.

WEBSITES

www.barcelonareporter.com Local news items in English.
www.barcelonarocks.com Music listings and news.
www.barcelonaturisme.com Official tourist authority info.
www.bcn.cat The city council's information-packed website.
www.bcn.cat/guia Excellent interactive Barcelona street maps.
www.catalanencyclopaedia. com Catalan history and geography. In English.
www.lecool.com Youth-oriented round-up of offbeat cultural events.
www.mobilitat.net Generalitat's website about getting from A to B in Catalonia, by bus, car or train.
www.renfe.es Spanish railways.
www.timeout.cat Comprehensive local listings magazine, in Catalan.
www.timeout.com/barcelona The online city guide.

Index

INDEX

INDEX

Advertisers' Index

Please refer to the relevant pages for contact details

Maps

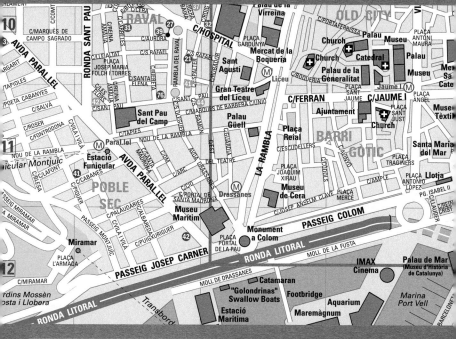

Legend	
Major sight or landmark	
Hospital or college	
Railway station	
Parks	
River	
Carretera	
Main road	
Main road tunnel	
Pedestrian road	
Airport	✈
Church	✚
Metro station, FGC station	Ⓜ 🌀
Area name	EIXAMPLE

Trips Out of Town

© Copyright Time Out Group 2009

50 km
25 miles

MEDITERRANEAN
SEA

334 Time Out Barcelona

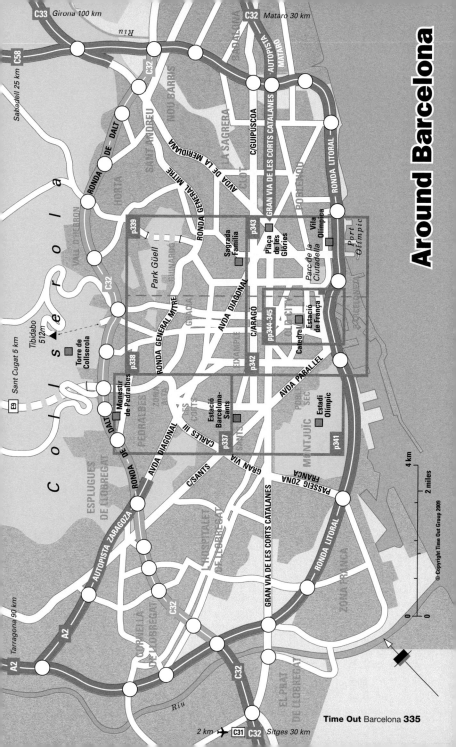

Around Barcelona

C33 Girona 100 km

C58 C32 Mataro 30 km

Riu

C32 AUTOPISTA MATARO

Sabadell 25 km

BADALONA

C/GUIPUSCOA

NOU BARRIS

SANT ANDREU

RONDA — DE — DALT

RONDA

VALL D'HEBRON

HORTA

C32

GUINARDO

RONDA GENERAL MITRE

AVDA DE LA MERIDIANA

CLOT

GRAN VIA DE LES CORTS CATALANES

RONDA LITORAL

POBLENOU

p339

Park Güell

p343

Sagrada Família

Plaça de les Glòries

Via Olímpica

Parc de la Ciutadella

Port Olímpic

BOGATELL

Tibidabo 512m

Torre de Collserola

C o l l s e r o l a

AVDA DIAGONAL

GRACIA

EIXAMPLE

C/ARAGO

p342

RONDA GENERAL MITRE

p338

Catedral

Estació de França

pp344-345

E9

Sant Cugat 5 km

RONDA — DE — DALT

Monestir de Pedralbes

PEDRALBES

ZONA UNIVERSITARIA

LES CORTS

AVDA DIAGONAL

CARLES III

C/SANTS

Estació Barcelona-Sants

p337

GRAN VIA

SANTS

AVDA PARALLEL

POBLE SEC

MONTJUIC

Estadi Olímpic

p341

AUTOPISTA ZARAGOZA

ESPLUGUES DE LLOBREGAT

L'HOSPITALET DE LLOBREGAT

C/SANTS

PASSEIG ZONA FRANCA

GRAN VIA DE LES CORTS CATALANES

RONDA LITORAL

ZONA FRANCA

A2 Tarragona 90 km

A2

CORNELLA DE LLOBREGAT

C32

EL PRAT DE LLOBREGAT

Riu

4 km

2 miles

0

© Copyright Time Out Group 2009

2 km C31 C32 Sitges 30 km

Time Out Barcelona **335**

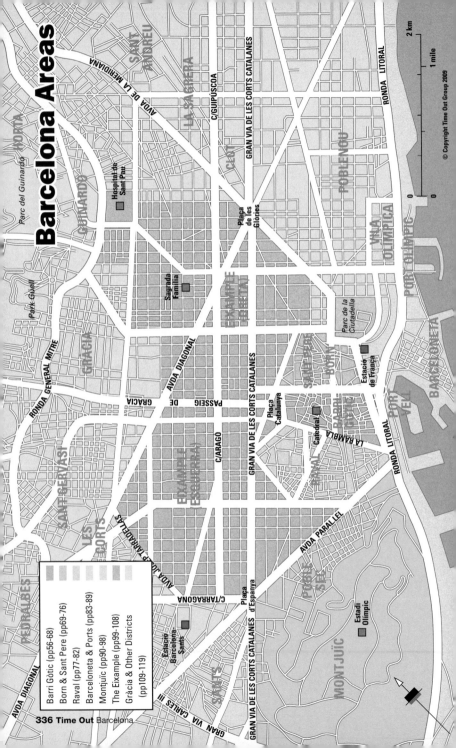

Barcelona Areas

PEDRALBES

HORTA

Parc del Guinardó

Parc Güell

GUINARDÓ

SANT ANDREU

AVDA DE LA MERIDIANA

LA SAGRERA

C/GUIPÚSCOA

GRAN VIA DE LES CORTS CATALANES

CLOT

Hospital de Sant Pau

Plaça de les Glòries

POBLENOU

Sagrada Família

EIXAMPLE (DRETA)

VILA OLÍMPICA

GRÀCIA

AVDA DIAGONAL

PASSEIG DE GRÀCIA

Parc de la Ciutadella

PORT OLÍMPIC

RONDA GENERAL MITRE

SANT GERVASI

C/ARAGÓ

GRAN VIA DE LES CORTS CATALANES

SANT PERE

BORN

Estació de França

BARCELONETA

Plaça Catalunya

BARRI GÒTIC

PORT VELL

LES CORTS

EIXAMPLE (ESQUERRA)

RAVAL

LA RAMBLA

Catedral

RONDA LITORAL

AVDA JOSEP TARRADELLAS

AVDA PARAL·LEL

PORT DE SEA

MONTJUÏC

Estadi Olímpic

AVDA DIAGONAL

SANTS

Estació Barcelona-Sants

Plaça d'Espanya

C/TARRAGONA

GRAN VIA CARLES III

GRAN VIA DE LES CORTS CATALANES

Barri Gòtic (pp56-68)
Born & Sant Pere (pp69-76)
Raval (pp77-82)
Barceloneta & Ports (pp83-89)
Montjuïc (pp90-98)
The Eixample (pp99-108)
Gràcia & Other Districts (pp109-119)

0   1 mile
0   2 km

© Copyright Time Out Group 2009

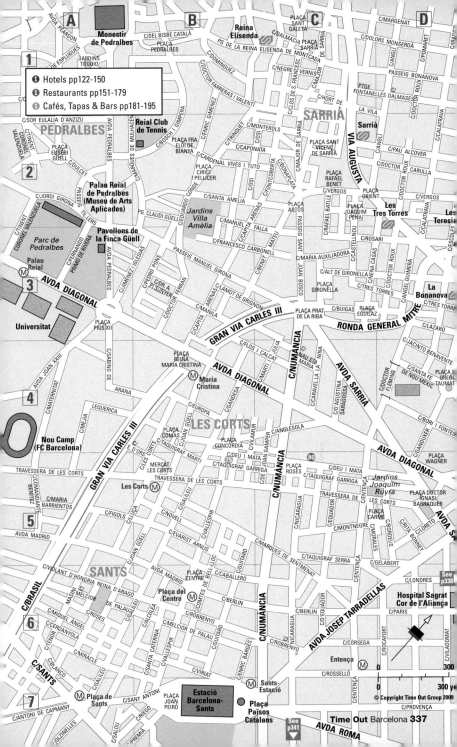

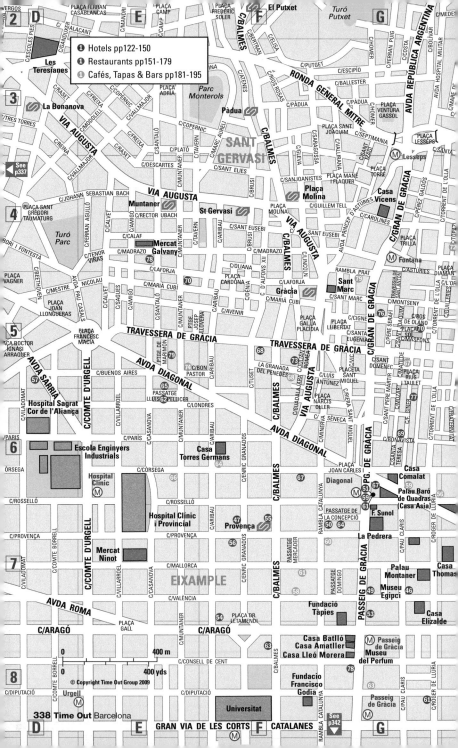

the Lobster house restaurant

6 menus at **€35** +VAT

Optional *A la carte* menu

A new concept of restaurant in Barcelona

Specialists in lobster, crayfish & prawns
All menus include:
Appetiser, two main dishes, dessert, bread & wine

Paris, 192 - 08036 Barcelona - T. 93 237 2444 - Metro Diagona

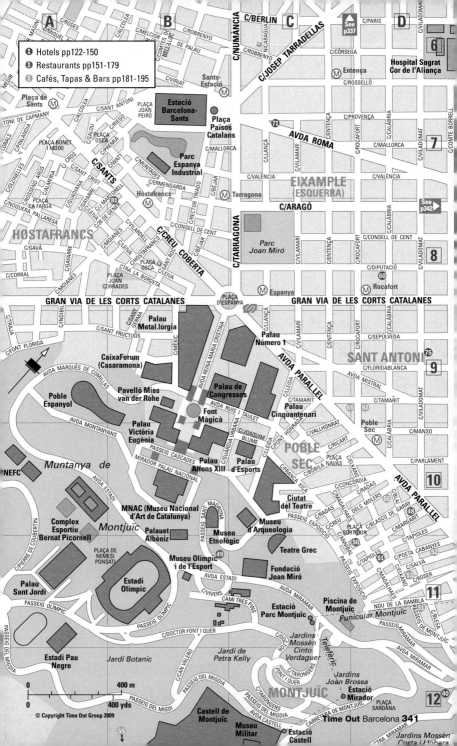

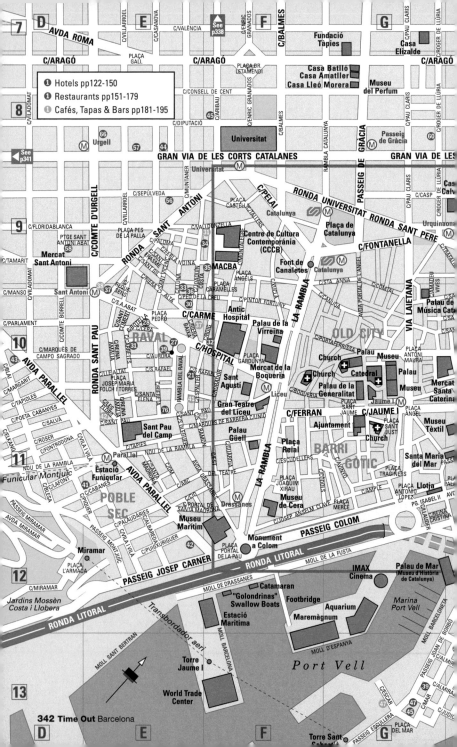

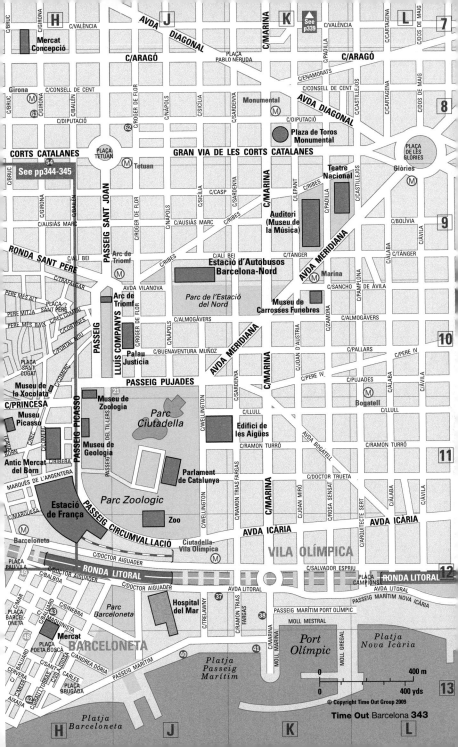

© Copyright Time Out Group 2009

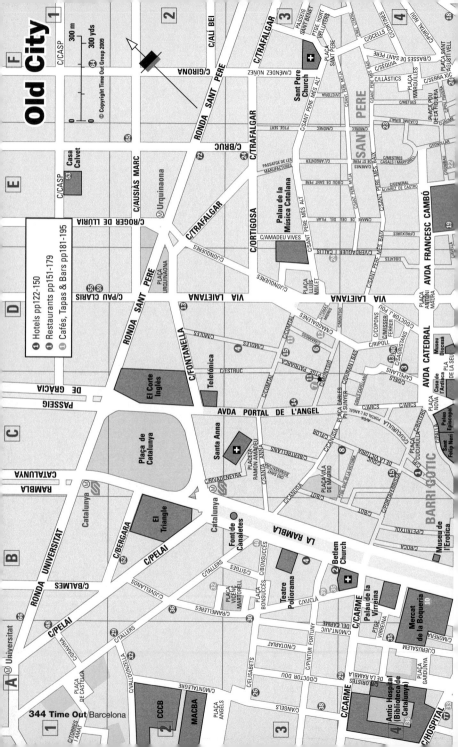

Old City

Hotels pp122-150
Restaurants pp151-179
Cafés, Tapas & Bars pp181-195

300 m
300 yds

© Copyright Time Out Group 2009

Street Index

STREET INDEX

STREET INDEX

STREET INDEX

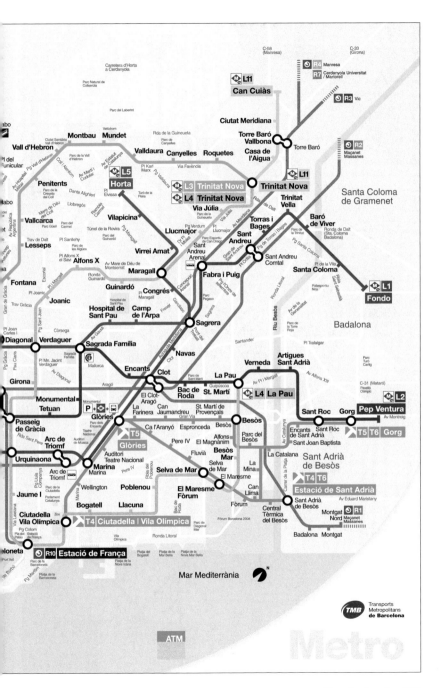

RENFE Local Trains

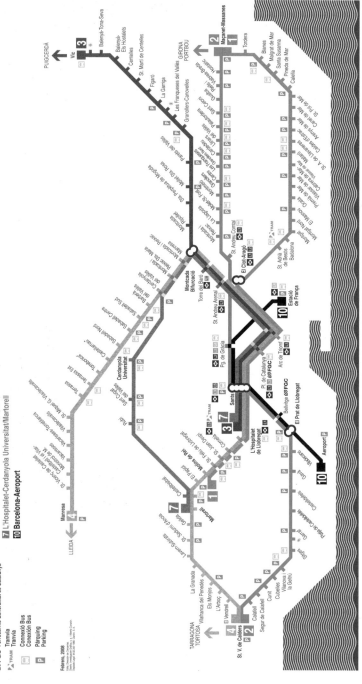